LESSLIE NEWBIGIN

Conversation by a South Indian road, around 1970
(Photograph used by permission of the Newbigin family)

LESSLIE NEWBIGIN

A THEOLOGICAL LIFE

Geoffrey Wainwright

OXFORD
UNIVERSITY PRESS
2000

OXFORD
UNIVERSITY PRESS

Oxford   New York

Athens   Auckland   Bangkok   Bogotá   Bombay   Buenos Aires
Calcutta   Cape Town   Dar es Salaam   Delhi   Florence   Hong Kong
Istanbul   Karachi   Kuala Lumpur   Madras   Madrid   Melbourne
Mexico City   Nairobi   Paris   Singapore   Taipei   Tokyo   Toronto

and associated companies in
Berlin   Ibadan

Copyright © 2000 by Geoffrey Wainwright

Published by Oxford University Press, Inc.
198 Madison Avenue, New York, New York, 10016

Oxford is a registered trademark of Oxford University Press.

Library of Congress Cataloging-in-Publication Data
Wainwright, Geoffrey, 1939–
Lesslie Newbigin : a theological life / Geoffrey Wainwright.
p.   cm.
Includes index.
ISBN 0-19-510171-5
1. Newbigin, Lesslie.   2. Church of South India—Bishops—Biography.
3. Ecumenical movement—Biography.   I. Title.

BX7066.5.Z8 N499   2000
287.9'4'092—dc21   99-045907
[B]

1 3 5 7 9 8 6 4 2

Printed in the United States of America
on acid-free paper

Preface

As rarely in modern times, the Church had in Lesslie Newbigin a bishop-theologian whose career was primarily shaped by his evangelistic and pastoral responsibilities and who yet made contributions to Christian thought that match in interest and importance those of the more academic among his fellow bishops and teachers. Their origin and destination in practice is what gave and continues to give such an extraordinary resonance to the oral and literary products of Newbigin's creative mind and loving heart. On any reckoning that takes seriously the ecclesial location and reference of theology, Newbigin must be accounted an ineluctable presence in his era.

Christian theology is more immediately a practical than a speculative discipline, and such speculation as it harbors stands ultimately in the service of right worship, right confession of Christ, and right living. Right practice demands, of course, critical and constructive reflection, and the best Christian theology takes place in the interplay between reflection and practice. That is why honor is traditionally given to those practical thinkers and preachers who are designated "Fathers of the Church." Most of them were bishops who, in the early centuries of Christianity, supervised the teaching of catechumens, delivered homilies in the liturgical assembly, oversaw the spiritual and moral life of their communities, gathered in council when needed to clarify and determine the faith, and took charge of the mission to the world as evangelistic opportunities arose. A figure of comparable stature and range in the ecumenical twentieth century was Lesslie Newbigin (1909–1998).

A Northumbrian raised in the Presbyterian Church of England, Newbigin went from his studies at Cambridge to service as a Church of Scotland missionary in India. He spent two lengthy periods on the subcontinent: first, from 1936 to 1959, as an evangelist, an ecumenical negotiator, and, from 1947, a bishop in the Madurai and Ramnad diocese of the newly united Church of South India; second, from 1965 to 1974, as bishop in metropolitan Madras. In between, from 1959 to 1965, he served as general secretary of the International Missionary Council at the time of its integration with the World Council of Churches. In 1974, he formally retired to Britain, but only in order to take a teaching position for five years at the Selly Oak Colleges in Birmingham and subsequently to act for almost a decade as pastor to a local congregation in a racially and religiously mixed area across the city. Besides being elected moderator of the United Reformed Church in the United Kingdom, Bishop Newbigin spearheaded the Gospel and Our Culture movement in Britain. In his second (or third) retirement in Southeast London, he figured as a national sage and finally prophet and continued toward the end of his ninth decade to accept, despite failing eyesight, numerous and multifarious speaking engagements. Throughout his life, his analytic penetration, his conceptual power, and his mental agility ensured the intellectual quality of his practical wisdom; and his ideas remain to be drawn upon by all those who still engage as he did in the tasks of commending the Gospel and defending the Christian faith, of the spiritual formation of individuals and the edification of the believing community, of reforming the Church and restoring its unity.

What confronts the reader of this book is a theological life in several senses. First, it is the life of Lesslie Newbigin himself, a life lived in faith, hope, and love, which are traditionally called the three theological virtues because they depend directly on God's presence in the human soul, Newbigin's was such a life in Christ. Second, this book is a theological biography in that it concentrates on the theological thought of its subject, always shown in relation to the contexts in which he lived and the ministries in which he engaged, always located in the broad tradition of churchly life and thought of which he was a part, and always examined for what the thought forged in Newbigin's life has to say to all times and places and to this time and place in particular. And third, the book is intended as itself a piece of theological writing, in a genre which can bear revival, namely theology as biography or biography as theology: it aims to instantiate a way of doing theology that takes sanctified life and thought seriously as an intrinsic witness to the content and truth of the Gospel.

Given the interweaving of those several strands in the book, it is important to indicate how they may nevertheless be distinguished. To clarify whose is what: the structuring of the book according to aspects of a life is mine, whereas of course the life whose aspects it presents is Newbigin's. Again, the places where Newbigin is being directly quoted or closely paraphrased—and I have provided for the reader much opportunity for firsthand contact with the subject's thought—are plainly set within my ordering of the material in relation to the classic themes and questions of Christian theology and my comments on his arguments in relation to the history of theology, doctrine, and dogma. And finally, I state quite openly when I am making developments and applications of Newbigin's thought that depend also on my own experience and reflection.

To elaborate a little on that last point, I am engaged in a continuing encounter with my subject that has lasted, on and off, for more than three decades. With a generational gap of thirty years, and at a much lower level of prominence on my part, I have shared many of the same interests as Lesslie Newbigin; my career has reflected, albeit palely, a few features of his own; and our paths have crossed at several junctures. I, too, was raised outside the Church of England, though as a Methodist, not as a Presbyterian. After my undergraduate studies at Cambridge, I trained for the ministry at Wesley College, Leeds, where I did some work (and the significance of this will emerge) on sacrifice in the Old Testament. My first encounter with Newbigin occurred when, as director of the Division of World Mission and Evangelism at the World Council of Churches, he came to lecture at the graduate school of the Ecumenical Institute at Bossey; I remember a German fellow student of mine being impressed that the bishop from South India could speak so incisively in an "unfootnoted" way. My overseas missionary service as a teacher and pastor in West Africa coincided with Newbigin's second major period of service in India. In the mid-1970s, we overlapped in Birmingham, where Newbigin taught missiology at Selly Oak and I taught Scripture and theology at the Queen's College. During that time we were both called on by Faith and Order at the World Council of Churches to address the current theme of local unity and conciliar fellowship. We both worked, in successive stages, on the ultimately unsuccessful plan for covenanting among the English churches. My move to the United States in 1979 still allowed me to roam the world in the cause of the unity and mission of the Church to which Bishop Newbigin continued his lifelong devotion. We corresponded over editorial projects of mine, to which Newbigin contributed readily with vigorous and substantial texts. He gave a series of lectures at Duke University, where I teach. Thus, although I was never an intimate of Lesslie's, we enjoyed over many years an easy rapport and saw eye to eye on many matters. It is from this fundamental sympathy of outlook, coupled with my admiration for Newbigin's life and thought, that this biography is written.

My study seeks throughout to show Newbigin's theology as it emerged in the varied contexts of his life and work. The introduction relates his life in a nutshell, so that the reader may have a constant reference to the times and places in which the theological activity is to be situated. The principal source here is Newbigin's autobiography, *Unfinished Agenda*, supplemented by correspondence preserved among his papers, by personal conversations with him, and by the reminiscences of others. Then the bulk of the book is arranged in order to exhibit the various facets of this jewel of a man: first and foremost as a believer and a disciple of the Lord Jesus Christ; then as an evangelist faithfully proclaiming to others the Gospel he had received; as an ecumenist passionate for the recovery of unity among divided Christians; as a diligent pastor and bishop in the Church of God; as a missionary strategist under the guidance of the Spirit; as a student of the world's religions and an interlocutor with their representatives; as a visionary who saw human society and the daily lives of people in light of the Kingdom of God; as a liturgist and preacher leading the assembled community to glorify God and find by grace a share in the life of the Blessed Trinity; as a teacher of Scripture and of the doctrinal tradition that interprets Scripture; and finally as an apologist for the Christian faith in the world of late modernity. The sequence of these chapters is in a very rough way chronological, for the aspects are displayed in the order in which they became specially prominent in Newbigin's life or in which a particularly important work was written or accomplished. Once such an aspect is introduced, the chapter may look back at earlier manifestations of that same interest on Newbigin's part and pursue the theme into the later stages of his career. My own evaluations occur partly in the course of the presentation and partly at the end of several chapters, where the continuing importance of Newbigin's insights may also be suggested. The conclusion of the book estimates Newbigin's place in the Christian Tradition, draws from Newbigin's example some lessons about the doing of theology, and offers, in the perspective set by its subject, some further material considerations concerning the big issues for churchly reflection and action in our time and into the foreseeable future.

 As I followed Newbigin's work over the years, I was impressed by the strength and consistency of his vision and its practical enactment; the impression was confirmed as I reread his writings and talked with him in preparation for this book. Newbigin offers, I believe, an authentic representation of the scriptural Gospel and the classic Christian faith. There is no question here of conducting a critique of Newbigin from a quite different standpoint. I have not even sought to tie up too firmly the occasional loose ends that may be observed in his thought, for that might tighten its texture beyond what is suitable. Certainly it has not been part of my plan to engage all the secondary and tertiary literature on Newbigin and the ambient issues. (In that regard, I have even resisted, though with difficulty, the temptation to read George Hunsberger's 1998 book, *Bearing Witness of the Spirit: Lesslie Newbigin's Theology of Cultural Plurality.*) What is present here springs from my own encounter, in person and on paper and in the results of his work, with a great man of God, theologian, and pastor.

When, in early 1994, I first mentioned to Lesslie Newbigin the project that was developing in my mind for such a book as this, he was hesitant about the prospect of a biography; but as I clarified my specifically theological intention, he wrote that "if anyone is to do it, I would certainly be happy that it should be you" (May 7, 1994). From that point on, he unfailingly gave me his prompt and detailed cooperation in correspondence, conversation, and the supply of continuing literary materials. He gave me ready access to all his writings and papers and permission to use them.

My other debts are nevertheless numerous. On a bright autumn morning, at a crucial point in the shaping of this book, I was received into his Bible Society office at the Selly Oak Colleges by Dr. Dan Beeby, theological and pastoral confidant of Lesslie Newbigin. Himself of Northern English Presbyterian stock and a former missionary in China and Taiwan, Dan Beeby told me that three things were necessary in order to understand what Lesslie was up to: some knowledge of the Reformed tradition, some experience in cross-cultural mission, and a streak of nonconformity. Dan has since commented generously on the complete manuscript of the book. The draft text was also carefully read by Martin Conway, a younger friend of Lesslie's whose kindliness was much appreciated by Newbigin. Martin made many valuable suggestions and saved me from some errors of judgment, although he and I, who have known each other since our Caius College days, differ at some points in how we interpret and evaluate Newbigin's work. Philip Butin and Telford Work, two of my *Doktorkinder*, agreed to furnish perspectives on Newbigin from the rising generation, and their contributions figure in the conclusion of the book. While he was writing his second thesis on Newbigin for the University of Helsinki, Jukka Keskitalo and I held a long conversation in a garden in Turku. Choon-Khing Voon employed her research skills in tracking down a number of documents that I had missed during my own sorting through the Newbigin archives lodged in the Selly Oak Colleges library. In my long association with Oxford University Press, Cynthia Read has always been a supportive editor, and she has become a cherished friend.

A score of people have helped with their memories of Lesslie Newbigin or the provision of texts and information otherwise hard to find: Gerald H. Anderson, Bishop Leslie W. Brown, Joan Cambitsis, Frank Clooney, Martin Cressey, Frank Davies, Simon Downham, Tom Foust, Dawn Fraser, Brian Goss, Dagmar Heller, P. J. S. Jesudoss, David Kettle, Eric Lott, Bruce McGreevy, Bishop Hugh Montefiore, John Newbigin, H. B. S. Rahi, Lamin Sanneh, Bishop Mark Santer, Terry Schlossberg, Mary Tanner, M. M. Thomas (*requiescat in pace*), Bernard Thorogood, Lukas Vischer, Hans-Ruedi Weber, Rita Wesley.

My thanks go to Cynthia Garver as production editor at Oxford University Press, and to Elaine Kehoe as copy editor. Proofs were read by my esteemed and dear colleague at Duke Divinity School, Karen Westerfield Tucker, and by J. Samuel Hammond, special collections librarian and university carillonneur. Any remaining lapses are most likely owing to my own obstinacy or oversight.

A Pew Evangelical Fellowship allowed me to extend my Duke sabbatical from a semester into a year, during which most of the research for this book was done. I am very grateful to the trustees and to the selectors.

The book is dedicated to Margaret, my companion along the way.

Durham, North Carolina   G. W.
Pentecost 2000

Contents

LESSLIE NEWBIGIN

Introduction

A MAN IN CHRIST

The Career

James Edward Lesslie Newbigin was born in Newcastle-on-Tyne on December 8, 1909, to Annie Ellen *née* Affleck, wife of Edward Richmond Newbigin, shipping merchant. According to Lesslie's autobiography, his earliest memories were almost all happy ones. His mother, a gentle person and an exquisite pianist, loved her children with a strength and constancy from which Lesslie never ceased to draw life. His father, a devout and thoughtful Christian and a radical in politics, took part in family outings to moors and fells and beach, and he satisfied the children's natural curiosity on all manner of subjects, as well as teaching Lesslie woodworking and model making. After local kindergarten and preparatory school, Lesslie went off to board at Leighton Park, the Quaker institution in Reading, Berkshire. From Bill Brown, the geography master, he learned to get to the heart of a big book so as to expound and defend its argument in debate. In chemistry classes, he was taught that "life is a disease of matter," and elsewhere he imbibed a broadly deterministic view of history; yet in his last year at school he gleaned from F. S. Marvin's *The Living Past* a vision of the human story as an upward striving toward growing mastery over all that stands in the way of man's full humanity. Lesslie ended up as senior prefect and remained grateful for the headmaster's advice not to overrate opposition or take it as directed against oneself. By this time he had abandoned the religious assumptions in which he had been reared, but he was prevented from dismissing the Christian faith as irrational by a reading of William James's essay *The Will to Believe* and of a book by a Presbyterian minister and family friend, Herbert Gray, which offered a lucid and reasonable exposition of Christianity.[1]

Having successfully gained entrance to Queens' College, Cambridge, Lesslie spent the first half of 1928 as an office boy in his father's business and there encountered both the excitement and the pains of a fiercely competitive economy. "Indelibly fixed in my memory," he wrote, was the occasion "when, by very rapid and accurate work, we secured an order ahead of our rivals and—a day or two later—learned that for the colliery which had lost the order this was the final blow. It closed, and hundreds of miners were thrown on to the street. Our small triumph was their colossal disaster. I began to see the reality of what I later learned to call 'structural sin.'"[2] After a summer trip to Germany, Lesslie went up to Cambridge in the Michaelmas term. Not very assid-

3

uously, he read for part one of the Geography Tripos but gave more time to music, debates, rock climbing, and the cultivation of friendships. Some of these latter occurred through the Student Christian Movement (SCM) as he began to explore the faith again. In the summer of 1929, while helping in a camp for the apathetic or desperate unemployed of South Wales, Lesslie was one night granted a vision of the Cross that reached to the depths of human misery and gave ground for fresh hope. His own new certainty now accompanied him on the evangelistic campaigns he took part in with fellow students. Visitors to Cambridge whom Newbigin met through the SCM included John R. Mott, father of the modern ecumenical movement; Jack Winslow, missionary from India; John Mackey, missionary from Peru; and William Temple, then Archbishop of York, who declared from the pulpit of Great St. Mary's that "it is possible to be comparatively religious but there is no such thing as comparative religion." "I was beginning," Newbigin wrote, "to have a thrilling sense of sharing in a worldwide Christian enterprise which was commanding the devotion of men and women whose sheer intellectual and spiritual power was unmistakable. I became, even as a second-year undergraduate, a reader of the *International Review of Missions*, and the Christian faith into which I was growing was ecumenical from the beginning."[3] He belonged to the Madingley Group, whose annual pilgrimage to the village after which it was named provided a focus for its regular prayer on behalf of Christian unity. The fledgling ecumenist secured his own ecclesiastical allegiance by being confirmed into membership of St. Columba's Presbyterian Church in Cambridge. At the SCM Swanwick conference in the summer of 1930, Newbigin heard an unexpected but inescapable call to the ordained ministry. Returning to Cambridge for his third and final year as an undergraduate, he read economics and heard the lectures of John Maynard Keynes.

To earn the wherewithal for his theological training, Newbigin found employment as an SCM staff secretary. Among the committee members in Edinburgh interviewing him for the job was Helen Henderson, daughter of Irish Presbyterian missionaries to India, with whom he fell in love there and then. They were to become colleagues in Glasgow for two years. Both were favorably considered for missionary service by the Church of Scotland, and Helen underwent the statutory year of training at St. Colm's College in Edinburgh; but the couple could not marry until Lesslie, having become a candidate for ordination under the Newcastle Presbytery, had completed his theological studies at Westminster College, Cambridge. From 1933 to 1936 he studied under John Oman and Herbert Farmer. His continuing SCM interests brought him into touch with J. H. Oldham, as well as William Temple, and so above all with the Life and Work movement, which, with Faith and Order, was to become from 1938 the World Council of Churches (WCC) "in process of formation." In May 1936 the Newbigins were formally commissioned by the General Assembly of the Church of Scotland for work in India, and on July 12 Lesslie was ordained by the Presbytery of Edinburgh for service as a foreign missionary. On September 26, 1936, Lesslie and Helen sailed from Liverpool for Madras.

1936 → India

After a month's voyage they docked at Madras and were immediately driven by car the thirty-six miles to their first home in the small country town of Chingleput. Newbigin wrote:

> That first taste of India was so vivid that it could never be forgotten—the soft, cool evening air, the lines of brightly lit stalls as we slipped out of Madras by the trunk road, the glint of light on polished brass water-pots, the graceful movement of women in their beautiful saris, and then the open country with the paddy fields and the big leafy trees fringing the road. On the way we had to stop because of a puncture and there was a chance to stand still in the darkness, smell the strange and delicious scents, listen to the symphony of the cicadas everywhere and watch the slow rhythm of the bullock-carts going by patiently, endlessly, through the night.[4]

For five months in Chingleput (where Lesslie helped with the English services on Sundays in the leprosy colony) and then four more months in the hills of Kodaikanal, the Newbigins spent a daily shift in learning Tamil, both the literary language and the ordinary language of the street and the shop. They were due to be stationed in Conjeeveram (later spelt Kanchipuram), but Lesslie's leg was smashed in a bus accident. After unsuccessful treatment in Madras, they set sail again for Britain. On November 14, 1937, Lesslie underwent in Edinburgh his tenth operation—a bone graft, after which osteomyelitis set in and amputation seemed probable. Friends prayed daily, and when the plaster was removed, the surgeon found that healing had begun. By the following February Lesslie was out of bed and by May he was walking on crutches. He had continued to study Tamil throughout his convalescence. In the further year that would be needed before final cure, he served as candidates secretary for the foreign missions committee of the Church of Scotland. In June 1939, the Newbigins' first child, Margaret, was born. On September 15 they left Newcastle, having seen Lesslie's father for the last time. On October 18 they finally arrived in Kanchipuram.

In a circular letter of April 1940, Newbigin described Kanchipuram as "one of the seven sacred cities of India, a place which has hardly a street without one or more temples, a place where Hinduism is at its strongest. The wonderful successes which the Church is having in certain parts of Indian society should not make one forget how massively resistant is the central core of ordinary caste-Hinduism."[5] In the city, with its 70,000 inhabitants and its annual influx of pilgrims for the great festival in May and June, Newbigin engaged with others in street preaching and in the distribution of gospels; he also shared with the head of a Hindu monastic community in the leadership of a weekly study group devoted to the Svetasvara Upanishad in Sanskrit and St. John's Gospel in Greek. As the district missionary, he undertook regular administrative duties and handled emergencies, besides touring the surrounding noncaste villages with Indian coworkers for pastoral and evangelistic purposes, making it his aim to strengthen local leadership in the congregations. The war years did not much disrupt the life of the Newbigin family, now augmented by the birth of Alison in 1941 and Janet in 1944. John would be born in 1947.

During the years in Kanchipuram, Newbigin became a representative of the South India United Church (SIUC) in the later stages of the negotiations that would allow the SIUC (Presbyterian and Congregationalist by origin), the Methodists (of British missionary origin), and the Anglicans to constitute the Church of South India (CSI). In what Newbigin called "the final struggle" toward unity, the decisions in the House of Bishops in the (Anglican) Church of India, Burma and Ceylon especially were touch and go, and during his home leave in 1946–47 Newbigin spent much time and energy not only in advocacy of the union among Scottish Presbyterians but also in defending the plan in the face of Anglo-Catholic opposition in the Church of England. The newly united Church was to be episcopal in structure (which worried many on the Reformed side), and all ministers from the founding denominations were to be recognized with little further ado as presbyters in the CSI (which meant in some Anglican eyes that those from the SIUC and the Methodists lacked priestly ordination). After positive final votes among the Methodists, the SIUC, and the Church of India, Burma, and Ceylon, the union was inaugurated in Madras Cathedral on September 27, 1947. Here is Newbigin's full description, in a circular letter written at the time, of what many ecumenists would regard as the highest moment so far in the recovery of visible unity, when Christian communities from the Anglican and some nonepiscopal traditions were for the first time brought together into organic union:

During the last few days of the week messages were coming in from almost every part of the world, and from an amazing variety of Churches and Christian societies, assuring us of their prayers as the day of union drew near. It made us all very conscious of the great company of people who were with us in heart and mind during the service, and we could not help also constantly remembering the presence of all those who worked so hard for this union and who now serve in the Church triumphant.

We [the bishops elect] set off together for the Cathedral at 7 on the Saturday morning. There had been rain the previous night, and it was a fresh, bright morning. A very large *pandal* [pavilion], seating about 2,000 people, had been erected beside the Cathedral, equipped with loudspeakers. The cathedral itself was, I believe, seated for about 1,500. According to the Madras papers there were 4,500 present, but I think 3,500 is more correct. Practically the whole of that number were in their seats from about 7.45 till 12.15, with only a short break between the two services when they could leave their seats. Yet when I asked some people if they were not tired, they repudiated the suggestion most indignantly. The whole of that great congregation seemed to remain in absolutely rapt attention to the very end. One had the overwhelming sense of a great company of worshipping people utterly taken up into the thing they were doing, made one by the presence of the living Spirit of God. When I was talking afterwards to a much-beloved Irish Presbyterian missionary who was there from North India, he summed it up by saying "The tide of the Spirit just rose and covered the walls." I don't think one could put it better.

The first service began with praise, prayer, the reading of St. John 17, and confession. Then an authorised representative of each of the uniting Churches came to the steps of the chancel, read out the resolution of the governing body of his Church accepting the union, and then turned and went to the Table and laid on it a signed copy of the Scheme of Union and a book containing the signatures of all the ministers of his Church assenting to the Basis of Union and accepting the Constitution. Each one knelt for a moment in silence at the Table as he and we commended to God this action of each Church in giving up its life to become part of a greater whole. Then there was a very solemn prayer asking for God's blessing on the union. Then the bishop presiding (Bishop Jacob of Travancore) came forward and read in ringing tones the declaration that the three churches were now become one Church of South India. Immediately there followed the Te Deum, and what a shout of praise it was! It was as if all the frustrated desire of these 28 years had at last burst through the dam and was pouring out in one irresistible flood. I think many found it hard to refrain from tears during that singing. ... We looked round at each other, and with each fresh face remembered again with a kind of start of joy that the walls between us were down and we were one Church. ...

When we had sat down, the five Anglican bishops came forward and presented themselves before the two senior ministers representing the SIUC and the Methodist Church. The Secretary of the Joint Committee read the declaration of their appointment to serve as Bishops in the united Church. They were then questioned as to their acceptance of the Basis of Union and Constitution, and knelt at the rails to be commissioned by each of the two ministers to exercise the office of a bishop in the congregations which had hitherto been part of these other churches. Prayer was offered for them, and then we sang "All hail the power of Jesus' name". Thereafter all the ministers of the three uniting churches were similarly questioned and commissioned to exercise their ministry in the Church of South India. Then with hymn, offering and prayer the first part of the service ended.[6]

At the age of thirty-seven, Lesslie Newbigin had been elected to serve as one of the first bishops in the united Church. During the second part of that liturgy on September 27, 1947, he received consecration to the episcopate.[7]

In a further letter, dated October 26, 1947, the new bishop described his diocese of Madurai and Ramnad thus:

The diocese of Madura and Ramnad exactly covers the Government districts with those names, which you will find on the map in the extreme South-East corner of India. It is an area roughly 100 miles each way, but not, of course, square. On its Western side it runs along the borders of the State of Travancore, and the border is marked by magnificent ranges of hills running up over 8,000 feet. These hills are largely uninhabitable jungle and are full of a great variety of wild animal life including elephants, tigers, cheetahs and the ubiquitous monkey. But there are valleys running up into the mountains where there are many villages, among which we have a considerable Christian population, and there is the famous hill station of Kodaikanal, 7,000 feet up and surrounded by lovely forests and rolling downs, the resort of holidaymakers from every part of India during the hot season. The greater part of the diocese is, of course, the plains area, stretching from the hills to the sea, and the great majority of the 50,000 in the diocese live in the plains. And the natural centre of the whole area is the ancient city of Madura.

You can find Madura on Ptolemy's map of the world. It is a very ancient city, and for long the capital of a famous kingdom. Throughout the Tamil country it is regarded as the cultural capital of the region. In the seventeenth and eighteenth centuries it was the scene of a famous Roman Catholic mission, and there is still a very strong Roman Catholic Church here. The American [Congregationalist] missionaries began work in 1834, at which time the population of the city was about 30,000. It is now about 400,000 and growing rapidly. The main reason for the rapid growth is the presence here of the [Scottish-owned] Madura Mills, and other modern [cotton-spinning] mills. They employ thousands of men and contribute to making the city larger and more wealthy. At the same time they naturally furnish material for difficult labour problems, and one of the first things that strikes a newcomer is the daubing of the Communist hammer and sickle on walls and houses everywhere. The control of the powerful labour unions is practically in Communist hands.[8]

Ecclesiastically, the diocese included not only the work of the American Board of Commissioners for Foreign Missions but also parts of the former Anglican diocese of Tinnevelly, where both the (high-church) Society for the Propagation of the Gospel and the (low-church) Church Missionary Society labored. Something of Newbigin's evangelistic and pastoral work is described in chapters 2 and 4, but here already may be repeated a story that he liked to tell about the hazards of a bishop's job in catholic-minded corners of the former raj:

On my first visit to the headquarters of the SPG area I confess to having been nervous. I need not have worried. I was escorted to the Church in a procession which included an Indian band, a brass band, a choir, an elephant borrowed from the temple, and a phaeton borrowed from the Rajah of Ramnad and drawn by a magnificent white horse, in which the bishop, garlanded with roses, was invited to sit. My Presbyterian upbringing asserted itself. I tried to protest. A senior member of the church, astonished, asked me what was the trouble. I said the first thing that came to my lips: "When our Lord went in a procession, He rode on a donkey." "Ah," was the relieved reply, "but He did that so that we could do this." The answer to that would have taken a long time, and I meekly sat down in the carriage, alternately trying to imagine what the Foreign Mission Committee of the Church of Scotland and the Standing Committee of the SPG would have said.[9]

Newbigin served as bishop in Madurai and Ramnad for some twelve years. By virtue of his own remarkable abilities, in combination with his episcopal standing in a Church that many were ready to view as a first fruit in a wider unitive process, he became during that period a prominent figure on the international ecumenical scene. He was a consultant to the inaugural assembly of the World Council of Churches at Amsterdam in 1948 ("Man's Disorder and God's Design") and chaired the high-powered and rambunctious theological "committee of twenty-five" that prepared the theme for the WCC's second assembly at Evanston, Illinois, in 1954, "Christ, the Hope of the World"; thereafter he was appointed to the central committee of the WCC.

In 1956 he was named vice chairman of the WCC Commission on Faith and Order and pressed that "the nature of the unity we seek" become a central question at the third assembly of the WCC to be held in New Delhi in 1961; in fact, he himself turned out to be the decisive drafter of the key paragraph in the description of ecclesial unity that would be adopted by that assembly.

Bishop Newbigin also had the delicate task of helping to keep communications open between the Church of South India and the worldwide Anglican Communion when, as a "special guest" of Archbishop Geoffrey Fisher, he attended the Lambeth Conferences of 1948 and 1958 (he came again in 1968, under Archbishop Michael Ramsey, as a "consultant"); but although some clarifications were achieved and, on the second occasion, 160 Anglican bishops received communion at a celebration of the CSI liturgy, yet these Lambeth Conferences were still not able to declare "full communion" with the CSI. Newbigin's disappointment was sharp and went deep. Had Lambeth been able to "give a cordial welcome to what had been done in South India," he wrote decades later in his autobiography, "the whole worldwide movement for unity among the Churches would have gone forward. The Anglican Communion would have fulfilled its true ecumenical vocation to provide a centre around which reformed Christendom can be brought together in unity and in continuity with the historic ministry of the universal Church. That opportunity was lost, and is not likely to come again."[10] From his days in Cambridge and in India, through his international activities, and after his retirement to Britain in 1974, Lesslie Newbigin made and kept many Anglican friends–Oliver Tomkins, Michael Hollis, Leslie Brown, Stephen Neill, George Bell, Hugh Montefiore, Martin Conway, Mary Tanner, and N. T. Wright, to name but a few from different generations—but there can be no mistaking his frustration at the institutional and corporate failure of Anglicanism to deliver its potential in the matter of Christian unity.[11]

In the 1950s, meanwhile, Bishop Newbigin became closely involved in the work of the International Missionary Council (IMC). In 1952 he participated formatively in the IMC's Willingen conference on "The Missionary Obligation of the Church." In January 1958, at the Council's assembly in Accra, he was elected—in his absence!—chairman of the IMC. He had already been sounded out for the full-time general secretaryship, a post which he was shortly afterward persuaded with some difficulty to accept. The CSI seconded him for five years "as a bishop of the Church of South India without diocesan charge, released for service with the International Missionary Council." Newbigin thus assumed principal responsibility on the IMC side for guiding the integration which he himself judged necessary between that body and the World Council of Churches; and after the integration was formally enacted at the New Delhi assembly in 1961, he became director of the Division of World Mission and Evangelism and an associate general secretary of the WCC. During these "bureaucratic" years (the word is laughably inappropriate in Lesslie's case, though he had considerable administrative gifts), he needed for a while to triangulate between London, Geneva, and New York. More significantly, he undertook extensive tours of Africa (1960), the Pacific (1961),

Latin America (also 1961), and the Caribbean (1962), as well as shorter trips to, say, Thailand and Japan and various parts of Europe and North America.[12] Old Africa hands may appreciate one vignette from Newbigin's visit to the Congo in October 1960:

> At about 11 p.m. we drove out to the Stanley statue to see the lights of Leopoldville [later Kinshasa]. It was a memorable moment for me, with all kinds of conflicting thoughts in my mind. Below was the vast sweep of the river, narrowing towards the rapids whose thunder formed the undertone of every other sound. To the right the glimmering lights of Leopoldville, the great expanse of the Stanley Pool dimly glimpsed in the moonlight. Across the river the lesser lights of Brazzaville. Above us towered the immense figure of Stanley looking out into the unexplored regions beyond. Around us a bunch of cheerful young Africans laughing and talking and occasionally giving a friendly slap to one of the lesser statues that form part of the monument. I suppose that much more history will have to unroll before we shall be able to see in one perspective the courage and vision of the white man's opening up of Africa, and the bubbling gaiety of the young Africa which the white man—to his perplexity—awaked.[13]

A single example must suffice to show the impact Newbigin's presence could have. It comes from the first National Conference of Australian Churches, held in Melbourne in February 1960. This account was written by David M. Taylor in the official report, *We Were Brought Together*:

> As far as it is possible for us to understand the mysterious workings of God's power, He made special use of Bishop Newbigin and of our study of 1 Peter. While all our distinguished overseas guests made their own special contribution to our fellowship and to our thinking, all willingly concede that Lesslie Newbigin was the outstanding personality of those ten days. And if we ask precisely what he did for us, it requires more than one man's pen to do him justice. Without taking away one whit from the glory and honour due to God Himself for the way He used His servant, we may express our gratitude to the Bishop for the way he made himself available as a channel through which the Holy Spirit might work.
>
> The unusual thing about Bishop Newbigin was the way he could talk freely and firmly about matters on which we are divided, yet instead of soon reaching the point where some of us would be gloating because we found that he was on our side, while others would be rejecting him, he spoke on and on, drawing from us all a continuing affirmative response. If we analyse why it was that this happened, we see it was no accident or chance, but the result of the combination of clear head, humble spirit, and long and careful search for truth. As we listened to him expounding the biblical doctrine of priesthood, for example, one by one we recognized our own blind spots. We saw that he was preserving everything we were anxious to defend, yet he was doing the same for others who came from other traditions. Bishop Newbigin is master of his subject and takes the greatest pains to find the most accurate way to express the spiritual truth given to him.
>
> Thus he himself set us an example in that very field to which he referred when at the end of the Conference he tried to pick out our greatest needs.

In his closing message he gently but firmly said our need is for better theology. In the Antipodes a common feature of our life is that we think we can get on without much theology. Large numbers of our people have it firmly fixed in their minds that theology is something obscure and far removed from the real needs of the common man. . . . One of the lessons we must not fail to learn from our Conference is this, that no man can speak clearly and convincingly on the problems that puzzle Christians today unless he really gives himself to the task of thinking theologically. Bishop Newbigin's fluency is the result of taking infinite pains, over many years, first to find "what the Spirit saith unto the churches," and secondly to find the exact word, and the right combination of words, in which to express this message.[14]

The early to mid-1960s were the years when Newbigin became most fascinated with the "secular theology" that had been adumbrated by Hans Hoekendijk and Paul Lehmann at the IMC Willingen conference in 1952 and that had come into fashion typified by a lopsided interpretation of Dietrich Bonhoeffer and his "religionless Christianity." Much more will be said about this in chapters 7 and 10, but it must be clear from the outset that Newbigin never bought heavily into this vogue, even while recognizing that the "worldly" reference of the Gospel had often been underplayed. Here is Newbigin's telling account of a significant occasion:

A crucial event was the conference called at Strasbourg in July 1960 by the World's Student Christian Federation on "The Life and Mission of the Church." It was the brain-child of D. T. Niles and Philippe Maury who believed, as I did, that there was an emerging theological consensus about the missionary nature of the Church and that the coming generation of student leaders could be captured and fired by the vision so that a new generation of ecumenical leaders could be prepared to take the place of those who were growing old. There was an immensely impressive array of speakers including even Karl Barth, but the event proved very different from the expectations. To quote the report in the WSCF's journal: "It must have been striking to everyone how much indifference there was to the theological issues and ecumenical achievements of an earlier generation." The convictions to which I and those of my generation—D. T. Niles, Visser 't Hooft and Philippe Maury—had come with much wrestling were dismissed, to quote the same report, as "pious talk and Geneva ideology". The new vision was of the world, not the Church, as the place where God is to be found. Consequently "the mission and renewal of the Church in our day depends on acceptance and affirmation of the secular world in place of traditional Christian tendencies to reject it." The most articulate exponent of the dominant mood was Hans Hoekendijk whose address called us "to begin radically to desacralize the Church" and to recognize that "Christianity is a secular movement—this is basic for an understanding of it."

On a theological level I had to recognize the big element of truth in what was being said, but I was acutely aware at the same time of what was being ignored or denied. . . . On a personal level I found the event very painful. It was painful to experience the contempt in which missions were held. . . . I did not yet know how far the decade that had just begun would take us from the lines on which my own theological development had brought me. I had been pleading for a "churchly" unity because I believed that God's purpose of reconciliation could not be achieved by a concatenation of programmes and projects unless these were leading towards the life of a reconciled family within the household of God. I was soon to learn that "churchly" was an adjective of abuse, and that the only way to be really part of God's work as understood in the 1960s was to leave the Church behind. The "secular decade" had arrived. The Student Christian Movement would not again in my lifetime be, as it had been, the most powerful source of new life for the ecumenical movement.[15]

The event that closed the secular '60s for Newbigin was the "shattering experience" of the fourth assembly of the World Council of Churches at Uppsala, where the ecclesiastical *soixante-huitards* took over the show—epitomized by a vaudeville artiste's singing of the satirical "there'll be pie in the sky when you die" to rapturous applause.[16] "The scars left on the body of the Church by that traumatic decade," wrote Newbigin fifteen years later, "will take a long time to heal."[17]

In 1965 Newbigin returned to India to serve as bishop of the Church of South India in Madras. In presenting to an international audience a series of meditations that he had originally given as communion addresses to his clergy and other coworkers during the nine years of his episcopal ministry there, Newbigin described the great city thus:

Madras is a city of some three million people, adding 100,000 to its population each year. About half of this annual addition is made by immigrants from the hinterland of the city—often young people who have managed to struggle through an elementary education in their village and have come into the city in search of work. For very many of these the first "home" is simply a sleeping place on the pavement. After a time, in company with others from the same village or area, they will perhaps manage to find a vacant site where a cluster of bamboo and thatch huts can be erected on some dark night when the police are looking the other way. They thus become part of the great company of slum dwellers, living in crowded clumps of unventilated huts, without water, light or sanitation—but with an unbeaten determination to come up in the world. The fortunate ones, where one or both of the members of the family can secure and hold a job in a factory, may eventually graduate to a small three-room house in one of the new residential estates. And they can dream that children or grandchildren will eventually qualify for one of the stylish bungalows which are to be seen, surrounded by their well watered gardens, but seldom more than a stone's throw from one of the slums.

The small town which grew up in the seventeenth and eighteenth centuries around the East India Company's Fort is now a great centre of both heavy and light industry. North, west and south of the city, stretching to a radius of 25 miles, there is a great belt of factories which together produce a substantial part of India's total industrial output including railway rolling stock, weapons, heavy and light vehicles, cloth, tyres, electrical goods and much else besides. Industry forms a very large part of the life of the city and has to have a large place in the thinking of the Church.[18]

The Church of South India diocese as a whole comprised almost one thousand congregations, with some 110 congregations in the city of Madras. For about fifteen of these last, the language of worship was English, and for most of the rest Tamil; their denominational backgrounds varied between Anglican, Reformed, and Methodist, but the majority of them used the forms of service developed in the CSI since union. The membership ranged "from the dwellers in the slums and on the pavements to the men and women who hold positions of highest leadership in government, business and the professions." Of the engagement of the Church with its urban location (the place "for" which it was present, as Newbigin would come characteristically to phrase it), he wrote:

> Like the Church everywhere, the congregations in Madras are tempted to turn their backs upon the world around them and to concentrate on their own concerns. Yet it can be said with thankfulness that there is a real measure of concern for and involvement in the problems of the city as a whole. Some—though by no means all—of the congregations have active programmes of direct evangelism. Some of them have responded to the call to enter into the problems of the slums, both with emergency help at times of disaster from flood or fire (very common occurrences) and with long-term programmes such as the provision of modern sanitation units for more than a dozen of the slums. The Church has also been able to cooperate with the Slum Clearance Board of the Tamilnadu Government in programmes for community development in the new housing units built to replace the hovels in which people had been living. Under the name of "Christian Service to Industrial Society" there is a programme aimed at helping Christians in industry—both on the management and on the workers' sides—to understand and fulfil their calling as Christians in the changing conditions of modern industry, and to awaken the Church to a biblical understanding of industry and its problems. A community Service Centre, operating on behalf of a number of churches, provides both training for service to society and an opportunity for men and women in many sectors of public life to equip themselves for Christian witness and service in the common life.[19]

Elements of Newbigin's episcopal leadership of the Church's social and evangelistic ministries in the metropolis are discussed particularly in chapter 4.[20] During this period the bishop also served as deputy moderator of the CSI (he was disappointed by a failure on the Lutheran side to constitute with the CSI a united "Church of Christ in South India"), as convenor of the National Council of Churches' Committee on Faith and Order (with the full-time help of a young Syrian Orthodox priest, he headed up an all-India study program that engaged the Orthodox, Roman Catholic, Mar Thoma, and Protestant churches and culminated in a residential conference at Nasrapur in 1972—"a very blessed occasion on which we found a deep unity of spirit even when we tackled very controversial issues"), and as a member (again) of the World Council of Churches' Commission on Faith and Order (at the Louvain meeting of 1971 he was reluctantly involved in launching the ecclesiologically ambiguous concept of "conciliar fellowship," but on the other hand he found himself enriched by participation in the section on the role of the handicapped in the Church).

Approaching the retirement age of a CSI bishop at sixty-five, Lesslie undertook with Helen their return to Britain by way of an overland trek. In September 1974 he began five years of teaching missiology and ecumenism in the Selly Oak Colleges in Birmingham. His audiences comprised British and other European students undergoing missionary training, as well as students coming from overseas churches for further study in England. A special and much appreciated feature of Lesslie and Helen's ministry was the Sunday afternoon tea parties they held for students in their home. As discussed at several points in this book, the scarcely retired bishop became much involved in the ecclesiastical and educational affairs of the city of Birmingham. In 1978–79 he served as national moderator of the United Reformed Church, the body into which his original Presbyterian Church of England had been integrated with the former Congregational Union/Church in 1972.

On settling again in his native land, Newbigin had been deeply struck by the mood of despair among the people and the moral decay in the country. Upon his retirement from Selly Oak, he responded to a challenge he had issued to the Birmingham district council of the United Reformed Church by himself accepting a call to the pastorate of a seemingly moribund cause in the shape of

> a small congregation of about twenty members which worshipped in a building just across the road from the Winson Green prison. It had begun 120 years earlier as a mission from the Handsworth Congregational Church to an area which was described as being bounded by the prison, the lunatic asylum, the London North-Western Railway and James Watt's famous foundry. Officially known as "Mary Hill" it was popularly described as "Merry Hell."[21]

The current residents came mostly from the Indian subcontinent and the Caribbean. Between January 1980 and September 1988 Newbigin ministered there; from September 1982 he had as his associate, at his initiative, a presbyter seconded by the Church of North India, Hakim Singh Rahi, who was fluent in Urdu and Hindi, as well as in Punjabi and English. The British Council of Churches invited Newbigin in the early 1980s to share in a working group of leading thinkers to prepare a major conference on Church and society initially foreseen for the year 1984; by an unpredictable providence, this led to his writing the first of his remarkable studies on the Gospel and Western culture, which were to add up to what he later called "the most intense years of missionary endeavour in my entire life," climaxing in the international conference of July 1992 at Swanwick that he saw—and had planned—as the event at which to hand on that torch to a wide range of younger Christian leaders. These years were, for Newbigin himself, the late stages in what had been a deep preoccupation of his since the 1930s with the relationship between Christianity and modern Western civilization and with the question—formulated since 1975 in terms borrowed from the retired Indonesian general T. B. Simatupang—"Can the West be [re]converted?"

These concerns went increasingly hand in hand with Newbigin's attention to Islam as the respected and more and more evident rival for the spiritual allegiance of Europe and much of the world.

Early in 1988, Newbigin returned to India for a WCC consultation arranged to "revisit" the Tambaram 1938 world missionary conference, and there he clashed sharply with representatives of the "Harvard school" in their approaches to the religions and found himself in a reprise of the part played by Hendrik Kraemer at Tambaram half a century before. After his third retirement, Newbigin continued to be in national and international demand as a speaker, although he largely confined his overseas travels to Europe and North America. In May 1989 he allowed himself to be cajoled into traveling to Texas for the second half of the WCC world conference on mission and evangelism in San Antonio and, once there, to give an off-program address late one evening that was attended by virtually the entire membership. Seven years later, it was with even more resistance and humility on his part that he was eventually persuaded to travel to Brazil for some days of the succeeding WCC world conference on mission and evangelism, in Salvador de Bahia in November 1996, when his eyesight had largely gone, and yet he gave, in two installments that had to be fitted into an already overcrowded timetable, what many present recall as the most valuable address of the entire event.

In 1992 Lesslie and Helen moved from Birmingham to London in order to be nearer to three of their four "loving and supportive" children. Out of their retirement home in South East 24, Lesslie kept up a significant ministry in local ecumenism. At his funeral service in Dulwich Grove United Reformed Church on February 8, 1998, it became clear to others, as Martin Conway reported, "what a remarkable role he had played in prayer, reconciliation, and inspiration between churches and their leadership of different denominations and races." Two quite different features from Lesslie's final years, which will surprise only those unaware of his lifelong attachment to music and his perennial openness to the presence and work of the Holy Spirit, were his association first with Nigel Swinford and the New English Orchestra and second with Holy Trinity Brompton (HTB), the London focus for a while of the Toronto Blessing. The links with HTB in particular merit further mention, and here Simon Downham, the curate who had the closest day-to-day relationship with Lesslie, has been most helpful.[22]

Downham says that although "HTB has come to be regarded in some circles as a flag-bearer of the so-called charismatic renewal, in practice its heart is for 'winning souls.' Indeed one might go so far as to say that our understanding is that the Spirit's work in our midst is precisely to that end. Perhaps that is the clue to Lesslie's surprise and delight at ministering here. There was none (or not much!) of the introspection that has discoloured so much of the charismatic renewal, but rather a passion for mission, even if our understanding of mission was not quite as sophisticated as those who wrote about mission would have liked." Downham recounts the original contact, made in the summer of 1994, in this way:

I had devoured Lesslie's work while studying Theology in Oxford, at Wycliffe Hall. I had suggested that he would be an ideal speaker to invite to Holy Trinity Brompton's holiday/teaching conference. His was one among several names. Sandy Millar, the Vicar of Holy Trinity, had a dream that he should invite Lesslie and quite late in the day rang to invite him. Lesslie, much to my surprise, agreed to come. The conference was taking place at a holiday camp in Morecambe in Lancashire, and Lesslie arrived having got himself through train and bus strikes from London to Morecambe. I remember meeting him and being apprehensive about what he would make of us and what we would make of him. He had been asked to talk about mission and culture. I remember him being introduced and before he'd said anything he was given a five-minute standing ovation. "After applause like that," he said, "I can't wait to hear myself speak." At once we took him to our hearts and it seemed he took us to his. He gave an hour-long learned exposition of the problems of preaching the Gospel in our western culture. Of course I'd heard the material before and had read much of it but was transfixed. More than that, many in our congregation with no theological background were transfixed. I remember one of our West Indians was leaving the conference hall at the same time as me and said "I don't think I understood half of that, but I know it's important and I'm going to buy the tape and make sure I understand all of it." Lesslie had that effect on us. It was an unlikely relationship, but the more seriously he took us, the more seriously people wanted to take the message he was bringing.

Picturing HTB as "a gushing oil well which simply needed capping," Newbigin returned many times to the church; here were "two hundred people attending his courses, all of whom were tertiary educated and involved in careers where their potential influence was not inconsiderable." He gave various series of lectures, preserved on audiotape, on St. John and Romans, on the major Christian doctrines, and on the Gospel in relation to the worlds of science, politics, and the religions. On one occasion he offered a particularly powerful and profound meditation on the Seven Words from the Cross.

Lesslie spent Christmas 1997 in the hospital with "an unexpected heart problem," as he put it in his last letter to me. He had been looking forward to traveling in mid-January to Birmingham in connection with the joining of Winson Green United Reformed Church with Bishop Latimer Anglican church in a local ecumenical partnership. His last journey, however, took another form. On Friday, January 30, 1998, the Lord took him closer to his eternal reward. Memorial services were, of course, multiplied. A year later, Lesslie and Helen were reunited.

The Character

Of middling height, sturdy build, and wiry manner, Lesslie Newbigin, in the words now of the anonymous obituary notice in the London *Times* (January 31, 1998), "was strikingly handsome and remained amazingly youthful in appearance well into his seventies." From my first meeting with him in 1963 to my last meeting with him late in 1996, the physical and mental impression he made on me was one of disciplined energy. Warmly acknowledging the personal impact of Newbigin on theology at King's College, London, in recent years, Professor Colin Gunton speaks of Lesslie as "something of a driven man."[23] As they met him in various arenas, many people sensed that the driving force was the Holy Spirit. "Lesslie in the flesh was quite as alluring as Lesslie in print," said Bishop Hugh Montefiore at the memorial service in Southwark's Anglican cathedral, and "one always knew that any advice he gave was both wise and prayer-laden." Lesslie, of course, did not parade his prayer life, but from glimpses we know that he always began "[his] morning prayers by singing a hymn—even if only under [his] breath," and that for a long time he "used Lancelot Andrewes' *Preces Privatae* as a guide in the quiet hour each morning."[24] "When he asked how you were," said Dan Beeby in his address at Lesslie's funeral, "you knew it was a prayer-backed question," which was exactly in keeping with the charge he laid upon his presbyters as bishop in Madras.[25] And in the obituary notice he wrote for the London *Independent* (February 4, 1998), Beeby recounted that to the very end Lesslie's "brilliance, pastoral care and missionary zeal were all present in the two 'sermons' he preached in intensive care a few days before he died."

"Humility," "kindness," and "courtesy" are words that frequently recur in people's characterization of Lesslie Newbigin. His habitual gentleness did not exclude firmness in argument. He recognized "impatience" as a trait in himself. On no more than a couple of occasions, Martin Conway recalls Lesslie's turning "terse" after a disagreement. Certainly he could be forthright. Hans-Ruedi Weber—in 1961 a young man on the way to becoming himself a distinguished missiologist and biblical expositor but hailing from a "Swiss village background and having no Oxford and Cambridge degrees"—accompanied Newbigin to the meeting in Samoa from which sprang the Pacific Conference of Churches:

> Early during the Malua meeting Lesslie took me aside and severely criticized something I had said during the first or second introduction to the Bible studies on Galatians. He felt that I had been carried away by rhetoric and had made Paul say things which were not in the text. (What exactly the point was, I no longer remember.) Lesslie was deeply worried about this, and in a brotherly but very firm way he corrected me. This small incident is certainly typical of the way Lesslie collaborated with others, and quite a few of his colleagues did not always like his frankness.[26]

Far more of Newbigin's colleagues, like Weber himself, let nothing impair their esteem and affection for the man.

Two collaborators who knew Lesslie Newbigin well in day-to-day work were Leslie Brown, a fellow missionary in South India, and Hakim Rahi, his associate pastor at Winson Green. Brown, who went on to become an Anglican bishop and archbishop in Uganda and then Bishop of St. Edmondsbury and Ipswich, wrote this to me: "Lesslie has been since then not only a dear friend but a hero. He was at my consecration in 1953, but Abp. Fisher wouldn't let him lay on hands. He was also with us in Uganda and took a quiet day for the bps before they elected me Archbishop. To see a true bishop I look at Lesslie."[27] Hakim Rahi wrote this: "For me to make any kind of comment about the ministry of Bishop Lesslie Newbigin is like a tiny lamp trying to comment about the sun. I am certain I can never find adequate words to describe that adorable person. It was sheer good luck or divine grace that gave me the rare privilege to work with him."[28] At a service of thanksgiving in St. Paul's Cathedral, London, for the golden jubilee of Newbigin's consecration to the episcopate in the CSI, Bishop Colin Buchanan recalled a very difficult time in his own life as an Anglican suffragan in Birmingham: "I was distanced from my own diocese and, in a caring way, Lesslie in effect became my bishop. So I owe him a personal debt which is over and above all that I learned from him as a theologian." The speaker concluded with the observation that "there is something wonderfully young in Lesslie—a touch perhaps of God's sunlit eternity."[29]

In his later years a number of article-length tributes to Newbigin's life and work had already appeared in quite varied locations: those, for instance, of Bernard Thorogood, then general secretary of the United Reformed Church, in the *International Review of Mission* (1990), of Martin Conway in the *Epworth Review* (1994), and of Tim Stafford in *Christianity Today* (1996).[30] The January 1990 issue of the *International Review of Mission* in fact contained a whole batch of shorter pieces, "In Tribute to Bishop Lesslie Newbigin," by a score of prominent ecumenists and missiologists, including Cardinal Jan Willebrands, Bishop Hans Joachim Held of Germany, Professor C. F. Hallencreutz of Sweden, Professor Charles West of Princeton, Dr. M. M. Thomas of Bangalore, and Dr. Pauline Webb of the BBC. To mark Newbigin's eighty-fifth birthday in 1994, a festschrift with international contributions was edited in India under the title *Many Voices in Christian Mission*.[31]

From this wealth of illuminating material two items may be picked out, both from Indian sources. The first is an anecdote from Bishop Sundar Clarke, Newbigin's successor in Madras, who affectionately called his predecessor "a bishop on the run":

> There had been heavy rains which had destroyed a number of houses, huts and school buildings. Without delay Lesslie rushed to these spots and found roofless schools and stunned, apathetic people. He called for a ladder, climbed it, asked the local people to pass him the leaves that had blown off, and began to thatch a shed to make into a school. It was a fascinating spectacle to see him so involved and exhibiting his faith and theology to a people who had lost not only their roofs but were also spiritually shattered. He did it and he got them to do it! In this sense he did theology and got people to do theology in life and in situations of need.[32]

The second, chosen partly to ward off accusations of "hagiography" of a kind that got the genre a bad name, is a very ambivalent piece by Paolos Mar Gregorios (Verghese), Syrian Orthodox Metropolitan of New Delhi, whose relationship with Newbigin had known tense moments over the years:

Lesslie Newbigin and I went to Geneva at about the same time—soon after the Third Assembly of the WCC in New Delhi, 1961. We were both from India—in different ways—but had met for the first time at the Assembly. He came from the missionary empire of the Western Church, and from the nation of my colonial masters. I had just been ordained an Orthodox priest, barely a month or so beforehand. I was in every sense a novice in the Church, having lived and worked in the world as a layman for the first thirty-nine years of my life.

Our positions in the WCC headquarters were similar. He was in charge of the division of world mission and evangelism; I was director of the division of ecumenical action. We were both associate general secretaries and met often with Dr. Visser 't Hooft, the general secretary. We started our work in the old "barracks" at 17 route de Malagnou, and I was excited about the prophetic pioneering that the WCC had already done for more than a decade by then.

I admired Lesslie for the lucidity of his linguistic expression, for the clarity with which he could present his case, for the transparency of his commitment to Christ and to the unity of the Church, and for the simplicity of his lifestyle.

But our backgrounds were so different from each other. I came from a Church that experienced the mission of the Western Church as a disruptive and in many ways destructive force. I came from a situation in which the Church was one until the Western missionaries came as colonists and conquered it by money and political military power. To me, the kind of mission the Western Church represented was the source of disunity and unbelief while for Newbigin it was the agent of Church unity. To me, Augustinian Christianity (both Roman Catholic and Protestant) represented a deviation from the teaching of Christ—a tragic deviation that has hurt humanity. For Newbigin, Augustine was a great Christian thinker, in fact the one thinker by whose standards other thinkers were to be judged.

So our views often clashed. Newbigin is a great teacher, and was a very popular missionary among the Tamil Christians of my land. Sometimes I felt he was treating me with a kind of paternalistic condescension, which he must have acquired in my country, living with doting Christian disciples.

The net result was that most of my ideas about what Christians should do in the world were politely ignored or actively countered, as coming out of innocent ignorance, out of lack of proper instruction by Western masters of Christianity.

This is a time to pay a tribute to a great Protestant soul who has dedicated his life to serving Christ as he knew and understood, a fruitful life of fourscore years. May God grant him many more years of selfless and humble service in the vineyard of the Lord.[33]

From among Newbigin's many human relationships two in particular may be selected for viewing from Lesslie's side: first M. M. Thomas, and then W. A. Visser't Hooft. Having met him a year earlier, Lesslie became properly acquainted with Madathilparamphil Mammen Thomas in 1942, the year in which "M. M." was rejected both for ordination by his Mar Thoma Church (because his politics were too radical) and for membership in the Communist Party (because he was not prepared to refrain from openly preaching the Gospel). Although M. M. was the younger by seven years, Newbigin later named him as the man he "would choose as guru in that difficult area of thought which deals with the meaning of the Gospel in politics, culture, and the inter-faith dialogue."[34] Thomas eventually became director of the Christian Institute for the Study of Religion and Society in Bangalore (from 1962) and chairman of the central committee of the World Council of Churches (1968–75). As will appear later in this book, Newbigin and he served each other frequently as sparring partners. "In a very rare measure," said Newbigin of Thomas, "he has held together the things which tear most of us apart. Deeply committed to involvement in the secular issues of our time, he has at the same time lived by a deep and growing personal faith centred in the risen Jesus. Realistic in his exposure of the sins of the churches, he has yet remained deeply rooted in and loyal to the Church of his own birth." The "coherent theological pattern" in Thomas "has had the risen Christ as its centre and the whole world as its circumference. To speak in Hindu terms, M. M. has held together in his own discipleship the way of action (*karma*), the way of wisdom (*jnana*), and the way of devotion (*bhakti*). We do well to thank God for this gift to the Church of our day."

Willem Adolf Visser 't Hooft, said Newbigin, "is widely remembered and honoured as the first General Secretary and (in large measure) the architect of the World Council of Churches. It is less often remembered that his central passion from beginning to end of his active life was for the missionary faithfulness of the Church."[35] Nine years older than Newbigin, "Wim" was from the start deeply respected by Lesslie as a senior colleague in the ecumenical institutions and became an increasingly close friend, as is evident in the many references to Visser 't Hooft in *Unfinished Agenda* and in correspondence between the two. Theologically, the two were related through their Reformed ancestry and through their appreciation of Hendrik Kraemer and (more slowly in Newbigin's case) Karl Barth. Newbigin heard especially Visser 't Hooft's repeated castigations of "syncretism," whether in the "national" churches of Europe or in the "democratic" churches of America or in unguarded attempts at "indigenization" in other cultures (Visser 't Hooft looked rather, with Kraemer, for "subversive fulfilment"). Visser 't Hooft's concern for the Church of Jesus Christ was that it might credibly witness across all frontiers to "the royal freedom of the Gospel"; the reach of the divine sovereignty into every sphere of life was not to be achieved by annexation of elements in the secular that stood in blatant contradiction to the Christian faith. Christianity was now in debate, even battle, with "scientific rationalism" and "neo-pagan vitalism." These themes resound also through Newbigin's thought and work.

The Reader and Writer

Given all Newbigin's multifarious activities, it is hard to think of him, for all the formidable energy he possessed, as an exhaustive reader, and certainly he did not feel it necessary to display his learning in footnotes to his own writings. Rather he appears to have made discerning choices among the literature that providentially came his way (sometimes with the help of friends) and then, by penetrating and receptive reading (with techniques learned from his geography master), to have made a critical and constructive appropriation of the ideas from such works as they suited the themes he was engaged on at the time and which would stay with him over the years.

Newbigin was, in fact, given to naming such-and-such a book as among "the three or four most crucial books" he had read. Thinking to make a count, I consulted Lesslie, and we arrived—by conversation, correspondence, and finally an audioletter he sent me as late as December 1997—at an agreed short list. When, as a young man, he was moving back "from unbelief to belief," he was convinced by William James's *The Will to Believe* that there were not three options—belief, unbelief, and agnosticism—but only two, to trust or not to trust, and that the will was involved in this decision. Eric Fenn's "little paperback" *Things and Persons* (1931) introduced him to Martin Buber's *Ich und Du* and "was quite decisive for the argument with scientific determinism, which up till then had seemed to me to present impassable barriers"; he was also reading G. A. Studdert Kennedy's writings during that period. While a theological student at Westminster College, Cambridge, Lesslie was turned by the study of James Denney's *Romans*, he said, from "theological liberalism" to a lifelong evangelical belief in the objective atonement wrought by Christ on the Cross. During the second half of the 1930s Newbigin was preoccupied with the relation of the Gospel to politics, and Reinhold Niebuhr's Gifford Lectures on *The Nature and Destiny of Man*, the first part of which he heard in Edinburgh in the spring of 1939, "brought together and consolidated the kind of thinking with which I had been wrestling during those years." Similarly, Hendrik Kraemer's *The Christian Message in a Non-Christian World* (1938) "consolidated and affirmed what I was not very coherently feeling my way to"; Kraemer's book continued to represent "a nodal point" for Newbigin's thinking. C. N. Cochrane's "brilliant" *Christianity and Classical Culture* (1940) helped Newbigin to grasp the decisive importance of the Nicene and Athanasian doctrine of the Trinity and how St. Augustine was able to build upon its foundation a new worldview that would shape the thought of Western Christendom for a thousand years. At the final approach, in the 1940s, to the union of the churches in South India, it was A. M. Ramsey's *The Gospel and the Catholic Church* (1936) which changed Newbigin's mind in favor of "the compatibility of a catholic belief in an historic succession with my evangelical belief about the Gospel." Newbigin read the "seminal" works of Roland Allen—*Missionary Methods—St. Paul's or Ours?* (1912) and *The Spontaneous Expansion of the Church and the Causes which Hinder it* (1927)—during the early years of his episcopate in Madurai, when he was confronted with congregations that lacked paid leadership and found that they were often the most lively, although he had already, during his time as a district missionary in Kanchipuram, been anxious to "win the local village congregations away from a wrong kind of dependence on the mission bungalow." J. H. Oldham had tried for many years to persuade Newbigin to read Michael Polanyi, the Hungarian scientist and philosopher of science, but Newbigin first did so with the Gifford Lectures, *Personal Knowledge*, fairly soon after their appearance in 1958; having once read the book, he resolved to reread it every ten years, and "certainly I have read it several times since." In the decade of the 1960s Newbigin got "a bit carried away by the enthusiasm for the secular" and was, as he later judged, too much influenced by the thesis of A. T. van Leeuwen's *Christianity and World History* (1964). After being repelled as a theological student by Karl Barth's writings, Newbigin became captivated by the man when he worked with him in person in the 1950s, and he resolved to read the *Church Dogmatics* in their entirety after his retirement; this he accomplished in 1974–75, having been led "by the grace of God to start with section four and then work backwards; otherwise I would never have survived."

None of the books Newbigin read in his later years seems to rank as "decisive," but his writings show that he was perfectly willing to pick up and run with ideas from a number of them, such as the tardily discovered classic by Paul Hazard, *La crise de la conscience européenne* (1935), Hans Frei's *The Eclipse of Biblical Narrative* (1974), Alasdair MacIntyre's *After Virtue* (1981) and *Whose Justice? Which Rationality?* (1988), Michael Buckley's *At the Origins of Modern Atheism* (1987), Carver T. Yu's *Being and Relation: A Theological Critique of Western Dualism and Individualism* (1987), or Christopher Kaiser's *Creation and the History of Science* (1991). Tom Wright, dean of Litchfield and New Testament scholar, has told me how Newbigin, when his eyesight was failing, had his "reading teams" work with him through Wright's *The New Testament and the People of God* and *Jesus and the Victory of God*. Newbigin found in such work the refutation of the historically and theologically "destructive scholarship of so many trends in the last thirty years" which Lesslie "knew in his bones couldn't actually be getting to the heart of the matter."[36]

Passing from Newbigin the reader to Newbigin the writer, we find that he wrote in many modes and idioms. He kept up a prolific correspondence, private, professional, and public. To give just one example from the latter domain: In October and November of 1989 he was exchanging letters with high officials of the Royal Mail in an effort to keep postal employees from obligatory work on Sundays at a time when the resumption of Sunday collections was being planned and the introduction of Sunday deliveries was being considered. Newbigin's epistolary margins were narrow; he reused the blank backs of older letters; he never liked to retire an envelope. It was not just when his eyesight failed that one needed to be aware of the keys that stand in proximity to those his fingers actually struck, although the postscript of a late letter to me both makes and illustrates the point: "My typing is an exercise of faith, but I hope grace will enable you to guess my intention in vases where I have hit the wrong key."[37]

Newbigin's prepared addresses or his incisive interventions could shape or turn a meeting. On one occasion he asked a president of the South African Methodist Conference whether he would like his speech "flavoured with sugar or with salt."[38] Newbigin was a master draftsman of ecumenical documents. We shall see him at work in the IMC Willingen conference of 1952 and in composing the description of unity that would be adopted by the WCC at the New Delhi assembly in 1961, and these two instances must stand for many. His clarity of mind, his fairness in summary, and his freshness and fluency with language all earned him trust. As anyone who has done the job will know, willingness to take on the drafting task also gives one—especially if one learns to be receptive of other suggestions rather than defensive of one's own first efforts—an unequaled influence on the final outcome.

On ecumenical occasions Lesslie could also craft limericks to "relieve the times of weariness." In *Unfinished Agenda*, he gives just one sample that captures some prominent figures from the time of a WCC Central Committee meeting during a hot and drowsy afternoon in New Haven, in 1957.

George Florovsky was making a very long and largely incomprehensible speech. Franklin Fry in the chair was maintaining a firm and soldierly appearance. Ernest Payne, the vicechairman, at his side, was visibly wilting. The following lines seemed to flow unbidden onto the pad on my knee:

> Florovsky is speaking again.
> His meaning is not at all plain.
> But while Franklin C. Fry
> Will never say die
> It clearly gives Ernest A. Payne.

Unfortunately D. T. Niles at my side saw, read, seized and passed the paper along the row. I don't think the chairman ever understood why the committee's decorum so suddenly disintegrated.[39]

In later years Lesslie compiled a collection prefaced thus: "I am normally a good sleeper. When occasionally sleep evades me, I concoct limericks. This gentle form of mental exercise is sufficiently interesting to banish boredom, but not so exciting as to produce unwanted stimulation. There is no hurry. If it refuses to come out right, there is always another night; if it does 'click' one drops off to sleep. Something accomplished, something done has earned a night's repose. It is a tranquilliser with positively no harmful side-effects." The collection took off from the names of places which St. Paul visited (or might have). Here are two examples with some theological significance:

The Final Equations

> A cosmologist living in Thrace
> said "Time's just a hiccup in space."
> At this Stephen Hawking
> said "Ah! Now you're talking,
> and God's just the grin on its face."

Original Sin

> The bad little boys of Apulia
> have a badness unique and peculiar.

> All moral instruction
> is met with obstruction,
> and rules only make them unrulier.

Some of Lesslie's limericks were read by family members at his funeral and memorial services.[40]

Newbigin's handwritten lectures—for instance, of the Bangalore series of 1941 on "The Kingdom of God and the Idea of Progress" or the Henry Martyn series of 1986 on "Church, World, Kingdom"—reveal that he did little or no stylistic revision, although he would sometimes make cuts of a paragraph's length for reasons of timing (he would write the estimated delivery time of a page at the top of page 1). His texts as printed could sometimes have profited from a little editorial tightening to avoid verbal repetitions or to lighten some lengthy prepositional phrases ("in terms of" and such). At its frequent best, however, Newbigin's published writing was vigorous and colorful; he could be trenchant, but his blade was a scalpel rather than a scimitar, curative rather than destructive.

Newbigin's bibliography runs to several hundred titles, depending on the categories of writing included.[41] The books, in particular, need to be located in their biographical and geographical circumstances. The first, *Christian Freedom in the Modern World* (1937), was written on board ship during the first passage to India; it was a critical response to John Macmurray's *Freedom in the Modern World*, which was receiving favorable attention in the British Student Christian Movement at the time but seemed to Newbigin antinomian in tendency. The need to "defend the South India scheme" in face of English Anglican critics in particular led to Newbigin's *The Reunion of the Church* (1948), which was republished in 1960 with an extensive new introduction that could draw on a dozen years of life since union in the CSI and answer the continuing criticisms. Newbigin's early years as a bishop in the CSI are recounted in *A South India Diary* (1951), published in the United States as *That All May Be One* (1952); many readers who encountered the text through the SCM's Religious Book Club testify to the profound impression made on them by this narrative combination of evangelism, ecumenism, and episcopal care. The author's formal ecclesiology in unitive, missionary, and eschatological perspective is found in *The Household of God* (SCM 1953), the book of his Kerr Lectures in the University of Glasgow, which achieved the status of a classic and was reissued as such by Paternoster Press in 1998. Newbigin's *Sin and Salvation* (1956) started life in Tamil as the bishop's aid for village teachers in the Madurai and neighboring dioceses and was taken up, in English, by the Religious Book Club.

Both *One Body, One Gospel, One World* (1958) and the inelegantly entitled *Relevance of Trinitarian Doctrine for Today's Mission* (1963), improved in the United States to *Trinitarian Faith and Today's Mission*, stem from their author's involvement with the International Missionary Council and the WCC's Division of World Mission and Evangelism, in whose successive employment he was during the period of the IMC's integration with the WCC. *A Faith for This*

One World? (1961) resulted from the William Belden Noble Lectures given in 1958 at Harvard, a place noted for its comparative studies in religion. *Honest Religion for Secular Man* (1966), the Firth Lectures at the University of Nottingham in 1964, show Newbigin at the height of his—never blind—flirtation with the ideas of the decade.

By the time of his Lyman Beecher Lectures at Yale in 1966, published as *The Finality of Christ* (1969), Newbigin was back in India as CSI bishop in Madras, where he also delivered *Christ Our Eternal Contemporary* (1968) as addresses to the Christian Medical College, Vellore. That was the venue, too, for *Journey into Joy* (1972). A collection of the bishop's communion homilies for his coworkers in Madras, first published there in 1974, was adopted by Archbishop Coggan of Canterbury for his Lent Book of 1977, *"The Good Shepherd": Meditations on Christian Ministry in Today's World.*

Newbigin's missiological teaching at the Selly Oak Colleges in Birmingham, where he served from 1974 to 1979, was deposited in *The Open Secret* (1978), which was republished in slightly revised form in 1995. His long-matured exposition of the Fourth Gospel, *The Light Has Come,* was issued in 1982, by which time he was serving as a local pastor in Winson Green. Newbigin's entry into the "1984" project of the British Council of Churches was marked by *The Other Side of 1984,* the themes of which were much more fully developed in his 1984 Warfield Lectures at Princeton Theological Seminary, *Foolishness to the Greeks: The Gospel and Western Culture* (1986). The desired "missionary encounter with modernity" became the subject of many shorter writings during Newbigin's final retirement. The most comprehensive statement of his thinking in the later years of his life is found in the book resulting from his Alexander Robertson Lectureship in the University of Glasgow, *The Gospel in a Pluralist Society* (1989). The continuing vigor of his thought finds expression in his last book, coauthored with Lamin Sanneh and Jenny Taylor, *Faith and Power: Christianity and Islam in "Secular" Britain* (1998). Meanwhile, backed by diaries kept and letters written over the years, Newbigin had in 1985 published his autobiography as *Unfinished Agenda* and then brought the business up to date with a postscript in 1993.

In dealing with writings composed by Newbigin over a period of sixty-odd years and in various cultural contexts, I have had to make certain decisions concerning grammar and typography when quoting from them. In general, British spelling and punctuation have been retained in quotations from works published in the United Kingdom or in India, whereas American conventions have been kept for works published in the United States. The reader will notice the trend of printers over recent decades to reduce pronouns referring to God from initial capitals to lowercase. On the other hand, there are indications that Newbigin himself continued to capitalize Gospel, Church, Kingdom, and Scripture, and I have standardized usage in that sense, particularly as it matches my own predilection. On the matter of gender-inclusive language, Newbigin wrote as follows in the preface to *The Gospel in a Pluralist Society* (1989): "Like all people who have used the English language I have until recently been accustomed to using the masculine pronoun inclusively to refer to both halves of the human family. That this is, for valid reasons, no longer acceptable to many readers poses a problem for the writer. To use both pronouns ("he or she") at every point can make sentences intolerably convoluted. I have therefore used both "he" and "she" inclusively and—I hope—impartially. I hope that this will not expose me to any serious charge of moral delinquency." Subsequently his preferred solution seems to have been to turn phrases so as to minimize the use of generic pronouns altogether. I have not made anachronistic changes where quoting or closely paraphrasing earlier writings. Bible quotations have been maintained in the versions originally cited by Newbigin. Where I make my own use of the Bible I have consistently cited according to the Revised Standard Version, thereby respecting the English-language translation that prevailed in ecumenical circles for a very long period in Newbigin's life. In leading the reader straight through a particular writing of Newbigin, I have usually not considered it necessary to give page references for every quotation; instead, I have provided a few landmarks that would allow the researcher to retrace the route in the originals.

The Theological Life

Newbigin theologized in the midst of practice and for its better pursuit. He never rushed into major projects or programs without consideration, and the lessons he learned in action he passed on to others. He preached what he practiced—or, like Chaucer's good priest, "first he wrought, and afterward he taught." As observed by Hans-Ruedi Weber, Lesslie "was an initiator and animator of ideas, of an ever new common search, and often also a sharp critic, based on biblical insights. He liked to be at the beginning of things, at the frontier of thinking and initiatives."[42] These engagements with new challenges were what lent punch and shifting nuances to Newbigin's thought and writing. The lineaments of his thinking, however, remained constant for sixty years, and as his ideas developed and expanded, the fundamental pattern continued to be readily recognizable. In this book I argue that Christ's atoning work constituted the center, set within an increasingly explicit trinitarian frame and persistently directed toward the goal of God's reign.

The confident believer is shown faithful to the sight of a cosmic Cross, expounding the entire work of Christ as our salvation from sin, and confessing the Resurrection as the foundation stone of a new creation. The direct evangelist is seen bearing individual and institutional witness to students, landless villagers, industrial workers, urban professionals, and modern intellectuals concerning the universal Gospel of the One who is the same yesterday, today, and forever. The ecumenical advocate appears tireless in the defense and encouragement of what makes for "the unity of all in each place" within the household of God as the congregation of the faithful, the body of Christ, and the community of the Holy Spirit. The pastoral bishop is watched exercising the cure of souls and the care of the churches in two South Indian dioceses and then on the local and national scene in Britain, setting an example to the flock in their own proper ministries among their neighbors. The missionary strategist is followed drawing implications from his experience as a foreigner in India for the cross-cultural nature of the global Church's task in fulfillment of its duty, at home and abroad, of letting people into God's "open secret." The religious interlocutor is heard in friendly yet firm debate with Hindus, responding to the challenge of Islam as a respected rival, and in sharp conflict with Western academic pluralists who seemed to him to have surrendered their birthright. The social visionary, passionate in his concern for living human beings, is observed clarifying the distinctions between the Kingdom of God and the idea of progress, between a Constantinian state and a Christian society, between welfare and justice, between liberty and license. The liturgical preacher presents on the ecumenical stage a drama of word and sacrament, whose directions he had helped to compose for the *Book of Common Worship* of the Church of South India, the whole being said and done to the glory of the Triune God. The scriptural teacher is discovered expounding the Bible as God's story with the world, interpreting the authoritative texts in light of the classic rule of faith, and inviting others to learn further with himself. The Christian apologist is caught puzzling over the relation between Christianity and modernity and then cutting through the ambiguities in order to offer in the Gospel a new-old alternative to other worldviews that always end up in either self-idolatry or despair, if not both.

The lens of Newbigin's life, work, and thought gives access to wider pictures, both retrospectively and prospectively. Retrospectively, Lesslie Newbigin instantiated the ecumenical movement for a good fifty years, and so some of the most significant and complex developments in the twentieth-century history of Christianity may be viewed through him: Faith and Order, Life and Work, Mission and Evangelism; the World Council of Churches; successes and failures in national and local unions; the *aggiornamento* of the Roman Catholic Church at the Second Vatican Council, and the consequent growth of bilateral relationships among the Christian world communions stimulated by the entrance of that Church on the ecumenical scene. All this was taking place, of course, amid one of the most agitated periods in global history, and the reader is invited never to lose sight of what can only be minimally recalled here: two world wars, the Communist revolutions in Russia and China, the rise and fall of the Soviet Empire, the decolonization of much of what has been regarded as "the third world," the staggering growth of science and technology, the decline in numbers and influence of the Western churches, the burgeoning of churches in parts of Africa and Asia, the reinvigoration and spread of Islam, the philosophical deconstruction of modernity, and so forth. The reader will remain aware of the geopolitical, ecclesiastical, and intellectual currents with and against which Newbigin swam.

Prospectively, movements and developments began that will continue to influence Church and world in the twenty-first century. Newbigin addressed several of them in their early stages, and insights and guidance may be found in his work for the ways in which Christians may regard these influences as they go forward. His life and writings, in fact, touch directly and powerfully on several of the most lively issues facing the churches and the theologians: the transmission of the Gospel along the axes of time and space, which raises questions of tradition and evangelization and the hermeneutical and communicational aspects of them; the relation between the Christian faith and competing worldviews; the emergent "clash of civilizations" on some sort of a religious basis; the current political, economic, and ecological ordering of the world in light of God's proclaimed and awaited Kingdom; the historic role of the Christian West, its slide into religious and intellectual apostasy, and its need for revitalization; the new geographical configurations of the Church, with the apparent southward shift in its center of gravity; issues of authenticity and multiculturalism at local and universal levels; the thriving of "independent" and "charismatic" companies of Christians and the tiredness of some older "denominations"; the forging of new theological alliances across continuing confessional and institutional lines, as between (say) "catholics" and "evangelicals"; issues of life, death, and conduct in the areas of bioethics and sexual morality. The reader may see all these matters, too, on the horizon in looking through the lens of Newbigin's theology.

Trying my hand at what Newbigin called "the lowliest of art-forms," I might provisionally sum up the subject of this book as follows:

A Presbyterian Bishop from India,
never short for theological ginger,
in the end did his best
to reconvert the West—
and bequeathed an *Unfinished Agenda.*

1

The Confident Believer

I have been crucified with Christ; it is no longer I who live, but Christ who lives in me; and the life I now live in the flesh I live by faith in the Son of God, who loved me and gave himself for me.

(Galatians 2:20)

Grasped by Christ

"Faith is the hand that grasps what Christ has done and makes it my own"; but first, "Christ has laid hold of me." That expresses the intensely personal character of the faith within which Lesslie Newbigin's own life was lived and in which all his more technical discussions must be situated. The particular formulation just quoted of what it is to be a Christian believer occurs in the book *Sin and Salvation*, which the bishop wrote in the 1950s for village teachers who, with little formal theological education, carried a heavy load in the pastoral care of several thousand rural congregations in the Tamil-speaking dioceses of the Church of South India.[1] The book was begun in Tamil, and when pressures of time necessitated a shift to English composition, the author adopted a style that would lend itself to translation into the vernacular. Addressing a situation in which both teachers and students needed a statement of the Gospel in its most basic form, the book contains the heart of the evangelical faith such as Newbigin himself had discovered it during his own days as a theological student in Britain in the 1930s and such as he would continue to commend it on his return to his home country in the 1970s. That faith undergirded his thinking, his practical ministry, and his entire existence. That is why this theological biography begins with an account of Newbigin as a believer: his faith—or more exactly the Christ whose grasp he returned—constituted the core of his identity and the substance of his message. Both comprehensive and concise, the Indian book will provide most material for the exposition in this fundamental chapter; but the systematic account of the source, object, content, and process of the gospel faith found in *Sin and Salvation* will be enclosed by the story of Newbigin's first arrival at that faith and by his later development of it as proper confidence in the universal sovereignty of the Savior.

29 ... *the Christ whose grasp we return*"

The evangelist speaks of what he knows. "I believed, and so I spoke," wrote St. Paul in 2 Corinthians 4:13–15, following the Psalmist; and so it was with Newbigin. Having been laid hold of by Christ and having grasped what Christ has done, like the apostle he testified in the Spirit of faith to the salvation which God has wrought in Christ and is waiting to extend by grace to more and more people so that the chorus of thanksgiving may swell to God's glory. In considering Newbigin as believer, we must therefore give attention both to the fact of his belief and to the content of his belief. Phrased in the terms of technical theology, the *fides qua creditur* and the *fides quae creditur* are coordinates: "the faith by which one believes" and "the faith which one believes" call for each other; the act of faith is directed toward the God who summons it and about whom the believer then may and must speak.

According to his own autobiographical account, Newbigin had by the end of his schooldays with the Quakers at Leighton Park "abandoned the Christian assumptions of home and childhood." That faith of some kind was not beyond the bounds of rational possibility was kept open for him by the reading of William James's *The Will to Believe*, picked up from his father's bookshelves.[2] As an undergraduate at Cambridge, he was attracted by friends into the company of the Student Christian Movement and learned to read the Bible and pray as a seeker. In his first summer vacation from the university he worked in a social service center run by the Society of Friends in the Rhondda Valley of South Wales; and amid the distress of miners "rotting for years in hopeless unemployment and destitution," and stimulated perhaps by a reading in William Temple, he saw in the night "a vision of the Cross, but it was the Cross spanning the space between heaven and earth, between ideals and present realities, and with arms that embraced the whole world":

> I saw it as something which reached down to the most hopeless and sordid of human misery and yet promised life and victory. I was sure that night, in a way I had never been before, that this was the clue I must follow if I were to make any kind of sense of the world. From that moment I would always know how to take bearings when I was lost. I would know where to begin again when I had come to the end of all my own resources of understanding or courage.[3]

Having become active in the Student Christian Movement at Cambridge, Newbigin was upon graduation appointed to its national staff in Scotland. In the deep economic recession of the early 1930s, his Christian concern addressed social conditions, but any tendency to limit the need to a temporal amelioration of human life was tempered by both a memory and a trip abroad that marked Newbigin deeply. While on a student mission from Cambridge to industrial Lancashire, he had "visited a tenement where three families had to live in a single small flat, and at least one of the men was dying of tuberculosis": "When I struggled to find words for that situation I knew once and for all that a merely humanistic hope was not enough. At that point my talk about a new social order was impertinent nonsense." The other experience took longer to acquire its proper interpretation. In 1932 Newbigin visited

Germany and was "taken in by the freshness and the vitality" of the National Socialist youth. When "the demonic character" of Nazism became obvious, the lesson made him, he said, ever thereafter "skeptical" toward claims by "the new wave" to be "God at work in the world."[4]

When, in 1933, Newbigin returned to Cambridge for three years of ministerial training at the Presbyterian Church's Westminster College, he managed to secure freedom enough in his program for a good deal of personal reading in exploration of the Christian faith. He settled on the Letter to the Romans as likely "the most complete and condensed statement of the Gospel," and the influence of that epistle of St. Paul's on his thought was to be lasting and profound.[5] He spent months with the Greek text, thereby acquiring the habit of familiarity with the original that was more common among theological students then than it has since become; and that practice certainly affected the Bible studies that he was to conduct as an important part of his several later ministries. Karl Barth's celebrated commentary on Romans, which in the aftermath of the First World War had signaled the shift in continental Protestant theology to a dialectical and eschatological version of the Christian faith, Newbigin found "incomprehensible" at the time, although he would later become deeply indebted to the mature Barth of the *Church Dogmatics*. Nor yet was he satisfied with the recently published commentary on *The Epistle of Paul to the Romans* by the English Congregationalist C. H. Dodd. Dodd took the wrath of God on which the apostle expatiates in the second half of the first chapter as "not a certain feeling or attitude of God towards us, but some process or effect in the realm of objective facts, an inevitable process of cause and effect in a moral universe." If, however, "'wrath' was only an anthropomorphic way of describing the consequences of sin," then according to Newbigin "'love' would have to be explained along the same lines." Coupled with Dodd's "demythologizing" of God's wrath was his preference for "expiation" over "propitiation" as a rendering of *hilasterion* in Romans 3:25, lest the latter term suggest "the placating of an angry God." Newbigin was more persuaded by the tougher route to affirming the love of God followed by James Denney, the professor of systematic and pastoral theology at the Free Church College in Glasgow, in his commentary on Romans in *The Expositor's Greek Testament*. According to Denney, who had published in 1909 a classic work, *The Death of Christ: Its Place and Interpretation in the New Testament*, the mercy of God does not discount the holiness of God that cannot abide sin, and the freely given gift of righteousness to the sinner comes at a price to God:

> Grace does not signify that moral distinctions are ignored in God's procedure: the righteousness which is held out in the Gospel is held out on the basis of the redemption which is in Christ Jesus. It is put within the sinner's reach at great cost. It could never be offered to him—it could never be manifested, or indeed have any real existence—but for the propitiatory virtue of the blood of Christ. Christ a propitiation is the inmost soul of the Gospel for sinful men. If God had not set Him forth in this character, not only must we despair for ever of attaining to a Divine righteousness; all our attempts to read the story

of the world in any consistency with the character of God must be baffled. ...It is a demonstration of His righteousness—that is, in the widest sense, of His consistency with His own character—which would have been violated by indifference to sin. And that demonstration is, by God's grace, given in such a way that it is possible for Him to be (as He intends to be) just Himself, and the justifier of those who believe in Jesus. The propitiatory death of Jesus, in other words, is at once the vindication of God and the salvation of man. That is why it is central and fundamental in the Apostolic Gospel. It meets the requirements, at the same time, of the righteousness of God and of the sin of man.[6]

Newbigin credited Denney's insights into Romans as the decisive factor in this "turning point" in his theological journey: "I began the study as a typical liberal. I ended it with a strong conviction about 'the finished work of Christ,' about the centrality and objectivity of the atonement accomplished on Calvary." Such passages from Denney as the one just quoted find echoes in Newbigin's *Sin and Salvation* and time and time again when he is expounding the Gospel as a believer and offering it as an evangelist for the response of faith.

Three Student Papers

An early theological exercise of Newbigin's was the exegetical paper he wrote at Westminster College for W. A. L. Elmslie in November 1935 on the Hebrew text of Exodus 30:11–16 (which is interpreted as the provision for a poll tax or levy for the initial construction of the tent of meeting—forerunner of the temple—where "atonement" is to take place).[7] Newbigin develops from the phrase *kopher naphshō* in particular a detailed consideration of the concept of atonement in the Old Testament. He notes that the verb *kpr* ("to make atonement") is never used in the Old Testament with God as its direct object (in the way in which pagan practice is to "appease the deity"). This is remarkable because (and this observation provoked from Elmslie the marginal comment of "excellent") "in view of the deep Hebrew conviction that all sin is ultimately sin against God, we might have expected that God would have become the natural object of this verb which denotes the covering or expiation of sin and its consequences. The fact that this is not so springs from the equally fundamental truth of the higher Hebrew religion, that God is one who himself undertakes to deal with and 'blot out' sin." Newbigin the student exegete goes on to make the theological comment: "It is, of course, the fact that both these statements about God are true that explains the difficulty of interpreting the word *kpr*. The complexities of its use reflect—as does much theological thought—the struggle of the human mind to hold together the facts that God is both Judge and Saviour, and simple solutions to the problem are apt to arise from the neglect of one of these two truths." When God is the expressed or implied subject of the verb *kpr* (as in Psalms 65:3; 78:38; 79:9; Isaiah 6:

7), the meaning is to blot out, purge, or forgive sin, and "the thought of God as the author of forgiveness quite overshadows the thought of Him as judge." In the ritual code of the second temple (included in what modern critical scholarship has designated the "P" writings), the agent of atonement is the priest, and the instruments are primarily and normally the bloody sacrifices of the sin offering (*hatta'th*) or burnt offering (*'olah*). Yet the system of atonement is not a placatory human invention; rather it is "provided by God Himself for His people, as part of the gracious act by which He redeems them out of bondage and makes them His children."

This thereby precludes any notion of "an absolute alienation of God from His people. Whatever be the things which stand between Him and them, God sees beyond them and provides for their removal." Yet this must not be taken in such a way as to infringe on either God's holiness or human accountability. In a passage which anticipates Newbigin's evangelistic style and the evangelical substance of his views on sin and salvation, on grace and faith, the Cambridge essay proceeds:

> Guilt is not something which can be simply removed as one wipes a dirty mark off the face of a child; no mere act of omnipotence can remove it from without, unless it is to destroy our moral responsibility. And we part company with the biblical conception of God if we do not allow room in our understanding of Him for wrath against the sinful. It is true that the Bible uniformly refuses to pretend that man can appease God's wrath, but it is certainly very far from the idea of a God who cannot be angry with sinful men. God in the Bible speaks to men in living converse according to their condition; He does not merely emit a stream of 'unchanging love' like a wireless broadcasting station which continues to radiate its programme according to a predetermined plan irrespective of what listeners there be and what they think of the programme. Such a conception of love is abstract and unreal and is certainly not biblical. . . . Forgiveness is not merely the washing away of defilement, physically conceived: it is a transaction between God and the guilty soul, and it is apparently regarded as delayed until certain sacrifices have been made by men in accordance with God's instructions.

I disagree

But "why must the 'way to God' be so stained with blood?"

The priestly code, says Newbigin, is seeking to answer the question of how the holy God can dwell in the midst of a people which is unholy. The message of the great prophets and the sequence of disaster upon disaster in the national life have led to a deeper awareness that the covenant by which the Lord binds himself to Israel contains inalienable moral demands. A proper consciousness of guilt recognizes that "atonement" is needed—and receives the assurance that its means have been graciously provided from the divine side to "bridge" the "gulf between God and His people." The blood of sacrifice expresses "that blend of tenderness and wrath which is redemptive love." Looking back, the Christian faith considers the death of Christ as the universal atonement between God and humankind that had been prefigured in the Lord's provisions for Israel: "What we see in the full light of the Cross is the

wrath of humans vs. wrath of God

perfection of that of which the ritual system was the dim outline—at once the gulf that sunders man from God and the graciousness of God who stretches out a redeeming hand even across that gulf. But because love must be known in deeds and not only in symbols, that perfect sacrifice had to be the sacrifice of Himself." So Newbigin concluded his Cambridge essay.

Thus far, faith has appeared as the acceptance of the *redemption* offered by God in Christ. Soteriology needs and supplies its epistemology: the theology of faith must also give an account—even if only after the event—of how we come to know the character of the God who redeems and his acts of redemption. Another Cambridge paper of Newbigin's from the same year, 1935–36, in fact allows a focus now on faith as the reception of *revelation*.[8] Essential to the Christian view of revelation, says Newbigin, is that God can be known only as self-disclosed (for "we know a person only as he chooses to reveal himself")—and yet may precisely so be known "as our own spirit is sensitive and trustful to respond to his revelation." Both divine grace and human knowledge must be so understood as to respect the nature of God and the condition of man: the relations of God and man must be so stated as neither to annihilate man nor to reduce God's revelation to a mere human discovery; and our knowledge, to be true, must on the one hand be "wholly our own inward understanding and valuing" and on the other hand be "wholly concerned with a reality external to our mind." A further vital point to be respected in a theological account of God's communication with us is the social constitution of humankind: "The revelation which is the key to our highest blessedness does not descend to us straight from heaven, but has to reach us passed from hand to hand of our fellow men along the chain of an historic community." That is why the Church is the location of—and the Bible is an instrument for—the reception of the divine self-disclosure.

In the Hebrew canonical scriptures, the revelations are concerned with "the nature of God," with "God's personal will for man," and with "the world from the point of view of man's duty to God." God—who is "so utterly transcendent, and yet so personal and therefore near"—speaks to cheer, to warn, to promise, and to guide. From the case of the prophets, above all, it appears both that God was most truly revealed in the heart and conscience of those who sought him and also that the message was always addressed to the entire people. Perhaps the deepest insight in the whole Old Testament came, says Newbigin, when Hosea "clung to the conviction that both the warring elements in his nature—the voice of judgement and the voice of affection—were true reflections of the heart of God. And that struggle," he continues, "was not resolved till the Son of God Himself bore its stress and conflict in His own body on the Cross." In the New Testament, however, agony and struggle do not have the first or final say: "the first word is good news, and the last word is praise." There is now "a light by which all is seen, and a truth by which all is judged."

What, according to the original testimonies, were the evidences and circumstances of this new and determinative revelation? On what grounds was it believed, and how was it understood? What was the relation of God's self-

disclosure to the human valuation of it? Newbigin again turns characteristically to St. Paul for the shaping of his answers. Human wisdom had allowed
itself to rest in the visible creation rather than glorifying its invisible Maker
(Romans 1:20–32), but now God is revealed through the foolishness of the
preaching (1 Corinthians 1:21)—by the proclamation, that is, of "a set of
historical facts," "how that Christ died for our sins according to the Scriptures, that he was buried, and that he has been raised" (1 Corinthians 15:
3f.). The New Testament places upon us, says Newbigin, "an almost terrifying
responsibility for recognising the light when it shines upon us." The light has
a self-evident authority to the single eye and the pure heart. The teaching of
the New Testament on the relation between revelation and faith may be
summed up in this way:

> On the one hand, God's purpose for man is made known not by the upreach
> of human moral and intellectual striving, but by the downreach of God's
> saving grace. On the other hand, saving grace achieves its end only as it is
> recognised and accepted by men's deepest insights, and it will take no other
> road. Our own unaided insight will not bring us to God; yet only as it accepts
> Him will He come to us; we only receive His light as we recognise it for the
> light; yet it may be very different from what we had expected. God's saving
> word is not spoken *through* our highest faculties; but it is spoken *to* them.

Newbigin finds support for his exposition among the Fathers of the Church.
For them, it is "the union of all [man's] faculties of heart and mind and will,
which alone can lay hold of the revelation"; but this faith, as Origen replies
to Celsus, is "only the religious application of that by which men can attempt
the enterprise of living at all."[9] According to St. Augustine, mankind is originally a creature of the supernatural order who, by the Fall, has become
imperfect; but it knows itself to be so, and there is that in the human which
seeks for the blessedness that cannot be had apart from God's gift. Augustine's
"restless heart" is likened by Newbigin to the stork and the crane and the
swallow of Jeremiah 8:7: as God has planted in these migratory birds an
unerring instinct for their home by which they can find their way, "so in us
He has planted an instinct for Himself which we have but to obey to find
Him." For the Protestant Reformers, "faith is itself the response of the human
soul to the divine self-disclosure, and in that response the revelation is received," revelation being seen as "the revealing of a purpose and the establishing of a personal relation." Karl Barth, however, is right that "the voice
that speaks to our religious insight is the voice of another person and another
will which confronts us with a question and a judgment which is emphatically not that simply of our own highest selves." Finally, God's revelation is
"the love which discloses its nature in the act of seeking its object," and the
human response is "the answer of heart and mind and will to the love that
is seeking [its object]."

Where, more precisely, do Church and Scripture enter as location and instrument for the reception of God's self-disclosure? They enter, says Newbigin,
as witnesses to the life of Christ, which was both the perfect expression of

God's love and the perfect response to that love and hence the reconciliation of humankind to God. The light of Christ's life reaches us through the Church as the community of those who, bound together in the love which Christ brought down, are "forever shedding that love abroad" in their own lives and "manifesting in the grace of Christlike character the reconciling purpose of God." The Scriptures are the record of God's purpose, of Christ's life, and of those transactions between God and humankind in which the Church was born.

G's purpose

Thus Christ's life, then and now, is the spring of holiness. A third thing becomes apparent about the nature of faith. Acceptance of *redemption*, in response to the *revelation* received, turns faith into the source of *sanctification* as Christ lives in the believer. A further early paper by Newbigin, again from the year 1935–36, brings out this third aspect of Christian faith. He addressed a summer conference of the Student Christian Movement at Glenalmond in Scotland on the theme of "The Remaking of Personality."[10] The transformation of the believer takes place "by the power of Christ," and more precisely "the power of Christ to remake personality is His power to make the slave free." In describing "the essential change that is involved in being a Christian," Newbigin once more follows the course of the apostle Paul with his constant reversion to the notion of freedom: "The law of the spirit of life in Christ Jesus made me free from the law of sin and of death" (Romans 8:2); "[w]ith freedom did Christ set us free; stand fast therefore, and be not entangled again in a yoke of bondage" (Galatians 5:1); "[w]e received not the spirit of a slave but the spirit of a son, whereby we take on our lips the words of Jesus and cry, Abba, Father" (cf. Romans 8:15).

The bondage from which Newbigin sees the believer liberated is not principally, in this paper, "the dark and terrible bondage which comes when man abdicates the moral rule of his own life and the reins fall into the tyrannous hands of what St. Paul calls the world rulers of this darkness, the spiritual hosts of wickedness," but rather the bondage that besets even—or, rather, precisely—"the man or woman who takes conscience and duty at their full value." That bondage comes to expression in three paradoxes: first, the necessary observance of general moral principles and the simultaneous need for a free and spontaneous response to each situation—there is a slavery of impulse as well as of repetition; second, the fact that desire for the improvement of one's character may be a selfish motive for action, a self-regarding intrusion into the doing of duty, and yet "a person is a more precious thing than a lifetime of good deeds"—so that although the most important thing about people is character, not good deeds, yet our motive for doing good deeds must be that they are good, not that they will improve our character; and third, the recognition that whereas, on the one hand, if the moral order has any reality and is not just a subjective delusion, we must always be seeking to conform to that moral order, yet, on the other hand, to seek to achieve that moral conformity by our own effort corrupts morality—both by corrupting motives (doing things to justify ourselves rather than because they are right) and by lowering standards (as though one could compensate for failures by doing "more" than one's duty next time). Could any paradox be more tragic than that, asks Newbigin: "The law is holy; it carries the stamp of its divine origin to the sensitive conscience; yet to be under the law is to be in bondage, and by the works of the law shall no man be justified."

If, then, personality is to be remade, it must be "from some source of succor beyond morality, for if one thing is certain it is that morality cannot by its own efforts remake itself." The deliverance from that predicament is what St. Paul gave thanks for in Romans 7:25: "I thank God through our Lord Jesus Christ." The remaking of personality began with the redemptive act of God in history, which we have already seen Newbigin expounding. And, with Luther, Newbigin says that "we no longer lack anything save faith to believe that it is so." The remaking for each person begins "as we give ourselves in penitence and faith to this God." The Gospel of Jesus Christ delivers us from the paradoxes of morality. It provides a completely different motive for the moral life, namely gratitude to God at the announcement that God has not waited for us to achieve what must be forever impossible but has forgiven us in spite of what we are and offered us the status of sons and daughters here and now. Rather than "hoping to be forgiven because of my good deeds," I am "in the joyful position of being able to do good deeds because I know I am forgiven." Again with Luther: "I will therefore give myself as a sort of Christ to my neighbour, as Christ has given Himself to me." Moreover, "we can cease to be directly concerned for the improvement of our characters, because when we have committed ourselves to God, He charges Himself with that responsibility": "Life as it confronts us, our daily portion of duty and discipline and endurance, is precisely what God"—"the God of the whole earth"—"has planned for that purpose." And finally, the Gospel brings freedom, too, because it "exerts its redirecting power in the springs of the will and not in the realm of external standards" and directs the will indeed "towards a person and not merely towards a set of moral principles." Through the Bible, "as the real living word of our Father, speaking from Spirit to spirit, by meditation upon which we may be guided in each day's tasks," the whole of life becomes "a living personal traffic with God whom by faith we discern behind the manifold experiences of life, and whose character is revealed to us in the Bible." Such is the source of "authentic Christian character," marked by

the love that comes from knowing that God loved us and gave himself for us, the joy that comes when He reigns in the heart, the peace that comes of knowing that all things are of Him, the humility that comes of knowing that we have nothing we have not received, and the austere self-discipline and absolute honesty and integrity in facing all life which comes from knowing that God's love is offered to us at the cost of a Cross, the passion of Christ, because God's honesty could not suffer sin to appear in anything but its true colours.

With that, the full circle has been made from faith as the acceptance of redemption through faith as the reception of revelation to faith as the source

but did Jesus have to die ???

of sanctification and back. The pattern will be repeated to the end of Newbigin's theological life. In one of his last writings, he declares that in the human situation left by the Fall, God's self-revelation "cannot be merely the communication of true information"; it

> can only be an act of redemption and forgiveness. . . . The death of Jesus is the final and conclusive manifestation of the fact that the human race has turned its back upon its Creator; it is, as Jesus said, the judgment of this world (John 12:31). And in raising the crucified Jesus from the dead, God the Father has inaugurated a new creation, a new era in which this alienated and rebellious world is given the possibility of a new being in love and obedience to the Creator.[11]

Already from those student papers, which in all likelihood have rarely seen the light of day again in the past sixty-odd years, it is apparent that Newbigin's faith was Christ-centered as to content, origin, and effect; and so it remained throughout his days. The trinitarian character of his doctrine of God and of his understanding of the relations between God and the world remained rather implicit in the early stages; but it became more explicit in the mature and comprehensive statement of *Sin and Salvation*, to which I am now about to pay major attention, as promised. A second feature to be noted about the early papers is Newbigin's concentration on the relationship between God and the soul of each person, "the inner citadel" as he called it in the Glenalmond address; and this again would henceforth stay constant.[12] However, the early papers contain enough asides on social and political matters ("the outworks," one might say) for it to be clear that Newbigin's concern for the mundane life had not been abandoned at the evangelical turning point in his theological journey; and the full integration of these things into a single vision would gradually be achieved. A third theme incipiently present in the early papers and awaiting further development was the ecclesial dimension of faith, that is to say, the Church as the location in which revelation is transmitted and received, redemption is offered and accepted, and holiness is nourished and lived out.

Ransomed, Healed, Restored, Forgiven

The exposition of *Sin and Salvation* in the Madurai book opens with the meaning of salvation, but since salvation resides in the fulfillment of God's initial purpose in creation, it is necessary to analyze first the predicament that is to be resolved if human beings are to find their place in that original plan. "Salvation"—Newbigin connects the Greek verb *sôzô* with the Sanskrit root *sarva*, taken to imply wholeness and found in many words commonly used in Tamil—means "making whole": its nuances, as Newbigin formulates them, are the healing of that which is wounded, the mending of that which is broken, the setting free of that which is bound. Salvation entails the overcoming of a number of contradictions in the actual condition of humankind.

1. "Man is in a state of contradiction against the natural world." The human body, like that of many animals, is made up of flesh, blood, and bones and depends for its existence on the right kind of food, water, air, and so on; yet human beings cannot be satisfied as animals are with sufficient food, water, shelter, and opportunities for reproduction. Being so made that only God can truly satisfy us, we humans have unlimited desires; but, not understanding the nature of our desires, we seek satisfaction by means of natural goods alone ("more of the same"), and the result is "a glutton, a drunkard, or a sexual pervert." Thus man "ruins himself."

2. "Man is in a state of contradiction against his fellow man." The human story abounds with fighting, hatred, and murder, nation against nation, class against class, race against race, generation against generation, sibling against sibling. Although all are aware that the result can only be misery, that without cooperation we must perish, and that love is the highest good that makes life worth living, yet the conflicts continue. All seeking their own good rather than the good of others, each is brought up against equally selfish others who are seen as threats to oneself. Divided within itself, "the human race, instead of being one united family, is constantly torn by fratricidal strife."

3. "Man is himself in a state of inner self-contradiction." Instincts revolt against the mind; the body disobeys the will; desires conflict with one another and with rational purposes. Above all, says Newbigin, echoing St. Paul at Romans 7:19, "there is in every man a great division between what he knows he ought to do and what he actually does, between what he is and what he knows he ought to be."

4. "Man is in a state of contradiction against God." This basic contradiction grounds all the rest. Humankind is a creature in revolt against its Creator, a creature that has cut itself off from the roots of its own being. Made in God's image, made for God and to do God's will, to live as God's child in humble, trusting obedience, humankind chooses rather to live otherwise, independent of God, relying on its own strength, wisdom, and virtue, and even when wishing to do right, seeking its own righteousness, its own glory, not God's.

This fourfold state of contradiction, says Newbigin, is in fact a state of bondage. Humankind is confronted and limited at every turn by hostile forces that are too strong: the power of evil in the world around, the power of sin in the soul, the power of death to put an end to life. Salvation can only take the shape of release from bondage, of liberation from servitude. It means deliverance into a divine kingdom where, in accordance with the Creator's original purpose, all people shall "live together in one holy family, as children of one Father, in a new-created earth and heaven." That is the opening vision from which Newbigin proceeds to give, according to the biblical story, a closer account of sin (its origins, its nature, its results) and of the salvation which

God prepared and provided, a salvation to be appropriated and finally to be consummated.

How did sin enter the world? Interpreting the early chapters of Genesis, Newbigin finds the creation of human beings in God's image to mean that "man's humanity" does not reside "in himself" but "in the relation between himself and God"; it consists "in living in a relation of trust and obedience towards God, and in God's love of him." In the divine Trinity of Father, Son, and Holy Spirit, "love is perfect and complete, because love is both given and received." As the creature of that Creator, humankind's very constitution contains the need for and possibility of love; our "essential nature is to be found in a reflecting of God's love." The first proper object of our love is God. And because humankind was altogether made in, by, and for love, human beings cannot themselves live alone. "The image of God," therefore, "is not seen in an individual man, but in man-and-woman bound together in love." But love "means both independence and dependence." That relationship between humankind and God was marked by the stewardship with which God privileged humans over God's earth *and* by the limit that God set in keeping the determination of good and evil to himself. In that situation, temptation begins with "distrust in God's fatherly goodness." This "unbelief" is "the very root and basis of sin." The next step is when "man wants to be God himself": "he wants to be able to rule his own life, to foresee the future, to determine what is good and what is evil, to be the centre of the world. That is sin full-grown." Because the essence of sin is unbelief, its opposite will be faith. Meanwhile there results the four "disharmonies," which were earlier called the four contradictions: the disharmony "within man himself" (Genesis 3:7, 12f. shows shame and the shifting of blame), "between man and nature" (Genesis 3:16–19 shows painful childbirth and burdensome work), "between man and man" (Genesis 4:1–15 shows Cain's killing of his brother Abel), and above all "between man and God" (Genesis 3:9f. shows the beginning of humankind's fear and attempted evasions, the running away from God even while pretending to seek God).

What has all this done to the image of God in which humankind was made? Newbigin borrows a parable from his friend Daniel Niles, just across the Palk Straits in Ceylon:

> On a still and cloudless night we may see the image of the moon in the water of a lake. So long as the water is unruffled by wind, and the moon not covered by cloud, the image will shine out clear and beautiful. But if a cloud comes between the moon and the earth, the image will disappear, or if the water is ruffled by wind, the image will be scattered and distorted. Thus the image of the moon in the water does not belong to the water in the same way that the image of the king on the coin belongs to the coin. The image depends upon a certain relation between the moon and the water. If this relation is broken, the image is distorted or lost.[13]

Newbigin goes on to spell out the nature and manifestation of sin in more detail, sticking closely now to the teaching of Jesus and the letters of St. Paul.

Sin is "a corruption of the very centre of human nature": "A good tree cannot bring forth evil fruit, neither can a corrupt tree bring forth good fruit" (Matthew 7:18). Evil things come forth "out of the heart" (Mark 7:21–23; Matthew 12:35), from the very soul. Thus "sin is not primarily a matter of the body," as the ancient Greeks taught and as is still common teaching in India. The most terrible sins are spiritual sins—unbelief, pride, self-righteousness—and it is from these that the body also is corrupted. Unbelief is the turning away from God to self. Instead of reaching out to grasp the love of God, human love turns inward (here Newbigin echoes Luther's *cor in se incurvatum*). But the self is a false god; and to make oneself the center of the world is to live a lie, and thence to fall into anxiety and into an ever-deepening spiral of the dishonesty that comes with self-assertion. "Sin creates blindness, but those who are thus blinded do not know that they are blind" (cf. John 9:39–41); or, as St. Paul says, "they hold down the truth in unrighteousness" (Romans 1:18). The worship of self, when the anxious self seeks security elsewhere than in God, may take the form of idolatry toward created things ① things or the work of human hands (Romans 1:23), whether of the sort that the Christians faced in the ancient world and that is still familiar in India or the sort represented by the deification of the nation or the state "as in Germany ② Nation in the time of Hitler." More often, however, the idolatry is "hidden in the heart," although lusts too show themselves in sensual behavior (Romans 1:24–27) and covetousness manifests itself in envy, strife, and murder (Romans 1:29–31; cf. Colossians 3:5).

The "situation which sin has produced" is, then, this. Sin is no mere illusion but has set us a real and terrible condition in which the outcome, left unattended, is death. Even God cannot put it right apart from man, because "the centre of the problem is man's guilt and responsibility." There are no excuses, for "this responsibility is the very essence of human nature," coming with the gift of freedom that characterizes personhood. Although circumstances may set up a temptation to sin, "I and I alone am responsible for my sin." And sin starts a train of consequences that even my repentance cannot stop: the repercussions continue into the lives of other people (even "spreading infectious diseases by unhygienic habits"), and I have wounded the loving heart of God. Nor do we sin alone: for many grievous sins a society may be corporately guilty, such as slavery, which has brought forth the harvest of sorrow, suffering, and death that sin always brings. As St. Paul teaches in Romans 5:12–21, the entire human race in fact is corporately implicated in sin against God: "The first sin started a train of sins that goes on right through the human race." We share in that sin of the race even before we commit actual deeds: we inherit a fallen, tainted nature, which lends temptation its power, and then each of us commits sins for which we are individually responsible, and every such sin increases the strength of temptation. Where the first temptation came from is, like sin itself, "a dark and terrible mystery." Jesus deflected the question, "Did this man sin, or his father, that he should be born blind?" and instead "manifested the works of God in him" by healing him (John 9:1–7). What is certain is that "man cannot save himself from sin," for there is no part of the human race which is free from sin and able to lift up the rest and no part of human nature which is free from sin and able to redeem the other parts. Pride and self-seeking corrupts even the desire for redemption, whether in the practice of religion or in the construction of morality or in the pursuit of ideals: "Man's effort to save himself becomes the most terrible form of sin. Self-righteousness is the most terrible contradiction of the love of God." Salvation—reconciliation to God and the renewal of human nature—is possible only from God, against whom the sin is committed. It will be a hard way: "It is because God is God that He resists sin, punishes it, and causes it to end in destruction and death. If God ceased to do this, He would not be God, and the world would be utterly destroyed. . . . If God were to treat wrong as though it were right, and lies as though they were the truth, that would be the end of all things." That God repels and resists sin is rooted in God's nature as holy love, and such is the source also for God's acts of mercy and grace. The Christian Gospel is "that mercy has triumphed over wrath, that there is a way for sinful men to be reconciled with Holy God." How God can "save the sinner while at the same time resisting and destroying his sin" demands telling the story of Jesus Christ.

Newbigin starts the tale by insisting that salvation is not to be gained by human study or even human prayer—as many people not only in India but also in the West are inclined to believe—but is brought only by "the acts of God," "mighty deeds," "actual events which have happened in history" at the hands of the Creator of all things, which then on the human side must be attended to, reckoned with, and believed in. Although both the sin and the salvation affect the entire human race, God's way of salvation "works through the choosing of a particular people, and finally of one man of that people." Such a way—of representative election—is certainly mysterious, and yet it can be seen as both possible and appropriate not only on account of our racial solidarity *en mal* but also because God "desires to knit together into one holy family the whole race of men broken by sin." The first call was to Abraham, for the sake of his people and finally of all nations (Genesis 12:1–3). Abraham believed God and obeyed (cf. Hebrews 11:8). In the long story that followed, however, "the seed of Abraham again and again forgot the purpose of their calling, again and again denied God and fell into slavery and ruin," and yet "God again and again recalled them and held before them the still-unfulfilled promise." Christians see in that history the preparation for the coming of Jesus as the Christ, through whom salvation will be accomplished and given to all who believe.

Newbigin follows the prophetic, priestly, and royal strands through the Old Testament, prophets, priests, and kings being the appointed mediators of God to his people Israel. Looking back, Christians see the prophets as witnesses to God's righteousness, but do not see the prophets producing it among the people: "Only when God himself became man, born under the Law and fulfilling the Law to the last limit, could the Law fulfil its work" (cf. Galatians 4:4f.). Looking back, Christians see the sacrificial system as a sign of the need for a way from sinful people to the holy God but as finally unable to provide that way: "That way could only be provided when the Son of God Himself came, to be both Priest and sacrifice" (cf. Hebrews 9:9–12). Looking back, Christians see earthly kingship, even at its best, as only a sign and witness to God's Kingdom, which it cannot bring in; and, indeed, it becomes the enemy of that Kingdom if it tries to do so: "The King himself had to come," and "because He refused every kind of earthly kingship," he was utterly rejected by those to whom he came (John 6:15; 18:11, 36). Thus the great themes of the Old Testament all "point beyond themselves," but their fulfillment could come only paradoxically. Yet the clue had already been present in the Old Testament. The failings and distress of the chosen people were to be taken upon himself by one who perfectly embodied Israel and, indeed, the entire human race for whose sake they were chosen. Mark 9:12 and Luke 22:37, among other passages, suggest that Jesus knew the meaning of Isaiah 53 as the provision of redemption through vicarious suffering: "God must save the world through the suffering, rejection, failure, defeat and shame of His Servant. The holy love of God can only make terms with the sin of men at the cost of suffering and death. . . . He Himself, both God and Man, came into the world as the true Prophet, Priest and King, to suffer and die for the sin of the world."

Newbigin goes on to expound the work of the Savior under the heading of John 3:16, the verse "which every Christian knows and loves": "God so loved the world, that he gave his only-begotten Son that whosoever believeth in him should not perish but have everlasting life." God the Holy Trinity, in whose tripersonal being "there is complete fulness of love," is, in his love for the world, the author of our salvation. What humankind could not do for itself, God has done. God's just wrath at sin was "not turned away by anything from outside of God: it was because God loved the world that He gave His Son to be its Saviour." When the Son came forth into the world to be our Saviour, he took our humanity upon him, under the power of sin as it was, and thus came under the sentence of suffering and death which is the wages of sin; yet he "remained and remains one with the Father in the unity of the Godhead." Fully human, he yet says and does things that only God can say and do, and so his identity is brought to light. "He lived a life of sinless perfection in the midst of sin. . . . Thus He met and overcame sin in our nature, from within the enemy's territory." The absolutely decisive battle took place on the Cross, and the victory was displayed in the Resurrection, which is the pledge of eternal life to those who believe: "Faith is the hand that grasps what Christ has done and makes it my own."

Newbigin's exposition of the meaning and effect of Christ's death draws first on the gospels and then on the epistles of the New Testament. Jesus taught that his death was necessary (Mark 8:31; 9:31; 10:33f.), accepted as the will of his Father (Mark 14:36). Arising from his self-identification with sinners (betokened in his submission to the baptism of John), Jesus' death is God's judgment on the world (as Luke's version of the parable of the wicked husbandmen makes especially clear, at 20:18). Jesus' death is a ransom, paid vicariously for lives that are forfeit (Mark 10:45), an atoning sacrifice that inaugurates a new covenant (Matthew 26:28). Jesus' death is the means of life to the world (John 6:51; 10:10f.; 12:24f., 32f.), and the way of faith is so to follow him as to share in his dying and new life: although Jesus did for us what we could not do for ourselves, he does not will that we should "stand back and leave him alone" but rather that we should "share with him in his redemptive agony."

After Christ's resurrection, his followers, having been redeemed and forgiven, reflected on his death; and so the apostolic writings launched the continuing enterprise of accounting for how the Cross accomplished what it did. In the epistles, the central point remains that the death of Jesus was a revelation of God's love: "God commendeth his own love for us in that, while we were yet sinners, Christ died for us" (Romans 5:8). Only such a costly act in and by the incarnate Son could allow for the forgiveness of sin without the abandonment of righteousness. The death of Jesus was a judgment on the sin of the entire human race, showing up the rule of sin in the world, meeting and overcoming evil with good, bearing the iniquity of us all—and its penalty (Romans 8:3; 2 Corinthians 5:21; Galatians 3:13). The blood of Jesus was the price paid for our redemption (Romans 3:24f.; 1 Peter 1:18f.), although the metaphor of ransom must not be pressed so far as to say that the price was paid to God or to Satan. The death of Jesus was the sacrifice of a life to God, the one perfect offering of love and obedience to the Father that alone could give us access again to the holy God (Hebrews 10:1–20). The steadfast obedience of Jesus to the point of death—through all temptation and agony—accomplished a mighty victory over the powers of evil (Colossians 2:15; cf. 1 John 3:18), so that "the name of Jesus on the lips and in the heart of a believer is enough to banish the power of Satan."

Having thus expounded the work of the Savior, Newbigin looks in the next chapter of *Sin and Salvation* at "how salvation becomes ours." Here he makes a move that already in the preface to the book he has avowed would be unusual in his—Reformed—tradition: instead of beginning with the inward and spiritual act of faith, he reverses the order and starts with the outward and visible fact of the Church. Two reasons are given for the switch, one biblical, the other related to his current experience in India:

> Firstly, it is the order which the reader of the New Testament finds himself following: the Acts of the Apostles come before the Epistles—the fact of the Church before the clue to its inner life. Secondly, it is the order which the non-Christian has to follow when he comes to Christ. What he sees is a visible congregation in his village. It is that congregation which holds out to him the offer of salvation. Only when he has come within its fellowship does he (usually) come to any deep understanding of its inner source.

The significance of this valuation of ecclesiology will become increasingly apparent in later chapters of this book, particularly those that treat Lesslie Newbigin as evangelist, as ecumenist, and as missiologist. Here it suffices to note that a more active part is attributed to the Church in the generation of faith than perhaps had been suggested when the Church was viewed as sim-

the Church as

ply the "location" of the acceptance of redemption, the recognition of revelation, and the growth of holiness.

The ecclesiological move had been presaged when Newbigin spoke earlier
of human solidarity in both sin and redemption: "Each one who has been
reconciled to God has to be the means by which others are reconciled. Thus
God's purpose is fulfilled by a visible earthly fellowship of men and women—
beginning with those whom He has first chosen, and spreading out to others."

Because love exists only in concrete relationships, the "centre of God's plan
for salvation is an actual community of men and women called by God for
this purpose. . . . They are called in order that through them God's love may
reach others, and all men and women be drawn together into one reconciled
fellowship." Newbigin now speaks very tangibly about the Church as the
"connection" between the work of Christ in Palestine two thousand years
ago and my sin and need for redemption today: "When we look at the record,
what strikes us is that the story of Jesus has reached us through a group of
men and women who were so closely bound to Him that their life could
almost be spoken of as an extension of His life." This is not quite the same
as calling the Church "the extension of the Incarnation," an expression about
which Newbigin expresses mistrust in other writings. Yet he speaks very

highly of the apostolic generation whose confession and experience he finds
recorded in the letters of St. Paul. They lived "in Christ" (a phrase used by
Paul scores of times), and Christ "lived in them" (cf. Galatians 2:20; Colossians 1:27; 3:4). When they spoke of Christ's death and resurrection, they
spoke of them "as events in which they themselves have shared" (cf. Romans
6:3f.; Colossians 3:1; Ephesians 2:5f.). Those who used this language "felt
themselves to be so bound up with [Christ] that what He had done had
become their own, so that when they came before God they came, so to say,
in the person of Christ—in His Name and as part of Him. They are His and
He is theirs. Their righteousness is not their own, but His [Philippians 3:9]
and so also is their wisdom and their holiness [1 Corinthians 1:30]. Everything that they have is His; their very existence is 'in Christ.' " And so
through the successive generations, what Christ has done "becomes mine
when I become part of this society, this fellowship"—become a member, that
is, of the Body of Christ, which is the Church.

Drawing on Acts 2:42, Newbigin enumerates "four links by which the
continuing fellowship is bound to Christ and His work, continually renewed
and redirected by Him." The first is the apostles' teaching, that is, the continuing proclamation according to the New Testament of what Jesus was and
is, what he has already done and will still do, a powerful word bringing home
to hearts afresh the mighty acts of salvation. The second is the breaking of
bread, "a participation in the body and blood of Christ" (cf. 1 Corinthians 10:
16), a continual strengthening of communion with Christ for those who by
their baptism have been identified with him in his death and resurrection.
The third is a new quality of common life, marked by mutual forgiveness and
upbuilding in love, a fellowship of reconciliation grounded in Christ's atoning
work. The fourth is prayer, based on what Jesus has done and promised, a

believing response to his self-offering, made in the confidence that our great High Priest has entered on our behalf into the Holy Place and ever lives to make intercession for us. Yet the mere performance of these things does not guarantee salvation: "Preaching may become empty talk; sacraments may be perverted into empty symbol or pagan magic; fellowship may give place to mere gregariousness; prayers may become lifeless incantations." The flesh must be quickened by the Spirit of God (cf. John 6:63).

The New Testament record tells how, when Jesus had accomplished his earthly work, the same Holy Spirit who had been in Jesus now fell upon his followers. From the day of Pentecost, they were empowered to preach the gospel boldly and do the mighty deeds of Christ. The Spirit became their common possession and the gift which unites all subsequent believers with Christ. The inner reality of our participation in Christ is thus twofold: "From God's side, . . . it is the Holy Spirit who unites us with Christ; from man's side, . . . it is faith which unites us with Christ."

Faith begins in the true repentance that only the sinless Christ could offer in solidarity with sinners, a repentance into which we may, like the dying thief, enter as we accept the justice of God's judgment on our sin. Having understood "the enormity of our sin," we may then at the Cross understand also "the infinite depths of God's love," who has himself in the Son borne the burden and penalty of sin, in order that we may in mercy be forgiven. Newbigin describes these realizations thus:

> We are humbled to the dust, and at the same time raised up and comforted. As we see the horror of our sin brought home to the loving heart of God, we cry: "How hateful I must be to God! Surely I am fit only for death." At the same moment as we see [Christ] deliberately bearing it all for our sake, standing on our side of the gulf, willing rather to be separated from the Father than to be separated from us, we cry in amazement: "How precious I must be to God! Surely He who has done this for me, will never let me perish." This double confession is something which is wrung from us by Christ's death. It is not that by an act of will I have decided to choose Christ as my saviour. It is that *Christ has laid hold of me* with this tremendous judgment and mercy and I am forced to cry out in shame and wondering gratitude: "Lord, I am a traitor fit to die; Lord, thou hast died for me, and I am thine for ever." This faith is, thus, wholly the result of what God has first done for me. It is not first an act of my will which is always seeking something for itself instead of seeking the glory of God. It is, so to say, the "Amen" which is wrung from the heart by this mighty act of Christ. It is the surrender of my will to Him, who alone can make my will free.[14]

Given the delicacy, in doctrinal history, of the question of the beginnings of faith, it is important to allow Newbigin to continue his exposition of the work of the Holy Spirit in the birth of faith in the human heart, mind, and soul:

> That surrender, that "Amen", is faith. And it is the work of the Holy Spirit. We cannot separate these two. From God's side, it is the work of the Spirit; from my side it is faith. Yet that faith itself is not my independent work; it is

the work of the Holy Spirit in my heart. Only God Himself has the power to bring my stubborn and rebellious will to the point of surrender. So that we must say that faith is the work of the Holy Spirit. At yet at the same time we ought also to say that it is through faith in Christ's work that we receive the Holy Spirit. It is when the Cross of Christ has shattered our self-sufficiency, humbled our pride, and raised us again from the dust by the power of His love—only when this has been done that the Spirit of God can flow into our souls and take control of us. While the fortress-wall of self-righteousness remains standing, God's Holy Spirit cannot flow in.

is it necessarily sequential?

Therefore we have to think always of these two things together—faith and the Holy Spirit, and both of them only through the work of Christ on the Cross. The Spirit brings home to our hearts what Christ has done for us, and awakens that response which is faith—the Amen of the soul to God's judgment and mercy. That humble response places the soul in the position where the life-giving stream of God's Holy Spirit can flow in to possess the whole soul. The Spirit creates faith, and faith receives the Spirit. But all this only through what Christ has accomplished on Calvary; the Spirit brings home to our hearts what Christ has done for us, through the preaching of the word of the Gospel, through the sacraments of baptism and the Lord's Supper, which He ordained, through the fellowship of His people, and through the prayers which they offer in His Name. . . . Faith in Christ is born in us when the fact of His crucifixion is brought home to us in word and sacrament, through the power of the Spirit. . . . The Spirit, working in and through the continuing fellowship and its various means of grace, both creates faith and also is known and received through faith. Thus by faith, in the Church, and in the Spirit, we are made partakers of Christ.[15]

After dealing thus with the Holy Spirit and the beginnings of faith, Newbigin goes on to expound three principal ways in which the New Testament describes the changes that union with Christ brings: regeneration (or rebirth), justification (judgment and forgiveness), and growth in holiness (or sanctification). The "new birth" is the creation of a new mind, a new heart, a new will, a recreation into the true image of God—a child of God through Jesus Christ. The new life is lived under the sign of justification, which means both to be judged (accepting the verdict which Christ bore on behalf of humankind) and to be forgiven (set, for Christ's sake, into the right relation with God). On the human side, that right relation is one of trusting, obeying, loving—having toward God the mind of Christ, the very opposite of unbelief which is the root of sin. This new life is "energized by the love of God in Christ" and, in the spontaneous, uncalculating "response of gratitude" to God's infinite love, starts to bring forth "good fruit." Yet although in one sense the changes brought by union with Christ in faith are accomplished in a moment, in another sense time is required. Old habits need to be mastered, new patterns learned. Conversion occurs once for all and yet has to happen daily afresh. There is a warfare still to be waged by believers, first against the "old man" in themselves but then also in "the good fight of faith," where as part of "the bundle of humanity" they "share in the travail of Christ's soul" and seek to extend reconciliation by acts of witness and service. All this is made possible only by the constant renewal of the mind through participation in the fellowship of God's people and in the means of grace with which it has been furnished.

Having shown the present incompleteness of salvation, Newbigin looks forward in a final chapter to its consummation. Present union of believers with God and with one another is a foretaste of perfect salvation. God gives a twofold assurance of future attainment: inwardly, the Holy Spirit is an "earnest" of the full inheritance (2 Corinthians 1:22; 5:5; Ephesians 1:13f.); outwardly, the resurrection of Jesus is a promise of the believers' resurrection (1 Corinthians 15; 1 Peter 1:3–5). The joyful assurance about the completion of God's saving work in Christ is what the New Testament means by hope. That hope includes longing, praying, working for the consummation of God's saving purpose for the whole world. The center of the picture is Jesus, who is not merely a product of our imagination but has himself promised to come again. God holds back the return of Christ in order that the Gospel may be preached and people have time to repent and be saved. For God's will is "that all should be saved. He does not will the destruction of any soul." (If "some Christians have taught that God created some men for the purpose of destroying them," that is based on "a misunderstanding of certain passages in Scripture" and "is certainly not the teaching of the Gospel.") That does not mean that all will surely be saved: "At the end we cannot deny the possibility that men—even the majority of men—may be left outside." We are to "strive to enter in by the narrow door" (Luke 13:23). If any are left outside, "it will be because—like the elder brother in the parable [Luke 15:28]—they are not willing to share the Father's fellowship on His terms."[16]

The resurrection of Jesus presaged the glory of a new creation. The whole Body of Christ, with all his members, is to be raised. But, as the cosmic range of the creation stories has shown from the start, nothing in the entire created world is, in fact, irrelevant to God's purpose: "None of it is mere scaffolding to be thrown away when the building is complete. He made it all in love, and He loves it all. Therefore the completion of His purpose means not only the resurrection, but also a new heaven and a new earth." The worldwide scope of the atonement which Christ has wrought between God and humankind is "the restoration of creation to its original purpose by the purging away of sin, . . . the restoring of all men and all things to perfect harmony and perfect joy, through the perfect love of God."

From some of Newbigin's very early papers, and then from the book *Sin and Salvation*, written while he was a bishop in South India, an account has been offered of his understanding—as a Christian believer and an ecclesiastical teacher who spoke whereof he knew—of the content, origin, and effect of faith: faith as the acceptance of redemption, the recognition of revelation, and the source of sanctification. There is a fourth aspect of faith that comes to the fore, in a shape conditioned by the new context, during the years since Newbigin's final return to Europe. The old question of assurance reemerges as the possibility of what Newbigin calls "proper confidence" or the nature of the "certainty" that attaches to faith. Where the general framework of the

Christian faith has been assumed, the issue has perennially arisen as to whether or not an individual Christian may properly be assured that he or she presently enjoys the favor of God and/or will attain eternal salvation. In face of a diminution in the cultural credibility of Christianity in the modern West, Newbigin now begins with the more basic need which believers have for a "proper confidence" in the truth of the Gospel as such, and the nature of the "certainty" of faith has to be expounded in this light. More attention will be given to the cultural circumstances in chapter 10, on Newbigin as apologist, but the essence of faith itself is clarified by the new discussion, and so these later moves on Newbigin's part demand treatment in the present and fundamental chapter on him as believer. They also provide a setting for discerning Newbigin's views on the traditional issues surrounding the assurance of faith. Representative writings are the book *Proper Confidence* and the article "Certain Faith: What Kind of Certainty?"[17]

Proper Confidence

In these later writings, Newbigin is much concerned with the relation between faith and knowledge. He notes that in modern parlance, following the philosopher Locke's definition, belief is "a persuasion of our own minds, short of knowledge."[18] With this is to be contrasted St. Augustine's *credo ut intellegam* (translated as "I believe in order to know"), which defines "a way of knowing that begins with the faithful acceptance of the given fact that God revealed himself in Christ." Newbigin draws on the Hungarian scientific epistemologist Michael Polanyi for the view that *all* human knowledge has a "fiduciary" character:

> Knowing always begins with the opening of our minds and our senses to the great reality which is around us and which sustains us, and it always depends on this from beginning to end. . . . All efforts to know must begin with something given. This given includes what we normally call the data, the facts that form part of the foundation from which our reason works. It also includes the tradition of knowing which has developed in a human community and which includes the language and all the conceptual tools used in that tradition. . . . In order to be informed, we have to make acts of trust in the traditions we have inherited and in the evidence of our senses.[19]

The Christian faith offers, says Newbigin, the most comprehensive of clues to reality, for it proclaims that the divine Word which creates and sustains all things has been made flesh in Jesus Christ. The primary witness to this act of God, this fact (*factum*), is contained in the Scriptures; and the interpretative tradition is borne by the Church, which is part of the story that it carries on toward its conclusion.

In the nature of the case, the faith-knowledge of created reality and of its Creator has several characteristics. Negatively put, it is to be distinguished from what is anyway the problematic "indubitable certainty" sought by Descartes, which rests within the mind of the thinking subject; and it may be conceded to the philosopher of the German Enlightenment, G. E. Lessing, that "accidental happenings of history cannot prove eternal truths of reason." Positively put, the Incarnation shows ultimate reality to be personal in nature, which means that it can be known only by self-revelation on the part of the Creator and by an answering response on the part of the human knower. Such knowledge comes by way of an inseparable trust and obedience toward the call of Christ, "Follow me." Any "personal knowledge is impossible without risk," for "trust can be betrayed." If ultimate truth is to be found "in a story that has not yet been finished," then "the certainty we have rests on the faithfulness of the one whose story it is": "We walk by faith, not by sight" (2 Corinthians 5:7). Thus when St. Paul wrote "I know whom I have believed, and I am sure that he is able to guard until that day what has been entrusted to me" (2 Timothy 1:12), one may note "two features of this kind of assurance which distinguish it from the ideal of certainty we have inherited from the Age of Reason":

> In the first place, the locus of confidence . . . is not in the competence of our own knowing, but in the faithfulness and reliability of the one who is known. The weight of confidence rests there and not with us. Secondly, the phrase "until that day" reminds us that this is not a claim to possess final truth but to be on the way that leads us to the fullness of truth. I do not *possess* the truth, so that I do not need to be open to new truth; rather, I am confident that the one in whom I have placed my trust, the one to whom I am committed, is able to bring me to the full grasp of what I now only partly understand.[20]

There is expressed the need for "grace alone" and the New Testament promise concerning the work of the Holy Spirit in leading the followers of Jesus into the fullness of truth.

What light, then, does this "proper confidence" throw on the question of assurance as put in the history of Christian theology? As a preliminary, it must be insisted that the increased attention devoted by Newbigin in the apologetics of his "later European" phase to epistemological issues concerning creation at large has in no way diminished his awareness of the human need for atonement and reconciliation to God: "We have to learn that we are lost and that we have to be rescued."[21] A purple passage in *Proper Confidence* recalls the God of the Bible in contrast with the religions of East Asia and elsewhere:

> No one who has been deeply immersed in the biblical narrative could ever again entirely escape from the presence of that One, God, so tender and yet so terrible, so passionate in his wrathful love and his loving wrath, forever calling on those who turn their backs on him, forever humbling himself in tender appeal, forever challenging his children to the heights of utter purity, and finally accepting the shameful death of a condemned sinner in order to open for us the gate of glory. There is absolutely nothing in all the world's sacred scriptures that can be compared for a moment with this.[22]

Thus Newbigin remains firmly located in the classic doctrinal tradition that— formulated in the Western terms of St. Augustine and St. Anselm, of St. Thomas Aquinas and the magisterial Protestant Reformers—recognizes the extreme gravity of sin and the gracious provision of redemption through the vicarious work of Christ.

The question of the individual believer's assurance concerning present acceptance before God and his or her final salvation has both pastoral and dogmatic dimensions. I offer a brief survey of some historically controversial issues so that the nuances of Newbigin's views may be better appreciated; these happen to be matters on which there has been considerable tension not only between Catholics and Protestants but also between Newbigin's Reformed tradition and my own Methodist. In medieval debate, Aquinas held that some might receive an assurance of salvation by the special privilege of a direct revelation from God, but that generally one had to be content with a measure of certitude concerning present pardon: in the face of self-delusion on the one hand or agnosticism on the other, the tests were hearing the word of God with joy, readiness to do good, a firm intention not to sin in future, and sorrow for past sins. The Protestant Reformers brought the issue to the fore with Luther's cry amid the uncertainties of an ecclesiastical system that appeared to make salvation dependent on human work: "Where do I find a gracious God?" Luther's discovery of justification by grace through faith alone confuted "that pernicious doctrine of the papists, that no one can know for certain (*certo scire*) whether he is in a state of grace," whereby they "utterly ruined the doctrine of faith, overthrew faith, tormented people's consciences, banished Christ from the Church, and darkened and denied all the benefits and gifts of the Holy Spirit"; and the faith which God gives can be described by Luther as "a living and daring confidence (*Zuversicht*) in the grace of God, so certain (*gewiss*) that for it one could die a thousand deaths; and such confidence and knowledge (*Erkenntnis*) of divine grace makes us joyous, bold, and cheerful toward God and all creation." Such fighting words provoked the Council of Trent, in its decree on justification, to reject any "certitude" about present forgiveness and final salvation that rested on "faith alone" or "*vana fiducia*." The moral dangers which Trent saw were presumption and antinomianism; but behind these stood concern for loss of ecclesial mediation in the process of salvation.[23]

Meanwhile, controversy occurred within Protestantism on these matters. Luther insisted, against the apparent subjectivism of the "enthusiasts," that salvation remains grounded "outside of ourselves" in the person and work of Christ and in the baptism by which God applies it and gives faith. For Calvin, objective certainty resides in the divine decrees of predestination and the implied gift of final perseverance; the subjective knowledge of being among the elect is afforded by the Father's call, the gift of faith in Christ, the daily blessings of God and the protection of Christ, and the sealing of the heart by the Spirit of adoption. The matter became controversial again during the Evangelical Revival of the eighteenth century: Wesley looked to the witness of the

Holy Spirit—both direct, in the enabling of believers to cry "Abba, Father" (Romans 8:15f.), and indirect, in the evidence of the fruit of the Spirit in their lives (Galatians 5:22f.)—and considered this present assurance of God's favor ("God is reconciled to me in the Son of his love") the "common privilege" of believers; but for Wesley, the promises of God were conditional and held good only so long as a person remained in the faith, which it was possible to lose. He distinguished between the "assurance of faith" (Hebrews 10:22) and the "assurance of hope" (Hebrews 6:11): "The plerophory (or full assurance) of faith is such a clear conviction that *I am now* in the favour of God as excludes all doubt and fear concerning it. The full assurance of hope is such clear confidence that *I shall enjoy* the glory of God as excludes all doubt and fear concerning this." The latter assurance Wesley held to be rarely given and to have no basis in, or provide any basis for, a consistent doctrine of final perseverance.[24]

These brief notations on the issues and options that have marked Christian thinking at the particularly delicate point of assurance have been meant to illuminate retrospectively the path which Newbigin followed in his exposition of the nature of faith in relation to sin and salvation; they allow him to be tracked—by the choices he made and the obstacles he avoided—within both the common and the controversial history of doctrine. The historically controversial questions surround the scope of salvation and, immediately connected with that, the respective roles of God and man in it. Newbigin, as we have seen, disavows any version of the doctrine of predestination that sees God as having "created some men for the purpose of destroying them." He holds to the original saving intent of God toward the human race as such, as it is expressed in the words of the apostle Paul at 1 Timothy 2:4: God "desires all men to be saved and to come to the knowledge of the truth."[25] Yet this does not guarantee that all will in the end be saved, as the "universalists" maintain; indeed, Newbigin contemplates that some, perhaps many, will finally be lost. He holds in any case that the universally sufficient work of Christ in redemption requires, to be profitable, the response of faith, which the Holy Spirit enables but which human beings in their misused freedom may refuse. Where the response of faith is made, Newbigin holds that God, who is faithful, is able to preserve believers until the last day and has in fact provided in the Church the means of grace to help them freely persevere. In none of this, however, and particularly in view of the fallen condition of humankind, does he present a facile view of human freedom such as threatens those who veer too far toward what in Western Protestantism is called Arminianism. Newbigin would appear to agree with those points in Calvin over which Wesley also agreed with him, namely "in ascribing all good to the free grace of God, in denying all natural free-will and all power antecedent to grace, and in excluding all merit from man, even for what he has or does by the grace of God."[26] In fact, Newbigin appears to escape the strictures under which the World Alliance of Reformed Churches and the World Methodist Council placed themselves when, in their dialogue document *Together in God's Grace*, they confessed that "both traditions have gone wrong when they have claimed to know too much about this mystery of God's electing grace and of human response."[27] With their strongly personalist cast and their attention to the subtly enabling work of the Holy Spirit, who is "the Spirit of faith" (2 Corinthians 4:13), Newbigin's views on the attainment of salvation ring true to the New Testament and its echoes in Eastern Christianity. Or, if the matter has to be put in the terms of Western Christianity: Newbigin appears to embody in his thought and practice both sides of A. Mitchell Hunter's dictum that "pious Arminians pray like Calvinists," ascribing all the glory to God, just as "pious Calvinists preach like Arminians," offering the good news of the Gospel to all.[28]

A Contemporary Faith

In his positive teaching in the area of salvation, Newbigin brings out several features regarding the content and exercise of faith that are especially appropriate in the contemporary situation. To begin with, he tells the tale of creation and redemption on a suitably grand scale. The cosmic scope of God's purposes and activity is well recognized and humankind properly located within them. Here Newbigin displays a breadth which has characterized the Eastern Christian tradition—both ancient (say, Maximus the Confessor's "cosmic liturgy") and more recent (take Alexander Schmemann's *For the Life of the World*)—more firmly than much of the Western tradition, which has often tended towards a fixation, rather than a concentration, upon the human creature. Biblically, the story of the Cross unfolds within the universal dimensions of Genesis at the origin and the expected summation of all things according to the Apocalypse. Newbigin's scriptural vision here respects the urgent ecological concerns of our time concerning the human stewardship of the earth and simultaneously refers them to their proper depth in the history of God with the world. According to Christian doctrine in its fullness, the destinies of humankind and of the rest of creation cannot be pried apart.

Next, Newbigin recaptures the character of God as it is rendered in the Scriptures. Insofar as modernity has retained vestiges of belief in the personal God of the Bible, the divine character verges on sentimentality and good humor. In terms of human salvation, there is often a casual reliance on the dying *mot* of the notable nineteenth-century German ironist, Heinrich Heine: "God will forgive me, it's his job." Newbigin recalls the biblical and traditional God of mercy and of wrath, the God of the *Dies irae* and of the *Kyrie eleison*. Concomitantly, he holds—with Scripture and the great Tradition—that true freedom entails for human persons our responsibility before God. Again, the two are not to be pried apart. Their proper conjunction is especially needed amid a modernity in which liberty has often degenerated into license.

Still further, modernity has witnessed in some quarters, and even among some Christians, a decline in the belief in an afterlife at all. Newbigin restores the eschatological dimension that is vital to the scriptural proclamation of salvation and its traditional understanding. The realistic basis for that is the resurrection of Jesus Christ, whereby the fruits of his redemptive death are displayed, Christ himself being the "first fruits" of the harvest: "If Christ has not been raised, your faith is futile and you are still in your sins. Then those also who have fallen asleep in Christ have perished. If for this life only we have hoped in Christ, we are of all men most to be pitied. But in fact Christ has been raised from the dead, the first fruits of those who have fallen asleep"(1 Corinthians 15:17–20). Such is necessary to the Christian expectation of eternal life. The prospect that "God will be all in all" (1 Corinthians 15:28) may be translated, as far as human beings are concerned, into the first exchange of the Westminster Catechism, with which Newbigin as an English Presbyterian had a lifelong familiarity:

> What is the chief end of man?
> Man's chief end is to glorify God, and to enjoy Him for ever.

Although the theme is present from the start, Newbigin's later writings in particular address the question of "purpose" in human life and, indeed, in creation at large, noting how modernity has lost the sense of "final cause" in the sciences and of worthwhile end in our (absurd?) existence. Theologically speaking, teleology and eschatology must never be pried apart: God has, Newbigin insists, both the purpose and also the power and the patience to accomplish it. God intends that the creatures—with human creatures in their appointed place—should come to share according to their kind in the superabundant love of the Holy and Blessed Trinity that is the ground of their making in the first place, and God works in grace to achieve that.

Correspondingly, Newbigin describes the attitudes that are appropriate to human beings, and to believers in particular, at the present stage in the story of salvation. They need special cultivation in our times. Gratitude is the first among them, such as may be expressed in the words of the general thanksgiving from the Book of Common Prayer:

> Almighty God, Father of all mercies, we thine unworthy servants do give thee most humble and hearty thanks for all thy goodness and loving-kindness to us, and to all men. We bless thee for our creation, preservation, and all the blessings of this life; but above all, for thine inestimable love in the redemption of the world by our Lord Jesus Christ; for the means of grace, and for the hope of glory. And, we beseech thee, give us thy due sense of all thy mercies, that our hearts may be unfeignedly thankful, and that we show forth thy praise, not only with our lips, but in our lives; by giving up ourselves to thy service, and by walking before thee in holiness and righteousness all our days; through Jesus Christ our Lord, to whom with thee and the Holy Ghost be all honour and glory, world without end. Amen.

On the heels of gratitude comes humility, for we do not deserve what God graciously gives. Lesslie Newbigin not only often enjoined these virtues in his writings but also unselfconsciously embodied them in his life. Such witness is conspicuous in our time, and perhaps in all times. It derives from and expresses a "proper confidence."

Finally, what emerges from Newbigin's vision, teaching, and practice as a Christian believer is that faith and works, body and soul, here and hereafter, individual and community, humankind and the rest of creation are all of a piece. "Hearing" and "obeying" the Word, *akouê* and *hup-akouê*, are inseparable. The Incarnation and Pentecost together confirm the spiritual character of flesh and blood. The Cross and the Resurrection bring eternal life out of present sin and death. Persons flourish in the social Body of Christ. The justice and peace of the new creation will embrace all in heaven and earth. The unifying factor is the Triune God, whose mercy overcomes his wrath for the achievement of a loving purpose whereby the forgiven and redeemed are freely given and freely receive a lasting share in the life and communion of the Holy and Blessed Trinity.

To hold on to these things and propagate them—Newbigin realized at the end of his life when the apostate decadence of "old Christendom" weighed heavily upon him—requires "learning afresh the skills needed for a true spiritual warfare":

We have to learn from St. Paul about this spiritual warfare and to learn how to put on the appropriate armour. The only offensive weapon he enlists is the sword of the Spirit which is the word of God—that apparently weak and powerless word of witness to Christ, which even in the mouth of an unworthy speaker, can become the mighty instrument of the Spirit to convict, to teach, and to guide. He speaks of the necessary means of defence—above all the shield of faith, that tough, stubborn commitment to the Gospel when so much opposition is arrayed against it. But, most important of all, Paul speaks of the constant, all-encompassing prayer which is the mightiest power of all.[29]

2

The Direct Evangelist

Since we have the same spirit of faith as he had who wrote, "I
believed, and so I spoke," so we too believe, and so we speak,
knowing that he who raised the Lord Jesus will raise us also
with Jesus and bring us with you into his presence. For it is all
for your sake, so that as grace extends to more and more people
it may increase the thanksgiving, to the glory of God.

(2 Corinthians 4:13–15)

Lifelong Practices

The believer's first commission is to the service of evangelism. The apostle
Paul, writing also for the evangelist Timothy, appropriated the words of Psalm
116:10 to say "We too believe, and so we speak," seeing in the testimony of
the two of them to the Gospel a vehicle for the extension of divine grace and
the inclusion of respondents into the community of those who give thanks
and glory to God. Bishop V. S. Azariah of Dornakal told the meeting of the
International Missionary Council at Tambaram in 1938 that when he toured
the churches of his Anglican diocese, he would have the baptized members
place their hands upon their heads and repeat the words of St. Paul at 1
Corinthians 9:16, "Woe unto me if I preach not the Gospel." The sentiment
was shared by Lesslie Newbigin and applied in the first instance to himself.
At the literary level, he wrote in his early years in India a study booklet for
the Student Christian Movement—it sold for two annas a copy—under the
title *What is the Gospel?*[1] While bishop of Madras in the late 1960s, Newbigin
published a series of addresses on *Christ Our Eternal Contemporary*, characteristically beginning with "We Preach Jesus" and leading toward "Conversion."[2] In the 1990s, Newbigin continued to commend the Gospel with *Truth
to Tell: The Gospel as Public Truth*, lectures he gave at the Western Theological
Seminary in Holland, Michigan, from which had come in years past several
of his missionary colleagues in South India.[3] At the practical level, Newbigin
himself engaged from beginning to end in what, with his friend the German
missiologist Walter Freytag, he called "direct evangelism."

Already during the long vacation of 1929, after his first year as a Cambridge undergraduate, Lesslie had participated in one of the "evangelistic cam-

paigns" that students undertook to industrial towns in the Midlands and the North of England. In these campaigns,

> the main programme was open-air preaching and visits to factories during lunch-breaks. It called for the ability to speak effectively from a soapbox in a crowded street, to stand up to heckling, and to meet the serious questions of working men and women. . . . For the campaigners it was an enormously fruitful, if sometimes frightening, exercise. I had been drawn into this good company before I can honestly say that I had something to give. But by the time we gathered in Preston in September I knew that I could at least point to the cross of Jesus as the ground of hope for every human being.[4]

During his three years as a theological student at Westminster College, Newbigin served as superintendent of the Sunday School at the York Street mission of St. Columba's Presbyterian Church in one of the poorer parts of Cambridge and learned "how to talk to children."[5]

Newbigin records two typical exercises in evangelism from his early years in Kanchipuram, first in the city and then in the surrounding villages. In Kanchi,

> I fitted a wooden box to the back of my bike and stocked it with cheap paperback copies of the Gospels which could be sold for one anna. Every now and then I would stop, prop up the bike, open the box and take out a Gospel to read. At once a small crowd would collect and within the next ten minutes some friendly conversations would have ensued and a dozen Gospels been sold. It was a good, simple way of communicating.[6]

Then there were the trips to the villages of the "Untouchables," when "a group of us would set off through the darkness, following winding tracks through the jungle or balancing on the narrow *bund* between the flooded paddy fields, with a paraffin lantern to light the way and sticks to deal with snakes."[7] A letter he sent home in April 1940 offers a vivid description of primary evangelism (such as I myself remember still from parts of West Africa in the late 1960s, where the pagan tokens would be fetishes and the gathering point the shade of a spreading tree):

> Early in January two men came to our Mission Hospital here from a village of which we had not heard, named Thirupanamur. They said they had come on behalf of their village to ask us to send someone to tell them about Christianity. The Hospital Catechist promised that someone would come, and two or three days later three of us set off to look for the village. After many inquiries, and much wandering about in territory which was new to all of us, we arrived after dark at the village. In the middle of the village was a small, well-built temple. To our surprise, the temple was immediately opened, a lamp brought, and ourselves invited to sit down inside. In a few minutes a large crowd was gathered round the porch of the temple, and the leading man, having made us sit down, spoke to us in words that reminded me of Cornelius welcoming Peter. In effect, he said: "We have invited you to come, and we are glad that you have come. Now here we are, and we know nothing

about Christianity, but we want you to tell us all about it from the beginning." The Catechist, whom by general agreement we had made our spokesman, replied by asking why they had invited us, and in particular how it came that they invited us into the temple. They answered that they had asked us because some of them had been in the Mission Hospital, and what they had heard and seen made them want to find out more about this Christian way. As for the temple, they were not using it, and they were wondering whether the idol was any use at all, or whether they should not go over entirely to the Christian way. So they asked us to tell them all about it.

It was wonderful to see the eagerness with which they listened. Here were people who were really in earnest, and their attention never wavered. The Catechist began from the idol in whose temple we were sitting, drawing from the people, by question and suggestion, their own admission of the futility of worshipping the work of their own hands. Then he went on to appeal to the sense in all of them of a supreme creator God, and to the common situation of guilt before Him. Then came the change from argument to announcement as he told them of Jesus, and of the life which He gives. When the meeting at last came to an end, the majority had expressed themselves as satisfied that this was the truth, and they wanted to be instructed further. They had responded to my suggestion of sending a teacher with the promise of house and food and welcome for him, and the unfettered use of the temple for Christian teaching and worship.[8]

Newbigin's ministry as a bishop in the newly united Church of South India contained features similar to "the old days in the villages around Kanchi-puram except that it was on a much bigger scale." By bus, bicycle, bullock cart, or on foot, he would visit some "very large village congregations, often including fairly prosperous farmers." From 5 or 6 o'clock in the morning until beyond midnight, he would move from village to village:

A typical visit began with an enormous and noisy reception complete with fireworks, bands, dancing and, of course, garlands and fruit; then a slow procession through the village, a service in the church and a public meeting outside to which the whole village came. In each place I preached first to help the congregation to understand the meaning of the union and then to commend to the village as a whole the One who has promised by the power of his atonement to draw all peoples to himself.[9]

When in 1980, at the age of three score years and ten, Newbigin became pastor of the United Reformed congregation at Winson Green, he found— amid all the differences—more than one resemblance between this part of inner-city Birmingham and what he had known in India. Many of the residents in the civic housing areas were in fact from the Indian subcontinent or from the West Indies. In English society at large, a "world whose values and beliefs are ceaselessly fed into every home on the television screen," Newbigin found a "very tough form of paganism" in the form of "a cold contempt for the Gospel which is harder to face than opposition." And "as I visited the Asian homes in the district, most of them Sikhs or Hindus, I found a welcome which was often denied on the doorsteps of the natives."[10] The pastor remained faithful to the style of direct evangelism he had practiced from his student and missionary days, employing both the personal approach and the public witness. From 1982 onward, he secured the colleagueship of Hakim Singh Rahi, a Punjabi- and Urdu-speaking presbyter loaned by the Church of North India, who reports that he constantly accompanied Bishop Newbigin on his visits to the families—"Asian, Afro-Caribbean and English alike"—of children associated with the Sunday School and Boys' and Girls' Brigades and that "sustained contacts were developed with parents of all the backgrounds." Then

> at Christmas, Good Friday and Easter, witness processions were taken out into the streets, and different persons preached at various points in the streets. Bishop Newbigin had excellent ecumenical relations with all the churches in the area; consequently all churches took part to some degree in these witness processions. Leaflets were given out and dropped into homes, with a short message in English, Urdu and Punjabi. Service times of different churches were given, and people were invited to the services. These processions often ended at a public park with open air preaching and singing.[11]

A prayer fellowship met on Saturday evenings to invite and nurture seekers. Candidates were prepared for baptism, "which always took place at the local reservoir with much praise to the Lord. Several families of Sikh background were baptized. New persons from English and Afro-Caribbean backgrounds started attending church services too." The heads of local schools often invited the bishop to speak to the students, Rahi reports.

The practical commitment of Newbigin to evangelism is thus apparent throughout his life as a believer and at various stages in his churchly ministry. Literary evidence supplies the details of the Gospel to which he bore witness. The three publications mentioned at the outset of this chapter—*What is the Gospel?* (1942), *Christ Our Eternal Contemporary* (1968), and *Truth to Tell* (1991)—illustrate both the consistent substance of his message and also his nuanced presentation of it according to the circumstances.

The Gospel for Indian Students

That the title of the booklet *What is the Gospel?* should take the form of a question indicates the approach adopted by Newbigin toward students in the Indian SCM. He directs them to the primary source in the Scriptures and invites them to firsthand engagement with the biblical texts in thought and discussion: "Only to those who thus wrestle with them will they yield their fruit." On examination of the Scriptures, the Gospel appears as "a statement of historical facts made by witnesses who believe and proclaim that these facts have a certain supreme importance." The first task, therefore, in tackling the question "What is the Gospel?" is to "study the earliest evidence as to the facts." In a scientific enquiry, the ultimate standard of authority is conformity to the observed data, which may come to us directly through our senses or may be refined by instruments or may be reported by trustworthy observers. In matters of historical fact we are bound to rely on the evidence of others. By our own insight we cannot *discover* historical facts, but we may be able to assess the reliability of the witnesses. Once "the facts" have been ascertained, the second step in tackling the question about the Gospel, says Newbigin, is to "open all our faculties of perception in the effort to estimate their importance." The choice in "matters of belief"—and we may properly choose only what we believe to be true—is "only rightly made by the use of all our faculties of perception—intellectual (the logical coherence of the belief with other experience), aesthetic (the simple impression which the belief makes on our minds), moral (its implications in practical living)." Newbigin's procedure in the booklet—as will be seen shortly in connection with what he writes on "the implied nature of God"—shows him to be aware that the two-step approach to the question of the Gospel may be overly neat. For our judgment concerning what count as matters of fact may be colored by our previous "background beliefs," and Newbigin himself in later writings will come to emphasize the fiduciary character of all our knowledge.[12] On the other hand, the impression made on us by data may well cause us to modify, or even radically change, our frameworks of interpretation (particularly if, as Newbigin will write in *Proper Confidence*, the *factum* of God's having acted in Christ "cannot form part of any worldview except one of which it is the basis").[13] In any case, Newbigin's later insistence on "personal knowledge"— the phrase he owed to Michael Polanyi's work in the 1950s—is adumbrated in the thesis of this early evangelistic booklet that the study will have borne its fruit "when 'The Gospel' is also 'My Gospel.' "

As the basis for fifteen sessions of study and discussion by the Indian students, Newbigin takes "the first recorded proclamation" of the Gospel, Peter's speech on the day of Pentecost. Acts 2:22–36 is found to contain the following elements: (1) implied views as to the nature of God; (2) a statement about the well-known facts of the life of Jesus of Nazareth (verse 22); (3) a statement about his death (verse 23); (4) a statement about his resurrection (verse 24); (5) a statement about who Jesus is (verses 25–32, 34–36); (6) a statement about the new powers that follow (verse 33). For each of the one or more sessions under those headings Newbigin supplies further biblical references to be followed up, his own reflections on the theme, and usually some suggested questions to start discussion.

The importance of background beliefs emerges immediately in the opening section on "implied views about the nature of God." Peter's speech presupposes "a God of action and purpose," which is indeed the view of the Bible as a whole. Attention is drawn to Psalm 106 (God is the controller of Israel's history), Isaiah 10:5–15 (God uses pagan nations as his instruments), Isaiah 41:1–29 (God is working out a glorious plan, but the gods of the nations are dumb and helpless idols), and to New Testament texts which present the Gospel as the story of God's decisive acts (Hebrews 1:1–4; Luke 20:9–18; John 3:16–18). This is sharply contrasted with Hindu thought concerning God:

Hindu thought for the most part conceives God as the timeless Absolute, for whom history can have no real meaning. For such thought, revelation is given in mystical experiences, when the soul sinks between time and circumstance and finds unity with the unchanging One. Particular events cannot reveal God: they belong to the world of variety and change which hides God from our eyes. To identify God's revelation with a particular person or event is simply to misunderstand what revelation is.

In the sharpest possible contrast to this, the Bible conceives God as personal will, actively engaged in forwarding His purpose in human history. Thus revelation is through concrete historical events and there is no revelation apart from such events. It is through what He does that He shows what He is. The Biblical view of God is thus precisely contradictory to the Hindu view of God at its central point. This is why the Old Testament is indispensable to the Gospel. Without the Old Testament, the New Testament is misunderstood in its fundamental presuppositions.[14]

Thus the Gospel message stands out in all its radical character: "In Peter's speech we have a recital of historical events which took place in a certain town of the Levant 2,000 years ago. Yet these events are confidently proclaimed as the decisive acts of God by which He has laid bare His purpose for the whole human race."

The questions which Newbigin then put for discussion to Indian students six or more decades ago have lost none of their importance either for seekers or for evangelists trying to reach such seekers in the contemporary situation. On the one hand, the religious quest is often marked by spiritualistic escapism; on the other hand, the secularist tendencies in intellectual and even popular culture favor an ultimate nihilism. Newbigin's questions were these: "Does God intervene in history? Is He equally present in all events, or are some events more particularly His deeds than others? Are questions of historical fact of vital significance in religion? Can you discern the purpose which is disclosed in the Gospel Drama as also at work in world history? In Indian history? In your own life history? Do you agree that the Old Testament is indispensable for the understanding of the Gospel?"

It would, of course, be unfortunate if the seeker or the evangelist remained stuck in what in one sense are prolegomena and in another sense are questions that may properly be answered only when the seeker has risked—and the evangelist offered—exposure to the Gospel in greater detail and more of its fullness, both in what it narrates and in the claims that it makes and the blessings that it promises. For even a provisional and tentative opening on the part of a listener may allow sufficient entry for a message that is able to challenge and transform unsympathetic or inadequate outlooks on reality. That is doubtless why Newbigin presses rapidly on to the Gospel story itself in setting forth "What is the Gospel?"

He begins with four sessions devoted to "testimony about the life of Jesus." Thereby he follows the pattern of the canonical New Testament itself: the Gospel writers—the four "evangelists"—tell first the life of Christ. They do so, of course, as believers in the present Lord; and it is only in critical modernity that such faith has been regarded as so grave a disqualification for the accuracy of their tale. At Pentecost, Peter could appeal to facts well known among his hearers in speaking of "Jesus of Nazareth, a man approved of God unto you by mighty works and wonders and signs which God did by him in the midst of you, even as ye yourselves know." Recognizing that later access to those events comes only through the written accounts, Newbigin maintains that "150 years of the most exacting literary criticism of these records has left them in their essentials vindicated as absolutely trustworthy evidence." Six decades later, and after a couple more "quests of the historical Jesus" conducted in large part according to the methodologically atheistic principles of modern historiography, there still seems no reason to reject the lineaments of such a "picture of Jesus" as Newbigin finds the Gospel writers drawing— although the claims that are made by or for Jesus, and the interpretations of his significance, must be decided at another level than that of factual reporting.

The ministry of Jesus is presented as the beginning of the awaited Reign of God. That was the burden of his preaching and the import placed on the healings and the exorcisms he performed (Mark 1:14f.; Luke 4:16–20; 7:18–23; 10:17–24; Matthew 12:22–29): "By word and act He claimed and proved, for those not spiritually blind, that the redemptive powers over evil which had been promised so long, were at work in Him" (note how Newbigin here recognizes that, then as now, spiritual discernment is needed in order to get the meaning of what is occurring). About Jesus' public conduct two things made a uniquely striking impression on his contemporaries, notes Newbigin: his authority and his self-abasement. On the one hand, the common people listened with astonishment to his authoritative teaching and marveled at the power of his word (Luke 4:31–37; cf. Matthew 5:21ff.; 7:24–29; John 12:44–50); a Roman officer recognized in him "the touch of soldierly authority" (Luke 7:2–10); and in the storm on the lake his disciples suddenly glimpsed in him a royal authority that dumbfounded them (Luke 8:22–25). On the other hand, Jesus scandalized the respectable by identifying himself with the lowest: he submitted to a baptism of repentance (Matthew 3:5f., 13–15); he ate and drank with sinners (Luke 5:29–32); he chose obtuse fishermen as colleagues; he washed the feet of disciples who themselves had quarreled about places of honor (John 13:1–14; Mark 10:35–45); being reviled, he reviled not again (1 Peter 2:23); he was born in a stable and died between two bandits (Luke 2:7; 23:32f; Matthew 27:38). "To have grasped fully in one field of vision the authority and self-abasement of Jesus," concludes Newbigin, "is to have grasped the Gospel."

Then, too, the attitudes of Jesus were marked by both severity and tenderness, even in direct juxtaposition, as in the sayings over children and the conditions of entry into the Kingdom (Matthew 18:1–14): to some religious leaders he says "Ye serpents, ye offspring of vipers, how shall ye escape the judgement of hell?" (Matthew 23:33); to the woman taken in adultery, "Neither do I condemn thee; go and sin no more" (John 8:11); to Peter who had thrice denied him, "Simon, son of John, lovest thou Me?" (John 21:15–17). "Ponder the Bible passages," invites Newbigin, "and come to grips with this paradox of the severity and tenderness of Jesus. You will not resolve it, but the effort to resolve it will take you to the very heart of the Gospel." The writer summons his students to follow out the episodes involving those closest to Jesus and those who claimed his help and to ask "whether you know anything greater than His patience, His delicacy of touch, His care for every individual, His utter self-giving and self-emptying. Across His relations with others the faintest shadow of self-seeking never passes." In this world, Jesus is the one occurrence of perfect love, love that is "a relation with people which requires of us that we think—not spasmodically but constantly—from the other's point of view, and yet at the same time never lose hold of the point of view of God who wants him, or her, to be perfect as He is perfect."

That sets the scene for Newbigin's treatment, next, of the New Testament's testimony about the death of Jesus. The fact of the death is incontrovertible; three interpretative themes are discerned for the students to pursue and discuss. First, Jesus' death is presented as a judgment on our world (Mark 8:27–31; Romans 1:18–3:18): "When perfect love appeared, men had to hound it to death," for in our world "there was no room for such a man—who upset everything and claimed everything, a king who yet refused kingship in the only sense in which men understood it." Humankind stands in "a treasonable and murderous conspiracy against God." But, second, the death of Jesus is "God's love in action" (Romans 5:6–11; 8:31–35; 2 Corinthians 5:14f.). For not only does the Cross show up the sinfulness of humankind, but it is also the place where divine love itself bears the judgment deserved by sin:

> The Cross is a judgement, and also a revelation of Love, and it is the one because it is the other. In the Cross we see the self-abasement of Jesus carried to the uttermost. He who exercises the authority of God becomes obedient to death. He dies of His own choice at the hands of those who only deserve death, and in the hour of death prays that they may be forgiven. By being what He is, He allows the fearful evil of all that they (and we) are to fall upon Himself. By so doing, He both shows how evil it is, and also lays the foundation of a new hope. When they have done all they can do, He still loves them. And—as always—He speaks with authority. What He says and does seems to come from God Himself. Can it be that God against whom we sin, and who punishes sinners, at the same time loves them enough to share the punishment and endure the wrath? That is what the Cross means, if we dare to believe that such authority is His.[15]

The third theme picks up from the response of Peter's hearers, pricked to the heart: "What shall we do?" (Acts 2:37). The death of Jesus is presented as "once for all": something decisive has happened which calls also for decision (Acts 4:11f.; Hebrews 10:1–18; Colossians 1:9–23; 2:8–15):

> God has done, once for all, the supreme thing that love could do, come down to our position and borne the shame and pain of our sins Himself. If God has really done this, we have no right to say "I will accept this till He does something better," nor to say "God ought to have done this, or something similar, in India, China, Europe, America." The only thing we can do is to

accept it finally for ourselves and then tell every creature that He has done this. *There* is God's salvation! Stand there, and accept or reject it! This is the message to every man of whatever nation, or language, or culture.[16]

The next three studies in the booklet are given to the biblical testimony about the resurrection of Jesus, for "everything said about the Cross is said because the resurrection followed it." The Resurrection—whose character as event is affirmed on the basis of Matthew 28 and 1 Corinthians 15:1–28 but not further investigated by Newbigin—is first of all the vindication of Jesus and his authority: "The impression that what He said and did was not from man but from God, instead of being proved an illusion, was proved gloriously true." Second, Jesus' resurrection sets his friendship on a new basis, exemplified by the *noli me tangere* scene with Mary Magdalene (John 20:11–18) and now extensible to "all, of whatever race or age." Third, the resurrection of Jesus "proves that the writ of God runs beyond death, and that He can raise victory and life out of defeat and corruption"; because there is a real Kingdom, which is not of this world, we can now for the first time "build in hope."

After the life, then the death, and now the resurrection of Jesus, the question, hitherto on the threshold, becomes unavoidable: Who was, and is, this Jesus? The answer offered in Peter's sermon at Pentecost is "Lord and Christ": "On the lips of a Jew, the first word meant at least this, that to Jesus a name was given which hitherto had been used only for God Himself; and the second meant that Jesus was the inaugurator of God's final victorious rule on earth and in heaven." To "the central question of the Gospel"—"Who say ye that I am?"—the New Testament records would require that the response be a confession in conformity with the following affirmations:

that Jesus believed Himself to be sent by God on a mission of redemption for men which was to be accomplished through His death; that He had a relationship with God which was unique and not shared by those with Him; that He did not wish to be proclaimed as Messiah during His life on earth, but to be recognized as such by each man's faith; that within a very short time of His death His disciples were proclaiming, and thousands of sternly monotheistic Jews were believing, that he was Lord and Christ.

Newbigin leaves his Indian students to discuss the question: "Does it make a serious difference whether we regard Jesus as an incarnation of God or as *the* incarnation of God?" His own affirmation of the uniqueness of Christ will run through his work and thinking as a missiologist, as a participant in religious dialogue, and as an apologist.

The study booklet ends with three sessions on "testimony about the new powers which follow." After the exuberant manifestation of the Holy Spirit at Pentecost, which had attracted Peter's hearers in the first place and which he interpreted as "the sequel of these divine events which have taken place among you," the Church came to reflect more soberly on "the new relationship between God and men, in which God gives Himself to men in a new way." First, the new relationship is marked by freedom: now that God has,

through the Son, won for humankind a salvation it never could have earned
or attained by itself, people may—"if they would give themselves to Jesus as
Jesus has given Himself to them"—feel and live and act with the joyful liberty
of God's children (Romans 8:1–17; Galatians passim). Second, the joy of salvation did not obscure its cost in the Cross of Jesus, and "gratitude produced
moral fruits not poorer but far finer than fear could ever do" (Romans 12;
Colossians 3:1–17). And "whenever in later times the same Gospel has been
rediscovered, the same new power to transform men and societies, to produce
practical results in personal goodness, social justice, and all kinds of adven-
turous energy for the sake of God's Kingdom, has been witnessed." Third, the
new powers created a new kind of fellowship, "the fellowship of the Holy
Spirit," the Church as "a body whose energizing life-blood is the love learned
from Jesus" (1 Corinthians 12–13; 1 John 4:7–21).

The Same Yesterday, Today, and Forever

So far, the story of Newbigin as evangelist has, naturally enough, paralleled
the story of Newbigin as believer: the Gospel faith—grounded in facts, held
in the heart, confessed by the lips, and lived in the life—is what has been
commended to others and proclaimed in the varied circumstances of his student days and the first encounter with India. With *Christ our Eternal Contemporary*, Newbigin is back in India, where, however, the traditional culture is
increasingly affected by modern developments. Through his intervening residence in Europe and his worldwide travels on behalf of the International
Missionary Council, Newbigin has "seen the West" again and observed its
tentacular grasp on the globe. In such circumstances, it is not surprising that
these tape-recorded meditations, originally delivered in July 1966 at the Christian Medical College in Vellore, show greater evidence of the engagement with
modernity that will so strongly mark—and in an ever more critical mode—
his evangelistic thought and activity for the remainder of his life.

Newbigin started his week's "teaching mission" in Vellore by recalling from
Acts 17 the apostle Paul's preaching of "Jesus and the Resurrection" before
the philosophers and religious devotees of Athens. Whereas the names of
ancient deities from the Acropolis are now merely names, the Name of Jesus
is still invoked by countless millions: decades of propaganda by the official
Russian Anti-God Organization have failed to extinguish that Name; and in
the new apartments in the industrial quarters of the Japanese city of Osaka,
the presence of a Bible is three times more common than that of a Buddhist
or Shinto shrine. Nor is it sufficient to picture Jesus, as in popular bazaar art,
with Buddha and Gandhi as "one of the great holy men of history," for such
a view leaves the world as it was and you as you are. The Jesus who is
preached by Christian evangelists, today as in St. Paul's day, is "the risen
Jesus." And

> if Jesus died and rose again, then we are at the beginning of a new world, a
> new creation. . . . He is One who has always created, who is always creating

and who is moving forward with the creation to that end for which, in the beginning, He was the agent. . . . He is this because He is the One who not only died, who not only suffered, who has not only gone down to the deepest depths of the human predicament, who has not only known the deepest darkness of pain and despair and defeat and death, to face them, master them, conquer them—He is the One who goes before us as the pioneer, the leader of the human march. In Jesus, and in Jesus alone, the ultimate depth and height of the human situation has been measured. He is the One who alone has the keys of death and hell.[17]

In the West, where the Name of Jesus has for many centuries been both celebrated and abused, "the dominant literature is informed by a total lack of faith, a total breakdown of any kind of sense of meaning in history, and even the theologians are announcing that God is dead." But Jesus cannot be tied to the vicissitudes of institutions that historically bear the name of Christian. He is "a living sovereign Lord," who appears "like a refiner's fire" (cf. Malachi 3:2), who "holds all things in His hands," and who alone "is able to break the seals and unroll the scroll of human history" (cf. Revelation 5: 1–10). Amid all the changes in the physical, biological, and technological conditions of human existence that both frighten and exhilarate people in modernity, Jesus is "the eternal contemporary," in whom "true meaning and proper use" is to be found, and who "beckons us forward into the future which He has prepared for the human race."

The second Vellore address treats the question "How do we know?" and designates it also as "the problem of authority." Although the personal character of knowledge marked Newbigin's thought from his days as a theological student, in this address he draws on the more recently published book of Michael Polanyi's Gifford Lectures of 1951–52, *Personal Knowledge.*[18] Knowing is "a skill which has to be learnt"; and if "all knowledge is acquired by the skill of learning," learning is "a skill which is exercised only in a community," which both enables and tests new knowledge. Advance in knowledge "involves commitment and therefore an element of risk," for ideas that are initially accepted on trust may, after a creative leap forward, need criticism. Knowledge, however, never leaves faith behind, for it remains necessary that an enquirer and explorer in a particular area continue to trust the best general knowledge available and the community which seeks to further it. That is where the importance of background beliefs again needs to be recognized—those "fundamental, underlying, unquestioned beliefs" that "to a very large extent we take over without even being conscious of them, as part of our culture, as part of all we learn without questioning."

Modernity is an age "dominated by a particular ideal of knowledge": "We are living in a time when the ideal of knowledge is a knowledge of the physical world which can in principle be reduced to mathematical formulae which can be, if necessary, stored in an electronic computer. That is the ideal of knowledge, and other knowledge is accepted as reliable in so far as it approaches that ideal." But in human history there have been other ideals of knowledge. One such is found in Indian classical thought, where "the knowledge of ultimate reality is to be found by withdrawal from all the experiences of the senses, from involvement in a world of visible and tangible and measurable things, by withdrawal into a world where, it is claimed, a deeper and truer knowledge of reality is to be found. . . . This concept of knowledge finds its assurance, its force of certitude, ultimately in that mystical experience of the unity of the conscious self," where "*athma* and *brahma* are one." Another, quite different, ideal of knowledge is embodied in the Bible, where "the primary meaning of the word 'to know' is to know another person" and knowledge comes "in the adventure of trust and commitment to another person" who "discloses his own mind and heart to me."

How, asks Newbigin, does such "knowledge of persons" relate to "our whole knowledge of the world"? Again he draws a contrast between the view of the Bible and the view of Indian sages (and Greek, as well). He notes in human development generally a passage in the perception of reality from incoherent multiplicity to unity. It is the passage from the gods and goddesses of the early Greek legends to the mental unity of the philosophers. In Indian terms, it is the road from the polytheism of the Rig Veda to the Vedanta, where "the key to unlock the mystery of the world is the power of the human mind to transcend and unify the whole of experience in a single consciousness." In this solution, "time ceases to have any ultimate significance": it is but "the movement of the circumference of a great wheel," whereas truth resides "at the centre where everything is at rest"; and consequently, "personality, the distinction between me and you, everything that is involved in the tension and clash of a personal relationship—everything that is involved in the Hebrew conception of knowing—is seen as part of the world of unreality which ultimately is not significant."

The road that the Bible records is very different. Although "there is plenty of evidence that the early Hebrews—the majority of people at least—thought of their god as one among the gods of the nations," from "that apparently unpromising beginning there has emerged a majestic conception of a living personal God who guides and rules all the nations and who is in fact the Creator and Ruler and Consummator of the whole universe." The clue is not found in the power of the mind to unify and transcend experience but in "the experience of a personal relationship of love and truth and faithfulness." The secret lies "in the existence of a Reality which is now present behind all the confusion of the visible world"; the secret resides "in the mind of him who has created all things and who will bring order out of all this chaos, who is indeed ceaselessly *engaged* in bringing order out of this chaos, who will in the end sum up all things in Christ." So here "time is of the essence of the matter," for "God is at work and doing something, and because he is doing something, the time which he takes to do it is real time." Moreover, "by means of actions in history" and their inspired interpretation, God "has shared his plans with us." We are part of that history, and the revelatory events (decisively, the exodus from Egypt, the captivity in Babylon and the deliverance from it, and the coming of Jesus and his dying and rising again) are summonses to people to commit themselves to God in return and to participate in God's work. Only as we so share do we _know_. That knowledge begins when Jesus "lays hold" of a person.

In the third Vellore meditation, Newbigin comes to "the fact of Christ"— "who Jesus is and how it is that He lays hold on us." The fact of Christ is "the starting point, whose justification will only be at the end, if it enables us to grasp the whole of our experience truly." It is a personal starting point, insofar as Newbigin alludes to Christ's having laid hold on him when, at a time of deep perplexity, he was given the vision of Christ's Cross as the one reality spanning the entire range of things.[19] But he insists that Christ mediates himself to us through a community and its Book. From the reliable records of the Gospels Newbigin paints for his audience a picture of Jesus in his humanity: a man who could be hungry, disappointed, exhausted, a marvelous storyteller and brilliant debater, tender with the outcast and fearless toward the local maharajah; who yet "assumes as a matter of fact that it is he who makes the final judgement upon all mankind," announces that the Kingdom of God is manifest in his deeds, and speaks of himself as the unique Son of the Father. Now as then, people confronted by Jesus are compelled to make a decision: "Either this claim is true, in which case we must worship him as Lord, or else this claim is false, in which case we must destroy him as a deceiver and blasphemer." Then, the practically unanimous decision was taken: "Crucify him." But "God reversed the unanimous verdict of men and raised him from the dead." In the resurrection of Jesus on the third day, "a new world was born. That was an event which can never be fitted into any other picture of the universe. It can only be believed as the foundation upon which a new understanding of the universe is built." In the face of it, one has now again to decide about Jesus, and whether we shall pass from being "misfits in this world which God has made" and enter the reconciliation that Christ, "truly man and truly God," has "accomplished between man and his Maker." Left with no other ground to stand on, we find that Christ "stretches out his hand and says, 'No, you shall not die. I died, so that you should not die. You shall live. That is my will; it is for that that I died. You shall live for me.'" The only response is "to give thanks with the whole of one's being, to offer back that which He has given." That, at least, was the response of the man on the other cross to whom Jesus said "This day you shall be with me in paradise" and made him "the first of the human race to be reconciled to God through Jesus Christ."

Newbigin then comes in the fourth Vellore address directly to "the Christian hope" as an answer to the question "Where do we end?" or at least "What is there to look forward to?" Death renders inadequate the modern individualism, whether irreligiously existentialist or religiously escapist, that makes history "a non-stop variety show, in which each of the actors comes on to the stage and does his bit and goes off, and what he does has no relation to what is done after him or before him"; death renders equally inadequate the Marxist collectivism in which, for the sake of "the cause," expendable workers become "like the shavings on the carpenter's floor which are swept up and burned when the job is finished." It would be a bleak choice between "finding significance in the history of mankind as a whole at the cost of losing any significance for the human person" and "finding significance for the individual human person at the cost of losing significance for the history of man as a whole." From the Bible Christianity draws the vision of reality in which, rather than human history being imprisoned within nature through a recurring cycle of birth and growth and decay and death, the whole world is taken up into a history from creation to the final consummation, the clue to which is the story of Israel and Jesus. Through the death and resurrection of the Suffering Servant and its proclamation, "a great multitude from all nations is being brought into a new fellowship of those who look eagerly forward to the coming in glory of a righteous kingdom, to the summing up of all things in Christ; not a return to the Garden of Eden, but the advance to a city, the Holy City into which all of the nations will bring their glory, their culture, their civilisation." It is "a corporate hope" for "the completing of God's whole creative purpose for the world," in which people from all intervening generations will have a place. Finding "its pattern and its security in the dying and rising of Jesus," the Christian faith consists in following "the same path of total commitment to the doing of the Father's will and the manifesting of the Father's righteous rule here in this world which He has made and which He loves and which He is bringing to its consummation, albeit a consummation which cannot be achieved except with a cleansing by fire." Because of our sin, egotism, and blindness, there is no direct route from our efforts to the kingdom of God; but, offered to God in faith, our actions become, in Albert Schweitzer's words, "an acted prayer for the coming of the kingdom"; and God "is able to keep what I have committed to Him against that day" (2 Timothy 1:12).

For Christians, Jesus has never been simply a figure in the receding past but always a present reality, who is indeed also to come. That is due to "the Spirit of God, the Spirit of Jesus, the Holy Spirit," who since Pentecost has been poured out upon the entire community of believers. Drawing on Romans 8 and other passages from St. Paul, Newbigin's next meditation expounds "life in the Spirit" as freedom (from futile attempts at self-justification), as sonship (neither mastery nor slavery, but confidence and obedience toward the Father who is Lord of all), as an inheritance (of which we already have the down payment but must await with patience the fullness), as witness (where our words and deeds allow the hidden rule of God to be glimpsed), fellowship (mutual care and help through the exercise of diverse gifts from the one Source), and, supremely, love, which is the outflow of Christ's love through us for others.

Under the title of "God in Experience," Newbigin in the sixth meditation addresses rather pointedly his original audience at the Vellore Christian Hospital, where, for all its Christian foundation, the staff, as well as of course the patients, might be Hindu or Muslim. He seeks to show that some of the hospital's seemingly—and perhaps indeed really—current secularist assumptions, paradoxically including at some level its religious pluralism, derive from the Bible and from Christianity. At least there is a correspondence between the belief that the entire human race is made in the image of God and the common purpose, freely accepted by all who choose to work there, that the hospital be "a place where the human person is cared for as a person, whoever he is, whether he be rich or poor, whether he be Muslim, Hindu, Christian, or whatever." Actively, "a human being in God's intention is"—according to the Christian faith—"a being who echoes, who responds to God's own unending gift of love," "a person who gives himself to his neighbour as God gives himself to us, a person who is responsible for his neighbour as God accepts responsibility for us." Newbigin then interprets thus the "strange sentence" of Dietrich Bonhoeffer, whose wartime writings were capturing theological attention in the 1960s:

> "God is calling us in our generation to live as if God did not exist." I believe that when Bonhoeffer said that, he was in line with the great prophets. He was referring to the forms of religion (especially perhaps the forms that belong to the days when we had a Christian sacral society, the days when Christianity was the established religion) and saying that we are being called to go beyond that, to go out into the ordinary secular world, not with a religious label on us, but simply to play our part as grateful sinners redeemed by Christ, in meeting the needs of men, not protected by any religious forms, not insisting that the label "Christian" be over us and all that we do, but simply, as it were, anonymously, going out into the ordinary world of men's needs, and there seeking to honour and serve all men.[20]

The lecturer goes on to recall, perhaps inexactly, a sentence from such a superficially different source as one of Oswald Chambers's devotional books concerning someone who was "so completely holy as to be absolutely unnoticeable." Non-Christians are invited "not to look at us Christians" but to "look at Jesus," especially "as He is given to us in the New Testament"; yet they must not ask Christians to "live in a night where all cats are grey," accepting "the dogma that all religions are really the same." The responsibility of Christians on the staff of the hospital is humbly to do the job for which God has chosen them, bearing witness—however unworthily—to Jesus Christ. In a "secular society," that will entail "a deepened personal religion," "a deeply experienced communion with God"—not as escape from the world, nor yet as exhaustive immersion in it, but as faithful, sacramental identification with Jesus Christ at his Cross and Resurrection, where "both the separation of God from the world and the identification of God with the world are at their absolute maximum"—and so as sharers in Christ's reconciling ministry (as John 17:15–20 pictures it).

There comes a point, says Newbigin, when discussion must yield to decision; and so he entitles the last of his talks "Conversion." That is a prickly subject, because religious conversion has sometimes taken place at the social level by cultural conquest and at the individual level by unfair arguments and tricks. Yet truth is decisively at stake, and Christians cannot accept either for themselves or for others what Newbigin again calls "the dogma"—which is popular among Indian intellectuals but which "under the cloak of neutrality" is in fact "a particular form of religious belief"—"that all religions are really the same." Conversions, therefore, need be neither meaningless nor wrong. The content and procedure of conversion that Newbigin puts forward is drawn from the Bible, both Old Testament and New. The prophets of Israel constantly call the people of the covenant to "return to the Lord," recognizing that only "a remnant will return" (Isaiah 10:20–22)—those "whose hearts the Lord has turned back" (1 Kings 18:37). John the Baptist, and then Jesus, tell the people to "turn their minds around"—to look in the right direction and see, says Jesus, that the kingdom has dawned in himself (Mark 1:15). Jesus chooses twelve to follow him and in due course become "fishers of men" (Mark 1:16–20; 3:13–19; cf. John 15:16). Three points are vital here for the understanding of conversion: "the call is addressed to all"; "those whom God actually converts are few"; they "are converted not for their own sake but for the sake of all." Then, by the preaching of the Gospel, the Gentiles are summoned—and the Holy Spirit enables them—to "turn from idols to the living God, who made heaven and earth" (Acts 14:15; 1 Thessalonians 1:4–10). Thus conversion, according to the New Testament, essentially involves three things: first and fundamentally, "a personal commitment to Jesus Christ as Lord and Saviour, the Son of God, 'who loved me and gave himself for me' "; second, "a pattern of conduct," a "disciplined freedom" in order "to be at the service of your neighbour"; and third, "a visible companionship," a community of people who are baptized into Christ's death and resurrection, abide in the apostles' teaching concerning Jesus, belong to a fellowship of his disciples known for their love of one another, break bread to share in his offering of himself to the Father, and join in the prayer which he taught. Today, the call to conversion is addressed first "to those who bear the name of Christ, but who have not made that personal commitment, or who have fallen away from it or grown slack and cold in it," and then also "to all who do not bear the name of Christ":

> to you also, my patient hearers of Hindu or Muslim or other faiths: You are already looking to Jesus, or you would not have come to these meetings. To be converted means for you, I think, to let Jesus have the last word in regard to your life, to let him have the full surrender of your life, to let him have the key that unlocks the inner chamber of your house. And if he comes in, he will show you the way by which he means you to walk, and give you the light that you need to walk in it.

And in a final exhortation, Newbigin reminds those who have started on the track that there is a cloud of witnesses urging them on to keep their eyes fixed on Jesus, who is the pioneer and perfecter of faith (Hebrews 12:1f.).

Although there are obviously many characteristic themes in these Vellore addresses and Newbigin's evangelistic zeal clearly does not flag, there is also at points an unfamiliar tone. Thus in the opening evocation of the "cataclysmic speed" of social and technological change, he wrote that "the truth is, if we will believe it, that all this exhilaration of change is but the reflection of [Christ's] urgent mission from the Father to set men free, to bring them to that adult maturity in which they can answer freely and intelligently the definite invitation to be the sons of God."[21] The addresses were originally delivered in the mid-1960s, during the heady days of theological enthusiasm for secularization. Newbigin would later regard his own mild succumbing to this trend as a temporary aberration. It preceded the cultural and ecumenical disillusionment of 1968 (the WCC Uppsala assembly—which Newbigin would regard as marking a disastrous turn away from the classic goals of ecclesial unity and evangelical mission—could only have occurred in the year of the "student revolution"). From the 1970s on, Newbigin continued to hold in high regard many of the achievements of science and technology—but adopted an altogether more somber outlook on the hegemonic pretensions of modernity.

Reconverting the West

In the third and latest sample of Newbigin's evangelistic writings, *Truth to Tell*, the author is not engaging in direct evangelism. The exercise is more oblique. In the context of the Osterhaven Lectures at Western Theological Seminary, Newbigin is addressing a Church hobbled in its own understanding of the Gospel that needs release from some of the assumptions it shares with the ambient culture in order to be able to preach the authentic Gospel to contemporary society and its denizens. The situation is the early 1990s, when many churches in the Western world were starting to respond to the call for "a decade of evangelism." Newbigin was concerned lest this be understood simply in terms of "revival," "a return to values that have been forgotten and need to be reaffirmed." Rather the Gospel calls for people—first the evangelizers and then the evangelized—"to believe something which is radically different from what is normally accepted as public truth." It invites a conversion not only of the individual heart and will but of the mind in its social setting, for the Gospel's own claim is to be a "public truth which ought to be acknowledged as true for the whole of the life of society." For the sake of evangelization in the contemporary situation, the nature and content of Christian belief once more need clarification. The exposition of faith that was encountered as *Proper Confidence* in the previous chapter is, in *Truth to Tell*, oriented toward evangelism: "I believed, *and so* I spoke."

Compared with the long centuries of Christendom, faith and the preaching of it now involve a different, and perhaps more basic, questioning of the reigning assumptions of public life. Much more will be said in chapter 10, on Newbigin as apologist, concerning his diagnosis of the history and condition of Western civilization. Here it suffices to note that Newbigin finds late twentieth-century Westerners caught between, on the one hand, the false objectivity of a rationalism that still enjoys the prestige accruing from brilliant scientific achievements and, on the other hand, a rebellious subjectivism that relativizes and fragments reality into what "seems meaningful for me." That dilemma is reflected in the Church by the conflicts between fundamentalists, who in some ways constitute a mirror image of "scientism," and liberals, who

Scientific rationism & meaning for me

privatize faith as the religious experience and opinions of individuals. In society at large, and perhaps in the penumbra of the Church, the situation is aggravated by the existence of a skepticism that—rejecting the preceding alternatives—doubts the possibility of knowing truth at all. Among an intellectual élite, a Nietzschean fashion is current that regards claims to such knowledge as merely a concealed assertion of power. "Deconstructionism" is the self-chosen name for a program that allows the Chinese thinker Carver Yu to make "literary despair" the opposite pole to "technological optimism" in his twofold characterization of contemporary Western culture, where in what Newbigin calls an "ultimate absurdity" all claims to speak of truth may appear untenable.

In this situation, says Newbigin, the Gospel may and must offer, as it did in the hands of Athanasius and Augustine during the collapse of the ancient world of Greece and Rome and its "plausibility structures," a new *archê*, a fresh departure from which to reconfigure the landscape. It is in the nature of the Gospel to do that, for "the resurrection of Jesus from the dead is the beginning of a new creation, the work of that same power by which creation itself exists" and hence "the starting point for a new way of understanding and dealing with the world." The Gospel itself does not change: "The story Peter tells on the day of Pentecost, the story he tells in the home of Cornelius, the story Paul tells to the church in Corinth as the one he had originally been told is recognizable as the same story." To allege its cultural remoteness in first-century Palestine as grounds for its unintelligibility today is "a denial of the fundamental unity of the human race": "The landless laborers of South India with whom I have had the privilege of sharing the Gospel are at least as culturally remote from me as are the New Testament writers. Yet they are perfectly able to understand and rejoice in the Gospel, although they certainly find their own ways of responding to it." Nor did the shock of a proclaimed resurrection await "the rise of the modern scientific worldview": "The fact that a man who has been dead and buried for three days does not rise from the tomb was well known even before the invention of electric lights."[22] Yet the Gospel claims to tell "news about things which have happened," "real events for which there are witnesses," and it would be the sheerest "cultural chauvinism" to suppose that our constructions of "what really happened," shaped as they are by our own cultural perspectives, "must necessarily displace that of the immediate witnesses," who must have the premier role in the conversation between the present and the past.

The content of the Gospel and the starting point of the new creation is "God's revelation of his being and purpose in those events which form the substance of the Scriptures and which have their center and determining focus in the events concerning Jesus."[23] As it has done in every traditional retelling and continuation of the story, the process by which knowledge of this revelation is appropriated corresponds, on the human side, to the process of scientific exploration as it has been described by Michael Polanyi, who wrote from the viewpoint of "a working scientist . . . who is trying to discover the truth rather than from the point of view of the professional philosopher who is dealing with claims to know truth": it involves "personal commitment in faith and personal judgment about evidence," all deployed in a community that provides rules and tools and requires that individual efforts—and ultimately the corporate enterprise itself—be subject to a procedure of "publish and test." In the case of the Christian claim that "Jesus is the true and living way," the publication and the test consist in "world mission"—understood as "exegesis of the Gospel," whereby the universal sovereignty and saviorhood of Christ is not only proclaimed by the Church but also learned in the risky struggle "to bring all the manifold works of learning and industry and politics and the arts into obedience to [Christ]"; and its truth will have been fully demonstrated only when "the Lordship of Jesus has been manifested in the lives of all peoples and in all sectors of human living." The "central claim of the Gospel" remains that "it is Jesus, the crucified and risen Jesus, who is alone the center around which alienated human beings can be drawn together in a reconciled fellowship."

For the proving of "the validity and power of the Christian faith" in public life it will be necessary to overcome in the Church a practical dichotomy—which in some ways is the reverse of the initial epistemological dichotomy—between liberals, on the one hand, who have been thought to have "substituted for the Gospel of salvation through Jesus Christ a whole range of social and political issues . . . on which the preacher was less well informed than many of the listeners," and fundamentalists, on the other, who have been thought to peddle "cheap grace" instead of making a call to follow Jesus in challenging the wrongs of the world. If the Church is "the bearer of the truth by which all human beings must live" and "the ethical implications of the Gospel [are] the law of the Creator with jurisdiction over the entire human family," then it is the public duty of the Church, in the light of the Gospel and in the face of society, to "unmask the ideologies" and "condemn reigning falsehoods" in order to present a better—because more truthful and evangelical—account and model of life and community. As the crucial thing to reject in contemporary Western society, Newbigin names an "idolatrous conception of freedom which equates it with the freedom of each individual to do as he or she wishes" that thus contradicts "the trinitarian faith which sees all reality in terms of relatedness": "In explicit rejection of an individualism which puts the autonomous self at the center and sees other selves as limitations on our freedom, we have to set the basic dogma entrusted to us, namely that freedom is to be found by being taken into that community of love given and received which is the eternal reality from which and for which all things exist." A genuine Gospel witness will be a "lay" witness, in the sense that it is the responsibility of each and every Christian in the universal priesthood (and training and equipment must be provided for those in specific areas of secular work and public life, where "plausibility structures" are shaped). As to corporate witness, "the most important contribution which the Church can make to a new social order is to be itself a new social order"; and "the basic unit of that new society is the local congregation."

Provided it is "a place where the Gospel is preached and believed," the local congregation is "the place where the truth is tested and experienced in the most basic way":

> The local Christian congregation, where the word of the Gospel is preached, where in the sacrament of the Eucharist we are united with Christ in his dying for the sin of the world and in his risen life for the sake of the world, is the place where we are enabled to develop a shared life in which sin can be both recognized and forgiven. If this congregation understands its true character as a holy priesthood for the sake of the world, and if its members are equipped for the exercise of that priesthood in their secular employment, then there is a point of growth . . . from which the subversion of the principalities and powers and the first shoots of a new creation can develop.[24]

The only title deeds of the local congregation are as "the local presence of the one holy catholic and apostolic Church that we acknowledge in the creeds." Therein resides the urgency of visible Christian unity in the truth of the Gospel.

The striking of that ecclesiological note both prepares for some summary remarks on the principles and practice of evangelism and heralds the following chapter on Newbigin as ecumenist.

Locality and Language

Newbigin came to speak of the local church as the church not in or of but *for* a particular place.[25] That turn of phrase signals two themes in his understanding and practice of evangelism: first, the local church is the primary instrument of evangelization; second, the church should neither be detached from the local culture (as though the culture were merely the ambience "in" which the church happened to be located) nor yet be absorbed by the local culture (so that the church became the possession "of" that culture), but rather the church is called to win and transform that culture for Christ.

The first insight was not easily acquired by one whose overseas ministry as an evangelist began under the direction of a board for foreign missions. Many years later, Newbigin testified gratefully to the new vision brought to him by "a lonely prophet" from the early decades of the twentieth century, the former Anglican missionary in China Roland Allen (1869–1947), whose writings he had encountered during the late 1940s: "I fought against his ideas, but it was a losing battle."[26] Allen's principal book publications were *Missionary Methods: St. Paul's or Ours?* (1912, 1927), *Pentecost and the World: The Revelation of the Holy Spirit in the Acts of the Apostles* (1917), *The Spontaneous Expansion of the Church, and the Causes which Hinder it* (1927), and *The Case for Voluntary Clergy* (1930).[27] Under the power of the Holy Spirit, whether in the apostolic period or in later times, the "spontaneous expansion of the Church" was typically due, said Allen, to the activity of a single zealous Christian spreading the word from a small congregation, which would then quickly "propagate itself" among the new group of converts by equipping them with the Gospel (through the Bible), the Faith (summed up in the Creed), the Sacraments (of Baptism and the Lord's Supper), and the Ministry ("local men ordained for the local church"); in turn, members from that new community would carry the Gospel further, and the propagation of the Church would continue. For all his emphasis on the "charismatic," Allen clearly remained a "catholic": his "Gospel," "Faith," "Sacraments," and "Ministry" correspond to the Lambeth Quadrilateral of 1888 (including "the historic episcopate, *locally adapted in the methods of its administration*"). It was from the cumbersome machinery of "the establishment" that Allen wished to free Anglicans and others in favor of practical apostolicity. During his formative years in China, Allen was learning, wrote Newbigin, to "prise the missionary calling loose from its colonial moorings";[28] and then through his writings he helped Newbigin and others to move toward a new pattern of evangelization that, in recognizing "the sovereignty of the Spirit as the true agent of mission," called for a radical reordering of ecclesiastical and ministerial practice. This was the message Newbigin delivered to the founding assembly of the East Asia Christian Conference at Kuala Lumpur in 1959 and which he tried a few years later to carry over to the global scale through the program of the World Council of Churches on "The Missionary Structure of the Congregation."[29] If Allen's ideas took a long time to gain acceptance (and then only patchily), that was not necessarily surprising or regrettable. Newbigin wrote in 1962:

> I have known in my own experience the long years of wrestling with these issues which were needed before a Church was willing to put some of Allen's ideas to the test. But those years of wrestling were not mere 'preliminaries'; they were not an unfortunate necessity arising from the slowness and dullness of committees and clerics. They were part of the essential thing that Allen was concerned about—the re-submission in each generation of the traditions of men to the Word and Spirit of God.[30]

That the results could be dramatic is clear from a story Newbigin narrates at first hand from rural South India: "In an area almost entirely pagan, the number of Christian congregations rose from thirteen to fifty-five in twelve years. The secret of growth was the spontaneous witness of the new Christians themselves."[31]

In 1994 Newbigin was still—or again—writing that "as churches of the old Christendom try to come to terms with the progressive paganization of the 'Western' world, they have not yet learned what Allen had to teach about mission, as an always fresh and surprising work of the Spirit." In two respects, in particular, a rediscovery of Allen's ideas could prove fruitful—"firstly in respect of the local congregation in the very discouraging mission fields of pagan Europe and North America. In England, certainly, a strong dose of Roland Allen's missiology would have a wonderful effect in loosening up the stiff joints and muscles of the typical congregation, of whatever denomination, and would bring a liberating confidence in the power of the Holy Spirit to

bring his own witness into the life of the world." A second significant contribution from Allen's ideas could—and should—affect the changing shape of
the ecumenical movement:

> During the past century this movement has been concerned with the rela-
> tionships between the main Christian confessions as they are organized lo-
> cally, nationally and globally. But we seem now to be in a situation where
> the growing edges of the Church are not in these bodies but in the increasing
> numbers of independent bodies of Christians: house churches, "independent
> Christian fellowships," "base communities," and so on. It seems to be in such
> movements that the signs of vitality are evident. In one respect they reflect
> Allen's central teaching about the role of the Holy Spirit in the life and growth
> of the Church. They generally lack, however, the other element of his teach-
> ing—the objectivity, given-ness and power of sacraments and the apostolic
> ministry linking them to the universal Church. Many in these movements
> seek to escape from the rigidities of the old "Christendom" patterns, but do
> not see, as Allen did, that one can cherish the elements of order which give
> coherence to the universal Church and yet be free from the heavy structures
> with which these elements have been associated during the centuries of
> "Christendom." It seems to me that it is in this direction that the movement
> for Christian unity must move in the immediately coming decades, and I
> think that the missiology of Roland Allen could powerfully contribute to such
> a development.[32]

Those thoughts will be picked up again in the next chapter, when consideration is given to Newbigin's contributions to the modern ecumenical movement and his reading of it, as well as to its prospects in the twenty-first
century.

The remaining theme of this chapter is the relation between evangelization
and the local culture. Newbigin's engagement with the modern West is discussed in chapter 10. At this stage, the focus falls on his ideas and practice
while in India, even if questions of what is now called "inculturation" are no
longer limited to the areas beyond historic Christendom. The case in point is
Tamil culture or, more personally put, Newbigin's evangelistic approach to
the Tamil people and their language.

The first fundamental clue, in two parts, is found in Newbigin's reaction
when, after more than twenty years of close acquaintance with South India,
he was in 1958 asked to accept nomination as general secretary of the International Missionary Council, a position that would entail residence in Europe and constant travel: "I did not want to go. I *loved the Tamil people and
country* and had *learned to be at home in their language and ways of life.*"[33]
When in June 1959 he did leave Madurai, Newbigin entered this in his diary:

> There was a great crowd at the station. At the end they just stood in a great
> mass and gazed and gazed at me till I felt I would weep. We sang (a Tamil
> lyric) and at last the train moved off and the group became only a blob in
> the distance. . . . There was a group at Kodai Road station with fruit and
> flowers and honey and they asked me to bless them before the train left. At
> Dindigul there was another big group with many presents. Then that was

left behind too, and as the train went on through the night I tried to face the fact that I was no longer their bishop. I realized that I loved them and that they loved me and I prayed that God would keep them.[34]

The Tamil language—which Newbigin had spent strenuous years in acquiring and perfecting—became the vehicle of his love for the Tamil people, for his proclamation of the Gospel to them, for the response of faith that some made to the message, and for the love that they returned to the messenger. In the early months of their first tour in India, Lesslie and Helen spent eight hours a day in study of the language: "We secured the services of the most successful Tamil teacher available, a redoubtable and colourful Brahmin named Ragavachariar. He was a brilliant teacher with a great love for the language and a very delicate ear for the precise nuance of meaning conveyed by a word or phrase. He helped us not only to read and speak Tamil but to see things through the eyes of a Hindu."[35] That simple report already makes two vital points in connection with the communication of the Gospel: the importance of sensitivity to the existing language of the hearers and of an empathetic understanding of their worldview.

Examples of reckoning with an Indian worldview—and challenging it in the name of the Gospel—have already been given in this chapter, and more will emerge in the discussion later of Newbigin as a religious interlocutor in chapter 6. As to language, even in his writings in English Newbigin would sometimes make a point on the basis of Tamil linguistic usage or correct a misunderstanding opened up by an earlier Tamil translation of the Christian Scriptures. At the beginning of his book *Sin and Salvation*, conceived (as was noted in the previous chapter) in Tamil, the author remarks:

> The words used in the Tamil Bible to translate 'sin' and 'salvation' are both unfortunate. The word *pavam*, which is used for 'sin', carries much less of the idea of personal guilt and responsibility and much more of the idea of misfortune than is proper for an equivalent of the biblical word 'sin'. And the word *ratchippu* means primarily providing support and sustenance. Dr. J. H. Maclean of Conjeeveram [= Kanchipuram], that great missionary of the Church of Scotland, used to say that the real meaning of the words used in the Tamil Bible at 1 Timothy 1:15 is 'Christ Jesus came into the world to provide free board and lodging for rascals'. The Hindu observer of our multitudinous philanthropic activities—and of our churches—is apt to think that he has understood that text.[36]

Or again, in expounding the biblical teaching concerning the Spirit, Newbigin regrets the choice of the Tamil word *aavi* that connotes "steam" rather than capturing the sense of the Hebrew *ruach* as "the mighty, mysterious wind out of the desert, of which one has to say, where does it come from? where does it go to? and yet when it is here, it is powerful, it shakes things, and we cannot escape it."[37]

Two or three stories from Newbigin's time as bishop in Madras will further illustrate the subtleties surrounding the relation between the Gospel and the culture to be evangelized. On Newbigin's return to India in 1965 to take up the metropolitan bishopric, he relates this concerning the service at his installation:

> Services in St. George's Cathedral had always been in English, as it was the temple of the old English establishment. I thought it was important to give the central part of my sermon in Tamil and the point of this was not lost, as the very full newspaper coverage next morning showed. Tamil came back easily, but I found that the movement led by C. N. Annadurai for the elimination of Sanskrit words in favour of pure Tamil and for a new style of sentence construction made my Tamil seem very old-fashioned. I therefore got the help of a teacher to steer me, in daily lessons, into a more acceptable style.[38]

In May 1967, C. N. Annadurai became the chief minister of the state of Tamilnadu, at the head of the Dravida Munetra Kazhagam party that was held together not so much by a political program as by devotion to the Tamil language and culture and that was officially committed to atheism. The latter commitment did not worry Newbigin, since "the gods whose existence they denied were, in my Christian understanding, no gods." In celebration of Tamil culture, the government organized an international festival that would entail the erection of a series of bronze statues along the Madras marina; lest a grave historical injustice be committed, an Indian bureaucrat encouraged Bishop Newbigin to commission and offer sculptures of two nineteenth-century English missionaries who had done the groundwork for the Tamil Lexicon and for the comparative grammar of the Dravidian languages. The sculptor's fee of 25,000 rupees was raised in small contributions from the Christian institutions in the state. The chief minister accepted the offer and eventually asked Newbigin to dedicate one of the statues: "And so on an evening in January 1968 I stood before an audience of 250,000 people on the Madras beach, with the Chief Minister and his entire cabinet, and delivered an oration in Tamil in praise of Dr. G. U. Pope, the Methodist missionary who had translated some of the Tamil classics into English and laid the foundation of the Tamil Lexicon." The other Englishman to be honored was Bishop Robert Caldwell, who had published a *Comparative Grammar of the Dravidian Languages* and demonstrated their independence from Sanskrit; and a third statue commemorated the eighteenth-century Italian Jesuit, C. J. Beschi. Wryly, Newbigin remarks that the episode is "a nice commentary on the popular view that the only work of missionaries has been to destroy native cultures."[39]

A third story concerns the celebration of the nineteenth centenary of the martyrdom of St. Thomas. "That the apostle Thomas came to India, that he was martyred, and that his bones lie buried under the Cathedral of Mylapore is, for most Indian Christians, an article of faith almost worthy of inclusion in the Apostles' Creed. Indeed there is," says Newbigin, "an impressive amount of evidence to point to the possibility that it may be so." Although the commemoration was organized by the Roman Catholic Church, Newbigin joined in to claim Thomas also as "a good member of the Church of South

India": "The whole celebration was a great witness to the City. There was a vast public meeting in the Island Ground where several ponderous addresses in English were lost on the audience, but the Chief Minister and I spoke in Tamil, and I think something of the meaning of the event was communicated. At any rate one of the Jesuit Fathers ran up to me at the end and embraced me and said 'I have been converted all over again!' "[40]

An ecumenical and a personal note may wind up these remarks on inculturation. In 1995 there appeared a new translation of the whole Bible into contemporary Tamil, sponsored by both the United Bible Societies and the Roman Catholic Church. Meanwhile, Lesslie Newbigin, living with impaired eyesight in his third retirement in Southeast London, benefited from the services of local *garagistes*, who read for him the Tamil letters that he still received from friends in India.

3

The Ecumenical Advocate

I do not pray for these only, but also for those who believe in
me through their word, that they may all be one; even as thou,
Father, art in me, and I in thee, that they also may be in us,
so that the world may believe that thou hast sent me.

(John 17:20f.)

The Movement for Mission and Unity

The modern ecumenical movement is conventionally dated from an event
that took place in the first year of Lesslie Newbigin's life and within a hundred
miles of his parents' Northumbrian home. A world missionary conference was
held at Edinburgh, Scotland, in June 1910 in order "to consider missionary
problems in relation to the non-Christian world." From that event sprang
both the International Missionary Council, formally constituted in 1921, and
(at least in the mind of Bishop Charles Henry Brent) the Faith and Order
movement, whose first world conference would gather at Lausanne, Switzerland, in 1927. In 1948—the agreement of 1938 having been delayed by the
Second World War—Faith and Order merged with the Life and Work movement from the 1920s to compose the World Council of Churches; and in
1961 they were joined by the International Missionary Council. "Edinburgh
1910" was chaired by the American Methodist layman John R. Mott, who
was already active in the World's Alliance of YMCAs and the founder of the
World's Student Christian Federation. The conference had an ecumenical
scope insofar as it represented missionary work in every part of "the inhabited
earth" (*oikumenê* in the Greek). It was embryonically ecumenical in another
sense in that it brought together leaders from at least the Protestant sector
of Christendom and set them on the track toward ecclesial unity (albeit there
were lacking yet the Orthodox and Roman Catholic churches; each of these
in fact claimed for itself alone ecumenicity in the sense of identity with "the
entire Church").[1]

In its direct concern with worldwide mission, Edinburgh 1910 determined
on the encouragement of self-governing, self-supporting, and self-propagating
churches in every region and the development of practical cooperation
through institutional forms. Yet, in some eyes at least, the accomplishment

of the mission required more than collaboration among the separate agencies. From the Edinburgh conference, Charles Henry Brent, an American missionary bishop in the Philippines, returned to persuade the general convention of the Protestant Episcopal Church in the United States to assume an initiative in bringing about "a conference for the consideration of questions touching Faith and Order" among "all Christian Communions throughout the world which confess our Lord Jesus Christ as God and Saviour." For the profoundest impediment to evangelization, some saw, consisted in those divisions among Christian communities that amounted to "the scandal of disunity": the Gospel of the world's reconciliation to God—as the apostle Paul formulated it in 2 Corinthians 5:19—could not credibly be proclaimed by communities unreconciled among themselves; and (more deeply yet) schisms between bodies variously claiming the status of "Church" are wounds in the Body of Christ, if not its dismemberment. Thus historically controversial matters of doctrine, worship, and pastoral structures—"Faith and Order"—would need to be settled among the churches on their way to the fuller unity that matched the Gospel and gave credibility to its proclamation. For it was Jesus himself who had prayed for his followers "that they all may be one; even as thou, Father, art in me, and I in thee, that they also may be one in us, so that the world may believe that thou hast sent me" (John 17:21). Correspondingly, global mission and ecclesial unity were twin and interactive concerns of the modern ecumenical movement throughout the twentieth century. Lesslie Newbigin was a leading player in both areas.

One of the mere eighteen "native Christians" scattered among the 1200 "foreign missionaries" and members of "home boards" at the Edinburgh conference was the Reverend V. S. Azariah, who spoke on "The Problem of Cooperation between Foreign and Native Workers" and who would later, as an Anglican bishop, play an important role in the formation of Anglicans, Congregationalists, Presbyterians, and Methodists into union as the Church of South India. Azariah thus constituted a personal link between Edinburgh 1910 and Lesslie Newbigin in the latter's role as a missionary in India, a participant in the final stages of the negotiations toward union, and one of the first generation of bishops in the newly formed CSI of 1947. After twelve years of episcopal ministry in the CSI, Newbigin was persuaded to become general secretary of the International Missionary Council and superintend the integration of that stream of the ecumenical movement into the World Council of Churches as the Division of World Mission and Evangelism. That integration was sealed at the third assembly of the World Council of Churches at New Delhi in 1961, and Newbigin stayed on for four more years as associate general secretary of the WCC, making from Geneva his continuing contribution to ecumenical thinking and practice concerning the mission and unity of the Church.

This chapter focuses on Newbigin's theology of the Church and its unity. It shows him principally as a union negotiator in India, as a defender of the South India plan of union both before and after the event, especially in the face of its Anglican detractors overseas, and as the persistent advocate of an "organic" model of ecclesial unity—the pattern he experienced in the CSI and sketched in the description he drafted for the 1961 New Delhi assembly of the WCC of "the unity which is both God's will and his gift to his Church" and hence "our task." His reluctant polemic in *The Reunion of the Church* (1947–48) still lets one feel the heat of the situation in which Newbigin forged also his more serene yet still positively impassioned ecclesiological classic of 1952–53, *The Household of God*. Newbigin is also seen in relation to efforts in favor of "home reunion" in Britain in the 1970s and 1980s; then to the new phase of ecumenism that blossomed after the Second Vatican Council with the "bilateral dialogues" in various permutations between the several world-wide confessional families or communions (in his case, the conversations between the World Alliance of Reformed Churches and the Anglican Consultative Council); and finally to the "paradigm shift" that has been detected at the World Council of Churches over the generation since 1968. The next chapter offers a theological presentation of Newbigin as bishop and pastor, with regard to both his practice and his understanding of ministerial order in the Church. This has proved to be a particularly problematic topic in the approach to structural unity among Christians, and Newbigin's insights are important as coming from one experienced in the care and discipline of the churches and the exercise of an office whose traditional duties include the guardianship of communion. The episcopal office also charges its holders with responsibility for superintending the evangelistic endeavors of their communities; and chapter 5 is given to Newbigin's theology of mission. His missiological thinking was formulated and developed in his two periods of service in India; it was nourished and tested on the global scale before, during, and after his time with the International Missionary Council and the World Council of Churches; it found sustained literary expression in *The Open Secret* (1978), written while he was teaching the subject at the Selly Oak Colleges in Birmingham.

Throughout Newbigin's theological understanding and practice, the concerns for the Church's unity and for its mission are inextricably interwoven strands, just as they run together through the center of the modern ecumenical movement. Theologically, Newbigin rooted the Church, its mission, and its unity all in the Gospel of God's reconciliation of the world to himself:

> That which makes the Church the Church is at the same time the thing which gives it its mission. That which makes the Church one is what makes it a mission to the world. Everything . . . which drives back to that one central fact which is the substance of the Gospel has the effect both of making the Church more truly the Church, and of making it more truly a mission to the world. The connection between the movement for Christian reunion and the movement for world evangelization is of the deepest possible character. The two things are the two outward signs of a return to the heart of the Gospel itself.[2]

The Church of South India

Moves toward ecclesial union in India began in the early years of the twentieth century with the coming together of communities sprung from the work of various British and American churches and missionary societies in the Reformed (Presbyterian and Congregational) tradition. This South India United Church (SIUC) received approaches from the Anglican side, first at the initiative of Henry Whitehead, Bishop of Madras since 1899, who advocated union on the basis of the 1888 Lambeth Quadrilateral of the Scriptures, the Apostolic and Nicene Creeds, the dominical sacraments of baptism and the Lord's Supper, and "the historic episcopate, locally adapted." Other Anglican leaders were V. S. Azariah, suffragan bishop in Dornakal from 1913, and E. J. Palmer, Bishop of Madras between 1908 and 1929, whom the Swedish missiologist Bengt Sundkler, in his history of the union process, was to call "the main architect of the Church of South India."[3]

An informal meeting between Anglicans and members of the SIUC in May 1919 drafted the Tranquebar Declaration that engaged its signatories to seek union along the lines of the Lambeth Quadrilateral and in fact contained "the essential elements of the later Scheme."[4] Although the local authorities on both sides welcomed the proposals and appointed official representatives to confer, a setback occurred when the Anglican bishops returned from the Lambeth Conference of 1920 with the news that the worldwide assembly of the Anglican episcopate had failed to "recognize the absolute equality of the Ministry" which the SIUC had stipulated between the partners. Yet the joint committee continued to meet and, through two decades of "negotiation by way of criticism and amendment," sense progress in its work on this most delicate issue. The Methodists, of British origin, entered the discussions in 1925, and in 1943 they became the first to approve the plan of union in its seventh and decisive edition of 1941–42. In January 1945, the general council of the (Anglican) Church of India, Burma, and Ceylon (CIBC) voted to allow the four South Indian dioceses of that church to enter the union, but a statement from the House of Bishops in June of the same year seemed to put an interpretation on that decision that was unacceptable to the other churches. It all turned on "the pledge" contained in the Scheme of Union to respect the conscientious convictions of congregations concerning the forms of worship and ministry to which they were accustomed: some Anglicans took this to mean that in no circumstances would a minister whose ordination had taken place in the Reformed or Methodist traditions be *appointed* to a formerly Anglican congregation; but the general council of the CIBC, after vigorous advocacy by Bishop A. M. Hollis of Madras, in January 1947 finally accepted the joint committee's interpretation of 1934–35 that the pledge protected the congregations rather from the *imposition* of a minister from another tradition (acceptance was by as narrow a majority as seven to six in the CIBC House of Bishops, but by thirty-three to seven in the House of Laity, and by thirty to twenty-two in the House of Clergy). By that Anglican acceptance the last obstacle was removed from the implementation of the decision taken in September 1946 by the general assembly of the South India United Church—by a majority of 103 to 10, with 7 abstaining—to enter a union that would be episcopally ordered while fully respecting the SIUC's existing ministry. The Church of South India, bringing together the fruit of Anglican, Congregationalist, Presbyterian, and Methodist missionary labors, was inaugurated on September 27, 1947; and Lesslie Newbigin was consecrated among its first bishops that day.

Newbigin had been in the thick of the negotiations during the last years before union. In 1942 he was elected convenor of the union committee of the Madras council of the South India United Church and in 1943 convenor of the union committee of the SIUC as a whole. In that capacity he worked closely with J. S. M. Hooper, the British Methodist secretary of the Joint Committee on Church Union in South India, who was called by historian Bengt Sundkler "the pilot of South India Union."[5] Sundkler refers to Newbigin's "eminent skill" at his task: "J. E. L. Newbigin was outstanding. With a background of solid Scottish theology and experience as a Student Christian Movement secretary, he became in India an expert Tamil linguist and evangelist. An exceptionally happy blend of youth, mature judgment and spiritual authority made his contribution unique."[6]

Opinions on the Scheme in Newbigin's own SIUC varied by region and according to the influence of the various missionary agencies. Newbigin promoted the debate through the publication of a sixty-page booklet in which five leading participants could develop their arguments for or against the Scheme. His own contribution, entitled "The Church and the Gospel," contained the results of a good deal of personal "theological wrestling," which he retrospectively described thus:

> I had serious difficulties with the Scheme in so far as it involved acceptance of the so-called "historic episcopate" as a necessary element in a united Church. The Church, as I understood it, was constituted by the Gospel, communicated in word and sacrament and evoking the response of faith. Ministerial order was therefore secondary and could never be put on the same level of importance as word and sacrament. On this I had some vigorous correspondence with my old Cambridge friend, Oliver Tomkins [later Bishop of Bristol], who insisted that the apostolic ministry was part of that which was given and constitutive of the Church and not to be separated from word and sacrament. What changed my mind was the reading of Michael Ramsey's book *The Gospel and the Catholic Church*. I found there a doctrine of the ministry which did not contravene but rested upon the biblical doctrine of justification by grace through faith, and I saw that the historic episcopate could be gladly accepted as something given by the grace of God to be the means of unity. But this meant that one had to reject at the same time any way of interpreting the historic episcopate which made it a *conditio sine qua non* of the fullness of grace. That was what some Anglo-Catholic theologians seemed to be doing.[7]

"The Reunion of the Church"

In May 1946 the Newbigins left India for furlough in Britain with, as we have seen, the outcome of the South Indian union scheme still undecided. Lesslie spent much of his time and energy commending the scheme among Presbyterians and Episcopalians in Scotland—and even more in defending it against its Anglo-Catholic critics in the Church of England who coalesced in "The Council for the Defence of Church Principles." The Anglican opponents included supporters of the Society for the Propagation of the Gospel, which had missionary work in India, and they were prepared to move for the excommunication of such Anglicans as would enter the CSI. In April 1947 Newbigin was freed by the Church of Scotland's foreign mission committee from his ordinary furlough duties as candidates secretary in order to respond to the continuing opposition through the writing of *The Reunion of the Church*, which was published in January 1948. Serendipitously, that book is accessible in a second edition, published in 1960, with a lengthy new introduction that allows the author to exercise hindsight a dozen years after the realized existence of the Church of South India. During that time the Anglican Communion had still not come to a common mind about the CSI, and debates had developed over plans and methods of reunion among comparable partners in North India, Ceylon, and West Africa. Newbigin was now able to underline once more the crucial character of the doctrine of justification by grace through faith in its ecclesial application, that is, in its qualification of the life and even of the structures of the Church; he was able to stress again the imperative of rendering and keeping the Church's teaching subject to the Scriptures as "the supreme and decisive standard of faith" and the appropriate manner of doing so; he was able to testify to the unifying power and effect of the episcopate in bringing Christians from several traditions together in a single body; and he took the opportunity to argue in favor of South India's process for integrating hitherto separate ministries in preference to reemerging Anglican-sponsored proposals elsewhere for "supplemental ordination" such as the CSI had rejected. These four themes may be viewed stereoscopically through the 1948 and 1960 editions of *The Reunion of the Church*.

It is Newbigin's contention, first, that "the Christian doctrine of justification by faith," which is "so central to the teaching of St. Paul" but is usually expounded in a primarily individualistic manner, provides a way for "understanding theologically the issues involved in moving from disunity to unity." For this to happen, the starting point for interpreting the thought of the apostle has to include his valuation of the fellowship of the Church "equally fundamentally" with the faith of the individual believer. From the beginning, it was the key purpose of Newbigin's book "to argue that the theological clue to the problem of the method of reunion lies in the fact that the Church has its being from the God who," according to Romans 4, "justifies the ungodly, raises the dead, and calls the things that are not as though they were." Apparently, only one reviewer of the first edition noticed the argument about justification by faith, and even he complained that it was out of place in a book on the Church. In the later edition, therefore, Newbigin returned to the charge.

The heart of *The Reunion of the Church* resides, then, according to its author, in the sixth chapter, "Justification by Faith." Here Newbigin sets out his doctrine of sin and salvation, of God's redemptive action in Christ and its human appropriation, in terms that were made familiar in the first and second chapters of this book. The atoning sacrifice of Christ, as God and Man, allows the holy and loving Father to forgive and restore sinners when, in and through Christ alone, they return with penitence, gratitude, and adoration to Him. Faith is "the acceptance of the grip of Christ's pierced hand upon the hand that pierced Him," it is "the soul's humbled and trembling 'Amen' to the revelation of the wrath and the love of the Lord God Omnipotent"—and it "involves a death and rebirth," a "new creation of the creative love of God Himself" and of "Christ's redeeming love." "This restoration to God *is* justification," and "good works are not its condition but its fruit," for "if God so loved us, we ought also to love one another." Yet this gift and this life we know at present only as a foretaste and earnest: "its power now works in us, but it is not yet fully realized"; the old self is dead and yet its works have still to be mortified; the "saints" are "yet still engaged in the struggle with sin in themselves." Now all this, says Newbigin, is just as true of the Church as it is of the individual believer, for the Church is "a communion of sinful souls with the Holy God." "The Church is both holy and sinful, as the Christian is both holy and sinful."

That "it is both holy and sinful" is the "fundamental paradox of the Church's being." This Newbigin asserts, even while affirming that "the Gospel only comes to us through the ministries of the Church" (the latter being a fact that causes Orthodox and Catholic theologians to refuse to ascribe sin to the Church, the "mother" of our salvation, even while recognizing that individual members may and do sin). Newbigin's recognition is that "we know the Gospel of God's redeeming grace through the fellowship of redeemed men and women," whose "mutual service and mutual dependence" remain in fact spoiled by "faction and division" springing from "carnality, from relying upon man rather than upon God." The "denominational" pride that springs from whatever combination of "historical correctness, evangelistic zeal or ethical achievement" can only be subdued "by the word of the Cross, before which no flesh can glory": "The word of the Cross to the Church is a summons to return in penitence and faith to Him in whom alone is our righteousness, to abandon confidence in everything save His mercy, and to accept and embody in our institutional life that unity with one another which is given to us in Him."[8] The Church "does not live by what it possesses and has inherited," says Newbigin in a phrase that may need a little nuancing; "it lives in the dynamic relationship of ever-new penitence and faith before the Cross of Jesus Christ, and its unity, its continuity, and all its spiritual gifts are the fruits of that."[9] The nuance is required insofar as Newbigin himself should be willing, in terms of his own thesis in this connection, to apply also to the Church at this point what he affirms of individual believers: "Faith places men in that relation with God for which men were created, and inasmuch as it becomes *the settled direction of their wills* it issues in *the remoulding of their whole lives* in conformity to the holy love of their Creator."[10]

It will be necessary to come back later to Newbigin's understanding—as already hinted, not uncontroversial—of the nature and history of the earthly Church between its birth at Easter and Pentecost and the expected return of Christ to bring it to completion. Meanwhile Newbigin was able to note in 1960 the positive judgment of the Roman Catholic ecclesiologist George Tavard concerning the Church of South India and its "dynamic" theology of the Church that Newbigin had done much to shape: "The CSI cannot be appraised only from the peculiarities of its organization; the implications of its theology must also be considered. For it is giving rise to a relatively new conception of the Church. According to this view the Church should be defined in terms of what it is becoming rather than in terms of what it is."[11]

The second theme that needed highlighting in the 1960 edition of *The Reunion of the Church* was that of the statement and the standard of faith. The Lambeth Conference of Anglican bishops in 1958 had recommended that the churches seeking unity in West Africa and the Middle East should look for an example to the scheme then being proposed in Ceylon rather than to the model already realized in the Church of South India. One of the differences lay in "the statement of faith" and the reference therein to the Scriptures as "the standard of faith." The chief cause of the Anglicans' concern appears to have been the impression left on them that the CSI's plan of union and subsequent constitution shortchanged the doctrinal authority of "the Church" and its "tradition" as the interpreter of Scripture and the preserver of orthodoxy: on the one hand, the "statement of faith," unlike that proposed in Ceylon, makes no reference to the Church "handing down" the Scriptures; on the other hand, notes appended to the statement in the plan (though not carried over into the constitution) expressly allowed to individuals "reasonable liberty of interpretation" in regard to the ancient Creeds. In chapter 8, the most bitingly forensic chapter, of *The Reunion of the Church*, Newbigin refuses to permit the question of the nature and identity of "the Church" to be begged—for, on what he considers a proper understanding of "the Church," the Church is indeed the locus in which the Scriptures by the working of the Holy Spirit fulfill their divine purpose, which can occur only when the living Lord is met by the free faith of people who have the liberty to err. "The Bible," he owns, "can only be understood in the fellowship of the Church." That Church, however,

> is not merely a historically continuous institution bound by the terms of its original articles of association. It is a fellowship in the living Christ through the Holy Spirit, living the daily renewed life of faith in the Redeemer but embracing the whole company of the faithful in all ages and all lands. Its appeal to the Scriptures is an appeal to the living Christ himself, in order that it may know, in the circumstances of the present, what His living Spirit has now to speak to it concerning His will. Its unity with those who have gone before does not consist in its being bound to the details of their practice; it

consists inwardly in its obedience to the same living Lord whom they obeyed, and outwardly in the maintenance, so far as that obedience permits, of continuity with them in one visible institution.[12]

As a matter of fact, says Newbigin, speaking precisely in the context of the search for Christian unity, the Church "is liable to error and has erred": that is manifest in the "factions and divisions," which, he has argued, are "signs of a relapse into carnality, into life after the flesh."[13] Resubmission by the Church to its Lord takes place by way of resubmission to the Scriptures because, through the testimony of his first followers, it is there that Christ is encountered in his person, his words, and his work, and there, too, therefore, that individuals and the gathered Church may and should take the responsibility of recognizing and accepting the Truth. Again:

> The *ultimate* standard of faith is the revelation of God in Jesus Christ. When we appeal from the present to that revelation we are not appealing from a later to an earlier phase in the development of a society called the Church. We are appealing to the Church's living Lord, who is alive in the Church today, whom alone we must obey, but who has made his nature and will clear to us by a work done for mankind at a certain point in history. To that point in history, therefore, we must go, not because it is earlier than the point at which we live but because it is the place where Christ has revealed Himself and wrought redemption for us. We do not go to the Bible to find the earliest forms of the traditions and rules of the Church. . . . We go to the Bible to meet Christ, our present and living Lord.[14]

Thus it is as means and norm of the encounter with Christ that the Scriptures serve, according to the constitution of the CSI, as "the supreme and decisive standard of faith"; and the implication is acknowledged that "the Church must always be ready to correct and reform itself in accordance with the teaching of those Scriptures as the Holy Spirit shall reveal it." The substantive thrust of Newbigin's argument is that it is on that very understanding and by that very use of the Scriptures that the divided denominations are coming together in obedience to the perceived will of their common Lord.

The "object" of faith is Christ and his work, taken of course in trinitarian terms. The *solus Christus*, on which justification by grace through faith and, properly understood, the *sola Scriptura* are based, has a further resonance in the context of the Church's witness amid India and its religions. Here again, though without going into detail, Newbigin asserts in the second edition of *The Reunion of the Church* the superiority of the CSI "statement of faith" over the version in the Ceylon plan for which the Anglican bishops had expressed their preference at the 1958 Lambeth Conference:

> The title "Redeemer of the world" does not safeguard the Christian faith in Christ as God. It could be used by a Hindu for the god of his worship. It is inadequate for the purposes of a credal statement of this kind. South India has corrected this by speaking of Him as "incarnate Son of God and redeemer of the world," and by adding the important (and in certain contexts essential) word "alone"; so as to read "by whom *alone* we are saved by grace."[15]

The third thread along which Newbigin was able to look back from the second edition of *The Reunion of the Church* to the first edition was that of episcopacy. As a Presbyterian, he himself came from one of "the great non-episcopal communions, whose traditions are so much bound up with resistance in the name of faith to episcopal claims." Yet, by the plan to which he had helped to put the finishing touches, some such denominational churches were "accepting not merely episcopacy, but the historic episcopate, the re-engrafting of separated life into the original episcopal stem"—and this "not grudgingly as the 'price of union,' but in the belief that episcopacy 'is needed for the shepherding and extension of the Church in South India'" (*Basis of Union*, 9) and as "an act of obedience to Christ's will that there should be 'a ministry accepted and fully effective throughout the world-wide Church'" (*Basis of Union*, 1).[16] And Newbigin was ready in 1947 "to plead with those who oppose the Scheme from the Protestant side to consider again whether our return to the unity of the one Body must not also be a return to that continuous ministerial succession by which the Church is visibly united through time and through space. So long as episcopacy is accepted and cherished"—as Newbigin found happening in A. M. Ramsey's *The Gospel and the Catholic Church*—"as the organ of the Church's continuing unity from the Apostles in Palestine to the Christian Churches in every land today, it will offer a centre round which the Church may be visibly re-united."[17] The reservation was that such an acceptance should not infringe the evangelically decisive principle of justification by grace through faith by making an historic episcopate a necessary, or even the sole sufficient, condition of the presence of the Church, valid sacraments, and a valid ministry. Newbigin saw that principle safeguarded in the union's provision that existing ministers from participant nonepiscopal traditions be recognized without further ado as presbyters in the CSI—a matter to receive further treatment in a moment. Looking back in 1959, after the CSI had been in existence for more than a decade and he himself had served as one of its bishops from the start, Newbigin observed earlier expectations to have been not merely met but exceeded:

> On the one hand, the Church is far more unified round the bishops than many of us expected. Undoubtedly many in the non-episcopal churches accepted episcopacy simply because it was one of the things without which union could not be had. Today I think it would hardly be possible to get a vote anywhere for a proposal to drop episcopacy, even as the price of a wider union. The position of the Bishop as the chief pastor of the flock in each area has become something that hardly anyone would wish even to think of abandoning. But, on the other hand, the Church has a far more open door to the non-episcopal communions than the written text of the Basis of Union suggests. Not only have ministers of the parent Churches been received freely and without question to minister in the CSI, whether episcopally ordained or not; ministers of other non-episcopal communions have also been received, and there has been no desire even to consider the question of ordaining them. This goes beyond the provisions of the Basis of Union. I can only interpret these two facts to mean that episcopacy is seen and valued as the visible centre of the process by which the Good Shepherd gathers together His own;

and that the desire to see this unifying and reconciling work extended and strengthened overmasters any desire to make claims for episcopacy which would exclude those who are willing to come into the one fellowship. The picture which these years of living together in the united Church have begun to open out for us is thus of a continuing process of reunion among Churches, with the historic episcopate as the visible centre round which the fellowship of the Church is gathered.[18]

The fourth theme, then, that Newbigin took up again in the extensive new introduction to the 1960 edition of *The Reunion of the Church* concerned the presbyteral status of ministers ordained in nonepiscopal traditions. The Lambeth Conference of 1958 had meanwhile commended the method of unifying ministries that was being proposed for North India and Ceylon by way of a mutual commissioning through prayer and the laying on of hands. To Newbigin this appeared dangerously close to the procedure of "supplemental ordination" that had been mooted for the CSI in the mid-1940s, opposed already at that time by Newbigin, and finally rejected by the CSI union despite the advocacy of Bishops Palmer, then in England, and Azariah.[19] In summing up his renewed opposition to such a procedure in 1959, Newbigin judged that the proposed mutual action in North India and Ceylon—where the "prayers and formulae are in all essentials those of an ordination service"—was in fact lopsided: it would be a means of satisfying (unacceptable) Anglican "doubts and scruples" concerning the validity of ordinations in the other churches, which do not themselves question Anglican ordinations. Moreover, the ambiguity of the rite (ordination or not?) would be perpetuated each time the rite was undergone by a minister from whatever denomination, Anglican or other, on entering the service of the united churches. None of this could happen without weakening for all parties the whole idea of ordination. Although one aspect of ordination is the transmission of the Church's authority (and there may indeed be need to enlarge the sphere of a minister's jurisdiction, especially when service becomes possible across former lines of division), the central act in ordination is a prayer for God to bestow the gifts required for ministry, and thereafter the Church acts in the faith that God has done so; and "if—as the ordinals of the undivided Church plainly imply—ordination is an act of God in response to the prayers of the Church, then the idea of supplemental ordination becomes impossible."[20]

In 1947, Newbigin could write prospectively thus in favor of the South Indian method over against the alternative of "supplemental ordination":

The Holy Catholic Church has not ceased to exist, defaced and divided though it is by our sin, and our ordination is to its ministry. It is true that owing to our divisions the authority of the whole Church is not behind our ordinations. But these divisions are but the manifestations of sin, and it is not for us to try to rationalize them and say that our ordinations are to one or other of the "branches" of the Church. The cardinal fact is that God in His mercy has not allowed our sinful divisions to destroy the operation of His grace, but has continued to give to the Church ministers empowered by His grace for the perfecting of the saints, for the work of ministering, unto the building up of the body of Christ. Our part is to recognize what He has so abundantly done, and to seek to restore that orderly unity of life which is His will for us and the fruit of the Spirit, whom He has given us. What has been lacking in authority will be made up by the constitutional acts of the uniting Churches in the act of union and by the United Church itself, but they will be of the category of authorization, not of ordination. And for the filling up of that which has been lacking in the needed spiritual gifts, the common life of the re-united body will provide abundant means.[21]

In 1959, strengthened by a dozen years of experience in the CSI, Newbigin's beliefs on this matter remained essentially the same:

It is possible to believe (as I do) that it is God's will that the Church should be episcopally ordered, and yet deny absolutely that episcopal ordination is essential for a valid ministry. For the being of the Church, and therefore the validity of its ministry, rest not upon the conformity of the Church to God's will, but upon the grace of God which justifies the ungodly. Once again we come to the doctrine of justification by faith. If episcopal ordination is essential to a valid ministry, then that ministry which is not episcopally ordained is not a valid ministry and has no way of becoming such except by receiving the ordination which it lacks. But if the true secret of the Church's being is that it is the place where God's supernatural grace takes hold of those who were no people and makes them His people, takes the prodigal and makes him a beloved son, takes the sinful man and the sinful body of men and makes them verily members incorporate in the Body of Christ for no worthiness of theirs but for His own infinite mercy; then one can *both* insist that episcopacy is God's will for the Church *and* at the same time acknowledge without any hedging or double talk that non-episcopal bodies are truly churches. That is the root of the matter. Conformity to God's will is not the pre-condition of fellowship with Him, but the fruit of it. God justifies the ungodly through Jesus Christ. That is the secret of the being of the Church as it is of the Christian man. Those who know that will rightly resist any plans for reunion which appear to found the being of the Church on any other foundation. Those who believe, as I do, that God wills His Church to be one body, united not only in word and sacrament but also in visible fellowship with a universal ministry credibly representative of that apostolic ministry which was its first foundation, must also listen to the apostolic teaching about justification by faith as our only standing ground in the presence of God. If they will do so, then we can look forward to a growing visible re-integration having the historic episcopate as its visible ministerial focus, a re-integration not in some distant hypothetical future but now in the decades immediately before us. This concern that the bearing of the doctrine of justification by faith upon the practical tasks of Christian reunion should be more seriously considered is the main reason for agreeing to the re-issue of this book.[22]

As acknowledged, it will be necessary to return to Newbigin's understanding of the nature, unity, and continuity of the Church. To appreciate the broader significance and importance of views elaborated in connection with South India, note must be taken of some ecumenical developments, or lack thereof, in the period between the first and second editions of *The Reunion of the Church*. It had been hoped that the CSI would be "a growing point for further union," not only in South India (both for "growing together" within the CSI, which certainly occurred, and for inclusion of Lutherans and Baptists, which did not) but also further afield. In Newbigin's words of 1947:

> It is a time for all the sundered parts of Christ's Church to be roused to a more active dealing with the intolerable scandal of division. . . . The uniting Churches believe that their small and local act of obedience will help to loosen the bonds that hold the Churches apart and will hasten the fulfillment of Christ's will that his Church should be one. . . . If the South India Scheme is recognized as a valid attempt, within the conditions of a particular part of the world, to restore the visible unity of the Church, then one cannot help feeling that the whole process of theological and ecclesiastical reintegration within the ecumenical movement will receive new impetus.[23]

In 1959–60 Newbigin tried to urge on the "parent Churches" of the CSI the need for their own reunion if the CSI was not to be "just one more denomination" and "a great and God-given opportunity wasted"[24]; and a further two decades on, after his return to Britain, he will be encountered still working toward "home reunion." That domestic tardiness was for the moment, however, relativized by the wider shift on the global scene that had taken place with the establishment of the World Council of Churches in 1948 and the excitement of the debates concerning its own ecclesial significance. Having become a figure of international stature, Bishop Newbigin played a leading part in those discussions and served as chief drafter of the description of unity adopted by the third assembly of the WCC at New Delhi in 1961. The new introduction to the 1960 edition of *The Reunion of the Church* expresses concisely what was at stake: the member Churches of the WCC, bringing with them their various ecclesiologies, were now bound together in a solemn covenant, confessing that "Christ has made us one, and He is not divided"; what, then, was the ecclesial significance of their new life together in the WCC and in national and local "councils of churches," and how was the present form of it—"a stepping stone which will not permanently bear our weight"—related to the final goal, the vision of which differed according to the starting points and ecclesial claims of the several member Churches?

The questions, then, for the ecumenical movement were: "What form of unity does God will for His people? And what is the method by which we are to move from our present disunity to unity in that divinely willed form?" Those questions remain. Newbigin's ecclesiological understanding and vision can be expounded both from the occasional and at times pugnacious book *The Reunion of the Church*, written in defense of the CSI, and from the more measured and systematic but still urgent and provocative treatise *The Household of God*, resulting from his Kerr Lectures of 1952 at the University of Glasgow. He stood by those basic views in all his later thinking and activity, and they retain their importance, whatever nuancing their application may require through the changes in circumstances during the intervening years.

Returning for the moment then to *The Reunion of the Church*, we may this time take the tack of noting which views of the Church, its unity, and its continuity Newbigin rejects and how he composes from the valid elements in each rejected position an account that he argues is more faithful to the Scriptures. Admitting the caricatural quality of each description, Newbigin designates one mistaken position Catholic and the other Protestant; their failure—and it is sinful—consists in driving apart what the New Testament correlates, the spiritual and corporeal nature of the Church. The "Catholic" position resembles that of St. Paul's opponents in the Letter to the Galatians, the "Protestant" that of the Corinthians whom the Apostle redresses.

On the one side, "the Epistle to the Galatians was addressed to people who were seeking in the outward rite of incorporation into the Israel of God an additional assurance of their salvation," but "to insist on outward and institutional continuity with 'Israel after the flesh' is to contradict the Church's nature."[25] This occurs when, characteristically, Roman Catholicism has held that belonging to the Church entails the acceptance of additional elements that do not belong to the essence of the Gospel but rather have accumulated in the course of a corporate history that has known its share of sin. Here Newbigin takes on, throughout the entire fifth chapter, the whole notion of the Church as "the extension of the Incarnation" such as Yves Congar had developed it in his pioneering book *Chrétiens désunis* (1937). It is impossible to ignore, Newbigin says, that "the Church as a society within history is made up of a multitude of human and sinful wills, and that the fact of incorporation in the Church does not here—*in via*—remove this sinful element": "Few forms of power can corrupt men so radically as spiritual and ecclesiastical power. Not only in Christians as individuals but also in the Church as an institution there are to be found marks of man's sinful will, not least in the fact that we are more conscious of the truth of this statement as it applies to other Churches than as it applies to our own." That last wry remark is then given pointed theological application as Newbigin declares in the face of Roman Catholic claims: "When [a Church] seeks to find the criterion of its status as a Church in the fact of its continuous institutional existence, it has abandoned the one standing ground that sinners have before God."[26]

On the other side, "the First Epistle to the Corinthians was written to people whose confidence in their own possession of the Spirit was destroying the unity of the Body":

> They were thus threatened with what might be described as the opposite perversion of the truth to that which threatened the Galatians. Their confidence that they were the possessors of the gifts which the Holy Spirit bestows upon believers was leading them into factions and jealousy, into extreme laxity on moral questions, into abuse of the Lord's Supper, and into the perversion of Christian liberty into a self-destructive anarchy. Factions had developed, each boasting the name of some revered leader and each—apparently—glorying in the possession of particular gifts. They were destroying the temple of God, the Church. They were denying the unity of the Body of Christ. They were misusing the Spirit's greatest gift, which is a love that never boasts, never envies, never seeks its own. The apostle uses of them a word that must have surprised and shocked them. He calls them "carnal". . . . [27]

It is difficult not to see adumbrated there the fissipariousness of Protestantism.

Noting that "a divided Church in the New Testament sense of the word Church is something illogical and incomprehensible, as illogical and incomprehensible as human sin," Newbigin proceeds to show how the two characteristic ecclesiologies—"Catholic" and "Protestant"—respectively deny the existence of disunity:

> The first type, represented in its most unambiguous form by the Roman Catholic Church, identifies one existing Church exclusively with the Church of the New Testament and regards other "Churches" as congeries of baptized persons to which God in His mercy has granted many of the gifts and graces of His Spirit, but which are not parts of the Church. On this view the Church is not divided. What has happened is that members have fallen away from it. The way of reunion is simply that they should return to it.
>
> The second type, represented by many Protestants, affirms that the unity of the Church is a spiritual unity, that outward unity of organization is not of the essence of the Church, and that true Christians are in fact united already. It sings with determination: "We are not divided, All one body we," and regards questions of "ecclesiastical joinery" as belonging to a lower level of spirituality than that upon which it becomes possible to make this affirmation. On this view, what is required is primarily an increase of cordiality among Christians, and the question whether or in what way this is to lead to institutional unity is a relatively minor matter.
>
> Each of these types of theory does justice to one aspect of the New Testament teaching about the Church—the first to the fact that the Church in the New Testament is one visible society, the new Israel, the holy temple in the Lord, in whom Christians are builded together for a habitation of God in the Spirit; the second to the fact that the Church in the New Testament is Israel after the Spirit, created and constituted by the union of its members through the Spirit in the ascended life of the Lord. Both fail, as it seems, to do justice to the effect of sin in severing the two things that God has joined, and both, therefore, in fact deny the existence of the real problem.[28]

An accurate and responsible account of the Church—its given unity, its actual dividedness, and its ecumenical vocation—depends on the proper correlation of Body and Spirit, which Newbigin proceeds to offer on the basis of a splendid exposition of St. Paul's First Letter to the Corinthians and other related passages.[29] The crux of the matter is this:

> When St. Paul calls the Corinthians carnal, his meaning is that they have fallen away from dependence solely on God and His grace and have begun to depend on possessions of their own, upon human leaders and the particular spiritual gifts which each has. Dependence upon the one Holy Spirit would have produced the visible unity of the one Body. Their divisions are the outward sign of their carnality, of the fact that they have fallen back on man. "After the flesh" and "after the Spirit" are contraries for St. Paul, but the Spirit and the Body are correlates. "In one Spirit were we all baptized into one body," he says (1 Cor. 12:13), and when he urges the Ephesians to guard the unity which they have in the Spirit (Eph. 4:3), he is not (as the following verse so clearly shows) speaking of a spiritual unity which is distinct

> from a bodily unity, but precisely of their unity in one visible fellowship which is the gift to them of the one Spirit. . . . The one Body is the counterpart of the one Spirit. . . . If the Body is divided, it is because Christians are not spiritual but carnal, not walking after the Spirit, but after the flesh.[30]

Or a little later, this time with St. John coming in to support St. Paul: "The Church is the society bound together in mutual love, the love of God shed abroad in the hearts of its members through the Holy Ghost which was given them through faith in Christ. It is both a unity in the Spirit and a corporeal institutional unity, and it is the second because it is the first, for he who says 'I love God' and does not love his body is a liar."[31] "Where love is real and deep and steady," Newbigin has said, "organization is the strong, living, bony system that gives the body power to act with determination and unity."[32]

That "sin still works in the Church"[33] is a function of the fact that "the Eschaton has entered history . . . yet the end is not yet."[34] As long as "the mystery of sin" lasts, the historical Church is affected by it and, even as "a colony of heaven," remains under God's judgment until his eternal purpose is accomplished at Christ's final appearing. "If there were no sin in the Church, there would be perfect congruity between the outward and the inward."[35] The Church comes closer to its proper nature and calling when, in penitence and faith, its divided parts make a common return to the Christ who has not ceased to hold them in his grace and when they accordingly let their broken unity be visibly and tangibly restored.[36]

One final feature of Newbigin's ecumenical ecclesiology that emerges from the very beginning in *The Reunion of the Church* is the prominence he gives to the local church, not simply as a general principle of ecclesial existence but precisely in its relation to Christian unity. The policy of comity among the Protestant missionary agencies—whereby they had agreed not to undertake work in territorial overlap—was of more than practical significance: not only did the spreading of resources allow greater geographical expansion in the proclamation of the Gospel, but also the concentration of Christian witness and presence into a single form in any particular place had important consequences both for the clarity of evangelistic testimony and for believers' own perception of the unifying power of Christ's redemptive work:

> In any one place—town or village—there is *normally* but one Christian congregation, and upon this one congregation rests the responsibility for the evangelization of the area allotted to it under the principle of comity. . . . The outsider is presented with a clear and simple choice between Christ and no-Christ, unconfused by conflicting interpretations of what to be "in Christ" means. The proper connection between the Gospel and the Church is visibly preserved, for the Church stands in the pagan community as a clearly marked society founded upon the Gospel in such a way that faith in the Gospel and membership in the Church obviously and naturally belong together. The Church stands as a visible and distinct community possessing the secret of reconciliation and offering this secret to men in its evangelism.

As Christians move about from place to place in the course of their employment, they are commended to the congregation in the place to which they go and are invited to identify themselves with it. This means that in a large town congregation there will be Christians coming from every sort of background of caste, class and denomination. There may be in one such congregation in South India men and women whose original affiliation has been Syrian, Lutheran, Anglican, Methodist, Presbyterian, Congregational, Baptist. There may be representatives of the highest and lowest castes of Hinduism. There will be an immense range of wealth and education. . . . In a South Indian country town they have all to face the choice between accepting membership of the one congregation which is there and being outside the visible membership of the Church in the place altogether. In other words, the question is raised with absolute simplicity and in a way which requires an answer one way or the other: "Is it sufficient for men divided on every other ground to have in common their redemption in Christ?"[37]

Such is clearly the background and source of Newbigin's insistence, at New Delhi 1961 and beyond, on churchly unity as entailing the Christian unity of "all in each place." This same idea would need to be adapted and applied also to "a typical Western city with its multitude of different denominational Churches," where in the current situation each group finds "its own group of like-minded people with whom to associate."[38]

Although Newbigin stresses a single congregation "in each place" (the phrase that became famous occurs already in 1947),[39] there must of course be a network of communion among such local churches. It was the very point of the South India plan, within its own geographical area, to allow the free and unquestioned circulation of Christians among the congregations as circumstances shifted them from one locality to another.[40] Ultimately, the communion among local churches has to be worldwide, for the Church catholic is precisely "a unity of persons in the Body of Christ, represented locally by congregations in which Christ is presented in the midst in Word and Sacrament."[41] That is why the goal of the ecumenical movement has to be "organic reunion" in structures appropriate to each geographical level, parochial, regional, global: "We ought to accept no goal short of the reunion of the Church, made visible in a local congregational life which gathers up into itself the full and many-sided richness of the whole Christian tradition."[42] Not only geographically but also confessionally, Newbigin could already in 1947 envisage—or at least think it right to pray for—such an advance in "the process of mutual comprehension, of reformation, and recovery" that would one day make reunion among Protestants, Catholics, and Orthodox a practical possibility. And "however far-reaching may be the transformation required both of the Protestant Churches and of the Roman and Eastern before union can be a matter even of discussion, there ought to be nothing to prevent our looking now towards the restoration to the whole Church of a visible unity with a central organ of unity such as Rome was for so many vital centuries of the Church's history."[43] In his encyclical letter of 1995, *Ut Unum Sint,* expressing now the "irrevocable commitment" of the Catholic Church to the ecumenical cause, Pope John Paul II invited other Christians to a "patient and fraternal dialogue" on the universal ministry of unity which the see of Rome claims to provide.

"The Household of God"

During the family furlough of 1952, spent in Edinburgh, Bishop Newbigin turned to the preparation of his Kerr Lectures on "the nature of the Church" that were to be delivered at Trinity College, Glasgow, in November of that year. Five years earlier, the Anglican theologian Alan Richardson had suggested to him that the ecclesiology implied in *The Reunion of the Church* could be expanded into a setting beyond the South India debate; and Newbigin now took the opportunity, enriched by his having shared in the life and ministry of the CSI from its inauguration, to propose a more systematic doctrine of the Church that might undergird the rapidly developing ecumenical movement focused since 1948 on the World Council of Churches. The resultant book, *The Household of God*, has achieved the status of a classic.[44] It was translated into French, German, Chinese, Japanese, and (*samizdat* format) Russian. A *peritus* at Vatican II reported that it had influenced the writing of "Lumen Gentium," the Council's dogmatic constitution on the Church.[45]

Newbigin started out with the dichotomy between Protestant and Catholic that had marked the thinking of the WCC's inaugural Amsterdam Assembly, but "as I dug into the biblical material," he reports, "I became more and more convinced that this twofold approach did not reach the heart of the matter, and that these two traditions would only accept each other's truth if there was brought into the debate a third element—that which lays stress on the immediate experience of divine grace and power. For a long time I hesitated about how to name this third element. Finally I used the name Pentecostal."[46] In fact, this move led the author to give a trinitarian structure to his book, as we shall see; and the reality of the Trinity, never of course absent from his earlier writings, gained a new prominence that was thereafter maintained in his thought and shaped it powerfully. By this attention to the Holy Spirit, Third Person of the Blessed Trinity, the way was paved for the extension of Newbigin's ecumenical interests and audience in two hitherto unfamiliar directions: first among the Eastern Orthodox, with whom he claimed at that stage only a slight acquaintance, and then later among the Pentecostals, whose style he had hitherto "regarded with the distaste of a well-educated university graduate."

The introductory chapter to *The Household of God* begins with Newbigin's reading of the current condition of the Church. The geopolitical circumstances are those of a global conflict recently ended, a developing cold war between East and West, and the incipient demise of the colonial era. The author's personal situation is that of a European located in India, a bishop who represents his newly united Church in the affairs both of the International Missionary Council and of the newly established World Council of Churches, where an eschatological mood is reflected in the theme of the impending second assembly, "Christ the Hope of the World." In his sketch of the context in which the churches are debating the nature of the Church, Newbigin refers to three phenomena in particular: "the breakdown of Christendom," "the missionary experience of the churches in the lands outside of the old Christendom," and "the rise of the modern ecumenical movement."

First, Newbigin indicates the consequences of the increasingly rapid dissolution of the thousand-year "synthesis between the Gospel and the culture of the western part of the European peninsula of Asia, by which Christianity had become almost the folk-religion of Western Europe." Although the modern missionary movement had at first appeared as the extension of the frontiers of Christendom, the spread and growth of an indigenous faith beyond the walls of the mission compounds in Asia, Africa, and the Pacific forced the question of the relation between the Gospel and culture and thus of the relation between the Church—as "the body which, in whatever cultural environment, lives by the Gospel alone"—and the society in which it is set. The distinctions thus made overseas, between Gospel and culture as between Church and society, also had to be drawn at home on account of "the rise of non-Christian forces, at first more or less accepting of the *mores* of Christendom while challenging its theology, but eventually launching a full-scale attack upon the whole ethical tradition of Western Europe and seeking to replace it by something totally different." Concomitantly, the loosening of old social ties and the proliferation of urban life had "atomized" the individual wherever "Western civilization" had reached and turned him into "a more and more anonymous and replaceable part, the perfect incarnation of the rationalist conception of man." Given the "appalling results of trying to go back to some sort of primitive collectivity based on the total control of the individual, down to the depths of his spirit, by an all-powerful group," it was natural that people in the postwar world, Christians among them, should ask: "Is there in truth a family of God on earth to which I can belong, a place where all men can truly be at home? If so, where is it to be found, what are its marks, and how is it related to, and distinguished from, the known communities of family, nation, and culture? What are its boundaries, its structure, its terms of membership? And how comes it that those who claim to be the spokesmen of that one holy fellowship are themselves at war with one another as to the fundamentals of its nature, and unable to live together in unity and concord?" These questions of Gospel and culture—and the intrinsic need for a unified Church to make an authentic witness—continue to run through Newbigin's thought in its successive phases.

The second factor named by Newbigin as setting the context for reflection on the nature of the Church is developments from the experience of Christian mission in lands in which the cultures are dominated by religions other than Christian. Whereas, in the "wider semi-Christian culture" of the West, individual Christians may still look to the churches to meet at least their "religious" concerns, the situation of the Church amid an ancient non-Christian culture such as Hinduism is quite different: having made a radical break with his inherited culture, the convert looks to the Church for "the total environment of his life"; the Church itself has to provide "a new kind of social discipline" for its members that will keep it as "a distinct body, separate from the pagan world around it," refusing to compromise its witness yet doing so in a way "which leads to Christian freedom and not to ecclesiastical tyranny"; the Church, too, in such a situation, has—even if some may argue that it does not belong to the real business of Christian mission—felt compelled to engage in all kinds of educational, medical, agricultural, and industrial service in order to demonstrate "not merely a new pattern of personal behaviour within the pagan culture, but a new pattern of corporate activity extending beyond the strictly religious sphere"; and, finally, with the Church as "a new community set in, and yet separated from, the ancient religious cultures of the non-Christian lands, the question of unity has become inescapable." Although confessional rivalries might almost have become for a time a tolerable luxury "within the assumed unity of Christendom," Christian disunity in a missionary situation is "an intolerable anomaly." Standing under Christ's abiding promise to draw all people to himself, the Church knows, when it "faces out towards the world," that it only exists as "the first-fruits and instrument"—a phrase that keeps recurring in Newbigin's ecclesiology—of the reconciling work of Christ, and that "division within its own life is a violent contradiction of its own fundamental nature":

Christ's reconciling work is one, and we cannot be His ambassadors reconciling the world to God, if we have not ourselves been willing to be reconciled to one another. It is the result of this deep connection at the heart of the Gospel itself that Churches which—within Christendom—had accepted their disunity as a matter of course, found that when they were placed in a missionary situation their disunity was an intolerable scandal. Out of this new missionary experience arose those forces by which the churches were drawn from isolation into comity, from comity into co-operation, and—in some areas at least—from co-operation into organic union.[47]

That already indicates the third factor stimulating the churches to ecclesiological reflection, debate, and action—the rise of the ecumenical movement. The inauguration of the World Council of Churches in 1948 brought about a new ecclesial reality. Declaring that "we are divided from one another, but Christ has made us His own, and He is not divided," the member churches—by their mutual covenant of foundation and by their commitment to "stay together"—had faced themselves with a question which each had to answer for itself and reflect on with the others: In what sense did "the Church Universal" exist beyond the boundaries of one's own community? The initial responses to that question and its eventual resolution entailed a vision—currently diverse but finally to be agreed—of the nature of ecclesial unity. The central committee's Toronto statement of 1950 made clear that entry into membership of the WCC did not require a church to surrender its own present claims, its assessment of other communities, or its view of the proper form of Christian unity. Yet life together in common study, mutual helpfulness, and developing spiritual relationships would make the Council not only a place for the discussion of differences but a shared instrument of witness, service, and the edification of the Body of Christ. Thus, Newbigin argues in 1952, the WCC "has itself a churchly character," and "it follows from this that, while we accept the statement of the Toronto document that the World Council is *in intention* neutral on the question of the form of the Church's unity, we cannot agree that it is neutral *in fact*, for it is itself a form of that unity." And then comes the crunch: "If the Council be regarded as anything other than a transitory phase of the journey from disunity to unity, it is the *wrong* form."

Abandoning "any pretence at speaking from a position of neutrality among the conflicting ecclesiologies with which we have to deal," Newbigin goes on to declare in his own name the vision of ecclesial unity that had been forged and tempered in his South Indian experience, which would through his pen be written into the New Delhi Assembly's 1961 description of "the unity we seek" and which he would continue to advocate and defend against any dilution:

> I believe that the divinely willed form of the Church's unity is at least this, a visible company in every place of all who confess Jesus as Lord, abiding together in the Apostles' teaching and fellowship, the breaking of bread and the prayers. Its foci are the word, the sacraments, and the apostolic ministry. Its form is the visible fellowship, not of those whom we choose out to be our friends, but of those whom God has actually given to us as our neighbours. It is therefore simply humanity in every place re-created in Christ. It is the place where *all* men can be made one because all are made nothing, where one new humanity in Christ is being daily renewed because the old man in *every* man is being brought to crucifixion through word, baptism and supper. Its unity is universal because it is local and congregational.[48]

On the one hand, Newbigin defines this unity over against the "Protestant" temptation of federalism:

> I am bound to believe that all conceptions of reunion in terms of federation are vain. They leave the heart of the problem—which is the daily life of men and women in their neighbourhood—untouched. They demand no death and resurrection as the price of unity. They leave each sect free to enjoy its own particular sort of spirituality, merely tying them all together at the centre in a bond which does not vitally and costingly involve every member in every part of his daily life. They envisage a sort of unity whose foci are not the word and sacraments of the Gospel in the setting of the local congregation, but the conference table and the committee room. They do not grapple with the fact, which any serious reading of the New Testament must surely make inescapable, that to speak of a plurality of churches (in the sense of "denominations") is strictly absurd; that we can only do so in so far as we have ceased to understand by the word "Church" what the New Testament means by it; that our ecclesiologies are, in the Pauline sense, carnal (1 Cor. 3:3–4). The disastrous error of the idea of federation is that it offers us reunion without repentance.[49]

When federation is considered the adequate goal, "Catholics" may be "provisionally justified in refusing intercommunion on those terms"; their refusal is a way of "maintaining their witness to the Scriptural truth about the nature of the Church which might otherwise be hopelessly compromised." Yet "Catholics" also face a dilemma: if, as they rightly believe, it is "of the nature of the Church to be one visible fellowship," and if, as they must, they believe that their own Church is that fellowship, then what account can they consistently give of the "sheer fact," as the ecumenically oriented among them have recognized, "that Christ is present in the other Churches"?

Newbigin's argument is that, in an actual situation of "stalemate" between "Protestants" and "Catholics," "the visible reunion of the Churches" will make progress only if some way can be found of "breaking through the theological impasse in regard to the doctrine of the Church." The insight he seeks to propound in *The Household of God* characteristically combines thought and action, mission and unity, the accomplished and the awaited:

> The Church is the pilgrim people of God. It is on the move—hastening to the ends of the earth to beseech all men to be reconciled to God, and hastening to the end of time to meet its Lord who will gather all into one. Therefore the nature of the Church is never to be finally defined in static terms, but only in terms of that to which it is going. It cannot be understood rightly except in a perspective which is at once missionary and eschatological, and only in that perspective can the deadlock of our present ecumenical debate be resolved. But—and this is of vital importance—it will be a solution in which theory and practice are inseparably related, not one which can be satisfactorily stated in terms of theory alone. There is a way of bringing the eschatological perspective to bear upon our present perplexities which relieves them at no cost to our selves, which allows us to rest content with them because in the age to come they will disappear. That is a radically false eschatology. The whole meaning of this present age between Christ's coming and His coming again is that in it the powers of the age to come are at work now to draw all men into one in Christ. When the Church ceases to be one, or ceases to be missionary, it contradicts its own nature. Yet the Church is not to be defined by what it is, but by that End to which it moves, the power of which now works in the Church, the power of the Holy Spirit who is the earnest of the inheritance still to be revealed. To say that the deadlock in the ecumenical debate will be resolved in a perspective which is missionary and eschatological is not true unless it is understood that that perspective means a new obedience to, and a new possession by, the Holy Spirit. It is a perspective inseparable from action, and that action must be both in the direction of mission and in that of unity, for these are but two aspects of the one work of the Spirit.[50]

The pneumatological dimension is what receives a new emphasis in Newbigin's writing.

Newbigin insists that he is speaking, all the while, of the Church as a tangible community. What constitutes the Church is invisible: it is the calling of God, the choice of the Lord, the work of the Holy Spirit. But what is constituted is "an actual, visible, earthly company," composed of those whom God is gathering, whether in a household, a city, a region, or the whole world. The power by which this congregation is constituted is "the divine love which loves even the unlovely and reaches out to save all," and to this community God has "committed the entire work of salvation." Yet this "visible Church is full of things which are utterly opposed to the will of God as it is revealed in Jesus": "The great Pauline words about the Church as the Body of Christ, the Bride of Christ, the Temple of God, are addressed to the actual visible and sinful congregations in Corinth and Asia Minor, and indeed are spoken precisely in connection with the urgent need to correct the manifold sins and disorders which the Apostle found in them." The notion of the earthly, historical Church as *simul justa et peccatrix* is one of the clues that Newbigin will follow in looking for an ecclesiology appropriate to the path from disunity to unity. This touchstone will be applied to each and all of three main ways which Newbigin detects of answering the questions: Where is the Church to be found? How are succeeding generations made participants in the atonement wrought by God in Christ? What is the manner of our ingrafting into Christ? Granting the caricatural nature of his threefold typology, Newbigin formulates a first answer, characteristic of classical Protestantism, that "we are incorporated in Christ by hearing and believing the Gospel." The second answer, characteristic of Catholicism, is that "we are incorporated by sacramental participation in the life of the historically continuous Church." The third answer, eventually to be designated Pentecostalist, is that "we are incorporated by receiving and abiding in the Holy Spirit." Each of these ecclesiologies has a "basis in Scripture and in the nature of the Gospel"; but each has resulted in distortions when its features are exaggerated to the neglect of the others.

In the three chapters expounding the three typical ecclesiologies, Newbigin takes first the Church as "the congregation of the faithful." Starting out from Jesus's opening invitation to "repent, and believe the gospel" (Mark 1:15), he shows how the summons to faith characterizes the progress of the Gospel and the constitution of the Church as the believing community in the Acts of the Apostles. Lengthy passages are then devoted to close readings of Paul's letters to the Galatians and the Romans: Newbigin interprets the epistles in classic Reformation style as the proclamation of justification by grace through faith—alone. To seek righteousness by the works of the law is to abandon the sole ground on which universally sinful humankind can stand, namely the sheer mercy of God made available through the redeeming work of Christ and the gift of the Holy Spirit. Except for a remnant, biblical Israel failed to understand the nature of the covenant which made it God's people: the foundation of the covenant was "a relationship of pure grace on God's side and pure trust on Abraham's." With Christ, "a new hour has struck. Out of the womb of the old Israel, the new Israel—Israel after the Spirit—is born." The "true seed of Abraham" are those, whether Jew or Gentile, who by faith lay hold of God's love and receive the Spirit of freedom and life which flows through the members of Christ's Body. That community exists "publicly," "upon the plane of history," with its rites of baptism and the Lord's Supper as visible signs of the grace and faith that constitute it.

That "central and essential strand of biblical teaching"—focused by the apostle Paul and reasserted by the Protestant Reformers—must, says Newbigin, be firmly grasped throughout the ecclesiological search. But Protestantism has in fact—perhaps for understandable reasons embedded in its origins—distorted the picture. In answering the question of how "Jesus Christ is presented to our faith who live nineteen centuries after his incarnation," Protestants have underplayed the active instrumentality of the Church as "the bearer of God's saving purpose." Against the view that the Church is simply "created from above by the work of Christ in the word and sacraments," it must be maintained that "the word is preached and the sacraments are administered in and by the Church as well as to the Church, and Christ, the Head of the Body, acts in them, both through and for the Church":

> The word and sacraments are never isolated events. They are never—if one may speak crudely—let down from heaven at the end of a string. We may agree that they are creative in relation to the Church, but they do not create the Church *de novo*, or *ex nihilo*. Every setting forth of the word and sacraments of the Gospel is an event in the life of an actually existing Christian Church. . . . We shall not question that they are the word and sacraments of Christ. But also we cannot close our eyes to the fact that, in their actual transmission and administration, and in the congregational life which forms their inevitable context, they are the words and acts of that particular Christian body.[51]

An episodic view of the Church as a recurrently repeated "event" leaves no room in the picture for "a continuing historical institution, nor for any organic relation between congregations in different places and times." Protestants have found it hard to accept that "what Christ left behind was a fellowship, and He entrusted to it the task of being His representative to the world." The circumstantial reason for this refusal may go back to Luther's struggle to reassert the Gospel in the face of a concretely existing Church that excommunicated him, but the fact is that he was thereby driven toward a notion of the "invisibility" of "the true Church" in a way that failed to apply precisely to ecclesiology the teaching that "justification by faith is the article by which *the Church* stands or falls": "By substituting at this critical point for the true and biblical dialectic of holy and sinful, a false and unbiblical dialectic of outward and inward, visible and invisible, Luther himself helped profoundly to confuse the issue of the Reformation."[52] The subsequent history of Protestantism—the conception of the Church's visible unity and social continuity having been largely destroyed—is "a tendency to endless fissiparation" for which penitence is ecumenically required. Withal, the setting of word and sacraments (understood "verbally") over against the continuing life of the fellowship has led in Protestantism, says Newbigin, to an "over-intellectualizing" of both the act and the content of faith. Theological disputes have proved needlessly divisive, and too much store has been set by theological statements as a means to unity. Although "true doctrine will always be vital to the Church's life," much "intellectual disagreement," painful though it may be, can be tolerable, and even mutually instructive, in the time before final clarification, provided it is contained within a unity that is essentially "a work of the Holy Spirit binding us to one another in the love wherewith Christ loved us."

The second of Newbigin's ecclesiological types is that of the Church as "Body of Christ." This ecclesiology concentrates precisely on the element that was weak in the first type: incorporation into Christ is achieved "primarily and essentially by sacramental incorporation into the life of His Church." A survey of the biblical basis unfolds as follows. Newbigin first affirms that "at the heart and centre of the earthly ministry of the incarnate Christ was the choosing, training and sending forth of a band of apostles"; they were to "represent" him in whom they had encountered God and in whom they found their unity. This is congruous with the fact that what binds the whole Bible story together is "the history of a people," chosen and redeemed by the Lord. This in turn is congruous with the fact that, scripturally, the life of the human creature is lived in a complexity of social solidarities. In turn, humankind in its "body-soul unity" is part of the whole created order, whose "material means" are used by God "to convey his saving power" as "an earnest and foretaste of the restoration of creation to its true harmony in and for God's glory, and of man to his true relation to the created world." Hence the sacraments, which embody both grace and responsive faith. All this grounds the utter appropriateness of St. Paul's presentation of the Church as the Body of Christ, which Newbigin then displays with acknowledged help from the exegetical studies of the Anglican J. A. T. Robinson (*The Body*, 1952) and the Roman Catholic Lucien Cerfaux (*Le Christ dans la théologie de saint Paul*, 1951). By baptism and faith Christians are joined with the body of Christ, crucified and risen, the fleshly body in which sin has been put to death and the spiritual body through which new life courses, "a Spirit-filled body in which the Spirit quickens even the mortal bodies of the members" (Romans 7:4–6; 1 Corinthians 15:45). There is, correlatively, only one such Body and one such Spirit (1 Corinthians 12:13; Ephesians 4:4). From the First Letter to the Corinthians it appears, with reference to both baptism (chapter 1) and the Lord's Supper (chapters 10–11), that "any breach in the unity of the Church was in violent contradiction to the very heart of the Gospel as Paul understood it": "For Christians to find other centres of common life than Christ, to call themselves by other names than His, is a monstrous absurdity, and in such circumstances the Lord's Supper will be an instrument of judgment upon them." A Corinthian congregation whose life was marked by grievous sins could still be addressed as "the body of Christ" precisely as the apostle's way of designating the ground, need, and possibility of its corporate amendment.

Newbigin next turns to "the long story of the Church" for indications that underline the truth in the biblical conception of "our membership in Christ" as "essentially membership in one undivided visible fellowship." He finds four such indications. First, the fact that Christianity is not a disembodied spirituality but life in a visible fellowship is confirmed by the history of renewal movements, which may begin by rejecting the hardened structure of an older body but rapidly develop their own organization and modes of succession. Second, even if there have been "occasions when a break in the continuing structure is—under the conditions created by human sin—inevitable if the truth of the Gospel is to be maintained," the formation of a new structure on the basis of "the particular doctrine of the reformer, or the particular spiritual experience of the group" has entailed the loss of "something essential to the true being of the Church"; the resulting body "lacks the richness and completeness which belongs to the whole catholic Church." Third, there is "the whittling away of the sacraments at many times and places in Protestant history"; "when we allow ourselves to be more rational or more spiritual than Christ who gave us these two sacraments" as the "visible and tangible means of his presence," seeking to "rise above the ordinary limitations of humanity," we "become something less than human" and lose "a certain simplicity and a certain awareness of ultimate mystery which belong to the very heart of man's true response to God." Fourth, it is common experience that the most satisfying personal relationships require a stable institutional context: "It is surely congruous with the whole nature of man that Christ, in giving us Himself, has given us a Church which is His body on earth and therefore marked by visible limits and a continuing structure, so that fellowship with Him should be by incorporation in it." Given all that, it follows that "disunity in the Church is no mere external crack on the surface of a solid reality. It is something which goes down to its very core."

To understand the Church as the Body of Christ is characteristic of Catholic ecclesiology. Newbigin next proceeds to show how in fact Catholicism has distorted the New Testament view of the matter. His central criticism is directed at the way in which Catholic thinking has denied the presence of sin in the Church, on the grounds that "since the Church is the body of Christ it cannot sin":

> No honest person can deny that the Church as a visible institution has in the course of its history been guilty of pride, greed, sloth and culpable blindness. Nor can we admit the possibility of easing the difficulty by making a radical distinction between the Church and its members. The "individual Christian" is such only as a member of Christ, and there is no meaning in saying that the body of Christ cannot sin but His members can. Nor, finally, does the New Testament leave us in any doubt that the church *does* sin. The words, "Ye are the body of Christ" and the words "Ye are yet carnal", were addressed by the same apostle to the same body of men and women [cf. 1 Corinthians 12:27 and 3:3]. The living Lord of the Church can say to a Church, "I know thy works, that thou hast a name that thou livest, and thou art dead." The Lord himself can remove the candlestick out of its place [cf. Revelation 3:1 and 2:5].

For a Church to claim, as is typical in Catholicism, to "have the plenitude of grace in itself" is to have "abandoned the Spirit for the flesh," for it is to have forgotten that its sole ground of standing is the sheer mercy of God; it is to have renounced the necessity and the comfort of hope, which is given by the Spirit who is the spirit of promise, the earnest, the foretaste of the completed victory of God (cf. Galatians 5:5). A true doctrine of the Church, says Newbigin, will match the "dark mystery of sin in the Church with a doctrine of the divine grace profound enough to deal with it without evasion" and will at least in some measure "explain how a body which by sin denies its own nature is yet accepted by God and used as the means of His grace."

There is one point in particular at which Newbigin sees the "carnality" of Catholicism's distorted ecclesiology most obviously expressed, namely the tendency to make of "apostolic succession" a necessary and, in the worst case, even the sole sufficient condition of being Church. Although "the natural result of unity will be continuity in the transmission of authority," breaches that were apparently necessitated by circumstances have evidently not prevented God from working in bodies outside the succession in ways that can be attributed to his "uncovenanted" or "extra-sacramental" mercies only at the cost of undermining the necessity of the Church itself:

> No one who is not spiritually blind or worse can fail to acknowledge that God has signally and abundantly blessed the preaching, sacraments and ministry of great bodies which can claim no uninterrupted succession from the apostles, but who have contributed at least as much as those who have remained in it to the preaching of the Gospel, the conversion of sinners, and the building up of the saints in holiness. Any theology which tries in any way to evade the most complete acknowledgment of that fact is self-condemned.

And even more polemically perhaps:

> What seems to be implied in so-called Catholic definitions of the Church is that while a Church may in other matters lose what belongs to its essence and yet be accepted by God as a Church, a Church which loses its continuity with the undivided Church forfeits completely its character as part of the Catholic Church; that though a Church be besotted with corruption, bound to the world in an unholy alliance, rent with faction, filled with false teaching, and utterly without missionary zeal, God's mercy is big enough to cover these defects and they do not therefore destroy its claim to be regarded as part of the Church; but that though a Church be filled with all the fruits of the Holy Spirit, if it lack the apostolic succession it is no part of the Church and all the mercy of God is not enough to make it so.[53]

The conclusion from this part of Newbigin's work was to be carried over into all his subsequent writing on the restoration of the Church's unity, and it proves interesting to note how even Roman Catholic teaching on the matter has developed in ways that move at least some distance in Newbigin's direction. Newbigin sums up his own position thus: "The Church in the New Testament is that real, visible, human fellowship in which Christ is alive in His members, and they are growing up into Him. Those who seek Him must find Him there and nowhere else, for the world—as over against the Church—lieth in the evil one. I do not think that it is possible to deny that the Church, so understood, exists in bodies which have lost the visible succession."[54]

Newbigin's third ecclesiological type is what he hesitantly calls the Pentecostal, which he expounds under the heading of "the community of the Holy Spirit." Here the answer given to the question "Where is the Church?" is "Where the Holy Spirit is recognizably present with power." The story of the apostolic Church, told in Acts and theologically and pastorally reflected in the Pauline and Johannine epistles, offers much evidence in its favor: "The Holy Spirit may be the last article of the Creed but in the New Testament it is the first fact of experience." Christ's revealing and atoning work having been completed, and the nucleus of his Church being chosen and ready, so that the "message and structure" or "faith and order" were already in place, still the breathing of the Spirit of God was awaited before the Gospel could be proclaimed and baptism be administered in Christ's name for the remission of sins: "In very truth it is the presence of the Holy Spirit that constitutes the Church" and "the Church is, in the most exact sense, a *koinonia*, a common sharing in the Holy Spirit." As time goes by, the emphasis in the apostolic Church appears to have shifted from the more spectacular gifts of the Spirit to the Spirit's more constant witness and more abiding fruits; but "there is no gainsaying the decisive place given in the New Testament doctrine of the Church to this experienced reality of the Holy Spirit's presence": "If any man hath not the Spirit of Christ, he is none of His" (Romans 8:9), and "Hereby we know that He abideth in us, by the Spirit which He gave us" (1 John 3: 24; cf. 4:13). In current ecclesiological terms, says Newbigin, "the Pentecostal Christian has the New Testament on his side when he demands first of all of any body of so-called Christians, 'Do you have the Holy Spirit? For without that all your creedal orthodoxy and all your historic succession avails you nothing.'" And then, interpreting expansively rather than restrictively the scriptural impossibility of dissociating the Spirit of Christ from the Body of Christ, Newbigin himself presses on "Catholics" the question "whether we are not departing altogether from the New Testament doctrine of the Body of Christ if we suppose that to acknowledge the presence of the Spirit of Christ does not involve any acknowledgment of the presence of His body."

Newbigin's next argument is, in fact, that the ecclesiological debate "has to become three-cornered." From the Pentecostal angle, the Protestant-Catholic dilemma is seen to be a false one. The exaggerated Protestant emphasis on evangelical message (insistence on precisely formulated doctrinal statements) and the exaggerated Catholic emphasis on corporate life (insistence on continuity of ministerial succession) are distortions resulting from a sinful separation between two fundamental and permanently valid truths: "It is not sufficient for the Church to point to itself and say, Here is the body of the Messiah. It must point beyond itself to Him who is sole Judge and Saviour, both of the Church and of the world. And yet the Church is not *merely* the witness to Christ; it is also the body of Christ. It is not merely the reporter of the divine acts of redemption; it is also itself the bearer of God's redeeming grace, itself a part of the story of redemption which is the burden of its message." What both sides have tended to forget is a third term: the Holy Spirit. Due attention to the Holy Spirit will bring message and life, faith and order, back together as they were in the beginning, when Christ endowed the apostolic band with the Spirit in order to represent him (John 20:21–23) and bear witness to him (Acts 1:8), preaching the Gospel to the world and incorporating believing respondents into Christ by baptism; for "the Church lives neither by her faithfulness to her message nor by her abiding in one fellowship with the apostles"—though both those strands must be tightly clung to—but "by the living power of the Spirit of God," by which alone we can abide in Christ's communion and bear witness to his grace. There is a revolutionary element in this Pentecostal vision; but in the New Testament it is taken for granted "*both* that the Holy Spirit is free and sovereign, able to work in ways that demand re-thinking of our traditional categories, *and* that He Himself gives to the Church the necessary gifts by which He may be known." Discernment of spirits is needed, and the tests are the confession of the incarnate Christ (1 Corinthians 12:3; 1 John 4:2f.) as well as the charity in which the seekers after truth are maintained.

This third ecclesiology suffers its own distortions, says Newbigin, when it isolates the truth of present experience from what has been given once and for all in "Christ's work in the flesh, the Scriptures, and the sacraments." The "extreme development" of such "non-historical mysticism" is perhaps to be found in Quakerism. But it is found also in any form of the doctrine of election which separates the relationship between each individual soul and God from the social and cosmic scope of redemption on the part of "a love which works on the plane of human history, mediated by the concern of man for man knitting men together into a visible community": there remains an element of ultimate mystery in why one was chosen and another not, but "if we cannot know for what *reason* one was chosen, we can most certainly know for what *purpose* he was chosen: he was chosen in order to be a fruit-bearing branch of the one true vine (John 15:16), a witness through whom others might be saved."

A further distortion which Newbigin detects in his third ecclesiological type is "the setting of ardour against order" (a phrase borrowed from John Mackay). It appeared in the Church at Corinth and has recurred. The prizing of the more flamboyant gifts of the Spirit may lead to the favoring of particular individuals, whose humility becomes forfeit. Rather, the Holy Spirit functions, according to apostolic teaching, as "the abiding and indwelling principle of life in a fellowship," the single source "of all those gifts which such a common life needs and of which the greatest is love." It follows, says Newbigin, that "a decisive mark of the Spirit's presence will be a tender concern for the unity of the body, a horror of all that exalts some human leader or some party into the place which Christ alone can occupy."

A final distortion occurs in the third type of ecclesiology when a proper recognition of "the real primacy of the local congregation" degenerates into "a proliferation of mutually irresponsible sects." The answer is not to be found in the imposition of a "large-scale organisation with its attendant evils of

mechanisation and bureaucracy." Rather, Christian reunion will be "the recovery of the true nature and quality of the Church's life as the visible fellowship of all who in every place call upon the name of the Lord Jesus," with
the local communities joined together in "binding obligations" by which each
"contributes its insight to the common seeking of the Spirit's guidance" and
"defers to the corporate insight of the whole body," so that Christ's redemptive
purpose may be expressed not only at the local but also at the regional and
finally the universal level.

Newbigin ends this chapter of *The Household of God* with a vision that in
1953 was decades ahead of its time. He called for the entry of the "Pentecostal" stream into an ecumenical movement hitherto largely confined to the
"Protestant" and the "Catholic." The latter two had been reluctant to face
the radical criticism they would have had to face from the Pentecostal side,
but, to break their own deadlock, they needed a new understanding and
experience of the Holy Spirit to which the Pentecostal might help them. For
their part, the fissiparous Pentecostals had something to learn from "the
growth of real charity between the great confessions" that provided "evident
tokens of the Spirit's working in the experience of the ecumenical movement."
Half a century later, the fear must be that the "mainstream" Western Protestantism that helped to shape the modern ecumenical movement has gone
into such decline that it will scarcely be around anymore to contribute to, or
benefit from, the developing relations between a biblically and spiritually renewed Catholicism, an Evangelicalism that is seeking the historical depth and
catholic range of the great tradition, and a Pentecostalism that has already
influenced the other two and has tentatively begun to occupy its own place
at the ecumenical table.

The two final and closely connected chapters of *The Household of God* deal
with the Church from an eschatological and from a missiological perspective
under the respective headings of "Christ in You, the Hope of Glory" (cf. Colossians 1:27) and "Unto All the Nations" (cf. Matthew 24:14). The theory
and practice of mission in light of the End is the focus of chapter 5 of this
book, on Newbigin as missiologist. At this point the focus remains on Christian unity. Newbigin argues that a truly biblical eschatology will unblock the
impasse on the road to ecclesial unity and that the two tasks of mission and
unity are mutually conditioning and "must be prosecuted together." Unity is
for the Church both a gift and a task when the Church realizes its nature
and function as the sign, foretaste, and instrument of salvation.

Eschatologically, the time of the earthly Church is stretched between the
completed events of Christ's death and resurrection and "the dissolution of
all things which must be before God's new heavens and new earth and all
the glory of His Kingdom can be revealed." The grip of Satan on humankind
has been broken by Christ's redemptive death, but because "the full revelation
of God's Kingdom must mean the obliteration of all that is opposed to it,"
Christ's victory "must remain hidden, for only so is there room left for the
free response of faith, hope, and love" by which we appropriate the victory
and enter the Kingdom. Newbigin proceeds to describe the Christian life

through a detailed analysis of Galatians 2:20: "I have been crucified with Christ; yet I live; and yet no longer I, but Christ liveth in me; and that life which I now live in the flesh I live in faith, the faith which is in the Son of God, who loved me, and gave himself up for me." The "self which is centred in itself" dies in order to "make room for the self which is centred in Christ." The Christian life is lived in the Spirit, and

> here the Pentecostal has surely been right as against both the orthodox Protestant and the Catholic: against the Protestant in expecting and welcoming wholeheartedly a real manifestation of the supernatural power of the Holy Spirit in the life of the believer in this present age; against the Catholic in recognising that it is only a foretaste which must never be allowed to blunt the keen edge of hope. Where he has been wrong is in failing to recognise that the supreme supernatural gift of the Spirit is love, and that therefore the proper counterpart of the one Spirit is the one body.[55]

It is the corporeal and corporate character of the Christian life that grounds Newbigin's application to the entire Church of what he says of the individual believer. Rather than thinking that it "possesses" the fullness of divine grace, the Church maintains its participation in the life of God only in "an ever-renewed dying to self," "a receiving of Christ's risen life which is ministered to us by the Holy Spirit in the word and sacraments of the Gospel and in the daily life of the fellowship which He rules," and "an ever-renewed pressing forward to the fullness of that which we have only in foretaste through the Spirit by faith." For the divided Christian communities this means that their measure of truth and their particular gifts will be properly maintained only through the sharing that comes by way of "the mutual losing of isolated selfhood to find it in the beloved," all in "penitent acknowledgement of our common failure to be what the Church ought to be" and in common reliance on the sheer "mercy of God, who 'calleth the things that are not, as though they were' (Romans 4:17)." In terms of ecumenical procedures, Newbigin considers that

> if we refuse fellowship in Christ to any body of men and women who accept Jesus as Lord and show the fruits of His Spirit in their corporate life, we do so at our peril. With what judgment we judge we shall be judged. It behoves us therefore to receive one another as Christ has received us. . . . To accept one another as we are does not mean leaving one another as we are. It is precisely the beginning of a process of mutual correction and of speaking truth in love to one another that is impossible so long as we do not treat one another as brethren.

A mark of the ecumenical calling will be "a determination to cease judging one another for what we are, and to build one another up in faith and hope and love into what God has called us to be."

Missiologically, the Church is the fellowship of those who, by God's representative election of them, have been called and commissioned by Christ to bear witness before the nations to himself and the redemption he has wrought, to bring people to the obedience of faith, until such time as the redemption has reached its intended universal and cosmic scope. Between the withdrawal of Christ's visible presence and his promised return for the consummation, the apostolic mission is carried out in the power of the Holy Spirit: "The gift of the Spirit, itself the sign and foretaste of the age to come, is the means by which the Church is enabled to lead this present age to its consummation, by bringing the Gospel to all nations." Under the Spirit, the life and witness of the Church becomes "the sign and first-fruit and instrument" of salvation. Ecclesial unity is essential to the Church's nature and task: "The Church's unity is the sign and instrument of the salvation which Christ has wrought and whose final fruition is the summing up of all things in Christ." That is so because salvation

> must be communication in and by the actual development of a community which embodies—if only in foretaste—the restored harmony of which it speaks. A gospel of reconciliation can only be communicated by a reconciled fellowship. . . . At each stage of the apostolic task, the Church's task is to reconcile men to God in Christ. She can only do that in so far as she is herself living in Christ, a reconciled fellowship in Him, bound together in the love of the Father.

Thus the intrinsic connection between the Church's mission and the Church's unity can be exhibited in a twofold way, positively and negatively: "firstly, in that unity is in order that the world may believe, and secondly, in that the act of witness sets the Church in the situation in which disunity is seen for what it is," namely, "a direct and public contradiction of the Gospel," a proclamation of our disbelief in the sufficiency of Christ's atonement. In terms of the ecumenical vision and goals, there can be no "resolute dealing with our divisions except in the context of a quite new acceptance on the part of all the Churches of the obligation to bring the Gospel to every creature," and no prospect "that the world will believe the Gospel until it sees more evidence of its power to make us one."

In 1952, at the conclusion of *The Household of God*, Newbigin summed up the ecumenical task concretely thus:

> Our task is, firstly, to call upon the whole Church to a new acceptance of the missionary obligation to bring the whole world to obedience to Christ; secondly, to do everything in our power to extend the area of cooperation between all Christians in the fulfilment of that task, by seeking to draw into the fellowship of the ecumenical movement those who at present stand outside of it to the right and to the left; and thirdly, to press forward unwearyingly with the task of reunion in every place, until all who in every place call upon the name of Jesus are visibly united in one fellowship, the sign and instrument of God's purpose to sum up all things in Christ, to whom with the Father and the Holy Spirit be all the glory.[56]

In 1961, at New Delhi, the third assembly of the World Council of Churches welcomed the institutional integration of the International Missionary Council into the WCC's own structures as its division of world mission and evangelism. Piloted by Bishop Newbigin, since 1959 general secretary of the IMC, the integration was a feasible way of joining the two organizations such as had been envisaged in *The Household of God* as an expression of the insepar-ability of unity and mission in the essential constitution of the Church.[57] That same assembly received into membership the Russian Orthodox Church and several other Orthodox Churches from Eastern Europe, thereby "drawing into the fellowship of the ecumenical movement" some who had hitherto stood outside of it, whether "to the right" or "to the left." Meanwhile, the Second Vatican Council had been convoked and was waiting to convene; and within a couple of years the conciliar decree *Unitatis Redintegratio* would sanction the official entry of the Roman Catholic Church into the ecumenical move-ment, although that Church has never sought membership in the WCC and its most significant ecumenical participation has taken the form of bilateral dialogues at global level with other confessional families and communions. In the pursuit of what Newbigin called "reunion in every place," the Faith and Order "survey of church union negotiations 1959–1961" reported on the progress of some fifty sets of conversations and plans toward unity that were being conducted or drawn up at national and regional levels on every continent.[58] Some of these were to result in "organic unions" such as New-bigin advocated in the light of Scripture and his experience in South India (so in Northern Rhodesia/Zambia, in North India and Pakistan, and in Aus-tralia), other schemes eventually broke down or were postponed, and others never set themselves such an ambitious goal as full visible unity.

"The Unity We Seek"

The New Delhi assembly of the WCC adopted a description of "the unity we seek" that was greatly indebted to Lesslie Newbigin's vision, persistence, draft-ing skills, and conciliar savoir-faire. He has already been seen calling for the WCC to move beyond the unstable "ecclesiological neutrality" set out in the Toronto declaration of 1950. In the 1950s, as a bishop of the Church of South India, Newbigin served as vice chairman of the WCC's Faith and Order working committee, a position he was obliged to resign on becoming a staff member at the International Missionary Council. His last meeting in the cur-rently pertinent phase of his connection with Faith and Order took place in the summer of 1959 at Spittal in Austria, where his paper on "churchly unity" led to the addressing of a minute to the Central Committee of the WCC recalling the historic inspiration and purpose of the Faith and Order Move-ment and requesting a reaffirmation of the cause of unity in the context of the WCC.[59] Something of a neologism (and the adjectival form never really caught on), the term "churchly unity" was intended to designate a unity that went beyond mere "cooperation." The Spittal minute contained, from New-bigin's pen, a paragraph that, after much debate in the plenary meeting of the Faith and Order commission at St. Andrews, Scotland, in 1960, was brought with very little change to the New Delhi assembly of the WCC in the following year and there adopted.[60]

The New Delhi statement, entitled "The Church's Unity," begins with a paragraph, drafted by Albert Outler, on the trinitarian ground of ecclesial unity that is entirely consonant with Newbigin's views:

The love of the Father and the Son in the unity of the Holy Spirit is the source and goal of the unity which the triune God wills for all men and creation. We believe that we share in this unity in the Church of Jesus Christ, who is before all things and in whom all things hold together. In him alone, given by the Father to be Head of the Body, the Church has its true unity. The reality of this unity was manifest at Pentecost in the gift of the Holy Spirit, through whom we know in this present age the first fruits of that perfect union of the Son with his Father, which will be known in its fullness only when all things are consummated by Christ in his glory. The Lord who is bringing all things into full unity at the last is he who constrains us to seek the unity which he wills for his Church on earth here and now.[61]

Then comes the Newbigin paragraph describing the unity for which "we believe we must pray and work":

We believe that the unity which is both God's will and his gift to his Church is being made visible as all in each place who are baptized into Jesus Christ and confess him as Lord and Saviour are brought by the Holy Spirit into one fully committed fellowship, holding the one apostolic faith, preaching the one Gospel, breaking the one bread, joining in common prayer, and having a corporate life reaching out in witness and service to all and who at the same time are united with the whole Christian fellowship in all places and all ages in such wise that ministry and members are accepted by all, and that all can act and speak together as occasion requires for the tasks to which God calls his people.

Another paragraph follows, acknowledging the limitations inherent in the preceding:

This brief description of our objective leaves many questions unanswered. We are not yet of a common mind on the interpretation and the means of achieving the goal we have described. We are clear that unity does not imply simple uniformity of organization, rite, or expression. We all confess that sinful self-will operates to keep us separated and that in our human ignorance we cannot discern clearly the lines of God's design for the future. But it is our firm hope that through the Holy Spirit God's will as it is witnessed to in Holy Scripture will be more and more disclosed to us and in us. The achievement of unity will involve nothing less than a death and rebirth of many forms of church life as we have known them. We believe that nothing less costly can finally suffice.

To the reader of this book, the themes and even the phraseology of the New Delhi text—except perhaps for some of the disclaimers in the last paragraph quoted—will be unmistakably familiar. Newbigin's contribution to the New Delhi statement, the subsequent influence of that statement, and Newbigin's continuing advocacy of its ideas have been described at first hand by Lukas Vischer:

The New Delhi statement on "The Unity We Seek" was largely due to Lesslie Newbigin's initiative. When I joined the staff, the draft statement was already being circulated. About one hundred theologians had been invited to offer their comments. My first assignment was to see the statement through the New Delhi assembly. I made a summary of the responses and suggested some changes of the text—very few because we were really eager to get Lesslie's draft accepted. It was at that time far from obvious that an agreement could be reached because many regarded the attempt as a departure from the principles laid down in the Toronto statement. But the assembly section on unity was prepared to go ahead. Lesslie was busy in another section [on witness] and could not follow the debate. Suddenly, during one of the sessions, he appeared at my side. The text read at that time "to form *a* fully committed fellowship." Turn it please into "*one* fully committed fellowship," he whispered. I did so and nobody noticed the change. The New Delhi statement had an enormous impact throughout my years in Faith and Order. Lesslie continued to emphasize that the unity of the local church was the real test of unity.[62]

After New Delhi the emphasis in Faith and Order, expressed at the fourth world conference held at Montreal in 1963, fell at first on the local aspect of church unity, epitomized in the phrase "all in each place." Soon, however, several factors provoked a shift of attention to the global aspect, which came to the fore in the desire recorded by the fourth assembly of the World Council of Churches at Uppsala in 1968 that "the members of the WCC, committed to each other, should work for a time when a genuinely universal council may once more speak for all Christians." As early as a speech given at the University of Chicago before the second assembly of the WCC at Evanston in 1954, Bishop Newbigin recognized the need for church unity to be both local and universal (and indeed transtemporal): "first that it must be such that all who are in Christ in any place are, in that place, visibly one fellowship; second, that it must be such that each local community is so ordered and so related to the whole that its fellowship with all Christ's people everywhere, and with those who have gone before and will come after, is made clear."[63] The substantial difficulty and delicacy involved in relating those two aspects was perhaps trivially reflected in issues of punctuation surrounding the New Delhi statement: in the Spittal minute the clauses corresponding to the local and the universal were still separated by a semicolon; in the New Delhi text itself they were deliberately held together by being simply "run on" ("all in each place who are baptized . . . and who at the same time are united with the whole Christian fellowship . . ."); in citing New Delhi, the Montreal report, in a move which Newbigin noted with regret but considered inadvertent and which may in fact simply reflect American typographical style over British, introduced a comma at the place of the old semicolon![64]

In any case, the factors that contributed to a shift in favor of the universal—and more particularly the form that it took—were not all to Newbigin's liking. Most important, "the massive presence of the Roman Catholic Church in the ecumenical movement from the 1960s onwards shifted emphasis from local schemes of union to bilateral dialogues between world confessions. It was obvious that the RCC as a single world communion should find its partners in the world confessional families. These thus assumed a much more prominent role than in the preceding decades."⁶⁵ Willy-nilly, part of the ecumenical impact of the Second Vatican Council was to "relegate the issue of local unity to the margin and bring back into the centre of the stage the development of theological discussion among globally organized organizations which show little sign of readiness to disappear."⁶⁶ More benignly, "the growing role of the Orthodox churches in the life of the WCC was giving wider recognition to the role of ecumenical councils in the history of the Church."⁶⁷ And so Newbigin, now back in the Faith and Order commission as Bishop of Madras, let himself be persuaded (though to his later regret) to help launch the WCC study of "conciliarity" as a mode of unity:

> At Louvain in 1971 I shared in the full meeting of the Commission on Faith and Order and was asked by Lukas Vischer to chair the section on "Conciliarity" and draft the report. I had great hesitation about accepting this, for I was sure that "conciliarity" would be seized upon as an alternative to organic union and therefore welcomed by those who wanted at all costs to preserve denominational identities. Unfortunately my fears proved to be well-grounded for, in spite of repeated statements by the WCC to the contrary, bodies like the Lutheran World Federation have enthusiastically welcomed a concept of conciliarity (further described as "reconciled diversity") which enables them to take part in councils of churches but to retain their separate sovereignty. I therefore regret that I was responsible for drafting the operative document.⁶⁸

By way of a consultation on "concepts of unity and models of union" held at Salamanca, Spain, in 1973, Faith and Order proceeded successfully to present to the section on "What Unity Requires" of the fifth assembly of the World Council of Churches at Nairobi in 1975 a text on conciliar fellowship as its "vision" for the form of "the one Church":

> The one Church is to be envisioned as a conciliar fellowship of local churches which are themselves truly united. In this conciliar fellowship, each local church possesses, in communion with the others, the fulness of catholicity, witnesses to the same apostolic faith, and therefore recognizes the others as belonging to the same Church of Christ and guided by the same Spirit. As the New Delhi Assembly pointed out, they are bound together because they have received the same baptism and share in the same eucharist; they recognize each other's members and ministries. They are one in their common commitment to confess the Gospel of Christ by proclamation and service to the world. To this end each church aims at maintaining sustained and sustaining relationships with her sister churches, expressed in conciliar gatherings whenever required for the fulfilment of their common calling.⁶⁹

The new attention to the conciliar connection that was to hold churches together as far as the universal level naturally raised afresh the question concerning the nature of the ecclesial units that were to be so joined in fellowship.

"A Fellowship of Local Churches Truly United"

"What is 'a local church truly united'?" was the title of the paper brought by Lesslie Newbigin to a small consultation in which he and I participated over a weekend in December 1976, at the Foyer John Knox in Geneva, under the dual auspices of Faith and Order and the WCC working group on renewal and congregational life.[70] This densely argued and passionately expressed text instantiates Newbigin's mature ecclesiology: it draws on his experiences as a rural pastor and preacher in India, a first bishop of the Church of South India after union, and later the episcopal head of the metropolitan diocese of Madras, a global leader in matters of Faith and Order as well as Mission and Evangelism, and finally a returnee to the modern West in the particular shape of the city of Birmingham, England. Strikingly prominent in this piece, compared with the ecclesiological writings of Newbigin's that we have already examined, is the attention given to language, race, class, and culture as elements to be negotiated in the question of ecclesial unity. In his generally positive "personal report" on the fifth assembly of the World Council of Churches held in Nairobi a year earlier, Newbigin declared that he had "come to feel that to talk of the unity of the Church only in terms of the problem of reconciling our denominational diversities is to miss the heart of the matter" and endorsed the section on "What Unity Requires" in its conclusion that "since Christ died and rose for us all, and his Church is to be a sign of the coming unity of mankind, . . . it follows that, in order to be faithful to our calling to unity, we must consider this calling within the wider context of the unity and diversity of mankind."[71]

In his Geneva paper, Newbigin does not, of course, treat lightly the matter of denominational division: it remains for him a blatant and disabling contradiction of the Gospel. He is adamant that a certain (mis)understanding of the notion of "ecclesial *typoi*" lately propounded by Cardinal Willebrands of the Vatican Secretariat for Promoting Christian Unity is incompatible with the scriptural requirements concerning the nature and form of the Church. It is a skewed use of "conciliarity" to think that it may justify "a form of unity in which varying 'types' of ecclesial bodies would continue to exist side by side in each local situation, fully recognizing one another, and meeting together from time to time for common counsel, but retaining their separate existence and continuing to develop their own distinctive 'styles' of worship, thought and life." The maintenance of separations determined by "the distinct 'types' of Christian discipleship which have developed in history on the basis of special experiences of individual Christian leaders or national churches, 'types' defined by such names as Anglican, Lutheran, Roman" seems to be "roundly condemned by the language of St. Paul in dealing with the Corinthian factions." Separations that are determined "by the past quarrels through which the Church has been divided" and that " take out of the past not the one name of Jesus but other names by which the identity of a congregation is to be defined," contradict "the promise of the Gospel that in Christ there is one mercy-seat where all people may meet and be forgiven and reconciled."

The positive thrust of Newbigin's paper is that the Church, both local and global, receives from its christological determination a missiological obligation that should direct all its forms and structures dynamically toward the eschatological goal of a universal reconciliation and renewal of mankind in God's reign. Beginning at the "local" level, Newbigin notes that the adjective, when applied to the Church, refers to the "place" where the Church is, not just as the latitude and longitude of the spot where a particular church happens to be but as its location "in the fabric of human society." The local Church is the Church *for that place*. There is both a soteriological and a sociological side to that:

> The Church is wrongly described unless it is described as the church *for that place*, and the meaning of the preposition "for" is determined christologically; that is to say, it is determined by what Jesus Christ has done, is doing and will do with and for the world as its author, redeemer and consummator. The Church in each place is the Church for that place, in the sense in which Christ is for mankind and for the world. Just as Christ is not understood unless He is understood as the Word by whom all things came to be, for whom they are, and in whom they are to be consummated, and as the Last Adam in whom alone mankind's destiny lies; so also the church in any place is not rightly understood unless it is understood as sign, first-fruit and instrument of God's purpose in Christ for that place. And in this sentence the word "place" must mean the whole secular reality of the place including its physical, social, cultural and political aspects.[72]

That last remark specifies that it must be "that" precise place that the local Church is "for."

The question is thereby raised of "the relation between the Gospel and culture," says Newbigin in a phrase that would come to summarize his major concern in the remaining twenty years and more of his life. The Church must avoid two "extremes" in its relations to the complex culture of a place: either "an uncritical identification with the secular reality around it" or "a merely polemical confrontation with it." Within the field of debatable options, difficult decisions have to be taken that are complicated by the changing character of the context. This is well illustrated in the historical account Newbigin gives of the churches' procedures with regard to caste in India when he is discussing the highly controversial question of whether the establishment and "existence of separate congregations in the same geographical area on the basis of language and culture may have to be accepted as a necessary, but provisional, measure for the sake of the fulfilment of Christ's mission":

> The story of the Church's struggle to come to terms with caste in India is a poignant illustration of the perplexities inherent in this question. The Portuguese made their first converts into marginal adherents of their own culture. They were *assimilados* co-opted into the foreign ways of thought, life and speech. The great Jesuit Robert de Nobili insisted that high-caste Indians

could be Christians without breaking caste, and the fruit of his work was a substantial Christian community drawn from the higher castes of Hinduism. Throughout the eighteenth century, missionaries—both Catholic and Lutheran—accepted caste as a social fact and did not think that they were called to contradict it. In the following century a new generation of missionaries, imbued with the ideas of the French Revolution, saw caste as a contradiction of human equality and demanded a total breach with caste as the condition of baptism. This has become the officially accepted view of the churches, whatever the underlying realities may be. Where the Church consists (as in many parts of the country) of an overwhelming preponderance of members drawn from one caste, this means that others can only become Christians at the cost of a total breach with their own kinship group. The missiologists of the "Church Growth" school deplore this and insist that—as a matter of missionary obedience—the Church should accept and welcome the organization of congregations of different castes in the same town or city. Most Indian Christians would utterly repudiate this suggestion as, in present conditions, a denial of the Gospel (rightly I believe). Yet, in situations of racial conflict, we have learned that the demand for integration may in fact be a demand for dominance by one group over another. The assertion of a separate identity may be necessary as the condition for the development of authentic response to the Gospel.[73]

Newbigin envisages such a—*provisional*, he insists—"separation for the sake of mission" in reference to his city of Birmingham, where people in all three of the social categories he will mention themselves inhabit, as typical of modern urban life, multiple "worlds" of residence, industry or profession, political or ideological commitment:

> The white middle-class suburban congregations of Birmingham, however devoted they might be, cannot and could not function as sign, foretaste and instrument of God's purpose or blessing for the immigrants or for the shop-floor workers on the Leyland assembly lines. There have to be communities where these and others can hear and see in terms of their own culture the words and signs of the Gospel. The Church is not truly local if it does not take these situations seriously, and if its forms do not provide for them.[74]

If, in some situations, the "local church" must "take the form of a plurality of congregations" composed "primarily (but never exclusively) of those of a distinct language or culture," such arrangements "must be understood as provisional, looking always to the unity which is the promise of the Gospel." Practically, three things at least are required: "first, full mutual recognition by which the distinct congregations accept and welcome one another, recognizing that their separate meeting represents no mutual estrangement but only the acknowledgment of creaturely distinctions of language and culture; second, total freedom of movement between those congregations and a full welcome for members of each at the meetings of all; third, structures which are explicitly designed to promote the growth in unity of those who are provisionally separated."

The unity which the local church must manifest, says Newbigin, "is an eschatological unity, the unity which will be fully manifest only when God has completed his purpose to sum up all things in Christ. The local Church will be a credible sign of that eschatological unity when it is moving towards it, and when it is already embodying a foretaste of it in its own actual life." That brings us to the catholicity—in both the qualitative and the quantitative senses of the term—that is a mark of the Church inseparable from its unity: the diverse riches of the one Gospel are required to be shared through an ecclesial fellowship that cannot finally be less than universal in space and time. This means that at any particular time and place and in any particular cultural setting, a particular congregation needs both the "correction" and the "support" that comes from being "knit by bonds of mutual recognition and mutual responsibility" with others who also worship and confess the Creator and Redeemer of all. "Conciliarity" may designate that "pattern of common life" in which we learn "with all the saints what is the length and breadth and height and depth of the love of Christ" (cf. Ephesians 3:18f.):

> Within this conciliar fellowship the legitimate and proper variety which must mark the Christian discipleship of different human communities inhabiting different 'places' is at the same time affirmed and controlled by the unity which is given in Christ himself. Thus the wider conciliar fellowship is not a substitute for unity in each place; rather it is the necessary context in which true local unity is to be progressively learned and experienced.

In the one direction, "where, as a matter of missionary faithfulness, there has to be a provisional separation of the congregation in order that the specific gifts of each human community may be brought to the feet of Christ, the wider fellowship of the regional or universal council provides the necessary safeguard against the tendency for these provisional separations to become absolute and permanent." Conversely, "the variety of the different local expressions of discipleship provides a safeguard against all tendencies to monolithic imperialism which, in the name of unity, crushes that blessed variety which God the Father has so lavishly bestowed on his creation."[75]

Newbigin's grand vision of ecclesial and human unity is summed up thus at the conclusion of his 1976 paper:

> What matters is that the Church should everywhere be recognizable as simply the new, the true humanity; as the place where every human being is given the freedom of his own home where he can know and love and obey God as his Father, and Jesus as his Lord in the power of the Spirit who is himself the living presence now of the blessedness to which all are called. In order that the Church may be this, it must be this in each place where human beings are, speaking to everyone in the language of his own humanity; but it cannot be this unless it is also this universally, unless the local fellowship truly embodies in its own life the universal love which is the being of the triune God and into which He would draw all creatures. The diversity-in-unity which is expressed in the word "conciliarity" must be the mark of the Church at every level from the local to the universal. Local unity and universal fellowship cannot be set against each other. Only if the Church at every level is moving towards the unity to which God calls all human kind is it true to its nature.[76]

Newbigin never neglected the local range of Christian unity during his later pastorate in Winson Green or even in his final retirement in Southeast London. Three instances remain to show how Newbigin in the succeeding decades thought about and worked toward Christian unity at the national level (in connection with the plans for a "covenant" among the denominational churches in England), at the level of those "globally organized confessional structures" that he viewed with such suspicion (for in fact he agreed to participate in the "bilateral dialogue" between the Anglican Consultative Council and the World Alliance of Reformed Churches), and at the level of the World Council of Churches (where he sought to recall the organization to the twin concerns of evangelical mission and visible unity such as had marked the ecumenical movement from its origins).

The Abortive Covenant of the English Churches

In 1969 and again in 1972 the governing bodies of the Church of England repeatedly rejected a scheme for unity that the Conference of the Methodist Church had each time approved. In 1972 the English Presbyterian Church and most of the Congregational Church joined together to constitute the United Reformed Church, which was encouraged to invite the other denominations to "talks about talks." These resulted in the setting up of the Churches' Unity Commission, to which I was appointed as a Methodist representative on my return from missionary service in Africa. Between 1974 and 1976 we formulated a set of "Ten Propositions" whose adoption would, it was hoped, form the basis of a covenant among the denominational churches to seek "visible unity in life and mission," starting with a mutual recognition of communicant members in good standing, the use of mutually acceptable rites of initiation into membership in the future, the mutual recognition of ordained ministries as "true ministries of word and sacraments," and the performance of all subsequent ordinations according to "a Common Ordinal which will properly incorporate the episcopal, presbyteral and lay roles in ordination." As expected, the Baptists and the Roman Catholics were not able to proceed, but by 1978 the Church of England, the Methodist Church, the United Reformed Church,ˑthe Moravian Church, and the Churches of Christ (Disciples) had, with varying degrees and points of qualification, reached sufficient agreement of principle to allow the establishment of a Churches' Council for Covenanting in order to work further on the terms and implementation of such a covenant. In this second phase, Bishop Newbigin served as a representative of the United Reformed Church, which became "a major preoccupation" for him during the years 1979 to 1982.[77] On his final return from India in 1974, Newbigin had inevitably been disappointed at the lack of progress toward church unity: "Thirty years ago we had been innocent enough to hope that three decades would be enough to enable the divided Churches in England to catch up with India."[78] Now the proposed covenant might signify at least some first steps toward visible unity among the participants.

Unsurprisingly, the most delicate points for clarification and negotiation proved to concern the recognition of ordained ministries and the historic episcopate. Newbigin had already traversed that ground in the case of South India. Within the Churches' Council for Covenanting, he accepted the interpretation of the contributing Roman Catholic observer, Fr. John Coventry, S.J., that in the act of covenanting the covenanting churches would be "neither affirming nor denying the sufficiency of their ministries, initiation rites and eucharistic celebrations up to that point" but rather be "defining their attitudes to each other *from that point on into the future*"—and then Newbigin added to Coventry the characteristic twist: "What we ought to ask is that we accept one another as sinners who have *not* fulfilled God's intention for His Church, on the basis of the fact that God in His mercy *has* accepted us; and that then (unlike those who say 'let us continue in sin that grace may abound') we set about together to order our common life more fully in accord with God's intention."[79] To avoid the danger that, *after* recognition, the denominations would simply continue their own "parallel" lives and ministries, Newbigin suggested a plan of "mutual responsibility" that would "commit the covenanting Churches to acting together *both* in ordination *and* in pastoral care in such wise that they would actually be growing together into unity from the start." From the point of covenanting, all future ordinations of presbyters and all "consecrations of bishops and the analogous actions by which (in URC terms) provincial moderators and others exercising similar pastoral responsibilities are set apart for their offices" would take place in joint services bringing together "large numbers of the faithful of all the churches," in which "the proper authorities of all the covenanting Churches would share"; from the point of covenanting, moreover, "organs would be created for the shared planning and pastoral oversight of the Churches in the appropriate units—dioceses, districts, provinces, etc.," whose business it would be "to lead the Churches in each place to the situation where shared life at the local level is normal." Newbigin summed up his suggestion thus:

> The basis of it all would be the *intention*, accepted by all, to move together towards a time when all the Covenanting Churches share the ministry of persons who perform the functions of personal pastoral oversight over an area larger than that of the local congregation, who share responsibility for leadership of the Church in teaching, evangelism and action, and whose ordination/consecration is such that it embodies the unanimous assent, prayer and authorisation of all the churches and is therefore within the historic ministry of the universal Church. This would in fact be the essential substance of the historic episcopate, and I cannot doubt that before long it would be clear that those who exercise this ministry are bishops and should be so described. But the substance is at least as important as the name.

In 1980 the CCC put forward in *Towards Visible Unity: Proposals for a Covenant* a plan that was entirely compatible with Newbigin's understanding and vision.

In the United Reformed Church, Bishop Newbigin undertook advocacy of the covenant plan as it was proposed and further clarified by the CCC. For instance, a document under the title "Which Covenant?" shows him in December 1981 making trenchant responses to criticisms that depended on false understandings of the proposals.[80] In 1982, however, the plan came to naught, ostensibly on account of differences both between and among the Anglicans and the United Reformed over whether the current generation of provincial moderators in the URC should receive episcopal consecration before continuing to exercise oversight as part now of a "college" with bishops of the other covenanted Churches; at issue, too, was the acceptability of women's ordination, as practiced in the other denominations but a much agitated question at the time in the Church of England.

Newbigin's disappointment in the English scene was deepened by the collapse of the proposals:

> The whole exercise and the character of many of the debates in which I was involved exposed in a painful way how great was the loss which had been inflicted on the Church by the virtual eclipse of the Student Christian Movement. I belonged to a generation which had been given their formative vision of the Christian life and received their Christian calling in an ecumenical setting. But now the majority of those in the Churches had been shaped either in a conservative evangelical setting where visible unity was not seen to be important, or in a merely denominational setting which had deprived them of the opportunity to form deep and trustful friendships outside of that setting. With the failure of the Covenant the whole movement which had begun with the Lambeth Appeal of 1920 seemed to have come to a dead end, and the united churches of the Indian sub-continent were marginal oddities rather than pioneers.[81]

Characteristically, Newbigin nevertheless glimpsed a ray of hope in the "local ecumenical projects" which from the '60s and '70s onward—my own first pastoral appointment had placed me in an Anglican-Methodist partnership on the edge of Liverpool—had been fostering cooperation and even coalescence at the congregational level and which would now have to continue without the easing of those denominational ties that, on the one hand, bind the localities into a wider ecclesial fellowship but, on the other hand, sometimes hamper them precisely because the denominations remain separate at the national level.

The International Anglican-Reformed Dialogue

Another way of tackling denominational differences is to start at the universal level, and it was no doubt because of what agreement at that level might make possible at national and local levels that Newbigin accepted the invitation to serve as a representative of the World Alliance of Reformed Churches in its bilateral dialogue with the Anglican Communion despite his grave suspicion of "globally organized confessional structures." The Anglican-Reformed

International Commission worked between 1981 and 1984 to produce a report entitled *God's Reign and Our Unity*.[82] It is acknowledged by himself and others that Lesslie Newbigin—as would in any case have been evident from the vocabulary and the style—was the principal writer of the final document; he had also contributed two papers to the earlier deliberations of the group, one on "Christ, Kingdom and Church" and the other on "Sacraments and Ministry."[83]

The more traditional, or "faith and order," background to this bilateral dialogue resided in the facts that the two communions had originated as distinct entities in the events of the sixteenth-century Reformation and then, following the developments of colonial and missionary history, existed cheek by jowl in many parts of the world and more recently entered upon schemes of union that had proved successful on the Indian subcontinent but collapsed in West Africa and Australasia. The newer factors were brought to the dialogue from churches in the Third World, where the emphasis fell on the need for a common "orthopraxis" in the face of desperate social, economic, and political conditions. In drafting *God's Reign and Our Unity*, Newbigin was able, in the one direction, to reassert the missiological and eschatological perspectives of the search for ecclesial unity that had marked his own thinking already thirty years ago in *The Household of God*: "If we seek for unity among Christians, it can only be in order that the church may become a more credible sign, instrument and foretaste of God's purpose to 'unite all things with Christ as head' (Col. 1:19f., cf. Eph. 1:10)."[84] And if, using now the terminology that Newbigin had endorsed from the 1975 Nairobi assembly of the World Council of Churches, "it is wrong to separate the question of church unity from the question of the unity of humankind," it is then also, in the other direction, "wrong and delusive to propose 'justice' and 'peace' as goals to be sought apart from a shared life in Christ":

> If "justice" is conceived as an abstract principle, the pursuit of it is a recipe for endless war, because all human beings overestimate what is due to themselves and underestimate what is due to others. Belligerents invariably claim to be fighting for justice. The Christian faith is that God's justice has been made manifest and available in the actual event of Christ's atonement, and that it is here at the cross that it can be received as a gift by faith and become the basis for actual justice among human beings. So also "peace" pursued as an abstract concept can only delude us. The most devastating wars are fought among the promoters of rival programmes for peace. The Christian faith is that God has made peace through Jesus "by the blood of his cross" (Col. 1:20), so establishing the one valid centre for the unity of the whole human family. But these statements are mere words unless they are embodied (even if only provisionally) in a visible community in which the righteousness of God and the peace of God are actually known and experienced in reality— even though it is only a foretaste of the full reality. The Church is not authorized or empowered to represent a justice and a peace other than the justice and peace offered to the world in the atoning work of Christ. But it contradicts its own nature and calling when its members are unable to live

together in a reconciled fellowship. Concern for the unity of all humankind is the only proper context for the quest of church unity, it is not a reason for abandoning that quest.[85]

With a sense of urgency about its theological task as "not so much academic as essentially evangelical," the claim of *God's Reign and Our Unity* was to have placed "a new emphasis on the unity of the human race as the goal of the Christian gospel, with the Kingdom of God restored as a focus for ecclesiology." The commission had worked within a "freshly discovered world-wide context and within the ultimate dimension of the Kingdom of God, in which creation and human community are renewed by the Spirit through their transformation in Christ" (interestingly, the World Council of Churches came to shift its terminology from "the unity of mankind" to the more dynamic "renewal of humankind").

The document first presents a basic ecclesiology under the heading "The Church: God's Apostolic People." Stressing the sheer grace of God toward "sin-stained humanity" and the intrinsic connection between the divine work of reconciliation and the unity of its beneficiaries and witnesses, a christocentric, trinitarian reading of the history of redemption comes to focus on the Church as "first-fruits of a new creation." Precisely because—and only insofar as—the Church is a "foretaste" of the universal and complete reconciliation of all things in Christ, it can be a "sign" and "instrument" of God's purpose. In this context, the quest for embodied unity is "one aspect of the Church's acting out of her unceasing prayer, 'Your kingdom come.' " It is thus false to set either evangelism or social justice or doctrinal truth against the search for unity: first, numerical growth cannot excuse continued division, for "the mere multiplication of cells, unrelated to the purpose of the body, is a sign not of life and health, but of cancer and death"; second, if the Church contradicts in its own life the social order which it is called to signify and provisionally embody, Christianity is "turned into a mere ideological crusade, and its actions for justice and peace are robbed of their essential and distinctive character, namely the presence here and now of the peace and righteousness of God freely given to sinful men and women"; and third, "all formulations of truth must be judged by their relation to the central reality of God's redeeming and reconciling work in Christ," and "we are more likely to reach unanimity as a result of accepting one another in Christ and then working out our differences in one fellowship than by giving them in effect a status higher than that of the one supreme truth given to us in Christ." On its way to the end of the age, the pilgrim Church journeys also to the ends of the earth, "sent to all the nations" in order that God's purpose may reach its full scope; and "as the Church goes out to bear witness to Christ among the nations, its own partial understanding of God's purpose is corrected and enlarged." That is also the perspective in which existing differences over sacraments and ministry inherited from ingrown ecclesiastical controversies can now be looked at afresh, for "where the Church is a small evangelizing community in a pagan society, ministry is primarily leadership in mission, baptism is commitment to that mission, and Eucharist is the continual renewal of that commitment."

Because there is but "one Christ," into whose "one body" we are baptized by "our one baptism," the "continued separation of our two communions is a public denial of what we already are in Christ"; and because "in the one man Jesus we see our common humanity taken up, redeemed, and given back to us so that we can share it together," baptismal fidelity requires the verbal and practical affirmation of "the full, equal and God-given humanity of every person" and militant opposition to "all that denies this shared humanity." Likewise, "participation in the Eucharist commits us to the ceaseless search for reconciliation among all for whom Christ died, and is incompatible with the exclusion of any person on grounds of race, sex, social distinction or culture as well as with the refusal to share material resources given by God for the benefit of all." Both the "ministry of the Church" and "ministry in the Church" can be adequately understood and practiced only within the mission of God, through the Son and in the Spirit, for the salvation of the world: "Leadership in the Church means leading others into the company of Jesus so that—in him and by the working of the Spirit—their lives may be offered to the Father, and also leading others into the world to challenge the dominion of evil in the name of Christ and in the power of the Spirit." Toward inherited ministerial forms "our duty is first to receive and cherish them with gratitude, and then to learn, as those before us have done, to adapt and reform them under the guidance of the Spirit in faithfulness to the apostolic witness, and in accordance with the missionary needs of our day."[86]

The two chapters on sacraments and ministry are followed by a final consideration of the "visible form of unity" that will best correspond to the character of the Church as "the provisional embodiment of an eschatological unity." Positive recall is made of the descriptions of local and universal unity offered by the assemblies of the World Council of Churches at New Delhi (1961), Uppsala (1968), Nairobi (1975), and, with a decline in coherence, Vancouver (1983); and of the respect for "the secular realities of each place" demanded by the 1976 Geneva consultation "Towards a Fellowship of Local Churches Truly United." It is forcefully declared that "we are not simply seeking a *modus vivendi* between two globally organized denominations which would continue their separate though reconciled existence." Rather, the search, with others also, is for "the emergence of reconciled local communities, each of which is recognizable as 'church' in the proper sense, i.e. communities which exhibit in each place the fullness of ministerial order, eucharistic fellowship, pastoral care, and missionary commitment and which, through mutual communion and cooperation, bear witness on the regional, national and even international levels."[87] Such churches "would express both the unity to which God calls his whole creation in Christ and the diversity which properly characterizes the human family as God intends it to be"; they would "express locally the whole of the catholic Church."

Sadly, it has to be admitted that Anglicans and Reformed have so far nowhere entered into organic unity with one another since the theological work done by the Commission. Was Newbigin right, then, to fear the futility of bilateral dialogues between confessional families or (in the term later preferred) Christian world communions? Their record of providing an enabling structure for local, national, or regional unions is not strong. Thus the dialogue between the World Alliance of Reformed Churches and the World Methodist Council, despite the encouragement given in its report *Together in God's Grace* (1987), has not led to further unions beyond those already existing, notably in Canada (since 1925), Zambia (1965), Belgium (1969/1978), and Australia (1977). The dialogue between the World Methodist Council and the Lutheran World Federation has, in *The Church: Community of Grace* (1984), provided a framework in which "fellowship in word and sacrament," though deliberately not "organizational union," has been achieved between Lutherans and Methodists in Germany, Austria, Sweden, and Norway. It would, however, be premature to dismiss the pattern of international bilateral dialogues before taking into account the reconfiguration of the ecumenical scene that was necessitated by the entrance of the Roman Catholic Church with the Second Vatican Council.

Although bilateral arrangements had allowed communion without full visible unity between, say, Anglicans and Old Catholics (since the Bonn Agreement of 1931), or between European Lutherans and Reformed (on the way to the Leuenberg Agreement of 1973), it was the appearance of the Roman Catholics that prompted the surge in bilateralism as a method of dialogue. Given its size and its self-understanding as a single universal body, the Roman Catholic Church could not have become a member of the World Council of Churches without radically affecting the structure, and perhaps the nature, of the WCC (the difficulty is indicated by the fact that since 1968 the Roman Catholic Church has twelve, but only twelve, official members in the Faith and Order Commission of the WCC out of a total membership of 120 on the Commission). The procedure of choice therefore appeared to be the establishment of bilateral dialogues between the Roman Catholic Church, on the one hand, and the various respective confessional families or communions on the other; and this in turn stimulated the setting up of dialogues between other pairs among the rest. Discussions could then center on the particular matters that troubled the respective relationships. The dialogues involving the Roman Catholic Church have tended to attract most energy and attention. Although these dialogues with Rome have been slower to produce the results than many, say, Anglicans or Lutherans would have wished, very significant theological groundwork has been laid for what may turn out one day to have important institutional effects. Here I must declare my own interest and involvement, having been since 1983 a member of the Joint Commission for Dialogue between the Roman Catholic Church and the World Methodist Council, and since 1986 its chairman on the Methodist side. What forms may finally be taken by any resulting increase in visible unity is not clear; but it seems possible that something might emerge between the tapestry of nationally or regionally united churches which Newbigin had in mind and the mere "reconciled diversity" of confessional families or the "communion of communions" which he considered inadequate. Thus, in its Nairobi Report of 1986, the Methodist-Catholic commission envisaged as one possibility in "ways of being one Church" that the various "ecclesial traditions" might figure as "religious orders, characterized by special forms of life and prayer, work, evangelization, and their own internal organization," but all set within a single structure of pastoral and doctrinal governance and a universal communion.[88] Newbigin would surely insist that such a development must occur without prejudice to the unity of "all in each place." He would also want it geared to the task of evangelization whose urgency was expressed by Pope John Paul II in his ecumenical encyclical *Ut Unum Sint* (1995).

Crisis Around the World Council of Churches

Lesslie Newbigin was connected with the World Council of Churches in one way or another from its inception to the time of his death. He attended the inaugural assembly at Amsterdam in 1948; and, as an elder statesman at the world conference on mission and evangelism held at Salvador de Bahia, Brazil, in 1996, he was received with a standing ovation and captivated the audience with an unscripted address that many participants judged to be the outstanding moment of the meeting.[89] In between, he served as an associate general secretary and the first director of the new Division of World Mission and Evangelism during the crucial period after the integration of the International Missionary Council with the World Council of Churches; and on either side of his years on the WCC staff he held membership in the Commission on Faith and Order. For over forty years he was in regular demand as a consultant and writer for World Council events and causes.

Bishop Newbigin was a delegate of the Church of South India to the fourth assembly of WCC held at Uppsala, Sweden, in 1968, the year of the Western cultural revolution. It was "in many ways a shattering experience":

> The plenary sessions were dominated by the realities of economic and racial injustice. The mood was one of anger. The well-drilled phalanx of students in the gallery ensured that the emotional temperature was kept high. It was a terrifying enunciation of the law, with all its (proper) accompaniments of threat and wrath. We were corporately shaken over the pit of hell. The word of the Gospel was hardly heard except, in a muted way, when a little band of Salvationists sang to us. More characteristic was the evening when Pete Seeger sang the well-known mockery of the Christian Gospel which affirms that "there'll be pie in the sky when you die," and the assembly sat in rapt silence and then applauded as though it were a new revelation of truth. How, I couldn't help wondering, could such a group be so easily brainwashed?[90]

The report of the section on mission ended by "reducing mission to nothing but a desperate struggle to solve insoluble problems. Obviously the Church itself was the major problem, and there was no enthusiasm for enlarging the membership of this dubious institution. Perhaps the best thing that could be said about the report was that it honestly reflected the profound confusion in the Churches about what mission is." Newbigin found some encouragement in the world conference on mission and evangelism held at Bangkok, Thailand, in 1973 under the title "Salvation Today" and, as has been noted, in the fifth assembly of the WCC at Nairobi in 1975; but as the years went by, he stood further back from the World Council of Churches and became increasingly critical of the directions it was taking.

Uppsala 1968, however, has been favorably regarded as the start of "a paradigm shift in the ecumenical movement" that now needs to be carried through to a successful conclusion; such was the program put forward by Konrad Raiser in his book *Ökumene im Übergang?* (1989), which turned out to be an election manifesto for his appointment as general secretary of the WCC in 1992.[91] An administrator and academic compared with Newbigin's pastoral bishop and cross-cultural missionary (with a dread of "becoming an ecumenical office-wallah"), a theological liberal compared with Newbigin's evangelical, Raiser almost inevitably personified much of what Lesslie Newbigin had feared could go wrong with the World Council of Churches, although in his literary controversy with him Newbigin sticks to the substantive issues raised by Raiser's theological positions. Documentation of the encounter includes Newbigin's lengthy review of Raiser's *Ecumenism in Transition* that first appeared in the periodical *One in Christ* and was reprinted under the title "Ecumenical Amnesia" in *The International Bulletin of Missionary Research*, a subsequent exchange between Raiser and Newbigin in that latter journal, and then finally a response by Newbigin to Raiser's public lecture at the bicentenary celebrations of the London Missionary Society in July 1995.[92]

The paradigm shift that Raiser detected in the ecumenical movement—and sought to promote—went from the christocentric to the trinitarian, from the history of redemption to the future of the planet, and from the Church to "the whole human household" and even "the one household of life." The author saw it as an expansion of horizons, but the crucial question—going beyond the historical matter of Raiser's having underestimated the breadth of the earlier vision—is the theological one of whether the loss of a concentrated focus does not in fact render the new vision vacuous.

The heart of Newbigin's criticism resides in his rejection of Raiser's dismissal of "christocentrism." "Plainly," says Newbigin, "a trinitarian perspective can only be an enlargement and development of a christocentric one and not an alternative set over against it, for the doctrine of the Trinity is the theological articulation of what it means to say that Jesus is the unique word of God incarnate in world history." "Of course, Raiser knows this well," Newbigin generously assumes, but is bound to ask whether in Raiser's thesis "the truth in the former paradigm is developed or obscured." The test is applied in three areas: the form of the Church's unity, the action of the Church in the world, and the obligation to mission and evangelism.

First, there is Raiser's argument that the model of the Trinity would replace a hierarchical and institutional model of church unity with a kind of unity whose ecclesiastical form is conciliarity and whose method is dialogue—"not dialogue as a means to an end," Newbigin glosses, "but as a way of life." Newbigin acknowledges that a full trinitarian framework is needed for the understanding of God's presence and work but notes that Raiser rarely speaks of the atoning Cross of Christ: "There can be no true understanding of Christian unity which fails to have at its centre the mercy seat, that place where— at inconceivable cost—our sins have been forgiven and we are able to meet one another as forgiven sinners who must embrace one another because we have been embraced by the divine compassion in Jesus Christ." A corresponding ecclesiology will not be content with dialogue as itself an adequate form of life but will see it as instrumental to "mutual correction in the light of God's revelation of himself in Jesus Christ as witnessed in the Scriptures." It will not "settle for mutual recognition and co-existence, for a relationship of conviviality but not of total mutual commitment"—for that is to make "the question of truth less serious than it is" and to "reduce the value of what it deals with." The mutual criticism is to be accomplished, of course, in the context of "mutual acceptance as those who have been accepted by God in his mercy towards those who fall short of his purpose"—which is to "see the entire Christian Church as a company which lives only by the grace of God to sinners, a company which does *not* possess in any of its divided parts the fullness of what is 'essential' but which God nevertheless in his mercy sustains as witness to and foretaste of his blessed reign." That company is not to be understood "as a wholly unstructured fellowship whose authority resides within itself" but rather as "a body of forgiven sinners who are still sinners even though forgiven" and therefore in need of an exercise of apostolic authority given to those chosen by Christ who "did not renounce lordship but defined it (John 13:12–14)."

Second, Raiser favors an extension of the *oikoumene* to include all "men and women struggling to become what they were intended to be in the purpose of God," with the ecumenical movement occurring "wherever Christians and others are one way or another seeking to work for the unity of mankind." This, says Newbigin, obscures "the necessary distinction between Church and world." A token of the difference in vision is Raiser's preference for the word "solidarity" over "love": " 'Solidarity' suggests"—according to Newbigin—"a too naïve acceptance of all human struggle as being directed towards the will of God"; it evokes a "1968" model—"owing not a little to Marxist thought"— which "interprets all situations in terms of the oppressor and the oppressed" and "the struggles of the oppressed as the instrument of redemption." After "the collapse of Marxism as a world power," says Newbigin, the World Council of Churches has as "one of its most pressing tasks for the immediate future" to "rediscover a doctrine of redemption which sees the cross not as the banner of the oppressed against the oppressor, but as the action of God which brings both judgment and redemption for all who will accept it, yet does not subvert the proper struggle for that measure of justice which is possible in a world of sinful human beings."

Third, Newbigin taxes Raiser's book with "total amnesia in respect of the missionary and evangelistic work of the Churches"—both historically and as a continuing obligation. Raiser speaks of "confession of faith and baptism" as the foundation of (Christian) ecumenism but shows no concern that "the great majority of the world's people have not made this confession and have not been baptised." "It is here," says Newbigin, that "the thoroughly Euro-centric character of the book becomes clear. No one shaped by experience of Asian and African religions could have written this. When Raiser says that 'awareness of religious pluralism is a development of the past twenty years,' it is clear that we are speaking within the horizon of European culture. The profound experience of the missionary movement over the past two or three centuries is ignored." If mission and evangelism were to be dropped from the WCC's agenda, then "the bringing of the International Missionary Council into the WCC would have to be judged as having been a mistake." Whereas deliberately "evangelical" churches and movements outside the WCC "are growing and showing increasing breadth of vision in their approach to the whole range of contemporary human problems," the bodies holding the doc-trinal position represented in Raiser's book are largely in decay. "A body which ceases to be concerned about communicating its faith to others is on the way to death. It would be heart-breaking," says Newbigin, "if the WCC should in truth become, what some already claim to see in it, only the organ of those parts of the Christian Church which are in decline. God grant it may not be so."

In his response to Newbigin's review, Raiser—who appears to have read very few of Newbigin's writings over the decades—reproaches his critic with the lack of an adequate trinitarian framework, specifically an appreciation of "the constitutive role of the Holy Spirit in understanding the Christ event," and charges him with failing to "admit either the challenge of religious plu-rality or the challenges arising from the threats to all natural life systems." Newbigin comes back, first, by recalling his own advocacy in WCC circles of the missiology of Roland Allen, "for whom the recognition of the work of the Spirit in mission was the very center," but notes that "the 'paradigm shift' of the 1960s ensured that the study [on the missionary structure of the con-gregation] was hijacked in the interests of the dominant ideology of the sec-ular. Thirty years later secularity is out and 'spirituality' is in. But there are many spirits abroad, and when they are invoked, we are handed over to other powers. The Holy Spirit, the Spirit of the Father and of the Son, is known by the confession that Jesus alone is Lord." (Raiser's trinitarian invocations, it may be observed, amount to no more than airy references to "Trinity"—materially undefined—as a form of Godhead and a "model of unity.")[93]

"Religious pluralism," says Newbigin, is as old as recorded history; the novelty is that the churches of Christendom have woken up to it. Whereas "the euphoria of Western colonial expansion, which was so often mixed in with missionary motives, enabled the Western churches to engage in world mission without seriously facing for themselves the question of the uniqueness and finality of Christ," now "the collapse of Western self-confidence and the corrosive effects of the 'acids of modernity' (Lippmann) produce a mood in which the recognition of religious pluralism puts a question mark against the absolute lordship of Christ." Precisely the issue to be faced is: "Do we look for the ultimate unity of the human family as the fruit of God's reconciling work in Jesus Christ, or do we have some other center to propose?" Newbigin himself engaged in interreligious dialogue from his earliest days in India but without abandoning "the assumption that Christians must make"—and have in fact made from the very beginnings of their preaching of the Gospel in the ancient world—namely, that "in Jesus God has acted decisively for the redemption of the world."[94]

That confession lies at the basis, too, of Newbigin's attitude toward the ecological crisis that Raiser falsely accuses him of neglecting:

> It has been a constant theme of my speaking and writing that the world dominance of the idolatry of the free market will, if not reversed, both disintegrate human society and destroy the environment. I regret that the immense labor of the WCC under the banner of 'Justice, Peace, and the Integrity of Creation' has had such meager results, because it has attacked the symptoms and not the cause of the malady. The ideology of the free market rests upon a doctrine of human nature that is directly attacked by the biblical faith. Idolatry cannot be countered merely by moral protest against its effects. It has to be tackled at its source. . . . We have to find ways of making known the fact that the incarnate, crucified, and risen Christ is Lord also of the economic order.[95]

After hearing the keynote address given by Konrad Raiser on the 200th anniversary of the London Missionary Society, more recently called the (Congregational) Council for World Mission, Lesslie Newbigin could not forbear from expressing his astonishment that the "Ecumenical Vision for the Twenty-First Century" painted by the current general secretary of the World Council of Churches failed to mention "the glorious Gospel of the ever-blessed God" that had in 1795 inspired a small group of Londoners, facing amid revolution and war the seemingly imminent end of the European social order they knew, to make provision for sharing the Christian message with the whole inhabited world for which it was intended. Seeing himself as having what he had called in his earlier exchange with Newbigin the responsibility of orientating a process that would "change the profile of the ecumenical movement," Raiser returned to his themes of the ecological crisis, the need for a pluralistic view of religion lest clashing claims to universal spiritual hegemony produce a fatal conflict among cultures, and the advocacy—allegedly according to the model of a divine trinity—of a global order of mutual relatedness expressed through a multitude of networks that would hold society together in nonhierarchical and nonoppressive ways. Newbigin lamented:

> There was no hint of any good news. For me, at least, if I were not a committed missionary, this presentation would have been simply crushing. What possible hope is there of reversing the ruin of the planet, reconciling the

warring ambitions of human communities, or creating truly communitarian societies within the lifetime of even the child born today? Without the Gospel, there could only be the response of crushing despair in the face of such a scenario.

Concerning the ecological crisis, Newbigin argued that Raiser's shift from an anthropocentric to a "life-centered" approach tended both to release humankind from its unique, God-given responsibility for the environment and to reduce the world to a biological sphere in which the last word in fact belongs not to life but to death: "Surely what is needed is not replacement of human responsibility by an appeal to the principle of biological life, but the repentance of humans who were entrusted with husbandry and have acted as rapists."

As to hegemonies, Newbigin recognizes that there have been imperialist moves for which Christians must repent, but it is a "return to the heart of the Gospel itself, to the crucifixion and resurrection of Jesus" that would provide

> the unique ground on which plurality can be safeguarded, since it is the ground for assurance that the total submission of all human wills to the will of God ('islam') is the true goal of human history, but lies beyond history. If there is no assurance that God's will finally prevails, there is no bulwark against total corruption, the slide into moral anarchy which we now witness in our society. But if God's final victory is within history, then those who claim to speak for God can allow no space for plurality. In other words, we safeguard plurality not by abandoning the universal claim of the Gospel but by affirming it as good news for all without exception.

Better yet: since "plurality cannot be the first and last word about society" (for fragmentation, shattering, and destruction always threaten), it must be asked "where is the centripetal force strong enough to hold together the communities drawn by the centrifugal power of their separate ethnic and religious identities"; and Newbigin's answer is "the good news that in the atoning work of Jesus Christ there is provided for us all that place, that 'mercy seat' where we can be reconciled to one another because we have been reconciled to God": "When those who are entrusted with that Gospel use it as a means for the coercion or subjugation of others, they subvert it. But to cease offering it to all peoples as God's invitation to a reconciliation which gives room for particularity, would be a betrayal of trust."

The way to a society of mutual relationship and responsibility—the third of Raiser's concerns—is not, says Newbigin, to be found along the route of "liberal democracies" as they have become and in the forms in which they seek to impose themselves upon the world:

> As the remaining traces of Christian belief continue to evaporate, and we become more and more certainly a pagan society in which there is no God and no Torah which sets an absolute limit to the freedom of the individual to pursue self-interest, there is nothing to prevent democracy from descending into tyranny. As the commissioned witnesses of the Gospel, we cannot be

content with simply advocating the desirability of a participatory society, much as we ought to do so. We are entrusted with a Gospel which can set people free from the tyranny of self-interest and can give to our tired society the confidence that a different kind of life is possible.

At the World Council of Churches, Konrad Raiser continued at the turn of the century to plow the furrow he had marked out in his book *Ecumenism in Transition*.[96] Upon Lesslie Newbigin's death in late January 1998, the writer of the announcement from the WCC declared that "his legacy will live on and continue to shape the ecumenical vision for the new millennium." The climate in which that occurs may depend less on the WCC than on Pope John Paul II's encyclical of Pentecost 1995, entitled precisely *Ut Unum Sint*, in which the Bishop of Rome reaffirmed the Catholic Church's irrevocable commitment to ecumenism as integral to missionary obedience, for lack of unity among Christians damages the credibility of a Gospel of reconciliation and love. The original vision of the modern ecumenical movement is thereby rejoined: "That they all may be one . . . so that the world may believe."

4

The Pastoral Bishop

I exhort the elders among you: Tend the flock of Christ among
you, exercising the oversight, not by constraint but willingly,
not for shameful gain but eagerly, not as domineering over
those in your charge but being examples to the flock.

(1 Peter 5:1–3)

Ministry in and of the Church

Lesslie Newbigin's entire career may properly be regarded as pastoral in the
broad and christological sense of the term: as he himself wrote of another
great missionary to India, C. F. Andrews (1871–1940), his life "has reminded
people in our day of the Good Shepherd himself."[1] More specifically and ecclesiastically, Newbigin served both local congregations and larger units of
the Church as the ordained representative of Christ "the Bishop and Pastor
of our souls" (1 Peter 2:24). In India, he first ministered pastorally as a district
missionary in town and villages; and then as bishop in the largely rural
diocese of Madurai and Ramnad, and later as bishop in the big city diocese
of Madras when he functioned also as deputy moderator of the Church of
South India, there fell to him "the care of all the churches" (2 Corinthians
12:28). In Britain, he spent most of his eighth decade as pastor of a small
congregation of the United Reformed Church in the inner suburbs of Birmingham, immediately after having led the whole denomination for a year
as moderator of its assembly. His theological reflections on the practice of
ministry and on the ordering of the Church not only were shaped by his
study of the Scriptures and the Christian Tradition but also grew out of his
experience in such diverse capacities and circumstances.

Chapter 2 of this book is devoted to Newbigin as an evangelist; another
treats him as a thinker on mission. In fact, he considered it an essential part
of the pastor's and the bishop's office to equip their people for witnessing to
the Gospel and to lead them in the apostolic task. So the themes of evangelism
and mission occur also in this chapter, but related now precisely to the ministries that are specially charged, under the Spirit, with feeding the flock of
Christ and exercising oversight among God's people. The emphasis at first is
practical, then moves to the constitutional; but these two aspects of Newbigin's theology of ministry overlap, for his understanding of practice was fun-

135

damentally shaped by the rites of ordination and by the doctrines particularly of the Reformed tradition concerning order in the Church, while his developing views on the institutional structure and discipline of life in Christ's Body owed much to his experience as a pastor and especially as a bishop in the Church of South India.

Two things must be made clear at the outset, as a reminder that Newbigin's theology of ministry fits within the entire vision that has already been described of the nature of salvation and of the place and function of the Church in God's story with the world. The first is that the authentic pastorate will never be for Newbigin merely inward looking. The principle is laid out in *The Household of God* (1953):

> When the eschatological and missionary perspective has been lost from the thinking of the Church, its task comes to be conceived in terms of the rescue of individuals one by one out of this present evil age and their preservation unharmed for the world to come. When this becomes dominant, the Church thinks primarily of its duty to care for its own members, and its duty to those outside drops into second place. A conception of pastoral care is developed which seems to assume that the individual believer is primarily a passive recipient of the means of grace which it is the business of the Church to administer. "The Church," then, comes to mean the paid ministry—and this may and does happen in Churches which claim to repudiate sacerdotalism. There is of course real truth in this picture. The sheep are to be fed by those whom the Lord appoints for the purpose. The faithful steward has to give their due portions to all the household. But when this is taken to be the whole truth, then we must point to other parts of the New Testament which stress the responsibilities of the whole body as a royal priesthood, as the body of Christ in which every member has its proper function. The root of the error lies in the failure to keep in view throughout the *whole* salvation of which the Church is the sign and first-fruit and instrument. If this is done, the Church will be delivered from the tendency to turn in upon itself and will always be turned outwards to the world. It will know itself to be wholly committed in every part to the task of witness to the world in word and in service. It will understand that participation in Christ means participation in His mission to the world, and that therefore true pastoral care, true training in the Christian life, and true use of the means of grace will be precisely in and for the discharge of this missionary task.[2]

What the "missionary thrust" of pastoral ministry implies for pastors is spelled out in a style characteristic of Newbigin in the document he drafted for the Anglican-Reformed International Commission, *God's Reign and Our Unity* (1984):

> 'Shepherd' in the Old Testament is the familiar title for the kings and other rulers who led their people, ruled them, guarded them and went before them into battle. The Good Shepherd in Jesus' language is the one who is willing for the sake of the sheep to meet the attacking wolves and give his life in the combat (John 10:7–15). And when Jesus entrusts to Peter the pastoral care of his flock he immediately tells Peter that it will entail learning to follow him on the way that leads to the cross (John 21:15–19).

Consequently, "ministerial leadership may be defined as following Jesus in the way of the cross so that others in turn may be enabled to follow in the same way."[3]

The second observation needed to set the soteriological and ecclesiological context for Newbigin's theology of ministry concerns his view of the Church as the company of redeemed sinners, people who continue to need forgiveness when the powers of darkness bring them into contradiction with their faith. The matter may be illustrated from what Newbigin relates—in connection with the approach to church unity in South India—of the "strain and stress" that occur when people of varying caste and class are joined together in the typical congregation of a country town consisting of "men and women who have nothing in common save their redemption in Christ":

> It means that quarrels are frequent and often bitter. It means that party spirit often disfigures the conduct of church business. But it does also mean that men are driven back to Christ and compelled to ask themselves again and again how much it matters to them that Christ died for them. If congregational life is not to dissolve altogether, men have to allow themselves to be driven back to this fundamental fact, that Christ died for them and for their friends and for their enemies—for on no other fact can the common life of the congregation hold together. The divisions between Christians are vividly seen for the sinful things they are, for a quarrel in a Christian congregation is such a plain and open contradiction of the Gospel by which it lives that so long as it lasts the members can only hang their heads in shame before the outsider. . . . The average church member in South India . . . is familiar with the spectacle of a quarrel in the Church, of real or imagined issues being made the occasion for party spirit, of the slow and difficult process of repentance and reconciliation as the village elders or the pastor plead again to both warring parties the sacrifice of Christ. He regards the issue of union as the problem of bringing to an end a particularly long and stubborn quarrel in the Church, and in that light he prays for reconciliation. Is he wrong?[4]

Clearly recounted from personal experience, and just as clearly applicable mutatis mutandis to most if not all local Christian congregations on the face of the earth, such a narrative should make it evident that Newbigin's theological reflections on ministry will not be offered in abstraction from the checkered realities of ecclesial life.

The Pastor

Newbigin has given the barest of accounts of his inward call to the ordained ministry of Christ and his Church. It took place in the course of a conference of the Student Christian Movement at Swanwick during the summer vacation of 1930: "There was a tent set aside for prayer. On an afternoon near the end of the week I went into it to pray. No one else was there. While I was praying something happened which I find it hard to describe. I suddenly knew that I had been told that I must offer for ordination. I had not been thinking

1936: ordained

about this. But I knew that I had been ordered and that it was settled and that I could not escape."[5] The path to ordination passed through a further year to complete his bachelor's degree, two years on the staff of the SCM in Scotland, and three years back in Cambridge studying theology at Westminster College. In June 1936 he was "licensed to preach the Gospel" by the Presbytery of Newcastle, and on July 12 he was ordained by the Presbytery of Edinburgh for service as a foreign missionary. His first tour in India was interrupted by a serious motor accident and the consequent need to return to Britain for surgery.

Only in October 1939 could Newbigin take up his first appointment as a "district missionary" based at Conjeeveram, or Kanchipuram.[6] In this stronghold of Hinduism, the single Christian congregation was composed entirely of professional people who had arrived from different parts of India on mission or government or other service, or of outcastes who had come to the city from the surrounding countryside. Extension work took place largely among the outcaste villages, where elementary schools might be set up with paid teachers or where the convert congregations would be "dependent on their own leadership and on the visits of the pastor and catechists."[7]

Declining to reduce his job to office administration as had become customary in many places,[8] Newbigin taught in the mission high school and preached in the streets of the city; he also spent much time touring the villages to visit the local workers, leaders, and parishioners and to speak in local congregations and evangelize in their surroundings; he set up annual weeks of Bible study, hymnody, and evangelistic practice for the uneducated leaders of village congregations;[9] and he organized monthly two-day sessions in Old Testament, New Testament, sermon class, and Tamil poetry for the paid workers.[10] There was no romanticism here:

> As I go round these village churches I have over and over again the overwhelming feeling that they are such stuff as cobwebs are made of. The ramshackle huts of mud and thatch which are their outward apparatus seem fitting symbols of something so apparently frail and impermanent as these little congregations, lost in the sea of timeless and changeless village paganism, divided often by long-drawn-out and futile quarrels, wounded by heartsickening falls from the ordinary Christian standards, crushed under a load of poverty and debt which no power on earth seems able to lift.

Yet the writer can immediately narrate several individual incidents among simple believers that "have cheered the eye of faith."[11] As a minister of the Church of Scotland, Newbigin did not yet bear the title of bishop, but he was in fact exercising general oversight over an area that included twenty or thirty assemblies of Christians who gathered around the Word and, when possible, the Sacraments, and who bore witness in manifold if imperfect ways to their neighbors.

Certainly the experience of the early years in and around Kanchipuram was not left behind when, after the church union, Newbigin became bishop in Madurai and then, after service with the International Missionary Council and the World Council of Churches, bishop in Madras. Cumulatively, the several periods of unfailing if diverse contact with local churches in their varied circumstances give firm grounding to the addresses which Bishop Newbigin regularly gave to the fifty or so presbyters of the Church of South India in pastoral charge of the 110 congregations of the complex city of Madras. Every month the bishop met with the clergy and "a number of women engaged in full-time church work" for Holy Communion, breakfast, and discussion of "some aspect of our common ministry." The theme was introduced each time by the bishop's sermon at the Eucharist; and a selection of these liturgical meditations, each based on a text of Scripture, was published as *The Good Shepherd*. This resource of distilled wisdom became available far beyond its origins when Donald Coggan, calling Newbigin "a bishop with a pastoral heart," adopted it as "The Archbishop of Canterbury's Lent Book for 1977."[12]

In revising the text for wider publication, the author removed some of the very particular references but otherwise allowed the Indian idiom to stand, believing that it would be most useful for readers elsewhere "to overhear remarks made in another context and to do their own 'translating' "—especially as "a greatly trusted friend in the parish ministry in England" assured him of their applicability there. Disclaiming, with characteristic modesty, any "profundity or originality," Newbigin expressed the hope that the book might

> help some readers to think about the many-sided ministry of the Church in today's world, a ministry which has—however—one centre. That centre is at the point where we are made sharers in the Body broken and the Blood shed for the life of the world. These addresses were given in the context of the celebration of the Eucharist. I believe that this is the proper setting for Christian teaching, and I hope that this setting may help to ensure that these talks, which deal with many different aspects of the ministry, direct attention to the one centre.

The thirty chapters begin with a pair that present Jesus as the permanent origin and model of a ministry whose redemptive efficacy no longer needs to be accomplished but only communicated and appropriated in a changing world. Ten chapters follow on the perennial tasks involved in nourishing and regulating the life of Christ's flock. Another ten deal with the training of Christians for witness and service in society at large. Three or four more treat the spiritual life and discipline of the pastor. Toward the end, three or four chapters revert to the broad questions of the salvation which the Gospel offers to the world. To summarize each of these occasional pieces would not be appropriate, but some prominent and representative themes may be picked out.

From the key text of John 10 Newbigin draws the all-controlling lesson that Christ, as the Good Shepherd, "expects his sheep to follow him. That means taking the road that Jesus took, the road that is marked by the Cross because it means bearing the *karma* of the world."[13] A true pastor, says Newbigin, "must have such a relation with Jesus and with his people that he follows Jesus and they follow him." People for whom Christ has become a living

reality will recognize the Good Shepherd's voice when they hear it issuing from the lips of an appointed pastor whom they have learned to trust as himself a servant whose love for the flock is shown in his knowledge of each one of them by name, "a uniquely precious person for whom Christ's blood was shed." The path is painful, for "to follow Jesus means to accept death and resurrection as the only law of life": the Cross is "the final 'No' to every human order that claims to be perfect and self-sufficient," but by "keeping close to the Cross," one may "receive constantly afresh the power of Christ's risen life, which is always power for radical renewal."

The first duty of the pastor, the bishop tells his presbyters, is to preach Christ, who is the Word of God made flesh and whose words therefore are the words of God, the words of eternal life (cf. John 6:68). By "the reading and exposition of Scripture," Christ "has to be put before men again and again in his flesh, in the concrete reality of his manhood—his life, his words, his deeds, above all his death and resurrection." The "business of the sermon is to bring the hearers face to face with Jesus Christ as he really is," which means as Savior (who "helps and delivers and comforts us") and as Lord (who "has the right to absolute rule over our lives"), so that hearers "are liberated from care about their own salvation in order to be totally at God's service for the world's salvation." Although brought up in a church that did not use a lectionary, the bishop commends its use for the way in which "wrestling with an uncongenial text can be the source of endless new insight." Wrestling also with "the trouble and pain and sin in the world around you, in the slums around your church, in the lives of your members" will make the words spoken in the pulpit "part of the obedience of you and your congregation to the living Lord."

Christ's word comes also acted in rite and sacrament. Leading the worship of Christ's people is a "sacred privilege," for the worship of God who is "utterly holy"—Newbigin bases his thoughts on Psalm 73—calls for "the highest exercise of all our powers," offering us now "a true foretaste of heaven and a preparation for its joys." Worship directed anywhere but to our Maker is idolatry, which dehumanizes and eventually enslaves. Christian worship both protects those who take part in it against the false standards and convictions of the world and also challenges and attracts outsiders by its testimony to what God has done for the redemption of the world in Jesus Christ. It is "the corporate action of a single body" in which "every member is involved and has to play its part." While the service will reflect "local and domestic interests," it should also be "recognizable as the worship of the universal Church, in which every Christian from any part of the world could meaningfully take part." The basic structure of Christian worship is displayed in the story of the disciples on the road to Emmaus (Luke 24:13–35): the living Lord gathers his people and meets with them in the ministry of the word and the breaking of the bread; he "first interprets to them the Scriptures as a continuous revelation which finds its meaning and focus in him, and then—through the bread broken and the cup shared—draws them into an actual participation in his dying and his life." The liveliness of corporate worship in Pentecostal congregations and the achievement by Roman Catholics in Tamil Nadu of active and intelligent participation in the liturgical assembly as instructed by the Second Vatican Council are held up by the bishop as examples for emulation by the CSI in Madras.

The next "vital and indispensable part of our ministry" is "the regular visiting of the homes of our people." The point is not to coddle the members but to love and respect each one as a child of God. God's cosmic purpose and universal missionary charge do not diminish but rather include his fatherly care for unique persons. Particularly in the anonymous society of a large city, the pastor may be for many "the only representative God has to minister his loving care." The bishop urges "regular prayer by name for each member of your congregation" as "the indispensable basis for good pastoral visiting." A satisfactory system of pastoral care requires also the development of small lay-led groups after the pattern of the old "cottage prayer meeting."

The pastoral ministry, says the bishop from the Reformed tradition, essentially bears a priestly character, understanding that the priest will "stand between man and God not as an obstacle but as a necessary helper": "The fact that the whole Church is called to a priestly ministry *necessitates* the priestly character of the ordained ministry. We who are ordained to the holy ministry are called to be priests *in order that* the whole body of believers may attain to its true priestly character." There should be no eagerness to bear the title of priest but rather an eagerness to *be* priests, as "faithful followers of the great High Priest, in order that all our people may also share in his priestly ministry to the full." Upheld by the priesthood of the Son of God, ministerial priests must also—counter to the docetic temptation to view Christ as a Hindu *avatar*—follow him in the humanity which Hebrews 4:14–16 shows to be his: they will share in the burdens, troubles and trials of their people, in order that "our people in their turn may be priests to their neighbours, so that the whole world may be brought at last within the grace and power of the eternal High Priesthood of Jesus."

The pastor—notes Newbigin, observing the quarrelsomeness of Christian congregants in India but perhaps not only there—regularly has to minister in a situation that pits against one another the righteousness and the peace that Scripture says should kiss each other (Psalm 85:10; cf. Matthew 5:9f.). "Where," the preacher asks in a particularly powerful address, "can we find the righteousness which does not become self-righteousness, and the peace which does not become appeasement?" The only place is "the Cross of Jesus Christ," where there stands over each one of us the accusation "Enemy of God" and the assurance "Friend of God." "To bring every situation into that presence means that self-righteousness is destroyed, but it also means that compromise with evil is made impossible," and so Ephesians 2:11–22 should be "our constant guide as we try to wrestle with the quarrels in our congregations"—accompanied by Philippians 2:1–11, where the Apostle marvelously expounds the self-emptying of Christ in face of the petty quarrels and jealousies of the Philippian Church, not hesitating to bring "tremendous theological truths to bear upon ordinary, mundane pastoral problems." In the "body" and "blood" of Ephesians 2 Newbigin finds eucharistic resonances and moves to 1 Corinthians 11 for the warning against eating and drinking judgment by "proclaiming the Cross as the one source of our unity" while "cherishing hatred against one another in our hearts." The bishop reminds his presbyters that "we are given authority under the discipline of our Church to exclude from communion those who persist in a malicious quarrel. Are there not times," he asks, "when we should be more ready to avail ourselves of this permission?" For "if we took the service of Holy Communion more seriously than we do, perhaps our ministry of peace-making could be the means whereby men and women are really brought into the presence of the crucified Lord, in whom alone righteousness and peace have kissed each other."

In a further meditation on pastoral discipline in the Church, Newbigin starts from the story of Jesus and the woman taken in adultery (John 8:3–11). The crucial moment takes place between Jesus and the woman alone: "The sinner is alone before him who alone can deal with her sin. . . . Jesus does not make excuses for her. She has sinned and she is warned not to sin again. But the divine mercy has forgiven her sin and given her time for repentance and amendment of life. This is what he alone can do, and he does it." From the story the bishop draws a general conclusion for disciplinary policy: there is a narrow path to be found between the dangers of rigorism (which may be a mark of self-righteousness on the part of the "accusers") and laxity (which leaves evil unchallenged, "comfortably established in the Church like a tenant who cannot be evicted"). Six principles are then laid out to guide pastors in their exercise of discipline. First, the authority to condemn and forgive belongs to Jesus alone, and ministers can only be "the agents and instruments of his holy and loving discipline," having of themselves no right whatever to judge the lives of others. Second, ministers of the Gospel are not to be "law-enforcement officers" usurping the functions of the state by means of fines or even corporal punishment. Third, in changing times, fixed rules need constant examination to see how well they "embody the holiness and love of Christ in the concrete situation of our society today" (Newbigin was thinking particularly of the relations between men and women, and between parents and children). Fourth, "we have to be quite fearless in tackling the sins of the rich and powerful" (Jesus "could refer to the ruling Rajah as 'that fox,' and to the leading ecclesiastical authorities as 'whited sepulchres' "). Fifth, the object of all church discipline is "that the person may be saved, may be forgiven, healed and restored to the Church's fellowship." Sixth, "[f]undamental to all church discipline is the fact that all who are called upon to exercise it—bishop, presbyter, elder, congregation—are forgiven sinners." When the minister, always himself unfit, is able to "lay hold afresh upon the fact of God's forgiveness," the minister can both recognize his solidarity with the sinner and long that the sinner, too, may know the joy of release. That may come only by way of a painful experience of estrangement, but the minister must not shrink from excluding the sinner from the fellowship if that is necessary for the sinner to "own his sin so that he may disown it."

It is a constitutional duty of presbyters in the CSI "to use every opportunity to preach the Gospel to non-Christians." Their own evangelizing activity is to be exemplary for the entire Church: "It is an essential part of our ministry," the bishop tells them, "that we are appointed to lead God's people in evangelism." Curiously, the name of evangelist has become used for "the lowest category of church worker—half-trained, half-paid and half-starved." Newbigin senses "behind the disrepute of the word evangelism" some symptoms of "a breakdown of faith in the Gospel": what should be the sharing of good news with friends has often degenerated into securing greater numbers and influence for the ecclesiastical organization; evangelism is corrupted when it tries to exploit the various weaknesses of others by sending evangelists "to backward villages, to slums, to people who are sick in hospital, to those in jail, to the hill tribes" but *not* to "the lawyers, the businessmen, the legislators." The remedy is to return to the way of the incarnation, of being "truly present with our neighbours, bearing with them the sin and sorrow of the world." But because we are not Christ himself, our presence and our deeds of love—while forming the "context" of our evangelism—are not enough but must be accompanied by "the naming of his name," the pointing to Jesus in such a way that people will see his Cross on Calvary and recognize him as Savior (cf. Romans 10:8–15). Newbigin testifies: "I have never felt the reality of the Gospel more fully than when I was regularly involved in a ministry to the condemned prisoners in the Madurai jail. It is in a situation where the Gospel is really being received as *news* that you understand what it is." That same news is also needed, he says, by the doctor, the government servant, the teacher, the professional administrator.[14]

The meditations on the pastor and evangelism are the route by which Newbigin approaches the theme of "presenting every man mature in Christ" (Colossians 1:23–29), of "equipping the saints" (Ephesians 4:11–13) who have been called "out of the world" in order then to be sent "into the world" for a ministry of witness and service (cf. John 17:11–23): "All truly pastoral ministry in the Church has as an essential part of its content the training of others to be ministers of Christ in the world. The test of our ministry will be the extent to which our people become ministers." That should start early in a Christian's life, as Newbigin reports of his practice in a small mass-movement area in Madurai: "The newly baptised converts who were being prepared for confirmation were expected after each period of instruction to go over to the next village and try to communicate to their neighbors what they had learned. When they had completed their period of preparation and were admitted to the full privileges of membership, it would be their privilege to present for baptism people of the neighbouring village whom they had prepared." In the more sophisticated situation of Madras, there was a task to "train our lay members who are playing key roles in the life of government, business and the professions to become ministers of Christ in these secular situations"; and not only so, but to "enable" church members for Christian witness in whatever their field of work or their neighborhood of residence. Newbigin recommends the creation of small, ecumenical, lay-led groups for Bible study, prayer, and mutual help, encouragement and exhortation.

The Church's ministry in the world is to be carried out both corporately and individually; it occurs through the congregation and its members. Congregations are not to be viewed, warns Newbigin, as private clubs competing to satisfy various religious tastes; they are to retain, even in India, enough of the sense of "parish" from old Christendom that they "take enduring responsibility" for a particular "area," a particular "bit of the world," which will be primarily geographical and residential (the village, the suburb, the neighborhood) but will also take account of such "segments" of secular society as the factory, the school, the office, the trade union, the professional association. Only by being firmly located within, and organically related to, the structures of the old creation can the Church be the "first-fruit, sign and instrument" of God's new creation. To be "in" and "for" its "parish" and thus fulfill its roles in God's plan for the salvation of the world, a congregation must follow out three biblical notions: it is to be "the humble servant of Jesus for the sake of its neighbours," "stooping down to do the menial tasks that a slave is expected to do"; it is to be "the witness to Jesus and his kingdom," pointing beyond itself to him, and "ready, in the wisest and most loving way possible, to tell its neighbours all about Jesus, through preaching, drama, the distribution of literature, and in any other way that seems appropriate"; it is to be "a priesthood on behalf of all its neighbours," "bringing the truth and love and peace of God to men who do not know God" and "offering up to God on behalf of all men the worship and prayer and obedience which are due to him . . . offering up to God the life of its whole neighbourhood that God's reign may truly become effective in the whole of its life."[15]

Newbigin devotes meditations to Christian ministry in four discrete areas of the common life: health care, social service, the search for social justice, and industry. Regarding the first, he notes that "a purely secular medicine is always finally defeated," for "in the end, of course, the patient always dies." Even when the whole person is viewed as "body and soul" and, better yet, as "person in community," the picture is incomplete unless health is related to salvation, to the coming of God's reign (cf. Matthew 9:2–8; 11:2–6; 12: 22–29). But just as there can be sick societies as well as sick individuals ("in more and more societies the greatest single cause of premature death is accidents on the roads"), so "there can be a healed and healing society, a society which brings health and wholeness to its members." Such the Church "is intended to be." Behind the ancient designation of the Eucharist as "the medicine of immortality" lies a picture of "the Church, its life centred in the Lord's Supper, as a healed and healing community in which the healing love of Christ flows out to heal the sicknesses of men" (cf. James 5:14–16 and, for contrast, 1 Corinthians 11:27–34). "Healing," the bishop tells his presbyters, "is part of our ministry as much as preaching and teaching are, for healing is an authentic sign of the presence of the kingdom of God. . . . The whole congregation is called to be a healed and healing fellowship, in which the healing love of God is ever at work to bind up the wounds of the members.

And beyond this, the healing work is to spread beyond the congregation into the community around it." Newbigin offers encouraging examples of Christians being called to pray in the homes of sick persons not belonging to the Church and of hundreds of church members in Madras volunteering to be trained as health visitors to homes and hospitals, thus building up "a whole new network of loving communication between the congregation and the community, through which the congregation can learn to exercise its function as a centre of healing."

The Church in Madras was engaged in "fairly extensive social work in the slums of the city." To meet human need is part of the obedient following of Christ (cf. Luke 4:16–19; 10:30–37; James 2:15f.). The point is not to earn merit (the Hindu idea of *punnyam*) or simply to offer "a bait to make people swallow our preaching." But the aim *is* conversion, properly motivated and understood. Christian deeds of mercy and liberation ought not to be part of a "contrived programme" with an "ulterior purpose" but rather "natural and spontaneous signs of the new reality in which we have been made sharers through Christ," for "those who have received so much cannot keep it to themselves." Precisely as "overflow in love to others," as "part of the reality and not something separate from it," however, the signs need words to interpret them. Verbal witness to Christ and his Cross is needed if (and here Newbigin harks back to his early experience among the unemployed miners of South Wales) people's deepest needs are to be met. Conversion to God's saving reign is most credibly invited when the followers of Jesus follow their Master's example in stooping down and washing feet.

Salvation, according to the Scriptures, includes political liberation, economic prosperity, social justice, civil peace, and happy family life (Exodus; Psalm 144; Micah 4:1–4), yet its "true kernel" is "fellowship with the living Lord," who says "I will be with you"; "the rest is the outward token of that inward reality." Furthermore, says Newbigin, "there is always in the background the eschatological vision of a totally new order which goes beyond anything that this worldly experience can show." Thus salvation is not only "both outward and inward" but also "both a present experience and a future hope" (cf. Romans 8:18–25). The search and struggle for social justice is always to be seen in that double tension. Recalling Isaiah 1:12–17, the message Bishop Newbigin wants brought home to the well-to-do congregations of Madras is that "the piety which can comfortably co-exist with flagrant social injustice is an abomination to God. Salvation is not a privilege which we can enjoy apart from our total commitment to God's battle with the powers of evil." Justification, or being right with God, is a free gift, which can only be received with wonder and gratitude; but "we can only receive that gift as we commit ourselves totally and irreversibly to the justice of God in action." The coming of Jesus to the house of Zacchaeus was "an act of pure kindness which had nothing to do with any merit of Zacchaeus"; but it was "when Zacchaeus made the decision to do justice to those whom he had robbed" that "Jesus said, 'Today salvation has come to this house'" (Luke 19:1–10). In the Holy Communion, "we are offered as an utterly free gift the bread and wine which are the body and blood of Christ—the food and drink of eternal life. But to receive them is to be totally committed to his passion, to become sharers in his broken body and his blood shed for the life of the world."

The theme of "mission to industry" leads Newbigin to make an interesting interpretation of "the nations" among whom the Church is commanded to make disciples by the one Lord whose sovereign authority covers all things (Matthew 28:18–20). Noting that "nations" in the modern sense of "states" would be anachronistic to the New Testament, he takes *ta ethnê* in the sense of "communities." He turns for an example to the German missionaries who brought the Gospel to "the Batak people" of Sumatra: they "took immense pains to study not only the language of the Batak people but also the whole body of customary law (the *adat*) by which the life of the whole people was moulded and held together" and "sought to bring the people as a whole, with their *adat*, into the realm of the Gospel where new powers were at work and new forms could be created." Their success suggests that the Church should also learn the *adat* of the "nation" of industry. It will not be principally a matter of "industrial chaplains" or "worker priests." Rather, every pastor with industry in his parish should familiarize himself with its *adat* and help train his members who are already at work on the shop floor or in the office to bear witness to Christ's "sovereignty over industry, to be the instruments by which that sovereignty is more and more fully exercised, and to be signs for men to see that his blessed reign is over the factory as it is over the field, the farm and the home."

Given all the responsibilities which Newbigin attributes to the pastor, the bishop appropriately offers also counsel regarding the spiritual resources and discipline that are needed to sustain the ministry and to enable a steady "growing up into Christ" such as befits his whole Body (Ephesians 4:14f.). The pastor is to be a student like the apostle Paul, who, man of action though he clearly was, instructed Timothy to bring him his "books, and above all the notebooks" (2 Timothy 4:13). Constant study is required both because of "the exceeding greatness of the God whom we preach" and because of "the vastness and variety of the human world to which our preaching is addressed." The former subject demands the careful study of the text of Scripture, the history of the Church's mission, and the developing understanding of the Christian faith which is theology. The latter kind of study—of the human world—is necessary if the Gospel is to be interpreted to people whose models of the world and of themselves are influenced by public events, the work of scientists and artists, the impact of press, radio and film, the performances of politicians, and the ways in which commerce and industry are run. Newbigin makes four suggestions for disciplined reading: "Always try to have one *big* book on which you are working"; "try to read original works rather than summaries or digests"; "always keep some Bible work going," using commentaries; "have some secular interests of your own," for they will keep your theology fresh.

Then there is "the hidden life of the pastor." "The more time we have to give to the ministry of public prayer," says the bishop, "the more time we need to spend in private prayer—in that kind of prayer where we go into our room and shut the door and pray to our Father in secret." Only as the branches abide in the Vine will fruit be borne (John 15:1–8). For "the life of Jesus to be reproduced in the life of the world" it is necessary "to make the words of Jesus our constant theme of meditation, to come back again and again to them, to listen afresh to them, to apply them to our situation as it changes each day." By "systematic and unwearying prayer for others and for the doing of God's will in the world" we become "fellow-workers with Christ, sharing in his unwearied intercession for all men." That is to be remembered when, in times of physical exhaustion or spiritual and moral frailty, or amid the stresses and strains of a quarrelsome congregation, the pastor must rely with the apostle Paul on the paradox of the cruciform Gospel: "When I am weak, then I am strong" (2 Corinthians 12:8–10; cf. 4:1–18).[16]

The "pastoral heart" from which flowed the bishop's addresses to the presbyters of Madras in the late 1960s and early 1970s had already been exercised in Newbigin's direct ministry to a particular congregation outside India and would be so again: while living in Geneva from 1962 to 1965 as a staff member of the World Council of Churches, he helped to form a "house church" in the developing apartment complex of Les Palettes, where he and his wife resided along with many newcomers of various nationalities; and after retiring at the age of seventy from teaching at the Selly Oak Colleges in Birmingham, he served from 1980 to 1988 as pastor of the United Reformed congregation at Winson Green in the inner suburbs of the city. From Geneva, Lukas Vischer, another member of the WCC staff living in Les Palettes, reports that the house church became "the nucleus" of the parish and that Newbigin was very much appreciated for his preaching in French, even though it was not unknown for him to exhort people to have a sound liver (le foie) rather than a sound faith (la foi).[17] Newbigin records that "in the end, true to the missiology of the time, the world provided the agenda":

> We formed a Tenants Association which proved to be an immense success. Under its auspices all kinds of activities began to flourish which brought the separate families together to serve each other, to teach each other's languages, to learn new skills and to resist the more outrageous extortions of the landlord. "The Palettes" began to be something of a human community and that was surely pleasing in God's sight. But the number who gathered to acknowledge the Source of all blessing was small.

On his departure from the city for Madras he was given "a parting gift and a warm expression of affection from the famous 'Compagnie des Pasteurs' of the Église Nationale de Genève."[18]

From Winson Green, Frank Davies, the church secretary, testifies to "the humanity and the unshakeable belief Lesslie displayed during his ministry" there. From "two churches" he made "one": the young people and their leaders had been worshipping on Sunday morning and the "small aging group of commuting worshippers" on Sunday evening but "with Lesslie's encouragement we changed the pattern to one combined act of worship on Sunday mornings" and "received great stimulus from all age groups worshipping as one family"; and "while Lesslie would be the first to admit he was no story teller to children," he held the attention of the boys and girls. Frank Davies calls the introduction of a weekly Bible study group in the winter months a specially memorable feature of Newbigin's ministry. Mention has already been made in a previous chapter of his evangelistic and ecumenical work in Winson Green. Following race riots in Handsworth he organized with the city fathers and the police a forum in the church for all community groups to meet. Almost ten years after Newbigin's departure from Winson Green, Frank Davis reported that "many folk who do not worship at our church still stop us in the street to enquire of the well being of Lesslie since he was so much respected by the people of the district of all faiths," and that he in turn got "frequent telephone calls from Lesslie to enquire of news of the church family."[19]

Two typescripts from the 1980s and 1990s show how Newbigin continued into the last decade of his life to reflect on the pastoral ministry in which he had for so long been active. The first, headed simply "Ministry," begins from John 20:19–23, in which the apostles on whom Jesus breathes the Holy Spirit and whom he commissions to forgive and retain sins are "both the first ministers and the first members of the Church."[20] Some have always been called within the Church to "a ministry in and to the Church, to enable the whole ministry *of* the Church in and to the world." To enable all Christians to "fulfill their ministry to the life of the secular world, the ministry *of* the Church *for* the world," leaders are required to set an example for imitation (cf. Hebrews 13:7). To be imitated, however, they themselves must first, like the apostle Paul, imitate Christ (cf. 1 Corinthians 11:1). To be a fisherman (John 21:1–14) and a shepherd (John 21:15–17), it is first necessary to be a disciple: "Follow me," Peter was told by the risen Christ, predicting "by what death he should glorify God" (John 21:19f.). Leadership in the Church always means "following Jesus in the way of the Cross, so that the whole Church may be enabled to follow and so, in turn, to draw others into the company of those who belong to Christ." "Here," says Newbigin with reference to such Pauline passages as 1 Corinthians 4:9–13, 2 Corinthians 4:5–12 and 6:1–10, and Colossians 1:23–25, "is the vicarious principle which is the very heart of the Gospel and therefore the very heart of the ministry: Christ died that the world might live; he sent his Church to share in his dying so that it might mediate his life to the world; he calls apostles and other ministers to be leaders in the same paradoxical way of the Cross, sharing the dying of Jesus so that the Church may share his life." That means also that just as "Jesus' concern is with the last and the least, with the hundredth sheep, with the least of his brethren," so the Christian ministry must be concerned that "no one is ignored, no one is marginalized, no one is pushed to the periphery."

The second late typescript is titled "Pastoral Ministry in a Pluralist Society."[21] Newbigin starts by showing that the Church was launched from its very beginning into a world of many religions and cultures. He turns to the pastoral ministry that is reflected and exercised in the canonical letters of the Apostles for five lessons on how Christians and Christian congregations should understand and comport themselves amid a similarly pluralist society today. First, the emphasis must be "on the need for absolute fidelity to the Gospel." The Gospel is an account of events that took place in the public world "under Pontius Pilate"; it is the story of the redemptive work of God for humankind in the incarnation, death, and resurrection of Jesus Christ (1 Corinthians 15:3; Galatians 2:20; 1 John 1:1). "Christianity" is "what we have made of these facts . . . a complex of thought and practice which embodies the ways in which, at different times and places and in different cultures, the Gospel has been understood and interpreted," and is therefore "a constantly changing and developing thing" with "no absoluteness or finality in itself." It is the unchangeable Gospel itself which must be retold, for if (as Christians believe) "almighty God has really done what the Gospel affirms he has done, then there is nothing in all the religious ideas and practices of the world that can be put into the same category as this." Second, the Apostles teach respect toward other religious communities, whether Jewish (for, according to Romans 9–11, the Church remains permanently indebted to the Jewish people as the recipients of the divine promises) or Gentile (for, according to Acts 14:14, 17:13, and Romans 2:14–16, "God has not left himself without witness in the hearts of any people"); but this does not relieve Christians from the responsibility of announcing to others the Good News of what has "now" taken place through Jesus Christ (Acts 10:34–43; 17:30f.; Romans 3:21–26). Third, and consequently, "pastoral ministry in a pluralist society must prepare Christians to be witnesses for the Gospel"—especially when opportunity is afforded by the unbeliever's questions (Acts 2:7f., 12, 37; 1 Peter 3:15). Fourth, "pastoral ministry in a pluralist society must include the kind of leadership which nourishes pluralist congregations," that is, "congregations in which men and women of very different social and ethnic backgrounds live together in harmony," for "only so can the congregation be an authentic representative of the Lord who said 'I, when I am lifted up from the earth, will draw all people to myself' (John 12:32)" (cf. Galatians 2). Newbigin rejects the "homogeneous unit principle"—long championed by Donald McGavran—that encouraged church growth through the gathering together of "people of the same race, caste, or social class." Fifth, pastoral ministry in a pluralist society requires great patience, the very "meekness and gentleness of Christ" (2 Corinthians 10:1); for even in the Church "people cannot be forced into a fellowship which unites them across the strong natural divisions of kith and kin, social group or class." While thus affirming the proper pluralism that should freely mark the Church as the redeemed community, Newbigin concludes with a reminder that Christians must "reject the pluralism which abandons truth, which says 'All roads lead to the top of the same mountain'"; for "there are many roads which do not lead to the top of the mountain but to the edge of a precipice," and "there is a broad road that leads to destruction"—the broad way that "fosters a lazy reluctance to make hard decisions between truth and falsehood."

The Bishop

Lesslie Newbigin was consecrated to the episcopate in St. George's Cathedral, Madras, on September 27, 1947, among the first nine new bishops of the freshly inaugurated Church of South India. "The figure of Christ rising from the tomb faced us as we knelt at the rails waiting our turn to kneel before the bishop presiding, and for me at least," he recounted, "it was the answer to the sickening sense of utter incapacity for the work for which I was being set apart. The laying on of hands was by three [Anglican] bishops and three presbyters from the SIU and Methodist Churches, and then each of us was given, according to ancient custom, the bible and the staff."[22] Some aspects of Newbigin's ministry as a bishop have already been displayed: he has been seen (particularly in chapter 2) as a direct evangelist and (in this chapter) as a teacher and encourager of his presbyters in the pastoral tasks they share with him. Other features also need to be brought to the fore from his exercise of the episcopate in Madurai and in Madras. Newbigin's own retrospective "reflections on the ministry of a bishop" suggest a template that allows all the various elements to be composed into a comprehensive picture of his understanding and practice of the ministry of a chief pastor.[23] The illustrative details are chiefly taken from his more or less annual circular letters to friends overseas, from his *South India Diary*, and from his autobiography *Unfinished Agenda*. Eight main lineaments shape the portrait.

First, Newbigin devoted a heavy proportion of his time and energy as a bishop to *visitation*. His first diocese, he reported in November 1949, comprised some 800 town or village congregations, organized into forty-eight pastorates. In October 1955, after eight years in Madurai, he was still enjoying "new experiences of this fascinating and varied world," usually spending "three days of each week on tour." Newbigin wrote in October 1948 that

> the Indian villager, whatever his ecclesiastical affiliations, likes to make the most of the visit of a "guru," and a bishop is, even though unworthy, given that status. But this means that one has the most wonderful opportunities for preaching the Gospel. One is met at the entrance to the village by the whole congregation with flags, drums and garlands. There follows a surging procession through the streets, punctuated by fireworks, and halted from time to time by a performance of whatever sword-dance or similar exhibition is locally traditional. Finally one reaches the church, and either in it or in front of it the whole village gathers. There is generally a service in church first, and then a public meeting outside when one has a chance of speaking to practically the whole village.

Leslie Brown recalls a stop he made with Newbigin in 1950 on the return drive from a youth conference in Kerala to the hill country of Kodaikanal:

> We broke our journey at the foot of the hills, where Lesslie had a confirmation. There was a small church building and little else. The Christians were already assembling; all of them worked in the paddy fields around the village. We had our evening meal, and then sat on the ground in front of Lesslie. He spoke to us in Tamil, and they were following his words with excitement and obvious complete understanding. They responded eagerly to his questions, and we went on in the moonlight for an hour and a half or two hours. Lesslie and I spent the night on two charpoys (string beds) under the stars, surrounded by the sleeping forms of the congregation. At five in the morning Lesslie baptised a Muslim convert in the river, accompanied by all the people. (He was Paul, who later became a canon of Nagpur and had a most splendid ministry among workers, starting a trade union for rickshaw men.) He was baptised there as he might have been killed if the ceremony had been known in his home town. Once more we sat on the ground while Lesslie led a Eucharist, in the course of which a large number was confirmed. Then they changed back to working clothes and returned to the fields. The atmosphere of love was almost palpable, and the affection between the bishop and his people evident. This experience has been the guide and compass of my own ministry as a bishop.[24]

That description of a visitation already incorporates several functions of episcopal ministry that figure in Newbigin's pattern, as will be seen in a moment. In the context of the newly united Church of South India, the episcopal visitation served with special intensity an ecclesiological purpose that by tradition attaches permanently to the office of bishop: "The continual visiting of each congregation by the bishop was the first way in which their unity in one Church became a reality to them." Or in more universal terms, as Newbigin again put it looking back: "I found that one of the important tasks of a bishop was to help local congregations to understand their real nature as local manifestations of the full reality of the catholic Church, not local branches of it"—for (borrowing the words of Ignatius of Antioch in his letter to the Smyrnaeans) "where the Lord Jesus Christ is present, there is the catholic Church."

The next four features in Newbigin's pattern of episcopal ministry were listed from the start in the description of the bishop's responsibilities contained in the Constitution of the CSI, and Newbigin insisted on them as his priorities from the moment of his assumption of the office.[25] Both in his see and throughout his diocese the bishop must be (in the order Newbigin adopted in his retrospective "reflections on the ministry of a bishop") a "leader in worship, in evangelism, in teaching, and in pastoral care." Concerning leadership in *worship*, Newbigin wrote:

> Worship is the central work of the Church, and everything else in its life has meaning and value as it finds its focus in worship. Therefore if the bishop is to be a leader of his people in their total discipleship, he must first of all be

a leader of their worship. One cannot even begin to think of the corporate life of the diocese without first thinking of those great occasions—especially ordinations—when the bishop has the privilege of leading the corporate worship of the whole diocese gathered together in its representatives. As I look back on the earliest days of the newly formed diocese of Madurai and Ramnad, it is to such occasions as these that I look as having given to the whole life of the diocese its emotional and spiritual focus, its centre of meaning and direction. It is from such acts of worship that everything else flows, and in them all the multifarious activities of the diocese find their true end. Everything is offered to God as an acted prayer for his Kingdom, and the bishop is the chief celebrant in this action. It is as such that he can also be the leader in all these activities which may otherwise become fragmented and meaningless.

Newbigin's letters and *Diary* show him continuing this leadership in worship at many points on his tours of the diocese, and in chapter 8 of this book he is seen propagating on ecumenical occasions around the globe the eucharistic liturgy he had helped to shape in the Church of South India.

As an indication of the bishop's leadership in *evangelism*, it may be enough to note from his annual letter of November 1949 that Newbigin had preached "about 275 times in the year" and to allow him to describe a baptism—after a year's preparation—of some 125 people at a village on the seacoast which could be reached only after mattocks and crowbars had been used to hack a way for the Ford through a trackless jungle:

By the time we arrived it was already dusk, and lamps had to be lit and shielded from the wind. The congregation of about 200 was drawn up in a semi-circle facing the water, and the service conducted from the waterside. Then the two presbyters and I waded out till we stood in two feet of water. Family by family they came out as they were called, and one by one they were immersed and signed with the cross, then escorted back to the bank where they dried and put on their new and spotless clothes. For two hours the baptising went on, till dusk had turned to dark, and the moon shone brilliant over the water, and the leeches and crabs had done what they could with six unprotected ecclesiastical legs. Then the brief conclusion of the service, and the procession back to the village. Next morning early, the newly baptised congregation was crammed into the little prayer house for its dedication. It was a crude enough affair of mud and thatch, but that eager throng of worshippers, with the glow of their baptism upon them, made it as glorious as any cathedral. I preached on Romans 6:3–4, though "preach" is not the proper word to convey the interplay of question and answer with which one must go to work in such a setting. "We were buried with Him through baptism"—Yes, of course we were, that just describes it!—"That like as Christ was raised from the dead, so we might walk in newness of life"—Yes indeed, everything is new from today. "Old things are passed away, behold they are become new."

Retrospectively Newbigin commented that episcopal duty is not fulfilled if the bishop merely encourages other people to evangelize: "The mission of the

Church requires leadership from in front, and the bishop cannot—like the Duke of Plaza Toro—lead from behind."

Then the bishop is called also to be a *teacher of the faith*. Newbigin recalls that he "spent a great deal of time in small residential gatherings of clergy and other church workers, generally doing straightforward Bible study with them." He looked on these occasions as "among the most precious experiences of [his] service as a bishop": "The study of the Scriptures together in the immediate context of pastoral and evangelistic experience always yields new and surprising treasures." Theology, says Newbigin,

> is rightly done in the context of worship and discipleship. The central place of theological teaching is the place where, in the midst of the mystery of the Eucharist, the minister seeks to interpret the words of Scripture to those who, having partaken of the Eucharist, will then go out into the world to live out in practice the action of the broken body and shed blood. This kind of theological teaching certainly needs illumination and correction by the work of those whose whole time is given to the scholarly study of the Christian tradition, but it must not be allowed to lose its central place in the life of the Church.

The bishop's leadership in *pastoral care*, according to the Constitution of the CSI, is displayed on the broadest scale in his ministering of the rite of Confirmation, and Newbigin's letters and *Diary* show him in conversation with the candidates: "These hours with the young people just before their confirmation are extraordinarily precious. It is not primarily that they give an opportunity for testing their preparedness, though that is important. The main thing is that one can get into really vital contact with a group of young people at a decisive moment in their lives," he writes apropos of a village "confirmation under a pipal tree."[26] As he circulates in his diocese, the bishop takes the opportunity, Newbigin writes in October 1948, "for meeting with the teachers and lay workers to discuss their problems and pray with them, for a long meeting with the Pastorate Committee to discuss all the affairs of the Pastorate, and for talking with the Presbyter in his home." In the Madras diocese as a whole Newbigin had 120 presbyters and found that he did not have the same "closeness of touch" as he had had with the fifty in Madurai and Ramnad, so that in retrospect he judged it "hard to see how a bishop can really fulfill his proper pastoral function in relation to the clergy if he has more than a hundred in his care." The bishop must also seek to settle quarrels (sometimes between the laity and their minister). In Madras he discovered an important part of the bishop's work to be "pastoral contact with those lay men and women who carry the main responsibility for the manifold works of the Church in education, medicine, and social service."

That thought brought Newbigin to the sixth item in his portrait of a bishop's ministry, namely the role of the bishop as the *representative of the local church to the secular world*:

> Even in a place like India, where the Church constitutes only a tiny fraction of the population, it is the Church for the whole nation; the bishop, therefore,

is not merely the pastor of the Christians under his care but also a representative of Christ to the whole secular community. I remember vividly the moment in Madras Cathedral when I was preaching at the service [in October
1965] in which I was installed as bishop. The representatives of the secular
press were not visibly enthralled by my sermon, but when I came to the
words "Jesus Christ is not the Head of the Christians, he is the Head of the
Human Race," pencils began to scribble vigorously, and this was the only
part of my sermon which was reported. I tried to practice what I had
preached, and I found that—once the secular authorities were convinced that
we cared about their problems and not just about our own—they welcomed
such help and counsel as we were able to offer.[27]

Well down the list of priorities, but nevertheless regarded as indispensable,
comes the bishop's job as *administrator*. The Church of South India adopted
the episcopate "in a constitutional form": "While some things can best be
handled by a bishop acting alone and in a confidential way," wrote Newbigin,
other matters "ought never to be decided except after full discussion in council
or synod." Although the bishop may be tempted toward autocracy (and may
even be encouraged by some of his clergy to adopt that style), and although
the bishop who "has earned the trust of his people" has "a great deal of
freedom available to him to take initiatives," he must "carry his council with
him," yet without becoming, on the other side, "a puppet manipulated by
parties in his council." The question for the bishop as administrator is: How
can the bishop serve to enable the conciliar bodies to function at their best,
and how can the councils enable the bishop to function at his best? "I have
never been able to agree," wrote Newbigin in later evaluating his experience,
"that presiding over a committee was an unspiritual occupation": "At its best
a committee meeting, rightly conducted, is a means by which small visions
are expanded by larger ones, so that conflicting wills are enabled to work
together; by which the detail of daily work is brought into the perspective of
a broader purpose; by which people's gifts and abilities are drawn out and
developed and harnessed to a bigger task." The point is to show the whole
enterprise as "an outcome of the life in Christ which is the central mystery
of the Church."

Finally, through the faithful exercise of leadership as himself a disciple and
servant of Christ, the bishop will become a *focus of unity*. Within the varied
life of the diocese, the bishop "can be a vital centre of unity, provided that
his office is seen not as a peg on which everything in the life of the Church
hangs, but as one part of God's manifold provision for the good of his
Church." More broadly, the bishop "is called to be a focus of wider unity
among all Christians and all people." Thus did Newbigin, ordained originally
as a Presbyterian minister, come to regard the office and ministry of a bishop
in the light of his episcopal experience in the Church of South India. With
that, the emphasis in the rest of this chapter shifts to Newbigin's views on
historically controversial questions of order in the Church.

Ministries Ordained and Lay

In the context of negotiating and defending the union of Anglicans, Presbyterians, Congregationalists, and Methodists in the Church of South India, Newbigin turned for an acceptable understanding of ordination to the Reformed tradition in which he himself had been ordained as a minister of the Church of Scotland. In *The Reunion of the Church* he cited in particular the ordination prayer from the ordinal of the Church of Scotland:

> Almighty God, most merciful Father, Who of Thine infinite goodness hast given Thine only Son Jesus Christ to be our Redeemer and the Author of everlasting life, and hast exalted Him unto Thy right hand, whence, according to Thy will, He hath sent down the Holy Spirit and given gifts unto men: we thankfully acknowledge Thy great mercy in bestowing upon us these inestimable benefits; and we humbly beseech Thee, SEND DOWN THE HOLY SPIRIT UPON THIS THY SERVANT, WHOM WE, IN THY NAME, AND IN OBEDIENCE TO THY MOST BLESSED WILL, DO NOW, BY THE LAYING ON OF OUR HANDS, ORDAIN AND APPOINT TO THE OFFICE OF THE HOLY MINISTRY IN THY CHURCH, COMMITTING UNTO HIM AUTHORITY TO DISPENSE THY WORD AND SACRAMENTS, AND TO BEAR RULE IN THY FLOCK. Impart to him such fulness of Thy grace as shall fit him more and more for the work to which he has been called. Give him counsel, understanding, and utterance, that he may boldly proclaim Thy word and will. Make him a light unto them that sit in darkness, a watchful and loving guardian over Thy fold, and a follower of the Good Shepherd Who gave His life for the sheep. Enable him to guide aright the people of his charge, and in all things to fulfil his ministry without reproach in Thy sight, so that he may abide steadfast to the end, and be received with all Thy faithful servants into the joy of his Lord. These things we ask through Jesus Christ our Lord, Who taught us to pray: Our Father, which art in heaven . . . [28]

"In the New Testament," says Newbigin, "the Church is the Body of the living Christ, and the ministry is the gift of the living and ascended Christ to the Church." Accordingly, forms of ordination from early times down to today make it explicit that "ordination is fundamentally an act of the living and ascended Christ in response to the prayers of His Church; that the Church acts, in this matter, as the hands of the living Christ." In fuller theological description:

> The Church [in ordination] acts in her true character as a society constituted by the union of her members in faith with the ascended Christ. In this faith she sets before Him the man whom she believes that He has called, and she lays her hands upon him in the act of prayer that Christ Himself may bestow upon him the commission and the grace that are required. And in the faith that He hears and answers, acting as His instrument, she commits to the ordained man the authority to act as minister of Christ to the Church. The prayer is a prayer of the whole Church and the hands are the hands of the whole Church which is His Body—not only of those now present, not even of those now living, but of all who have gone before everywhere and always.

It is the hands that bear the unmistakable authority and commission of the whole Church that must be laid on the head of the ordinand, in token that the prayer that is offered is in truth the prayer of the whole Church—is indeed, "through Jesus Christ our Lord," a part of the one undiscordant offering of perpetual prayer which is made by Christ and by the Church in Him.

If, in spite of "our sinful division," Christ in his mercy does not disown "the hands that are stretched forth to ordain and the prayers that ascend in the act of ordination," that gives no permission to "continue in sin that grace may abound." In 1983–84 Newbigin was able to carry into the report of the Anglican-Reformed International Commission, *God's Reign and Our Unity*, exactly the view of ordination to priest, pastor, or presbyter that he had defended against various Anglo-Catholic attacks upon the CSI in 1947–48:

Ordination is the act which constitutes and acknowledges this special ministry of representation and leadership within the life of the Church both locally and universally. In the act of ordination, the Church in Christ prays to the Father to grant his Spirit to the one ordained for the office and work to which that person is called, accompanying the act with a sacramental sign which specifies by the imposition of hands the one for whom prayer is made, and—in faith that the prayer is heard—commits to the person ordained the authority to act representatively for the universal Church in the ways proper to that particular office.[29]

The entire Church is "a holy priesthood," Newbigin successfully argued in 1983–84 as he had in 1947–48, and "the rule that the celebrant at Holy Communion shall be an ordained minister is a *rule of order*."[30] He wrote in *The Reunion of the Church*:

The essential matter is that the dispensing of the Sacraments shall be so ordered that it visibly expresses the truth that what is done is the act of Christ in His Church—the whole Church in earth and in heaven. . . . We do not know precisely when or how or by whom it was first established in the Church that the celebration of the Sacraments should be confined strictly to those who have been ordained for the permanent exercise of that ministry, but it belongs to the whole nature of the Church, and of the Sacraments that some such rule of order in the matter must have become established from a very early stage, even if not from the very beginning. It is not an accident of history, but of the essence of the Church, that this ministry should be both conjoined to the permanent exercise of pastoral responsibility in the Church, and also connected with a sucession of authority binding the Church in all ages and all places into one. Yet it remains still a rule of order, derivative from and subordinate to the fundamental truth that the whole Church is a sharing in the heavenly High Priesthood of Christ.

In *God's Reign and Our Unity* it is concisely stated: "The presidency of the ordained person [at the Eucharist] does not depend on his possessing a priesthood which others lack; it depends upon the good ordering which is essential to the life of the Church as it exercises corporately the priesthood given to it by the one who is alone the good High Priest."[31]

If, in some Protestant traditions, "lay celebration" has been demanded as "an indispensable evidence of adherence to the doctrine of the priesthood of all believers," that very demand seems to "imply the belief that the celebrant is *exclusively* the priest" and thus to "rest upon precisely the very error which it is sought to resist."[32] Where "lay presidency" has been temporarily authorized in order to meet the exceptional needs manifest in a shortage of ordained ministers, the proper course is "to take all necessary steps to see that provision for regular celebrations of the Holy Communion is made as soon as possible without further breach of the Church's rule."[33]

Newbigin was among the first in the Church of South India to press for the ordination of local leaders in the villages, so that each congregation might come to understand and present itself more clearly as an instantiation of the Church catholic. Such ordained ministers would preside at the regular celebration of the sacraments and be in a position to lead and enable the entire congregation in its evangelistic task according to missionary principles and methods such as Roland Allen was coming to persuade Newbigin were those of St. Paul. In 1951 Newbigin wrote:

> I believe that we have got to extend the volunteer principle much farther than we have done. I myself believe that if the Church is to be really rooted in the country and to Christianize the country through and through, our present pattern will have to be drastically modified. I think we ought to have an ordained Presbyter in every village, who would normally be a villager himself, earning his living with his hands, but sufficiently trained to be able to read and explain the Bible intelligibly, and to conduct the liturgy with understanding. I think there should be, further, a peripatetic ministry of teachers, on whom we could rely for instruction of the people in the faith in a systematic way, which might include both paid Presbyters and also the "faith" workers who are already so popular a feature of church life. Further, there should be a fully trained and paid ministry of people—including a very much larger number of bishops than at present—with ultimate responsibility for the life and worship and teaching of the Church. . . . I do not want to reduce the number of fully trained and paid ministers, but I want greatly to increase the ministry and make it more local and indigenous. I think something like what I have outlined is in line with the experience of the church in its first thousand years in Europe, and even now in vast areas, and that our present pattern, the creation of the mercantile societies of the post-Renaissance West, is quite unsuited to the field we are working in.[34]

As bishop in Madurai, Newbigin set into operation a training program for several hundred volunteer leaders, whose congregations became "more lively and more active in evangelism"; he developed an annual Village Workers' Almanack that he had first begun producing in Kanchipuram, providing "teaching suggestions and material for every Sunday in the year."[35] Despite hesitations on professional and educational grounds, the diocese in 1954 secured from the CSI synod the authority to prepare these village leaders for ordination, but only a few completed the course before Newbigin's departure in 1959, and his successor disapproved of the program and terminated it.

On his final return to Britain decades later, Newbigin supported the moves being made in several denominations toward a "supplementary," "non-stipendiary" ministry.[36]

From all that has been said so far it will be obvious that, for Newbigin, the ordained ministry properly functions not to exclude or replace but rather to enable the varied ministries of all Christians and the corporate ministry of the whole Church. The ordained minister does this primarily by leading in the way of discipleship, by prayer and pastoral care, by setting an example in witness and service, and by instruction and counsel in determinate areas. Besides their gathering with and as the entire people of God for worship, the witness and service of most other members of the Church is rendered chiefly in their various locations in the life of the world—in their "family relationships," in their "daily work," and in "responsible participation in secular organizations" (as the Consitution of the Church of South India came to formulate it).[37]

"All baptized Christians," wrote Newbigin in a paper prepared for the 1983 meeting of the Anglican-Reformed International Commission, "are called to exercise this [common] priesthood in the course of their daily avocations in the secular world, offering to God their love and obedience, and showing forth to others the love of God in Christ." He did not favor the pairing of the terms "clergy" and "laity" insofar as it "suggested a sharp distinction between two different classes of Christians." Rather, the function of the "special" ministries is to lead the "general": "The language of leadership emphasises the fluidity of the boundary without surrendering to a fashionable kind of egalitarianism which denies the necessity for leadership. A good leader might almost be defined as one who does *not* draw a boundary to separate himself from others, but is eager that others should follow so closely that they in turn become leaders for others."[38] "A minister does not," Newbigin told the United Reformed Church when commending the proposed Covenant among the English churches, "cease to be a layman when he is ordained. The ministry is not a separate body from the whole people of God (Greek *laos*)." This applies even when the minister speaks and acts in ordination: "The minister is a lay person chosen and authorised to speak [and act] on behalf of all the lay persons, of whom he is one."[39]

Episcopacy and the Historic Episcopate

Two related but distinct matters were involved in the constitution of the Church of South India in 1947, namely "episcopacy" and "the historic episcopate"; that is to say, the benefits of an episcopal pattern for the ordering of the united Church's life and the continuation of the episcopal succession such as Anglicans believe themselves to enjoy. Lesslie Newbigin had already been persuaded before the union that the maintenance or recovery of ministerial succession in the episcopal line corresponded to the nature of the Church as a visible society stretching from the events of Easter and Pentecost to the awaited Return of Christ. Through his own experience in episcopal ministry in the CSI he came also to see the practical value of a constitution that made a bishop the chief pastor of a diocese. Newbigin became and remained an ecumenical advocate for both episcopacy and a historic episcopate, commending them particularly to churches that hitherto had not had them but now—usually in unity negotiations with Anglicans—had the chance to adopt them. As was seen in chapter 3, such an adoption was not to take place in a way that unchurched bishopless bodies in respect of their previous history, for that would be to offend against divine grace already granted and manifest.

Newbigin propounded his position in the English situation in the 1970s and 1980s, when several churches were exploring the possibility of a covenant for visible unity and when local ecumenical projects of varying kinds were being established. In his "Reflections on the Ministry of a Bishop" he testified again to the influence of Michael Ramsey's *The Gospel and the Catholic Church* in bringing him to see "the ministry of bishops in continuity with the ministry of the apostolic Church" as "one element in the proper form of the Church as a single society continuing through the centuries." And when he "went behind Ramsey to read F. D. Maurice," it became much clearer to him, he says, that "episcopacy was to be received and prized as a gift and a fact, rather than as a doctrine." As a "given order of ministry" that allowed, just as the rite of baptism does, for "considerable diversity" of interpretation, "the historic episcopate could be seen as a magnet which could draw the scattered parts of the Church into unity, not as a touchstone by which to judge between the true Church and its counterfeit." Newbigin remained convinced that "if the Lambeth Conference had been able to give a straightforward blessing to what had begun in South India, the way would have been open for a great movement of unity."[40] The issue and the opportunity will arise again if and when sufficient rapprochement occurs between the churches of the Reformation or more recent fruits of the Gospel, on the one hand, and the Roman Catholic or Orthodox churches, on the other.

Concerning the structure and exercise of episcopacy as a constitutional form, Newbigin reveals that in the Church of South India—composed from Anglican, Presbyterian, Congregational, and Methodist traditions—each diocese was allowed a certain latitude to "work out its own detailed practice in the light of the local traditions and experience," albeit within "an agreed framework" that was provided by the written constitution and a synod composed of the bishops and of representative presbyters and laypersons from each diocese.[41] In later years, Newbigin moved toward formulating the elements that were needed in ecclesial governance as "personal," "conciliar," and "corporate."[42] In *God's Reign and Our Unity* (1984), the Anglican-Reformed International Commission's report, of which Newbigin was admittedly and recognizably the chief drafter, the terminology finally adopted was that made widely familiar by the Lima document of WCC Faith and Order on *Baptism, Eucharist and Ministry* (1982), namely the "personal," the "collegial," and the "communal." The Anglican-Reformed text of 1984 reads thus:

> To the extent that ministry conforms to Christ, it reflects the character of
> God as revealed in the incarnation. As God in Christ deals with us in a
> personal way, so all ministry must have a *personal* character, providing in a
> specific person a focus for the unity and witness of the community. As God
> calls us into a reconciled fellowship, so all ministry must have a *collegial*
> character—exercised not by one person alone but in shared responsibility
> with colleagues. As the Church is the body of Christ quickened by the Spirit,
> so the ministry must have a *communal* character, so that every member is
> enabled to exercise the gifts which the Spirit gives and so that the whole
> community is, as far as possible, associated in the process of teaching and
> decision making. And as the work of Christ was that of the servant Lord who
> gave his life a ransom for many, so these three characteristics must combine
> in a ministry of service to the world for which Christ died.[43]

While the three elements can be found in the Presbyterian and Congregational traditions at local level in the shape of a pastor surrounded by a group
of elders and/or deacons and the assembly of the church, Newbigin—and the
report—nudged the Reformed traditions toward considering the moderator of
a district or regional council or synod as a "bishop-in-presbytery" in order to
enhance the "personal" dimension at that level—without, of course, making
of the bishop (in Newbigin's words) "the king-pin upon whom the whole
being of the church depends" in such a way that, as has sometimes happened,
"the element of corporate responsibility is marginalized or negated."[44]

I may sum up this chapter and prepare for the next with some late thoughts
of Newbigin on "ministerial leadership for a missionary congregation."[45] It is
the ordained minister's business "to lead the whole congregation as God's
embassage to the whole community." Two striking series of pictures are offered, the first from the film *The Gospel According to St. Matthew* by the Italian
Marxist director Pier Paolo Pasolini:

> It shows Jesus going ahead of his disciples, like a commander leading troops
> into battle. The words he speaks are thrown back over his shoulder to the
> fearful and faltering followers. He is not like a general who sits at headquar-
> ters and sends his troops into battle. He goes at their head and takes the
> brunt of the enemy attack. He enables and encourages them by leading them,
> not just by telling them. In this picture, the words of Jesus have a quite
> different force. They all find their meaning in the central keyword, "Follow
> me."[46]

And then from "the picture of apostolic leadership in the Church" given in
the portrait of St. Peter in the last chapter of the Fourth Gospel:

> Peter is first presented to us as an evangelist. He is a fisherman who, however,
> catches nothing until he submits to the Master's instruction. When he does
> so, there is a mighty catch which he brings, with the net intact and as the
> fruit of his work, to the feet of Jesus. Then the image changes and Peter is a
> pastor to whom Jesus entrusts his flock. He can so entrust it because Peter

loves him more than all. But then, finally, the image changes again. Peter is a disciple who must go the way the Master went, the way of the cross. He is not to look around to see who else is following. He is to look one way only—to the Master who goes before him. Ministerial leadership is, first and finally, discipleship.[47]

5

The Missionary Strategist

> And Jesus came and said to them, "All authority in heaven
> and on earth has been given to me. Go therefore and make
> disciples of all nations, baptizing them in the name of the Fa-
> ther and of the Son and of the Holy Spirit, teaching them to
> observe all that I have commanded you; and lo, I am with you
> always, to the close of the age."
>
> *(Matthew 28:18–20)*

The Foreign Missionary in India

In September 1936 Lesslie Newbigin set sail from Liverpool to India for what
proved to be the last decade of missions under the old regime. A world war
later, in which soldiers from the subcontinent had fought on the side of the
Allies against the Axis, India gained its independence from the British crown,
on August 15, 1947. Six weeks afterward, on September 27, 1947, the
Church of South India was inaugurated as a united and autonomous body
resulting chiefly from the missionary labors of British Anglicans, Presbyterians, Methodists, and Congregationalists—and of the American Board of Commissioners for Foreign Missions—over the previous century and a half.

At his first arrival in Chingleput, Lesslie had been greeted as a sahib and
escorted to the palatial bungalow provided for him and Helen: "It was as
though we had stepped out of the life of the twentieth-century student into
that of an eighteenth-century country gentleman." Even more of a shock was
what they saw of the relations between missionaries and their Indian colleagues: "There seems to be no question of getting alongside them and sharing their troubles and helping them spiritually. We drive up like lords in a
car, soaking everybody else with mud on the way, and then carry on a sort
of inspection, finding all the faults we can, putting everyone through their
paces. . . . One thing is as sure as death: surely they won't stand this sort of
thing from the white man much longer." Although some of what he and his
wife saw of the work of Mission and Church impressed them very much,
Newbigin tells of a fundamental problem in "the unwillingness of missionaries
to entrust full responsibility to the Indian leaders whom they had trained"—
and in "the corresponding irresponsibility on the other side." In the early
1940s, as a "district missionary" based in Kanchipuram, Newbigin learned

to rough it somewhat, at least in the surrounding caste villages and especially in the settlements of the Untouchables that could be reached only by bullock cart or on foot. When young Indian Christians returned from military service, they were found to have developed gifts of leadership, even evangelistic leadership among their peers, and it was clear to Newbigin that "the village congregations and the Church as a whole could never again revert to a position of dependence on the Mission."[1]

In January 1945 Newbigin published a rather revolutionary vision for the future of "the ordained foreign missionary in the Indian Church."[2] Instead of functioning from his residence on the mission compound as primarily an administrator for "a heavily financed and highly centralized organization based on paid agents," the minister from overseas would reassume among local congregations the preaching and pastoral offices for which he was ordained. Following the incarnational principle of identification with those to whom he is sent, he will work "as a member of the Church in India and as its servant," for "comradeship with the Indian Church cannot be complete so long as the missionary cannot accept, along with his Indian fellow-minister, the spiritual authority of the Church which he is himself committed to build up." Receiving spiritual help from mature local Christians and placed in challenging posts suited to his talents, the new young missionary must be ready in humility "rather to take his place as a junior member in an Indian fellowship than to be the leader and pioneer of new enterprises on his own." Only after learning the vernacular of the Church and coming to know the ordinary life of its congregations and its homes will the missionary be properly in a position to contribute to the needed training of other pastors and preachers. Such few missionaries as will temporarily remain in administrative jobs should perform them so as to encourage and help their local colleagues and successors. Full as it is of "fragrant memories of missionaries who were truly fathers in God to multitudes of people," the Indian Church, as it starts to rule itself, will need to accept that the support and strength it continues to expect will have to be given in ways that do not weaken its own independence and sense of responsibility.

By mid-1945 the mission council was persuaded to hand over Newbigin's job to a local colleague, but his own request for appointment to a place usually occupied by an Indian pastor met with refusal. Instead he was "withdrawn upwards into a superior administrative post created for the purpose." At least it allowed him to become familiar with the self-supported but introverted and fractious SIUC congregations of Madras City, where the development of "Church" in relative independence from "Mission" had led to "the complete absence of evangelistic outreach." He would return there in 1965, when "through a larger unity, under episcopal leadership, these quarrelling congregations were to be brought into a real missionary engagement with the life of the city."[3]

It was toward the end of Newbigin's first decade in India that he started to wrestle with, and gradually accept, those ideas of Roland Allen concerning "spontaneous expansion" that have already been seen in chapter 2 to mark his own understanding, practice, and policies of evangelism. They were to influence also his thinking on mission when, without for a moment abandoning his emphasis on the local, Newbigin developed into a missiologist at the global level. This chapter is devoted to showing Newbigin as a theorist and strategist of mission in the time of his direct association with the International Missionary Council and the World Council of Churches and then as a teacher both at the Selly Oak Colleges and beyond.

The International Missionary Council

Originating in 1921 as an outcome of "Edinburgh 1910," the International Missionary Council had by the time of its world missionary conference at Tambaram in 1938 made very clear the global character of the Christian Church. When the IMC convened a world consultation at Whitby, Ontario, in 1947, the extent of what Newbigin called the "spiritual damage" done to "the old Christendom" by the Second World War could not yet be assessed, and "the complete extinction of the colonial pattern was still in the future." The mood at Whitby was one of "renewal and advance," of an "expectant evangelism" in the confidence that the world was eager to hear the Gospel. It was thought on both sides that "the problem of the relation between missionary bodies in the West and the 'younger Churches' which were the fruit of their labour in the East and South" could be settled through a "partnership in obedience" by which each would accept an equal responsibility for cooperation in mission based on its distinctive gifts. The focus remained on the task in the traditional "mission lands"; it was not yet evident that the "younger Churches" should be partners with the older in the (re)evangelization of Europe and North America.[4]

As a young bishop in the new Church of South India, Newbigin attended the inaugural assembly of the World Council of Churches at Amsterdam in 1948, where the accent in the section on the missionary and evangelistic task of the Church fell on responsibility to one's immediate non-Christian neighbor rather than on proclamation "to the ends of the earth." But by the time he took part as an invited speaker in the "enlarged meeting of the committee of the International Missionary Council" at Willingen, Germany, in 1952, it was clear that a profound rethinking of the nature of "the missionary obligation of the Church" was under way. In the changing geopolitical circumstances, "missions" in the old sense and in the plural were perhaps already a thing of the past, while a sense was emerging that the Church's participation in the singular mission of God to the world could occur only "under the Cross" with its judgment and mercy, for—as Norman Goodall put it in editing the volume from the Willingen conference and echoing the contributions of Max Warren and Reinold von Thadden—"the moments at which the whole gathering felt itself most surely under the leading of God and held in the power of His Spirit were those in which the Cross and its 'hiddenness' were the focus of worship and the theme of exposition."[5]

Newbigin's address at Willingen was entitled "The Christian Hope," a theme with which he was also at this time occupied as a chairman and a drafter for the group of twenty-five theologians charged by the central committee of the World Council of Churches to prepare a text for the forthcoming second assembly of the WCC.[6] Both personal and corporate in range, the Christian hope for God's Kingdom—which is itself both historical and transcendent in scope—is sure because it is anchored, said Newbigin on the basis of 1 Peter 1:3–5, in the resurrection of Christ, the hidden victory of crucified love, and is sustained by the gift of the Holy Spirit in whose power the works of God are done in anticipation of the final consummation of the new creation. Because Christ "is the new Adam, because He is the maker of all and the lover of all, this Gospel is to be preached to all nations and to every creature. Witness is to be borne to all. All are to be reconciled." The Kingdom of God is not ours to build, but "all our labour and all our witness" are committed to the Savior as a "visible prayer for the hastening of the coming of His Kingdom."

Newbigin's chief contribution to the Willingen meeting, however, characteristically came in his drafting of common texts. It was a difficult task, because the conference was not ready to adopt the line forcefully propounded in the theological group by the Dutchman Hans Hoekendijk and the American Paul Lehmann—an attempt, as Newbigin put it later, to "swing missionary thinking away from the 'church-centred' model which had dominated it since Tambaram and to speak more of God's work in the secular world, in the political, cultural and scientific movements of the time."[7] Newbigin was called on to rework the group's report and produced a "Statement on the Missionary Calling of the Church" that was then adopted "with some enthusiasm" by the whole meeting.[8] It bears a fivefold structure.

First, under the heading of "the missionary situation and the rule of God," the challenge of "other faiths of revolutionary power in the full tide of victory" is noted (Soviet and Chinese Communism are not named) and confession is penitently made of "our share of responsibility for the terrible events of our time"; yet "we preach not ourselves but Christ crucified," which is "to human seeming a message of death, but to those who know its secret, the very power of God." With "the battle set between God's hidden Kingdom and those evil spiritual forces which lure men on towards false hopes, or bind them down to apathy, indifference and despair," there is "no room for neutrality in the conflict."

Second, in grounding "the missionary obligation of the Church," Newbigin introduced in all but name a notion that was to make its fortune in the next two decades, namely that of the *missio Dei*, whereby the origin of mission was traced to the Father's "sending" of the Son and the Spirit into the world for its redemption, moves that were rooted in the very being of the Triune God. "The missionary movement of which we are a part," Newbigin's text reads, "has its source in the Triune God Himself. Out of the depths of His love for us, the Father has sent forth His own beloved Son to reconcile all things to Himself, that we and all men might, through the Spirit, be made one in Him with the Father in that perfect love which is the very nature of God." The duty and the authority of the Church to bear witness everywhere rest on a series of facts confessed in the historic Christian *regula fidei*:

> i. God has created all things and all men, that in them the glory of His love might be reflected; nothing therefore is excluded from the reach of His redeeming love.
>
> ii. All men are involved in a common alienation from God, from which none can escape by his own efforts.
>
> iii. God has sent forth one Saviour, one Shepherd to seek and save all the lost, one Redeemer who by His death, resurrection and ascension has broken down the barrier between man and God, accomplished a full and perfect atonement, and created in Himself one new humanity, the Body of which Christ is the exalted and regnant Head.
>
> iv. On the foundation of this accomplished work God has sent forth His Spirit, the Spirit of Jesus, to gather us together in one Body in Him, to guide us into all truth, to enable us to worship the Father in spirit and in truth, to empower us for the continuance of His mission as His witnesses and ambassadors, the first-fruits and earnest of its completion.
>
> v. By the Spirit we are enabled both to press forward as ambassadors of Christ, beseeching all men to be reconciled to God, and also to wait with sure confidence for the final victory of His love, of which He has given us most sure promises.[9]

After that comprehensive confession of faith, the essential and obligatory participation of the Church and of Christians in the "mission of God" is given strong and explicit expression: "We who have been chosen in Christ, reconciled to God through Him, made members of His Body, sharers in His Spirit, and heirs through hope of His Kingdom, are by these very facts committed to full participation in His mission to the world. That by which the Church receives its existence is that by which it is also given its world-mission. 'As the Father hath sent Me, even so send I you.'"[10]

Third, "the total missionary task" is then spelled out. The Church is sent by God "to the ends of the earth" ("No place is too far or too near. Every group of Christians is sent as God's ambassadors to the people in its immediate neighbourhood . . . [and] is also responsible for the proclamation of His kingship to the uttermost parts of the earth"), "to all nations" ("to every social, political and religious community of mankind," including "those who deny or rebel against the reign of Christ"), and "to the end of time" ("in every moment and every situation," seeking out "opportunities for advancing the mission of the Church," and interpreting the catastrophes which destroy that mission as "judgments of God which are the other side of His mercy"). The boundaries that the Church's mission transcends "can no longer be identified with national frontiers, and certainly not with any supposed line between the 'Christian West' and the 'non-Christian East'"; the mission involves "both geographical extension and also intensive penetration of all spheres of life."

Any Christian may be called to missionary service anywhere in the world and must at that time be ready to "leave land and kindred and go."

Fourth, the Church's "solidarity with the world" is presented as living incarnationally in identification with the world, "not only in its perplexity and distress, its guilt and its sorrow, but also in its real acts of love and justice— acts by which it often puts the churches to shame." Wherever a church "divorces its deeds from its words, it destroys the possibility of communicating the Gospel and presents to the world an offence which is not the genuine offence of the Cross."

The fifth section—on "discerning the signs of the times"—replaces some of the brasher claims of the rejected version concerning "the revolutionary movements of our time" with a more modest account of the ability of "the eyes of faith" to perceive "the sovereign rule of Him who is Saviour and Judge of all men . . . in the great events of our day, in the vast enlargements of human knowledge and power which this age is witnessing, in the mighty political and social movements of our time, and in countless personal experiences of which the inner history cannot be revealed until the Last Day."

In sum, Newbigin, although somewhat perplexed by his colleagues Hoekendijk and Lehmann, was like them predisposed by his Reformed faith to affirm the present sovereignty of Christ over and in "the world"; and in the 1960s he would for a time share to some extent the enthusiasm of another Dutchman, Arendt van Leeuwen, for "the secular."[11] Moreover, Newbigin was ready on occasion to quote the then-famous dictum of Emil Brunner that "the Church exists by mission as a fire exists by burning";[12] and he consistently advocated the intrinsic relation between ecclesial body and missionary society that called for and grounded the eventual integration of the World Council of Churches and the International Missionary Council. Yet Newbigin would never relinquish the position from which, in *The Household of God* (1953), he criticized Hoekendijk for "overstressing the truth [concerning "the fundamentally missionary nature of the Church"] to the point of defining the Church solely in terms of its missionary function." Newbigin holds fast to the ecclesially essential character of worship and fellowship even while the Church is still *in via*: "Worship and fellowship, offering up praise and adoration to God, receiving His grace, rejoicing in Him, sharing with one another the fruits of the Spirit, and building up one another in love are all essential to the life of the Church." Precisely because the Church is the "first-fruits" of the Kingdom, it can be a "sign" pointing beyond itself to that Kingdom and an "instrument" in God's hands toward its realization. The Church "is both a means and an end, because it is a foretaste." Practically, mission must "spring from and lead back into a quality of life which seems intrinsically worth having in itself. If we answer the question, 'Why should I become a Christian?' simply by saying 'In order to make others Christians,' we are involved in an infinite regress. The question, 'To what end?', cannot be simply postponed to the *eschaton*."[13]

If "an unchurchly mission is as much a monstrosity as an unmissionary Church," then the question of ecclesial unity is unavoidable, for "the means by which the good news of salvation is propagated must be congruous with the nature of the salvation itself," so that the Church's task of reconciling people to God in Christ can only be accomplished "in so far as she is herself living in Christ, a reconciled fellowship in Him, bound together in the love of the Father."[14] Therewith we return to the connection between mission and unity that has characterized the modern ecumenical movement from its beginnings—and to Newbigin's third contribution to the Willingen meeting of 1952. On behalf of the central committee of the World Council of Churches at Rolle in 1951 and in fraught circumstances (for there were strong disagreements over "the visible forms in which [ecclesial] unity is to be expressed" and over "the manner" of Christ's awaited "final victory" and "its relation to what we may rightly hope for within history"), Newbigin had already drafted a report on "The Calling of the Church to Mission and Unity"; and now he was able to secure at Willingen the adoption of a statement under virtually the same title that contained the theological gist of the earlier one. This conjunction, he reported, helped to create the climate for the later integration of the IMC and the WCC.[15]

The Rolle text had enunciated the principle that "because the Gospel is one and the world is one," unity should be a mark of the Church as both the bearer and the fruit of the message. The word "ecumenical" properly describes "everything that relates to the whole task of the whole Church to bring the Gospel to the whole world." Historically and theologically, the missionary movement and the movement toward unity are "interdependent"; the "obligation to take the Gospel to the whole world" and "the obligation to draw all Christ's people together" are "indissolubly connected" because they rest on Christ and his work, "in whom the Church has its being and its task," for those whom Christ makes members of his Body become "members one of another and [are] committed thereby to partnership in His redeeming mission." To the extent that they had acquired different constituencies, the World Council of Churches and the International Missionary Council needed, the Rolle text argued, to have their enthusiasms brought together. On the one hand, introverted churches needed to realize "the essentially dynamic and missionary character of the Church": "As we see how many churches in our own day are being stripped of many things which have been regarded as necessary—such as buildings, funds, institutions, and privileged positions— we are led to believe that God is in this way forcing His Church to come out into the open and to commit itself afresh in a dynamic encounter with the world." On the other hand, the time had come for the modern missionary movement, which had despite its imperfections been such a "mighty work of God's Spirit," to seek remedy for defects transmitted to its offspring in the shape of "division of the Christian witness among non-Christian peoples," "confusion of the unchanging Gospel with the particular cultural, economic and institutional forms of the older Churches," and continuing financial dependency that served "to prop up relatively static younger Churches rather than to make new advances for the Gospel." The much less discursive Willingen text includes the following apodictic paragraph:

The love of God in Christ calls for the threefold response of worship, unity and mission. These three aspects of the church's response are interdependent; they become corrupted when isolated from each other. Division in the Church distorts its witness, frustrates its mission, and contradicts its own nature. If the Church is to demonstrate the Gospel in its life as well as in its preaching, it must manifest to the world the power of God to break down all barriers and to establish the Church's unity in Christ. *Christ is not divided.*

At the Evanston assembly of the World Council of Churches in 1954, Newbigin was elected to the central committee of the WCC, and he became one of the WCC representatives on the joint committee of the WCC and the International Missionary Council. At its Herrenhalb, south Germany, meeting in 1956 the joint committee proposed that the parent bodies should consider integration. Newbigin presented the case to the WCC central committee at New Haven, Connecticut, in 1957, where he had both to counter the deep suspicions of the Orthodox ("for whom 'mission' meant destructive proselytising by irresponsible Protestant sects") and to defuse some of the tensions between "the younger people who were revolting against the 'colonial' style of missions and the older ones for whom they were sacred." In 1958 Newbigin became chairman, and in 1959 general secretary, of the International Missionary Council and hence leader of the IMC team on the joint committee with the WCC. "But from whichever side I had to speak," he reports, "I was convinced that integration was necessary."[16]

Newbigin's key writing in this connection was *One Body, One Gospel, One World: The Christian Mission Today.*[17] Prepared for, and then revised after, a three-day consultation held at Oxford in September 1958 between leaders from the mission boards and from the "younger Churches," the text represented Newbigin's own views rather than being an official statement of the International Missionary Council; but it was widely circulated in several languages and became "a rallying point for discussion about the proposed integration."[18]

This short book of fifty or so pages began with Newbigin's analysis of "the present situation of Christian missions." In a world in which Christianity had not penetrated to any significant extent into the ancient religious cultures of Asia, in which Islam remained "as completely resistant to the Gospel as ever," and in which global Communism faced the Christian mission with "an aggressive opposition undreamed of fifty years ago," the missionary movement had undeniably suffered a "loss of momentum." Internally, many Western Christians had concluded that the spread of the faith would best be left entirely to indigenous churches and that any useful "service abroad" would take the form of a "fraternal worker" in some other capacity than that of an evangelist. The crisis was not to be met, however, by a reversion to the methods and mood of the nineteenth century. John R. Mott's vision of "the evangelization of the world in this generation" had been rendered inept by geopolitical developments. In a world "divided into colossal antagonistic power-blocks and always trembling on the brink of an all-annihilating war," a more appropriate vision might be crystallized as "the whole Church with one Gospel of reconciliation for the whole world." If "the Christian world mission holds the secret that can make mankind one family," its appeal will become attractive to a new generation only on condition that "the form and structure both of our churches and of our missionary operations" are made to conform to the pattern of "one fellowship, one Gospel, one world." For that to happen, "the deep dichotomy between the sending and the receiving end of 'missions'"—which has resulted from the "infection" of even the noblest service by the "cultural and economic domination" characteristic of "colonialism"—must be healed, and churches and Christians everywhere must learn again that "the Church *is* a mission."

The first step is a return to the Bible, "to the fundamentals of the Gospel, in order to lay hold afresh upon the real sources of the Christian mission"— "to God's revelation of Himself, to learn afresh, by the guiding of the Spirit, what is our duty for today." The "unchanging basis" is found in the notion of mission as the Church's "continuation of the work of Christ through the Holy Spirit" (Luke 4:18f.; John 20:21f.; Acts 1:8). The Church is "the place where the fruit of Christ's mission is already present in foretaste and as an earnest of that which is to come." It is from the Church's "common life" (*koinônia*) in the Holy Spirit that "both service and evangelism spring," the new reality of the Holy Spirit's active presence being "the primary witness, anterior to all specific acts whether of service or of preaching." Thus "the whole life of the Church has a missionary *dimension*, though not all of it has mission as its primary *intention*." Notably, "the Church's worship, the perpetual liturgy in which she is joined to the worship of the heavenly hosts, is directed wholly to God for His glory; and yet it has a missionary dimension, and may in certain circumstances (as for instance in the Church of Russia today) be in fact the most powerful possible form of witness." The Spirit's manifold gifts equip the Church for many ministries in the world, and, binding them together by the preeminent gift of love, the Spirit "wills to carry on His mission through the cooperation of all in one harmonious unity" for witness to Christ as Lord. The "fellowship created by the Holy Spirit is both local and universal," and "the place where the Christian is directed to meet his Lord is in his neighbour," both near and far. In reaching to the ends of the earth, the mission prepares for the end of the world, when the end of man and of creation will be fully revealed. From these scripturally based theological convictions Newbigin then drew seven "principles for action today," which should not imply "passing judgement on the obedience which our fathers rendered in their day" but only the assumption of "our own responsibility for obedience in the different circumstances of ours."

First, "the Church is the Mission": there should be no separation between Church and Mission either at the sending or at the receiving end; if, in the old Protestant world, "missionary societies" were at first needed because of blindness to "the missionary implications of churchmanship," the "obedience of the missionary pioneers has now awakened many churches" to the universal commission of Matthew 28:18–20; and, in the areas of reception, the proper fruit of mission is immediate churchmanship among the converts and the assumption in turn of the ecclesial obligation to mission.

Second, "the home base is everywhere": what makes a missionary is "the crossing of the frontier between faith in Christ as Lord and unbelief"; although there is likely thus "a missionary task on every man's doorstep," the involvement of all Christians in some appropriate and proportionate way in the crossing of geographical frontiers does not become redundant, for it testifies to the universal scope of the mission, to the fact that the Gospel always comes "from outside," and to "the true foreign-ness of the Church" as "a colony of heaven" (though not, as it has often appeared, "a colony of some white race").[19]

Third, "mission in partnership": although there is a "fundamental equality of standing between older and younger churches" as instantiations of the Body of Christ, the younger churches will in many situations continue to need help and advice as they assume their adult responsibilities for mission in what may be in their area "a huge unfinished evangelistic task"; if a debilitating sense of dependency on the older churches is to be avoided, there needs to be common planning of programs, an opportunity for younger churches to find fellowship among themselves as "sister churches in the adjacent parts of the world," a willingness on the part of the younger churches also to undertake "foreign missionary work" (for "this would give them a sympathetic insight into the problems with which mission boards in the older churches have been wrestling for many decades"), and a psychological and spiritual readiness on the part of the older churches to "welcome in their midst missionary activity" from the younger churches and thus receive the "riches" which are "the special possession" of the latter.

Fourth, "mission and inter-church aid": here would arise in any integration between the World Council of Churches and the International Missionary Council an organizational question that demanded theological clarity concerning "the relation between these two forms of Christian action." As Newbigin saw it:

> Missions, beginning with the simple obligation to make Christ known to the non-Christian nations, have been led to a point where they can conceive of their task only as the task of the whole Church to make the Gospel known to the whole world by a witness which includes both word and deed. Inter-church aid, beginning with the needs of stricken churches in Europe [during and after the Second World War], has been led to a point where it defines its task as nothing less than the strengthening and renewal of all church life in all continents and a ministry to human need throughout the world. How are these two activities, so different in their origins, traditions, and methods, and yet so largely overlapping in their aims and spheres of operation, to be related to one another within the total life of the Church, and of an integrated council of churches?[20]

The dividing line could no longer be geographical, as between Europe and "the under-developed countries," nor could it fall between "evangelism" and "service," for those were united in Christ's own ministry and belong together within the total witnessing life of his Church. Seeing that "our supreme concern at this hour must be for a fresh missionary advance," Newbigin argued that an integrated council would need "a point of concentration for the missionary *intention*" that marks those activities which directly seek to bring people from unbelief to faith and safeguards against the loss of "the missionary *dimension* which is proper to the whole life of the Church"—even in those activities that are best described as compassionate service.[21] Theological differences—which did not always fall between people associated with "mission and evangelism" and those associated with "inter-church aid"—meant that working relationships would remain strained after the integration of the IMC and the WCC: "The dilemma with which I constantly wrestled," says Newbigin, looking back on his time at the integrated Council, "was how to achieve a permeation of all the activities of the Council with a missionary concern, and at the same time to preserve and sharpen a specific concern for missions as enterprises explicitly intended to cross the frontier between faith and no-faith."[22]

Fifth, "the role of the missionary": here Newbigin points to the unconscious irony of the phrase "mission station" and invokes the principles of Roland Allen in favor of the missionary as a pioneer who moves quickly on after equipping his converts for evangelism. There is still a place, writes Newbigin in 1958 in *One Body, One Gospel, One World*, for "the foreign missionary," though his vocation must be worked out in cooperation with the Church on the spot (the example is given of "several young missionaries who have been able to convince the church of their vocation to pioneer service over the frontiers of the church's life, and who are now engaged in fresh missionary advance along lines for which no Indian worker was ready, and yet in perfect loyalty to and fellowship with the Indian Church"). Admitting that some tasks allow for short-term service and yet wishing to preserve the value to the whole Church of vocations to "life-long and total commitment," Newbigin floats the idea of an "ecumenical *order* of men and women committed to life service as missionaries and available for service (for longer or shorter periods) wherever they may be most needed"; after the model of some religious orders in Catholicism, one might envisage also, for Christians working abroad in government or industry and ready to make "voluntary and informal witness" alongside the organized missionary activity of the Church, a "loosely knit 'third order' which would give to such 'non-professional missionaries' a real spiritual unity with those who were committed to life-long service at the disposal of the Church." The slow progress of official ecumenism, coupled perhaps with the change of mentality that affected many young Christians in the secular '60s, allowed that suggestion to run into the sand; but it may be that, in changed circumstances, its time is still to come.

Sixth, "cooperation in mission—local, regional, global": Newbigin rejects for the Church the organizational model of "headquarters" and "branches." The proper concern is that "the Church should be—universally and locally—recognizable as one reconciled fellowship offering to all men everywhere the secret of reconciliation to God through Jesus Christ." Thinking and action best begin locally and regionally. Consultation and cooperation in mission should be furthered by conciliar structures at those geographical levels in order to lessen the risks of centralization that attend the global structure that is nevertheless necessary if the universal unity of the Church is to be made manifest.

Seventh, "cooperation is not enough": "The unity that Christ wills for us is something more than cooperation. It is a unity of being—the new being of the new man in Christ." That is the ontological basis for the rhetorical question which Newbigin puts yet again: "How can we, unreconciled to one another, proclaim one reconciliation to the world?" The historically divisive questions of faith and order need urgent treatment: "It is a matter of seeking together penitently and patiently such a common understanding of our common salvation, that men in every land may hear the authentic voice of the Good Shepherd, undistorted by our racial and national and denominational egotisms." Not "more and more elaborate forms of merely administrative and organizational unity" are needed but "the true unity of life in one fellowship centred in the Word and Sacraments of the Gospel." And so Newbigin concludes with a statement that anticipates the description of "the unity we seek" that he would draft for the New Delhi assembly of the World Council of Churches: "For myself, I do not believe that we can be content with anything less than a form of unity which enables all who confess Christ as Lord to be recognizably one family in each place and in all places, united in the visible bonds of word, sacrament, ministry and congregational fellowship, and in the invisible bond which the Spirit Himself creates through these means, one family offering to all men everywhere the secret of reconciliation with God the Father."[23]

World Mission and Evangelism

On Sunday, November 19, 1961, at the opening sessions of the New Delhi Assembly, the integration of the International Missionary Council with the World Council of Churches was sealed,[24] and Lesslie Newbigin was consequently transmuted from general secretary of the IMC to director of the new Division of World Mission and Evangelism in the WCC. In Geneva, as elsewhere, there was taking place a swift shift of mood and even of substance. Newbigin later recollected:

> The kind of Christian statements which were accepted in the 1950s and which arose out of the understanding of the Gospel to which I had come were no longer accepted. We were into the decade of the secular. The world, not the Church, was the place where God was at work. It was far more important to get people involved in action for justice and development than to have them converted, baptized and brought into the Church. The world of the secular was not only the most important object of attention: it was perhaps the only world there is.[25]

Newbigin's own brief and mild flirtation with the secular temptation at the ideological level is recounted in chapter 10, in which he figures as "the Christian apologist"; and his vigorous engagement with the everyday needs of humankind, more programmatic perhaps from his time as bishop in Madras (1965–74), is described in chapter 7, in which he appears as a social critic and builder. Meanwhile, Newbigin's uphill struggle during his four years on the staff of the WCC is reflected in a jotting of the six "convictions" he listed for himself during a "retreat" on August 9, 1962:

1. That it matters supremely to bring more people to know Jesus as Saviour.
2. That our responsibility in the political order arises out of the love command.
3. That it does not arise out of the expectation of being able to anticipate the establishment of any particular social or political order.
4. That the New Testament teaches us (a) not to expect success in our cause; (b) to expect the sharpening of the issues and the coming of antichrist; (c) that there is no hope apart from Christ.
5. That "Rapid Social Change" thinking has not developed any coherent theology and is in danger of identifying the movement of revolution with the work of redemption.
6. That in so far as it distinguishes these two things, it fails to show a clear understanding of the sense in which being in Christ is different from and transcends involvement in "Rapid Social Change."[26]

Newbigin saw the principal task of his division as the provision of "a focus of concern for evangelism among all the multifarious and fruitful operations in which the WCC was involved all over the world." But the incomprehension of many of his WCC colleagues when he spoke of "the unfinished evangelistic task" indicated that there was bound to be controversy around the theme of "Witness in Six Continents" for the first world conference sponsored by the new division in Mexico City in late 1963.[27]

The title "Witness in Six Continents" was a way of recognizing what Newbigin the missiologist had been arguing at least since the Willingen meeting a dozen years earlier, namely that the "home base" of the Church's mission is worldwide and the "mission field" likewise. (Already himself "at home" in both Western Europe and Southern Asia, and having started to gain familiarity with North America in the course of several visits in the '50s, Newbigin had undertaken as general secretary of the International Missionary Council major tours of Africa in 1960 and of the Pacific and Latin America in 1961; and as editor of *The International Review of Missions* he would compile extensive surveys of missionary developments during the years 1962–64.)[28] But the questions of the "mood" and, more important yet, the "substance" of the witness to be made in six continents would not necessarily be answered at Mexico City in ways that entirely suited the director of the Division of World Mission and Evangelism.[29] What perhaps pleased Newbigin most at the Mexico City conference was the "magnificent restatement of the call to missions" issued by W. A. Visser 't Hooft, general secretary of the WCC, under the cry "Missions as the Test of Faith."[30] In his own account of the conference a few years later, Newbigin used a title that retrospectively sharpened the specifically missionary focus: "Mexico and Mission to Six Continents."[31]

The first of the four sections at Mexico City dealt with "the witness of Christians to men of other faiths." Since 1956 a joint study between the WCC and the IMC had been in process through regional centers on "The Word of God and the Living Faiths of Men"; but Newbigin considered that the section at Mexico "failed to achieve any significant fresh insights," a fact which he attributed in part to "the profound crisis of faith in the Western churches." Much more will be said on the topic of the Gospel and the world religions in the next chapter, in which Newbigin figures as religious interlocutor.

The second and third sections at Mexico treated "the witness of Christians to men in the secular world" and "the witness of the congregation in its neighbourhood." In their respective ways, the discussions in each of these areas made clearer than ever before that the "mission field" included, with their specific problems, Europe and North America just as truly as it stretched over the other continents. Concerning secularity, North Atlantic theologians and Asian theologians, whether in Boston or in Tokyo, were pushing—albeit from different starting points and with somewhat different aims—for the recognition that "God is somehow at work in the secular events of our time, beyond the bounds of the Church." Concerning witness to the neighborhood, a study set in motion by the New Delhi assembly was examining "The Missionary Structure of the Congregation." Given his stress on the local church and his advocacy of the missionary methods of Roland Allen (and of St. Paul, as Allen interpreted the apostle), Newbigin naturally saw promise in this study, but he later considered it to have been waylaid by the spirit of the times. He had

> hoped that integration [between the IMC and the WCC] might provide the opportunity to bring into the thinking of ordinary church people new models of ministry and congregational life directed more to mission than to mere maintenance. The study programme on "The Missionary Structure of the Congregation" was intended (at least in my mind) to stimulate new thinking among the older churches about mission and ministry as essentially charismatic realities—gifts of the sovereign Spirit. But other spirits were abroad. The *zeitgeist* was too strong. The study process was carried into the powerful currents of the "secular" decade, and for many people the only fruit of its labour which is remembered is the slogan "The world provides the agenda," a phrase which pointed to an important truth but could be, and was, very easily misunderstood . . . and help[ed] to persuade many Christians that both Church and ministry were irrelevancies.[32]

The fourth section at Mexico City considered "the witness of the Christian Church across national and confessional boundaries." The international and ecumenical dimensions of mission were favorite causes of Newbigin's, and he welcomed the expressed willingness for speedier "joint action both on a world scale and in local situations," the tokens of which were to be the provision of funding for the ministry of healing and for Christian literature (by analogy with the existing Theological Education Fund).

Newbigin would declare, concerning the Mexico City conference of 1963, that "underlying all the wrestling there was a profound sense of confidence in the sufficiency of God and the finality of the Gospel."[33] Yet when he came to write, for the second volume of the *History of the Ecumenical Movement*, a chapter entitled "Mission to Six Continents," he would begin with the stark sentence that the two decades from 1948 to 1968 "were a period in which the foreign missionary movement of the non-Roman Catholic Churches faced the most profound crisis of its history" and end with the blunt recognition of the internal "crisis of faith in the Church," on whose "outcome will depend the possibility of faithful proclamation": "The course of the next stage in the world-wide mission of the Church will depend upon the recovery by the Church of clarity regarding the gospel which it has to proclaim."[34] At this midpoint in the presentation of Newbigin as missiologist, his description of these crises needs to be outlined before attention can pass to the theological remedies and practical policies he came to propose in the last three decades of his life. Allowing for some mutations in the critical factors meanwhile and for the further effects they have wrought, Newbigin's diagnoses retain a claim to accuracy even today, and his evangelical prescriptions could still prove beneficial to wider areas of the Church.

Newbigin named six factors that made for crisis in mission in the period 1948–68, four of them more external to the Church and two of them more internal. The first was "the dismantling of the colonial empires." Although it is far too simple to view missions as "the spiritual and cultural aspect of western colonialism," it is a fact that for a century and a half "the colonial systems of the western powers provided for the most part the political and cultural framework within which missions operated in most parts of what is now called the 'third world'"; and the rapid removal of the framework "could not fail to shake profoundly the whole missionary movement, even though the discerning missionary leaders had been for many years advocating and preparing for the liberation of the dependent peoples, and even though the work of missions was itself one of the most powerful forces preparing for that liberation." The second factor was "the end of missions in China" as a result of the Communist revolution. In that connection, perhaps the most searching questions arose from the fact that the Communist government had been able to "accomplish many of the reforms for which missions were the early advocates but which they were not strong enough to complete"; and, more generally, questions were thus raised regarding "the relation of the Christian world mission to the whole world-wide process of secularization, and to the exercise of political power." The third factor was "the growth of a sense of global human interdependence." While countervailing separatist movements were already leading to "the break-up of nations or to acute conflicts within them," the emergence of a "global village" or "world parish" was removing some of the frontiers whose crossing had been a vital part of the Christian mission. The fourth factor was a concept of "development" that had emerged whereby the Western powers sought to expand a kind of "welfare state" as far as the poorer and hitherto exploited lands, and "many former supporters of missions began to feel that 'development aid' was the modern equivalent for the missionary activities of the past."

The two more internally generated factors were "the growth of the ecumenical movement" and "the crisis of faith in the West." Certainly, "a profound reexamination of the nature of the missionary movement" was necessitated by a new self-awareness on the part of the "younger Churches" as equal members of the World Council of Churches, developing regional links among themselves and international relations with other bodies than their parent missions and assuming responsibility for the propagation of the Gospel in their own lands and elsewhere. Those ecumenical moves should sooner or later benefit the Church and its missionary tasks. An altogether different kettle of fish, however, is the "profound crisis of faith within the Western Churches [which] has led to a loss of conviction that there is anything in the Christian faith which is so vital that without it men will perish." Newbigin points to a "long-term questioning of the very foundations of faith" that has been endemic to "Protestantism ever since the eighteenth century." The "dissolution of Christendom" was well under way by the middle of the twentieth century; and fifty years later—and not only in the lands of the Reformation—the question of what Newbigin was calling "the meeting of the Gospel with the anti-traditional secularized societies of the West" has become increasingly acute. During the last twenty-five or thirty years of his life Newbigin devoted his remarkably resilient energies largely to seeking an answer to that question.

The Open Secret

The dogmatic frame of Newbigin's missiological thinking in his final phase was set by the doctrine of the Trinity that had helped to shape his ecclesiology in *The Household of God*. A trinitarian missiology was inchoately implied already in the Willingen notion of the Church's mission as participation in God's mission to the world through the Son and the Spirit. By the time of New Delhi, Newbigin recognized the growing necessity of "a Trinitarian, rather than a purely christological understanding of the missionary task," such as had dominated *One Body, One Gospel, One World*: "Only a fully Trinitarian doctrine would be adequate, setting the work of Christ in the Church in the context of the over-ruling providence of the Father in all the life of the world and the sovereign freedom of the Spirit who is the Lord and not the auxiliary of the Church."[35] Starting from the draft in his awkwardly titled pamphlet of 1963, *The Relevance of Trinitarian Doctrine for Today's Mission*,[36] the bishop used the years of his teaching at the Selly Oak Colleges in Birmingham to develop what were in his own eyes still only the "sketches for a missionary theology"; published as *The Open Secret* in 1978, they became, by the (lightly) revised edition of 1995, "an introduction to the theology of mission." Taken as a whole, this work that was more than thirty years in the making may in fact represent Newbigin's most comprehensive and systematic literary contribution to Christian theology, stretching as it does over all the dogmatic topoi in its reflection on the engagement of the Gospel with the contemporary world.[37]

The trinitarian brochure of 1963 began with "today's mission" and the "hesitancy," the "perplexity," in which the churches—insofar as they had been persuaded that the Church is "not so much an institution as an expedition sent to the ends of the earth in Christ's name," an "embassage of the whole people of God to the whole world"—now practically found themselves at this juncture in human history. Newbigin detected three situational factors in what he stopped just short of calling the "crisis" of mission. First, the expansion of Christianity in Asia and Africa that had marked "the great century" of missions—and which had implied for some a view of the "Christianization of the world" in substantial continuity with the general course of human progress—was now largely arrested, notably by the loss of China, and many formerly Christian lands in Eastern Europe had also come under the control of Communist governments hostile to the faith. Second, more and more realms of life were being taken over by secular systems of thought and organization so as to shrink the area in which the Christian faith was recognized to hold authority. Third, Christian missions were stagnating in face of the apparent imperviousness of the old religions of Southern Asia and the Islamic territories. Theologically, the "uniqueness, sufficiency and finality of Jesus Christ as the one Lord and Saviour of the world" was being called into question—not only outside the Church but within—as people became increasingly aware of the fact of religious pluralism (and even Christians worried about the potential divisiveness of their exclusive claims for Christ in a world needing unity) and as the dynamic movements of national liberation, scientific discovery, cultural renaissance, and religious revival beyond Christianity compelled Christians to examine the relation between what God had done in Christ and what God was doing in the life of humankind as a whole. Newbigin set the historical situation and the christological question in eschatological perspective. By New Testament teaching, Christians

are called upon to recognize the signs of the times—that is to say the signs of the last days which follow the coming of Jesus and point to his coming again. In the light of what Jesus has done they will understand that war, tumult, persecution and suffering, the appearing of false messiahs and the manifesting of the antichrist with all his deceitful powers, are not evidence of defeat for the Christian cause, but are among the things which "must come to pass." . . . The coming of the Messiah precipitates the crisis of human history. In him God presents every man, and the whole of mankind, with the possibility of receiving or rejecting the end for which he created all things. The whole of human history, after the coming of Christ until his coming again, is the pressing of this choice to the final issue. And the Church is the body which understands this, which is called to bear witness among the nations to the real meaning of the events amid which we live, and thereby present to all men and nations the concrete alternatives of acceptance or rejection.[38]

The resources for the Church's missionary understanding and practice today were to be found in a binding of itself afresh to the strong Name of the Trinity.

Though without attributing a formal authority to the patristic teachers and councils except as they drew out the implications of Scripture, Newbigin found a historical precedent and a substantive norm in the early Church's articulation of a fully trinitarian doctrine of the God it proclaimed in the Gospel amid the struggle with the pagan world:

> The Church had to articulate the Christian message of God's Kingdom in a world which interpreted human life mainly in terms of the interaction of "virtue" and "fortune." Put in terms more relevant to our day, human life was interpreted as the interaction of man's intelligence, skill and courage with the forces of his environment. It is significant that the Church found itself driven to articulate the Christian message in this situation in terms of trinitarian doctrine, and that, during the period in which the intellectual struggle took place to state the Gospel in terms of Graeco-Roman culture without thereby compromising its central affirmation, it was the doctrine of the Trinity which was the key to the whole theological debate. It was in terms of this doctrine that Christians were able to state both the unity and the distinctness of God's work in the forces of man's environment and God's work of regeneration within the soul of man. The vehemence of the doctrinal struggles which centred on the formulation of the trinitarian doctrine, and especially on the question of the relation of the Son to the Father, is evidence of the centrality of this issue for the whole Christian witness to the pagan world of that time.[39]

Although the doctrine could be more or less taken for granted during the centuries of Christendom, its importance leaps to sight, Newbigin attested, when the Gospel is brought to non-Christians. Newbigin here drew on his experience of evangelism in Indian villages. When the name of Jesus is preached, it must not be as still another god among many, nor yet, however, as the name of the one God who is vaguely sensed behind all the gods as creator and judge. Rather, "one cannot preach Jesus even in the simplest terms without preaching him as the Son. His revelation of God is the revelation of 'an only begotten from the Father,' and you cannot preach him without speaking of the Father and the Son."[40] Moreover, as the evangelist, and retrospectively his converts, discover ways in which the hearers have been prepared to receive the Gospel, they will recognize these things as the prevenient work of the same Spirit who made the preaching his instrument and continues to work in those he has enabled to believe. On these bases, Newbigin's proposal was to acknowledge the necessity of a trinitarian starting point for a fresh articulation of the missionary task in the "pluralistic, polytheistic, pagan society of our time."

Newbigin proceeded by devoting a chapter to each of the three situational factors that figured in the current predicament of the Christian mission. In

"Missions and the Shape of World History," the focus falls on God the Father's creating and consummating purpose. In "Missions and the Secularization of Human Life," the clue is provided by the incarnate Son. In "The Pattern of Missionary Advance," the energy is supplied by the Holy Spirit. In all three chapters the full range of God's trinitarian reality and work is kept in sight.

In relating mission to the shape of world history, Newbigin noted that God's fatherly care, sustenance, and rule of all things was at the heart of Jesus's teaching and that, as the Son, Jesus had submitted himself wholly to the Father's ordering of events. To that ordering belonged the coming of the Son as "the event by which the Father has chosen to bring all things to the point of decision, to the issue of judgment and salvation." That event was extended in the mission of the apostles who were "sent into the world not as the agents of the Father's rule, but as the witnesses of it." It is the Spirit who, through the speech, actions, and suffering of the followers of Christ, bears witness to "the real meaning of the things which happen in the world, so that—*in relation to these things*—men are compelled to make decisions for or against God." Newbigin notes that "the most sustained and explicit New Testament statements of the relation between the mission of the Church and the events of world history are to be found in the apocalyptic sections of the first three Gospels and in the discourses at the end of the fourth Gospel." Christ's coming means judgment, separation, polarization; and these texts "project this process of polarization prophetically through history," extending it through time by the witness of the Church. The process has now reached universal dimensions as, thanks to the spread of the Christian message, a linear conception of time has displaced cyclical notions and provoked "belief in the possibility of a corporate salvation for mankind as the goal to which human affairs move." Secularized forms of the biblical hope of God's Kingdom take shape as messianic movements, which may bring good gifts, "yet in so far as they claim to offer total welfare to men, and claim therefore men's total allegiance, they become bearers of evil ultimately more fearful than those from which they liberated men": "The coming of the true Messiah leads to the appearing of the false ones. . . . The offer of God's salvation precipitates the offers of salvation on other terms than God's." The nations are confronted ever more sharply with the choice between "the true purpose of the Father to sum up all things in him through whom they were created" and the substitutes for that purpose. Conflict is to be expected, rather than a gradual ascent to a perfect world. The calling of Christians is "to continue through history the ministry of Christ, looking up to the Father as those who share his Sonship, accepting the Father's disposition of events as the form in which their mission is to be accomplished, rejoicing in the presence of the Spirit who gives them the foretaste of God's completed purpose and therefore confronts the world with the most powerful witness to that purpose and with the necessity to accept or reject it." Preceded, guided, and accompanied by the Holy Spirit who is one with the Father and the Son, the Church's mission within God's timing and pleasure is to bear faithful and responsible witness to the hidden and promised divine Kingdom in every new human situation and community until God should finally establish it.

In the next chapter Newbigin placed the secularization of human life under the banner of the incarnate Son. Whereas for the fifteen centuries of Christendom both the carriers and the addressees of the Christian message had operated on the assumptions of a sacral society, the modern liberation of the individual from local and religious control is making Christian faith and discipleship increasingly a matter of personal decision. Liberation turns into perfect freedom, Newbigin asserts, only when the service of Christ is accepted; for otherwise the secular individual falls into a new kind of bondage, to anonymous powers, economic forces, hidden persuaders, reasons of state, and the rest. The withdrawal of more and more areas of human life from the direct control of religion should not be allowed to make of the Gospel a mere offer of private salvation; for the Gospel announces precisely the redemption of the world. The New Testament shows Jesus and his followers accepting the political, social, and economic institutions of their time as part of the Father's provision for the preserving and ordering of human life. To view the authorities and institutions as created through Christ and for Christ means, on the one hand, that they have no absolute autonomy and, on the other, that the Church is to be subject to them rather than seek to rule them. Christ's rule over the various spheres of life is for the moment hidden, manifested only by the work of the Spirit. It will often be displayed by lay people who, in the name of Christ's redemptive victory, challenge the existing structures of government, industry, commerce, and culture where they have been corrupted by sin and who witness to the true purpose for which God created them. These men and women will need both the support of the local worshiping congregation and the fellowship to be found in vocational associations among Christians in the fields of their daily work.

The "pattern of missionary advance" is properly pneumatological; and, Newbigin argued in the next chapter, the Church was being given, by changing historical circumstances, an opportunity to learn afresh the primacy and sovereignty of the Holy Spirit in mission. By largely following the currents of colonial power in Asia and Africa, modern missions had created financially and spiritually dependent churches rather than the "spontaneously multiplying Christian communities" that were produced by "the missionary methods of St. Paul" (as Roland Allen would have it). The conviction of the apostle, ever eager to move on, was that "the Holy Spirit of God is himself the missionary," "the essential resource for witness and growth," and "the source of truth and holiness" in the rapidly established new congregations. From his Indian experience Newbigin knew both the immobilizing effects of a legalism and a professionalism that resulted from imported patterns of ethics and education and also, at least incipiently and by contrast, the release of energy that could come from trusting the Spirit to form the conscience of the converts and raise up various types of ministry among the simple and unlettered. The permanent point of reference remained, of course, the Gospel of the Cross of

Christ, where God's strength is found in weakness. The Holy Spirit brings people to confess the lordship of Christ crucified and risen and binds them to him in the fellowship of his body. Adopted in the Son, believers are enabled by the same Spirit to acknowledge God as Father and to discern, in a measure, God's will for the world and thus to share in the groaning and travailing of the whole creation with hope and with a sense of direction: "The presence of the Spirit in the believer's heart enables him to trust the creative and providential power of the Father to direct all things towards the glorifying of the Son."

In trinitarian sum, "the mission is not ours but God's":

> We are invited to participate in an activity of God which is the central meaning of creation itself. We are invited to become, through the presence of the Holy Spirit, participants in the Son's loving obedience to the Father. All things have been created that they may be summed up in Christ the Son. All history is directed towards that end. All creation has this as its goal. The Spirit of God, who is also the Spirit of the Son, is given as the foretaste of that consummation, as the witness to it, and as the guide of the Church on the road towards it. The Church is not promised success; it is promised the peace of Christ in the midst of tribulation, and the witness of the Spirit given out of the church's weakness and ignorance. For the future it has Christ's promise: 'It is your Father's good pleasure to give you the Kingdom.' And for the present it has his assurance: 'Be of good cheer, I have overcome the world.'[41]

In *The Open Secret* many of these themes were reworked in a more systematic way.[42] The principal developments were as follows: introductory chapters updated the description of the contemporary situation and indicated that the fundamental question was that of the authority of the mission; three new chapters brought up front the biblical bases of the mission as proclaiming the Kingdom of the Father (mission as faith in action), sharing the life of the Son (mission as love in action), and bearing the witness of the Spirit (mission as hope in action); consideration of God and world history was now conducted under the headline of divine election; the liberation ambiguously manifested in secularization was turned in favor of mission as action for God's justice; the pattern of missionary advance was now treated in relation to three issues currently agitated in missiological discussion, namely church growth, conversion, and culture; and a new final chapter set the Gospel among the religions (a theme that is reserved for chapter 6 of this book).

In describing the background of missiological discussion in the late twentieth century, Newbigin both deepened the historical picture and acknowledged the severity of the internal debates. The five modern centuries of concomitant colonialism and evangelization were to be seen as the movement of Western Christendom to break out of an Islamic encirclement which had turned Europe into something of a large ghetto and precluded missionary advance; but in a world that has lately rejected the power and influence of the Western nations, missions must now learn to go against the stream and rediscover from the earliest Church what it means to bear witness to the Gospel from a position not of strength but of weakness. Even the benefits brought by Western science and technology do not ensure automatic acceptance of Western cultural goals, whose relation to Christianity is in any case ambiguous; but the almost universal "revolution of rising expectations," whether fired by French, American, or Marxist models, has made it indispensable for contemporary missiology to face the question of "the inner relationship between this expectation of a new world and the Christian gospel of the reign of God."

Twentieth-century missiology had begun, as displayed at the world missionary conference of Edinburgh 1910, with "a still unshaken confidence in the future of Western civilization as the bearer of the gospel to the 'backward peoples'"; the Jerusalem conference of 1928 had noted the renascence of the ancient religions and the global impact of Western secularism; the Tambaram conference of 1938 had responded with a concentration on Christ and on his worldwide Church as "the people entrusted with the gospel and called to do battle with a paganism which was showing its power in the heart of the old Christendom." An ecclesiocentric view of mission helped to imprint the missionary vocation on the mind of the Church. But, following the straws in the wind at Willingen in 1952, the Strasbourg conference of the World's Student Christian Federation on "The Life and Mission of the Church" in 1960 saw the emergence of "a radically secular interpretation of the *missio Dei*" and heard a call "radically to desacralize the Church." Now "mission was primarily concerned with the doing of God's justice in the world, not primarily with increasing the membership of the Church." The grown-ups at the fourth assembly of the World Council of Churches at Uppsala in 1968 "accepted a definition of mission which identified it primarily with action for humanization in the secular life of the world"; and concurrently, and perhaps rather oddly, there developed a new attitude toward the world religions as also spheres of God's action in history, calling for dialogue and partnership to replace an evangelism that was now often equated with proselytism. Tensions increased between the "ecumenical" and the "evangelical" approaches to mission, although the evangelicals began also to take concerns for ecclesial unity and social justice into account, while the WCC Nairobi report of 1975 on "Confessing Christ Today" attempted a holistic call both to personal conversion and to action for God's justice in the world. In *The Open Secret* Newbigin made his most sustained constructive contribution to a debate which had still not subsided by the end of the twentieth century.

The theological discussion of mission begins with "the question of authority." The question is posed not only by adherents of other faiths but also from within the Church. Newbigin declares that the Christian mission cannot be justified by appeal to any other commitment, such as its service to human unity, development, or liberation. It is rather the practical working out of an ultimate commitment to a person who embodies God's authority in the life of men. It is performed "in the name of Jesus." To confess Jesus as Lord is commitment to "a belief about the meaning of the whole of human experience in its entirety, namely, the belief that this meaning is to be found in the person of Jesus Christ, incarnate, crucified, risen, and destined to reign over all things." Individual Christians participate in the Church's mission as the community continues to live out this faith in wider and wider areas of reality, reaching the entire public life of the world—"its philosophy, its culture, and its politics no less than the personal lives of its people." I can make this confession, says Newbigin, "only because I have been laid hold of by Another and commissioned to do so" (cf. 1 Corinthians 9:16–17). "You did not choose me," said Jesus to his apostles, "I chose you and appointed you that you should go and bear fruit" (John 15:16). The true understanding of mission requires the central biblical doctrine of election, in which the company is chosen by God not for privilege but for responsibility.

To conduct mission "in the name of Jesus" is to share in "the mission of the Triune God." In the pages of the New Testament Jesus appears from his baptism as the herald and bearer of the divine Kingdom now starting to manifest itself, as the obedient Son of the Father, anointed by the Spirit to bring forth justice to the nations, even to the sin-burdened humanity with which he identifies himself and whom he calls to repentance. When his baptism had been completed on Calvary, the way was open for his chosen apostles to receive the Spirit's anointing, to be acknowledged as God's children, and to be sent out in Christ's name to carry God's Kingdom to the peoples. In the Greco-Roman world, this involved the intellectual task of showing how the scientific dichotomy between the intelligible and the sensible and the historic dichotomy between human virtue and external fortune had been healed by the incarnation and atoning work of the Son and the continuing gift of the Spirit, so that "God himself is involved in the suffering of history" and "through the Spirit the Christian can share this suffering, knowing that in doing so he is in touch with the very being of God himself." The resultant doctrine of the Trinity formed the basis of a "new world view that would shape the thought of Western Christendom for a thousand years," a "new way of making sense of the world, not just by speculative science, but by practical wisdom." That essential faith, says Newbigin, has to be restated in fresh ways in each cultural situation, always in dependence on the original biblical sources and with the knowledge that it cannot be verified by the axioms of existing cultures but will rather offer new possibilities for human life as it really is. As the acting out of a fundamental belief, the Christian mission entails the constant reconsideration of that belief in the light of its exercise and "in dialogue with every other pattern of thought by which men and women seek to make sense of their lives." The rest of Newbigin's book looks at the Christian mission as the acting out of the fundamental belief that God has revealed himself as Father, Son, and Spirit.

The biblical story concerns first the Kingdom of the Father, and mission appears as its proclamation or "faith in action." God's sovereignty extends over all that is, and therefore we are talking about the origin, structure, meaning, and end of the universe and of all human history within the history of the universe. The biblical story tells of "the carrying forward to its completion of the gracious purpose which has its source in the love of the Father for the Son in the unity of the Spirit." Over the course of the Old Testament, the focus is narrowed to the smaller and smaller remnant who are chosen to bear the blessing that remains intended for a recalcitrant humanity until finally the beloved Son himself appears in order to announce the Father's impending reign. By his parabolic words and deeds and by the supreme parable of the Cross, he "bears witness to the presence of the reign of God, not by overpowering the forces of evil, but by taking their full weight upon himself." Simultaneously hidden and revealed, this mystery of God's reign in seeming weakness and defeat can be perceived only by those to whom the Spirit gives faith and whom he chooses to proclaim abroad the good news of a new creation whose firstfruits is the resurrection of Christ. Viewed from this angle, mission is "the acting out by proclamation and endurance, through all the events of history, of the faith that the Kingdom of God has drawn near. It is the acting out of the central prayer which Jesus taught his disciples to use: 'Father, hallowed be thy name, thy Kingdom come, thy will be done on earth as in heaven.'"[43]

Second, the story is unfolded as "sharing the life of the Son," with "mission as love in action." In Jesus the divine Kingdom was not only proclaimed but present: it had "the name and face of the man from Nazareth"; and that is why the primitive Church "preached Christ," having been commissioned by him and enabled by the Spirit to do so as his continuing body in which his death and life were manifested (cf. 2 Corinthians 4:10). The Church is the "society in which the life of the crucified and risen Jesus lives on and his mission continues, not only as the proclamation of the Kingdom but as the presence of the Kingdom in the form of death and resurrection." Receiving God's forgiveness and peace by virtue of Christ's atoning death, the Church— as itself "the place where the reign of God is present as love shared among the unlovely"—offers the secret to others (cf. John 20:19–23): "By inviting all humankind to share in the mystery of the presence of the Kingdom hidden in its life through its union with the crucified and risen life of Jesus, the Church acts out the love of Jesus which took him to the cross."

Mission is not only the proclamation and the presence of the Kingdom but also, says Newbigin, the prevenience of the Kingdom in both time and space. As "bearing the witness of the Spirit," mission is, in the third place, "hope in action." The same Spirit who anointed Jesus was, after his exaltation, given to his followers as, in the language of Paul, the "cash deposit" that pledged the final settlement, "the advance installment which will make them the living evidences of the reality which is promised." As the free, sovereign agent of mission, the Spirit is seen, in the Acts of the Apostles, to go ahead of the Church, guiding, surprising, and changing it (the conversion of Cornelius is also a "conversion" of Peter in favor of the Gentile mission). The Spirit, as advocate, defends those who witness to Christ and confutes their adversaries, "proving to the accusing world that its fundamental religious and moral convictions are wrong and proved wrong by the work of Jesus" (cf. John, chapters 14–16). With the Spirit as the source of hope, the Church can "work and wait with both eagerness and patience for the fullness of what God has promised for his whole creation." "By obediently following where the Spirit leads, often in ways"—Newbigin insists also from personal experience as a missionary—"neither planned, known, nor understood, the Church acts out the hope which it is given by the presence of the Spirit who is the living foretaste of the Kingdom."[44]

Within that trinitarian framework Newbigin proceeds to discuss some theoretical and practical problems of mission. The first issue is that of the Gospel and world history. Israel and Jesus represent a "scandal of particularity" when, among the many nations and the billions of human beings who ever lived, claims are made for their universal significance; the central question concerning missions is the relation of God's universality to his particular deeds and words. That such "universality and particularity do not contradict one another but require one another" is accounted for by "the doctrine which permeates and controls the whole Bible, the doctrine of election": "The one (or the few) is chosen for the sake of the many." In contrast to Hindu and idealist notions of a monadic soul that needs neither other persons nor a created world for the achievement of its true destiny, the Bible shows the human as made by the Triune God in his image for "a life of mutual personal responsibility in the context of a shared responsibility for the created world"; it is this life which is "the object of God's primal blessing and of his saving purpose." The gift of salvation is therefore bound up with our openness to one another, conveyed by the transmission of the blessing from chosen bearer to intended recipients. Concretely, the Letter to the Ephesians shows little companies of believers elected in the beloved Son by sheer grace and entrusted with passing on the secret of God's goal to unite the whole creation in Christ. The emissaries have no ground for boasting, and their own salvation is linked to that of those to whom they are sent. That the biblical story is "part of the unbroken fabric of world history" and "the place in the whole fabric where its pattern has been disclosed, even though the weaving is not yet finished" is a Christian claim which challenges and relativizes all other understandings of reality; it can be raised only on the basis of faith in Jesus as the Alpha and the Omega in whom the beginning and the end are revealed, and it can be made good in the context of the actual secular history of the present hour "only through actions in which this confession is embodied in deed—and in suffering. If the Christian confession is true, the Acts of God do not cease with the Acts of the Apostles."[45]

The next issue for mission thereby emerges: What are the actions by which the believing community will fulfill God's purpose for it as the community chosen, called, and sent with a view to the salvation of the world? Newbigin's answer is given in a chapter devoted to "mission as action for God's justice" understood as the making visible of the prayer "Thy will be done." Newbigin observes that the Gospel has always prompted its bearers to heal the sick, feed the hungry, school the young, help the helpless. The forms of social service engaged in by missionaries during the colonial period had since been continued under the more secular guise first of "technical assistance" and then of "development"; but by the 1970s the mood in what had by then become known as the Third World shifted to a more revolutionary one of raising the people's consciousness to seek deliverance not only from political but also from economic and cultural oppression. Arising first in Latin America and represented by such figures as Gustavo Gutiérrez on the Catholic side and José Míguez Bonino on the Protestant, liberation theology found its primary model for salvation in Israel's exodus from Egypt and sought to interpret the work of Christ also in terms that denied the separation of two histories, sacred and profane, and instead located the history of salvation at the very heart of human history. Newbigin agrees that "to know the Lord" is "a matter of doing justice and mercy in concrete situations" (cf. Jeremiah 22:16) and that "there is no knowledge of God apart from the love of God, and there is no love of God apart from the love of the neighbor" (cf. 1 John 3:14–24; 4: 8). Theologically, Newbigin sympathizes with Gutiérrez's placement of three different "levels" of liberation within "a single, all-encompassing salvific process": in political liberation the oppressed struggle against the oppressors; in cultural liberation people assume responsibility for their own destiny; in spiritual liberation Christ delivers sinners and restores them to fellowship with God. But Newbigin considers that liberation theologians have been led by their indebtedness to Marxism—in reaction perhaps against the ancient religious view that looks for salvation outside of history—into missing the proper relation between "liberation of the person" and "political and cultural liberation."

Measured by the Bible, Marxism is inadequate, nay wrong, in its eschatology, its anthropology, and its epistemology. Eschatologically, Marxism has no answer for the dark mystery of death but rather uses or discards successive generations in the process of creating a new world ("Stalinism is not an accidental outcome of Marxism, it is the logical development of it"). By contrast, the Gospel delivers us from the dilemma of "meaning for the human person at the cost of denying meaning for history" or "meaning for history at the cost of denying meaning for the human person." Death, for the Bible, is the wages of sin, the outward sign that neither I nor my achievements nor the institutions nor the civilization of which I am a part are of themselves fit for the Kingdom of God. The good news is that in Jesus Christ God has dealt with sin and death and "opened up a way on which I can travel towards the holy city knowing that the end of the journey will be a real consummation both of my personal journey and of the public history in which I have shared." Given the Spirit as a foretaste of the life of that city, I can in trust "lose myself in the service of God's cause, knowing that though I cannot create the city, God can raise up both me and my works, purged in the fire of judgment, to take a place in the life of the city. . . . I can live fully the life of a real person, part of the real world of society, history, and nature, and know that, because Christ is risen, my labor in the Lord is not futile (1 Cor. 15:58)." Newbigin expounds the strongly trinitarian chapter of Romans 8 to show the correspondence between the "inward working of the Spirit in the hearts of believers" and the "outward working of the Father who orders all things in the cosmos towards the fulfillment of the purpose for which he has called them," so that "the community of those who follow Jesus is called to share in the struggle for liberation as those who are full of eager and patient hope: eager, because they have already tasted the freedom to which God calls all; patient, because God can be trusted to complete that which he has begun."[46] The cost may be martyrdom, for the New Testament Apocalypse views history under the sign of the Cross. It was "the Constantinian dream" to imagine that the Church could be the agency through which God's order is established in history; nor is there much biblical basis for an ascending evolutionary process, à la Teilhard de Chardin, by which the cosmos arrives at its goal. The modest calling of the Church is "to be the witness to a grace and justice, which challenges, judges, and redeems the structures in which we embody our hopes for justice."

Anthropologically, the chief failing of Marxism resides in its "extreme moralism." For the Marxist, evil is always external to himself, the "class enemy," whereas "the oppressed and exploited"—and their self-identified representatives—are "the exclusive bearers of truth and righteousness." Because there is no truth or righteousness *over* them to judge them, there is no room for forgiveness and reconciliation, and the door is open to ruthless tyranny when power shifts. By contrast, "the Church can only represent the righteousness of God in history in the way that Jesus did." In the Eucharist, "the Church has to learn to live by the grace which forgives but does not condone sin and under the judgment which exposes sin and yet keeps open the way of repentance." That is why Newbigin rejects, ever so gently, the overhasty call from some liberationists to break eucharistic fellowship with those oppressors who are also Christian.[47]

Epistemologically, Marxism fails by rewriting the history of science, and indeed of all knowledge, in terms of the class struggle. Borrowing from Michael Polanyi's *Personal Knowledge*, Newbigin shows how, by the casting of moral passions in the form of scientific affirmations under a façade of objectivity, "the self-interest of the proletariat is impregnated with a supreme moral value which cannot be questioned because there is no locus of truth outside of proletarian praxis." That is why the critical theologian will be suspicious when Míguez Bonino, claiming that "action itself is the truth," bases action on a "scientific" analysis of the sociopolitical situation that is derived from Marxism. One does not need to adopt a metaphysical idealism, Newbigin writes, in order to deny Míguez's statement that "there is no possibility of invoking or availing oneself of a norm outside praxis itself." Admitting with Míguez that "we always read a text which is already incorporated in a praxis, whether our own or someone else's" does not alter the fact, says Newbigin, that "the text of Scripture does function and has constantly functioned as a source of judgment upon the praxis of those who have the Scriptures in their hands." And we depart from those Scriptures altogether

> if we put gospel and 'scientific analysis' side by side so that the latter becomes the primary and independent source of our understanding of what is the case and what is to be done. . . . The obedience to which the gospel calls me and apart from which I cannot know God is obedience to the personal calling of Jesus Christ in and through his community. The ultimate model, in terms of

which I am to understand what is the case and what is to be done, is furnished by the biblical story. This does not obviate the necessity for a scientific analysis of the political-cultural-economic reality in which I am involved, but this analysis cannot take the place of the fundamental model provided by the biblical story and cannot therefore be the ground for excluding from the communion of Christ's community those who do not accept it.[48]

In a paragraph inserted into chapter 8 of *The Open Secret* in the revised edition of 1995, after the sudden collapse of the Soviet empire, Newbigin both hinted at the persistence of Marxist thought in some intellectually nostalgic quarters—which makes his analysis of its import for theology of more than past interest—and called the attention of theologians and the churches to the critique of "unrestrained capitalism" that had now become more necessary than ever:

> The collapse of Marxism as a world power at the end of the 1980s has to some extent discredited this way of thinking, but it has not solved any problems. The ideology of the free market now has nothing to limit its claims. There is now no visible countervailing power. There seems no sign of a check to its relentless advance. And its destructive potential, both for the coherence of human society and for the safeguarding of the environment, are formidable. The ideology of the free market has proved itself more powerful than Marxism. It is, of course, not just a way of arranging economic affairs. It has deep roots in the human soul. It can be met and mastered only at the level of religious faith, for it is a form of idolatry. The churches have hardly begun to recognize that this is probably their most urgent missionary task during the coming century.[49]

Newbigin's thought and work as a social critic and builder are treated in chapter 7.

Meanwhile, Newbigin proceeded, in *The Open Secret*, to discuss a trio of interconnected issues to do with Christ's Church as the bearer of missionary advance. Resources and energies were mostly being put into maintenance, and many churches showed little enthusiasm for forward movement. In appreciative and critical engagement with Donald McGavran, then of the Institute of Church Growth in the School of World Missions at Fuller Theological Seminary, Newbigin treats the questions of (1) numerical growth among Christians in relation to the message of the Kingdom, (2) the meaning of conversion in relation to its ethical context and content, and (3) the complex relation of Gospel and Church to culture.

On the first question, Newbigin agrees with McGavran that the specific task of the missionary is to introduce the Gospel and then move on, rather than "build a bungalow" and establish the oxymoron of a "mission station." In the line of Roland Allen (for years now Newbigin's literary mentor), provision should be made as quickly as possible for the word of the Gospel to be preached and the sacraments of the Gospel to be administered by an indigenous ministry which links the new community to the wider fellowship of the Church but has not been subjected to an educational and cultural campaign that seeks at great cost to replicate the conditions and styles of the "sending" churches. But against McGavran and with Allen, Newbigin distinguishes between rapid *spread* and rapid *growth*. Recognizing the joy that attends increasing numbers, as in the early chapters of the Acts of the Apostles, Newbigin nevertheless observes that the Epistles (of a Paul pressing on to the ends of the earth!) show much more interest in the new communities' faithfulness and in the integrity of their Christian witness, while the Gospels, including Luke's, show joy at the finding of even one lost sheep (Luke 15:3–7) and do not make the coming of God's Kingdom at all dependent on the number of those—"the little flock"—who expect it and pray for it (Luke 12:32; 18:8). Moreover, the evidence of Christian history is ambiguous in the matter of "people's movements" whereby whole social groups are encouraged to make corporate decisions for the Gospel. On the one hand, there are such groups as the fisherfolk of the Coramandel coast—the Paravas—who were baptized en masse in 1534 as a condition of Portuguese protection from Muslim raiders and were instructed only eight years later by Francis Xavier but have remained among the most vital Christian communities of India; on the other hand, "the Church is least recognizable as the body of Christ when it is growing rapidly through the influence of military, political, and economic power" or "when it is chiefly concerned with its own self-aggrandizement." In Newbigin's Pauline vision, once the missionary has brought to birth a confessing community as the firstfruit of the Gentiles in a particular area, it quickly becomes that new community's adult responsibility to spread the Gospel among its neighbors. Newbigin cites his experience of evangelism in South Indian villages, where the Gospel spread and living churches multiplied and grew when leadership was entrusted to local Christians.

As to the second issue, Newbigin agrees with McGavran that missionaries must beware of imposing their own culturally conditioned ethics as prerequisites for acceptance of the Gospel and entrance into the Church, a danger threatening from both the bourgeois and the liberationist directions; Allen condemned that as legalism. But whereas McGavran thought years might properly elapse between (in his terminology) "discipling" and "perfecting" (or "teaching them to observe all that I have commanded you"), Newbigin believes that conversion and obedience cannot be separated even for a moment: the outward reorientation of conduct in all areas of life belongs in a single action with the inner reorientation of heart and mind. However, the missionary must be ready to trust Christ and the Spirit, speaking through the Scriptures, to direct the ethical content of salvation at any time or place. The Spirit may spring surprises through new kinds of obedience, and other parts of the Church should be prepared to have their own patterns corrected and enlarged by the fresh insights of converts. Newbigin cites from John V. Taylor the nineteenth-century case of the first converts among the young men at the court of the Kabaka of Buganda: whereas the missionaries laid great stress on the necessity for the immediate abandonment of polygamy as a condition for baptism, the converts felt the demand of the Gospel on their consciences as calling for humility, for a willingness to share the work and hardship of the poor, and for the end of slavery.[50]

The third issue, which underlies the previous two, is that of the relation between the Gospel and culture. Modern German missiologists—Gustav Warneck (1834–1910), Christian Keysser of New Guinea (1877–1961), Bruno Gutmann of Tanzania (1876–1961)—laid stress on the preservation of social cohesion through the conversion and baptism of whole communities rather than of individuals, but the dangers of *Blut und Boden* are obvious, says Newbigin. Sociologically, all organization is subject to change; theologically, it is intolerable to ascribe to elements in the created world a finality which belongs only to Christ. Newbigin's position is that all the "powers"—political orders, laws, customs, traditions—must be brought to the Cross of Christ, where they all combined to destroy him but where in fact he "established a place where we are directly related to God himself, a place, therefore, from which we have the freedom to judge, criticize, and challenge the powers"; and only so may they be set in the service of Christ. McGavran's talk of "adapting" Christianity to every piece in the magnificent mosaic of human cultures forgets, sociologically, the facts of cultural mutability and mutual permeability. And, although one may "have to recognize that at certain times and places such institutions as slavery, polygamy, the dowry system, and the capitalist system exist as an integral part of the culture of a society and that the Christian convert cannot separate himself from them without ceasing to be part of that society," one may nevertheless hold, theologically, that "other ways of ordering the economic, marital, and political life of society are better and that there is an obligation upon Christians to seek to change these elements in a culture. The fact that something is part of a particular culture does not mean that the Christian can give it unconditional endorsement."[51] Whereas McGavran appeared to think that in, say, the Madras of three million inhabitants, the quarter of a million Christians should, in the interests of the effective evangelization of their Hindu neighbors, be organized in separate groups according to their caste origins, Newbigin joins with the majority of local Christians in judging that such a policy would run counter to the essential witness of an evangelical ethic concerning the unity of all in Christ.

As itself the "sign, instrument, and foretaste of God's purpose for all human culture," the Church must avoid both accommodationism and intransigence in aiming so to "live, act, and speak within each culture that its words and its deeds and its life communicate in a way which can be understood as the judgment of God upon that culture and his promise for it." Missiologically, Newbigin illustrates his point by way of the idioms of language and conduct. Concretely, "a three-cornered relationship is set up between the traditional culture, the 'Christianity' of the missionary, and the Bible." There is no single, predictable pattern of development. Both the bringer and the receiver may be changed in various ways as the Scriptures are allowed to operate critically on each in the course of the interaction, the entire process being further complicated in modern times by the growth of both a global culture and an ecumenical Christianity. On the fundamental assumption that the Scriptures embody "the given revelation with its center and focus in the person of Jesus Christ," a hermeneutical discussion is called for, in which matter Newbigin

INTER-
FAITH
DIALOGUE

showed himself years ahead of narrowly Western biblical and theological scholarship. His insights—described earlier—into the relation between particularity and universality provide the framework for learning "to confess the one Lord Jesus Christ as alone having absolute authority and therefore to acknowledge the relativity of all the cultural forms within which we try to say who he is." Hermeneutics will return to the fore in the presentation in chapter 9 of Newbigin as scriptural expositor and dogmatician.[52]

Mission in Late Modernity

The pattern of *The Open Secret* constituted the stable background for what Lesslie Newbigin continued to think, speak, and write on missiological matters in the 1980s and 1990s. Christocentric trinitarianism remained Newbigin's confessional stance in his missiological reflections. He still addressed the global scene while bringing an ever sharper focus to bear on the West. Relativism was the common ideological bogey, whether he was treating the question of the world religions or tackling the skepticism of late modernity. There was geographical and cultural overlap, too; for the presence of Islam was making itself more and more felt in Europe at the same time as Western religious thinkers were celebrating religious pluralism, and the secularism of old Christendom was at various levels affecting almost the entire globe. Several associated themes were expressed in the question from the Indonesian soldier and theologian T. B. Simatupang that Newbigin had been fond of quoting ever since he had heard the general mutter it under his breath at the 1973 Bangkok missionary conference on "Salvation Today": Can the West be converted? In a lecture entitled "Mission Agenda" at the 1992 Trinity College celebration of the centenary of the Dublin University Mission to Chota Nagpur, Newbigin said:

> Looking at the total situation of Christianity in the contemporary world, that is the most urgent question, and for two reasons. Firstly, because it is modern, post-Enlightenment western culture which, in the guise of 'modernization,' is replacing more traditional cultures all over the world; and second, because that modern western culture has a unique power to erode and neutralize the Christian faith. It is the most powerful, the most pervasive, and (with the possible exception of Islam) the most resistant to the Gospel, of all the cultures which compete for power in our global city.[53]

Chapter 6 shows Newbigin as religious interlocutor, and chapter 10 as the apologist of the Christian faith in the midst of an apostasizing Western civilization. Meanwhile, from Newbigin's many occasional writings and addresses on mission in the last two decades of his life, a selection is presented of three or four pieces that arose from his continuing informal association with the Division of World Mission and Evangelism in the World Council of Churches, to which is added a couple of articles written for the *Occasional/International*

Bulletin of Missionary Research issuing from the independent Overseas Ministry Study Center.

In 1980 the WCC conference on mission and evangelism was held at Melbourne, Australia, under the title "Your Kingdom Come." In preparation for that meeting Newbigin composed a series of lectures that were first delivered at the Theological Seminary of the Swedish Covenant Church in Stockholm and later published in Britain as *Your Kingdom Come* and in the United States as *Sign of the Kingdom*.[54] Newbigin welcomed the Melbourne theme for several reasons. First and foremost was the primacy of the Kingdom of God as the central theme of Jesus' preaching and action and the corresponding fact that the question of the manner and form of the reign of God—raised biblically by the dual strand in the Old Testament of Yahweh as Israel's true and transcendent King and the promise and expectation of a messianic ruler—had been answered, surprisingly, in the Person of Jesus: "The Kingdom now had a name and a face, the name and the face of Jesus." That fact itself had a number of consequences. One was its challenge to "the timid privatization of religion which has become so general in Western Christianity," for the gift and claim precisely of *God* embodied in Jesus Christ cannot be less than universal in range and comprehensive in scope. On the other hand, the personal embodiment of the Kingdom in Jesus also corrected ideological trends to turn the Christian mission into a cultural or political program in favor of "social progress" or "progressive capitalism" (as represented by the American "Laymen's Enquiry into Foreign Missions" of the 1930s) or of abstractly or Marxistically conceived "liberation" and "justice" (as had become popular in the secular '60s); for such is to turn into law the gospel that in Christ the Kingdom has graciously drawn near: "The people to whom the Kingdom is promised—the halt and the lame, the blind and deaf, the lepers and the outcastes— are *not* by any means the proletariat in Marxist terms. They are not the possible bearers of revolutionary justice. They are more akin to Marx's *lumpenproletariat*, from whom no revolution comes." A further chance afforded by the Melbourne theme was that of clarifying both the distinction and the inseparability between Church and Kingdom: "From the beginning the announcement of the Kingdom led to a summons to follow and so to the formation of a community. It is the community which has begun to taste (even if only in foretaste) the reality of the Kingdom which can alone provide the hermeneutic of the message." That it is the crucified Lord who is the presence of God's Kingdom in wisdom and power (1 Corinthians 1:18–25) and that the answer to the disciples' question concerning the Kingdom is the Father's sheer gift of the Holy Spirit (Acts 1:6–8) means that the Church's part will be to share faithfully in the tribulation of Jesus and the secret of his victory over death and thereby provide through its words and deeds and the corporate life of the fellowship the locus and the occasion of the sovereign Spirit's witness to the Kingdom (cf. John 20:19–23). In that sense, the Church may become "a sign of the Kingdom," continually pointing men and women beyond itself to Jesus and inviting them to personal conversion and commitment to him and always remembering that the Kingdom's coming can never be a human achievement but only the granting of a prayer.

In 1986 Bishop Newbigin returned to the Church of South India in order to conduct Bible studies for its synod meeting on the theme "Mission in Christ's Way." His addresses were later published by the World Council of Churches in the approach to its international missionary conference held at San Antonio, Texas, in 1989 under the title "Your Will Be Done: Mission in Christ's Way."[55] The original ecclesial context of the addresses was one of a vital tension between vigorous evangelism and radical movements for social and political justice. To suggest a framework in which this tension could be creative and not destructive, the speaker reworked much of his current missiological thinking into the shape of meditations on a series of scriptural texts. In formal terms the result is a remarkable display of skill by the experienced pastor and teacher in conveying the deepest truths in the simplest terms. The bishop's thesis was that the Church's mission is founded and modeled on Christ's own mission. From Mark 1:14–18 he showed first the "news-flash" of Jesus' announcing that the reign of God had drawn near to the world, summoning people to the "U-turn" of a total mental revolution, and calling those whom he has chosen to believe so that they may become the means of calling others to accept God's reign, hidden from sight but present to faith in Jesus; and then from Matthew 10:1–8 he shows Jesus sending out his disciples to heal and to exorcise, their preaching serving to interpret the signs of the dawning Kingdom. In Acts 1:6–8 the lesson from the risen Lord is that the Kingdom is God's reign, not our program; and the gift of the Holy Spirit, though only a foretaste of the final Kingdom, is what makes the Church the place of witness through the faithful words and deeds of its members. John 20:19–23 shows the crucified and risen Jesus launching the disciples—as the embryonic Church and ministry—into the wide world as those who participate in his passion and witness to his resurrection (cf. 2 Corinthians 4:7–12), neither withdrawing into a religious sanctuary nor engaging with the world on its own terms but offering "a totally uncompromising yet totally vulnerable challenge to the powers of evil in the name and in the power of the kingship of God present in the crucified and risen Jesus," continuing through the Spirit to "liberate those who are in the iron grip of unforgiven sin" and bring them the peace of God that humbles pride. Finally, Matthew 28:18–20 shows the authority and presence of the victorious Christ who, by the Holy Spirit, impels and equips the bearers of the Gospel not to make "carbon copies" of themselves but to call people in every tribe, caste, and clan into a new kind of life that encompasses and transforms both the hearers and the evangelizers.

After "Your Kingdom Come" and "Your Will Be Done," Newbigin expressed the hope that the World Council of Churches would convene a missionary conference on "Your Name Be Hallowed."[56] Much missionary talk in the past century, he there said, has been "terribly Pelagian":

Whether the emphasis was upon the saving of individual souls, or on the shaping of more truly humane cultures, or on the righting of social wrongs, the overwhelming emphasis has been upon missions as our program. From the New Testament I get a different impression. There, it seems to me, mission is an overflow of gratitude and joy. The center of the picture is not the human need of salvation (from sin, from oppression, from alienation) but God and God's immeasurable grace. So the central concern is not "How shall the world be saved?" but "How shall this glorious and gracious God be glorified?" The goal is the glory of God.

This doxological thrust brings Newbigin back, in his Dublin lecture of 1992, to his perennial concern for the "thousands of local congregations, communities of worship where God is glorified and the love of God flows out in spontaneous service and witness to the community":

If God indeed has done what, in all our liturgies, we affirm that he has done, then that is the most tremendous fact which must be told as public truth in every culture and in every generation. . . . But our telling of it is corrupted when we think in terms of our success rather than in terms of the glory of God. . . . We [properly] tell the story as an act of love and gratitude to God, that our blessed Lord may see the travail of his soul and be satisfied. . . . Recent surveys in England about how people in contemporary society come to faith in Christ have shown that the overwhelming proportion come through the witness of a local congregation. And we can never forget that during the seventy years in which the churches in the Soviet Union were denied all possibilities of witness and service outside the walls of the Church, it was the witness of authentic worship which drew to Christ men and women shaped and formed from cradle to university by an atheist ideology. In those years there was little possibility for the Church to be domesticated in the culture. The contrast was too sharp. Perhaps we can learn from their experience how to live and tell the story in the midst of our modern, scientific, free-market culture in such a way that the story recovers its sharp cutting edge. If we can do that, we shall perhaps render the greatest service that we can to the total mission of Christ in this global city.[57]

The domestic captivity of the Western Church was, in fact, a major theme in the surveys of missiological issues that Newbigin contributed to the *Occasional* (renamed *International*) *Bulletin of Missionary Research* at the start of the 1980s and the 1990s—or, as he put it in a paper given before a German missionary conference at Arnoldshain in 1988: "Instead of allowing the Gospel to challenge the unexamined assumptions of our culture, we have co-opted Jesus into our culture by giving him a minor role in what we call the private sector."[58] Looking forward into the 1980s,[59] Newbigin started from the theme of contextualization, which had been made a catchword by the Theological Education Fund. The term had become favored over "adaptation" (which might imply that the message brought by the missionary was the unadapted Gospel, the pure truth unadulterated by any cultural admixture) and "indigenization" (which sought to interpret the Gospel through traditional elements in the receptor cultures when the people were in fact turning away from these). Western missiologists were "debating with intense earnestness the questions which arise from the effort to 'contextualize' the Gospel in all the cultures of mankind from Peru to Papua," but Newbigin found no missiologists devoting "the same intense and sustained attention to the problem of finding the 'dynamic equivalent' for the Gospel in Western society as they are giving to that problem as it occurs in the meeting with peoples of the 'Third World.' " The case was, however, that "it is in the West that the Church appears to be continuously losing ground," becoming "the typical product of our Western 'enlightened' culture to which the Gospel appears irrelevant nonsense." What is obvious to a returned missionary, Newbigin observed, is that "English Christianity is a prime example of syncretism. Christianity as practised in most of our churches does *not* call in question the basic assumptions of the normal Englishman. Christians are *not* distinguishable as people who obviously live by different commitments from their neighbors. And I should doubt whether it is normal on the other side of the water to find that the churches are regarded as centres of 'un-American activities.'" Newbigin summed up the issue in a phrase borrowed from a senior missionary to India and former principal of Madras Christian College, A. G. Hogg (1875–1954): "challenging relevance." Newbigin wrote:

> The Gospel must be heard as relevant. It must speak of things which are real things in the life of the hearer. It must therefore begin by accepting his issues, using his models, and speaking his language. But relevance alone is not enough. The Gospel must at the same time challenge the whole world view of the hearer. It must cause him to question things that he has never questioned. It must bring him to the place where he hears spoken to his whole world of understanding and experience that word of grace and judgment which marks the end of one world and the beginning of another, a death and a new birth.

Throughout the 1980s, as is told in chapter 10, Newbigin himself devoted his best spiritual and intellectual energies to that kind of "contextualization" of the Gospel in relation to "the powerful paganism of our Western world."

Looking into the 1990s, Newbigin found the question even more urgent as "old Christendom" continued to disintegrate while technology originating in the West was locking increasing numbers of urbanized people around the globe into a single financial, economic, ideological, informational network and the challenge of Islam to both Christianity and Western culture was becoming more acute.[60] Although Newbigin hoped for a resolute attempt to clarify the content of the Christian mission on the part of theological minds which come to the Bible from cultures unencumbered by the controlling assumptions of modern Western thought, he directed his own work closer to home by seeking to imbue Western Christians with a "proper confidence" in the Gospel that would allow them both to accept forgiveness for their degree of complicity in colonialism and to recover their lost nerve to live and tell again the story that challenges every other account of reality, whether from the ancient religions or from the skepticism of modernity.[61]

From Tambaram 1938 to Tambaram 1988

Two more engagements from the last decade of Newbigin's life may be narrated to close this chapter on his role as missiologist and prepare for his appearance in the next as religious interlocutor: a return to Tambaram, India, in 1988 and attendance at the WCC conference on world mission and evangelism held in San Antonio, Texas, in 1989 under the title "Your Will Be Done: Mission in Christ's Way."

In 1988 he was invited by the World Council of Churches to return to India for its celebration of the fiftieth anniversary of the international missionary conference of Tambaram 1938. The event took the form of "a small consultation on the relationship of dialogue and mission, as these impact on Christian understandings of relations to people of other faiths." In the postscript to the updated edition of *Unfinished Agenda*, Newbigin comments briefly and poignantly: "It was not an easy meeting for me, since the gathering included several very powerful representatives of a (so-called) pluralist theology, particularly Wilfred Cantwell Smith and Diana Eck. I found myself fighting the same battle that Hendrik Kraemer had fought at Tambaram fifty years earlier."[62]

Tambaram 1938 had been particularly notable for two reasons. First, the conference had affirmed that the unfinished task of evangelization was "the task of the whole Church for the whole world." Evangelism was the business of the entire Church, home and abroad, ministerial and lay, missionary and local, women and men. If the slogan elsewhere in the ecumenical movement at the time was "let the Church be the Church," then in this connection it meant "the Church is mission." It has been seen that Newbigin regarded recognition of the missionary nature of the Church and the churchly character of mission as a lasting acquisition from Tambaram into the next generation. But what was the composition of "the whole world" to which the Gospel was addressed? With that question appears the second reason for the significance of Tambaram 1938. Under the powerful impact of the book-length study on "the Christian message in a non-Christian world" that had been solicited from the Dutch Reformed missiologist and lately missionary in Indonesia, Hendrik Kraemer,[63] the conference of 1938 addressed the theme of "The Witness of the Church in Relation to the Non-Christian Religions, the New Paganisms, and the Cultural Heritage of the Nations." Given Newbigin's remarks about Tambaram 1988, the statement of Tambaram 1938 on these matters needs recalling at some length.[64]

First, note is taken of the indirect influence of Christianity—"both positively and negatively"—on the ancient religions in particular: certain social, moral, and even spiritual progress among their adherents is here ascribed to their recent contacts with Christianity, but the revival and reform of the religions has often been linked to aggressive and even idolatrous nationalism; with the spread of modernity all have felt the disintegrating effects of Western materialism and secularism, and the compensatory growth of new pagan cults is a rebuke to the failings of Christians. Then the following consequences are drawn for "the witness of the Church in this new world situation":

> The end and aim of our evangelistic work is not achieved until all men everywhere are brought to a knowledge of God in Jesus Christ and to a saving faith in Him. Therefore, in this changing world we must re-affirm the message which is our witness to His grace. Our message is that God was in Christ reconciling the world unto Himself. We believe that God revealed Himself to Israel, preparing the way for His full revelation in Jesus Christ, His Son, our Lord. We believe that Christ is the Way, the Truth and the Life for all, that He alone is adequate for the world's need. Therefore we want to bear witness to Him in all the world.
>
> There are many non-Christian religions that claim the allegiance of multitudes. We see and readily recognize that in them are to be found values of deep religious experience, and great moral achievements. Yet we are bold enough to call men out from them to the feet of Christ. We do so because we believe that in Him alone is the full salvation which man needs. Mankind has seen nothing compared with the redeeming love of God in the life, death and resurrection of Christ. What He is for us, judge and redeemer, teacher and friend, brother and Lord, we long to see Him become also for others.
>
> Our knowledge of God through Christ as Holy and Compassionate Love going forth impartially to all His erring children leads us to expect that everywhere and at all times He has been seeking to disclose Himself to men. He has not left Himself without witness in the world. Furthermore, men have been seeking Him all through the ages. Often this seeking and longing has been misdirected, but there are evidences that His yearning after His children has not been without response.
>
> As to whether the non-Christian religions as total systems of thought and life may be regarded as in some sense or to some degree manifesting God's revelation, Christians are not agreed. This is a matter urgently demanding thought and united study. For we believe that all religious insight and experience have to be fully tested before God in Christ; and we see that this is true as well within as outside the Christian Church. Christ is revolutionary: He brings conversion when we meet Him, from whatever point we may have started. Paul said: "What things were gain to me, those I counted loss for Christ."

Practically, the Church is called on by the Tambaram statement of 1938 to take several steps for the sake of its witness: to interest itself in the religious life of others in order to find intelligible ways of commending the Gospel to them without impairing its integrity; to gain a fuller understanding of other religious faiths as total systems of life, with a view to distinguishing between good and evil elements in them and integrating what is valuable into the life of the new Christian community; to appropriate the contributions of traditional cultures for the development of indigenous forms and the enrichment of the Church universal; to cooperate with non-Christians in all good works, thereby "expressing in service our ultimate loyalty to Christ"; to improve the quality of Christian group life so that "the presentation of the Gospel [may] be made effective by the witness of the local church as a household of God";

to find a fuller expression of Christian unity, in order to remove the scandal presented by a divided Church and to be able to speak with a single voice against the wrongs of the times.

Many of the themes from Tambaram 1938 will be recognized as having occupied Newbigin throughout his career as a missionary and missiologist, but the sentence most pertinent to our present concern is the declaration that Christians are not agreed on "whether the non-Christian religions as total systems of thought may be regarded as in some sense or to some degree manifesting God's revelation." By the time of Tambaram 1988 there had taken place, in World Council of Churches circles and elsewhere, a resurgence of that "(so-called) pluralist theology" which not only answered that question in the affirmative but rejoined the Laymen's *Re-Thinking Missions* Report— produced in 1932 under the chairmanship of Harvard professor W. E. Hocking—in regarding "other religions" as equally valid paths with Christianity in a common, and ultimately converging, quest for salvation. It was in the face of this that Lesslie Newbigin felt the obligation to reaffirm "the uniqueness, decisiveness, sufficiency of the Gospel," his Kraemerian christocentrism now set within the explicitly trinitarian framework that he had been constructing in his ecclesiological and missiological thinking over the past thirty-five years.

Bishop Newbigin's opening sermon to the 1988 consultation in the chapel of Madras Christian College stood under the Pauline text of Romans 10:12– 15 that brings together "the universality of God's grace" and "the specificity of mission" as "the telling of the story of the Son of God who loved us and gave himself up for us."[65] Tambaram 1938 was to be gratefully celebrated in that light. It had been significant for four reasons. First, at a time when old "Christendom, the family of nations that had called themselves Christian, [was] falling into the demonic power of new pagan ideologies" and "the Nazi war machine was trampling over the whole European continent and destroying everything that had been treasured as, at least in intention, a Christian civilization," the meeting at Tambaram provided a sign of hope by embodying "a new Christendom, a family of Christian churches in every continent and in every culture"—what Archbishop William Temple would call in his Canterbury enthronement sermon of 1942 "the great new fact of our time."

Second, Kraemer's book had been an implicit repudiation of the attempt "to domesticate the Gospel" within European and American cultures. Kraemer "did not claim uniqueness for Christianity, which is a changing, variegated and ambiguous human phenomenon" but rather for "the events that form the substance of the Gospel." This came as a great liberation from the syncretistic confusion between the Christian faith and national identity or the values of Western civilization. Although it is intolerable arrogance to claim uniqueness and finality for one's own religious ideas or experiences, it is treason to our fellow human beings if we keep quiet about the *fact* that "almighty God, creator and sustainer of all that exists in heaven and on earth, has—at a known time and place in human history—so humbled himself as to become part of our sinful humanity and to suffer and die a shameful death to take away our sin and to rise from the dead as the first-fruit of a new creation." One can, of course, deny the story, says Newbigin, but if it is really true, "how can I agree that this amazing act of matchless grace should merely become part of a syllabus for the 'comparative study of religions'?" Rather, "it can only be the starting-point, the pre-supposition of all our struggle to understand the world, including our struggle to understand the world of religions."

Third, Tambaram 1938 marked the firm and decisive affirmation that mission is the responsibility of the whole Church. Here the preacher pays tribute to Bishop Azariah of Dornakal, "one of the most influential figures at the conference, who in his own ministry had shown what it means to be a missionary church," who saw equally that "missions must be churchly" and who accordingly urged the necessity for bringing together the work of Faith and Order and the work of the International Missionary Council.

Fourth, the final reason for thankful remembrance of Tambaram 1938, Newbigin said, was its emphasis on theological education, which at least started the missionary societies and churches along the road to a pattern of ministerial training that would no longer be dominated by theologies too much shaped by the European synthesis of Gospel and local culture but rather "equip the leadership of churches everywhere for their task of confessing Christ in the idiom and language of their own cultures."

Although the ostensible theme of Tambaram 1988 was "Christian Witness in a Pluralistic World," the hidden agenda may have been the currently controversial issue of the relation between mission and dialogue, or more precisely between the Christian "mission" and "dialogue" with people of other faiths. In any case, the official record of the meeting shows that the questions discussed were of the following kind: Are revelation and salvation found also outside the Church or even outside of Jesus Christ? Do other religions and movements also have a valid "mission"? Do Christians have things to learn from people of other faiths? How may people of every allegiance live together peaceably and constructively in a single world?[66]

The two participants whom Newbigin singled out as particularly representative of the outlook he rejected were Wilfred Cantwell Smith and Diana Eck, both associated in their generations with the Center for the Study of World Religions at Harvard University. Calling attention in their papers at the consultation to "other voices" from Tambaram 1938, both bluntly stated they considered Hendrik Kraemer to have been fundamentally wrong and, on the basis of their own experience of testimonies received in dialogue with other believers, they forthrightly affirmed "God" to be revealingly and savingly encountered by "Hindus, Muslims, Buddhists, and the rest," who have also been given missions by this same God.

In the reported discussions, Lesslie Newbigin asserted the singularity of God and therefore of reality and of the human story. The "clue to follow" was provided by "those acts which have their centre in the life, ministry and death of Jesus Christ," which "focus" the "ultimate meaning of human history." Newbigin was there operating with an epistemology of objective reality and subjective apprehension which he believed to be grounded in Christ himself in his cosmic capacity. Recorded in colloquial style, he said:

> The Greek civilization for all its glory finally perished through a failure of nerve, because at the end of the day the struggle to know the truth was given up as hopeless and Greek civilization relaxed into polytheism and syncretism. And it was the Christian Church that challenged that with the confident affirmation that the ultimate reality is to be known, and it is to be known in this man Jesus Christ. The Logos became flesh, and it was that challenge which finally replaced the disintegrating culture of the classical world. I think that we are exactly in that position now in our Western culture. Western culture has lost its nerve. It no longer has any confidence in the capacity to know reality, and therefore we can only speak of what is true for me, and what is true for you. I think one of our greatest tasks is to recover the capacity to affirm the truth as a matter of belief. All knowledge has both a subjective and an objective pole, and our situation is that these have become dissociated. All knowing has a subjective pole that involves my attempt to grasp reality in terms of the information that I have received and the understanding I have been given, but it involves my personal passionate commitment to understand reality. It has an objective pole. In that sense, it is my belief, but it is my belief that this is true. It is the reality that I believe I am in a measure able to grasp, always subject to revision. And of course the test of objectivity of your faith is not that you can prove its truth from any other source. You cannot prove ultimate truth. It is the essence of the matter that we are seeking, probing, open to new understanding, but that we believe that we are in contact with reality, so that we cannot be content with this kind of polytruth that says what is true for you is not necessarily true for me. Then we are all in a world where in the twilight all cats are grey. I think this fundamental crisis of the Western world is the background of all our present discussion about dialogue. And if that is ignored we shall miss the bus.[67]

It is precisely because Islam has such a confident fiduciary framework for knowledge—its own—that Newbigin came to consider it the chief rival of the Christian faith as the twentieth century turned toward the twenty-first.

Concerning the implications of his stance for mission, Newbigin stressed at Tambaram 1988 the prevenient and often surprising witness of the Holy Spirit, asserting that "the witness of the Spirit is to Christ" while recognizing that the relation of "the work of the Spirit to Christ is a very vital issue that needs a lot of exploration." He quoted his old friend D. T. Niles to the effect that "Jesus walks ahead of the Church, but it is the Church he walks ahead of": "Among the many spirits at work in the world, the distinguishing mark of the Holy Spirit is the confession of Jesus." Newbigin objected, for instance, to the tendency to give "an abstract noun like justice an ultimate status" that is refused to the person of Jesus, when in fact justice has to be defined in reference to "the Lord Jesus Christ, in whom the justice of God has been fulfilled in a way that undercuts all our understandings of justice and makes possible a world in which we are able to seek justice and to forgive one another." In their constant christocentrism, trinitarianly understood, there became evident the underlying closeness between Newbigin and another participant in the Tambaram anniversary, his old sparring partner M. M. Thomas, about whom more is said in chapter 7.

Shortly after the Tambaram anniversary meeting of 1988, Newbigin set out some wide-ranging "reflections on the history of missions" in preparation for the world conference on mission and evangelism that was to be held in San Antonio, Texas, in 1989. He recalled the meeting of the previous year, when

> strong voices were heard that appeared to deny the centrality of Jesus Christ and to support other models for human unity. In the earlier debates about mission, passionate as they were, there was never any question about the centrality of Jesus Christ. I do not think that the WCC can continue to play any significant role in the world missionary task if it does not adhere firmly to its basis. This is not one of the issues on the agenda of San Antonio, but it will certainly have to be faced. But the San Antonio meeting has the immense advantage of being able to build on the remarkable Ecumenical Affirmation on Mission and Evangelism approved by the WCC's central committee in 1982. This splendid statement is a worthy outcome of these years of debate and (sometimes) confusion, and should set the parameters for ecumenical thinking for many years to come.[68]

Urgent in tone, the ecumenical affirmation commended by Newbigin was in effect an enriched reaffirmation, in a new time, of the themes that had marked his own work with the International Missionary Council. The document is biblically based, christocentric, and trinitarian; it links evangelism, service, and social action; it associates common witness and the unity of the Church; it is both local and global in range; it is oriented to God's Kingdom and aims at God's glory. The address of the Gospel, it says, is both singular and communal: "Each person is entitled to hear the Good News. The call to conversion, as a call to repentance and obedience, should also be addressed to nations, groups, and families." On "witness among people of living faiths," the document declares that "life with people of other faiths and ideologies is an encounter of commitments. Witness cannot be a one-way process, but of necessity is two-way; in it Christians become aware of some of the deepest convictions of their neighbours. It is also the time in which, within a spirit of openness and trust, Christians are able to bear authentic witness, giving an account of their commitment to Christ, who calls all persons to himself."[69]

At the San Antonio conference itself, Newbigin's "evening address" brought to the attention of a worldwide audience his call for "a missionary encounter with modernity." This theme occupies chapter 10, but it may be adumbrated here. "The most important dialogue for us now," he said, "is the dialogue between the biblical understanding of the human story and that understanding of the human story which is dominating Western culture and increasingly the culture of the world. I am seeing it as the crucial missionary task that we challenge and claim the high intellectual ground of our Western culture, the ground that rules our public life." In the active life of the churches in Britain, Newbigin judged that "the ministers and people are more devoted, more committed to the Gospel than was normally the case a hundred years ago; they are much more involved in the political and social implications of the Gospel than they were a hundred years ago." He asked:

> Why is it, then, that the Church tends to be so defensive, and even so timid in the faith, before the claims of what we call modern culture? The answer is that we have allowed ourselves, we have allowed the Gospel, to be co-opted into a subordinate position in this world of values where it cannot challenge what is called the world of facts. We must recover the courage to recognize that it is this world of so-called facts that we have to challenge, and where we have to claim the high ground. We have to do as St. Paul says in his letter to the Corinthians, "to bring every thought in captivity to Christ."

The task is an intellectual one, Newbigin will insist, but it affects every local church that seeks to understand itself and the world through the biblical story.[70]

Meanwhile, the study of Newbigin's missiological thinking follows in chapter 6 the theme of his engagement with the religions, where the theoretical and practical relation between evangelism and dialogue becomes crucial.

6

The Religious Interlocutor

So Paul, standing in the middle of the Areopagus, said: "Men of Athens, I perceive that in every way you are very religious. . . ."

(Acts 17:22)

First of all, then, I urge that supplications, prayers, intercessions, and thanksgivings be made for all men. . . . This is good, and it is acceptable in the sight of God our Saviour, who desires all men to be saved and to come to the knowledge of the truth. For there is one God, and there is one mediator between God and men, the man Christ Jesus, who gave himself as a ransom for all, the testimony to which was borne at the proper time.

(1 Timothy 2:1, 3–6)

In India

Two passages in Newbigin's writings from thirty years apart will raise the themes of the Gospel's relation to adherents of other religions than the Christian and of his own understanding and practice in the matter over half a century and more. The first passage occurs in the address given by Newbigin under the title "Mission Agenda" at Trinity College, Dublin, in 1992 on the occasion of the centenary celebrations of the Dublin University Mission to Chota Nagpur: "The globalization of human society has, very naturally and properly, led missionary societies to move away from the one-directional model of mission to a model which emphasises sharing, listening and dialogue. My own life-time as a missionary has been in the context of this shift and I have shared in it to the full." Newbigin immediately went on to declare, "There is a wide gap between the way inter-faith conversation happens when it is conducted in Tamil among people who have never been through an English educational process, and the way it is conducted among those, Indian and European, who share the same kind of academic formation."[1] The second passage dates from 1963 and Newbigin's programmatic reflections on "Trinitarian Faith and Today's Mission":

In what terms shall we affirm the uniqueness, sufficiency and finality of Christ without either denying the reality of his working in the world or blunting

204

the sharpness of the challenge which he puts to every man to choose? It is at this point, I believe, that the real difficulties lie for those in the Asian Churches who are trying to reopen a living dialogue through which the Gospel can be commended to men of other faiths and of no faith. In the older Churches of the West it may well be that syncretism is the real danger; there seem to be many who think it only natural that the usual list of religious allegiances—Roman Catholic, Protestant and Jewish—should be extended as the occasion arises to include Hindus, Muslims and Buddhists also. But this kind of syncretism is not a living danger in the Churches of Asia. Here the danger, as their leaders have often pointed out, is "ghettoism"—a practical withdrawal into the position of a tolerated and static minority, a cultural and religious enclave within the majority community. Correspondingly the great need is to find ways of breaking out of this isolation and of entering into real dialogue with the men of other faiths who are wrestling with the problems of the modern world and who are seeking resources to meet its demands. . . . What is needed now, if there is to be a living dialogue with men of other faiths, is that we should see how God's unique and saving revelation of himself in Jesus Christ enables men to interpret what is happening to them and to respond to the calling of God in the midst of the life of the world."[2]

The formal point here is the nature and purpose of dialogue.

The substantive point, of course, is the status and value of the world religions in relation to Christianity and to the Gospel. In one set of circumstances—those of living practice—we shall observe Newbigin directly in his approach to the adherents of other religions. In another set of circumstances, we shall see Newbigin in debate with Western or Western-educated academics on the matter. His experiences in these two types of situations feed into each other, and they help to shape Newbigin's views on the relation between evangelism and dialogue. Concerning the practical engagement with adherents of other religions, the story runs from Newbigin's years as a missionary among Hindus in India through his time as a teacher, pastor, and citizen in multiethnic, multicultural, and multireligious Birmingham to a final concentration on the presence of Islam in the West and its worldwide range. Concerning the more theoretical debates, it appears from the way Newbigin engaged with the discussants that Western-educated academic religionists shifted their interests over the decades from a search for human unity by way of the commonalties between the religions to the advocacy of a mutually complementary pluralism. What Newbigin says early on about the higher Hinduism and the unity of religion will remain important throughout this chapter as the theme finds a reprise in the criticisms he later addresses to the Western academic affirmation of religious pluralism which, despite differences of terminology, he regards as bearing some fundamental resemblances to the higher Hinduism. In both practice and theory, Newbigin himself remained constant in his attachment to the comprehensiveness, centrality, and finality of Jesus Christ in the areas of creation, redemption, and consummation, while locating Jesus Christ theologically in an increasingly explicit trinitarian framework.

Substantial access to Newbigin's approach to Hindus and Hinduism during his Indian decades is to be had only through his own accounts, both contemporary and retrospective.[3] We have already seen Newbigin as a young missionary doing the work of an evangelist in the sacred city of Kanchipuram, preaching in the streets and selling copies of the Gospels at an anna apiece, as well as undertaking the simplest presentation of the scriptural story through team evangelism in the surrounding villages of the Untouchables. Take now an episodic encounter on a country bus as the new bishop in Madurai is quizzed about his business. When he states the object of his journey, the conversation takes a theological turn, and all feel free to join in:

> Even the V.I.P.s in the front seat beside the driver turn round to cock an ear at the conversation. There is every variety of response from the open-eyed wonder of the villager who has never heard of the Gospel, to the blasé scepticism of the college graduate who has seen through it all. A prosperous-looking Brahmin begins a mocking imitation of a missionary preaching in Tamil: "Ah, rascals, dolts, tramps and vagabonds, come to us and we will take you in." Tamil has no words which really mean "to save sinners". Apart from Christ, how could it? The words in the Tamil Bible could equally be translated "to provide free board and lodging for rascals". That is one of the inescapable problems of evangelism. The Brahmin has made a good hit and gets a good laugh for it. I am wondering how to reply when an unexpected ally turns up. A young farmer, sitting on the bench behind, leans forward and tackles the Brahmin. "I know all your nonsense. 'All religions are the same,' you say. 'All roads lead to God.' It is not true. If you want to go somewhere you have to get into the right bus. If you get into the wrong bus you get to the wrong place. If you want salvation you have got to have the religion that gets you there. That's Christianity." The Brahmin was not expecting this and is silenced. It is quite good fun teasing a missionary, but decidedly less edifying to argue about religion with an obvious outcaste. The farmer tells me his story, how he became a Christian, how he learned to be a good farmer, how he has developed fruit farming. Here is his place now. There are his fruit trees over there. He shouts to the driver to stop and gets down, shoulders his bundle, and tramps off through the fields to his house. The Brahmin is a little sorry for his attack and we have a good talk.[4]

As he moved through the years of his episcopate in the Madurai diocese, Newbigin observed "a change of consciousness" occurring "in the communities of Christians who lived in the outcaste quarter of hundreds of villages. People who had lived for untold centuries as serfs were learning to think of themselves as children of God." In his own thinking the bishop found himself starting less with the preaching of faith as the individual's access to salvation and putting the emphasis more on the local Christian community as the unbeliever's first point of contact with the redemptive work of Christ. The message could still be formulated as turning from idols to serve the living God, with a hope fixed on his Son (cf. Acts 14:15; 1 Thessalonians 1:9f.). When Newbigin returned to India as bishop in Madras, his encouragement of the churches to social service in the slums was not undertaken without making it plain to Hindu civic officials that "we were concerned about conversion, but that conversion should mean more and not less concern about

one's neighbours. I was happy that our contribution was so warmly welcomed."[5]

Especially important for Newbigin's reflection and practice was the conversation and study he shared with Hindu scholars during his early years in
Kanchipuram. This experience clearly marked him throughout his time in
India and remained with him to the last years of his life, as is evident from
the weighty passage he devoted to it in his autobiography:

> Kanchipuram was and is a strong centre of traditional Hindu learning, and
> I was privileged to enjoy the welcoming friendship of the scholars who gath-
> ered in the *math* or monastery of the Ramakrishna Mission. Along with the
> head of that community I shared in the leadership of a weekly study group
> in which we studied alternately the Svetasvara Upanishad and St. John's
> Gospel. We sat, Indian fashion, cross-legged on the floor and the leader in
> each case read the Scripture in the original language—Sanskrit or Greek—
> and expounded it, after which there would be an hour or more of questioning
> and discussion. These sessions were extremely rewarding for me. I would like
> to think that they also had some value for my Hindu friends. Certainly none
> of them became a Christian and I did not become a Hindu, though I learned
> to see the profound rationality of the world-view of the Vedanta. I well re-
> member how I astonished the Swami by saying that if it could be shown that
> Jesus had never lived and died and risen again I would have no alternative
> but to become a Hindu. He thought that only a lunatic would allow his
> ultimate destiny to hang upon a questionable fact of history which—even if
> it could be proved—belonged to the world of *maya*.
>
> The Ramakrishna Mission follows in general the school of Vedanta, but
> one member of the group was a respected teacher in the school of Visishtad-
> vaita, the theistic form of belief which stems from the teaching of Ramanuja.
> This has been called "India's Religion of Grace" and has many close parallels
> with evangelical Christianity which had been explained in Rudolf Otto's book
> with that title. This scholar was kind enough to give many hours of his time
> to initiating me into the teachings of this school. At the end I had to confess
> (contrary to my expectations) that Hendrik Kraemer's criticism of Otto's as-
> sessment was justified (*The Christian Message in a Non-Christian World*, pp.
> 168–73). Even this profoundly moving and gracious form of religious devo-
> tion had its roots and its only support in the human need for salvation, not
> in a divine act of redemption within the real history of which this human
> life is a part.
>
> I am bound to say that as I reflected on these long discussions on religious
> subjects with gracious and helpful Hindu friends, I became more and more
> sure that the "point of contact" for the Gospel is rather in the ordinary
> secular experiences of human life than in the sphere of religion. I had not
> then read Karl Barth and did not know that "religion is unbelief", but I was
> certainly beginning to see that religion can be a way of protecting oneself
> from reality.[6]

Time and time again in his writings, Newbigin reverted to the contrast
between the cyclical conception of time found in Hinduism (and other idealist
worldviews) and the linear movement of history in the Old and New Testa-

ments (and their realist derivatives, whether sacred or secular).[7] As the creator, redeemer, and consummator of all things seen and unseen, in whose purpose lay their origin, under whose governance their course ran, and to whose glory their salvation would finally redound, the God of Jesus Christ offered liberation from fate and sin both within the present substantial world and in his completed Kingdom. Contact with the biblical faith, direct or indirect, was in modern times starting to change Indian views of reality in a historical direction, and it was a crucial question whether the shift would be received in its full and authentic evangelical form or rather in the distorted and truncated secular forms of Marxism or capitalist progress. Late in life, Newbigin recalled before a German audience the observations on personhood and history frequently expressed to him by a Hindu friend, a Brahmin scholar, who had made a deep study both of the Bible and of the sacred scriptures of India: "I cannot forgive you Christians for the way in which you have misrepresented the Bible. You have introduced it to us as though it were a book of religion—of which we have plenty in India already. It is not. It is, as I read it, a quite unique interpretation of universal history and, therefore, a unique interpretation of the human person as an actor in that history."[8]

A very concrete issue concerning the relation of Christianity and Indian religions arose during Newbigin's Madurai episcopate in the field of children's education. In his letter home of October 1955,[9] the bishop writes favorably of the Madras government's introduction into the village elementary schools of the Gandhian pattern of basic education centered on craft and community in order to meet children's fundamental needs of love and work. However, in the basic training schools for teachers a form of daily common worship, modeled on Gandhiji's ashram prayers, had been made a more or less compulsory part of the syllabus. Students were being required to learn about, and in some cases join in, the celebration of the great festivals of all the religions, the aim being to build up loyalty to a community that transcends more particular loyalties that were felt to be divisive. "This creates," wrote Newbigin, "a conflict of loyalties for Christians. Some sincere Christians believe that they can play their part in the service of the nation by taking part in this sort of worship. The vast majority feel that it is impossible. . . . The CSI has put forth an official statement for the guidance of its members, advising Christian students in basic schools that they cannot take part in the 'common worship', and also suggesting positive ways in which they may make their contributions to the life of the School." The matter prompted Newbigin to recall the opinion expressed by Hendrik Kraemer on a visit a few years earlier that "the real meeting between the Gospel and Hinduism had not yet taken place." Important as questions of caste, evil social customs, and even polytheism and idolatry were, such things would hardly be defended any longer by educated Hindus. The crucial question was that being raised in the practical daily decisions having to be taken by ordinary citizens and by ordinary students in basic schools: "Is there a way of reconciliation with God, and therefore of mutual reconciliation among men, apart from Jesus Christ?" Again, the urgency is obvious to Newbigin of a Christian unity to end the grave compromise brought by ecclesial divisions to evangelical witness on behalf of Christ the Reconciler.

The case of the Indian schools occupied Newbigin enough for him to introduce it into his formal lectures at Chicago and Harvard in the 1950s. Issues of religious education in public schools would reemerge in the very different circumstances of the city of Birmingham twenty-five years later.[10]

At Chicago and Harvard, at Yale and Cambridge

In the 1950s Newbigin lectured at North America's two academic centers most famed for their interest in religion as a genus. On the occasion of his attendance at the second assembly of the World Council of Churches that met at Evanston, Illinois, in August 1954 with the theme of "Christ the Hope of the World," Newbigin delivered at the University of Chicago the Thomas Memorial Lecture under the title "The Quest for Unity through Religion."[11] In November 1958 he gave the William Belden Noble Lectures at Harvard University. Just before the third assembly of the WCC at New Delhi in 1961 confessed "Christ the Light of the World," Newbigin's Harvard lectures were published in book form as *A Faith For This One World?*[12]

Newbigin began his Chicago lecture by recalling the remarkable impact made by Swami Vivekananda at the Parliament of Religions held in that city in 1893: "The Lord," the Swami had said in his address, "the Lord has declared to the Hindu in his incarnation as Krishna, 'I am in every religion as the thread through a string of pearls.' " That was the first announcement of the claim of renascent Hinduism, Newbigin noted, to know itself by revelation to be "not merely a religion, and not merely a world religion, but *the* world religion—the religion within which the truths of all other religions had already been included and transcended." The belief that in essence all religions are one has become in India an axiom of thought, as displayed in the new basic schools. Jesus is readily recognized by Hindus as an incarnation of the one universal religious principle, but the exclusive claims made for him by Christians are dismissed as spiritually primitive, socially sectarian, and culturally imperialistic. Whereas the liberal Christians of the Laymen's Foreign Mission Inquiry and its report, *Re-Thinking Missions* (1932), had still to look forward to the growth of all religions into "unity in the completest religious truth," the higher Hindu already occupies a standpoint that knows all contradictions between the religions to be merely apparent and all religious forms to be merely relative, partial, and temporary. They are but varied refractions of the truth in the visible and tangible world that has itself no final reality. The "That art Thou" of the Chandogya Upanishad means, for the Vedantin, that pure selfhood is the ultimate reality at the heart of all existence. "Our real self is the supreme being," it was put by Sarvepalli Radhakrishnan, sometime Oxford don and later vice president of India. Liberation from the toils of "maya" comes by withdrawal of the mind from the world of sense perception, then concentration on one object of meditation, and finally dissolution into a single unitary "intransitive" awareness where "the soul, holding itself in emptiness, finds itself possessing all."

What is involved in "seeing the real" (as Radhakrishnan phrases it) is a mystical experience (which Newbigin considers it would be impertinent to doubt) that then issues in the philosophical and theological claim (which becomes, Newbigin this time insists, just as open to criticism and debate as any other philosophy or theology) that "the reality behind all the manifold appearance and all the ceaseless change which our five senses report to us is one undifferentiated and unchanging spirit and that that spirit is identical with our own spirit." Moreover, the claim to be, in the country of the blind, the only one who can see in turn implies "a fundamental intolerance in the Hindu position no less than in the Christian." The "almost infinite" tolerance of Hinduism stops short—with perfect self-consistency—at "the one assertion which Christianity is bound to make, namely, that the Supreme Being has, once and for all, revealed himself in a historic person; that truth is to be found only by relating one's self to him; and that he is the center around which the unity of mankind here in history is to be built." The question becomes: "Is the Hindu"—or mutatis mutandis the Christian—"view of religion true, and can it provide the means of unity for mankind?"

A decision regarding truth—in this case the relation of ultimate reality to the multiplicity of phenomena—is, in the last resort, a matter of faith, Newbigin argues. In any case, the nature of unity and the means of attaining it will differ radically between Hindus and Christians. Hinduism offers "the negative unity of tolerance," suited to a way of salvation for the individual that has no organic relation to any particular historical events or to any visible historic community; the Christian faith proclaims "the positive unity of love," grounded in what took place in Palestine under Pontius Pilate and offering not merely the cessation of strife but "the creation of a new community," and so the Church is part of the creed, "organic to the Gospel." Because "the character of the once-and-for-all event governs the character of the unity which it creates," the death of Jesus which effects atonement between God and sinful men is the God-created basis for mutual forgiveness among mutually hostile human beings and "the reconciliation of persons in their totality to one another." That is why ecclesial unity is urgently necessary to the credibility of the missionary proclamation, "Christ the hope of the world": "If the world is to be made one in Christ, the world must be able to see the nucleus of that unity embodied in some sort of visible unity." In reflecting on the proper form of that unity, Newbigin already anticipates the gist of the description that he formulated for the New Delhi assembly of the WCC: "First, it must be such that all who are in Christ in any place are, in that place, visibly one fellowship; second, it must be such that each local community is so ordered and so related to the whole that its fellowship with all Christ's people everywhere, and with those who have gone before and will come after, is made clear. That will mean at least this: a ministry universally recognized and visibly linked with the ministry of the Church through the centuries."[13]

Moving from Chicago in 1954 to Harvard in 1958, Newbigin used the opportunity of the five William Belden Noble lectures to enlarge the picture while retaining the same lineaments. The first chapter of *A Faith for This One World?* describes "the end of Christendom and the rise of a world civilization." With the halting and reversal of colonialism, it is not only the political and cultural tide that flows against the West but also the religious, for the modern missionary movement had coincided with the expansion of the white races of Europe and North America across the globe, and the spread of the Gospel had not been clearly differentiated from enlightenment through Western education. Enjoying a renascence stimulated precisely by the invasion of Western culture, Asian cultures are becoming confident to take into their own use what the West brought rather than letting themselves be displaced by it. India particularly is offering to the entire world the political pattern of a "peaceful coexistence" grounded in the "infinitely stable and infinitely flexible" tradition of Hinduism with its serene possession of the full-orbed truth—and this in the face of a West that has discredited itself by war and cinematic sex. At the same time, the science and the technology which is indubitably a product of the West appears as a detachable product that is potentially the property of all people everywhere.

Although the new world civilization was formed in the matrix of Western Christendom, it may be that the mother died in childbirth. But Newbigin wonders whether the infant can survive without the spiritual sustenance provided by its parent. Can science and technology permanently coexist with the view that the visible world is an illusion and that time is but a wheel spinning around a motionless center? (In Tamil country, the cycle recurs every sixty years.) Or will the notion of purposive change—which drives the scientific world civilization and derives from the Bible—transform "India" from within? From a Christian viewpoint, Newbigin argues, the development of a single world history may be seen as a providential move whereby all the nations are being brought into the range of God's decisive act of judgment and mercy as they are confronted with the critical choice between Christ and "the ruler of this age" in their search for "total welfare" in a "new age." In any case, says Newbigin, the emergence of "a common world civilization" ineluctably poses the question of the origin and destiny of humankind as a whole, of the meaning of human life itself—and that is a religious question.

Three proposals for a universal faith are examined in Newbigin's next chapter. First he brings back India's vice president, S. Radhakrishnan, and his "religion which transcends race and creed, yet informs all races and creeds"—and is substantially the higher Hinduism of Ramakrishna Paramahamsa; and again the practical case of the basic schools is described. The next to be criticized is Arnold Toynbee and his Harvard lectures on *Christianity Among the Religions of the World* (1958) and, last, Harvard professor William Ernest Hocking and his *Coming World Civilization* (1958). Both are taxed with importing from Christianity the notion of "self-sacrifice" or "suffering love" as the ultimate nature of things and then cutting a "Christ concept" adrift from Jesus and his story. "On the question whether the word Christ is or is not indissolubly and finally riveted to the name of Jesus," says Newbigin, "hangs the whole issue between life and death for man." Only "if it be a fact that in Jesus the God who created all things, the Lord of glory, humbled himself to die as a criminal for the sin of the world, and that having died he rose again as victor over death" is it "possible to believe and to preach that— in spite of all appearances to the contrary—love rules the world." There is no pride in the Christian claim to uniqueness but only a common invitation to all people to meet at the one place—the Cross of Jesus—where God has provided for righteousness and peace to kiss and where reconciliation is achieved through forgiveness. Newbigin's third and fourth chapters explore the nature and content of that message which, while offering the world its chance of unity, makes "even the future existence of human civilization a secondary question."

Those chapters represent an expansion of what Newbigin had written on "The Duty and Authority of the Church to Preach the Gospel" for the Amsterdam assembly of the WCC in 1948 and the even more concise formulation of the historic Christian rule of faith in the "Statement on the Missionary Calling of the Church" drafted at the Willingen missionary conference in 1952.[14] The authority of the Christian message resides in its source, in the name and fact and person of Jesus, not in its promise to answer the problems of a divided world. Not merely the auxiliary to one's hopes and fears for oneself and the human race, Jesus confronts people with the question of whether he is truly the bringer and presence of God's Kingdom, "the sovereign Lord of all mankind, the conqueror of sin and death, the cause and cornerstone of the universe." The "total fact of Jesus Christ," an event which occurs in and controls history, bringing one era to a close and opening another, must be understood within a cosmic frame. So Newbigin sets out in chapter 3 "the presuppositions of Christ's revelation"—first, "the faith that the God in whose name Jesus has come is the Creator of all things, the sovereign Lord of time with power to bring one age to an end and to declare the coming of a new one" (the biblical doctrine of creation); second, "the faith that mankind, created in God's image, is fallen from its true estate and involved in a common sin against the creator" (the biblical doctrine of sin); third, "the faith that what God is doing in Christ is the culmination of a plan which begins with the choosing of a people to be his own people, to be his witnesses and the agents of his purpose for the world" (the biblical doctrine of election). The first of these presuppositions is affirmed in contradiction to all polytheisms (which would seek savior gods to help us against the mysterious and dangerous forces of the universe), gnosticisms (in which the inward and spiritual alone is truly real), and creaturely claims to absolute authority (which end up destroying human freedom and integrity). According to the second presupposition, it is only by the Cross of Jesus that "the total rebellion of the human race against its maker is unmasked, judged and forgiven" and the self-righteousness of all ethical and religious efforts to please God revealed and rejected, so that salvation comes entirely as God's gift (Newbigin contrasts this with the reply made by a devout Vaishnava to his question, "What is the ground of your assurance that God is ready to forgive you?": "If he wouldn't, I would go to a God who would"). In the third presupposition, the biblical doctrine of election is, as we saw in the last chapter, Newbigin's answer to the question of particularity and universality and rests on belief in a personal God who is shown in Christ to be free to act for the furtherance of his purposes and chooses to do so in a way that requires us to receive salvation through our neighbor (and again the impediment of division among Christians is castigated).

In chapter 4 Newbigin develops "the content of Christ's revelation." Christ's coming was "the coming of a new reality, namely, the presence of the living God himself among men," and thereby "the inauguration of a new era in human history in which the ancient promises are fulfilled and the Spirit of God is given to man." After his disciples have been made anew by being brought to share in his death and resurrection, the "spontaneous overflow of love out of hearts full of the love of God in Jesus Christ" is "the divine mission to the world of which the Church is the instrument." The Holy Spirit in the Church, however, is an earnest, a foretaste, "a real instalment but not yet the whole." The Church is a pilgrim people, journeying to the ends of the earth as it travels toward the promised land of God's complete reign. Its witness hastens the universal consummation when the painful tension between having and hoping will be fully resolved. "The Church has the duty and the authority to preach the Gospel to the whole world," says Newbigin, "not only because in it the new reality of God's era is present, but also because in it the nature of the end to which human history looks is known, known on the basis of revelation. The Church looks to and bears witness to a real end of history, an end which is in the future and which we do not yet see but to which, according to St. Paul, we are nearer than when we first believed."

Newbigin then proceeds to expound the biblically derived notion—both teleological and eschatological—of "an end of history." This is set against the absence of all history in a cyclical worldview, against the reduction of history as such to a natural "process" by the removal of the category of purpose, against the collectivist idea of "progress" by which intervening generations become merely instrumental to a new social order they will never see, and against the individualist distortion of the drama of the whole human story into "a non-stop review, providing the setting for a series of solo items after which each of the players goes off and receives his bouquet privately in the wings." Christian eschatology is consistent with a transcendent God who "calls the whole created order into being, sustains it in being, and has power to bring it to its proper end. And the coming of Jesus is the revelation of that end within the created order; in him the Creator who is both the beginning and the end was present among men, and by the operation of the Holy Spirit he is still present in the community of believers"—until sin and evil are finally overcome, the dead are raised, and the world is re-created as new heavens and a new earth. For the rest of history, the choice for humankind is between Christ and antichrist—"this 'Big Brother' of George Orwell who offers all men security and peace, who claims to be able to produce a total, all-embracing world order complete with concentration camps and gas ovens for the recalcitrant." Newbigin recalls from Albert Schweitzer, "The Christian's every action will be a prayer for the coming of the Kingdom." The Church's urgent mission takes place under the mercy of God in "the time given for the Gospel to be made known to all men so that they may repent and believe and turn to God."

The fifth and final chapter of *A Faith For This One World?* spells out some practical missiological implications of a view of mission as "the mission of the whole Church to the whole world" such as we saw in our preceding chapter. They include the observation that "the churches of the old Christendom imperatively need the help of Christians who have learned to confess Christ in the midst of the worlds of Hinduism, Buddhism and Islam. They are already experienced in facing issues which are new for Western Christians."

In April 1966 Newbigin gave the Lyman Beecher Lectures at Yale University Divinity School, later used the substance of them in altered form as the James Reid Lectures in the Divinity Faculty of Cambridge University, and eventually published the material after further revision as *The Finality of Christ*.[15] This work was thus produced in the thick of the "secular '60s," and it certainly attributed value to the secular, although in a more cautious— and indeed substantially different—way than did the enthusiastic proponents of "the secular meaning of the gospel" (to borrow the title of a book of the time by Paul Van Buren). At the same time, however, the long-time missionary to India warned that "in spite of all that has been written from within the cultural situation of Western Europe, it would be unwise to conclude that the end of religion is a foregone conclusion." Indeed, the first full chapter of the book is titled "Christianity Among the Religions," and only in the next chapter does Newbigin come to "The Gospel as a Secular Announcement."

Newbigin's chosen purpose in the book, he tells us in the introduction, is not to *demonstrate* the "finality of Christ" but, much more modestly, to "explore what it means to claim finality for him" as the Christian faith has done. Today the claim can be made only in the face of several ostensibly countervailing factors: the overwhelming impression given by science of the vastness of space and time that makes the earth a mere speck of dust and human history a fleeting moment; the scientific method that makes all "conclusions" tentative and only starting points for further research; the development of a historiography that emphasizes the relativity of particular epochs; studies in the world's religions that show Christianity to be one of a broader family of religions in a common human culture that may in any case be looking elsewhere for unifying values; the "acute bad conscience of Western man" that shuns any thought of continuing to impose his traditional faith and morals on postcolonial peoples. Furthermore, Newbigin considers it necessary to his project, as should be the case in all interreligious discussion, to declare his own standpoint: he is not claiming to operate from "outside religion" with an "impartiality" toward the various religions that is often rooted in a theory that all religion is illusion; nor does he share either that total agnosticism or that stupendous superiority of vision that are implied when in this connection the fable is told of "the King of Benares who entertained himself and his court by putting an elephant in the midst of half-a-dozen blind men and asked them to tell him what it was. One got hold of the trunk and said it was a rope; one of the leg and said it was a tree; one of the ear and said it was a winnowing fan–and so on."[16] Newbigin's starting point, which he finds intellectually justified by Gerard van der Leeuw in his *Religion in Essence and Manifestation* (1938), is avowedly "within one of the religions," seeking to enter understandingly into the religious convictions of others and search out common ground and yet obliged—as all religions in principle are—to offer an interpretation of the others in relation to one's own ultimate loyalty.

The procedure by which Newbigin discusses the question of "Christianity among the religions" is that of a commentary on positions taken at the successive international missionary conferences of Edinburgh 1910, Jerusalem 1928, and Tambaram 1938, and the literature surrounding them. Edinburgh recommended knowledge and charity on the part of Christian missionaries toward "the non-Christian religions," affirming their "nobler elements" as stepping-stones to better things, because they "disclose elemental needs of the human soul which Christianity alone can satisfy" and "in their higher forms plainly manifest the working of the Spirit of God." This attitude is both possible and necessary, it was said, because "Jesus Christ fulfils and supersedes all other religions." Empirical Christianity may even be enriched by what it learns through sympathetic' contact between Christians and people of other faiths, although the treasures were in fact already contained in the Gospel and only waiting to be discovered. This general position, says Newbigin, was stated by J. N. Farquhar in a book that made Christ "the fulfilment of each of the highest aspirations and aims of Hinduism" (*The Crown of Hinduism*, 1913) and more recently by Raymond Panikkar in *The Unknown Christ of Hinduism* (1965), in which Hinduism appears as "the starting-point of a religion that culminates in Christianity" and, thanks to the hidden presence of Christ, was the means of salvation provided for the people of India before the arrival of historical Christianity. Newbigin raises a number of questions: May not some elements in, say, Hinduism (e.g. the "courage," as Aurobindo calls it, to worship the evil principle of the universe—Durgha—as well as the good) remain incompatible with the Christian faith rather than being "completed" by it? May not the "nobler" elements in the non-Christian religions actually constitute a "Pharisaic" block to the recognition of Jesus? Is it possible to agree on a list of evidences for the activity of the Holy Spirit in the non-Christian religions?

Jerusalem 1928, dominated by the rise of secularism, looked for "spiritual values" in the non-Christian religions—including secularism itself, viewed for this purpose as a "religion"! In the conference's closing message, a welcome was offered to secularism insofar as it undertook "the disinterested pursuit of truth and of human welfare," just as Islam was appreciated for its "sense of the Majesty of God and the consequent reverence in worship," Buddhism for its "deep sympathy for the world's sorrow and unselfish search for the way of escape," Hinduism for its "desire for contact with ultimate reality conceived as spiritual," and Confucianism for its "belief in a moral order of the universe and consequent insistence on moral conduct." A group of continental European theologians rejected this "Anglo-Saxon" procedure of establishing comparisons and contrasts between the "values" in the non-Christian religions and Christianity and insisted, in a way which Newbigin finds nearer to the language of the Bible and to the reality of Christian experience, that the business of Christians is to announce the Gospel of redemption through Jesus Christ, recognizing that acceptance of this Gospel means a radical break with even the best of the values of the non-Christian religions and a total conversion to Christ.

Tambaram 1938 was obliged to face the challenge made by Hendrik Kraemer, fresh from his missionary service in the Dutch East Indies, to the liberal North American "rethinking" of missions contained in the "Laymen's Report" of 1932. In *The Christian Message in a Non-Christian World*, Kraemer drew a sharp distinction between "Christianity"—which as a "religion" can claim no absoluteness or finality—and the revelation of God in Jesus Christ, which is sui generis. Newbigin endorses the distinction between empirical Christianity and the Gospel but (later in his own argument) questions, on ecclesiological grounds, whether it is possible to separate them as neatly as Kraemer did; and he (already at this point) questions, on epistemological grounds, whether it is possible to press the dichotomy between revelation and religious experience as far as Kraemer did.[17] But if, as Newbigin maintains, revelation has not occurred until God's revelatory act has been in some measure understood and accepted on the human side (which is "religious experience"), then the "sublimity" of religious experience that Kraemer can admit in a non-Christian must in reverse, Newbigin argues, mean that there has been some self-disclosure from the side of God. That there is some continuity between non-Christian experience of God and the experience of God which is given through Jesus Christ has been the working assumption, Newbigin observes, of Bible translators in choosing an existing word to render "God" (elsewhere Newbigin acknowledges his indebtedness on this point to conversation with Eugene Nida, longtime translations secretary of the American Bible Society). Still, the *discontinuity* will be greater than the continuity if, as Newbigin believes, the content of the revelation in Christ is not "timeless truth" or the character of God "himself" apart from his purpose and promise but rather a constitutive enactment of that promise on its way to fulfillment in the consummation of God's total purpose for the world.[18]

In transition to his next chapter, Newbigin suggests, even insists, that "the 'light that lightens every man' shines not only, perhaps not even chiefly, in man's religion" but "rather we may see it shining in the ordinary fidelities of home, business and national life": "The answer which Jesus gave to the question, 'What must I do to be saved?', was the story of the Good Samaritan, in which the two religious figures are plainly on their way to perdition, while the non-religious person is in the way of salvation." Some clarification is required here. When Newbigin says that the "point of contact" between the Gospel and non-Christian persons is "normally" found in some experience of their "secular life" *rather than* in some element of their "specifically religious" belief and practice—and indeed that "Jesus himself found his 'point of contact' with his hearer in the secular rather than in the religious field"—he is understanding "religion" in the limited sense of prayers and rites. But when religion means, as it does elsewhere for Newbigin, a fundamental worldview or an ultimate loyalty, then such a distinction between religious and secular will no longer work, for in that case religion is comprehensively present in every nook and cranny of "ordinary human experience."[19] A related question arises when Newbigin affirms, as he does throughout the rest of *The Finality of Christ*, the "secularization" brought by Western culture as the *liberation* of more and more areas of life and the world—presumably from *false* religion— where responsibility is now given to people to choose for or against Christ or God's action in history; for these decisions are surely themselves "religious" in the sense of total outlooks or definitive commitments.[20] In further clarification of Newbigin's terminology, it must also be noted that, unlike the more radical intramundane "secular theologians" of the 1960s, Newbigin held to a living, transcendent God who acts graciously toward the world and has in store for humankind a communal, death-defeating destiny under new heavens on a new earth.

In the following two chapters, then, Newbigin presents "the Gospel as a secular announcement" and Christ as "the clue to history," substantially in the same way as he had done in *A Faith For This One World?* and would do again in more developed trinitarian fashion in *The Open Secret*. Christ's coming was the effective announcement that God's comprehensive purpose for the whole world and the whole of human history—not simply a new religious doctrine or even a message perfecting the religious teaching of the ages, nor merely a new secular program or even a political theocracy—was now being brought to fulfillment in and through his presence and work. The placing of the announcement as an event at a particular point in "secular history"— beginning while Quirinius was governor of Syria and ending "under Pontius Pilate"—belonged to its very character: "The occurrence is the essence of the message," for the Gospel "refers to an event which is determinative not only for the human soul, but for nature and history in their totalities." Thus "nothing can displace the concrete historic figure of Jesus Christ from the centre of the Christian religion," and a consequence of the Incarnation is "the drawing of all men out of a non-historical form of existence into a single global history." Christ is "the clue" that "the deepest meaning of history lies in the fact that in it God, who *is*, is wrestling with the estranged and rebellious wills of men, until his own perfect love is embodied and reflected in a redeemed and restored creation"[21] Although disastrous mistakes of judgment may be made, as by the "German Christians" concerning Nazism, yet for the believer (says Newbigin, risking his own list of evidences for the activity of the Holy Spirit not so much in "the non-Christian religions" as rather in the "secular world"), the disclosure of God in Jesus Christ is determinative of his interpretation of all the events of history. Wherever he sees men being set free for responsible sonship of God; wherever he sees the growth of mutual responsibility of man for man and of people for people; wherever he sees evidences of the character of Jesus Christ being reflected in the lives of men; there he will conclude that God is at work, and that he is summoned to be God's fellow-worker, even where the Name of Christ is not acknowledged. By contrast, wherever he sees the reverse process at work, men being enslaved, mutual responsibility being denied, and the opposite of the character of Christ being produced in men; there he will recognize the work of the Devil and will know himself summoned to resist.[22]

The last sentence indicates, of course, that the exercise of responsibility in the larger areas of freedom allows not only for "constructive action in history" in alignment with God's purpose but also for "more and more disastrous rebellion against God," so that the conflict between Christ and antichrist is both sharpened and cast on to a larger screen.[23]

In the closing chapter of *The Finality of Christ* Newbigin returns to the question of continuity and discontinuity between the Gospel and other religions in a discussion of conversion—the point at which a claim for Christ's finality becomes actual and threatening because it implies a summons to ultimate loyalty. Newbigin had already allowed that there may be "a real communion between God and the believer in non-Christian religious experience" but equally had maintained that such pious individuals—being still under the grip of an original sin that makes human religion "self-righteous" and so hostile to the truth of God—are wrongly oriented in regard to the Gospel and the Kingdom as these announce and embody God's comprehensive purpose for historic humankind and the cosmos. Retrospectively, they may eventually come to believe that "it was the true and living God who was dealing with them in the days of their pre-Christian wrestlings," but such a realization can only come *after* a "radical repentance and conversion from all pre-Christian religious experience."[24]

Newbigin is well aware that interreligious conversion, especially in a Christian direction, is frowned on by sensitive spirits in the West, and that "the sincere Hindu at his best will advise the Christian or Muslim to strive to become a better Christian, a better Muslim, rather than urging him to become a Hindu," it being generally preferable to seek the common spiritual reality along the path for which one's religious and cultural training has prepared one. Yet Newbigin's conviction regarding the finality of Christ leads him to look for people's conversion to Christ's Lordship. In a biblically based and baptismally focused exposition, Newbigin spells out in chapter 5 the three components of such conversion. Conversion comprises from the start: (1) "an inward religious experience" of "being turned around in order to recognize and participate in the dawning reality of God's reign"; (2) entrance into the "visible fellowship" of a community—itself culturally diverse but held together through the apostolic word, the baptismal water, the table of the Lord, and a life of service (Acts 2:41f.)—that is sent, though not for its own aggrandizement, "to preach repentance to every man and to all nations" (cf. especially Romans 10:9–15); and (3) acceptance of a new and common pattern of conduct that is both personally transformative and "relevant for the doing of God's will and the fulfilment of his reign at this particular juncture of world history."

Lastly, Newbigin takes up from an earlier point in the book a discussion of salvation, which is the topic on which much intra-Christian debate concerning "other religions" centers.[25] He will not allow that "the vast multitudes who have never been presented with the Gospel call for conversion and commitment are thereby necessarily excluded from participation in God's ongoing and completed work," but neither will he tie God to a "referendum principle" whereby "since the unbelievers in all the range of human history are far more than the believers, it follows that God saves on other grounds than faith." Although by no means dismissing the question of the individual's present state and future destiny, Newbigin's approach is rather to refocus attention on the glory of God, on participation in the Church as the sign, earnest, and instrument of God's total plan of salvation, and on the ultimate achievement of God's cosmic purpose. Newbigin says:

> The proper question is not: Are there few that be saved? The question is: Who is doing the will of God? To speak of the finality of Christ is not, primarily, to speak of the fate of those who do not accept him as Lord. It is to say that commitment to Christ in the fellowship of those who share the same commitment is the clue to a true participation in God's purpose for his whole creation. The privileges to which conversion is the gateway are not exclusive claims upon God's grace; they are the privileges of those who have been chosen for special responsibility in the carrying out of God's blessed design. Their joy will be not that they are saved, but that God's name is hallowed, his will done and his reign perfected.

Not being permitted to anticipate the last judgment, the Christian must bear the tension inherent in the divine "arithmetic" of a biblical God who "cares for the unique individual, the last and least," who is "not impressed by majorities," and yet who "will be all in all" when "all things will be restored to the unity for which they were created in Christ." To claim finality for Jesus Christ is not a speculative assertion either that the majority of people will one day be Christians or that all others will be damned. Rather, "it is to claim that commitment to him is the way in which men can become truly aligned to the ultimate end for which all things were made. The Church which believes this will not be afraid to address confidently to every generation and every people the call which it has received from him: Follow me."

In Birmingham

On his return to Britain in the mid-1970s, Newbigin met religious pluralism not only as an observable fact but also as a theological stance. Arriving at the Selly Oak Colleges to teach missiology and ecumenics to students both coming from and going to other parts of the world, he found in the city of Birmingham a principal gathering point for Hindu, Sikh, and Muslim immigrants from Asian and African countries in the former British empire; and in the University of Birmingham he encountered the presence of Professor John Hick, who, after *Christianity at the Centre* (1968), had with *God and the Universe of Faiths* (1973) moved from christocentrism to theocentrism as a stage on the road to his "Reality-centredness" of the 1980s. These social and intellectual signs of the passing of Western Christendom were matched by the decline of ecclesiastical practice even among those who were culturally Christian and by the loss of confidence even among Christian believers concerning the truth and sufficiency of an evangelical worldview that had now been rejected by the very modernity which it had in part made possible.

Chapter 2 presented Newbigin in his seventies as the pastor in the inner Birmingham suburb of Winson Green engaging in direct evangelism toward non-Christians. Chapter 7 presents him again undertaking service to the wider multicultural and multireligious community. In immediate and practical connection with the matter of pluralism, Newbigin quickly involved himself in the debate—which also included John Hick—concerning the Agreed Syllabus of Religious Education put out by the City of Birmingham in 1975 for use in its public schools. (Hick indeed had been the chief writer of the syllabus; he was eventually replaced by Newbigin as one of the church representatives on Birmingham's Standing Advisory Council on Religious Education.)[26] The religious instruction and school worship mandated by the national Education Act of 1944 had been understood in a Christian sense (with provision for the withdrawal of children by nonobservant families); but the massive presence in the city schools of children from Hindu or Muslim homes now made this assumption improper and unworkable. The new syllabus was directed "towards developing a critical understanding of the religious and moral dimensions of human experience and away from attempts to foster the claim of particular religious standpoints"; and very specially, Newbigin comments, "there seemed to be great anxiety lest any child should become a committed Christian as a result of religious education."[27] When it was said that pupils were to study religions "objectively" as aspects of different cultures, not to accept any of them as true accounts of how things are, Newbigin saw this as the spurious objectivity that not only, epistemologically, overlooks the fiduciary character of all knowledge, including knowledge in the natural sciences, but also, sociologically, reflects the commitment of a consumerist public to a supermarket choice among virtually equivalent brands of religion. Whereas the city fathers were chiefly upset about the inclusion of Marxism as one of the "stances of living" to be studied, Newbigin thought that the passion thereby aroused—it being plain that "Marxism is a living faith about what is really true and can never be relegated to the position of an aspect of culture to be studied dispassionately along with Polynesian *kava* ceremonies and Indian *puranas*"—showed up the false premises of the general debate.

Newbigin returned to the question of religion in schools after the passing of the national Education Reform Act in 1988. In a paper on "The Place of Christianity in Religious Education,"[28] he deconstructed the dichotomy between "indoctrination" and "science," or the "confessional" and the "critical" approaches to teaching religion, showing it to depend on the false division between "facts" and "values" that is characteristic of modernity: physics both rests on certain beliefs and supposes that there is truth to be established beyond "private opinion," and, Newbigin argued, it is *not otherwise* with religions. A forceful reminder had been issued by Muslim leaders in Britain who

> complain that they are required to commit their children to an educational system which teaches as truth what they believe to be false. They are not, of course, here making any reference to what is called "RE". They are referring to the curriculum as a whole, which teaches that the world is to be understood apart from the hypothesis of God, that "religion" (whether Moslem or Christian or whatever) is a matter of private opinion, not a matter of truth. They justly complain of the arrogance of those who are so blinded by the assumptions of our culture that they cannot see that what they teach as "facts" conceals a whole credo which a Muslim must reject. In my opinion Christians ought to have made this protest long ago. . . . Whatever we do in schools, children are being taught to believe some things and disbelieve others. The question "What is the truth?" cannot be permanently evaded.

To teach Christianity, or any other religion, as one of the "varieties of religious experience" is already to set aside its truth-claim in favor of another view of "what is the case." To concentrate on "religious experience" is, says Newbigin, "like devoting all attention to one's spectacles while ignoring the text one is asked to read."

If it then be asked whether one can teach only the religion one believes to be true, Newbigin offers three conditions for doing otherwise, drawn from his experience of teaching Hinduism to college-of-education students. First, do not conceal one's own religious commitment or pretend that one has a neutral, objective standpoint, for there is no such thing. Second, encourage the pupils to immerse themselves in the writings of the religion being taught, suspending their critical judgment and trying to see how those writings deal with problems every human being has to wrestle with. Third, and only then, encourage the students to discuss the issues raised and begin to form their judgments. A *sine qua non* is to make clear that religion is concerned with questions about truth.[29] Newbigin, it seems to me, is here formulating rules that are also appropriate for mutual acceptance in interreligious dialogue.

Besides this participation in the civic debates occasioned by the fact of religious pluralism, Newbigin contributed in his Birmingham years and his London retirement to the academic and ecclesiastical discussion around the theological significance of the multiplicity of religions and particularly the struggle for a Christian theology of religions and for an appropriate understanding and practice of evangelism and dialogue. Attention will be given mainly to five fairly short texts composed by him across this period: "Interfaith

Dialogue," written in November 1975 for the Division for World Mission and Ecumenism of the Lutheran Church in America;[30] "The Gospel among the Religions," which figures as the last chapter of *The Open Secret* (1978);[31] "The Christian Faith and the World Religions," Newbigin's contribution to the volume of essays I edited in 1988 to mark the centenary of *Lux Mundi* under the title *Keeping the Faith*;[32] "Religion for the Marketplace," one of a number of responses gathered by the Indian Roman Catholic theologian Gavin D'Costa in 1990 to *The Myth of Christian Uniqueness* that had appeared from a California symposium under the aegis of John Hick and Paul F. Knitter;[33] and "Religious Pluralism: A Missiological Approach," which was included in the 1993 volume of *Studia Missionalia* from the Gregorian University in Rome.[34] Here, too, belong the chapters "The Gospel and the Religions" and "No Other Name" in Newbigin's *The Gospel in a Pluralist Society* (1989).[35]

Although the proportions vary among these pieces and there are nuances to be noted, it is possible to treat them synthetically because Newbigin in all of them reverts to three principal themes or tasks. First, he considers the various attitudes adopted by Christian theology past and present to other religions and, after an appreciative and critical review of historical and contemporary positions, expresses his own judgment on the matter of the Gospel in relation to non-Christian religions. Second, he reflects on what effects the theological judgment has on the understanding and practice of evangelism and of interreligious dialogue, remembering that experience in those two activities—in the case of some of the theologians and certainly in Newbigin's own case—has already fed into the theological attitudes adopted. Third, Newbigin engages particularly with the "Western scientific" position, which, ironically arising within Christendom, makes religion a "private affair" having to do with personal values rather than public truth and accordingly grants its ideological favor to a "relativistic pluralism" among an endless variety of "religious preferences"; this last is the position which, with the possible exception of an unquestioning exclusivism on behalf of Christianity, Newbigin finds most radically wrong.[36]

Amid and Against Religious Pluralism

Religious pluralism is an undeniable historical *fact*; it was known as a theological *problem* to the earliest Church, but Western Christendom was not obliged to confront it—except in the shape of Islam at its circumference and "except for the unsolved enigma of the Jewish people" in its midst, as Newbigin put it in 1993—until modern times brought a widespread awareness of the rest of the world *and* supplied, with the development of Enlightenment rationalism, a normative intellectual framework for a relativistic account of the various religions that systematically undermined the certainty of the Christian faith concerning the absoluteness of Christ; it was into this intellectual framework that the detailed substantive information gleaned in the nine-

teenth century by the "scientific study of religion" was also fitted. Set out by
Newbigin in varying degrees of completeness and in varying sequence, his
historico-theological typology of Christian attitudes to non-Christian religions
includes positions that may be arranged as follows.[37]

In the exclusivist camp, it is held that other religions are wholly false and
that Christians have nothing to learn from them. Newbigin objects that the
sensitive Christian mind, enlightened by Christ, will recognize and rejoice in
the spiritual fruits displayed in other believers, with whom Christians have
sometimes lived in friendship; that the use of indigenous names for God by
missionaries and Bible translators among the newly evangelized implies a
belief that the discontinuity cannot be total; and that John 1:9, although not
mentioning religions, speaks of Jesus as the light that enlightens every man—
so that, in short, it is impossible for the Christian to say that people outside
the Church are quite lacking in truth and goodness. Newbigin notes that
Justin Martyr, in his second-century *Apology*, distinguished between pagan
religions, which were demonic counterfeits to the Christianity whose rites
they might resemble, and pagan philosophy, where a Socrates or a Plato was
used by the Logos to lead people away from demons to the light. The valid
insights here are, first, that the sphere of religion is indeed the battlefield *par
excellence* in which evil exhibits a captivating power that human reason and
conscience surrender to; and, second, that the points of highest ethical and
spiritual achievement, where non-Christians most resemble Christianity, are
the very places at which the religions find themselves threatened by, and
therefore reject, the Gospel, saying "We see" while blotting out the light (cf.
John 9:41).

Moving toward a more inclusivist position, it has been held—as early as
Eusebius of Caesarea in Constantine's time—that other religions are a "preparation" which Christ comes to fulfill. This view was abundantly represented
at the Edinburgh Missionary Conference of 1910. Apart from the difficulty
raised earlier in reference to those religious beliefs and practices that clash
with Christianity or the Gospel, Newbigin brings against the *praeparatio evan-
gelica* view the more general observation of Rudolf Otto that different religions
turn on different axes. "The questions Hinduism asks and answers," says
Newbigin, "are not the questions with which the Gospel is primarily concerned. One does not truly understand any of the religions by seeing it as a
preparation for Christianity. Rather, each religion must be understood on its
own terms and along the line of its own central axis."

Two more recent subsets of an inclusivist position are, first, those which
rank other religions, either on account of their general character or on account of certain features in them, by their approximation to Christianity; and,
second and somewhat better in Newbigin's eyes, those which look for the
proximity and presence of Christ to people in other religions. Among the first,
the Jerusalem Missionary Conference of 1928 highlighted particular "spiritual
values" in the several religions that matched those in Christianity, where they
are all to be found in their proper balance and relationship; yet, as Newbigin
notes, the same final report of that conference went on to say that Christ is

not merely the continuation of human traditions, for coming to him involves the surrender of the most precious among those traditions, and the "values" of the religions do not together add up to Him who alone is the truth. More severe repugnance is provoked in Newbigin by the variant found in Pope Paul VI's 1964 encyclical *Ecclesiam Suam*, in which the world religions are viewed as concentric circles gathered around the Roman Catholic Church, and other Christians, Jews, Muslims, other theists, other religionists, and atheists are located at increasingly greater distances from the papal midpoint. Newbigin repeats that the religions must be understood "from within," and stresses that this model in particular fails to do justice to the paradoxical fact that it is precisely those who are in one sense closest to the truth who are in another sense the bitterest opponents of the Gospel. The standpoint of Karl Rahner with his notion of the "anonymous Christian" is the version of inclusivism that receives Newbigin's most detailed theological critique. Besides failing to take the beliefs of others on their own terms, the most serious weakness in the Rahnerian approach resides in its exclusive (!) concentration on the fate of the individual soul, compounded by the presumption, often moralistically expressed, of knowing who will be saved—it is "persons of good will," the "sincere" followers of other religions—on the Last Day.[38] More sympathetic treatment is offered by Newbigin to two scholars "who, while unambiguously affirming the centrality and decisiveness of the Christ-event, also take a generous view of the world's religions but are not preoccupied with the question, Can the individual non-Christian be saved?" But he finds in the practical proposals for a mutual permeability of ritual between the Church and other religious communities made by Kenneth Cragg's *The Christ and the Faiths* (1987) and M. M. Thomas's *Risking Christ for Christ's Sake* (also 1987) a confusion between a "Christ-principle" and "the Christ-event" that forfeits the particularity of the biblical story and of the witnessing task to which the Church is elected and to which it is committed by its ultimate belief concerning human nature and destiny.[39]

The theoretical position which Newbigin in his theological judgment cannot abide—although he seeks to distinguish it from what may be the "personal faith" of its holders such as John Hick or Wilfred Cantwell Smith—is the affirmation of religious pluralism (not, obviously, the mere recognition of the factual existence of multiple religions, but the theological or ideological valuation of the fact). A form of "provisional pluralism" was already represented by the Laymen's Report on Foreign Missions of 1932, in which the several religions, including Christianity, were seen as converging toward a common fulfillment in what was called "the Kingdom of God" but looked, quips Newbigin, "remarkably similar to the generally accepted goals of progressive capitalism at that point in history."[40] But quite new in Christian thinking, without prejudice to the adjective Christian, is the blatant affirmation, on a permanent footing, of a "rough parity" or better between the world religions. Such a view may have been held in philosophical Hinduism, on the basis either of agnosticism about the divine or of a superior mysticism that already knows the secret of cosmic unity; and it may have prevailed in that period of the Roman Empire of which Edmund Gibbon said that all religions were to the people equally true, to the philosophers equally false, and to the government equally useful. But in *The Myth of Christian Uniqueness* it has now been advocated as the proper counterpart to properly "nonabsolutist christologies." When Tom F. Driver writes, in what Newbigin calls a fitting conclusion to that book, that "inasmuch as God has different histories, then God has different 'natures,'" Newbigin roundly declares him "a polytheist in the ancient mold" (having earlier recalled the Hindu concept of the *ishta devata*, the god of one's choice); but he can also say, in anticipation of what will become in the *Studia Missionalia* article of 1993 a more sustained critique of "postmodernism," that "chaos has come again, and there will be nothing left except the will to power of the competing human projects."[41] It will be necessary to return to Newbigin's critical engagement with the views of religion held in modernity and late modernity, but for the moment this typology must be closed by reference to the attitude that Newbigin clearly views with most sympathy.

"Biblical realism" was the phrase Hendrik Kraemer used to designate his own approach to the question. Kraemer recognized that empirical Christianity shares many of the characteristics of a religion but considered the Gospel, as the announcement of a unique event whereby "God opened a way of reconciliation where there was no way before," to be sui generis, calling for a response from every human being. He did not deny the universal graciousness of God toward all people or conclude that all non-Christians are eternally lost; but he certainly insisted on the Church's inalienable responsibility to make known to all peoples the mighty event in which God offers reconciliation to the entire world hitherto consigned under sin (cf. Rom. 11:32). There was no failure here, Newbigin says, of logical rigor, but only a readiness to let the Bible frame the issues instead of expecting the Bible to answer the questions we formulate.

Newbigin is thereby led into stating his own theological standpoint from which to approach people of other faiths; and he begins by sketching in five acts "the central plot in the drama of salvation."[42] First, "the whole cosmos and the whole human family is the creation of a wise and loving God," whose tender mercies are over all his works; and "there is no human being in whose consciousness there is not some trace of God's presence and goodness." Second, there runs through the creation "a dark mystery, a perversion, an apostasy, which results in the alienation of human being from its source"; the depths of this alienation and the horror of this mystery are decisively exposed when "those human achievements which reflect the universal goodness of God—the religion and morality, the law and the political order, which claim to represent God's purpose of righteousness—are the weapons turned against the incarnate Lord to destroy him." Third, the human apostasy and God's dealing with it are carried out in actual historical events, God working by election through the particularities for the sake of his universal purpose; finally the Elect One dies to bear and bear away the sin of the world. Fourth, the Crucified is raised from the dead and commissions chosen witnesses to testify to his victory over the dark power, which will find a consummation that "gathers into one glorious event both the story of every human soul and the story of all the nations"; the witnesses will be "corporately a sign, because a first-fruit, of that consummation," living as the "suffering servant of God" and "a learning community, not pretending to possess all the truth, but having the promise that, as they bear witness among all the nations, the Spirit will lead them into all the truth" ("Every translation of the Gospel into a new language involves necessarily some development," yet "the Church is not led into the fulness of the truth simply by theological reflection" but rather "as it allows the Holy Spirit to challenge the world's assumptions about sin and righteousness and judgment as it moves into one human culture after another"). Fifth, a judgment is still to come. The Church's being "the sign and first-fruit of God's purpose to save all" neither entails the exclusion of those who lived without knowledge of the story nor ensures that all in the end are necessarily saved. According to the New Testament, it is possible to miss the way and be lost; and three things are clear about the final judgment that will have to be faced: first, it will be in accordance with what each one has done in regard to the will of God (cf. Matthew 7:21; 2 Corinthians 5:10); second, the warnings about judgment are directed chiefly against the over-confident; third, there will be surprises. Premature judgment by the Church is precluded (1 Corinthians 4:5). When asked whether those who are saved will be few, Jesus deflected speculation about others to a challenge facing the self: "Strive to enter by the narrow door" (Luke 13:23f.).

On the basis of such a faith Christians may, and should, enter into dialogue with other believers. This basis in faith implies certain presuppositions about the exercise that the Christian must make clear to the potential partner.[43] They arise from the fact that the Christian "cannot agree that the position of final authority may be taken by anything other than the Gospel." Thus no decisive appeal can be made to a court of independent, free-floating reason understood as external and superior to religious experience. Nor can it be conceded as an unexamined assumption that there is a common core of reality within all the varieties of religious experience ("The real is one, though sages name it variously," as a voice from the *Rig Veda* puts it). Yet again, there can be no subordination of the dialogue to the practical need for political and social unity at whatever level. Rather than Jesus' revelation being "one of a type," "susceptible to interpretation in categories derived from other ways of understanding the totality of experience," Jesus is for the Christian "the source from whom his understanding of the totality of experience is drawn and therefore the criterion by which other ways of understanding are judged." The case will not be otherwise with the Hindu, the Muslim, the Buddhist, or the Marxist, whose respective faiths provide them with their basis for understanding experience and judging other ways of understanding, including the Christian. "The integrity and fruitfulness of the interfaith dialogue depends in the first place," says Newbigin, "upon the extent to which the different participants take seriously the full reality of their own faith as sources for the understanding of the totality of experience."

The overarching *purpose* of dialogue for Christians, Newbigin says, must be witness to Christ, as they expect also their interlocutors to witness to the object and content of their own faith. Witness to Christ may occur in several ways and with various results. As the nonChristian partners relate their experience, the Christian participants, believing in the universal operation of God through the Word who brings life and light, may be able to discern signs of God's gracious goodness and rejoice in their neighbors' response to them, thereby enriching their own faith and perhaps that of the others; or, in listening to their interlocutors, the Christians may be brought to see failings in themselves and thus receive God's judgment and correction from the lips and lives of the others. Conversely, when Christians tell the story of Christ, though without seeking to "ferret out the hidden sins and deceptions" of their hearers or pressure them into accepting the Christian religion, it may happen that the Holy Spirit, who is the primary witness to Christ, will convict and persuade the non-Christians.

How, it may be asked, is such dialogical witness to Christ related to evangelism, which is normally defined as direct proclamation of the Gospel (though that be may labeled proselytism by its addressees and even by those Christians who strangely discountenance the idea of conversion)? In his Henry Martyn Lectures, given at the University of Cambridge in 1986, Newbigin sought to defuse the mounting intra-Christian debate on the matter by a shift in terminology and by relocating the question from theoretical discussion to everyday life: "ordinary human conversation" is the preferred modality.[44]

> Whether we like it or not, preaching in its original sense of announcing a forthcoming event, telling good news, is and has been from the beginning part of the Christian style. . . . If you have important news to tell about a forthcoming event, you have to tell it. It will not emerge in the course of conversation. But of course conversation follows. All missionaries have been involved in conversation and were certainly total failures if they were not. But they did not usually dignify this with the name of dialogue. I have recently been reading the delightful reminiscences of a former colleague—E. O. Shaw—with whom I shared the work of village missionary. He writes about conversations with Hindus in the temple, on the street, walking in the country, as a guest in Hindu homes. His heart is warmed by the good things in the life of simple Indian farmers and shopkeepers which the conversations bring to light. And quite naturally he talks about Jesus and shares with his friends something of the Gospel. These are ordinary human conversations, and they are the stuff of missionary life. And not only of the life of people set apart for a special calling as missionaries. Most of the worldwide spread of Christianity has been the result of millions of conversations of this kind, carried on by ordinary people in the course of ordinary daily life. What presuppositions make such a conversation possible? Not surely that I the Christian am saved, that my partner in conversation is lost unless I can, somehow, through the conversation bring him to accept Jesus as Lord. How could any ordinary human conversation take place on that basis?

In his 1993 article in *Studia Missionalia* on "Religious Pluralism: A Missiological Approach," Newbigin returned to the more technical debate, in which in fact attention usually centers on the question of individual salvation, in which the pluralists naturally favor dialogue to the virtual exclusion of evangelism, and in which the "interreligious dialogue" envisaged seems to be at an expert level. Newbigin, as we have seen, accepts the propriety and benefits of interreligious dialogue at all levels, but not, he repeats, as "a substitute for evangelism." How, then, are the two related? Such dialogue "should not be seen as an occasion for evangelism, but rather as the proper precondition for it," in the sense, it seems, of establishing human contact and of helping Christians, by what they learn of others, to frame the Gospel intelligibly and pertinently for their hearers when the opportunity for evangelism arises. It is important that "the Christian participant in such conversations is, and *is known to be*, fully committed to and loyal to the Church which is publicly preaching the Gospel and calling people to conversion and faith" in "Jesus Christ as Lord of all."[45]

Christians have, according to Newbigin, a trinitarian framework for their understanding of interreligious dialogue with other believers, and this should govern their practice of it.[46] The key is found in John 16:12–15, in which it appears that "the Father is the giver of all things," that "they all belong rightly to the Son," and that "it will be the work of the Spirit to guide the Church through the course of history into the truth as a whole by taking all God's manifold gifts given to all mankind and declaring their true meaning to the Church as that which belongs to the Son."

First, Christians participate in dialogue with others in the belief that all share a common nature as those created by the one Father, by whose kindness we live, to whom we are all responsible, and from whose purpose we may expect a common blessing. Christians will be eager to receive and learn what God has given and shown to their partners equally made in the divine image. The meeting will take place, not as "the encounter of pure naked spirits," but in "a common world," "a shared context of things," and at a particular time in an ongoing history that Christians believe to be under God's providence and rule—so that the meeting will be among people facing the demands and opportunities of this moment and place: "It is in this open encounter in the field of contemporary decision that true dialogue takes place," and it "may, and often should, lead into common action on many matters of public life."

Second, Christians participate in dialogue as members of the body of Christ, the body sent into the world by the Father and the Son to continue the mission of Jesus. They are therefore vulnerable, as he was: "The true disciple will be exposed without defense in his dialogue with men of other faiths and yet will remain bound to Jesus." Most profoundly, the Christian must be ready for a *kenosis*, a self-emptying: "Much of his 'Christianity' may have to be left behind in this meeting. Much of the intellectual construction, the piety, the practice in which his discipleship has been expressed may have to be called in question. The meeting place is at the cross, at the place where he bears witness to Jesus as the Judge and Savior both of him and of his partner." That risk explains why the dialoguing Christian needs to be deeply rooted in

Christ through being deeply rooted in the life of the Church—its worship, teaching, sacraments, and shared discipleship.

Third, Christians participate in dialogue "believing and expecting that the Holy Spirit can and will use this dialogue to do his own sovereign work, to glorify Jesus by converting to him both partners in the dialogue." The Christian may in some respects be convicted and changed by God through the non-Christian partner, and vice versa. How, at the human level, the critical calling into question of the other—which Newbigin reports as being desired also from the Hindu side by R. Sundarara Rajan of Madras—is to be distinguished from a direct attempt to "convert" or to "evangelize" remains unclear when Newbigin makes this point.[47] In any case, it is the Spirit who, taking all the gifts of God and showing them to the Church as the treasury of Christ, "guides the Church from its limited, partial, and distorted understanding and embodiment of the truth into the fullness of the truth in Jesus who is the one in whom all things consist (Colossians 1:17)"—and one of the Holy Spirit's own indispensable gifts is that of discernment, for not every form of vitality is his work.

As promised, we now revert finally in this matter of religious pluralism to Newbigin's critical engagement with its adoption as a theological or ideological stance among Western, or Western-educated, academics. In the last chapter Newbigin was observed at Tambaram 1988 clashing with Wilfred Cantwell Smith and Diana Eck, who fill the first part of that bill. In written allusions,[48] the old India hand deals more gently with Stanley Samartha and Christopher Duraisingh, on whom (it may be surmised) influences both from Hindu philosophy and from the current Western academy have been more pervasively at work than among many Indian Christians.[49] It was, however, to John Hick that Newbigin regularly addressed his most pointed criticisms from the mid-1970s onward, evident in chapter 10 of *The Open Secret* and continuing through his lengthy review of the Hick-Knitter symposium in D'Costa's *Christian Uniqueness Reconsidered*.

A clue to the gravity of the issue between Newbigin and Hick is found in Hick's assertion that "Christianity must move emphatically from the confessional to the truth-seeking stance in dialogue."[50] This sentence epitomizes precisely the basic mistake made by modern thought when, with its epistemological dichotomy between "facts" (which are purely objective) and "values" (which are purely subjective), it forgot the *fiduciary* character of all human knowledge that yet has its referent in a given *reality*. What Hick minimizes as "dogma" (e.g., "Jesus Christ is Lord of all") is rather, says Newbigin, the faith-claim on the basis of which the Christian seeks for further truth—which "is to be found in a life of obedient discipleship to Jesus Christ as he is to be known through a life lived in the community of disciples, in faithfulness to the tradition about him, and in openness to all the truth which may be discovered in the history of the human race." When Hick speaks, in *God and the Universe of Faiths*, of "a shift from the dogma that Christianity is at the centre to the *realisation* that it is God who is at the centre,"[51] he is implicitly making his own philosophically idealist conception of God ("Transcendent Being") the central essence of all religions and claiming "the scientific outlook" (which arose when Europe awoke from its "dogmatic slumbers") as the unchallengeable basis of knowledge on which he thinks to stand. "The Hickian revolution," says Newbigin, "is a move from a view centered in the objective reality of the man Jesus Christ, to a view centered in my own subjective conception of ultimate reality."[52] Newbigin was very fond of citing the dictum of André Dumas, the French Reformed theologian, that every proposal for human unity which does not specify the center has as its unacknowledged center the beliefs and interests of the one who proposes it.[53] Newbigin's alternative was supplied by Galatians 2:20: "I no longer live but Christ lives in me."[54]

There is "a sad irony," wrote Newbigin already in *The Open Secret*, about Hick's writing as he did "just at the time when the foundations of 'the modern scientific world view' seem to be crumbling, when the culture of the Western white man which dominated the world fifty years ago is visibly sinking into nihilism."[55] In his 1993 paper in *Studia Missionalia* Newbigin picked up the academically fashionable notion of the "post-modern," which for him represented the further "progress" of the self-destructive tendencies of "modernity" with its Cartesian epistemology based on radical doubt and its abandonment of the category of purpose in sole favor of efficient causality. As Nietzsche had foreseen, the outcome was a nihilism in which "truth" was a function of self-interested power. As an ideology, says Newbigin, religious pluralism is part of this "more fundamental pluralism," which "denies the possibility of making any universally justifiable truth-claims on any matter, whether religious or otherwise." The chaotic *décentrage* of reality precisely contradicts—and is contradicted by—the Christian confession of the crucified and risen Christ as the one in whom all things cohere (Colossians 1:15–20), who by his reconciling work draws all people to him (John 12:32) and displaces the self-centered wills of a deeply corrupted human nature (Galatians 2:20). Newbigin recognizes, indeed affirms, that the story of Christ—not a myth but ontologically grounded in real history—can fundamentally be told only on its own terms (for a "non-confessional" or putatively "neutral" language subordinates it to another view of reality). Never in their own strength and never in their own right but rather under the sovereign empowerment and correction of the Holy Spirit who is the primary witness, it is the business of Christians, by their words and deeds, their lives and deaths, to tell the story of Jesus Christ in such a way that they (to borrow on Newbigin's behalf a term that had currency in some postmodernist circles) "out-narrate" the stories told by those whose ultimate commitments reside elsewhere—and this for the achievement of the Father's purpose, and so to the glory of the Triune God.

In graphic sum: Newbigin's faith embraced the Gospel's "scandal of particularity." This was being refused when, in a Hindu monastery, veneration was offered on Christmas Day before a picture of Christ in his place alongside other divine figures, or when Jesus was ranked among "the great holy men of history" in "a picture which used to be very prominent in the coffee shops in the bazaar—a picture with three figures in it, in one corner Buddha under a tree, in another corner Jesus on the cross, and in the middle Gandhi."[56] It was being refused also when Western academic religionists reduced the cross to a cipher: "I cannot accept," wrote Newbigin, "the widely prevalent custom of putting the cross in a whole series of symbols of the world's religions. The cross is not a mere symbol like the OM often used to denote Hinduism, or the crescent denoting Islam. The crucifixion of Jesus was an event in history, the mighty act of God by which at infinite cost he reconciled the fallen world to himself and rescued it from perdition. To suggest that there is a reality more inclusive than this is to deny it."[57]

In the Face of Islam

Already during his African tour of 1960, Newbigin sensed with local Christians "the threat of Islam" in Nigeria, Ghana, and Uganda, and he was strategizing about the coming of Christians from Pakistan and Indonesia, preferably converts from Islam, in order to counter the appearance of Christianity as the white man's religion.[58] Over his final years Newbigin manifested a new preoccupation with Islam, occasioned both by the growing presence of Muslims in Britain ("More Muslims than Methodists," it is said, and perhaps more than practicing Anglicans) and by the increasing impact of Islamic nations in the political world. In a late conversation he remarked that the Muslims had taken over Hyde Park, having in mind not so much the nearby mosques as the soapbox orators at Speakers' Corner.[59] On the one hand, Newbigin respected Muslims greatly on account of their confessional stance, the frank recognition of their faith-commitment as the basis for action in public affairs and for their entire dealing with reality. On the other hand, he also believed Islam to be profoundly wrong in its divergence from the Christian story: "At many points," he said in his Henry Martyn Lectures of 1986, "Christianity contradicts the strongest affirmations of Hinduism, or answers questions which Hinduism does not ask. *And this is even more obviously the case if we consider Islam.*"[60] It is this twofold fact—the shared principle of fiduciary knowledge and the discrepant content of actual belief—which makes Christianity and Islam, in Newbigin's eyes, such serious rivals.

The rivalry may be played out in various ways. In the ailing nonscientific part of Western culture (for "the scientific part of our culture continues to flourish because it does not accept pluralism, it does *not* assume 'the parity of all scientific views'"), the relativism that seeks to evade the question of truth and error is a sign of impending death. Such relativistic pluralism, wrote Newbigin in 1990, "will simply crumble in the presence of a confident and vigorous claim to know the truth—such a claim as Islam is at present making with increasing vigor in the contemporary world."[61] Or concerning another area of existence: During the Cold War period, wrote Newbigin in 1992,

the world was divided between two power blocks based on rival ideologies, both products of the Enlightenment. Today one of these ideologies is over-

whelmingly dominant. It is locking even the smallest communities into a
more and more tightly knit fabric of economic and financial relations. After
the collapse of Marxist communism as a world power, the only effective challenge to this global system comes from Islam which rejects both ideologies
and seeks to create a world order based on the revealed will of God as interpreted by the Prophet. As the capitalist free-market system runs into deeper
crisis, I think Islam will be, in the twenty-first century, perhaps the major
contender for global power.[62]

In his 1993 paper on "Religious Pluralism: A Missiological Perspective," Newbigin referred to the brief excitement in the English-speaking world over

the writings of a US civil servant named Francis Fukuyama, who claimed
that with the collapse of Marxist socialism as a world power, we had reached
the end of history. There were no more great battles to be fought. The future
belonged to the victorious liberal free-market economies of the West. All the
world would come to recognize that this is the only future for humanity. He
did make passing reference to Islam as a possible contender for world dominance, but no reference—as far as I know—to Christianity as a possible
player in this game.[63]

In 1996 the scholarly historian Samuel Huntington forecast for the twenty-
first century a clash between the civilizations based on Christianity and those
based on Islam.[64] The irony of that, in Newbigin's judgment, would be that
"the civilizations based on Christianity" had now largely apostasized from
their foundation in the Gospel.

Two points may be made here in the perspective of Newbigin. First, if a
destructive clash is to be avoided, there needs to be dialogue between Christians and Muslims of the kind that Newbigin considers the most suitable for
Christians to engage in with other believers. "The way of discipleship," he
said in his Henry Martyn Lectures,

is a matter of action, and not only of thought. Therefore I think that the
most fruitful kind of interfaith dialogue is one in which people of different
faiths or ideologies who share a common situation and are seeking to meet
ordinary human needs, are enabled to share the insights which their different
beliefs give them for contemporary action. It is in this situation of active
discipleship, where we cannot take refuge in established formulations of doctrine but have to probe new and unexplored territory, that we learn what it
means to trust Jesus as the way, the truth and the life and as the one who
can lead us into the truth in its fulness.[65]

The second point is that Christianity, if it is to play its role in the discernment of God's will in light of Christ's story, will need an ecumenical renewal—
not only in the West but certainly there, with the help of Christian missionaries from more thriving places—so that it may everywhere bear its authentic
witness in relation to those chronic and critical problems that now affect the
entire globe as a result of the spread of the "acids of modernity" (a phrase
Newbigin liked to use from Walter Lippmann). The complex question of the
Christian faith and Western culture is the theme of chapter 10, in which
Newbigin is treated as the apologist.

Meanwhile, to end this chapter on Newbigin as religious interlocutor, his late concentration on Islam may be illustrated by an incident, a speech, and a book.

The incident was the publication in 1989 of the novel *The Satantic Verses* by the Indo-British writer Salman Rushdie, the explosion of wrath in the Muslim community at its blasphemy, and the incomprehension of the Western intelligentsia, which could hear the outcry only as an attack on freedom to publish. Although Newbigin deplored the "order to kill" (*fatwa*) issued by Iranian ayatollahs, he could look on the absolutists for liberty of publication only with a mixture of astonishment and pity at their failure to understand "the explosives they are playing games with." The freedom classically championed by Milton and his like demanded as its corollaries commitment to truth and the exercise of responsibility. "If Rushdie's work is stating a truth which is more precious to him than life," wrote Newbigin, "then he is right to stand by it and pay the price. But freedom without responsibility to the truth becomes mere nihilism." To view the offense of blasphemy as no more than injury to the feelings of a few people who choose to adhere to the Christian or some other religion is part of the modern illusion that a society can exist without any publicly shared belief about the truth. "The explosion of Muslim wrath," said Newbigin, "ought to be seen by Christians as a sharp word from the Lord about our failure to challenge the public life of our society with the Gospel"—and that, of course, "not because a nation with no shared belief about the truth will simply crumple [*sic*] under the assault of real conviction, but for His sake who died on the cross that all might have life." And there Newbigin adverts to "the fundamental difference" between Christianity and Islam: "Muslims have shocked us because they regard blasphemy as a terrible crime. I believe they are right in their judgment but wrong in their response. For Muslims it is impossible that God himself should have accepted death on a charge of blasphemy; for Christians it is the centre of God's saving work. That dictates a totally different kind of response, but it does not allow us to regard blasphemy as a matter of indifference."[66]

The speech that shows Newbigin at grips with the challenge of Islam was his address on "The Gospel in Today's Global City" given at the relaunching of the old mission department of the Selly Oak Colleges as the School of Mission and World Christianity.[67] In it he interpreted the rise of "religious fundamentalisms," whether Islamic, Hindu, or Christian, as "a cry for life" among people finding that the secular worldview—an ambiguous and ambivalent product of Western Christendom that has degenerated into hegemonic secularism—is not finally sustainable. That, he said, was the context for "the beginnings of Muslim fundamentalism in this country":

> The majority of British Muslims are living in the most deprived areas of our large cities and experience at first hand the worst results of the secular ideology. For there does not seem to be any logical stopping place on the slope which leads a purely secular society into a pagan society. As Nietzsche so clearly saw, if there is no God anything goes. All attempts to base effective moral norms on an atheistic philosophy are bound to collapse. The result is

the society with which we are becoming familiar, in which there are no landmarks, no fixed points of reference, no public belief about the purpose of human beings, only the need to gratify every immediate want. When some young Muslims uncompromisingly reject allegiance to this kind of society and insist that the rule of God over all human life be acknowledged, I am amazed at the complacency with which many Christians seem to accept a secular society as one in which they can be content to live. Where there is no God, life becomes finally meaningless and senseless. We may work ourselves up into a froth of indignation over the sticky mess of violence, drugs and gang warfare. But should we not realize how far down the slope we have gone when a British Prime Minister takes prime time on television to announce the latest jewel in the crown of our statecraft—a lottery? . . . We may disagree with our Muslim fellow citizens about the manner in which we understand God's exercise of his rule over human life. However, we cannot, I believe, ignore the very sharp questions which Islam puts to our cosy co-habitation with the secular society: Do you believe that God is Lord over the public life of society, its economics, its politics, its culture? Or do you believe that his rule is limited to the Church and the home?[68]

Believing the truth of the Gospel, Newbigin goes on, the worldwide Christian fellowship is constrained to proclaim the universal reign of Jesus. Yet bloody conflicts, though they may not be explicitly religious wars, are occurring—in Bosnia, Nagorney Karabagh, and Chechnya—at the friction points between the old territorial religions of Islam and Christendom. Might, then, the proclamation of Jesus lead us back into the age of religious wars? No sane person would desire that. But because, within the limits of human history, all truth-claims can and will be challenged, we must have the courage to maintain and confess the truth even in the midst of conflict:

This means that we have to recover the concept of spiritual warfare and struggle, of jihad (to use the language of our Muslim fellow-citizens), but not the kind which leads to the crusade. How can we ensure that this latter does not happen? Only by going back to that which is the centre of the Gospel, namely the cross of Jesus Christ. Only if we constantly remember that when Jesus sent his disciples out into the world, he first showed them his hands and his side. The scars of his passion are to be the authenticating signs by which the Church is recognized as his representative. Here the fact that the worldwide Church which is now the true base for the worldwide mission is not the strong, wealthy, arrogant old Christendom of Europe, but a fellowship of believers scattered throughout the world, often in minority situations, often suffering under harsh persecution, always requiring personal courage to share their faith with their neighbours—all this should help to save us from the errors which we deplore in our past. It is from these communities, I believe, that we in the old Christendom must learn afresh the skills needed for a true spiritual warfare.[69]

Although Newbigin always said that "dialogue is not enough," it would be a pity if either Christians or Muslims forswore between them the kind of inter-religious dialogue that Newbigin had earlier advocated on matters of common public concern.

That kind of relationship between Christians and Muslims is, in fact, envisaged by Newbigin in the book that must finally be mentioned. One of his last literary undertakings was his contribution of the first and fourth parts to a four-part book whose original title was apparently *A Christian Vision for Society*.[70] The book was published after Newbigin's death as *Faith and Power: Christianity and Islam in "Secular" Britain*.[71] The second part gives an account by Lamin Sanneh—a Muslim who became a Methodist (and then a Roman Catholic)—of Islam as a total religious, juridical, political, and cultural entity, especially in its relation to Christianity. The third part of the book was an account by the journalist Jenny Taylor of what is happening in various sectors of British national life as a result of ignoring religious belief as a factor in society and concentrating entirely on race as the key—and "all this with special reference to Islam." More is said in chapter 7 about Newbigin's contributions to this collaborative work in the presentation of his social thought and practice, and in chapter 10, which treats him as a Christian apologist in the midst of secular culture. Here only three points need be noted that Newbigin makes in connection with Christianity and Islam.

The first is this: "To the question 'What kind of society?' our Muslim fellow citizens have their answer. Through the network of mosques (now more than 2,000 in the UK) and through the teaching that is there provided for their young people, they seek to maintain the integrity of their society in a world which they (with much justice) perceive as pagan. The firmness of their stance contrasts with the relative timidity with which Christian leaders occasionally challenge the norms of British society. It is indeed of much ironic significance that, as commentators have noted, the proposal to portray Jesus as one of the characters in the TV show *Spitting Image* had to be vetoed because of the indignant protests not of the Christians but of the Muslims. Christians' protests can be ignored, not those of Islam."[72]

Second (and one needs to know that "naturalistic" became Newbigin's preferred word for "secularistic" or "scientistic"): "In our present situation in Britain, where Christians and Muslims share a common position as minority faiths in a society dominated by the naturalistic ideology, we share a common duty to challenge this ideology, to affirm that it can only lead our society into disintegration and disaster, and to bear witness to the reality of God from whom alone come those 'norms' that can govern human life, that 'dharma' which can give order to the chaos of human passions. Here Christians should be both encouraged and challenged by the much more vigorous testimony of Islam."[73]

Third, Newbigin asserts, and will argue, that the Christian faith in Christ's Cross both excludes coercion and provides the basis for true freedom: "During their long histories, both Christendom and Islam have sought to establish the absolute hegemony of their faiths over whole societies. Christians have, for the most part, been so chastened and humiliated that they have learned the bitter lesson and should never again be tempted to go down this road. It is not clear that Islam has been through the same experience. What is becoming clear is that in the last analysis it is only the Gospel that can provide the basis for a society which is free, but in which freedom does not lead into disintegration and destruction. The reason for this lies in the unique character of the Gospel itself. It is in the fact that God's decisive revelation of his wisdom and power was made in the crucifixion of the beloved Son, that in his resurrection from the dead we have the assurance that, in spite of all appearances, God does reign, that in the commission to the Church we have responsibility to bear witness throughout history to its end that God does reign, and that until the end God has provided a space and a time in which the reconciliation of our sinful race is possible, not by coercion but by freely given faith, love and obedience."[74]

That brings us to chapter 7, which treats Newbigin's social vision. Glimpses of that vision have already been caught, for the social dimension was never far away from Newbigin's thinking and practice from first to last. The key text introduced here for the first time is the unpublished Bangalore lectures of 1941 on "The Kingdom of God and the Idea of Progress." Human society on this earth is to be viewed always in the light of that final and heavenly City whose builder and maker is God.

7

The Social Visionary

I saw the holy city, the new Jerusalem, coming down out of
heaven, prepared as a bride adorned for her husband.

(Revelation 21:2)

So then, as we have opportunity, let us do good to all men,
and especially to those who are of the household of faith.

(Galatians 6:10)

Britain in the 1930s

What, for the Christian, is the relation between faith and works? What, for
the Church, is the relation between evangelism and service? What, for the
Christian and for the Church, is the relation between Christianity and society
at large, or between Christianity and politics? The first question had occupied
St. Paul and St. James and was crucial for Catholics and Protestants in the
sixteenth century. The second question has been much debated in twentieth-
century missiology. The third question presents itself perennially, although its
appearance varies according to historical circumstances. The three questions
operate on different levels, but the planes intersect, for each question touches
on soteriology (the doctrine of salvation), on ecclesiology (the nature and
vocation of the Church), and on eschatology (the doctrine of God's kingdom),
and all have broadly to do with ethics. A single situation or event may bring
all three into play. My purpose as usual is to follow Newbigin's thought and
action on the complex issues involved.

We may begin with Britain in the 1930s, looking at the content and the
circumstances of Newbigin's return from youthful intellectual wanderings to
the faith in which he had been raised, at his personal association as the
decade progressed with a number of prominent social thinkers, and at the
book he wrote on the boat the first time out to India, which shows him
reflecting on the Western world that, far from leaving behind, he would find
transmogrified in the increasingly urbanized and modernized East. Next, his
two major periods in India will be examined, starting with the detail of his
early and direction-setting Bangalore lectures on "The Kingdom of God and
the Idea of Progress" (1941), and then following through his running debate
with M. M. Thomas on humanization and salvation in the historical context

of nation-building, bearing in mind all the while Newbigin's social and political engagement while CSI bishop in Madurai and Ramnad (1947–59) and later in Madras (1965–74). Following his return to Europe, Newbigin will be located on either side of the Orwellian date of 1984, in a decadent Britain that he saw as epitomizing the decline and fall of Western Christendom. That will leave for examination what he meant by his late talk of "a Christian vision for society" or even "the vision of a Christian society."

Lesslie Newbigin's adult commitment to the Christian faith took place in response to a vision vouchsafed to him while he was engaged during a university vacation in a social service project of the Society of Friends among unemployed and destitute coal miners in South Wales. The Cross that he saw reached down from heaven into the depths of human misery yet promised life and victory to the entire world that its arms embraced. From his ship-owning father Lesslie had inherited a left-of-center concern for workers' lives and conditions; and when his own outlook, from his interpretation of the Scriptures and an encounter with wasting disease and death, took a firmly evangelical turn, he did not abandon his social and even political interest in the temporal welfare of his human neighbors. The Christian faith might be about more than this world, but it was not about less. Lesslie was his father's son in "always struggling with the question of how to apply his Christian faith to the day-to-day issues of business and politics."[1]

The first level at which the hearer of the Word is summoned to be also a doer of the Word is, of course, that of immediate personal encounter. From the time when he was a Student Christian Movement secretary in Glasgow (1931–33), Newbigin tells the following tale:

> One night I was accosted in the street by a beggar who asked for money for a night's lodging. He named a sum. As laid down in the Sermon on the Mount, I gave him twice the amount. After he had walked a few yards and had had time to recover from the shock, he came back and asked for a much larger sum. I did not have that amount, much less double the amount, on my person. But the teaching of the Sermon on the Mount was clear. I gave him my address and told him to call next day. He did, and that was the beginning of a relationship with George King which was to last until he died long after I had gone to India.

That friendship forced Newbigin to "think through the meaning of the Sermon on the Mount and its relation to the Christian message as a whole," and he thereby became prepared to "receive and understand the teaching of Reinhold Niebuhr when it came across [his] mental horizon."[2]

In Glasgow Newbigin made contact with George McLeod, then parish minister of Govan and later founder of the Iona Community, and with McLeod's help organized a conference to expose his SCM students to the situation of the workers and the workless of the Clyde shipyards and to McLeod's vision of the Church's response.[3] In these early and mid-1930s, Newbigin's reflections on the social implications of the Gospel reached out to include also international politics. How could they not, when "to those who were politically alert it seemed that the capitalist system was collapsing," and "social-isms of various hues"—including Soviet Communism—"posed a challenge which it was impossible to ignore, not a threat but a hope and a promise"? And the League of Nations, to which many Christians had looked "after the senseless slaughter of the 1914–18 War," was proving useless in face of the invasion of Manchuria by imperialist Japan, the attack on Abyssinia by Fascist Italy, and eventually the sweep through the Rhineland, Austria, and Czecho-slovakia by Nazi Germany. Newbigin found his pacifism called into question, especially by the impossibility of peace without justice (whether the problem be political injustice among nations or "the endemic injustice of the capitalist system," since R. H. Tawney had made him see "an inescapable contradiction between Christianity and capitalism"). But he would never lose the vision of the Church as "a foretaste of the new world" that he formulated with his colleague Arnold Nash in a statement on international peace for the SCM in 1934:

> We have, faintly adumbrated yet real and unquestionable, a foretaste of the new world for which we look: it is the Church. The Church is deeply divided by barriers of belief, of race and of class: nevertheless it is in a real, if partial sense, a supranational centre of unity and loyalty. This unity does not consist in similarity of opinion, of programme or of temperament: it is the unity born of God's act of love in Christ received and answered in its members. Apart from that relationship to God there is no Church and therefore no kind of unity. But where it exists there is a bond which can bind together men and women of vastly different belief and practice, race and class. "We speak that we do know." In that bond lies the hope of peace and the meaning of peace.[4]

A few traces of Newbigin's social and political interests show up in the essays he wrote as a theological student at Westminster College, Cambridge (1933–36). In an Old Testament paper of November 1935 on Exodus 30:11–16, for instance, he comments thus on verse 15:

> In the moment when God reviews His people, every soul stands naked before Him, and there is no room for reliance on anything that wealth can bring. This is the root of the democratic convictions which found their way into English politics in the seventeenth century from the practical religious ex-perience of the Independent and Presbyterian congregations, the only basis on which a belief in the equality of men can be successfully defended. Com-pare the famous remark made in the discussions between Cromwell, Ireton, and the army leaders: "I think that the poorest he has a life to live in England as well as the richest."[5]

Outside the curriculum Newbigin led a study, in which he tried to engage dons as well as students, on "The Kingdom of God and History." His interests in the SCM, both at Cambridge again and at the national level, brought him the acquaintance of such ecumenically significant figures as John R. Mott, Hanns Lilje, Hendrik Kraemer, and (most relevant to this present chapter) William Temple and J. H. Oldham. Both of these latter were engaged in the Life and Work movement, and Newbigin was "drawn into enthusiastic involvement" in the ideas Oldham was developing about Church, community, and state. Oldham in fact unsuccessfully attempted to dissuade Lesslie from going to India in 1936 so that he might instead help in the preparations for the World Conference of Life and Work to be held at Oxford in 1937 under the title "Church, Community and State."[6]

Unexpectedly back in Britain during 1938–39 on account of a serious bus accident in India, Newbigin found his pacifism finally disintegrating in face of the British policy of appeasement toward Nazi aggression, even while his reading of Indian history brought him a greater awareness of "the elements of sheer greed and violence which had marked the rise of British power in India." He regained contact with Joseph Oldham and was invited by him to take part in September 1938 in a meeting of The Moot, a group of prominent thinkers that gathered regularly—and at the time confidentially—to "reflect upon the human situation from a Christian and predominantly lay perspective." Convened by Oldham, the group included T. S. Eliot, Middleton Murry, Karl Mannheim, Walter Moberly, Gilbert Shaw, H. A. Hodges, John Baillie, Alec Vidler, Eric Fenn, and William Paton. Newbigin's response, as a "contribution from the younger generation," to a paper by Middleton Murry apparently displeased Oldham, but I have found no record of the substantial debate.[7]

Meanwhile Newbigin had written and published his first book, *Christian Freedom in the Modern World*. Composed on board the *City of Cairo* during the first voyage eastward in October 1936, and its preface signed at Chingleput, South India, the book was published by the SCM Press in February 1937.[8] It had developed from Newbigin's address at the 1936 Glenalmond summer conference of the SCM,[9] and from an earlier sermon of his on Luke 7:36–50 (the significance of which will emerge shortly). The book was intended as a reply to the philosopher John Macmurray's *Freedom in the Modern World*, which, whatever Macmurray's personal faith, seemed to Newbigin to undercut the Christian moral vision. Macmurray's work was being well received in SCM circles (as would also happen with the New Morality of the 1960s), and Newbigin felt an obligation to show its shortcomings.

In a move that, like it or not, aligned him with Feuerbach, Marx, and Freud, Macmurray sought in the name of freedom to replace a morality of law, duty, and obedience, which he considered mechanical and impersonal, by a morality centered on friendship and personal communion. Newbigin countered that, in personal relationships, trust depends on a common commitment to moral law. He recognized "the perils of conscientiousness": it could lead to attempts at self-justification and self-improvement, which in fact not only divert attention from doing the good for its own sake but also scale down the moral standard of man's "infinite obligation to goodness" by concessions to past failures and adjustments to future feasibilities; such, in fact, is bondage to a misused law. Yet "the significance of conscience" remained, in that conscience was—despite the limitations of its social and psychological conditioning and hence its need for further instruction—the channel by which God entered into the human situation as people faced choices and undertook actions (which is precisely what "makes a man an individual and a person"). Newbigin held no brief for what he called the "pharisaism" characteristic of "later Judaism" and "later medievalism," which today also obscured the Gospel both for its putative witnesses and for its potential recipients; but the Law itself, far from being abandoned, needed rather to be recognized in its original function of *torah* or teaching: "The Hebrew word *Torah* conjures up not the abstract conception of moral law, but the picture of a personal God forever watching over His people, teaching, guiding, rebuking, confronting them with His commands, in a most real and pungent personal directness." Thus the moral obligations of the Law are the expression of the personal will of God in self-communication to humankind; they summon people to personal response; and so they constitute the only secure basis for a life of friendship and communion both with God and among those made in God's image.

For a genuinely Christian understanding and practice of freedom, said Newbigin, both sides of the paradox have to be maintained: "The morality of obedience to duty by itself leads to bondage, and yet simply to eliminate obedience to duty from the good life is impossible." Or, in St. Paul's terms: "The Law is Holy" but "By the works of the Law shall no flesh be justified." "The life of a Christian," says Newbigin, is a "new and distinct and unique thing," which "solves the paradox of law and freedom by taking account of the reality which underlies the idea of moral law without falling into the self-contradiction of legalism." For, as St. Paul puts it: "Now apart from law a righteousness of God has been revealed, being witnessed by the law and the prophets, even the righteousness of God through faith in Jesus Christ, . . . whom God set forth, a propitiation by faith. . . . We reckon, therefore, that a man is justified by faith apart from the works of the law. . . . Do we then make law of none effect? God forbid; nay, we establish law" (Romans 3:21–31; Newbigin follows closely the Revised Version of the Bible). God from his side— from the side of the objective moral order—has provided the solution which man from his side could not, being himself the problem. Announcing the redemptive action of God in Jesus Christ, the Gospel "proclaims a quite new fact as the basis of a quite new motive. The new fact is forgiveness, and the new motive is gratitude."[10]

Because the Christian life "springs from the Cross of Christ, it carries with it the assurance that the law was no mere human imagining, but the true expression of God's mind, so that God Himself could forgive us only at this tremendous cost":

> To accept forgiveness as it is offered on Calvary is not to make our conscience less searching and active in its condemnation of us, but to make it infinitely more so. God is not one among the forces operating in the world, but the Creator and Ruler of the world, whose will is what we call the moral order, and whose wrath this dark world reveals because He will not allow sin to go on its way forever unchecked. Yet Christianity announces that God Himself came down amongst us and shared to the uttermost the bitter fruit which in

His government of the world is the harvest of sin—shared its agony and suffering and even desolation. Christ died for our sins—that is the new fact, the new datum which Christian morality has to work on.[11]

And Newbigin goes on to expound the "morality of gratitude" in contrast to "legalistic morality" as he sees them embodied in the story of the woman who burst into the house of Simon the Pharisee to pour out on the feet of Jesus her ointment and her tears (Luke 7:36–50):

On the one hand the Pharisee, a paragon of legalistic morality, the man to whom little is forgiven because he has fought for and won the right to regard himself as a good man; on the other the woman, who knows that the tatters of her morality can never cover her, but has met and accepted the miracle of forgiveness in Christ. His is the morality of law, with its well-defined rules and its reasonable demands; hers is the morality of gratitude, which can find no act of outpoured devotion too unreasonable or extravagant to express itself. "Thou gavest me no water for my feet; she hath wetted my feet with her tears. Thou gavest me no kiss; she, from the time I came in, hath not ceased to kiss my feet. My head with oil thou didst not anoint, but she hath anointed my feet with ointment." Jesus the Son of Man, who knew what was in men, discerned behind the extravagant devotion of the woman the great reality of a forgiven heart. Equally certainly He discerned behind the chilly courtesy of Simon the Pharisee a heart hardened and made cold by the conviction that it needed no forgiveness. The Christian life is not morality pushed a little further than would otherwise be possible. It is a new growth springing from a new root. It is the outpoured gratitude of a forgiven sinner.[12]

The Gospel, says Newbigin, "liberates great emotional energies of love and gratitude and directs them towards one end—the service of Christ." The joy does not remove the duty. "Beloved, if God so loved us," says the Apostle, "we also ought to love one another"; and Newbigin comments: "The love of one another does not spring up in us willy-nilly as a result of God's love for us; it passes through by way of the human conscience and the human will." Therefore, "duty belongs to the road which Christians must travel." Only at the goal will duty have been fully taken up into the spontaneous and sustained response of perfect obedience. At the universal realization of God's will, the glorious liberty of God's children, which is now enjoyed in foretaste, will be complete.

What purchase on everyday reality could those words, written on the boat out to India in 1936, still have by September 1939 when Newbigin set sail eastward again and "the modern world" in which "Christian freedom" was to be exercised found itself embroiled in the conflict that would become the Second World War? Without at all abandoning his concern for the individual in ordinary living, Newbigin was now led by circumstances to the expanded theological task of locating the perennial principles of social and political ethics, both in reference to the all-embracing question of the meaning of history and with precise regard to the present juncture in the human story. The result was his Bangalore lectures of 1941 on "The Kingdom of God and the Idea of Progress."

India from the 1940s to the 1970s

Newbigin set great store by "The Kingdom of God and the Idea of Progress." The four lectures given at the United Theological College in Bangalore were never published, but Lesslie insisted several times that I read them, even when the handwritten text proved difficult to find, and then to decipher. The lectures do indeed display the permanent lineaments of all his subsequent reflection of both principle and concrete detail on social and political ethics.

The lectures begin with the ironical observation that the people of Europe, filled with the conviction that they were the born leaders of men, had over three or four centuries spread their ideas and their wares over almost the whole world so as to create a strange new city-civilization of universal dimensions—and now the originating center of this civilization had turned into a Dark Continent, with the roar of gunfire, the cries of tortured prisoners, and the strident shouts of the mob orator all audible in its concentration camps. Did this civilization—in whose dress the Christian faith had largely been propagated and one of whose seminal ideas was that of progress—itself have any future at all? Newbigin sets himself to disentangle the idea of progress and criticize it from the angle of the authentically biblical reality of the Kingdom of God.

The idea of progress is basically the idea that human society has become better and will go on becoming better; ignorance and wrong can be, and gradually will be, eliminated from human life, until a time shall come when men shall live together in perfect brotherly love, equipped with perfect knowledge. In "These things shall be," the hymn of John Addington Symonds (1840–1893) so oddly included in many Christian hymnals, *man's* moral growth and *man's* mastery over the world are central; man is to become godlike, and earth is to become paradise—and this consummation is presented not as a hope only, or an aspiration, but a destiny. In contrast to classical Christianity, which regarded man as a sinner, radically corrupted, and unfit in himself for paradise, the idea of progress supposes that man's essential goodness needs only to be "educated," that is, drawn out of him and trained. Whether in its eighteenth-century rationalist form as individual improvement or in its nineteenth-century romantic form as social development, this belief in the upward march of history could, of course, only have arisen where history is believed to be real, and that is how it became possible on Christian soil, which in this way differed fundamentally from the Greco-Roman and Indian civilizations, in which the main intellectual traditions sought the real in the changeless. But the idea of progress developed through the detachment of the historical character of reality from its strictly theological origins in the biblical picture of God as "not a changeless and impersonal absolute, but an active will, seeking, calling, leading, punishing and forgiving." Biblically, it is their significance for God that makes events real, and history is the sphere in which the acts of God are accomplished and His will is being executed in judgment and mercy. The human story, therefore, is enclosed within the purpose and rule of God, and its consummation will not be by a natural process but by the final establishment of God's Kingdom in face of the powers of evil.

Newbigin's criticism of the idea of progress then proceeds in this way. In stable social conditions, the growth of knowledge and the mastery over nature may be cumulative; but, unless it be tautologously assumed that developments generally take a right direction, "progress" depends on "the will of men to direct these greater powers to good or to evil ends," and there is in fact precious little evidence of the progressive achievement of a "good will" among humankind as "a source of action steadily directed to good ends." Rather, "the human will retains its paradoxical character as being capable at the same time of the most glorious heroism and of the basest evil"; and the greater man's growth in power, the deeper the possible disaster. Besides the question-begging assertion that progress is an immanent law of history and the empirically falsifiable claim that progress has been a historical fact, the idea of progress may also take the form of a faith in the possibility of a better world in the future; but this, too, breaks down insofar as it treats intervening generations of individuals as mere means toward the future end of a perfect society. Those "bright visions of earthly utopia which gladdened the eyes of men in the eighteenth and nineteenth centuries have led directly to the pitiless and dehumanizing idolatries of the twentieth."

But is there, Newbigin wonders as he moves into the second lecture, a Christian corrective to this last version of the idea of progress, whereby the gradual attainment of a better, and finally perfect, society on earth may be accompanied by a belief in the personal survival of death that allows for the full fruition of the individual? Newbigin himself seems to have toyed briefly with this idea in *Christian Freedom in the Modern World*: against "the Nazi philosophy of race and blood" and "the Marxist materialist interpretation of history," he there allows for a "profoundly different Christian understanding of progress, which is based on the awareness that God can speak to us even in the sinful present, summoning us forward through the unconditional claims of duty to a better future"—where the "better future," without excluding "the hopes and aspirations of the individual man," nevertheless seems located in a continued earthly history.[13] In the Bangalore lectures, however, "the idea of progress" in any ultimate sense is dismissed on several grounds. First, there is the "absurdity" of two perfect societies, "one on earth, from which all but the final generations are shut out and where they enjoy the perfections which they have not striven for but simply walked into, the other beyond death, where all the preceding generations who are baulked of that earthly kingdom which they strove for, enjoy as a kind of reward for their labours and as a substitute for their disappointed hopes the bliss of heaven." Second, an earthly society existing under the biological conditions of decay and death and the spiritual sense of transience and loss cannot satisfy the thirst for perfection. Third, the other side of the deal, whereby "the individual soul may quit the whole travail and labour of God's purpose in the world and enjoy a merely individual experience of heaven," contradicts the corporate hope of the Gospel, robs human history as a whole of its meaning, and in modern times in particular leaves us without guidance in all those concerns of life where we can no longer treat face to face with our neighbor but must negotiate the powers of large anonymous organizations. The remainder of the Bangalore lectures are devoted to uncovering the biblical reality of the Kingdom of God as an eschatological reality that gives history its meaning in both its individual and its communal dimensions, while rejecting the idea of progress.

The proclamation of the New Testament is that in Jesus Christ the advent of God's heavenly rule on earth has begun; the order of evil, corruption, and death is being brought to an end; the promised new age has dawned. The coming of Jesus into the world, by which the character of God's Kingdom had been once and for all revealed and its powers set free among men, would (it was expected) be speedily consummated by his second coming to judge the world and finally to establish and complete God's Kingdom. The future completion would bear three main features. First, it would entail a "cosmic renewal": "It is neither to an otherworldly heaven nor to a gradual improvement of earth that the New Testament looks forward, but to a divine act in which all created things are to be renewed." Second: the full establishment of God's Kingdom begins with a day of judgment, "at which men will be judged according to their deeds, and by which their ultimate admission to or exclusion from the blessed Kingdom will be decided." Third, the general resurrection—of which Christ's rising from the dead is the firstfruits—means that the life of the final Kingdom will not be just an extension of life in the corruptible body of humanity which with all its achievements is doomed to die, but rather a new life given by God, fit for the new age.

Newbigin starts the third lecture by reasserting a "literal" eschatology against those scholars who, having by correct exegesis shown the degree to which the Kingdom is already realized in the first coming of Christ, then take the disastrous theological step of reducing the futurist references to the level of "symbol," understanding for example the day of judgment as "symbolic of the eternal spiritual fact that we all stand perpetually under the judgment of God" and should therefore "seek perfection now at every moment in concrete obedience to the will of God." "Take away the literal fact," says Newbigin, "and the symbol vanishes": "Only if there be real belief that an end is coming, will that end qualify what goes before it with the peculiar beliefs and feelings which we call eschatological." The root of the mistake, he says, resides in not allowing that time can be a reality for God. But then, why pray, if God cannot alter the future (though not undoing the past)? "Time," Newbigin argues, "is the creation of God, but it is a real creation of which he takes account as he does of the rest of creation." It is "the self-communication of God's will, grasped by faith here and now, which enables us already to live in the light of its final goal." Hope, which sustains the moral struggle, can itself be sustained only by confidence in the final triumph of God, the assurance that what "ought to be . . . ultimately shall be." "I do not see," declares Newbigin, "how the vital truth of Christian ethics that God's judgment is the final judgment can have any validity at all, unless it be true that the end of the time process is an effective judgment by God, in which, by virtue of his justice and his power as creator, right values are vindicated and wrong values condemned, and the dichotomy between 'what is' and 'what ought to be' finally ended." Here the objection of the "symbolists" has probably shifted: in Christ and his revelation, it is sometimes said, the idea of divine punishment or retribution is superseded. "What is revealed in the Cross," Newbigin counters, "is the piercing paradox that God who punishes sin and will punish sin, Himself bears the punishment, and thereby it is made possible for the sinner to repent and turn to God in faith." That, for Newbigin, is "the heart of the Gospel."

A third objection raised against the futurist eschatology is that the idea of an "arbitrary point," at which God decides to "stop the loom and take a pair of shears and cut right across the texture of human history," implies the termination of yet unfulfilled possibilities and thus the partial failure of God's purpose. Newbigin snaps back that if history is not a "continual developing process" but rather "a growth of good and evil side by side," then "a catastrophic eschaton might not be arbitrary but necessary": "We know how within history itself we see evil forces growing, organizing themselves with greater and greater power until they overshadow the whole world and men begin to ask whether there is a God in heaven at all. May that not be a microcosm of history itself? May it not be that the time will come when the long struggle of good and evil can lead no further and the final overthrow of evil and the consummation of all the long travail of goodness becomes necessary? If this be the true reading of history, then the consummation of God's purpose can only come by the destruction of evil and cosmic renewal such as the New Testament envisages." The dreadful day will not be arbitrary, but *right*—such as right has been revealed in Jesus Christ, through whom we may learn of it; in whom we may know ourselves, though deserving condemnation, forgiven; and from whom therefore we may catch a love that is big enough to contain wrath, too, a love which "alone is redemptive, because it is an echo of the mighty, wrathful, pardoning, suffering love of God Himself."

The proper eschatological hope, then, is "the hope of a new world, a re-created universe in which the travail of history shall find its completion and its rest." The fourth Bangalore lecture draws out some implications from that picture. Among other things, they allow Newbigin to ground the solution which he had already proposed in the second lecture to the problem of the relation between individual and corporate salvation when the realities of history are taken seriously in both cases:

> The Gospel as proclaimed in the New Testament is the publication of the divine plan to sum up all things in Christ, according to St. Paul's definition. The hope set before us in the Gospel is fundamentally corporate, not individualistic. To imagine that the individual soul may, so to speak, simply quit the whole travail and labour of God's purpose in the world and enjoy a merely individual experience of heaven seems to me untrue to the spirit of the Gospel. We can certainly believe that there is for the individual a higher and more blessed sphere of service beyond death, but I do not think we can believe that the individual can enter into the full blessedness of God's Kingdom apart from

the full consummation of that kingdom as it concerns all men, and all creation. It is of the essence of that Kingdom that its joy is the joy of communion. That joy cannot be complete till the fellowship is complete. It awaits, therefore, the full completion of God's purpose. We know that it is one by one that men must yield their obedience to God. But the full end of that obedience, the entry into the joy of God's perfected family, must necessarily be the act and experience of all together, and not one by one. The Kingdom cannot be enjoyed in full till all share it, because it is the Kingdom of love.[14]

In the fourth lecture Newbigin then expounds "the doctrine that death and resurrection are the connective terms between this present life and the recreated life of the new age." Every individual and every human institution must die; and even the best work of our hands and brains and the best of our social achievements have still about them the taint of sin that death confirms. But just as all that Jesus had done in the days of his flesh seemed on that dark Saturday to be buried in final failure and oblivion, yet on Easter Day was by God's might raised to new life and power, so

all the faithful labour of God's servants which time seems to bury in the dust of failure, will be raised up, will be found to be there, transfigured, in the new Kingdom. Every faithful act of service, every honest labour to make the world a better place, which seemed to have been forever lost and forgotten in the rubble of history, will be seen on that day to have contributed to the perfect fellowship of God's Kingdom. . . . Whoever is faithfully seeking, whether as an engineer, an economist, a politician, a craftsman, a teacher, or a friend, to overcome that which militates against true human fellowship and to create such fellowship in great ways or in small, may be assured that even though all the visible results of his labour perish before his eyes, it is no more lost than he is himself if he dies in faith. The outward implements of fellowship will perish; but in the day when the perfected people of God are gathered together in the fellowship of the Kingdom, he will know that his work was not in vain.[15]

By Christ's victory over sin and death we are assured that "death is not the last word, but that God in His power and mercy is able out of the corruption and death of men and of man's social institutions, to raise up that perfect, incorruptible society which is our true goal."

The barriers of sin, failure, corruption, and death mean that "there is no straight line of development from here to the Kingdom." Yet there is no utter disconnection. Christians are not to wait passively for the full realization of God's Kingdom at the final resurrection. Christian action in this world is to be understood, with Albert Schweitzer, as "a prayer for the coming of the Kingdom": "Christian action, done as in the sight of God, for His sake, acknowledging that He alone is final judge, and that the Kingdom must be His gift—such action," says Newbigin, "is a kind of prayer offered to God that He may hasten His Kingdom. It is a prayer that He can and will answer, because it is one where praying itself makes us and the world more fit to receive the answer. It is action done in hope of God's Kingdom and directly committed to God." Gratitude to God for the reconciling work of Christ impels the believer to acts of love toward the neighbor, which are committed to God as a thank-offering, in the sure hope that they will not be lost. That is how the apostle Paul understood his ceaseless labors: "I am persuaded that He is able to keep that which I have committed unto Him against that day" (2 Timothy 1:12, KJV). In the end it will not be a case of "I have succeeded," but "God's will has been fulfilled. Thanks be to God."

Having observed that by far the greater part of the problems facing humanity in the technical, economic, and demographic conditions of modern life are problems calling for political solutions, Newbigin asserts the impossibility of a Christian's avoiding politics. Political action means action in relation to, and in collaboration with, large bodies of people. Because it is necessary to decide between a very small number of politically possible alternatives, Christians find themselves working with others who do not share their motives or ultimate aims; and the tensions must be borne. Given an authentically Christian view of history and eschatology, the Christian will in practice exert his influence "rather against the tendency to exercise the imagination in making blueprints of a new and perfect world order, and in favour of efforts of a humbler kind to deal concretely with existing evils and put them right." In terms reminiscent of Reinhold Niebuhr, who had in 1939 delivered his Gifford Lectures at Edinburgh on *The Nature and Destiny of Man*, Newbigin declares that the Christian's

> realism about the nature of history as a concomitant growth of good and evil will prepare him, on the one hand, for using force against those who selfishly resist the common will in the name of private rights; he will not imagine that his programme will be carried through simply by the force of its own reasonableness. On the other hand, the same realism will prevent him from supposing that if only the existing world order can be demolished and a new and rational one imposed in its place, the real problems of human life will be solved. He will know that each advance will bring with it fresh problems, but he will, it seems to me, exercise his influence in favour of tackling and removing actual evils as and when it becomes possible, rather than in favour of utopian dreams.[16]

Although political action is obligatory, it is "not the only means, and probably not the most fundamental means," says Newbigin, "by which society will be changed." He suggests that "the biggest social consequences of Christianity have originated in movements which did not begin by aiming at social reform at all." But social engagement, arising from the evangelical command to love the neighbor and issuing in political action when opportunities arise, may have transformative effect: "In so far as we can do for the outcaste villages of India what John Wesley did for the downtrodden labouring classes in Britain, we shall transform India as surely as his movement transformed Britain." The earthly results may be transient, but Christians ought to be "the strength of every good movement of social and political effort," for they "have no need either of blind optimism or of despair," knowing what they do about the New Jerusalem, God's holy city coming down from heaven, to which there is no direct road but which shines out as the sure goal.

The ideas set out in the Bangalore lectures of 1941 provided the theological basis on which Newbigin would both continue his social and political reflection and conduct an ecclesial and public ministry as a bishop in postwar independent India. It was on the occasion of the Bangalore lectures that Lesslie first met a man who would become a lifelong friend: a lay member of the Mar Thoma Syrian Church of Malabar and a social thinker who would serve from 1968 to 1975 as moderator of the WCC central committee, Madathilparapil Mammen Thomas. In paying tribute to the bishop at his sixtieth birthday celebrations in 1969 (the Indian *shastiabapurthi*), "M. M." provided an insider's insight into Newbigin's theoretical and practical contributions to the social and political concerns of Church and nation in India.[17] He recalled Newbigin's emphasis on evangelical forgiveness, which was both the answer to Macmurray's total dismissal of moral law and, on the other hand, the alternative to judgment as the ultimate source of Christian prophetic ministry; he appreciated Newbigin's biblical realism and eschatology over against both liberal utopianism and fundamentalist indifference to politics. As a bishop, Thomas noted, Newbigin had pursued his basic concerns of building congregations, making them missionary-minded, experimenting with new patterns of ministry, and developing the ministry of the laity in secular society; and, although he had sometimes regretted that Newbigin's theological pursuits had focused on matters of ecclesial unity, Thomas acknowledged that Newbigin

never lost touch with the fields of religion and society, as it was inherent in his concern for mission. And he was always prepared to enter these fields with zest, in the light of the needs felt and insights received as a bishop of his church. He did it whenever the life and mission of his own church demanded. It was thus that he grappled with Gandhi's Basic Education in South India, entered into dialogue with the religious and social doctrines underlying it, and transformed the Church's participation in it as a means of Christian contribution to genuine education at the basic level. Thereby he showed how creativeness outside the Church could be received as part of the Church's own life. And he pursued his concern for the ministry of the laity in society as part of the ministry of the Church itself. More recently he has been attempting to challenge Christian people to get trained for social work in large numbers and to give those who are engaged in such training an understanding of the theology of society. . . .

Newbigin's contribution to the discussion of theological issues underlying Christian participation in nation-building was vital. More especially: on the relation between fellowship, evangelism, and service of the Church in society, on the basis of cooperation between Christian and Non-Christian in it, and on the Christian understanding of the State, a good part of the statements which went into the book *Christian Participation in Nation-Building* came out of his mind and pen. And the question of what God is doing in Asian nationalism, which has been raised in his books and in the EACC meetings on various occasions, has been a topic of continuous discussions between us. I have always taken seriously his warnings that one should not seek to identify the movement of God in Christ with other movements of a secular or religious nature, or to fit it into them, even while I have insisted that the question of discerning the meaning of these other movements in the light of what God has done, and continues to do in Christ in modern history, is vital. We have debated this at various times and have found that are our concerns are the same, though we often differed in emphases. He of course has a theologian's fear of translating eschatological and evangelistic insights into the historical meaning of the concrete political and social revolutions of our time for the humanity of men. . . . [But] I know for certain that he has continued to struggle to interpret the technical and social revolutions of our time in both their missionary and their social-human implications. His book on the Trinitarian conception of Mission is an attempt at comprehending the secular and the evangelistic aspects of Christian Mission in their interrelatedness.

We shall encounter M. M. Thomas again later, in the matter of what he saw as a shift in Newbigin's theology of the secular after his return to Britain in 1974. Meanwhile, we may take up three of the issues at which his 1969 tribute to Newbigin hints: the participation of Christians in nation building; the relationship between evangelism and service; and what would turn out to be a public debate between Newbigin and Thomas on the theme of "salvation and humanization."

The first is nation building. In ecumenical social thinking after the Second World War and during the demise of colonialism, it became broadly accepted that, even though imperialist and totalitarian nationalisms had been largely responsible for two global conflicts, yet national sovereignty, cohesion, and construction were indispensable in "the awakening of people to the dignity of their selfhood," so that "no self-awakened people in the modern world of nations could bypass the stage of nationalism and internationalism, with all their ambiguities, as they struggled towards other and higher expressions of community and selfhood"; but by the time of its assemblies in Bangkok (1968) and Singapore (1973), the East Asia Christian Conference (now the Christian Conference of Asia) recognized the inadequacy of "nationalism" as an ethos to bring social justice to the peoples of Asia (perverted as it had been by power elites in their own countries, who then used the theme of national security to preserve their own acquisitions), and so the accent shifted to support for popular liberation.[18]

Throughout the period of nation building in India, Newbigin's underlying concern was to let the Gospel have free course, so that its benefits, both direct and indirect, could be brought through the Church's preaching, its deeds and institutions of compassionate service, its responsible criticism and wise advisement of political authorities, and its modeling of a community of reconciliation and the transcendence of race and caste—all the while letting the Church's global catholicity bear witness to the provisionality of the nation-state. In his practice on the social and political fronts, Newbigin's letters home at the time—and later his autobiography—show him engaged with the Church in coping with famines, floods, and cyclones and seeking to strengthen the fragile village economies; he also spent long hours with the many millworkers among his church members in the city of Madurai who, "with little understanding of the issues," identified with the Communists against Congress, and the bishop tried "both to defend them against the police and also to help them see that Communism would not achieve what they hoped for."[19] In constructive thought, many of the theological foundations laid down in the composite volume on *Christian Participation in Nation-Building*—mentioned by M. M. Thomas and compiled by him—are clearly characteristic of Newbigin and often use his phraseology, although they are not of course peculiar to him: Christ as universal creator, redeemer, and judge, by whose life, death, and resurrection "God has radically altered the direction and course of history"; the Gospel as "the proclamation of the Kingship of Christ over all areas of the life of mankind, a Kingship which today is seen and declared by faith, but will be openly manifested at the end of times"; the Church as the community of forgiven and forgiving sinners and thus a model for all division-transcending community; worship, evangelism, and service all as integral to the life and mission of the Church; the dignity of every individual as that of a person made in the image of the personal God and a brother or sister for whom Christ died; both love and law as indispensable to the moral life; civil society as being "given a certain measure of autonomy by God," and the State as having before God, in the conditions introduced by sin, the responsibility to protect freedom, maintain order, and promote justice; biblical realism as the safeguard against both utopian hopes and paralyzing despair in the time before the end.[20]

There was, of course, from the beginning a prudential advantage for Christians in affirming the "secular" character of the Indian constitution in the sense that any establishment of religion would inevitably have been of a Hindu kind. A straw in the wind was the withholding of government assistance from Christian children in state-aided Church schools and its restoration if the family reverted to Hinduism;[21] and in chapter 6 we saw Bishop Newbigin taking up the matter of religious practices in the basic schools.[22] Yet Newbigin judged that "no nation can hold together in the modern world without some master-idea," and that for India the choice appeared to fall between Communism and "the Gandhian system, which draws much of its power from the deep feelings of the ordinary Hindu about his way of life."[23] From 1957 onward Newbigin the theologian started to develop most strongly his notion of the Gospel as itself a "secular" announcement that confronted the world and all its inhabitants with the choice between Christ and antichrist, between obedience to God's will and refusal of it, between alignment with God's Kingdom and exclusion from its enjoyment. In his autobiography, Newbigin reports how in that year of 1957, in preparation for a lecture he was to give in Switzerland, he

> spent the entire night hours on the plane from Bombay to Rome reading right through the New Testament and noting every reference to "the world". The result of this was to set my mind moving in a direction in which it was to travel for the next ten years. My thoughts for the past decade had been centred in the Church. This fresh exposure to the word of God set me thinking about the work of God in the world outside the Church. The result was a lecture in which I advanced the thesis that "what we are witnessing is the

process by which more and more of the human race is being gathered up into that history whose centre is the Cross, and whose end is the final judgment and mercy of God."[24]

In chapter 10 especially, we look again at the movement in Newbigin's thought on the oscillating notions of the secular, secularization, and secularism.

Second of the three hints from M. M. Thomas's tribute to Bishop Newbigin is evangelism and service. Newbigin did not find the relationship between evangelism and service an easy matter to settle, even though he was absolutely convinced that the Church and the Christian had to engage in each. In writing on "The Duty and Authority of the Church to Preach the Gospel" for the Amsterdam assembly of the WCC in 1948, Newbigin found it appropriate to think separately about evangelism and service while asserting that neither of them could be separated from the nature of the Church. Besides the duty of preaching the Gospel to the world, the Church has the duty to do everything summed up in the command to love the neighbor:

> The Church—acting corporately and through its individual members—has to go out to men where they are, in their need and pain and bewilderment, to get under their loads and help to bear them, to find men where they lie wounded, bind up their wounds and bring them home. It has also to do what is in its power—corporately and through its individual members—to bring all the common life of men, their economic and political systems, their family life and their social customs, under obedience to Christ. And the Church has to do these things, not with an eye on possible conversions, but because these are the things love must do.

If evangelism and service are confused, "the Church's works of love lose something of their spontaneous and disinterested quality and come to be assessed primarily for their value in winning converts." On the other hand, "the preaching of Christ will be vain if it comes from men and communities in which the signs of Christ and love are lacking."[25] Yet, as Newbigin seems to have later found more need to caution, there are dangers also in a reverse direction if service and evangelism are either separated or confused. He put the warning epigrammatically on a return visit to the CSI Synod in 1986: "Words without deeds are empty, but deeds without words are dumb." To fail to name Jesus and speak of God's Kingdom would be to pretend that our own acts of kindness or actions for justice could achieve that much greater and more glorious thing of which they are merely the signs.[26]

Perhaps Newbigin's clearest theological account of the relationship between evangelism and service sprang from reflection on his experience as bishop in Madurai. Thus at the end of the 1950s in *A Faith For This One World?* he declared evangelism and service to be related to one another not directly but rather by their common relation to "the new reality, the presence in the world of the Holy Spirit of Christ in a new community which is the body of Christ." This matches the fact that "in Christ's own ministry both the preaching of the good news and the manifold works of mercy are alike treated as the manifestation of the presence of the new age." The comprehensive category now is "witness": both word and action, both evangelism and service "can be used by the Holy Spirit for the total work of witness to Christ when they belong to and spring out of the life of the new community which the Spirit creates." Deeds of loving service are even "the first outward mark of the presence of the new reality in the world," but they are properly "a spontaneous outflowing of the love of God for men" and "not a matter of conscious missionary strategy"; and yet the word must be spoken, for "the Church must point always beyond its own good deeds to the deeds of God," which means preaching Christ and his Cross to every man and woman in every generation. Although this account is clear at one level, it nevertheless leaves the same kind of psychological question that arose in connection with Newbigin's account of evangelism and dialogue: how may one hope for the other's conversion to Christ as a *result* of witness—whether by dialogue or by service—without making it part of one's conscious *aim*?[27]

From the time of Newbigin's later episcopate in Madras we have already seen him, in *The Good Shepherd*, addressing his clergy in Madras on the practical inextricability of evangelism and service. Those homilies allow glimpses also into the social and political aspects of his own ministry in the metropolitan city.[28] His experience in Madras expressed and reinforced his conviction that the duty of Christian service extends to both private and public action. Without further explicating the relationship between the two, he proclaimed in *The Open Secret* the necessity of action both compassionate and structural: "To work for the reformation of structures, to expose and attack unjust structures, and, when the point is reached, to work for the overthrow of an evil political and economic order, is as much a part of the mission of the Church as to care for the sick and to feed the hungry. Part of it, but not the whole; and if the legitimate call to political action is allowed to replace the call to compassionate service, then the Church has betrayed its Gospel."[29]

A final qualifying note to all the activism of what has been said so far on the theme(s) of evangelism and service is sounded in a contribution Newbigin made to a Faith and Order study on "the handicapped and the Church." He takes "the handicapped" as those people, men, women, and children, who "suffer from any kind of deprivation—physical, mental, social or material—which is not at this moment curable with the resources and skills available to us" and then, under the paradox and dramatic irony of the evangelical text "He saved others, Himself He cannot save" (Matthew 27:42), Newbigin expounds the christological source not only of "a faith that rebels" but also "a faith that accepts." Handicapped members of Christ's Body

are not primarily a problem to be solved by the rich, the comfortable and the strong. They are the bearers of a witness without which the strong are lost in their own illusions. They are the trustees of a blessing without which the Church cannot bless the world. Their presence in the Church is the indispensable corrective of our inveterate tendency to identify the power of God with our power, the victory of God with our success. Because they keep us close to the reality of the Cross, they can bring to us also, if we are willing to see, the light of the new day which dawns from beyond our horizons and which is close to us in the Resurrection of the Crucified.[30]

Third and last of the hints from M. M. Thomas in 1969 is salvation and humanization. The debate centering on M. M. Thomas's book *Salvation and Humanisation* and Newbigin's lengthy review of it took place in 1971–72, but the fundamental issue had long been discussed between the two under various guises and would continue to be.[31] In the immediate background stood the recent WCC assembly of Uppsala 1968, which Newbigin interpreted— despite a valiant drafting effort by John Taylor—as a disastrous triumph of "humanization" over "salvation."[32] Globally, the ecumenical situation was so grave that the bishop could speak of "the real schism which is developing in our time within the Body of Christ—between those who see obedience to Christ primarily in terms of the call to manifest the reign of God in the secular life of the nations and those who see it primarily in terms of the offer of salvation to all men within the fellowship of the believing community."[33] Newbigin affirmed the legitimacy of both concerns and insisted on the necessity of finding the right relationship between the two. Both he and M. M. Thomas saw the differences between themselves as differences of emphasis, but Newbigin clearly thought that Thomas in the Indian situation, in his keenness to recognize the work of Christ in social movements for "humanization" on the part of Hindus and secularists, was in danger of forfeiting the essential nature and indispensable task of the Church as the locus and witness of "salvation," the Church as "the nucleus, the first-fruit, the sign, and the instrument of God's purpose to unite all things in Christ."[34]

M. M. Thomas, who had recently written a book under the title of *The Acknowledged Christ of the Indian Renaissance* (1970), was able to detect "a Christ-centred fellowship of faith and ethics" emerging both in places within the Hindu religious community and among secularists, where, as Newbigin also recognized, there was "a struggle to find the truly human, to find the form of belief within which man's historical existence can be meaningful and at the same time his personal existence be seen to have a meaning which is not exhausted by his participation in the historical process"; what Newbigin could not allow was that acceptance of Christ as a "Principle" (as among some Hindus), let alone the simple search for "a new path" (as among some secularists), could be called "faith" in an evangelical sense or seen as a substitute for "the actual experience of liberation through the grace of the Lord Jesus Christ accepted as personal saviour." Many in India, says Newbigin, "have come to accept Christ as the embodiment of the true goal for humanity ('the Law'), but find no necessity to commit themselves to him as the Saviour and Liberator from bondage ('the Gospel')." The "tremendous impact of the personality and teaching of Jesus upon Indian society" has "provided a vision and standard of true humanisation," and this is an instance of how "God uses the Law as one of the instruments of his saving work"; yet the Law itself is not a way to freedom, for freedom can come only as a gift from the Gospel of forgiveness. Missiologically, Christians can be "fighters for freedom" only because they are "bearers of freedom." That means being part of a visible fellowship, where through worship and prayer, through the word and sacraments of Christ's death and resurrection, there is constant renewal of a living relation with Jesus himself. Movements for humanization "will become trapped in legalism and self-justification if they are not being opened up to encounter with Jesus Christ himself as a living Person." The Church retains the responsibility of evangelism as "the open and explicit proclamation of Jesus as Saviour and the invitation to men to be committed to him in the fellowship of the Church." For all its shortcomings, the empirical Church remains the company of "those who participate in the struggle for humanisation not merely as those who are obeying a command or following an ideal, but as those who have already received (even if only in foretaste) the gift of humanisation—the priceless gift of being already a child of God and a brother of Jesus Christ."

Paul Loeffler's intervention in the debate allowed Newbigin to state his position with a sharpness that had been forsworn in his desire to interpret as benignly as possible his old friend "M. M.," whose christocentric commitment he never for a moment put into doubt. Loeffler, in fact, urged Newbigin and Thomas not to resolve their differences so quickly but rather to polarize their tension. Drawing on Ferdinand Hahn's *Das Verständnis der Mission im Neuen Testament* (1963), he suggested that they reflected two distinct christologies and missiologies that it had been the mistake of Constantinianism to "lump together": the first, a "Lordship Christology" characteristic of Mark and Matthew, was focused on Christ as the bringer of the "Kingdom," and mission consisted in the urgent announcement of the Kingdom's beginning by a small team of messengers to the nations; the second, a "Saviour Christology" characteristic of Luke/Acts and Paul, was focused on Christ as the locus of "Justification," and mission consisted in bringing people into the community of the saved where the new life is manifested and available. The alleged mistake of the later Church was to "narrow down" and "de-eschatologize" the "cosmic event of the *basileia* in process" and make it "identical with the purpose of saving persons generation after generation." In reply, Newbigin did a masterly job in showing that the themes of Kingdom and salvation, the cosmic and the ecclesial, belong together integrally in each of several strands in the New Testament witness; and that, whatever the historic faults of Christendom, the two "approaches" are held together by theological necessity. "The mission of the Church," says Newbigin,

must be seen both as witness to the Kingdom, to a reality which far transcends the Church, and as the invitation to men to enter into that community within which the power and reality of the Kingdom is already at work, even though only in a provisional way. . . . The whole point, surely, of the New Testament is that the reign of God has entered into history, first in Jesus Himself and then in the company of people which he gathers round him. Not that this company represents the final realisation of God's reign; on the contrary, it looks forward to that final realisation, praying, longing and working for it, carrying the hope for it always as the secret of its being, and for that reason being always a witness to its reality in the world. But the New Testament surely teaches that the Church can be such a witness only because the Holy Spirit, who is Himself the real witness, is present as the secret of the life of the Church; and the presence of the Holy Spirit means peace with God, wholeness, forgiveness and joy now.[35]

Britain Around 1984

Bishop Newbigin returned to his native Britain on his retirement from the see of Madras in 1974. For decades he had observed the decline and demise of Western Christendom, but he was nevertheless profoundly shocked when he came actually to live again in one of its former strongholds. When asked what was the greatest difficulty he faced in moving from India to England, he would reply: "The disappearance of hope." That condition showed itself in the twin symptoms of intellectual skepticism and moral cynicism, both of which derived from and contributed to the spiritual or religious apostasy by which the Enlightenment departed from the Christian faith. Newbigin summoned the churches to "a missionary encounter with our culture."

In 1981 the British Council of Churches initiated a study process that aimed at the holding of a national conference in 1984. It was thought that people would be pondering the state and direction of British society in the year that had acquired proleptic significance from George Orwell's futuristic novel of a generation ago about the maintenance of personal integrity in a perverted society under a totalitarian regime based on the lie, the linguistic expression of which was "newspeak": *Nineteen Eighty-Four*.[36] The size of the task ahead and the range and depth of specialist preparation needed required that the date be delayed for the conference that would mark, as it were, the grand opening of the project. In the meantime Newbigin, "being retired and having the time," drafted—within ten days, the rumor goes—a substantial paper intended to arouse interest, to clarify the issues, and to shape the agenda of the conference. After subjection to comment and criticism from thirty collaborators, the revised text was circulated around the British Council of Churches and published as a small book with the title *The Other Side of 1984: Questions for the Churches*.[37]

Newbigin sketched out five areas for "exploration," in which a challenge to thought and action might eventually be launched to society at large from the standpoint of the Christian faith. The most fundamental task was located in the area of epistemology or the questioning of contemporary assumptions about what is involved in knowing.[38] Despite the awe-inspiring technical achievements of modern science, science does not give, and does not properly pretend to give, a complete answer to the question of "how human beings are enabled to come to a true understanding of, and a practical relation to, the realities within which human life is set." Yet the belief that the methods of science are the sufficient key to knowledge in all its fullness has brought us to the brink of disaster. The Enlightenment's exaltation of radical doubt as an epistemological principle needs challenge from the biblical vision that places at the center a relationship of trust in a personal reality greater than ourselves. Science needs to be brought into a framework in which "ethical considerations are not merely external regulators of the results of scientific work" but are present from the start, "because all knowing is an activity of persons responsible to God and to one another." Much more will be said about epistemology in chapter 10, in which Newbigin appears as the Christian apologist. Meanwhile, his four other areas for exploration may be introduced in their pertinence to the matters of individual, social, and political ethics such as have been the concern of this chapter.

The first of the areas is the understanding of what it means to be a human person.[39] The Enlightenment saw the individual as an autonomous center of knowing and judging, with the right to develop one's potential limited only by the parallel rights of others. Any sort of heteronomy was excluded in principle, and the ideal of equality in rights made practical dependence on another incompatible with human dignity. The challenge from the biblical vision arises from the constitutive character of relatedness for the human, of which the governing principle is not an atomic equality but a personal mutuality, and the watchword is "Be servants one of another": "In this vision, human persons find their dignity when they surrender their autonomy to one another, and lose it when they place their 'equal rights' at the centre. And the centre which holds the whole 'frame' together is the God who enters into a covenant of faithfulness with men and women created to mirror divine faithfulness by their faithful relatedness to one another." Newbigin wonders what would be the implications of this vision for current economic systems, whether "free" or "socialist." Is a different ordering of economic life possible?

The next area for exploration concerns the goal of human life.[40] The "pursuit of happiness" is faced by the biblical vision that happiness is a gift of God, not a human achievement. The Beatitudes promise happiness "to those whom most people today would count most wretched." There can be hypocrisy in the questioning of Western affluence by those who enjoy it, but there is futility in imagining that "development" for the whole human race might consist in enabling the rest of the world to catch up with the affluent minority: "If the herd is rushing down the steep slope into the abyss, perhaps the laggards are to be congratulated." Rich and poor together need to reflect on models of world development that will acknowledge the mutual responsibility of all, safeguard real human dignity, and free everyone from the illusion of consumerist "happiness."

Next in line for questioning is the role of civil government.[41] Whether resting on a transcendent or on a populist legitimation (as in the cases of the American and the French revolutions respectively), modern governments have claimed or been given a greatly expanded role in responding to the universal desire for life, liberty, and the pursuit of happiness. When it is seen as the duty of national governments to implement those "rights," people have loaded on their governments historically unprecedented weights of responsibility for securing human happiness. Because no government can deliver what it promises or what is expected of it, cynicism results. Needed, for instance, are "ways of expressing the mutual responsibility which all must share for the welfare of all in a more personal and face-to-face manner than is possble within the inevitable bureaucratic constraints of state-organized welfare." We shall soon look a little more concretely at Newbigin's views on the welfare state.

The last in the sample list of areas for exploration is "our vision of the future."[42] The Enlightenment gave birth to the hope of an earthly utopia that would be achieved—whether gradually (in Liberalism) or by revolution (in Marxism)—by the emancipation of reason and conscience from the shackles of dogma and by the application of the scientific method to the exploitation of nature and the ordering of society. Most today have ceased to "think hopefully about any earthly future. But without hope action is impossible and life ceases." The biblical vision, says Newbigin, offers a hope for the future that is "both firm and realistic." It rejects those false messiahs who "pretend to offer total welfare on terms other than those which are offered to those who follow Jesus on the way of the Cross"; it includes the final victory that is assured by Christ's Resurrection but that "lies beyond the death and dissolution of both our persons and our societies." Like the action of the imprisoned Jeremiah in buying a plot of land in enemy-held territory, our present actions will appropriately be "signs of hope": "The hope is not just for personal salvation, it is for the accomplishment of God's whole purpose in nature and history; and therefore the actions will be actions in the public as well as the private sphere."

The whole "1984" project was, of course, bound to provoke the question: "Have we a mandate to 'meddle in politics'?" Newbigin offered here[43] a brief justification for the Christian engagement in the political sphere that he would then develop further in one of his Henry Martyn Lectures at Cambridge in 1986 under the title "Church, World, Kingdom."[44] "Christian discipleship," wrote Newbigin in the 1984 booklet,

> is a following of Jesus in the power of his risen life on the way which he went. That way is neither the way of purely interior spiritual pilgrimage, nor is it the way of realpolitik for the creation of a new social order. It goes the way that Jesus went, right into the heart of the world's business and politics, with a claim which is both uncompromising and vulnerable. It looks for a world of justice and peace, not as the product of its own action but as the gift of God who raises the dead and "calls into existence the things that do not exist" (Rom. 4:17). It looks for the holy city not as the product of its policies but as the gift of God. It looks for the city "whose builder and maker is God", but it knows that the road to the city goes down out of sight, the way Jesus went, into that dark valley where both ourselves and all our works must disappear and be buried under the rubble of history. . . . What is required is a faithful discipleship, following Jesus on the road he went, and living by the hope of which his resurrection is the outward pledge and the gift of the Spirit the inward foretaste. Such discipleship will be concerned equally in the private and in the public spheres to make visible that under-

standing and ordering of life which takes as its "fiduciary framework" the revelation of himself which God has given in Jesus. It will provide occasions for the creation of visible signs of the invisible kingship of God.[45]

In terms of systematic theology, Newbigin then appeals—in *The Other Side of 1984*—to a biblical doctrine of the human that rejects the ancient and Indian dichotomy between soul and body in favor of an embodied personhood that connects each of us with the world of nature and the world of other people. Further, it is not the case that, in those areas of our human living which we do not submit to the rule of Christ, we remain free to make our own decisions; rather, we fall "under another power." Such happened when, with modernity, economics became regarded "as no longer part of ethics but as an autonomous science governed by immanent laws to be discovered by analysis and induction," and there arose "the myth of the 'invisible hand' which could ensure that the sum total of individual self-seeking would add up to general welfare." We shall come in a moment to the concrete case of Newbigin's views on the "free-market economy." Meanwhile he declares the principle: "The decision for Christians is not whether or not to become involved as Christians in public affairs. It is whether our responsibilities in the public sphere are to be discharged under the kingship of Christ or under the dominion of the evil one." Nevertheless, a distinction is to be drawn between the activities of individual Christians and the actions and pronouncements of the Church as an organized body. The witness of the Church will depend principally on the day-to-day behavior of its members, who as citizens are constantly shaping public life in one direction or another; and the Church will be wise, says Newbigin, to concentrate on assisting its members to form their own judgments and limit its official declarations to matters in which great ethical issues are at stake. In any case, neither the Church nor Christians should identify in an absolutist fashion with any particular political program, although by discussion and argument they should try to discern the relatively better course of action in light of the righteousness of God revealed in Christ, and they should certainly reject options that are totally incompatible with discipleship to Christ. It is not escapism but precisely the realism of Christ's cross and resurrection that comes to expression in the third of Newbigin's Henry Martyn Lectures: "The Church has a real purchase in the world's life only insofar as it finds a point of reference beyond the life of this world. Only the hope which enters into the inner shrine behind the curtain provides with an anchor which cannot be moved by any storm or tide."[46]

From the very start of the "1984" project, Newbigin was well aware that its impingement on public policy might be seen as "an invitation to return to the ideology of 'Christendom'": "If the Christian revelation is to be taken as the framework for understanding and action in the public sphere—in politics, economics and social organization—how can we avoid falling again into the 'Constantinian' trap?"[47] Although he deplores "the absurdities with which the Emperor was hailed as almost a second Christ," Newbigin judges that at the historical moment of Constantine's conversion, there was no realistic alternative for the Church to "express its faithfulness to the Gospel which is a message about the universal reign of God" than by making "the experiment of a Christian political order." The fruits included "the creation of 'Christian Europe' out of which the modern world has been born," but the experiment finally "ended in the hopeless strife of the religious wars." The Enlightenment then provided a new "fiduciary framework" for Europe's public life. Even though that is now collapsing, there is, says Newbigin, "no way back to the Constantinian alliance between Church and state." Nevertheless, Christians and the Church must overcome the separation between the public and the private which they had too easily accepted from the Enlightenment, whereby the churches had become "privileged societies for the spiritual development of their members with a view to their ultimate blessedness in another world." What the churches need is "a return to the biblical vision of the last things which must govern all our secular obedience":

> Those parts of the New Testament which are usually called "apocalyptic" have naturally seemed strange and uncouth to privatised churches, but they point us to the essential issues. They offer no basis for a doctrine of earthly progress. They do not encourage us to look for the establishment of justice and peace on earth as the result of our effort. They point rather to more and more terrible conflict. But beyond that they promise justice and peace as the gift of God, and they therefore call for a patience and endurance which can remain faithful to the end. They are—in fact—the projection on to the screen of future history of that pattern which Christians have learned from the life, death and resurrection of Jesus.

What Jesus did was to "challenge the public life of the nation, at the time and place of its most passionate sensitivity, with a claim to kingship which was at the same time quite uncompromising and completely vulnerable. The claim was rejected and he was destroyed. But God raised him from the dead (an event in public history which our privatised religion has naturally converted into a purely psychological experience of the disciples) as the sign and pledge of the fact that the claim stands even though it is rejected by the world." Correspondingly, the actions of Christ's followers in the midst of this world will figure as tokens of a hope that derives from the divine promise of Christ's final victory and the manifestation of God's reign under a new heaven on a new earth. The present intellectual task is to expound the "fiduciary framework" within which Christian thought and action operates and which is offered to the world as "a new starting point for understanding and coping with experience." This must be accomplished in a genuine, and therefore risky, dialogue with people who have other fiduciary frameworks, whether religious or "modern." Such dialogue is "part of the ultimate commitment of faith," which "always means risking everything." With what he came to call "proper confidence," Newbigin confesses: "Because of what I believe about Jesus Christ"—that He "is the Word of God and is therefore the truth and the beauty and the goodness of all other faith or beliefs whatsoever"—"I believe that this open encounter can only lead both the Church and the other partners in the dialogue into a fuller apprehension of the truth."[48] Although "the 'Constantinian' establishment effectively identified the Christian dogmatic framework with the supreme political power," the Church "must never again aspire to the political and social power that the Constantinian establishment gave it"; for by its nature the Gospel brings freedom, can only be received in freedom, and is a summons to freedom.

In chapter 10 we return to the conference that eventuated from the "1984" project and to its aftermath. Meanwhile, we look at a couple of broadly ethical issues that Newbigin himself addressed during his British "retirement" and then conclude this chapter with a late word from him on "a Christian vision for society" or even "the vision of a Christian society."

First and internationally, there is the free-market economy. Even before 1990 and the collapse of Marxism (which Newbigin had rejected for its ideological utopianism) and of the Soviet empire (which he had condemned for its practical totalitarianism), Newbigin had voiced fierce moral criticism of "unrestrained capitalism" and the effects of its global spread. In 1983 he wrote:

> An international economic order which works steadily and inexorably to divide the world into a rich sector which expects to become richer with each year that passes, and a poor sector which sinks ever deeper into poverty, is in flagrant contradiction to the will of God as revealed in Christ. There can be legitimate differences of opinion about alternative possibilities for the ordering of the economic life of the nations, but when the cause of Christianity is identified with the resolute defence of the existing capitalist structure, if necessary by the use of nuclear weapons, then the question about the limits of permissible diversity, the question of apostasy, has to be raised.[49]

In fact, the ideology and practice of the free market—driven by the covetousness which the Apostle Paul called idolatry—will by Newbigin's forecast in his final years become, with Islam, one of the two great global rivals to the Christian faith in the twenty-first century.[50]

The other issue for the moment, following very much from the matter of the free-market economy and applying Newbigin's concerns to the domestic case of Britain, was the crisis of the welfare state. This may be examined in some detail, because it became for Newbigin the litmus test for the Christian character of a social and political vision. In the 1992 postscript to his autobiography, he wrote:

> During the decade of the '80s I continued to wrestle, very ineffectually, with the problem of relating the Christian faith to public issues. In 1984 I was invited to give the Gore Lecture in Westminster Abbey on "The Welfare State: A Christian Perspective" and I spent many months on reading in preparation for this. I was only beginning to understand the dimensions of the changes that were being forced through under the leadership of Mrs. Thatcher. . . . Things which had been simply taken for granted in the years following the War were being swept aside. The idea that we have obligations to fellow-citizens, that public service is a good way to spend one's life, and that public

consensus is something to be sought—all these were swept contemptuously
aside in favour of commitment to private gain. Market forces were to have
final sovereignty over our lives. People would only work effectively if they
were subject to the pressures of a competitive market. Teachers, doctors,
nurses, social workers and others in public service could not be trusted to
acknowledge good professional standards; they had to be bribed or threatened. . . . Long-term planning, such as only governments can afford, was to
be replaced by the rush for short-term profit. We were out of the era of
pragmatic politics and into an era of ideology. We were seeing (at a less
violent level) a replay of what happened in the 1930s when British people,
with their long liberal tradition, simply could not grasp the dimensions of
what was happening in Italy and Germany. We had been thinking of Britain
as a secular, liberal democracy. It was only slowly that one began to see that
the terms of the Church's mission had to change. We were dealing not with
a political programme but with an ideology. We were coming into a confessional situation.[51]

Newbigin began his Gore Lecture by reasserting the Christian contribution—made by such men as R. H. Tawney, William Temple, and William
Beveridge—to the conception and implementation of the welfare state in Britain in the second quarter of the twentieth century.[52] The welfare state's
coming into crisis in the 1980s revealed the absence—by then at the latest—
of a publicly accepted doctrine of human nature and destiny to undergird it,
said Newbigin. In political terms, the crisis arose from the fact that the welfare
state "is an attempt to found a social order based on the satisfaction of needs
upon an economic order based on the satisfaction of wants." Critics on both
the political Right and the political Left shared in their divergent ways the
mistaken assumptions of the Enlightenment concerning the human being as
an autonomous individual with an absolute right to determine for oneself
where one's happiness lay: people decide what is "right for them." From the
Right, the view is that "the competing, conflicting and co-operating actions
of individuals, each pursuing happiness as each conceives it, will work towards the general good through a process in which each will have to bear
the consequences and reap the fruits of his actions. Any drive to impose
equality will destroy liberty and undermine the personal initiative without
which society cannot be healthy." From the Left, rights are defined in terms
of needs rather than wants: every person has the right "to have basic human
needs met, with the corollary that a society which fails to meet these basic
needs is an unjust society and that the government of such a society has
forfeited its legitimacy." Newbigin's argument is that rights have no basis or
meaning "unless there is an accepted juridical framework in terms of which
rights are established and defined, [and] unless there are people and institutions which have a socially acknowledged duty to supply what is claimed as
a right." Ultimately, that means unless "the universe is sustained by a righteous God"; but that is a "dogma" which both Right and Left in a secular,
pluralistic society reject, because ultimate beliefs are there a matter for "private opinion," not "public truth."

Meanwhile, against the Right: a farmer, for instance,

could not grow a single grain if it had not been for a whole world of supporting and sustaining realities—including the society which bore him, sustains him, taught him the skills of husbandry and provided him with the possibility of a secure and stable existence. There is no one, and can never be any one, who can claim exclusive entitlement to the fruit of his labours. A model of human behaviour is fundamentally false which starts with the solitary individual and tries to calculate his rights and entitlements over against the rest. That is to put myth in place of reality. Whatever else may have to be said about the pursuit of happiness, this point must be made: that happiness for the self pursued apart from the happiness of all is a mirage, the pursuit of which can only lead into the wasteland. Adam Smith's famous invisible hand, which mysteriously overruled human activity in such a way that the selfish pursuit of individual happiness would automatically lead to the welfare of all, must be accounted one of the most malignant of the idols, the no-gods, the vanities against which the Bible so consistently warns us. We have enough experience of the actual working of laissez-faire capitalism to know that this is so.

And again:

Economic man as assumed in the textbooks of economics which I studied as an undergraduate represents the devil's intention for man. . . . Economic man is assumed to have one purpose: to secure as much gain for himself as possible with the least expenditure of effort. Once this is accepted, the rest of classical economics follows. Work is not a shared participation in the creative activity of God; it is a cost item in a profit and loss account. . . . It has no purpose except production and consumption. It has become purely cyclical and therefore meaningless.

Meanwhile, against the Left: "No proof has been given that needs create rights, unless indeed there is a just ruler of the universe; but in that case one would have to enquire about his purposes for the human person, which would in turn determine what real needs are." Without a recognized standard and instance of adjudication between needs, "the belief that needs create rights can only tear a society to pieces, for it allows selfishness to operate unchecked under a mask of moral indignation": "Justice means giving to each what is due, but it is of the essence of the fallenness of human nature that I overestimate what is due to me and underestimate what is due to others. And so we fight one another for justice with all the fervour of a moral crusade, and it eludes us while we tear the fabric of society to shreds." Newbigin affirms the "minimal needs" of life and liberty but asserts that a more-than-biological, "properly human" life needs also "respect, honour, love"—and "these needs are precisely those which cannot be made the basis of a demand for rights." To claim these "needs" as a "right" is "to destroy the possibility of having them met," for "these things do not exist except as they are freely given."

There is another set of "disastrous" consequences deriving from the Enlightenment separation between the public and the private. In a critique whose phrasing seems more directed toward the Left, even the Christian Left (perhaps because better might have been expected from that quarter), but which could also be addressed mutatis mutandis toward the Right, Newbigin mentions almost en passant in the Gore Lecture some issues that he tackled in other places:

> To suppose that you can have collective justice without personal integrity is folly. What God has set forth in Jesus Christ is the reality by which all human life, public and private, is to be tested. We justly earn contempt if we use the language of Amos and Isaiah to denounce irresponsibility in the ordering of public life, but are unwilling to challenge with equal clarity the irresponsibility of contemporary sexual ethics, the slaughter of unborn infants for mere convenience, and the easy dissolution of the most sacred bonds of marital fidelity, parental authority and filial obedience which are the very stuff of true human community.[53]

That last passage from the Gore Lecture of 1984 serves to indicate, of course, the source of the vision which, Newbigin believes, the Church has the responsibility of putting before society for its good: the revelation of God in Jesus Christ. The Christian understanding of human nature and destiny is that "man's chief end is to glorify God and enjoy Him for ever," which is to say that "human beings are created in love and for love, created for fellowship with one another in a mutual love which is the free gift of God whose inner life is the perfect mutuality of love—Father, Son, and Spirit; that happiness consists in participation in this love which is the being of God; and that participation in it is made possible by the justifying work of Christ and the sanctifying work of the Holy Spirit." "In the light of this given reality," says Newbigin, "all projects for the pursuit of happiness as the separate right of each individual human being are exposed as self-destructive folly, and all definitions whether of want or of need are to be in the light of this—the one thing needful, which is to be, along with one's brothers and sisters, on the way which does actually lead to the end for which all things were created and in which all human beings can find their blessedness." Mutual charity is the calling of forgiven sinners.[54]

The "struggle for justice is always necessary among sinful human beings," and "we struggle for more justice in a world where absolute justice cannot be, " but "we live by grace as debtors to the charity of God." "The poor," says Newbigin, "are not given to us as those who have to be encouraged to join us in the race after futility," but to "remind us that we are off the track," that it is "we, the affluent, who are in desperate need": "We who are rich must share the bread and so share the blessing." Our society "has to accept the need for corporate and personal repentance, for a recognition that we have been pursuing vanities."[55] With that challenge, the Gore Lecture ended. Elsewhere Newbigin declared that for such a call to be issued and responded to, there are needed "companies of people in every community who have love to spare for others because they have been dearly loved," bodies of worshiping Christians who—"ransomed, healed, restored, forgiven"—"live by grace and therefore become a source of grace abounding for those whose lives are short of grace."[56] We may even have to wait, he said, "for another St. Benedict to show us how to create the living cells for a new kind of body politic. Without such a fresh vision of what it is to be human beings together, the future for our society is dark."[57]

A Christian Vision for Society

In the last chapter of *Foolishness to the Greeks* (1986), Newbigin lays the biblical, historical, and theological foundation of what he will call "a Christian vision for society" or even "the vision of a Christian society."[58] Newbigin asks whether "to go with Jesus on the way of the Cross must mean to be on the side of those who suffer from the powers of the established order and not of those who wield those powers? Can one who goes the way of the Cross sit in the seat of Pilate when it falls vacant?"[59] The answer is not simple: "According to the Pauline teaching, the principalities and powers, which can become the agents of evil, and which were unmasked and robbed of their pretensions to absolute authority when they put Jesus on the Cross, are nevertheless created in Christ and for Christ and still continue to function after Christ's decisive victory, yet only under his authority (Col. 2:15; 1:15–16; 1 Cor. 2: 6–8)," and "the continuing existence of these powers, sustaining an order—albeit with much distortion and corruption—in which some measure of justice and freedom are secured, is a work of God, who in his mercy gives a time and space for men and women to recognize the true kingship, to repent, and to believe. These powers are ordained by God and are to be respected. They are appointed, as Paul says, to punish the wrongdoer and to reward those who do well. Thus the Christian is not to seek justice for himself by taking the law into his own hands, for there is one appointed by God to establish justice, a servant of God for your good, as Paul says (Rom. 12:17–13:4)."[60]

Newbigin draws the conclusion that, at the juncture in history "when the classical vision faded and the pagan empire disintegrated, it was right that those who had been given a new vision of the eternal order through the Incarnation of the Son should accept the responsibility of seeking to shape public life in the power of that vision. The attempt to create a Christian civilization, to shape laws consonant with the biblical teaching, to place kings and emperors under the explicit obligation of Christian discipleship—none of this was wrong. On the contrary, to have declined these responsibilities would have been an act of apostasy. It would have been an abandonment of the faith of the Gospel." And so: "By the same token, the Church today cannot without guilt absolve itself from the responsibility, where it sees the possibility, of seeking to shape the public life of nations and the global ordering of industry and commerce in the light of the Christian faith. . . . Most certainly when the Church enjoys freedom and influence, and when it includes a large part of the population in a democratically ordered society, it cannot be absolved from this responsibility." The Church has the God-given duty of reminding the civil government of its God-given responsibilities, including a responsibility "to reflect in all its ordering of society the justice of God—a justice that is primarily embodied in covenant relationships of mutual responsibility."[61]

The distinction between Church and state must be maintained ("and would have to be maintained even if every citizen of the state were also a member of the Church," for "Church and state have different tasks"). Above all, there must be no coercion of faith. That is where, according to Newbigin, the error of "Constantinianism" lay. The question of coercion, or even restraint, on behavior is also a delicate one. Newbigin of course recognized that it was not the case even in medieval Europe that all conducted themselves in accordance with Christ's teaching. He might, therefore, himself have done better to avoid, especially in present circumstances, the ambiguous notion of "a Christian society" and stuck rather to his other phrase, "a Christian vision for society."[62] A correspondence can in that case be established with Newbigin's ecumenical and missiological notion of the local church as the Church "for" the place: the Church and its social vision are placed there "for" the society.[63]

For the Church to play its proper role in such a society as modern Britain, said Newbigin, seven things will be required.[64] First, the Church will need to recover a biblical eschatology in place of the notion of "progress." Second, it will need to encourage religious tolerance, though not religious neutrality. Third, it will need to foster a "declericalized" theology, in which issues are "wrought out at the coal face." Fourth, there is needed "a radical theological critique of the theory and practice of denominationalism"—which is "the social form in which the privatization of religion is expressed"—in favor of what the Reformers sought, namely, "to restore the face of the Catholic Church." Fifth, the witness of Christians from other cultures is needed in order to correct the vision of home Christians who have long engaged in a "comfortable syncretism," "an illegitimate alliance with false elements in their [own] culture." The sixth requirement is for "the courage to hold and to proclaim a belief that cannot be proved to be true in terms of the axioms of our society" or of "our modern scientific culture." Seventh, the Church will need the grace and glory that overflow from its gathering as a community of praise in face of the re-creating God who raised Jesus from the dead.

A Christian Vision for Society was, according to a note to me from Lesslie Newbigin, the original overall title for the book that he produced in company with Lamin Sanneh and Jenny Taylor and which appeared after his death under the title Faith and Power: Christianity and Islam in "Secular" Britain.[65] The argument "is directed, in the first place, to Christians"; and—in explicit contrast to the document Changing Britain produced by the Board for Social Responsibility of the Church of England, which tried to appeal to the widest possible consensus that could be found on moral issues among the people of many faiths and ideologies making up British society—its basis is the assumption that "the Christian Gospel, with all its uniqueness and specificity, has validity for all people, and that failure to recognize the crucial significance of religious beliefs is causing and will continue to cause confusion, misunderstanding and alienation at all levels of national life."[66] Newbigin's own contributions developed ideas he had expressed in a paper of 1994 on "What Kind of Britain?"[67] For all the difference in circumstances, he was willing to invoke the inspiration of T. S. Eliot's *The Idea of a Christian Society* (1939) in countering D. L. Munby's *The Idea of a Secular Society* (1963). In chapter 10 of this book, Newbigin is presented as the Christian apologist amid a post-Christian Western civilization in which, internally and externally, Islam is the Christian faith's chief challenge and rival as an alternative to the prevalent paganism. The issues to be mentioned now are those that point most directly to Newbigin's views on what might almost be called, echoing the Indian experience, "Christian participation in nation-rebuilding."

Newbigin is clear that "only a fool can deny the evidence of disintegration in contemporary British western society."[68] The spiral of drugs and violent crime is a prominent symptom, as is the collapse of family stability. The underlying cause is the privatization of "values" that are divorced from onto-logical and moral realism (what really is the case with the world, and what is objectively needed for human flourishing—or simply what is right and what is wrong). A "secular society" in the Enlightenment mode is incapable of "creating the 'values' for which it seeks," for its own basic presupposition is the rank individualism of "autonomous rational man" who owes nothing either to God or to his fellows. That way lies anarchy and, as Newbigin frequently pointed out, the situation becomes ripe for a dictator to arise with totalitarian claims to provide a solution. Newbigin is willing to argue that "the secular societies which have developed in Western Europe since the Enlightenment have been able to survive [only] because of the very strong residual Christian element in the European tradition. Whatever may be the language of the public forum, the sense of the reality of God and of his commandments, and of Jesus and his saving work, is still so widely diffused in the European mind that it has protected us from drawing the full logical conclusion to the secular thesis."[69] Sooner or later, however—and now sooner rather than later—the question of truth has to be faced.

A society, then, cannot forever maintain an alleged neutrality in its basic beliefs concerning humankind. What course should Christians and the churches follow in a country in which there remains a vestigially established national Church, in which Muslims seek to extend the *umma* (Islamic world) or realize the *khilafa* (Islamic state), in which many in the population are at their respective intellectual levels secularist in the sense of "scientistic" or "naturalistic," and in which the official statistician reckons religion among "leisure activities"—all the while remembering that State coercion of belief or suppression of other beliefs, besides being practically impossible, is theologically incompatible with the Gospel?[70] "We are," wrote Newbigin in 1994, "in a confessional situation—that is to say, a situation where we are required personally to state our beliefs and to stand by them in the public arena. I believe that the Gospel is truth, and therefore that it is public truth, and therefore that it must determine the kind of society which we seek to nurture."[71]

That will mean, first, that the churches must set their own house in order at the level of faith.[72] Abandoning "the futile and self-destructive attempt to domesticate the Gospel within the collapsing ideology of 'modernity,' " they must recover "a coherent doctrine of the authority of Scripture, one which neither imposes on Scripture a concept of authority derived from the Enlightenment (the Bible as a body of indubitable factual statements), nor treats Scripture merely as an interesting collection of ancient documents illustrative of the history of human religions." Further, "the Church has in the ecumenical creeds of the first centuries a sufficient adumbration of her message: I think we have a right to know whether the clergyman who recites them in public worship believes in them or not."

Then, toward the state, and in face of the "demoralising of politics": "The Church has the right and duty to remind the governing authorities of the origin and the terms" of the civil power's "God-given authority for the limited purpose of sustaining righteousness and punishing wickedness and thus maintaining justice."[73] This cannot and must not infringe on the doctrine and practice of religious freedom, which "remains one of the most remarkable and radical achievements of the Age of Reason" and is entirely consonant with the Gospel whose acceptance can only be by "a personal response of faith and commitment and the deepest personal level." It is, in fact, "the Judaeo-Christian tradition" that grounds "the liberal state" when it "ascribes to the Creator the gift of the right of all people to life, liberty, and the pursuit of happiness."[74]

So then, in society at large, there needs to be "a sufficient number of Christians active in public life to shape the day-to-day discussions which lead to policy decisions. In a society which is both religiously plural and politically democratic, it is obvious that Christians will not always succeed in convincing others. But they should have the confidence to bring their Christian faith openly and unapologetically into the public debate."[75] Because the debate takes place not only in local and national politics but also in the worlds of industry, commerce, medicine, science, and the arts, there need to be developed agencies through which Christians in the various areas of public life may together think through the hard decisions that have to be made every day.[76] The area of public education is particularly important—because it is in the schools that the beliefs of the young about humankind and all reality are largely shaped—and particularly difficult, given both the entrenched illusion of "secular education" as alone "factual" (a view which in fact favors "secular*ist* humanism") and the new influence vigorously exercised by Muslims on and in the system. The aim must be "to create a public educational system which will train future citizens to live in mutual respect and mutual responsibility while acknowledging their differences in fundamental belief."[77]

Unshriven guilt about the past sins of "Christendom" is paralyzing. But pardon allows and empowers the penitent, Newbigin testifies, to proclaim afresh the death and resurrection of Christ (and the concomitant truths about history and eschatology that Newbigin developed, as is seen in this chapter).[78] If, as Christians, "we seek, as we ought to seek, a privileged position for the

Christian faith in the public domain," says Newbigin, "this is not to exclude or prohibit beliefs but to provide the only foundation upon which freedom of belief is in the long run possible."[79] For what are the alternatives? Negatively in one direction, the liberal doctrine of the state runs into self-contradiction, for without a transcendent grounding for the rights of an individual against the collective, or of a minority against the majority, the collective must prevail over the individual and the mob must eventually rule; and an agnostic in-difference—masquerading as tolerance—toward all religious beliefs undercuts its own foundation, for if the truth about the meaning and purpose of human life is something in principle unknowable, then there are no grounds for defending the liberal doctrine against any other doctrine of human nature and destiny.[80] Negatively in another direction, Islam "from its earliest begin-ning has sought for an earthly rule of God in which the truth of God as revealed to the Prophet would be embodied in, and enforced by, supreme political power"; Islam leaves no room for Allah's will ultimately to be denied even within this world's history; "dissent is un-Islamic"; and "I do not wish my grandchildren," says Newbigin, "to live in an Islamic state under the totalitarian rule of the *sharia*."[81]

Positively, "freedom of religion" is grounded in the Christian Gospel. It is of the essence of the Gospel that it be *freely* received in the time which the God who in his sovereign power and wisdom saved humankind by the Cross and Resurrection of Christ graciously allows for repentance, faith, and the learning of freely-given obedience before the final establishment of his rule under new heavens on a new earth.[82] Correspondingly, says Newbigin, "hu-man society can only flourish if there is vigorous and continuous struggle for the truth."[83] The Christian also has thereby to learn more of the truth. Be-tween Christ's coming and his return, "we are to put upon us the whole armour of God, and to fight not against human beings ('flesh and blood') but against those spiritual powers which so subtly, and yet often so blatantly, take over the great institutions and movements of public life"; and, looking forward "with eager longing to that Christian society which is the final goal of all God's creative and redemptive love," we are called on to "seek on earth a society which, as far as may be granted to us, reflects the glory of the city to which we look forward."[84]

There, in summary, we find what distinguished Newbigin's thought from much that passed for Christian social ethics in the second half of the twentieth century. Constantly and explicitly he set the practical matters of politics, eco-nomics, culture, and morals in the grand sweep of the biblical narrative and creedal confession concerning creation, fall, redemption, and consummation. That allowed him to be genuinely hopeful rather than naively progressivist, to be soberly realistic without being cynical or quietist. Human activity does not build God's Kingdom, but no constructive effort or achievement will be finally lost. God keeps it for the heavenly City and final Kingdom that em-braces people from every time and place.

8

The Liturgical Preacher

May the God of steadfastness and encouragement grant you to
live in such harmony with one another, in accord with Christ
Jesus, that you may with one mind and one voice glorify the
God and Father of our Lord Jesus Christ.

(Romans 15:5f.)

The South India Liturgy

At the heart of the Church's life stands the assembled congregation, where
the communication of the Gospel takes place through word and sacrament,
and the response of praise and prayer is made to the Triune God. That such
corresponds to Newbigin's understanding and practice is clear from the fre-
quency with which he returned to the point in so many different contexts.
Nevertheless, his formal theological statements concerning preaching, baptism and the Lord's Supper rarely exceed a page or two in length. In this
chapter, therefore, Newbigin is shown principally as the practical liturgist and
preacher. The presentation of his sacramental doctrine is reserved for later in
the chapter, and his theological approach to the Scriptures and his literary
exposition of them until the following chapter. During the 1950s and 1960s
Bishop Newbigin was frequently invited at international ecumenical meetings
to preside over the celebration of the Holy Communion according to the order
of the newly united Church of South India that he himself had helped to
compose, and he was often asked to preach on important ecumenical occasions around the world. He thus played a part in familiarizing the Church at
large with a eucharistic rite that was a firstfruit both of the ecumenical movement and of the liturgical movement that was starting to reshape the worship
of Catholic and Protestant churches alike; and he was able to set the
twentieth-century concerns for evangelical mission and ecclesial unity in their
proper doxological frame.

In the years following the Second World War, the eyes of both liturgists
and ecumenists turned toward South India, where the ecclesial union of Anglicans, Methodists, Presbyterians, and Congregationalists was inaugurated in
St. George's Cathedral, Madras, on September 27, 1947. The CSI was being
given the opportunity of creating a liturgical life that would simultaneously
bring together the best inheritances of the constituent traditions, begin to

place Christian worship in the context of the local cultures, and put into practice the ideas that were being advocated worldwide in the movement for the reform and renewal of the liturgy according to scriptural, patristic, and pastoral principles. The most significant rite to be developed was the CSI *Order for the Lord's Supper or the Holy Eucharist*, which was published in 1950 after its first use at the Church's Synod of that year, then underwent minor revisions in 1954 and 1962 (for inclusion in *The Book of Common Worship*, 1963), and in 1972 made the somewhat greater shift from "Thou" to "You" in the address to God.

As was seen in chapter 3, some English Anglicans in particular had difficulties with the theological basis of the CSI union and with the status of its ordained ministry and the constitution of its episcopate; and the same was the case, though perhaps to a lesser degree, with the liturgical formularies that were produced and adopted in the CSI. But many liturgical scholars, including the Roman Catholic Louis Bouyer, hailed especially the eucharistic rite of 1950/1954/1962;[1] and Colin Buchanan, in his encyclopedic collections of the Anglican liturgies produced between 1958 and 1975, considers the CSI service to have made such a marked impression on the shape and contents of several of them that one may speak of them as a "family" of rites deriving from it.[2] The influence of the CSI eucharist extended, in fact, to liturgical revisions then being undertaken also in other Protestant churches in the English-speaking world.[3] Its example eased the way for the adoption of several features much appreciated in the liturgical movement. Most important was the recognition that word and sacrament belong together in the fullest form of Christian worship. Next came the construction of the sacramental part of the service according to the four actions highlighted in *The Shape of the Liturgy* (1945) by Dom Gregory Dix, the Anglo-Catholic scholar who was one of the most vociferous opponents of Anglican participation in the South India unity scheme: the "taking" of the bread and wine (the offertory), the "blessing" of the bread and wine (the eucharistic prayer), the "breaking" of the bread (the fraction), and the "giving" of the consecrated bread and wine (the communion). More detailed acquisitions included the provision for solemn entrances with the Bible and with the bread and wine at the start of the two parts of the service that focus on word and sacrament respectively; the reintroduction, after many centuries, of a regular reading from the Old Testament before the Epistle and the Gospel; the use of prayers in the litany form, with the full congregation making responses to the minister's biddings; the retrieval of the ancient hymn "Holy God, Holy and Mighty, Holy and Immortal: have mercy on us"; the exchange of the greeting of peace among the entire assembly, the gesture taking the form of a touching of the hands in the Indian style; the formulation of the Benedictus qui venit as "Blessed be he that *hath come and is to come* in the name of the Lord"; the inclusion in the eucharistic prayer of an anamnesis ("Wherefore, O Father, having in remembrance the precious death and passion, and glorious resurrection and ascension, of thy Son our Lord, we thy servants do this . . .") and an epiclesis ("And we most humbly beseech thee, O merciful Father, to sanctify with thy

Holy Spirit, us and these thine own gifts of bread and wine, that the bread which we break may be the communion of the body of Christ, and the cup which we bless the communion of the blood of Christ"); the insertion of congregational acclamations into the presidential prayer (notably "Thy death, O Lord, we commemorate, thy resurrection we confess, and thy second coming we await"); and the making of the fraction into a distinct action between the eucharistic prayer and the communion.[4] Domestically, the CSI liturgy of the Lord's Supper proved to be a unifying factor in the new church: it was reported after almost half a century that "there are few congregations where this is not the normal Sunday service for the eucharist"; and "liturgical conservatism" (or a recognition of the need for ritual stability which has been ignored by denominational bureaucrats in many Western churches) ensured that "it is the liturgy of 1950 (minimally revised in 1954) that now provides most CSI congregations with a sense of ecclesial identity."[5]

Insider accounts of the early work of the CSI liturgy committee have been provided by A. M. Ward, T. S. Garrett, and L. W. Brown (convenor of the committee and Newbigin's friend, previously mentioned in chapter 4).[6] Ward described himself and his colleagues as "for the most part liturgically illiterate," and Garrett declared that "not a few of us have acquired a considerable amount of liturgical knowledge *ex nihilo* in the course of undertaking the projects set us." What part did Lesslie Newbigin play in the disciplined liturgical creativity of the CSI?

In the first place it should be noted that Newbigin belonged, with J. S. M. Hooper and Bishop V. S. Azariah, to the small group appointed before the union to draft the Service of Inauguration that would eventually take place on September 27, 1947.[7] Although lacking in places the rhythms that mark skilled liturgical composition, a prayer specific to the occasion reveals in the form of thanks and petition how the moment was oriented to both the mission and the unity of the Church, and all to the glory of God and the final establishment of the divine Kingdom:

Almighty and everlasting God, who alone art the author of unity, peace and concord, we thank Thee for the Churches in this our land and for Thy grace in choosing us to be members in Thy Church. We bless Thee for our fellowship, and for our rich inheritance. We praise Thee for Thy messengers from other lands who brought the gospel of Thy kingdom to this land, and for those who have faithfully proclaimed it to succeeding generations, and for all who have prayed and laboured for the union of Churches, especially in South India. Thou hast heard the prayers of Thy people and blessed the labours of Thy servants, and hast brought us to this day for the glory of Thy name. In obedience to thy will and led by Thy Spirit, as we accept one another as fellow members and fellow ministers, do Thou strengthen the bonds between us and unite us and make us one body, Thyself, O Christ, being its head. Make us all of one heart and one soul, united in one holy bond of truth and peace, of faith and charity. Grant that this Church may ever be zealous in commending Thy glorious gospel to the millions in this land, that India may find in Thee the goal of all her seeking and the fulfilment of her noblest aspirations. Hasten the time, O God, when throughout the world there shall be one flock, one shepherd, and in the name of Jesus every knee shall bow, and every tongue confess that Jesus Christ is Lord. Amen.

From the start of his episcopate Newbigin took seriously the constitutional provision of the CSI that the bishop be "a leader in worship" in his diocese. In a letter of October 13, 1948, to "dear friends" at home, the Bishop wrote:

> One of the questions which I had to answer at my consecration was this: "Will you diligently acquaint yourself with the various forms and methods of worship used in your diocese, and so advise the ministers and congregations committed to your charge that this Church may offer such worship as will be worthy of God's majesty and love, and a witness to those around them?" This is a matter in which the fact of our union has forced us all to think afresh about the things in religion in which above all else are we rightly conservative, and I have found it harder here than anywhere else to discern the right path. Some things which were most manifestly not worthy of God's majesty and love I have tried to change. Most ministers and congregations desire earnestly that we should come in course of time to a large measure of common practice. Yet—especially in the service of Holy Communion—hasty change is intolerable. We have begun by trying to study together some of the great liturgies of the Western and Eastern Churches, both ancient and modern. Meetings for the whole diocese have provided occasions for careful experiment, though even this has sometimes caused offence. Yet I have no doubt that we are moving forward, and that in this realm as in many others we are being led through tension and difficulty to deeper obedience. It is a constant comfort to remember that we did not unite because we wanted to, but because we believed that it was the plainly revealed will of our Lord.[8]

In his early years in Madurai, it seems that Newbigin himself drew on the "clear and firm liturgical tradition of a Reformed type" that he knew from the Church of Scotland's *Book of Common Order*, needing to set an example both for those schooled in "the vague New England liberalism" brought by American Congregational missionaries who had been the chief workers in the area and also for those who in reaction tended toward "an unthinking copying" of the liturgical practices legitimately retained by the former Anglicans in the diocese.[9]

Bishop Newbigin was appointed by the CSI Synod to its new liturgy committee, whose initial purpose was "more to monitor liturgical developments in the dioceses than to produce fresh material for the whole Church."[10] By November 1, 1949, however, Newbigin was writing to friends at home:

> We have begun to make progress in the matter of liturgy. The Synod Liturgical Committee has prepared a draft of an order of service for the Lord's Supper, to be used in the first instance at the meeting of the Synod and also— if approved—on other occasions where it is desired. The draft has been sent to liturgical experts in many Churches and countries and has been intensively discussed in the dioceses. Our own diocesan liturgical committee spent a day and a half on it, and these discussions did more—I think—to open up real communication between our different traditions than anything I have yet experienced since the union. The order as finally approved will doubtless be published in due course, so I shall not attempt to describe it.[11]

And then in a similar letter of October 28, 1950, he reports that

> the Order of Service for the Lord's Supper or the Holy Eucharist (to give its full title) was used for the first time at the Synod in January, and is now being translated into the vernaculars. Its publication and gradual coming into use are very big events in the life of the Church of South India. Of course, it is only used now occasionally, especially on Diocesan and Synod occasions. But every use increases one's appreciation of it. I am more and more sure that we have something of immense value in this liturgy, and that it will increasingly come to have a central place both in our worship and in our teaching. In this Diocese there is real eagerness for the increasing use of this common form of worship at the central point of the Church's life. I am more and more sure that the church needs to have *both* a fixed order of worship for its central common acts—embodying in the fullest and most perfect possible form the whole meaning of the whole Church in these acts, *and* a vast amount of thoroughly free and spontaneous praying and witnessing in small groups each shaped naturally by the experiences and characters of the people in them.[12]

Newbigin pays tribute to "the inspired leadership" of Leslie Brown in the process of composing the eucharistic liturgy. Individual contributions to the composition are not easy to trace, but there are a few hints in Newbigin's writings about his own part in it, and there are a number of touches characteristic of him in the final product. Directly, he recounts Leslie Brown's excitement at discovering the beautiful Mozarabic or Old Spanish *Adesto* prayer, "Be present, be present, O Jesus, thou good high priest, as thou wast in the midst of thy disciples": Brown "rushed into my bedroom (where I was having a mild illness) to ask how we should end it, and [I remember] my proposing 'and be made known to us in the breaking of the bread.' "[13] That prayer, in fact, was taken into the CSI liturgy for saying by the presbyter and people together immediately before the presbyter summons the people to the eucharistic prayer with the "Lift up your hearts." Less directly, it may be noted that the offertory prayer in the CSI liturgy, although it may (as T. S. Garrett remarks) echo the "prayer of the veil" in the Syrian liturgy of St. James, employs the theme of Hebrews 10:19f. in a usage familiar to Newbigin from the prayer at the unveiling of the bread and wine in the Church of Scotland's 1940 *Book of Common Order*. The CSI prayer runs "Holy Father, who through the blood of thy dear Son hast consecrated for us a new and living way to thy throne of grace . . ." and is cited by Newbigin in *Sin and Salvation* as he expounds the work of the Savior: "Because of our sin, we cannot of ourselves offer an acceptable sacrifice to God; He alone can do that. But because He has done so in the flesh, that is as a man, and because He unites us to Himself in His human nature, we can do so in and through Him. That is part of the meaning of the service of Holy Communion, and that is why in the Church of South India Liturgy we use those words from Hebrews at the beginning of the Service of Breaking Bread . . ."[14]

It is noteworthy that the "common preface" in the eucharistic prayer of the CSI encapsulated the entire sweep of salvation history in a way that was unusual in Western liturgical history but matches the "rule of faith" such as we have seen Newbigin setting it out through creation, fall, redemption, and new creation: "It is verily meet, right, and our bounden duty, that we should at all times, and in all places, give thanks unto thee, O Lord, Holy Father, Almighty and Everlasting God; Through Jesus Christ our Lord, through whom thou didst create the heavens and the earth and all that in them is, and didst make man in thine own image, and when he had fallen into sin didst redeem him to be the first fruits of a new creation."[15] Nor, given the centrality of the Atonement for Newbigin, can it be accidental that—in the manner of the Anglican Prayer Book of 1662, which Newbigin affirmed as the "starting point" for the CSI liturgy over against the Syrianizing enthusiasms of some colleagues—the eucharistic prayer later insists on Christ's "one oblation of himself once offered, a full, perfect, and sufficient sacrifice, oblation, and satisfaction, for the sins of the whole world."[16]

Finally, the introductory rubrics of the CSI liturgy indicate that "the word 'hymn' should be taken to include any sung prayer or praise, such as a 'lyric'" and express the hope that "in the Indian languages all the sung part of the service may be set to suitable Indian music." Newbigin loved Tamil Christian lyrics and encouraged their use in worship. He saw to it that village teachers and local catechists received instruction not only in Old and New Testaments and preaching but also in Tamil poetry.[17]

What, then, was the structure of the CSI eucharistic liturgy that Newbigin helped to compose, that met with the admiration of liturgiologists of several ecclesial traditions, and whose celebration he presided over on numerous ecumenical occasions? Using technical terms for brevity's sake, one may outline its order from the 1954 version thus:

THE PREPARATION
Hymn or Psalm
Entry with the Bible
Collect for Purity ("Almighty God, unto whom all hearts be open," as in 1662 BCP)
The Greater Gloria ("Glory to God in the highest . . ."),
    or "Holy God, Holy and Mighty, Holy and Immortal: have mercy on us,"
    or Litany of the Lamb (based on Revelation 5:12f.; 5:9bc; 7:10, 12)
Call to Self-Examination and Invitation to Confession
Prayer of Confession
The Comfortable Words (Mt. 11:28; Jn 3:16; 1 Tim. 1:15; 1 Jn 2:1f., as in 1662 BCP)
Prayer for Forgiveness or Absolution

THE MINISTRY OF THE WORD OF GOD
Collect of the Day
Old Testament Lesson
Psalm, or hymn
Epistle
Gospel

Sermon
Nicene Creed
[Announcements; Collection; Hymn]
Litany of Intercession
The First Benediction (2 Cor. 13:14)
The Dismissal of Non-Communicants ("Those who leave shall leave now")

THE BREAKING OF THE BREAD
Sentences (Ps. 133:1; 1 Cor. 10:17; Ps. 27:6)
The Peace
Hymn
Bringing of Bread, Wine, and Alms to the Table
Offertory Prayer ("Holy Father, who through the blood . . .")
"Be present, be present, O Jesus, thou good High Priest . . ."
Eucharistic Prayer:
  Sursum Corda
  Preface ("It is verily meet, right, and our bounden duty . . .")
  Sanctus and *Benedictus qui venit*
  "Truly holy, truly blessed art thou, O heavenly Father, who of thy
    tender mercy towards mankind didst give thine only Son Jesus
    Christ . . ."
  Institution Narrative
  Acclamation ("Thy death, O Lord, we commemorate . . .")
  Anamnesis ("Wherefore, O Father, . . . we thy servants do this in remem-
    brance of him, as he hath commanded, until his coming again, giving
    thanks to thee for the perfect redemption which thou hast wrought for
    us in him")
  Acclamation ("We give thanks to thee, we praise thee, we glorify
    thee . . .")
  Epiclesis
  Doxology
  Amen
Lord's Prayer
Prayer of Humble Access ("We do not presume," slightly adapted from 1662
  BCP)
Fraction
Communion ("The body of our Lord Jesus Christ, the bread of life"; "The
  blood of our Lord Jesus Christ, the true vine")
Agnus Dei, or other communion hymn
Prayer of Thanksgiving and Self-Oblation (two versions, each using scriptural
  [Rom. 12:1f.] and BCP phrases)
The Second Benediction ("The peace of God, which passeth all understand-
  ing," as in 1662 BCP)
Hymn, *or* part of Psalm 103, *or* Nunc Dimittis.

Bishop Newbigin will normally have presided, as the rubrics recommend,
from "behind the Table, facing the people." While Anglican priests still at
that time celebrated eastward (if "catholic") or at the north end of the table
(if "evangelical"), Newbigin was familiar from the Church of Scotland with
the westward stance that the liturgical movement was starting to restore to

the Roman Catholic and Anglican communions as the "basilican" position, whereby the presiding minister faced the congregation across the altar; and here again the CSI pioneered the way.

A number of ecumenically significant celebrations of the CSI liturgy are recorded by Bishop Newbigin in his autobiography. In September 1952, at a meeting of the committee of twenty-five that was charged with the theological preparation of the Evanston assembly of the World Council of Churches, he presided at the Lord's Supper on the Lord's Day, with Karl Barth as the preacher, in the chapel of the Ecumenical Institute at the Château de Bossey, near Geneva. At the Evanston assembly itself in 1954, "a very great number" received communion at the celebration of the CSI liturgy, and the bishop received "many testimonies that it had been one of the great moments of the Assembly." At the Lambeth Conference of the bishops of the Anglican Communion in 1958, the CSI was not officially represented, but Newbigin was invited by Archbishop Geoffrey Fisher as his guest, "so that there might be a celebration of the Holy Communion with the CSI liturgy which, of course, all the bishops would be free to attend if they wished to, and certainly some would wish to communicate": "I was delighted to accept this invitation," Newbigin reports, "and the service took place on the morning of 18 July. As fellow-ministers I had Leslie Brown, then Bishop of Uganda, E. C. John studying in Cambridge, and V. Gnanamuthu working in a Methodist circuit. About 160 of the bishops received communion, the first four being the two English Archbishops (Fisher and Ramsey), Sherrill, Presiding Bishop of the US Church, and Yasiro of Japan." In 1960 Newbigin presided at a celebration of the CSI liturgy in Grace Cathedral, San Francisco, at the launching of the "Blake-Pike" proposals for unity among the several mainline denominations in the United States (what became the Consultation on Church Union). In his homily he expounded 1 Corinthians 10:16–17 to show the Eucharist as both a source of unity and ipso facto a threat of judgment when participation in the bread and the cup is not accompanied by "a deep and solemn resolve to live, to work, and to pray without ceasing until those divisions by which we dishonor our one Lord are done away."[18] Sadly it must be reported that, forty years on, the hopes of COCU remained unfulfilled.

Less formally, Newbigin tells how, while he was on WCC business in the Soviet Union in the early 1960s, he was asked to celebrate the CSI liturgy in a bedroom of the Intourist hotel in Odessa; sixteen Orthodox clergy attended, and "the hotel servants were eager in helping to arrange the room for the service." On Pentecost 1963, as part of the celebrations to mark the fourteen hundredth anniversary of the landing of St. Columba on Iona, "on a bright and windy day with a glory of colour that only Iona can display," in the abbey church Newbigin "celebrated the CSI liturgy with ministers of the Scottish and English Churches who could not otherwise share communion." Beside him at the table stood the moderator of the Church of Scotland, the Episcopal bishop of Edinburgh, and the Anglican bishop of Durham: "As I gave the chalice to each of them," he wrote, "I felt overwhelmed by the significance of what was happening against the quarrel between bishop and presbytery which has rent history for so long." In 1973, during his last year as bishop in Madras, Newbigin received the visit of Michael Ramsey: "To have the Archbishop of Canterbury stand with me behind the Holy Table in Madras Cathedral and to join with him in celebrating the eucharist according to the CSI order was something that filled me with happiness. As I remembered the battles of the past and the absence of the Church of England from the great act of union twenty-six years earlier, I felt I could really say *Nunc dimittis.*"[19]

Since those years, the role of the CSI eucharistic order as a liturgy for ecumenical occasions has been overtaken by the so-called Lima Liturgy, which was developed as a by-product to give ritual expression to the doctrinal convergence attained in the WCC Faith and Order Commission on the themes of Baptism, Eucharist and Ministry. Having chaired the drafting work on "BEM" at the commission meetings in Bangalore (1978) and Lima (1982), I may perhaps be allowed to say that the texts of the Lima Liturgy are much too strongly thematized toward the particular occasion of their production to be suitable for more general liturgical use and that I still prefer the CSI rite that gave me my first living contact with that freshly united church when as a Cambridge undergraduate I attended a eucharist celebrated by a CSI missionary-presbyter on furlough. What the ecumenical reception of the CSI liturgy and then of the Lima Liturgy shows, however, is the felt need of a widely acceptable eucharistic order that can be used by churches on the way to that unity which "is being made visible" along the lines sketched by Lesslie Newbigin for approval by the New Delhi assembly of the WCC in 1961.[20]

In India itself, it has been argued by some missionaries and local theologians of a later generation that the CSI liturgy of the early years did not go far enough in the direction of "Indianization." Work at the United Theological College in Bangalore, led by Eric Lott and Christopher Duraisingh, produced *Worship in an Indian Context: Eight Inter-Cultural Liturgies* (1986); and "An Indian Liturgy for Celebrating the Eucharist" from that booklet, little changed, was accepted as "An Alternative CSI Liturgy" and celebrated at the General Synod in 1986.[21] In 1998 it was reported that the alternative liturgy was "mostly popular in the theological colleges;"[22] I observed its use, however, by the CSI bishops at the Lambeth Conference in that same year. According to Eric Lott, Lesslie Newbigin as appointed preacher refused to allow its use at the London CSI Day (September 27) in 1989 or 1990; and on a similar occasion in 1997 in celebration of the fiftieth anniversary of the CSI, Newbigin began his sermon by condemning the alternative "Affirmation of Faith"—which he had witnessed in use at a celebration of the Alternative CSI Liturgy by Christian Aid—as unfaithful to the Gospel because by it the Church did not "proclaim with sufficient clarity the Name of Jesus in relation to the second person of the Trinity."[23] Eric Lott opines that "although theoretically Lesslie could write about the inevitability of faith being clothed in particular cultural life," he had little notion of "why many Christians wholly faithful to the revelation of God-in-Christ find the 'inculturation' project so compelling." From the other direction I have the copy of a letter from the presbyter-in-charge and members of St. George's Cathedral in Madras expressing "shock" and "pain" at the "blasphemy" of a prayer "cutting at the root" of Scripture and Creeds that had been used—admittedly not from the Alternative Liturgy—at the CSI Synod in 1992: "O God the parent of our Lord Jesus Christ and our parent, you who are to us both Father and Mother . . . we see your compassion in Jesus. He gives content to the Hindu name for you—Siva, the kindly one. He gives significance to the Muslim address of you—Allah, the merciful. He embodies in the Godhead what the Buddhists worship in the Buddha—compassion itself."[24] Newbigin's attitude in these matters must be set in the context of his basic positions as a believer and dogmatician concerning creation, fall, redemption, and consummation, his understanding and practice as an evangelist and religious interlocutor, and particularly the sharp contrast he saw between the fundamental ontology of the Bible and the ontology characteristic of Indian thought and religion (so that he will have been offended already by the reformulation of the first article of the creed as "faith in one God, Source of all life, *greater than all names and forms, our inmost Self*").[25]

What was probably Newbigin's last celebration of the Eucharist according to the liturgy of the Church of South India occurred on August 31, 1997, when he characteristically made the journey to Milton Keynes to attend the farewell for P. J. S. Jesudoss, a young layman who had served as a missionary to Britain from the CSI, indeed from the diocese of Madurai and Ramnad. Bishop Lesslie, his eyesight almost gone, presided from memory at the old service of the Lord's Supper that he knew by heart.

The Form of Sound Words

Paper evidence of Newbigin's preaching exists in the form of the briefest handwritten sermon outlines and in the form of full typescripts from special occasions. From the time of his pastorate of the United Reformed congregation in Winson Green, Birmingham, his colleague Hakim Rahi reports that Bishop Newbigin was "gifted to put his ideas across in the layman's tongue." Carefully avoiding "complicated theological phraseology, he preached profound messages from the Word of God. He never read his messages, but used an outline to keep his thought consistent. He always looked into the eyes of the people while preaching, which secured full attention from his audience. He made use of his vast reservoir of experiences in India in his sermons. The people were greatly blessed."[26] From an acquaintance of almost forty years with Newbigin, Martin Conway singles out the Christmas sermon which the Bishop preached in 1975 to the London Tamil congregation: "I had heard him preach often enough in English, when he was invariably clear, intelligent and trenchant. But the impression he made while preaching in Tamil was rather different: majestic, evidently gripping and authoritative, yet utterly loving and at the service of those people."[27]

Those testimonies concerning the oral word and manner may now be borne in mind as we look at the substance and style of some fully scripted sermons and addresses of varying kinds from a number of very different contexts: ecumenical inaugurations and anniversaries, Indian cathedrals, British university churches, BBC "God-slots."

On the great occasions, Newbigin tended to concentrate on the event itself and let the very brief scriptural text of his sermon figure almost as a motto for the participants to take home as a memento. In preaching before the synod that brought the Congregational and Evangelical and Reformed churches together as the United Church of Christ at Cleveland, Ohio, in 1957, Newbigin used John 12:32—"I, when I am lifted up from the earth, will draw all men to myself"—to speak of the character, motives, and purposes of Christian unity and of this ecclesial union in particular.[28] It would be wrong, he said, to undertake a mere "organizational merger" that grounded unity in anything less than the "putting away of those things which hide from the world the sufficiency of Christ's atonement," "the true focal point at which the scattered fragments of humanity can be made one." The act of union must be an act of penitence, of obedience, and of witness: penitence, because division has been a public contradiction of the Church's fundamental nature, and even rightly precious traditions of devotion and practice, insofar as they have degenerated into "corporate pride," must be surrendered for the pearl of greater price as tested by the Word and the Spirit; obedience, because to deny the new relationship that Christ has opened up among all people by his death is to deny Christ himself, and only by constant return to the Cross is it possible to reconcile differences in the all-embracing charity of Christ; witness, because the drawing together of "this insignificantly small section of the human race is of no real significance if it is not in the context of the all-embracing missionary purpose" of Christ, "whose arms were stretched out between the nails of the Cross to embrace the whole human race"—"a fresh experience of the power of His atoning love" will surely give a fresh assurance and an enhanced credibility to the proclamation of the Gospel of reconciliation that is as needed in old Christendom as it is in Hindu India. Almost half a century later, the United Church of Christ may be ready to give another hearing to the preacher it chose for its inaugural synod and the evangelical message he never ceased to deliver in the intervening years.

Another American sermon was preached at the Riverside Church in New York in May 1960 in observance of the fiftieth anniversary of the world missionary conference of Edinburgh in 1910.[29] Taking Philippians 3:13b–14 as his text, Newbigin declared that there was a proper looking back to be done in gratitude (for the vision of mission and unity given to the ecumenical pioneers) and in penitence (for the loss of those evangelicals who believed that "the ecumenical movement" had "surrendered matters vital to the faith once delivered to the saints"); yet the main thing, as with the apostle and as with the Edinburgh pioneers, was to "press on towards the goal." At the impending integration of the International Missionary Council with the World Council of Churches, the institutional factors must subserve the causes of mission and unity. Present everywhere, the "expeditionary" Church in every locality must consider itself the "home base for a world missionary task," in which hitherto strangers become now partners and go forth together not to expand a particular culture but to bear joint witness across all frontiers to the one Savior of the world. That can only be convincingly done by "the whole healed and reconciled fellowship," for the question is rightly put: "What is the fellowship into which the evangelist is inviting the convert?" The preacher thereby hinted at the description of churchly unity that he was helping to prepare for the New Delhi assembly of the WCC in the following year. Meanwhile, however, he summoned his hearers to imitate the apostle in his personal participation in the passion of Christ, without which "all that we say about mission and unity remains mere clap-trap."

In June 1989 Bishop Newbigin preached in Philadelphia at the 200th general assembly of the Presbyterian Church USA.[30] The assembly's theme was "Continuing the Journey," and the preacher took as his text the words of Jesus "I am the way" (John 14:6). Newbigin set Jesus as the true way in contrast to the way of the world in the two hundred years since the French revolution of 1789, which had been the explosion into public life of "ideas that had been forming in the minds of scholars and thinkers throughout the eighteenth century" and "offered the possibility of understanding and managing the world without the hypothesis of God." The modern world—and the Presbyterian Church USA has perhaps not been entirely a dissenting minority—has believed in technical "progress" without ultimate "purpose." But now, said Newbigin in an image he often borrowed from Michael Polanyi, the "fuel" of the Christian tradition has burnt out in the "oxygen" of rationalism. The preacher therefore called for a return to Scripture as a radically alternative interpretation of the entire human and cosmic story, "because the beginning and the end are embodied in this man Jesus who is present in the midst of the story." Without ignoring even in an homiletical context the questions concerning biblical authority that occupy us in the next chapter, Newbigin rhetorically asked the PCUSA, "Can a church claim to stand in the Reformed tradition and at the same time talk about continuing the journey without explicit reference to the Bible as the guide-book?" We can "continue the journey" not because we can see the end or find the way for ourselves but because the way has been offered to us by the scriptural Jesus, "who has gone through the curtain of death and come back to be for us the way through the curtain." We may follow Jesus a step at a time along "that frontier which runs through every situation between the reign of God and the usurped dominion of evil, to challenge the powers of evil in the power of the kingdom and to accept the cost of the challenge." Newbigin would soon express his support for the movement of "Presbyterians Pro Life" in the Presbyterian Church USA.[31]

The typescripts are extant of Newbigin's sermons at St. George's Cathedral in Madras on the tenth anniversary of the inauguration of the CSI (1957) and at the London celebration of the fortieth anniversary of the united Church (1987).[32] The bishop's text on the former occasion was Hebrews 3:12–14 with its background in Numbers 14:21–23. The theme was trust in God's power to complete the work He began. Thanks were due for God's gift of an "impossible" union ten years before, and for many blessings since, namely "a liturgy which is increasingly precious to us and which has already come to play an important part in the life of the ecumenical movement," "a Women's Order which is proving more and more a means of grace to the whole Church," "new insights into God's will for His Church which may illuminate the road ahead for Christendom as a whole." Yet the hopes expressed in the Basis of Union with precise reference to "the Church of South India" were being thwarted by stubborn and unbelieving hearts: quarrels springing from unredeemed passions (cf. James 4:1–3) were disrupting the "closer fellowship" that should make the Church "a true leaven of unity in the life of India"; selfishness and indifference were detracting from the exercise of the Church's responsibility before God for the nation "in our evangelism, in our service, and above all in our intercession." The preacher challenged his hearers concerning "the integrity of our commitment," hammering home from his chosen text that "we share in Christ, if only we hold our first confidence firm to the end."

In a different time and place, in London thirty years later, the retired bishop was able to give thanks "for the way in which the Church of South India has continued to grow steadily, for the vigour of its witness in many fields, for the role it plays in the world-wide ecumenical movement, and above all for the faithful witness of so many thousands of ordinary Church members which never fails to gladden the hearts of all who visit the Church." Yet his theme here was to rework the connected concerns for unity and mission deriving from Jesus's prayer in John 17:19–26—which had inspired the creation of the Church of South India forty years before—into the changed intellectual and spiritual climate of the West in 1987. Newbigin is disappointed that churches which in India "have been living together in dynamic harmony for forty years" are "here separate" still, and that "splendid phrases like 'reconciled diversity' and 'conciliar fellowship'" are used as "polite ways of covering the intention to do nothing which will upset our existing arrangements." More fundamental still, and underlying the shift away from the goal of "organic unity," is the change in thinking about the Gospel. Even among the leadership of the Church, evangelization is "widely regarded as offensive and imperialistic"—an attitude that exemplifies the mood of relativism "which has become the most obvious feature of contemporary western culture, and which has penetrated deeply into the life of the churches." "We are invited," says Newbigin, "as the Church of the first centuries was persistently invited, to tone down our categorical statements about Jesus and accept the fact that ours is only one possible point of view. We are told to talk less about Christ and more about God, as though we had access to more reliable information about God than what is given to us in Jesus, Jesus in whom all the fulness of godhead was pleased to dwell. We cannot accept this. We are here as Christians, and the Christian Church exists, because the Christians of the early centuries declined this invitation to become part of a religious stew." The "profound inner connection" between "the loss of conviction about unity" and "the loss of conviction about the Gospel" resides in this: "The unity for which Christ prays is a unity such that the world, beholding it, will be convinced of two things—that Jesus is the one sent by God, and that his company is the place where God's love is known as the great reality. . . . The company that is constituted in the name of Jesus will be the place where the love of God is actually known, tasted, and enjoyed. It will be the place where all human beings of whatever sort and kind will know that they are at home in the house of the one Father." Therefore, "we must speak what has been given us to speak, that there is one Shepherd, the one whom the Father has sent to gather into one all his scattered flock; that we know him because he has called us and made us his own; and that we must speak of him because the love of Christ, the good Shepherd, reaches out to every human being." This brief sermon thus demonstrated the substantial consistency and deep continuity of Lesslie Newbigin's entire theological career, even if the emphasis in the Indian years fell on unity and mission, whereas his predominant concern in the decades after his return to Britain addressed "the Gospel and Western culture" (a theme which had in fact occupied him in Britain during the '30s).

We have sermons preached by Bishop Newbigin in the University Church of St. Mary the Virgin, Oxford, twenty years apart, the first in the evening of Sunday, April 24, 1960, the second as the University Sermon in the morning of Sunday, February 1, 1981.[33] The former, based on 2 Timothy 1:12, runs along a time axis to speak of "The Hope of the World"; the latter, based on Colossians 1:18–20, follows a space axis in meeting the terms for the Ramsden Sermon on "Church Extension."[34] In the sermon of 1960 Newbigin remarked on the irony that at a time when "Asian and African politics become increasingly messianic with every year that passes, Europe and America seem to be entering a period when the pagan religions of escape from this world begin to cast their ancient spell upon men wearied and disillusioned by incessant change." The preacher used a favorite Pauline text—"I know whom I have believed, and I am persuaded that he is able to keep that which I have committed to him against that day"—in order to commend as the true hope of the world the God of Jesus Christ, before whom our lives are not an "enterprise" doomed to disappear but an "offering" which He is able to raise beyond death into a final Kingdom that will gather up, in a personal and corporate destiny, those from every generation who have passed this way and what they have entrusted to Him. In the sermon of 1981 Newbigin acknowledges the ambiguity of what one historian called "the sacramental character of the British Empire" as an instrument of Providence for the extension of the Christian Church among all peoples. Although imperial history certainly played its part in bringing about a truly worldwide Church, the demise of colonialism should allow Christians to regain the sense that they are sent on mission by the risen Christ who showed to his apostles his hands and his side, for he had reconciled the world to God "by the blood of his Cross." Mission is not so much a matter of "extending" the Church as rather the Church bearing faithful witness to Christ, suffering for its active challenge to the powers of evil, and thereby becoming "the place where the sovereign

Spirit of God both convicts the world and teaches the Church, so that the Church is moved a little nearer to that which it is called to be—a sign and foretaste of the unity of all mankind under the headship of Christ." Among the shifts that Newbigin noted in that sermon was that betokened by the impact of the African bishops at the Lambeth Conference of 1978. "There is every probability," he concluded, "that by the end of this century, if any of the continents can be called a Christian continent, it will be Africa. By contrast one must already say, I think, that the most aggressively pagan of the continents today is Europe."[35]

Texts remain of three sets of brief meditations delivered by Newbigin on BBC radio's "Thought for the Day" or "Prayer for the Day."[36] For a week in Lent 1985 he offered simple teaching on prayer on the basis of Psalms 3, 4, 5, 6, and 7. In prayer we commit our problems and perplexities to God, for only God can disarm the powers of evil. In prayer we give thanks to God, for He alone is truth and goodness. In prayer we come to God with *our* requests, and His answers teach us what *He* wants. In prayer we come penitently to God, so that we may receive afresh the gift of what God wants us to be— forgiven, and thus free to forgive and to love. In prayer we throw away our accumulated rubbish and let it burn in the blaze of God's glory, whose light shows us things as they really are. In a second, undated series, Newbigin expounded the address and the first three petitions of the Lord's Prayer. Christians dare to go through life, in the midst of things that contradict God's fatherly rule, saying "Our Father" because Christ goes before us and shows us the way. Because of all that God is and has done for us in Christ, "it is our joy first of all to pray for the honouring of his name, the doing of his will, the coming of his reign." To pray, amid the powers of this world, "Thy Kingdom come" is to ask God "to complete what he has begun in the resurrection of Jesus, to give us the renewed creation which is the true end of all creation." To pray "Thy will be done" expresses a readiness to allow God's answers to shape our longings and our actions in better ways than we could foresee.

The third series of radio talks drew on memories of friends from Newbigin's Indian days. First, there was Asirvatham, a convicted murderer who had been converted and baptized in jail and then on release had confessed before the congregation in his own village the miracle of God's love for him and "taken, with the rest of us, the bread and wine which are the body and blood of Jesus given for sinners, respectable and disreputable alike": he became the bishop's companion and help on a difficult journey and thus reminded him that "the first may go last and the last come first." Next there was Esther, a college student who had drawn the bishop into visiting the shelter that she and other Christian women had set up for the disabled and the destitute, and "I found that I needed to go from time to time to share in that community of the very poor because, through them, I learned something about the power of God which is present not in what we call power but in what we call weakness." Then there was Paul Kadambavanam, whose baptism had meant the choice between the blood of Christ and his mother's tears. He had continued with his small income to support his Hindu mother; in the end there was a total reconciliation, and "he has now a much bigger family of men and women who owe a new life to him."[37] Finally there was Sundar: he had been born into a good and privileged Hindu family, but on seeing a festival procession of local Christians, the poorest of the poor, he had been persuaded by the joy and dignity in their faces that he must throw in his lot with them, for "this was the real revolution that puts the last first, the bottom at the top."

These practical instances of Newbigin as a preacher may be rounded off by a couple of more theoretical reflections of his on the homiletical task. The first comes from a lecture on "Preaching Christ Today" delivered at Overdale College, Birmingham, in 1979.[38] If preaching is nowadays devalued, Newbigin observes, the reason lies first in the inflation of verbal currency in a society of mass communication; nevertheless, the word can retain a seminal power, even if long hidden, when it testifies to the Word who made the world. A second reason for the unpopularity of the preacher's calling resides in the contemporary revolt against the monologue; but a preacher may be guarded against the clericalist distortion by imitating the apostle who saw himself simply as a "peon" of Christ (1 Corinthians 4:1), a "steward" bound to discharge his responsibility to his Master and authenticated by the sufferings of Jesus in his own life. As a servant of the Word, the preacher's job is not to propagate personal ideas but to expound the open Bible; and the use of a lectionary will help keep the preacher in an instrumental position through having to wrestle with initially uncongenial texts. The preacher "announces" Christ, in whom the reign of God has become a present reality. Christ is both Savior and Lord, to be preached "both as the one who delivers me totally from guilt, from fear, from anxiety, from all the terror of the future, and as the one who calls me into total obedience, calls me to take up the cross and follow him through the world, calls me to be a partaker in his body broken and his blood shed for the world." That is to put Gospel and Law in their right relation. As the presence, words, and works of Jesus were "all one reality—the life of God in action," so the preaching of the word cannot be understood in isolation from the life and work of the preacher and the congregation, for the Church is "the continuing of Christ's mission into the world," bearing with Him the world's sin and sorrow and pain and thus becoming "a sign and first-fruit and agent of the kingdom."

In a late article written for a dictionary of preaching under the heading "Missions,"[39] Newbigin noted that preachers in the West must now work in a missionary situation also, where "the Bible is no longer authoritative Scripture, and the name of Jesus, freely used in swearing, does not refer to any well known person." Whereas the foreign missionaries of the past had first to insert themselves deeply into the mental world of their hearers in order to probe behind their unquestioned assumptions with a call to a new allegiance, and in doing so subverted familiar terms by using them to communicate a message that radically questioned those concepts (the "challenging relevance" exemplified by A. G. Hogg in his *Karma and Redemption*), today the preacher must seek to retrieve the specificity of a Gospel that has been syncretistically "absorbed into the relativism, individualism and narcissism of Western culture": "The task is to recover the full meaning of the words we use in Christian discourse, and that can only happen when the Bible, in its canonical wholeness, recovers its place as Scripture." Preaching, wrote Newbigin, is "the communication of factual news": "In a society which has a different story to tell about itself, preaching has to be firmly and unapologetically rooted in the real story."

The Sacraments of the Lord

Newbigin's entire ecclesiology bears a sacramental ring. "The sacraments belong to the very essence of the Church," he wrote in *The Reunion of the Church*: "It belongs to the nature of the Church that it exists in a visible and institutional form. Christ has given to it the two sacraments which He instituted to be both signs and means of His grace towards sinners. These are at the heart of its existence as a visible institution. The one Bread is the centre of the Church's visible unity—a centre given to it by Christ Himself. Baptism is the visible mark of incorporation in the life of the crucified and ascended Saviour."[40] From *The Household of God* onward, Newbigin characteristically speaks of the Church—using terminology that belongs historically in the area of sacramental theology—as the "first-fruits" of God's Kingdom and therefore also the Kingdom's "sign" and "instrument."[41] The Lord's eschatological gifts of baptism and Eucharist—embodiments of the evangelical Word that always accompanies in spoken form the material act—both give the Church its identity and set the Church its task.

According to the most elementary teaching in *Sin and Salvation*, Christ gave to his followers "baptism as the sign, means and seal of their identification with Him in His death and resurrection for men. As He, in His acceptance of the baptism of repentance for sins, identified Himself with men, and accepted the cross, so He invited those who believed in Him to be baptized into Him, not a mere sign of cleansing, but, henceforth, a sign and means of union with Him in His death and resurrection for men."[42] A few pages later, the author takes the Church's practice of infant baptism as a "reminder" that "the work of God the Holy Spirit in recreating us as children of God begins before we have any conscious understanding of it"; but although "we can never fully understand how this regenerating work is done," it is "our task to seek more and more to understand it, to yield ourselves consciously to Him, and so to allow Him to bring to full stature the new nature which He has given us."[43] In *The Reunion of the Church*, Newbigin had made clear that "the nature of infant baptism is to be explained in terms of the life of the Church to which it is the entry, not the nature of the Church's life in terms of infant baptism."[44]

The most important texts for Newbigin's doctrine of baptism in particular occur in two discussions of conversion dating from the late '60s and early

'70s. The first one figures as the last chapter of *The Finality of Christ* (1969).[45] With India in mind (but similar questions arise also elsewhere), Newbigin sets out to refute the notions that conversion to Christ (1) is simply an inward religious experience, which (2) need and perhaps should not separate the convert from his or her natural family and even religious (say, Hindu) community, and whose most important result (3) is not the aggrandizement of the Church but rather the adoption by the individual of "the right positions on the great issues of war and peace, of social justice," and so on. Newbigin argues that it is precisely baptism as understood and practiced in the New Testament that, in concretizing and individualizing the call of God in Christ to repentance and discipleship (with the implication that the hearer was not hitherto in the right way), places the respondent in a visible community that provides companionship and guidance in the new pattern of conduct which is relevant for the doing of God's will and the fulfillment of his reign at this particular juncture of world history. To the question "Cannot the Hindu become a sincere follower of Jesus Christ without breaking his solidarity with his own people by baptism?" Newbigin offers a response by reversing the question: "Can a Hindu who has been born again in Christ by the work of the Holy Spirit be content to remain without any visible solidarity with his fellow-believers?"—and the answer he provides is "No." According to the New Testament Scriptures, baptism is where the convert, Jew and Gentile alike, calls on the name of the Lord Jesus, which is the condition of salvation (Acts 2:38; Romans 10:8–13). "True conversion," Newbigin says, "involves *both* a new creation from above, which is not merely an extension of the existing community, and *also* a relationship with the existing community of believers." Peter baptized Cornelius and his household on whom the Holy Spirit had fallen at his preaching—and, in admitting these Gentiles to the Church, changed the Church in accordance with God's purpose of offering salvation to the whole world. In history, of course, the embodied fellowship remains "liable to be influenced by all the accidental—and potentially sinful—facts of human cultural and political life"; and in contemporary India the "Western" character of "Christianity" and the misdeeds "perpetrated during the past two hundred and fifty years in Asia by persons professing the Christian religion" present obvious stumbling blocks to Hindus attracted to Christ. The solution, however, is not to drop baptism, but rather to recover a more scriptural sense and practice of what it means to be Christian (cf. Acts 2:41f.):

> Whatever content has been loaded into the word "Christian" through the centuries of sinful church history, the proper meaning of the word is: one who is baptized, who regularly shares in the Lord's Supper, who abides in the teaching of the apostles through faithful study of the Scriptures, and in their fellowship through his participation in the common life of prayer and service. In that sense of the word, I would encourage a believing Hindu to become a Christian. I will not say to him: "Become one of us, a Christian like me and follow all the habits and customs you see among the people called Christians." Nor will I say to him: "Remain a Hindu and worship Jesus

in the context of Hindu faith and practice." I would want to say rather: "Be a Christian in the sense which I have defined, and let the Holy Spirit who has brought you to Christ teach us too what it means to be a Christian."[46]

That represents at least an implicit call to reform of the Church; and Newbigin will argue, in the other text to be treated, that the beginning may consist in "a recovery among Church members of a true understanding of their own baptism."

The second text, in fact, is a typescript headed "The Church and the Kingdom," dated July 1972, and apparently remaining unpublished; it responds to papers and discussion surrounding a consultation on "Conversion and Baptism" held in November 1971 under the aegis of the Christian Institute for the Study of Religion and Society, Bangalore.[47] In contesting the New Testament exegesis of Christopher Duraisingh, Newbigin comes to make the following positive statement concerning baptism:

> The fundamental reason why we baptize is because Jesus was baptized, and because this baptism of Jesus was the foundation of all that he did. It is abundantly clear from all the strata of the New Testament that the baptism of Jesus by John was understood by the early Church to have been the starting point of "all that Jesus began to do and to teach." But it was more than a mere chronological starting point; it was in a real sense the initial act which contained the whole in germ. When Jesus came as one anonymous member of a great multitude of men and women seeking the cleansing of baptism for their sins, he was accepting that which could only be completed in the Cross. This is why Jesus speaks of his death as the baptism which he has to accomplish (Luke 12:50). . . . It is because Jesus is thinking of that total immersion in the sin and sorrow of the world which was initiated in his baptism in Jordan, carried out in his ministry, and consummated in his dying on the Cross. This is the "one baptism" to which a later New Testament writer refers [cf. Ephesians 4:5]. What Jesus offers to his disciples (although they do not then understand what the offer means) is that they will share this baptism (Mark 10:38f.). He is saying exactly the same thing when he tells them that they will share his cup—and this is what he tells them they must do at the Supper.[48]

Nor, "Karl Barth notwithstanding" (the allusion was to the then recently published baptismal fragment of *Church Dogmatics* IV/4), does Newbigin allow the exegetical separation of water baptism from Spirit baptism:

> John's baptism was confessedly only water baptism—a sign pointing to a reality that was to come later. When Jesus was baptized in water, the sign and the thing signified came together; he was baptized in the Spirit. No doubt what happened was different from what John expected. When he spoke of the Coming One baptizing with the Holy Spirit and fire, he was probably thinking in traditional terms of the messianic fire of judgment and catastrophe. When the Messiah came, he fulfilled the expectations in an unexpected way by taking the catastrophe upon himself. Instead of inflicting a baptism

of catastrophe on others, he accepted it for himself. After this we speak of
one baptism, baptism in water and the Spirit (John 3:5) as the way into new
life. . . . That *is* life in the Spirit, and to speak again of two baptisms is to go
back on the incarnation.

Theologically, it must be recognized that "we are part of a culture which
sharply separates the inward and mental from the outward and sensible, and
we struggle to find ways of relating them. The Bible belongs to a different
world, and can speak without embarrassment of one body, one Spirit, one
faith and one baptism—all in the same breath." If the meaning of baptism
has become lost or distorted, it is no solution to abandon the rite; rather, its
significance must be regained.

Admittedly, says Newbigin, "baptism is constantly and tragically misunderstood in the Christian community. It is regarded as a rite, sometimes almost as a piece of magic, by which one is separated from the Hindu community and assured of eternal safety within the fold of the Church." Truly
understood, however, baptism "is the rite by which we are committed to
Christ in his acceptance of the karma of humanity. It is therefore the rite in
which, by identification with Christ, we are committed to accepting as our
own all the concerns of men, their sin and their sorrow, as well as their
triumphs and their joys." When people "see in the life of the baptized community that kind of life which is both love for the world and separation from
the world, love for the world without being conformed to the world, that love
which embodies the holy love of God—then they will understand what baptism means." Most fundamentally, baptism is "a sign of the eschatological
Kingdom. By it we are admitted to a partnership with Jesus in accepting the
sufferings which are the birth-pangs of the new creation." Recovering baptism, the Church "may recover its true life, a life with all men for all men in
the name of Jesus" and perhaps gain "a fresh openness towards the working
of God in groups and movements outside the church through which God's
kingly and fatherly work is going on."

That was the context in which Newbigin responded also to the suggestion
made by Duraisingh and others that "Hindu Christians" could be admitted
to the Eucharist without baptism. It was being suggested that "in order that
those who confess Jesus as Lord may *not* be a distinct religious community
but may remain part of, and loyal to, the Hindu religious community, we are
to dispense with baptism. But, in order to express the solidarity which such
believers have among themselves, we are to retain the Eucharist." Newbigin
counters that the fundamental meaning of the two sacraments is the same:
"they are both sacramental means by which the believer is made one with
the dying and rising of Jesus." There are therefore no grounds for abandoning
the traditional understanding and practice of baptism as "the once-for-all rite
of incorporation," and Eucharist as "the repeated rite of renewal."[49] And, in
any case, is it not "the Eucharist above all which emphasises the socially
binding character of the commitment to Jesus?": "Can a body of men and

women repeatedly participate in the Lord's Supper and still maintain that they are not a distinct religious community? I should have thought not." The wider implication for the Church appears to be that the recovered understanding and practice of baptism and of the Eucharist will go together—and in such ways as to make both the distinctiveness and the power of the Gospel plain.

Concerning the Eucharist, Newbigin's most basic teaching is again found in *Sin and Salvation*. Drawing on Acts 2:42, Newbigin describes "the breaking of bread" as a mark of the apostolic fellowship and of the continuing Church:

> Jesus, knowing that words alone were not enough, had given to His disciples the simple ordinance of the Supper. Taking common bread and wine on the night of His passion, He had shared them with His disciples and told them: "This is my body", "This cup is the new covenant in my blood", and had bidden them take them in remembrance of Him. He wanted them to be not mere spectators of His passion, but (after His resurrection) to be taken up into it, made sharers in it. He alone could make the perfect offering to the Father for them; but the result of that should be that through Him they would also offer themselves in perfect penitence and obedience to the Father. This simple sacrament was to be the sign and means whereby they should do this. In St. Paul's words it was "a participation in the body and blood of Christ". He gave them this sacrament for their continual strengthening of their fellowship with Him.[50]

From the first Lord's Day on, the Lord's Table was the place at which Christ made the partakers of his body and blood "members incorporate in His risen life by participation in His dying"—and "the visible sign of bread broken together" became for the Church, wrote Newbigin in *The Household of God*, "the centre of its ongoing life."[51] That is why also "the centre of all our personal religion as Christians," said Newbigin in *Christ Our Eternal Contemporary*, "is the sacrament of Holy Communion where, week by week, we are invited to be identified again with Jesus, in his dying and rising"; and, accepting the invitation "to renew our communion with Christ, in whom God, who is not of this world, has come to the world, to be its Saviour," we are made "sharers with him in that reconciling ministry."[52]

Such high privileges and responsibilities require that the Church exercise a careful eucharistic discipline. In his letter of October 13, 1948, to friends at home,[53] Newbigin wrote as follows on the basis of his first year as a bishop in the newly inaugurated CSI:

> The Church of South India has laid upon the bishop the responsibility of excommunication and suspension from Holy Communion. Yet manifestly it is in the hands of the local congregation that the primary responsibility for the maintenance of Christian discipline lies. It is they who have to make the offender feel that he has separated himself from Christ's fellowship, to bring him to repentance, and to be the visible means of restoring him to that fellowship. Yet often the local congregation has been afraid to tackle the sinful member and the story of the Corinthian Church has been repeated. It is here

that—as it seems to me—a true marriage of congregationalism and episcopacy is most clearly needed and clearly possible. I am thankful to say that many congregations do faithfully try to discharge their duty in both its aspects, and are the means of bringing sinners to repentance, to confession of their sin before the fellowship, and to restoration. Yet it is also true that there are many cases in which the more distant authority of the bishop is needed to arouse a congregation to do its duty and to prevent flagrant evil from becoming permanently lodged in the church, and this authority sometimes has to be exercised even at the cost of grievous trouble within the local church. One can only say that, when one gets into this situation, the New Testament becomes luminously relevant at every step.

Much later, in *The Open Secret*, Newbigin tackles the question of excommunication in relation to what was by then called "structural sin."[54] Can the oppressor and the oppressed share together in the Eucharist? Some theologians of liberation were arguing that the oppressors must first disgorge their ill-gotten wealth before they could communicate at the Lord's table. "There are," says Newbigin, "situations where the oppression is so clear and blatant that this judgment must be made." But to make such a judgment is a very perilous undertaking, for "in every society, in every nation, even in every family, there is an element of oppression. We are all so made that we are conscious of the oppression of others and unconscious of the ways in which we oppress. Can there be any limit to the mutual excommunication which would follow if this principle came to be accepted?" Content with neither an escapist withdrawal from the life of society nor an arrogant equation of a particular political program with God's own justice, Newbigin asks "Is not the eucharist the point at which we acknowledge the fact that we are all in sin and that we are accepted only by grace? Must this not apply even to the great matters of justice between classes, between owners and peasants?" To be sure, "the Church lives in the midst of history as a sign, instrument, and foretaste of the reign of God"—but only as enabled by "being constantly reincorporated into Jesus' saving action through baptism and the eucharist and through the preaching and the hearing of the Word, which explains these and applies their meaning to the actual situation": "We have to learn in each situation to act and then to commit the action in faith to God our Father, in and through Jesus Christ who has taken away the sin of the world by his cross, following the leading of the Holy Spirit who alone can give us the wisdom to discern the way. . . . In every situation the Church must call all people—oppressor and oppressed alike—to that commitment to Jesus Christ which is expressed and sealed in baptism and continually renewed in the eucharist."

A final statement of Newbigin's sacramental theology is found in the paper he wrote for the 1983 meeting of the Anglican-Reformed International Commission under the title "How should we understand ministry and sacraments?"—much of which made its way into the 1984 report of the commission, *God's Reign and Our Unity*.[55] The author begins by drawing a contrast between the ways in which baptism, Eucharist, and ministry were understood and practiced in the Scriptures and in the earliest centuries of the Church and, on the other hand, their understanding and practice among the Anglicans and the Reformed, whose traditions were "formed in the 'Christendom' era, in a society presumed to be Christian." "In the former situation," Newbigin writes, "ministry is primarily leadership in mission, baptism is commitment to that mission, and the eucharist is the continual renewal of that commitment. These two rites are aptly designated by the word for the soldier's oath—*sacramentum*. In the 'Christendom' situation, ministry is primarily pastoral care of established communities, baptism is usually administered as a *rite de passage*, and the eucharist is the feeding of the community with the bread of life." Although he does not suggest that the traces of Christendom can be dismissed or the internal life of the Church neglected, Newbigin's tacit purpose is the preparation of both Anglicans and Reformed to face together "a missionary situation in which the Church is a small evangelizing movement in a pagan society."

Baptism and Eucharist must be considered together, for they belong inseparably with one another: "In baptism we are incorporated into the one baptism of Jesus begun in Jordan and completed on Calvary. In the Supper, that incorporation is renewed again and again." In both, Christ is present "in the power of his risen life." Three things may be said about both in theological exposition: first, each "antedates the Church and is constitutive of it"; second, word and action are held together in each; third, each can be rightly understood only in terms of the Holy Trinity. In his theological exposition Newbigin draws heavily on the doctrinal text of Faith and Order, *Baptism, Eucharist and Ministry* (1982), implicitly taking it as the current best in scripturally based ecumenical thinking.[56]

First, baptism derives from the prior event of Christ's own baptism, when he was anointed by the Spirit from the Father, and declared to be the Son; and only after Christ's own victory over evil had been completed on the Cross could he return and bestow on his disciples the gift of the Spirit so that they in turn might become part of the movement of liberation from sin, in which those who repent are through baptism made members of Christ, anointed by the same Spirit, and acknowledged as—in Christ—children of the Father (Acts 2:38; Romans 8:14–17; 1 Corinthians 12:13; Galatians 3:27). Thus not only baptism antedates and constitutes the Church, but the Eucharist also "is constitutive of the Church before it is an action of the Church." At the Last Supper Jesus gave his uncomprehending disciples a command to "do this"; and it was only subsequently "as they obeyed this command that those same disciples who had proved faithless deserters in the hour of Jesus' passion came to know that he was alive and that he was sharing with them his risen life": "The act of simple obedience to a command which could not be understood when it was given was the effective means by which the Church came into being and came to know the secret of its strange 'hidden' life—'always carrying in the body the death of Jesus, so that the life of Jesus may also be manifested in our bodies' (2 Corinthians 4:10)."

Second, word and action belong together scripturally, "while both our traditions have been formed in a society which separated them." In the New Testament, the preaching and the mighty works form a mutual accompaniment. In baptism, "the act speaks, and the word is acted." At the Supper, "the word may be elaborated and developed into many words, as the millions of eucharistic discourses from those of the New Testament to the present day demonstrate. But the words illuminate and expound the act or else they are vain; and the act equally is vain without the words which constitute it an effective sign: 'This is my body given for you; this is my blood shed for you.' " Newbigin accordingly puts a question to each of the two confessional traditions: "Do Reformed Christians remember that the proper context of Christian preaching is the eucharist? Would preaching not be different if this was always remembered? And do Anglicans remember that the 'word' called for as an integral (not optional) part of the eucharistic liturgy is not a little moral homily, much less a chat about current affairs, but an exposition of the mystery of what is being done in the action which accompanies it?"

Third, by the baptism of Jesus—the "foundation event which marks the beginning of the Gospel"—"the Triune God has taken up into his own being the sinful history of the world"; and once Christ's baptism has been victoriously completed on Calvary and, after his resurrection, the Spirit of his victory released, others may be baptized in the Triune Name and set on the way to "follow Jesus in his engagement with the prince of this world." The Eucharist, says Newbigin, is then "the continual renewal of our baptism"; and he proceeds to expound the second sacrament in a fully trinitarian way that works some of his own characteristic phraseology into the Lima outline:

> Jesus consecrated himself to the Father, and the eucharistic prayers and actions are addressed to the Father in thanksgiving for all that he has done and is doing in creation and redemption and in the surrender of love and obedience to him. These prayers and actions are done in the name of Jesus the Son. The eucharist is an act of *anamnesis*, not as a merely mental operation in which one who is no longer present is remembered, but as obedience to the command which Jesus has given to the church as the condition of his living presence. The words and actions of the eucharist are spoken and done "in Christ". And it is by the operation of the Spirit that Christ is made present to us in the eucharistic meal. The invocation of the Holy Spirit (*epiklesis*) is therefore a proper and necessary element in the action of the eucharist. In the eucharist the Church is enabled by the working of the Holy Spirit to offer its life in and through the perfect sacrifice of Christ to the Father and so to receive and abide in the life of the risen Jesus. Its life in Christ through the Spirit thus becomes the foretaste, first-fruit and pledge of the kingdom of the Father. United with Christ in the eucharist, the Church offers to the Father its intercession for all creation and for all humanity, an intercession which is summed up in the words spoken at the climax of the eucharistic prayer: "Your name be hallowed, your kingdom come, your will be done on earth as in heaven. . . ."

The Glory of God

In an address on "The Evangelization of Eastern Asia" presented to the East Asia Christian Conference at Bangkok in 1949, Newbigin spoke of the Church as always having "two simultaneous duties":

> It has firstly to strengthen and make more real the citizenship of all its members in heaven. In word and sacrament, in prayer and communion, it must be leading its members to an ever-deepening in the eternal order. It must lift up its members week by week into the heavenly places until they know more and more certainly that heaven is indeed their home, and the love and joy and peace of heaven become their very life. In this task the Church will often have to leave the world behind. Even the interested inquirer may be puzzled and repelled. The Church's worship may seem to him unintelligible. Yet, if the Church fails to do this, it is liable to become salt without savor, a mere dressing up of human desires and fears in the language of faith.
>
> Secondly, and all the time, the Church has to involve itself and all its members more and more deeply in all the affairs of the world, to be engaged up to the hilt in all its temptations and sorrows, its shame and despair, its strife and labor, its struggle with disease, injustice, and every manifestation of evil; and in all this to bear about in the body the dying of the Lord Jesus, that the life also of Jesus may be manifest in it. It is always relatively easy for the Church to do one of these things and neglect the other. Its task is to live in the tension of loyalty to both tasks, and in that place, in that tension, to bear witness to the Gospel.[57]

Among the practical suggestions that Newbigin offers, the first is this, making an allusion to the movement for liturgical renewal that was starting to affect the livelier of the European churches:

> I put first the strengthening of our churches in worship. I am sure that liturgical renewal is fundamental to the discharge of our evangelistic task in this day. If we are to make more vivid and real to all our members their citizenship in heaven, the very first essential is a strong liturgical life, which, week after week, and year after year, will bring all our members into vital remembrance of the fundamental truths of the faith, and which will make a way for the feet both of learned and unlearned, both of weak and strong, together to enter into God's holy place and to behold his glory. There is much evidence to show that it is along this line that God is bringing new strength to many of the churches in Europe. I do not think that we in Asia have yet taken this part of our evangelistic task sufficiently seriously. I am sure that it is fundamental.[58]

There is here an evangelistic *purpose* attaching to worship in Newbigin's thought; in another context he can observe the evangelistic *result* of the radiance emanating from the worshiping congregations of the Orthodox Church in the oppressive conditions of Soviet Russia;[59] elsewhere again he can see Christian worship as a possible *occasion* for the Holy Spirit's work of conversion in the hearts of unbelievers.[60] Yet it is clear that Newbigin did not regard liturgy as merely *instrumental* to mission. That worship was for mission not only a source but also the goal—with the liturgy of the earthly Church in history already a substantial anticipation of life in the final Kingdom—is clear from the criticism we saw Newbigin addressing to J. C. Hoekendijk in *The Household of God*:

> The Church is both a means and an end, because it is a foretaste. It is the community of the Holy Spirit who is the earnest of our inheritance. The Church can only witness to that inheritance because her life is a *real* foretaste of it, a real participation in the life of God Himself. Thus worship and fellowship, offering up praise and adoration to God, receiving His grace, rejoicing in Him, sharing with one another the fruits of the Spirit, and building up one another in love are all essential to the life of the Church. Precisely because the Church is here and now a real foretaste of heaven, she can be the witness and instrument of the kingdom of heaven. It is precisely because she is not *merely* instrumental that she can be instrumental.[61]

The eschatological character of the Gospel, its finality and its universal scope, is what justifies and requires the Church's "absolute claim in respect of *doxa*, of who is to be worshipped, glorified, and obeyed": the only proper object of human devotion is the God of Jesus Christ.[62] The appropriate course for redeemed creatures is grateful self-offering to their Creator and Redeemer,[63] and their "eucharistic ethic" takes its place within the salvation which is nothing short of participation in the life of the Triune God.[64] Thus Newbigin rejoins the classic declaration at the start of the Westminster Catechisms: "Man's chief end is to glorify God, and to enjoy him for ever." Or, as St. Irenaeus put it: "The glory of God is man alive, and the life of man is the vision of God." Moreover, humankind's participation in the life of the Triune God can—by the nature of God and by the nature of humanity—only be communal in character; and the glorification that befits God's Name comes from those who, in the one Spirit, "live in such harmony with one another, in accord with Christ Jesus, that they glorify with one mind and one voice the God and Father of our Lord Jesus Christ" (Romans 15:5f.): so it is the liturgy of the Heavenly City—where songs of divine praise resound from all, and the guests feast at the Messiah's marriage table—that orients not only the mission of the Church but also (Newbigin's other great and conjoint concern) its unity. The vision is well expressed in a passage from *God's Reign and Our Unity* that bears all the marks of Newbigin's hand:

> As in the Old Testament, so also in the New, the work of gathering all the nations to become God's people and to worship him from whom their life comes, is the work of God himself. It is the presence of the Spirit, foretaste of the eschatological Kingdom, which constitutes the effective witness to Jesus. The human occasions for the Spirit's work include both words and deeds, all springing from and expressing the life of the one body which lives for the praise and adoration of God. Where there is a shared life centred in the worship and service of God the Father, rooted in Christ as he is made known

to us in Scripture, interpreted in the teaching of faithful witnesses all down the ages, and sustaining the free exercise of the Spirit's varied gifts of speech and action among all the members, there the sovereign Lord, the Spirit, both gathers the peoples and leads the Church into fuller understanding.[65]

As the years went by and Newbigin agonized more and more over the disintegration of Western Christendom, he returned again and again to the liturgical assembly as the place where the Church has rehearsed the biblical story, entered into it and allowed its life to be shaped by it, and drawn others into being part of it. Thus, in *Proper Confidence*, he wrote:

> The community of the Christian Church understands itself and the human and cosmic history of which it is part in terms of the biblical story. Its being and life are incomprehensible apart from this story. Its liturgical actions are the reliving of this story. . . . The Gospel, the account of God's actions for the creation and redemption of the world, is always in narrative form: "The Word became flesh," "God so loved the world that he gave his one and only Son . . . ," and so forth. The ecumenical creeds are also in narrative form. Above all, the Bible, taken as a whole and in its canonical form, is a unique interpretation of cosmic and human history in which the human person is seen as a responsible actor in human history, always being called to respond to the initiatives of the one who is both Creator and Savior. . . . It would contradict the whole message of the Bible itself if one were to speak of the Book apart from the Church, the community shaped by the story that the book tells. . . .
>
> Christian discipleship, like all human activity, is embedded in a tradition and cannot live apart from that tradition. . . . For the Christian tradition the supremely authoritative memory is that embodied in the Bible, and the supremely authoritative practices are the sacraments of baptism and the eucharist. These together define what Christianity is and, conversely, are rightly understood only in the context of the Christian tradition. The ways in which people are drawn into the Christian tradition are enormously various but always include living contact with members of the Christian community. At some point, the new disciple is introduced to the Bible and learns to know it as an integral part of the Church's liturgy and (if the new disciple is literate) as something for private reading. It embodies the story that shapes and interprets the community.[66]

But whereas for a thousand years and more in Europe, "as a continually lived narrative, of which contemporary life was a part, the narrative gave shape to public life,"[67] now the book and the church and the liturgical practices have lost their sacred status through being placed in an allegedly more comprehensive story or worldview that "accounts for" them.[68] How Newbigin dealt with Scripture in the context of modernity and "a missionary encounter between the Gospel and our culture" will be told in the next two chapters. This chapter may be concluded with Newbigin's conviction concerning the "community of praise."

Amid the skepticism of contemporary society, reverence, admiration, and love will inevitably, says Newbigin, be countercultural.[69] Nevertheless—or rather precisely—it is from the worshiping community that Christian witness will proceed as a "spontaneous overflow," "the radiance of a supernatural reality":

> That reality is, first of all, the reality of God, the superabundant richness of the being of the Triune God, in whom love is forever given and forever enjoyed in an ever-new exchange. It is secondly the overflow of that love through the presence of the Spirit of God in the life of the community that lives by faith in Christ. It is said of this superabundant glory that it has been given to believers in order that they may be recognizable as a community where the love of God is actually tested and known (John 17:20–23). That is what makes the Church a place of joy, of praise, of surprises, and of laughter—a place where there is a foretaste of the endless surprises of heaven.
>
> In my own experience I have been touched by the evidence of two very different communities of faith into which men and women are being drawn out of the grey wastelands of a secularized and disenchanted world: the Pentecostals and the Russian Orthodox. Different as they are from one another, they have this in common: their life is centered in the action of praise—praise that is literally "out of this world" and is by that very fact able to speak to this world. Where this is present, the radiance of that supernatural reality is enough to draw men and women into its circle.
>
> I write these words at the season of Easter, the event that is the despair of a certain kind of rationalism but the starting point for a new rationality. The event of the resurrection, the empty tomb, and the risen Lord breaks every mold that would imprison God in the rationalism of a fallen world. But it is the starting point for a new kind of rationality, for the possibility of living hopefully in a world without hope, for the perpetual praise of God who not only creates order out of chaos but also breaks through fixed orders to create ever-new situations of surprise and joy:
>
> > When the Lord restored the fortunes of Zion,
> > we were like those who dream.
> > Then our mouth was filled with laughter,
> > and our tongue with shouts of joy.
> > Then they said among the nations,
> > "The Lord has done great things for them."
> > The Lord has done great things for us;
> > we are glad. (Psalm 126:1–3)[70]

9

The Scriptural Teacher

> Attend to the public reading of scripture, to preaching, to
> teaching.
>
> *(1 Timothy 4:13)*

The Authority of the Bible

The importance of Scripture in the life, teaching, and practice of Lesslie Newbigin will by now be apparent. While he was a theological student at Westminster College, Cambridge, the Epistle to the Romans, as commented on by
James Denney, was instrumental in bringing him to evangelical faith; and
the essay he wrote there on Exodus 30:11–16 treated in the Atonement—
the human need for it and God's gracious provision of it—a theme that he
would never abandon. In offering comprehensive teaching during his Indian
years, whether as a young missionary to students (as in *What is the Gospel?*)
or as a bishop to local pastors and lay workers in the diocese of Madurai (as
in *Sin and Salvation*) or to intellectuals at the Christian Medical College in
Vellore (as in *Christ our Eternal Contemporary*), it was always to the Bible that
Newbigin turned, both for the big picture and for the details of doctrine. As
an evangelist, he proclaimed the Gospel by way of the gospel stories. His
ecumenism was governed by the prayer of Jesus according to John 17. His
missiological thought rested on the history of creation, redemption, and consummation as told from Genesis to Revelation and summarized in the grand
theological vision of St. Paul. His attitude toward the religions was shaped by
his early engagement with Hindu scholars at Kanchipuram in the common
study of the Upanishads and the Fourth Gospel. In ethics, he took his New
Testament cues from the synoptic theme of the Kingdom of God and from the
epistolary theme of the new life in Christ. Liturgically, Newbigin held that
word and sacrament belonged inseparably together, and he demonstrated his
conviction by his homilies on appointed lectionary texts in the context of the
Eucharist when as bishop in Madras he regularly gathered his presbyters and
women workers around him. As the pastor of a small congregation in Birmingham in the course of his eighth decade, he preached, as his colleague
said, "profound messages from the Word of God." At various stages in his
career, Newbigin was in great demand as a leader of Bible studies.[1] Daily Bible

reading nourished his private devotions: "I more and more find," he wrote in 1992,

> the most precious part of each day to be the thirty or forty minutes I spend each morning before breakfast with the Bible. All the rest of the day I am bombarded with the stories that the world is telling about itself. I am more and more skeptical about these stories. As I take time to immerse myself in the story that the Bible tells, my vision is cleared and I see things in another way. I see the day that lies ahead in its place in God's story. I can then go into the unpredictable happenings of the day knowing that I will not be lost.[2]

In Newbigin's view, the crisis of faith in the modern West was bound up with the question of biblical authority. He put the matter plainly in the chapter of *Proper Confidence* devoted to "Holy Scripture."[3] If the Enlightenment involved "a shift in the location of reliable truth from a story to a set of eternal laws capable, in principle, of mathematical statement, and independent of accidental happenings in history," then it was inevitable that the Scriptures of the Old and New Testaments—hitherto regarded as the locus of reliable truth and its final arbiter—would retain only such authority as withstood an examination according to "the criteria developed in modern scientific work." The principles followed by rigorous practitioners of the so-called historical-critical method were the three enunciated by Ernst Troeltsch in 1898: first, methodological doubt (because any conclusion is subject to revision, historical inquiry can never achieve absolute certainty but only relative degrees of probability); second, analogy (historical knowledge is possible because all events are similar in principle, and we must assume that the laws of nature in biblical times were the same as now); third, correlation (the phenomena of history are interrelated and interdependent, and no event can be isolated from the sequence of historical causes and effects). Newbigin enters the threefold countercritique that the criterion of radical doubt is inoperable (because all claims to knowledge rest on some unquestioned assumptions), that the denial of uniqueness in favor of "the almighty power of analogy" is itself impossible to prove (and so there is reason to keep at least an open mind regarding Christian claims about the incarnation and the irruption of God's Kingdom), and that the reduction of all explanation to efficient causality makes an arbitrary exclusion of the notion of purpose (whereas a "hierarchy of levels of explanation" need not stop short at the human phenomenon of the free exercise of our will in performing bodily acts but can even allow for God "effecting his will in the events of history"). These arguments are presented in more detail in the next chapter in discussing Newbigin as an apologist for the Christian faith in face of modernity and its particular "plausibility structures." Here it suffices to note, first, that Newbigin allowed the value of historical investigation when properly conducted; second, that he considered the fundamentalist response to historical criticism misguided in that it remained within a framework set by the Enlightenment; and, third, that Newbigin himself proposed and employed ways of reading Scripture that were more in accord with traditional methods and the nature of the texts.

Even the investigations of the historical critics have been helpful, says Newbigin, by their illumination of the ways in which the biblical material was
formed: the disentangling of its various strands has shed light on the long
tradition, both oral and written, in which each of its parts took shape. What
emerges, in Newbigin's judgment, is sufficient to discountenance fundamentalism: "At every point in the story of the transmission of biblical material
from the original text to today we are dealing with the interaction of men
and women with God. At every point, human judgment and human fallibility
are involved, as they are in every attempt we make today to act faithfully in
new situations. The idea that at a certain point in this long story a line was
drawn before which everything is divine word and after which everything is
human judgment is absurd." The epistemological mistake of fundamentalism
lies in its captivity to modern concepts of objectivity, facts, and certainty, as
though biblical authority would collapse if a single factual error were to be
admitted in the Bible.

The proper approach to the Bible, Newbigin proposes, is one that matches
what occurred at the launching of the Christian story into the classical world
of antiquity:

> The Christian story could not fit into and be judged by the assumptions that
> controlled classical thought. It had to be recognized as itself a new starting
> point for thought. By the same token, we have to recognize that we must
> allow the Bible to provide us with its own account of what it means to speak
> of the word of God. We have to learn by the actual practice of living with
> the Bible how and in what ways God speaks. In the words of the Prayer Book
> collect, we have to hear, read, mark, and learn and inwardly digest the Bible,
> taking it wholly into ourselves in a way that shapes the very substance of
> our thinking and feeling and doing. It is less important to ask a Christian
> what he or she believes about the Bible than it is to inquire what he or she
> does with it.[4]

Such practices occur, of course, within the historic Christian community that
is informed and interpreted by the biblical story into which it is, as the
Church, incorporated.

The variety of material in the Bible offers ample exercise for the critical
faculty of the serious reader. "How," asks Newbigin, "is the ferocity of
Joshua's campaign to be reconciled with the Sermon on the Mount? How is
the exclusiveness of Ezra and Nehemiah to be reconciled with the universal-
ism of Ruth and Jonah? How do we relate Paul's description of the Roman
power as God's servant (Romans 13) with the identification of the same power
with the work of Satan in Revelation?" The basis on which faith answers
those questions is that "the word of God is Jesus Christ": "On this basis, the
reading of the Bible involves a continual twofold movement: we have to understand Jesus in the context of the whole story, and we have to understand
the whole story in the light of Jesus."[5]

On the one hand, Jesus cannot be detached from the whole biblical story
without becoming a mythical figure. Rather, "in his teaching and in his ac-

tions he speaks and acts as one who brings the story of God's dealing with Israel to its point of crisis and decision. And the apostolic preaching is not the announcement of a new religion but the announcement that the God of Israel has now fulfilled his promises and declared his whole purpose for all the nations." The God of Israel and of Jesus Christ is the God of "a holiness that rejects all compromise with evil and a generosity that seeks and saves the lost":

> As we live with the tension between the awesome holiness of God and his limitless kindness and as we bring this tension always to the person of Jesus himself in whom these seeming opposites are held together in a single life and death of judgment and mercy, we are led into a knowledge of God. To be more precise, we are enabled in growing measure to be admitted into that intimacy that Jesus had with his Father, an intimacy he spoke of when he said that no one knows the Father except the Son and those to whom the Son makes him known (Matthew 11:27; Luke 10:22).

On the other hand, the entire story from Genesis onward has to be read as "having its true interpretation in the total fact of the incarnation—the birth, ministry, death, resurrection, and glory of Jesus." Jesus did not make the Father known by way of "infallible, unrevisable, irreformable statements." Rather, he "formed a community of friends and shared his life with them"— and then "left it to them to be his witnesses." Under the guidance of the Holy Spirit, the Spirit of the Father and of the Son, they would interpret the meaning of his words and deeds, his life, death, and resurrection, and be led "into the truth as a whole." Newbigin insists that

> we are *not* required to choose between two alternative ways of understanding Scripture: either an objective account of the words and deeds of God or a subjective record of the religious experience of the writers. The prophets and apostles of the Old and New Testaments belonged to the same world as we do, a world in which knowing is a matter of the commitment of personal subjects to the clearest possible understanding of the reality of which we are a part. The Church has defined the boundaries of Scripture as canonical and thus as having a position of decisive authority within the entire ongoing tradition, but that does not mean that the conditions governing all human knowing of God do not apply within the biblical canon.[6]

The reader, then, needs to "indwell" the biblical story in daily life and there converse with the God whose character is revealed in the Bible:

> We grow into a knowledge of God by allowing the biblical story to awaken our imagination and to challenge and stimulate our thinking and acting. What we cannot yet understand or accept must nevertheless be allowed to challenge us to more daring thought and commitment. . . . This sense of the ineffable mystery of God does not arise out of metaphysical speculation about the vastness of things; it arises from the contemplation of the story of God's dealing with his people. The mystery is not so much a metaphysical one as

a moral one. It is the mystery of a holiness that can yet embrace the unholy. It is the mystery of the divine love for the unlovely. It is the mystery of grace.

In the long run, says Newbigin, we "are shaped by what we attend to."[7] Attention to the Bible above all else will save us both from a closed mind (for there remains much to be explored in the light of Jesus as the Word of God incarnate in our history) and from "a mind open at both ends, a mind which is prepared to entertain anything but has a firm hold of nothing": "The Christian is called to be a pilgrim, a learner to the end of her days. But she knows the Way."

What Newbigin there wrote toward the very end of his life in *Proper Confidence* he had urged ten years earlier in a 1985 contribution to the Forward Policy Group of the United Reformed Church on "The Role of the Bible in our Church."[8] There he recognized his indebtedness to Hans Frei of Yale for the notion of the Bible as "realistic narrative" that "renders the character" of God (*The Eclipse of Biblical Narrative*, 1974) and to Peter Stuhlmacher of Tübingen for his "hermeneutics of consent," whereby "the biblical texts can be fully interpreted only from a dialogical situation defined by the venture of Christian existence as it is lived in the Church" (*Historical Criticism and Theological Interpretation of Scripture*, 1977); and he wondered how it might be possible, without recovering "the pre-critical innocence of Indian or African villagers," to "find a way *through* this objectifying, post-Enlightenment culture, to a new innocence, to what Ricoeur calls 'a second naïveté' [*Essays on Biblical Interpretation*, 1980]." Arguing that "our job is not so much to understand the text as to understand the world with the help of the text,"[9] Newbigin described the Church's situation with regard to the Bible and the world in this way:

There is a community which bears witness that the character rendered in the Bible is the true reality from whom all reality comes.

The community knows that this is not something on which we expect everyone to agree or to be capable of conviction; it will be contested.

The community knows that the story has to be continually retold in the light of new situations, because God is the living God who does new things.

The community looks forward to a day when the truth will be so fully manifested that all will see; but it does not try to anticipate that day; it waits with patience.

As a former moderator of the United Reformed Church, Newbigin then made the following practical recommendations:

Give the Bible a more central place in our deliberations (as we are now beginning to do in the General Assembly).

Encourage the habit of preaching from a lectionary, so that the preacher is delivered from the tyranny of his own ideas and his own moods and is challenged by parts of Scripture which he might not himself choose.

Encourage the habit of daily Bible reading at home, with proper aids.

Challenge the biblical scholars to address themselves to questions which go beyond (not bypassing) the critical questions—to ask how the authority of Scripture is to be interpreted in the political and ethical dilemmas which face our society; a beginning has been made with the conference of biblical scholars under the auspices of the Foundation for Study of Christianity and Society.

In the rest of this chapter I first give a few examples, of very different kinds, of Newbigin's procedures with Scripture, culminating in his masterly exposition of St. John's Gospel. Then I return in more detail to the understanding of history that Newbigin finds in the Bible itself and correspondingly considers apt to govern the use of the Bible. Finally I describe the overall pattern and trace some particularly prominent themes of Newbigin's dogmatic vision, remembering that, for him, the Scriptures constitute both the source and the permanent norm of the Church's doctrinal tradition and that the creedal confessions and conciliar decisions of the historic Church continue to supply a hermeneutical key to the Scriptures.

The Reading of the Text

As distinct from his constant practice of weaving biblical references and allusions into his pastoral teaching and doctrinal reflection, three examples are given of Newbigin's more sustained exposition of particular passages or parts of Scripture in quite varied contexts. The first is his interpretation of the Book of Jonah and of Romans 9–11 in the course of treating the theme of election in its missiological implications. Then I look at a series of much more popularly oriented Bible studies based on Acts 1:6–8, John 20:19–23, and Matthew 28:18–20. Finally the fruit of half a lifetime's engagement with the Fourth Gospel will appear in Newbigin's commentary, *The Light Has Come*.

This is how, in *The Open Secret*, Newbigin renarrates in a multilayered fashion the story of Jonah as the instantiation and embodiment of God's "universal purpose of blessing" as it is patiently pursued—in narrowed focus but undiminished scope—in the face of human faithlessness:

The covenant of Noah is not revoked. The promised blessing is, in the end, for all the nations. Abraham, Israel, the tribe of Judah, and the faithful remnant are the chosen bearers of it.

Bearers—not exclusive beneficiaries. There lay the constant temptation. Again and again it had to be said that election is for responsibility, not for privilege. Again and again unfaithful Israel had to be threatened with punishment *because* she was the elect of God. "You only have I known of all the families of the earth; *therefore* I will punish you for all your iniquities" (Amos 3:2). The meaning of Israel's election and of her misunderstanding of it is depicted with supreme dramatic power in the story of Jonah, which is perhaps the most moving interpretation of the missionary calling of God's people to be found in the Bible. Jonah (Israel, God's chosen people) is called to go and bear witness in the midst of Nineveh (Babylon, Rome, the pagan world with all its awesome power and wealth). Jonah cannot face the challenge. He seeks to evade it and escape from the pressure of God's calling. He thinks he has succeeded. He sleeps soundly (the Church somnolent) while God whips up a raging storm and the pagan sailors devoutly pray for deliverance. It is the pagans who have to summon Jonah to his prayers. When lots are cast, Jonah is forced to confess his guilt. But he also confesses his God—"the God of heaven who made the sea and the dry land." Jonah is ready to pay for his sin with his life, but the conversion of the pagan sailors by this improbable missionary has already begun. They labor to save Jonah and they pray to the Lord. But Jonah must be thrown to the sea. The corn of wheat must fall into the ground and die. The elect must suffer. The Church must lose its life.

But out of death there is a resurrection. A penitent and restored Jonah goes to speak God's word to the pagan world, and his obedience is met by a stupendous miracle. There is universal repentance. The pagan world has been humbled. But Jonah is utterly disappointed. The heathen are not to be punished after all. What justice can there be in a world where God is so absurdly generous (cf. Matthew 20:1–16)? What is the point of missions if hell is going to be unnecessary? Jonah is frustrated and angry. He settles himself on the edge of the city (was it—as a Tamil friend of mine has suggested—the mission compound?) "to see what would become of the city." And we are left with the picture of Jonah sulking while God pleads with him for Nineveh, that great city with its thousands of innocent babies and its dumb animals—God so tenderly pleading for the pagan world and Jonah so sullenly wrapped up in his own self-pity.

It is Jonah who must take God's message to Nineveh. He is the elect bearer of God's promise of blessing for the nations. No one else can bring the blessing. But the election and the promise are for Nineveh, for the nations, not for Jonah alone. As God's chosen one he must suffer. God will not let him off. But God will also not let him go. For God does not cancel his calling.[10]

Eventually, "the focus is narrowed down to one who bears the whole purpose of cosmic salvation in his own person and who is hailed as the beloved Son in whom the Father is well pleased." That is "the beginning of the gospel" (Mark 1:1). Newbigin thus affirms the newness of the New Testament. But when the atoning work of Jesus has been completed through his death and resurrection, his followers become the bearers of God's old and unrelinquished purpose of universal blessing. This, then, is how Newbigin interprets Romans 9–11. Notice that just as the story of Jonah was given a christological and ecclesial reading, so also now, for all the difference made by the incarnation of the Son and his unique sacrifice, the Church and salvation are given an "Israelite" reading:

The unbelief of his own kinsmen is the source of Paul's deepest perplexity and anguish (Romans 9:1–3). They *are* God's chosen, God's covenant people, God's beloved (9:4–5). Yet even in his covenant faithfulness God always retained his freedom—the sovereign freedom of the creator over his own works (9:6–29). In fact, Israel has been guilty of trying to turn the covenant into a contract, of trying to establish a claim upon God based upon their own fulfillment of the law (9:30–10:17). And therefore God has hardened their hearts. It is not that he has rejected them (unthinkable thought!) but that he has hardened them (10:18–11:10). Does that mean that, being unbelievers, they will be destroyed? Perish the thought! No! The purpose is that through their rejection of the Gospel it may reach the Gentiles, and so they in turn will receive it back from the Gentiles (11:11–16). But this means that the Gentiles must equally recognize that they have no claim against God. The unbelief of the Jews has created the possibility for Gentiles to be received by a miracle of pure grace ("contrary to nature") into the life of Israel. If they now begin to "boast over the branches"—that is, to imagine that their faith gives them a claim upon God which the unbelieving Jews do not have— then they too will be cut off from the life of the true Israel (11:17–24). Thus, though God's tactics may seem strange, his strategy is clear. It is to destroy every claim in order to leave the way clear for grace. It is to thwart every device for turning the covenant into a contract. It is "to consign all men to disobedience that he may have mercy on all." Thus the unbelief of Israel does not mean their final rejection; it is part of God's wonderful strategy. The purpose is both that "the full number of the Gentiles [shall] come in" *and* that "all Israel shall be saved" (11:25–32). This salvation can only be in mutual dependence and relatedness. The corporate nature of salvation is a necessary part of the divine purpose of salvation according to the biblical view that no one could receive it as a direct revelation from above but only through the neighbor, only as part of an action in which he opens his door and invites his neighbor to come in. The reader might have objected that there was a flaw in the argument, for whereas "the nations" could only receive salvation through Israel, the elect nation, Israel itself would apparently receive the gift directly "from above," and not from the neighbor. But in fact, says Paul, Israel will receive the gift of salvation only by opening her doors to the "heathen."

It is here in this argument of Romans 9–11 that the inner consistency of the biblical doctrine of election becomes most clear. There is no salvation except in a mutual relatedness which reflects that eternal relatedness-in-love which is the being of the triune God. Therefore salvation can only be by way of election: one must be chosen and called and sent with the word of salvation to the other. But therefore also the elect can receive the gift of salvation only through those who are not the elect. The purpose of God's election for salvation in Christ is nothing other than the completing of his purpose of creation in Christ. It has in view, not "the soul" conceived as an independent monad detached from other souls and from the created world, but the human person knit together with other persons in a shared participation in and responsibility for God's created world.[11]

In November 1984 Bishop Newbigin gave three Bible studies in Edinburgh at a Church of Scotland conference on world mission and unity. The theme was "The Sending of the Church" according to the pericopes in Acts 1, John 20, and Matthew 28, where the risen Lord commissions his apostles.[12] The substance of the studies was taken up again in the presentations made to the Synod of the Church of South India in January 1986 on "Mission in Christ's Way."[13] They are cited again now for the particular purpose of illustrating Newbigin's imaginative ways with Scripture—philologically, historically, dramatically.

First, Newbigin's explanation of the word *arrabôn* in New Testament references to the Holy Spirit:

It is an interesting word which was apparently used by shopkeepers to denote a payment of cash in advance as a pledge of commitment to pay the full amount later. I learned from one of our mission students at Selly Oak that the same word is still used by the shopkeepers in Cairo. If you want to buy a suit, you bargain about the cloth and the style and then the tailor will ask you to put down a reasonable amount of cash in advance as the pledge that you are going to pay the bill when the suit is finished. This is the word Paul uses for the Holy Spirit. It is an advance payment on Kingdom account, so to speak. It is not just a promissory note, an I.O.U. It is real spendable cash and you can go and buy yourself a drink with it. But it is much more than that; it represents the reliable assurance of much more to come. So with the gift of the Spirit. It is not just a promise; it is a real foretaste of the joy and freedom and peace of God's reign. It is real, to be enjoyed here and now. But it is also much more than that; it is the pledge, the guarantee, the proof that the fullness of God's reign in all its glory is on the way. It is the *apéritif* before the heavenly banquet—good and refreshing in itself, but much more—the assurance that the meal is really going to come.[14]

The point is, of course, familiar to any student of the New Testament in Greek. Newbigin's way of making it to a popular audience follows exactly the style of a patristic homiletician.

Second, there is an example of the so-called counterfactual technique employed by some historians to bring out the significance of what did in fact happen by contrasting it with what might have occurred but did not. Newbigin sets up two "roads not taken" by Jesus:

During the only visit that my wife and I have ever paid to the Holy Land, there was one day that I shall never forget. It was the day when we visited two ancient sites on the shores of the Dead Sea—Massada and Q'mran. The first, Massada, is the mighty fortress built by Herod on a gigantic outcrop of rock towering two thousand feet above the surrounding desert. This is where the Jewish freedom fighters, the Zealots of Jesus' day, made their last stand against the Roman legions in AD 73 and finally perished in a mass suicide. The other, Q'mran, is the place to which the Essene community withdrew into the desert to pray for and prepare themselves for the coming of the Messiah. As I reflected on these two visits on the same day, I realized that each of them represented—so to speak—the terminus of one of the roads that Jesus might have taken. When it was clear that Israel had rejected his message of the Kingdom, there were—humanly speaking—two ways that he might have taken. He might have taken the road of the Zealots, active armed struggle to end the cruel oppression. That road ends in the tragic grandeur of Massada—the place where the state of Israel now takes its elite armed forces for their final vows of allegiance. Or he might have taken the other road and withdrawn his disciples into the desert to pray for and prepare for the Kingdom that God would bring in his own way.

Jesus did neither of these things. He did something different from both. He rode, with his disciples, into the heart of the sacred city when thousands were gathered to celebrate national liberation, the time and the place of maximum political tension and hope. But he rode on an ass. It was an unmistakable claim to kingship, yet equally unmistakably it was a claim made in total vulnerability. In that last great acted parable of Jesus lies the secret and the paradox of mission in his way. It is the way the Church must go. It is neither withdrawal from the world into a religious sanctuary; nor is it engagement with the world on the world's terms. It is something else. It is a totally uncompromising yet totally vulnerable challenge to the powers of evil in the name and in the power of the kingship of God present in the crucified and risen Jesus.[15]

The third example is a case of that "performance" of Scripture which Nicholas Lash in a seminal essay called the Church's primary or fundamental way of "interpreting" or "rendering" the story that is told in the biblical texts that are read and heard and already enacted in a ritual genre in the liturgical assembly.[16] Newbigin goes back to his time in South India:

Thirty years ago, when I was a bishop in Madurai, I had a visit from a village of which I had never heard, to say there were twenty-five families wishing to be baptized, and would I come and baptize them? I looked the place up in the map and found that it was actually not in my diocese but a few miles over the border in the Trichy-Tanjore diocese. I wrote to the bishop there, told him of the request, suggested that it must be the result of evangelistic work by members of the church there, and invited him to deal with it. He replied that he had never heard of the place and that he knew of no evangelistic work in that area, and that I had better go there myself. I did so, and after a day in the village was able to piece together the story behind the request. It was a drama in four acts.

Act I saw the visit of a team of development workers who helped them to put down a well, install an electric pump, and get a good clean water supply. The leader of the team was a Christian engineer, a good man but not much of a communicator. He told them he was a Christian, and they saw that he was a good man. That was all. End of Act I.

Next, a few months later, one of the villagers went to the neighboring town to make some purchases and a colporteur sold him a copy of the Gospel of St. Mark. He began to read it, became interested, and started discussing it with his neighbours who gathered round him to hear him read. End of Act II, with no visible change.

Some months passed, and an independent evangelist paid a visit to the village. As is the manner of his tribe, he preached a fiery sermon, stayed the night in the village, and left behind a tract that said: "If you die tonight, where will you go?" The villagers decided that the matter was more serious than they had thought and that further investigation was called for. So (and this is Act IV) they sent word to a village five miles away where there was a Christian congregation. "Will you please tell us," they asked, "what is all this about this man Jesus?" It happened that one of the members of the congregation (all of them landless labourers) had had an accident and was unable to do field work. The congregation decided to send him over to the other village, to spend a month with them answering their enquiry.

The result was a group of twenty-five families as ready and eager for baptism as any that I have seen.

If you had assembled the engineer, the colporteur, the evangelist and the coolie for a seminar on missionary methods, they would probably have disagreed with each other—perhaps violently. Unknown to each other, each had done faithfully the work for which the Holy Spirit had given the equipment. The strategy was not in any human hands. And I, as the bishop, was kept right out of the action until the moment came when I was given my duty to do.[17]

The narration of the episode clearly reveals Newbigin's belief in the divine Author-Director who is able to weave into the continuing drama on the universal stage the "bit parts" that are played by a very diverse company of actors who have all learned their roles from the same basic script.

At last we reach Newbigin's "exposition of the Fourth Gospel" in *The Light Has Come*.[18] This book of some three hundred pages is its author's most sustained literary production and his most elegantly written. It is the matured and polished fruit of a long and deep engagement with the text that the Fathers called "the spiritual Gospel" and which has frequently brought out from its students their very best work. It is evident that Newbigin lived in close communion with this Gospel at least since the time of the mutual and common studies that he and the Hindu scholars made of it and the Svetasvara Upanishad during his years in Kanchipuram. To read Newbigin's exposition of St. John in the context of his own many and varied, and often occasional, writings is to discover what constantly shaped and nourished his multifarious reflection and activity over a good half-century and to see how in turn (but only then in that reverse movement) his own intellectual and practical experience gave him insights into the Gospel that he was finally able to offer to others in the succinct form of this exposition. This is the classic work that I would most urge my readers to approach next if they have not already come across it in their encounter with Newbigin. My own purposes here lead me to present only Newbigin's preface as a statement of his principles and procedures and to allow his treatment of John 1:1–18—what he himself calls "the overture"—to adumbrate the great themes of the Gospel and his exposition of it.

Newbigin begins his preface with an apologia for adding to the "constantly growing cataract of literature about the Fourth Gospel," especially as "one who is no expert in the field" (as "scholarly" commentators to whom he is indebted, our characteristically modest author mentions Westcott, Hoskyns, Bultmann, Dodd, Barrett, Cullmann, R. H. Lightfoot, Brown, and Lindars). The book has grown, he says, out of his attempt to be faithful to his commitments made when he said yes to the questions addressed to him at his consecration as a bishop in the Church of South India: "Do you accept the Holy Scriptures as containing all things necessary for salvation, and as the supreme and decisive standard of faith? Will you be diligent in the study of the Holy Scriptures, praying for a true understanding of them, that you may be able to feed your people with the bread of life, to lead them in accordance with God's will, and to withstand and convince false teachers?" Other commitments may be brought to the study of the text; they are not his, but he has experienced two of them in particular, knows their fascination, and must be aware of the critical questions that are put to the text from those standpoints. From his "long involvement with the world of Hinduism," he has felt "the immense power and rationality of the Vedantin's vision of reality"; and at the time of the final writing, his ear is even more especially trained on a Western world characterized by "the methods, models, and axioms of post-Enlightenment historical science" that have also furnished "the prior commitment" of many academic students of the biblical text over the past two centuries. He himself is "a twentieth-century European with a university education" and therefore in some sense "belongs" to the modern Western world; yet he is "also"—and indeed determinatively—"a Christian believer with commitments to the ecumenical fellowship of believers in all cultures (including some for whom the 'modern' world view is a bundle of strange myths)." Certainly the critical questions posed from a modern standpoint must be heard, but there is no need to accept the assumption that modern scholarship "is necessarily in a position to understand better than the original writer what really happened and what Jesus really intended": "What is necessary above all is to expose the presuppositions behind the questions so that there may be an open encounter between the ultimate commitments on both sides, between the word and the world." "My task," says Newbigin, "is to make clear to myself and (if possible) to others the word which is spoken in the Gospel in such a way that it may be heard in the language of this culture of which I am a part with all its power to question that culture."

Such an enterprise is possible, Newbigin asserts,

> only because of the promise recorded in the Fourth Gospel, a promise of which the Gospel itself is one of the first-fruits, that the Holy Spirit would—after the victory of Jesus over the ruler of this world—bring the words of Jesus to the remembrance of his disciples (14:25f.), bear witness to Jesus (15:26), expose the fundamental errors of the world (16:8–11), and guide the disciples into the truth about him and about the world (16:12–15). These promises are part of the preparation of the Church for its missionary encounter with all the varied communities and cultures of the world. These are real encounters by which both the world and the Church are changed. . . . The enterprise, therefore, has to be conducted in and with the Church and at its service, depending upon the faithfulness of God towards those whom the Church calls to this ministry of study and teaching.

It is Newbigin's intention that the Gospel be studied in light of its own stated purpose. As a "witness to Jesus Christ, the presence of God in human history and therefore the source of truth and life," the Gospel may be expected to bring the reader "under the power of the truth who is Jesus Christ" so that he may "believe and receive the gift of life in the name of Jesus (20:31)." Newbigin characterizes the work of the Evangelist thus:

> The Fourth Evangelist gives evidence of accurate knowledge of conditions in Palestine in the time of Jesus, and his accuracy about matters of local detail has not been disproved. While he is more concerned to draw out the theological meaning of the things he records than to place them in chronological order, there is no reason to disbelieve the historicity of the things he records.

If his purpose is avowedly theological (20:31), the heart of his theology is that the word became flesh—that is to say, became part of history. However, the Gospel as we have it is not a mere collation of traditional material. It is the work of a powerful mind which has shaped the material into an intricately wrought and massively coherent pattern.

If we do not know the identity of this writer, or even of "the beloved disciple" on whose testimony the work rests, the (perhaps deliberate) effect of that "silence" may be to direct us to what is said and its truth.

One final point to be noted from Newbigin's preface is that "the frequent references to other parts of the Bible are an integral part of the exposition." What contemporary literary critics call intertextuality is traditionally practiced by Christian readers of the Scriptures on the grounds of their canonical unity. Especially interesting, in my estimation, are not only the typological connections with the Old Testament and the synchronic comparisons with the Synoptic Gospels but also and above all the correspondences which Newbigin establishes between the Fourth Evangelist and that other powerful theological mind, the apostle Paul.

Newbigin's treatment of John 1:1–18 in a dozen pages may be taken as a single sample of his exposition. This overture announces the theological themes of life, light and darkness, truth and glory that will be developed in the course of the Gospel; yet the introduction of John the Baptist's witness allows also the "very ordinary, matter-of-fact piece of human story" to begin without a break at verse 19: "The timeless sayings of the Prologue are deliberately not separated from but intertwined with plain narration of history, because it is in this history that the eternal reality of God is present, active, and manifest. We are not dealing with an idealist philosophy for which actual happenings can be at best only illustrative; we are dealing with events of history, and therefore events belonging to a particular place and time, in which that which is before all time and place is present as the life and light of God himself."

The story of Jesus "is about a man among men," who had been seen, heard, and touched (1 John 1:1); yet when the tellers told their tale, the hearers everywhere were driven to ask, "But who then is this Jesus?" The missionary can begin only by using words which have some meaning for the hearers. Confronted with the problem of "beginning to explain that which in the end must be accepted as the beginning of all explanation," the Fourth Evangelist chose to call Jesus "the Word," a term that could "evoke many different images: the creative word of Genesis, the word of God in the mouth of prophets and evangelists, the *logos* of the Stoic philosopher and of the various schools of thought which sought to use that word as a point of fusion between Greek and Hebrew thinking." Newbigin says: "Only when the reader has come to know Jesus himself will he be able to understand that it is Jesus who is the word, that in him all things were created and in him all things hold together (Colossians 1:16f.), that he himself is the gospel which is preached, and that it is in his name 'that there is life' (John 20:31)." Meanwhile, the opening words of St. John's Gospel "alert the reader to the fact that the story he is going to read has a meaning which will radically redefine even his most fundamental terms": "The most fundamental of all words, the word 'God,' will have to be redefined in view of the fact that he—Jesus—was in the beginning with God and was from the beginning God, and that he is himself the word of God, a word which is not merely declaratory but creative and life-giving."

Since "all things were made through him," the dichotomies that dominated the ancient world (and again much of the modern) are eliminated, especially that between "material" and "spiritual." It is the same with life and light or truth:

> The life of God given to men in Jesus—in his life, death, and resurrection and in the coming of the Spirit—is at the same time understanding of how things truly are. It is participation in the truth. These cannot be separated. The first act of God's creation was in the words "Let there be light," and when St. Paul describes what the coming of Jesus means, he says that the God who said "Let light shine out of darkness" has shone in our hearts to give the light of the knowledge of the glory of God in the face of Jesus Christ (2 Corinthians 4:6). The coming of Jesus is not an event which has to be subsequently interpreted. He is the bearer both of life and of light, and the two are not to be separated, for the life of God is also the light of truth.

Death and darkness remain on the cosmic and human scene and constitute the background of the Gospel story, right up to Judas's betrayal (13:30) and the world's continuing ignorance (17:25f). But "darkness cannot be as such a subject for research; it is simply darkness. It is what confronts one who turns away from the true source of his being, tries to find meaning elsewhere, and is thereby plunged into meaninglessness." It is the business of light to banish the darkness, which neither comprehends nor overwhelms it: the coming of "the light which shone in Jesus, and which shines on as the name of Jesus is proclaimed throughout the world," means judgment by the Creator of all, but its purpose is to create faith (12:46) and so bring salvation (3:16–21; 8:12; 9:5; 11:9f.; 12:35f.). "The light which shines on every human being," Newbigin argues, is none other than Jesus:

> There is no other light. There are not different varieties of light. There is only one light, namely, that which enables us to see things as they really are. And things really are as they are shown to be in the light of Jesus, because he is the word through whom they all came to be. It follows that all men, whether they believe or not, live under the light just as they live by the creative word of God. And thus it follows that when a person turns in faith to Jesus Christ he meets not a stranger but one whom he recognizes as the one in whom he was loved and chosen before the foundation of the world (Ephesians 1:4).

That the light was rejected at his coming not only by "the world" but by "his own people" makes visible "the terrible paradox of human existence in its most piercing reality": " 'Religion' in its purest and loftiest form is found to belong to the area of darkness" (cf. John 9:39–41). Yet darkness could not have "the last word," for "the word of God which is both light and life, both understanding and power, is the word of *God* and therefore not without effect." By a divine act, not by flesh and blood (cf. Matthew 16:17), God gives a new birth to those whom he enables to believe: "The coming of Jesus into the world of 'flesh and blood' was the fresh creative act of God himself, and it has as its result the existence of a company of men and women whose life is a kind of extension of his, a new life which is no achievement of human desire or power, but a sheer gift of God."

In the incarnation, "God himself in his creative and revealing being has become man." God has "pitched his tent" (Greek *eskênôsen*) among us, and his "glorious presence" (Hebrew *shekinah*) has been seen "tabernacling among men" (cf. Exodus 40:34–38; Zechariah 2:10). Believers see the true glory of God "in the figure of a slave washing the feet of his disciples, and finally offering up life itself in obedience to his Father's will": "It is not by a masterful exercise of power to control the world's affairs but by the humble obedience of a son, even to the point of death, that Jesus glorifies God and is glorified by God (12:27–33; 13:31f.; 17:1, 4f.)." "Not the self-glorification of a supreme monad which egocentric man fashions in his own image, a celestial reflection of man's own self-glorification, but the ceaseless and limitless giving of love and honor to the other within the one being of God—this alone is the true glory."

Over and over again, says Newbigin, the saints of Israel had testified that the Lord is "abounding in steadfast love and faithfulness"; and now, in a man "full of grace and truth," believers "have seen that which Moses longed to see but could not see face to face (Exodus 33:18–23), have seen what Moses could only hear proclaimed (34:6), the true glory of God who is alone the fullness of steadfast love and faithfulness." They can testify that in Jesus Christ, now explicitly named and titled for the first time in the Prologue, they have "seen in flesh and blood what flesh and blood cannot see," for "the only Son, who is in the bosom of the Father, he has made him known" (John 1:18), and whoever has seen the Son has seen the Father (14:8f.). Good gift as the Torah was—"the gracious and true teaching that was to guard and guide Israel," a "custodian until Christ came" (Galatians 3:24)—it could only promise life (Deuteronony 30:16), not give it (Romans 7:10). The gift has now been made in person, and so fully that "the whole community of believers is caught up in a chain-reaction of grace, grace becoming the opportunity for more grace so that they are together 'filled with all the fullness of God' (Ephesians 3:19)."

The Prologue ends in verse 18, says Newbigin, with "what is in effect a restatement of its opening": "Jesus *is* God's word. There is, therefore, only one way to know God, and that is to attend to his word. All men share the longing to know the ultimate secret of their life. Without this they are in darkness. The 'good news' which John is about to tell is that the light, the only light there is, has come into the world, that the word of God has become flesh in the man Jesus Christ, and that here, therefore, in this life, God has made himself fully known. For the beloved Son, who is the word of God, is God, and only God can make God known."

The World's Story

In his keynote address to a regional conference of the Bible Societies at Eisenach, Germany, in April 1991, Newbigin said this:

> If we take the Bible in its canonical wholeness, as we must, then it is best understood as history. It is universal, cosmic history. It interprets the entire story of all things from creation to consummation, and the story of the human race within creation, and within the human race the story of the people called by God to be the bearers of the meaning of the whole, and—as the very centre—the story of the One in whom God's purpose was decisively revealed by being decisively effected. It is obviously a different story from the stories that the world tells about itself. . . . All telling of history involves the selection of significant events out of the billions of things which have happened. To call an event 'significant' implies some belief about the meaning of the story as a whole. How do we know the meaning of the story while we are still in the middle of it? It is flattering to ourselves to teach world history as the history of civilisation, since it implies that we, the civilised people, are the point of the story. The Bible contradicts that belief and affirms that the meaning of the story has been revealed by him who is the author of the story. It follows that my own life has meaning, has significance, only as I seek responsibly to live as part of this story. And I have to live it as part of the people whose story this is. The Bible is the book of this people, and these are the people of this story.[19]

That paragraph sums up much of what Newbigin had recently said in the central portions of his Alexander Robertson Lectures at the University of Glasgow in 1988, which appeared in book form as *The Gospel in a Pluralist Society*. There the chapters in the relevant sequence were entitled "Revelation in History," "The Logic of Election," "The Bible as Universal History," and "Christ, the Clue to History."[20] Speaking of Christ and his Gospel as "the clue to history" was a familiar trope in Newbigin's work since the late 1960s and *The Finality of Christ*.[21]

In the book of the Robertson Lectures, Newbigin opens the discussion on revelation in history by establishing what is at stake when Christianity—in contrast to the religions originating on the Indian subcontinent which depend on what is held to be accessible to every human being apart from reference to any particular events in the past—insists on the "happenedness" of the story told in the New Testament. If, he says, your relationship with God—your salvation—is necessarily bound up with your acceptance of the part God assigns for you in his purpose for the world, then "your relationship with God cannot be separated from those acts in which God has revealed and effected his purpose for the world":

> You will understand your own life as part of a story which is not a story made up by you, not just the story of your decisions and actions, but the story which is being enacted under God's creative and providential control in the events of contemporary history. It will be of the very essence of the matter that the events and places which you read in your Bible are part of

the real world and the real history—the same world in which you live, and the same history as this in which you now participate and which is being chronicled with more or less understanding of its meaning in the daily bulletins in press and television.[22]

Indispensable to Christianity, the idea of God acting in history finds a partial analogy in the free actions of humans, as does the notion of the exercise of a personal will which makes some words and deeds more revelatory of character than others. Moreover, Christianity's specificity as (in Alasdair MacIntyre's terminology) a "tradition of rationality" taking its rise in a particular series of events in history places it in no worse case than any other tradition of rational discourse. True, there can be no appeal to a tradition of rationality drawn from elsewhere in order to justify the Christian belief that in the story told in Scripture and celebrated in the Church "God was acting in a unique way to communicate and effect his purpose for the human race and the created world"; but what is now accepted by an act of faith itself looks toward the end of history, when it must (and will) be justified (or not). Personal and corporate commitment to the Christian faith is saved from mere subjectivity by being made (in a phrase borrowed by Newbigin from Polanyi) "with universal intent": "I am bound to publish it, to commend it to others, and to seek to show in the practice of life today that it is the rational tradition which is capable of giving greater coherence and intelligibility to all experience than any other tradition."

Inherent in the biblical story, says Newbigin, is a "logic of election." God is always the initiator, who chooses, calls, and sends particular people. It corresponds to the character and purpose of God that I must "depend on another for that which is necessary to my salvation." In contrast to both the Indian and the modern Western views, there is in the Bible "no attempt to see the human person as an autonomous individual, and the human relation with God as the relation of the alone to the alone." Mutual relatedness "is not merely part of the journey toward the goal of salvation, but is intrinsic to the goal itself": "In order to receive God's saving revelation we have to open the door to the neighbor whom he sends as his appointed messenger, and—moreover—to receive that messenger not as a temporary teacher or guide whom we can dispense with when we ourselves have learned what is needed, but as one who will permanently share our home. There is no salvation except one in which we are saved together through the one whom God sends to be the bearer of his salvation." Election is thus in the first place for the sake of the other, and only thereby for my sake: "It is the universality of God's saving love which is the ground of his choosing and calling a community to be the messengers of his truth and bearers of his love for all peoples. . . . Neither truth nor love can be communicated except as they are embodied in a community which reasons and loves."[23]

It is in Jesus—and what happened when our human nature was taken by the one in whom and through whom and for whom all things exist—that the meaning of God's election becomes clear:

It is, as Paul says [in Romans 9–11], that God has consigned all to disobedience that he may have mercy on all. The Cross of Jesus is the place where all human beings without exception are exposed as enemies of God, and the place where all human beings without exception are accepted as beloved of God. No one is excluded from the scope of that prayer: "Father, forgive them, for they know not what they do." It is for all. And yet just as the universal and unbounded grace of God could only be made known through this historic deed wrought out at one place in the world and at one point in history; just as it could only be the action of God's grace by having the concreteness, the particularity, and therefore the limitedness of one particular happening which can only become known to others if it is told by one person to another; so also it is made known not by some cosmic spiritual illumination but by being communicated to certain specific men and women who had been chosen as witnesses and prepared beforehand for that role. . . . The logic of election is all of one piece with the logic of the Gospel. God's purpose of salvation is not that we should be taken out of history and related to him in some way which bypasses the specificities and particularities of history. His purpose is that in and through history there should be brought into being that which is symbolized in the vision with which the Bible ends—the Holy City into which all the glory of the nations will finally be gathered. But—and of course this is the crux of the matter—that consummation can only lie on the other side of death and resurrection. It is the calling of the Church to bear through history to its end the secret of the lordship of the Crucified.[24]

Having been let into the secret of the cosmic story by its Author already in the middle of it, the Church "was then sent out into the world to carry the secret into the life of the world, always reappropriating and reinterpreting it in the light of new circumstances." Because "the understanding of God's action in history remains always a matter of faith and never of indubitable knowledge," it is no surprise that there has been debate and struggle when each generation, guided by the original witnesses, has sought to interpret the events of its time in the light of what has been disclosed in those particular events through which God chose to reveal and effect his purpose; but the Church has Christ's promise of the leading and teaching of the Holy Spirit, by which it will be enriched as the Gospel spreads in time and space (John 14–16).[25]

The biblical story has its climax, or (as Newbigin sometimes says) its turning point, in the incarnation, ministry, death, and resurrection of the Son of God, "and if that story is true, then it is unique and also universal in its implications for all human history; it is in fact the true outline of world history."[26] The biblical story furnishes "a clear vision of the goal of history—namely the reconciliation of all things with Christ as Head—and the assurance that this goal will be reached." It is this goal—and the hope which it nourishes—that allows Christians to speak of "the meaning of history" and the meaningfulness of action in it. The advantage of the authentic Christian vision over other goal-oriented histories that may be ideationally derived from it, whether progressivist, nationalist, or Marxist, is the horizon it sets of an intergenerational society—anticipated in the communion of the saints—beyond the individual's death and the end of racial history. Christ, says Newbigin, "is coming to meet us, and whatever we do—whether it is our most private prayers or our most public political action—is simply offered to him for whatever place it may have in his blessed Kingdom." The present hiddenness of the Kingdom—leaving room for the conversion of the nations—entails a period marked both by suffering and by the "powers of healing and blessing which, to eyes of faith, are recognizable as true signs that Jesus reigns." God is patient, but the unveiling will not be held back for ever; and, quoting from Hendrikus Berkhof's *Christ the Meaning of History* (1966), "the joy of the great beginning removes all alarm about the delay in the end."

Newbigin concludes these chapters with a passage that recalls perhaps the hiking holidays that his autobiography shows him to have enjoyed in his younger days:

> When the disciples were perplexed and could not understand why Jesus was to leave them and go alone to his death, he told them that he himself was the way by which they were to follow (John 14:1–6). One can always travel hopefully if there is a reliable track and good ground for believing that it leads to the destination. The track on which we walk is one that disappears from sight before it reaches the destination. We may have a vision of the peak we are aiming for, but we do not see the track all the way to it. It goes down into the dark valley of death, and we, with all our works, go that way. We can go forward with confidence because Jesus has gone that way before us and has come back from the deep valley. If he is himself the track, we can go forward confidently even when the future is hidden. We are not lost. We have a reliable track.[27]

Journey's end is in fact the Holy City, in which the dichotomy created by death between the private and the public worlds is healed. For as the book of Revelation portrays it, the new Jerusalem is "the consummation of all public history," "the goal of the whole story of civilization, which is the creation of the true city": "It is perfect in beauty and unity. And into it all the nations of the earth will bring their treasures. The achievements of human civilization, art, technology, and culture are not obliterated. All that is unclean is excluded, but all that is worthy will find its place as an offering to the King of kings." At the same time, "the Holy City is the place where the journey of each soul finds at last its goal": "The throne of the Lamb shall be in it, and his servants shall worship him; they shall see his face, and his name shall be on their foreheads" (Revelation 22:3f.).

That, then, is how Newbigin valued and read and expounded the Bible, not as "another book of religion," but as containing, in the words of a learned Hindu friend whom he liked to quote, "a quite unique interpretation of universal history and, therefore, a unique understanding of the human person as a responsible actor in history."[28] The main lines of Newbigin's understanding of the biblical story as universal history were already evident—and set against the account of the human story rendered in modernity—in his Bangalore lectures of 1941 on "The Kingdom of God and the Idea of Progress."[29]

In the early 1960s, as will be related in the next chapter, he swerved a little to the side, although he was never quite happy in the company of the radical proponents of secularization. Fully back on course by the later '60s, he affirmed as clearly as ever before the transcendent reality of the grace, the judgment, and the hope in which the human story—in all its historical concreteness—is held by the Triune God.[30] The direction was then consistently maintained from *The Open Secret* to *The Gospel in a Pluralist Society* and beyond.

Given thus Newbigin's view of the authority, nature, content, and use of the Bible, it is not surprising that his dogmatics—his account of the Christian faith as normatively held in the traditional and traditioning community of the Church—should bear such a markedly narrative cast. The deliberately doctrinal work of Newbigin is the business of the remainder of this chapter.

The Rule of Faith

In *The Reunion of the Church* Bishop Newbigin defended the nascent Church of South India against the criticisms made by its Anglo-Catholic detractors in England concerning the section on "The Faith of the Church" in the Basis of Union.[31] The text read:

> The uniting Churches accept the Holy Scriptures of the Old and New Testaments as containing all things necessary to salvation and as the supreme and decisive standard of faith; and acknowledge that the Church must always be ready to correct and reform itself in accordance with the teaching of those Scriptures as the Holy Spirit shall reveal it.
>
> They also accept the Apostles' Creed and the Creed commonly called the Nicene, as witnessing to and safeguarding that faith; and they thankfully acknowledge that same faith to be continuously confirmed by the Holy Spirit in the experience of the Church of Christ.
>
> Thus they believe in God, the Father, the Creator of all things, by whose love we are preserved;
>
> They believe in Jesus Christ, the incarnate Son of God and Redeemer of the world, in whom alone we are saved by grace, being justified from our sins by faith in Him;
>
> They believe in the Holy Spirit, by whom we are sanctified and built up in Christ and in the fellowship of His Body;
>
> And in this faith they worship the Father, Son and Holy Spirit, one God in Trinity and Trinity in Unity.

The critics claimed that the authority of the Church and its tradition in the interpretation of Scripture was not made clear, and that the acceptance of the Creeds was undermined by a footnote (not in fact carried over from the Basis of Union into the Constitution of the CSI) to the effect that there was no intention "to demand the assent of individuals to every word and phrase in them, or to exclude reasonable liberty of interpretation, or to assert that those Creeds are a complete expression of the Christian faith."

Regarding the footnote, Newbigin argued that the very nature of faith as personal response to the living Christ requires freely assumed responsibility on the part of the individual believer, and that—ecclesially—"to insist that reasonable liberty of interpretation be safeguarded is not to destroy the power of the Church to confess the faith, but to safeguard the condition of its doing so." The latter point is developed by Newbigin in the following way: The Church has the responsibility "to declare to every generation what is the faith, to expose and combat errors destructive of the faith, to expel from her body doctrines which pervert the faith, and to lead her members into a full and vivid apprehension of the faith"; moreover, since "thought is never still," the Church is obliged "continually to re-think and re-state its message" (here, Newbigin says, the Roman criticism of a simplistic appeal to the Vincentian canon—"*quod ubique, quod semper, quod ab omnibus creditum est*"—has force). But

> the Church can only discharge this duty as the true embodiment of the Holy Spirit if she is—through all her members—awake and alert to the truth. It is true that there are churches which have so evaded the duty of articulate confession that they have become, like jelly fish, incapable of moving in any direction but that of the tide; but there are also examples of churches which have so identified faith with blind submission to authoritatively prescribed formulae that they have become but petrified fossils, having the form of a Church but not its life.

The Church cannot discharge her responsibility "except she encourage in all her members the personal appropriation of the faith for themselves, and for this she must have due regard to liberty of opinion in matters which do not enter into its substance." The footnote was not designed to "facilitate the entrance of error" but rather to "secure the widest possible diffusion of that personal faith which issues in the love of God with all the heart and mind and strength, and by which the Church lives and is edified and empowered to commend to every generation Him who called himself not tradition but Truth."[32] In point of fact, and "perhaps especially in a pagan land," it is "one of the high moments of the whole act of worship" when, in response to the Gospel as the heralding of God's mighty acts, the people rise and in an act of corporate confession "joyfully affirm their faith in God and in the mighty acts that He has wrought for them." The bishop expresses confidence that the ecumenical creeds will continue to be so used in the Church of South India.[33]

Regarding the authority of Scripture in, over, and for the Church: Newbigin readily admits "that the Scriptures of the New Testament are documents written by the Church in the Church for the Church, that the fixing of the canon was accomplished long after other elements in the Church's tradition were fixed, and that the most recent criticism of the four Gospels themselves has shown how profoundly the experience of the Church has modified this material in the course of its oral transmission. That is all indubitable, and it is a reminder to us that the Bible can only be understood in the Church." Nevertheless:

While the fixing of the canon of the New Testament was the work of the Church, it was not that the Church chose a collection of books which best expressed her doctrines, but that she chose those books which had the highest claim to be true records of the testimony and teaching of those who had been "eye-witnesses and ministers of the Word." The basis of the Church's claim against the heretic was the uninterrupted tradition of public teaching in the great apostolic sees. The Church choosing the canon was not like a book-lover selecting a library on the basis of his tastes; it was like a court sifting evidence in order to obtain the most reliable account of what really happened. The controlling fact was that Christ had lived, taught, done mighty works, died, risen again and appeared to His disciples. The appeal was to those who could claim either to have seen and heard and handled these things, or to have been in direct contact with those who had. The canon of Scripture is the direct result of that appeal. The selection of the canon is the work of the Church, but it is the expression of the fact that it is the actual event of God's work in Christ which is the supreme and decisive standard for the Church.

"The appeal to Scripture," Newbigin concludes, "is not an appeal to the first chapter of church history. It is an appeal to the events in which the Church's living Lord wrought the salvation by which she now lives." "The Bible," he says,

is to be understood in the fellowship of the whole Church, but the traditions of the Church are to be judged in the light of the Bible. The Church is the sphere of the presence of the Holy Spirit, but the gift of the Holy Spirit is the fruit of the hearing and receiving of the Gospel. The Church cannot, therefore, regard the promise of the Holy Spirit as delivering her from the obligation of submission to the authority of those Scriptures in which the events which are the content of the Gospel are set forth. . . . These [events] are her supreme and decisive standard of faith, and to these she must ever turn, knowing that as she exposes herself afresh to the Gospel of which the Scriptures are the record, she will receive afresh the guiding of the Holy Spirit as to the present will of her Lord.

Newbigin's nuancing of the CSI Constitution will be noticed: It is finally "the revelation of God in Jesus Christ," or "God's redeeming act once for all at a point in history," to which the Scriptures *bear witness*, that is "the ultimate standard of faith."

Newbigin's reading of the Scriptures clearly took place according to the "rule of faith" that found narrative and ontological expression in the Apostolic and Nicene creeds. Historically, the ancient creeds may have developed in a complex interaction between the transmitted apostolic writings, the catechetical, baptismal, and liturgical practice of the Church, and theological reflection in the face of arising questions. Theologically, the Apostolic and Nicene creeds are taken by Newbigin as faithful summaries of the biblical story and true statements about the triune God who is its author and the principal agent in it; they constitute a point of reference for all engagement with particular passages of Scripture. For Newbigin, the Nicene *homoousion* is of decisive importance: the Christian narrative stands or falls with the identity of Jesus Christ, the Word made flesh, the eternal Son who became man for our salvation. That identity lay at the heart of the Gospel which Newbigin sought to commend in his evangelistic practice and missiological thinking; it was the foundation of his apologia for the Christian faith in the encounters with both religious pluralism and skeptical modernity.

In *Trinitarian Faith and Today's Mission* (1963–64), we discover Newbigin linking the early "doctrinal struggles about the mutual relations of the Son and the Father" with "the battle to master the pagan world-view at the height of its power and self-confidence" and then going on to show how the preaching of Jesus to Indian villagers still forces the question of Jesus' relation to the "one God behind all the gods."[34] In *The Open Secret* (1978) Newbigin returned to *homoousia* as a case of the language of contemporary philosophy being used by Christian theologians to overturn and replace the axioms of thought in ancient classical culture.[35] After several generations of ecclesial reflection on the question "Who is Jesus?", the terminology adopted by the Fathers and the Councils of the fourth century allowed a clear statement of the Christian conviction that "the being of the Son and the being of the Spirit are not something intermediate between a remote and ultimately unapproachable Supreme Being and the known world of nature and history"—which in turn provided a basis for a new way of understanding the human situation and the world. "The ultimate reality, according to this new view, is not to be understood as a timeless, passionless monad beyond all human knowing, but as a trinity of Father, Son, and Spirit"—and, for all the intellectual effort that has gone into the doctrinal clarification of the christological and trinitarian confession, this understanding "is not the result of speculative thought" but "has been given by revelation in the actual historical life and work of the Son."

Neither the revelation nor its doctrinal expression can be understood, much less verified, by reference to the assumed axioms of classical thought: "It is verified only by the action of the Holy Spirit present in the witness of the martyrs. But accepted by faith it becomes the basis of a new way of making sense of the world, not just by speculative science, but by practical wisdom."

> Thus, on this new basis the dichotomy between the sensible and the intelligible worlds is healed, for God himself has actually been made flesh. The Son who offered the perfect sacrifice of loving obedience to the Father on the cross is not the Father, but he is truly God as the Father is God. The being of God himself is involved in the suffering of history. And through the Spirit the Christian can share this suffering, know that in doing so he is in touch with the very being of God himself (Romans 8:18–27).
>
> Likewise the dichotomy between virtue and fortune is healed, for the Christian who thus shares in the travail of history also knows that God works everything for good to those who love him (Romans 8:28). His life here in the midst of history is thus not a hopeless battle against fate, but the faithful following of Jesus along the way of the cross in loving obedience to the Father whose rule is over all. A wholly new way is opened up to accomplish what classical science and philosophy could not accomplish—a way of grasping

and dealing with the reality of human life as part of a meaningful history within a world created and sustained by the God who had revealed himself in Jesus and who continued by his Spirit to guide the followers of Jesus into the fullness of truth.[36]

In Newbigin's 1993 essay entitled "Religious Pluralism," the decisive importance of the fourth-century formulations is expounded in terms of the sole sovereignty of Christ. The early Church refused to accept a position as one of many tolerated religions of personal salvation within the public framework of an imperial cult. And "when the emperor finally bowed to the one who is truly Lord, and Constantine was baptized," still "the struggle did not end":

> It continued in the arena of theology and philosophy. The long and often arcane battles of the patristic period were, at heart, battles about the question of whether Jesus is Lord in this absolute sense. For Greek philosophy to accept the full meaning of the apostolic message that the *logos* was identical with the man Jesus of Nazareth required nothing less than a complete abandonment of fundamental dualisms of matter and spirit, of time and eternity, of visible and invisible. One could, without a total break with traditional philosophy, accept the idea that Jesus was *like* God (*homoiousios*) but not that he was one in being with God (*homoousios*). The historian Gibbon mocked at the spectacle of Christians fighting over a diphthong, but that apparently minute difference concealed a whole difference between surrender to an ultimate pluralism and acknowledgment that God has actually made himself known by presence in the stuff of human history. If it is true that God has done this, then this has to be the starting point of all fundamental thinking and the criterion by which all ultimate truth-claims are judged. The whole existence of the Christian faith hung on that diphthong.[37]

"The Church," asserts Newbigin, "can never go back on what was then decided"; yet "it is not enough for the Church to go on repeating in different cultural situations the same words and phrases. New ways have to be found of stating the essential trinitarian faith, and for this the Church in each new cultural situation has to go back to the original biblical sources of this faith in order to lay hold on it afresh and to state it afresh in contemporary terms."[38] That is what Newbigin attempted to do in the religious and philosophical context of India, which he saw as bearing some deep resemblances to the Greco-Roman world. In later life, he devoted his principal energies to the same task in the late modern West. Thus in *Truth to Tell* he asserts the need of "affirming the truth in the Church" as a condition of "speaking the truth to Caesar." Invoking the prescient book of Romano Guardini, *The End of the Modern World*, written immediately at the end of the Second World War amid the rubble of a ruined Germany, Newbigin agrees that the Church "has no alternative but to go back to its old dogmatic roots," for, with the rapid erosion of the remnants of Christian culture, it is now clearly the case, as Guardini foresaw, that "Christianity will once again need to prove itself deliberately as a faith which is not self-evident; it will be forced to distinguish itself more sharply from a dominant non-Christian ethos."[39]

Newbigin's comprehensive restatements of the faith according to the "biblical sources" and the "dogmatic roots" assume various literary genres. In a paper written in preparation for the inaugural assembly of the World Council of Churches at Amsterdam in 1948, Newbigin answered the question "What is the Gospel?" according to a fivefold schema that followed the sequence of salvation history: creation, fall, election, redemption, and consummation. An even briefer version—substantially the same, but with a slight variation in the distribution of the material—is found in the text drafted at the Willingen meeting of the International Missionary Council in 1951; its dimensions hardly exceed those of the various summary statements of the "rule of faith" or "canon of truth" made by St. Irenaeus in the course of his books "Against the Heresies."[40] A fuller display of the same basic soteriological pattern is made in the little book on *Sin and Salvation* which Bishop Newbigin wrote in the 1950s for rural teachers in South India.[41] Two further examples may now be given in a little more detail, both again from quite different contexts and in quite different formats. The first, *Journey into Joy*, transcribes a series of six talks given while Newbigin was Bishop in Madras to students and staff of the Christian Medical College, Vellore, in October 1971. The second is a series of articles contributed in 1988–89 to the United Reformed Church's magazine, *Reform*, the typescript of which, lodged in the Selly Oak archives, bears Lesslie's handwritten notation "My nearest approach to a 'Dogmatics'?"

The Vellore addresses were apparently directed to friendly seekers. Borrowing an image from the shipbuilding industry of his native Tyneside, Newbigin conducted an exercise in "compass adjustment" for an age in which societies were lacking an agreed definition of the good they set as their goal. *Journey into Joy* is presented as an invitation to pursue a line of inquiry. At the very start, Newbigin relates the youthful vision vouchsafed to him amid the miseries of the mining valleys of South Wales, where he saw "the Cross of Jesus Christ as the one and only reality great enough to span the distance between heaven and hell, and to hold in one embrace all the variety of humankind, the one reality that could make sense of the human situation." Having spent the subsequent years in the quest himself, he now invites his listeners to share with him "in exploring the meaning of the Cross of Jesus Christ for the journey that we have to make."[42]

In *Journey into Joy* Newbigin is not seeking directly to prove the truth of the Christian faith but rather to show the possibilities it offers those who are willing to give it a try. Although Newbigin does not himself make the point explicitly, his exposition follows—with one interesting switch that will be noted—the sequence of the classical creeds of the Church. Chapter 1 treats, in a rough correspondence to the Church's confession of the sole Creator, "the mystery of life and faith in God." Life is a mixed experience: beside beauty, health, friendship, kindness, courage, there are ugliness, discord, betrayal, transience, sickness, and finally death. The biblical story of Job confronts the fact that "there is a mass of bitter human experience to contradict all the things that seem to make life worth living" and make us question "whether there is any meaning at all" or whether life is not rather "just 'a tale told by an idiot, full of sound and fury, signifying nothing.' " If it is asked who is responsible for this mess, Hindu religion proposes first a multitude of gods and goddesses who control the different sectors of life, but ultimately all falls under Fate or Karma. Amid ancient religions only Judaism "dared to assert that this whole visible, natural world, as well as whatever invisible worlds there may be, is created and ruled by one God who is good and wise and holy. And when disaster following disaster fell upon the Jewish people, they still clung to that belief, interpreting these disasters as being not a defeat for God, but rather as God's punishment for their sins. That is something absolutely unique in all human history." In the face of all the evil and irrationality in the world, God's goodness and rationality can be vindicated only if there is a plan, a purpose, a hope, on the part of the one responsible, in which "your response, your belief, your commitment to the plan, your loyal participation in carrying it out—these are all essential elements in the rationality of things"; and in Job, in the Psalms, and above all in Isaiah's songs of the suffering servant of the Lord, there are clues that "the ultimate secret is nothing other than the patient and long-suffering love which bears the sin of the world and bears history itself to its glorious conclusion." Here we have, in substance, the first article of the creed, concerning "the Almighty," "the Maker of heaven and earth, of all things visible and invisible," "the Father" whose Son will be the Redeemer confessed in the second article; and here, in act, the initial *credo* or *credimus* would be an affirmation by believing men and women that they had accepted their place in God's plan and were cooperating toward its full and final realization.

Chapter 2 explores the meaning, for the line of thought being pursued, of "the life and teaching, death and resurrection and subsequent place in history of one man who belonged to the Jewish people and who was the heir of their faith." At the center of his story "there is an event which challenges, more sharply than any other event in history, the view that this is a rational and just world": Jesus—who went about doing good, who healed the sick, who befriended the outcasts of society, who forgave sins on behalf of the God he called "My Father"—"was executed by crucifixion and thereby branded by his contemporaries as an accursed criminal and an enemy of God. How is it that this event, the most irrational and unjust event in all recorded human history, has become the central point of the faith that human history is being guided towards the fulfilment of a just and rational purpose?" The first thing to be said about this, Newbigin avers, "is that we know about Jesus because he was raised from the dead." Practically all we know about Jesus was "written by those who believed that Jesus had died and had been raised from the dead; and it would not have been written otherwise." Although the Christian faith stands or falls with Jesus' resurrection and is inexplicable without it, "the story of the resurrection is not told in the New Testament as the story of a victory which wipes out the defeat of the Cross. On the contrary, there is great emphasis laid on the fact that the risen Lord is the crucified one." What happened on Calvary was that "this one and only man who has ever lived in total fellowship, trust, and obedience towards God, met the concentrated power of human sin, and in committing everything totally and simply into his Father's hands, bore it all to the end, praying for his murderers, and finally committing himself into his Father's hands, whom he had loved from the beginning." That it was precisely this man whom God raised from the dead means that "the God whom Jesus trusted as his Father is real, more real than death," that "this God who is the real God is the God whose nature was reflected and revealed in what Jesus was, did, and said," and that "the thing Jesus began to do must go on":

> He is the Messiah, and God's rule is manifested in his life and deeds and words. This, then, is the clue to the future. In the language of the Easter hymn, "The powers of hell have done their worst." The ultimate depths of evil and irrationality have been plumbed by the death of Jesus. There is absolutely nothing more that the powers of evil can do; there is nothing more to be feared. We can with sure confidence join ourselves to him and share in his continuing work of making the Father's will known and done throughout the whole creation.

The resurrection, "if it is true, is the starting point of a wholly new way of understanding and organizing our experience"—and with that, we are into the third chapter of *Journey into Joy*, and the third article of the creed: "New Life in the Spirit." It is a life marked by peace and forgiveness, by freedom from the power of sin and trustful obedience toward God, by joy and by love. Newbigin certainly recognizes that the new life is a life in community; but where one might now, in a creedal sequence, expect him to talk more fully of the Church, he takes up St. Paul's idea of the Holy Spirit as the *arrabôn*, "the earnest of our inheritance," in order to speak of hope and thus move immediately in an eschatological direction. That matches the author's stated intention to convey his faith that "in Jesus Christ we are given the direction for our lives, which is also the direction in which God intends to lead the whole creation, and which, therefore, can give meaning to our individual lives."

Accordingly, the fourth chapter is headed "Hope for the World." Biblically, hope corresponds to God's promises. God invites people to trust his promises and thus "reach after" the good things he has in store or "set out in pursuit of them." Not being the ground of our hope, the world as it is can legitimately be the object of our protest—and of our transformative work in suitably modest cooperation with God's plan. The final hope, beyond individual death and the history of the human race, is for the transgenerational society of God's new city in a renewed cosmos, containing all our achievements that have survived the fire of judgment. That is how Newbigin expounds "the resurrection of the body and the life everlasting," "the resurrection of the dead and the life of the world to come."

Thereupon the author returns in chapter 5 to the Church, "a committed people." It is because the Church has been given a "foretaste" and is itself a "first-fruit" that it can be an "instrument" of God's Kingdom. "If God is leading the world in the direction indicated by the cross and resurrection of

Christ Jesus," there must be a "body of committed people who are ready to go that way and to take the rest of mankind with them." Having been "redeemed from mankind as first-fruits for God and the Lamb," they "follow the Lamb wherever he goes" (Revelation 14:4). As Newbigin had said at an earlier point in the book, "In a twilight world where people are lost and asking their way, a few people marching together in one direction with the light of hope and expectation on their faces will surely prompt others to ask 'Where are you going?'" Those who have shared with Christ the "one baptism for the forgiveness of sins"—and continue to share through the bread and the cup in the holy things of his body and his blood (the "communio sanctorum")—are commissioned to bear witness to him in the world through a life of service, of sacrificial suffering, of words and deeds that signify and enact God's Kingdom, of mutual care and concern, of inviting fellowship, and of worship that keeps the focus unshakably on God, "who wills that all things and all men shall come to perfect unity in Jesus Christ, who has promised that this shall be so, and who guides both our personal lives and the life of the world to that end.

In the final chapter, under "The Path of the Disciple" and the text of Romans 12:1f., Newbigin once more ties closely together the two components of the "credo" or "credimus," namely, the "faith which is believed" (*fides quae creditur*) and the "faith by which one believes" (*fides quâ creditur*)[43]—for "if doctrine and life fall apart, God's purpose remains unfulfilled." At the hinge between the dogmatic and the practical parts of the epistle, St. Paul's "therefore" in Romans 12:1f. is like the coupling between an engine and the train: "If it is not there, the engine may blast off with a magnificent volume of steam and a thundering noise, such as only a perfectly orthodox theologian can produce, but the passengers remain sitting in their carriages with no chance of going anywhere." If there is no link between Christian doctrine and "my personal life, my family, my career, my ambitions, my fears, my hopes," then "the talk is just so much escaping steam." Those who have "learned God's secret" through the words and deeds of Christ, his dying and his rising, will become discriminating and articulate nonconformists with respect to this world and will seek by a discipline of prayer the will of God for their daily lives as well as their long-term future, always reckoning with God's intention to bring his whole creation into unity in Christ. And in the words of John Keble's hymn:

> If on our daily course, our mind
> Be set to hallow all it find,
> New treasures still of countless price,
> God will provide for sacrifice.

For the very joys which God already freely gives us are not meant for covetous hoarding but rather for glad returning, until in getting and giving we finally reach—perhaps through darkness and perplexity—the supreme joy, which is "to share both the richness and the generosity of God. . . . The end is not a

private joy but a social joy. It is the joy of God and his people together."
When Jesus has "the joy of knowing that all for whom he died have come
home," then he will "see the travail of his soul and be satisfied" (Isaiah 53:
11).

"My Nearest Approach to a Dogmatics"

The series of eleven articles, written for *Reform* magazine in 1990 and limited
to some 800 words each, rehearses in simple and compact form the basic
teaching which the reader of this book will have seen Newbigin constantly
offering over fifty and more years. Our present interests reside with the comprehensive structure, the topical sequence, and the internal cohesion that
characterize this miniature summa. Put in technical terms (which the author
himself largely avoids), the pattern is as follows: (1) Scripture; (2) God the
Holy Trinity; (3) Providence; (4) Atonement (Incarnation and Redemption);
(5) Pneumatology; (6) Ecclesiology; (7) Sacraments; (8) Worship and Prayer;
(9) Eschatology; (10) Religions, Truth, and Salvation; (11) Mission in the
World.

1. The Bible tells "God's story and ours." Compared with a "modern" ver-
    sion of world history in which everything "led up to our kind of civili-
    zation," this "alternative" world history "sets the human story in a cos-
    mic frame, between creation and consummation"; and the clue to the
    meaning of the whole is provided not by universal reason but rather by
    God's choice of a particular people, and finally one man of that nation,
    who stands at the center of "the story of the infinite patience and the
    awesome holiness of the creator and lord of all who will never give up
    his purpose to bring the world he has made, and the human family to
    whom he has entrusted its care, to the glory he has planned for us."
    Christians "live in" the biblical story, and "living in it, we learn to cope
    with the history in which we share, because we have seen the point."
2. While there are "rumors" of God among all peoples, Christians begin not
    from "my idea of God" (say, "a monarch in the sky"), but rather from
    what the New Testament writers witness to, namely, "that God was pres-
    ent in the fullness of his being in the man Jesus; that this Jesus understood
    himself to be the Son of his Father 'who is in heaven' and whose rule
    embraces all creation; and that the Spirit, by whom Jesus was conceived,
    led, and sustained, would, through his final act of loving obedience to
    the Father, be communicated to all who would give their lives to him."
    This "triune God" allows our thinking to overcome the disjunction of
    "spiritual" and "material," and "the disjunction of our personal purposes
    from what seem to be the meaningless accidents that befall us": "As I
    allow myself to be taken into the crucified and risen life of Jesus and daily
    offer my life through him to the Father, the Spirit enables me to find in
    all the 'accidents' of life the guiding and providing hand of the Father."

That is a way of "personal knowing, which is love," a sharing in "the communion of Father, Son, and Spirit."

3. Rejecting the Enlightenment view of the universe as a closed, mechanical system, Newbigin takes the human experience of willed, purposeful action as an analogy of "the guiding hand" of God, who according to the Bible is "in charge" of his creation. His final purpose can be known only if he reveals it, and this he does "by actual happenings in the world, happenings which his Spirit interprets to our spirits." "There are enough horrors and disasters in the Bible to furnish an atheist with all the arguments he needs," and supremely "when the holiest of all is condemned to death on a cross." "What followed on the third day is what gives us the confidence to say with Paul that God works all things together for good to those who love him." That proves true "when we follow Jesus in challenging all that denies God's love and take the consequences."

4. Our experience of wickedness in the world makes us ask how God can be both merciful and just. The Old Testament "unfolds the story of God's agony as love and wrath struggle within him": "As we read on, we see more and more clearly that the wounds of our wickedness are in the heart of God. We are prepared for the time when these wounds must become visible in the body of a man like us." The death of Jesus is "the sacrifice made by a sinner to God who is offended, yet it is God who offers the sacrifice"; it is "God's judgment on sin, and yet it is God who bears the judgment." The wounded body was raised from the dead "by the power of God who *is* in charge." The resurrection of Jesus is "the turning point of history," the beginning of "a new creation," "the birth of a new order." This event inaugurates a "paradigm shift" in which one "can begin to make sense—even joyful sense—of this (otherwise) meaningless world of sin and death" and "venture out into the new open world into which the risen Jesus leads us."

5. The new creation, in the power of God's Spirit, is both "a reality of history" (Acts 2) and "an inward experience" (John 20:22). The Holy Spirit is "the cash-on-deposit" for God's Kingdom, "the pledge of glory," a first but real "gift of God's power and wisdom now," making it possible "to believe in, to hope for, and to work for the full unveiling of God's rule for the whole creation." The Holy Spirit is the principal and convincing witness behind the words and deeds of the Church as it learns more and more of the truth through pursuit of its missionary commission to bring new peoples to Christ.

6. The Church was launched by the Spirit into the world in order to continue the mission of Jesus—by announcing God's Kingdom and teaching people its ways, and by performing the mighty works of healing and deliverance that belong to it. Because the Church is itself first "a community in which the freedom and joy of the Kingdom are already tasted and celebrated in praise and adoration," it can also be "a sign of the Kingdom, pointing beyond itself to God's love and holiness" and "an instrument which God can use (among other instruments) for doing his

will in the world." The Church is "a company of forgiven sinners," even "a bunch of escaped convicts"; it is maintained only by "the paradox of grace." Christians "confess belief in 'one holy catholic and apostolic Church.' But the Church is divided, sinful, sectarian, and lazy about its mission. We can only continue to confess this faith because God is mighty and merciful and is able to raise the dead and 'call into existence things that do not exist' (Romans 4:17)." Yet "it is a terrible thing to abuse God's mercy and think we can get away with it"; in particular, a claim to "spiritual" unity must not be as "an escape from actually sharing a common life." Rather, the pentecostal Spirit is given us "in order that we may be in active truth one, holy, catholic, and apostolic."

7. The sacraments are given to the Church by God as his "pledges of faithfulness." As "the centre of their new life," the Lord's Supper "holds together" those who are "committed to Christ." "Baptism is the act through which we are committed to follow Jesus on the way of the cross. The Supper is the act in which that same commitment is continually renewed." It is not "a private party" but "belongs to the universal fellowship," so that the person presiding should be authorized "not just by a small group but by the wider fellowship." "As God's word had to be spoken in the flesh and blood of a human being, so our incorporation into his life involves these visible acts." They are "simple acts which we can do as he commands us, even when our faith is feeble."

8. Sunday worship is "the most obvious public thing that the Church does." In the present time of spiritual decay, the exercise of reverence bears striking testimony to "what should be the heart of all human life." Like the Emmaus story in Luke 24, the Church's classic liturgy is given its shape by the exposition of Scripture and the breaking of bread that mediate the presence of God in Christ. It is filled with prayers of adoration, confession, and thanksgiving. "Worship in the congregation," Newbigin finds, "needs to be nourished by the daily practice of reading and thinking about what is given in the Bible. The rich tapestry of poetry, story, prophecy, and vision that fills the Bible gradually enables me, as I read it in the context of daily duty, to be grasped more and more by the wonder of God's dealing with me, the terror of his just anger and the marvel of his endless mercy": "It takes a whole lifetime to begin to learn how great and glorious God is. We shall need eternity to learn it all."

9. Hope is central in the New Testament, taking its origin from Jesus' announcement of the Kingdom of God and then from his own resurrection. Newbigin contrasts the Christian expectation first with that of the Brahmin who taught him Tamil (where the word "hope" does not exist, for "what will be will be, and wanting something better won't change it"), then with the modern notion of progress to be achieved by human planning, and finally with postmodern despair: "If you accept Jesus' call to follow, and accept the witness of Easter morning, then you will know that the new world is coming because you have seen its dawning." There will be no world of peace and perfect justice on this side of death or before

the end of human history. But Christians look forward with confidence to "the holy city coming to us as a bride adorned for her husband, perfect in beauty and splendour, a city into which all that is good in human history is gathered and perfected, and from which all that is evil is excluded." That vision starts to affect our conduct from this moment on.

10. Discussion of the relation of "the other religions" to Christianity is skewed if everything is put in terms of "Who is going to be saved?"—for obsession with this question is an expression of selfish individualism. The real question is "What is the truth about the human situation?" Christians claim to have in Jesus "the master-clue": "To confess Jesus as the 'true and living way' gives us the freedom and confidence to explore everything that claims to be real, knowing that it all belongs to him." Knowing the wideness in God's mercy, one can "rejoice in all the signs of God's grace at work in the lives of people of other religions or of no religion," and yet—in the face also of God's judgment on human sin, there is no substitute for the story of God's redemptive love in Jesus Christ (Acts 10: 34–48). The path of life is "marked by the footsteps of Jesus as he went from Bethlehem to Calvary. Because we know that this path is to be trusted, we want to call others to come with us on the way."

11. The Church's mission in the world, according to 1 Peter 2, is that of a holy priesthood with a double task: "to declare the wonderful deeds of God" and "to offer up spiritual sacrifices to God through Jesus Christ." Like "an X-ray photograph which makes visible the hidden bone structure of the body," Christians "are to make visible the hidden rule of God in the world," while also accomplishing "all those moment-by-moment acts of love and obedience which God puts in our way to offer." The Church "is *for* the world," not by "letting the world set the agenda" but rather by "fulfilling God's agenda for the world." The Christian life is lived between the Lord's Day assembly (where "we gather to renew our membership in the body of Christ, the one great High Priest" and "offer up the whole life of the world to God through Jesus"), the "secret altar" ("where, day by day, we offer to God through Jesus every bit of our lives, our most secret thoughts and our most public actions, and where we receive afresh through Christ God's ever-new gift of grace and mercy"), and "our daily work to make manifest God's blessed rule to the whole world."

Such is what Newbigin, a former moderator, sought to teach the members of the United Reformed Church in a series of magazine articles in 1990. In 1993 a (very) different moderator—Donald Hilton—addressed the general assembly on the basis of his commitment to a theological liberalism that would make a question mark the symbol of his vision for the United Reformed Church. Newbigin came back with a pamphlet on the internal inconsistency of the liberal tradition—"*A Decent Debate about Doctrine*": *Faith, Doubt, and Certainty*.[44] Meanwhile, this chapter concludes with an attempt to grasp the gist of Newbigin's teaching and thought.

The Gist of It

Of Newbigin's teaching and thought it may be said that the Atonement constitutes its soteriological center, the Trinity its theological frame, and the Kingdom of God its teleological direction. It was not quite so from the start of
Newbigin's writings. Atonement and the Kingdom, yes, from Newbigin's days
at Westminster College and the early years in India until the very end of his
life; but it took a little longer for the full significance of trinitarian doctrine
to dawn on him. In a late essay entitled "The Trinity as Public Truth," he
provided the following retrospect:

> In my own theological training, the doctrine of the Trinity played a very
> minor part. Of course it was not denied or questioned, but it had no central
> place. As I entered into the discipline of theological studies, the doctrines that
> gripped me, that glowed warmly in my mind so that I wanted to preach
> them, were concerned with grace, reconciliation, the Kingdom of God, and
> the last things. In the *magnum opus* of my revered theological teacher, John
> Oman, there is no reference to the Trinity. In my own experience, trinitarian
> doctrine came alive when I read classical scholar Charles Norris Cochrane's
> book *Christianity and Classical Culture* (1940). It is a study of the movement
> of thought from Augustus to Augustine, from the zenith of classical culture
> to its eclipse. Cochrane showed me how the trinitarian doctrine provided a
> new paradigm for thought, which made possible the healing of the dualisms
> that classical thought had been unable to overcome—the dualism between
> the sensible and the intelligible in the world of thought, and between virtue
> and fortune in the realm of action. The doctrine of the Trinity, in other words,
> was not a problem, but the solution to a problem that classical thought could
> not solve.[45]

Although for Newbigin the human predicament was not limited to sin and
its effects, and although he construed no easy correspondence between the
distribution of suffering and sins committed, yet he certainly saw sin and sins
as centrally frustrating to God's good purposes for humankind and to the
fulfillment of the human calling and destiny. The early Cambridge essay put
on display the human need of atonement and the divine provision of it: in a
costly triumph of mercy over wrath, the holy God, who is of purer eyes than
to behold iniquity, himself supplied the means of atonement through the redemptive death of Jesus, whose benefits become available to penitent believers
who allow themselves to be grasped by the risen Christ and transformed into
his likeness through the new life that the Holy Spirit gives. This was the "sin
and salvation" that Newbigin preached and taught as an active evangelist
and bishop. Reconciliation to God, and the consequent reconciliation among
believers and finally throughout humankind, was what, for Newbigin, constituted the Church, imposed the ecumenical vocation to unity, energized the
missionary obligation, and governed the conduct of Christians toward adherents of other religions and in the secular world. That same soteriological
concern remained as the sometimes hidden core in all the work of apologetics

that the older Newbigin undertook, as will be related in the next chapter, amid the sin-sick society of the West in the last quarter of the twentieth century. "The human situation will be radically misunderstood," wrote Newbigin in *Truth and Authority in Modernity* (1996), "unless we take account of what is told in the Christian tradition about the Fall" and "the corruption that has stained our story":

> When we speak of finding in Jesus the clue to the meaning of the whole human story, we are not speaking of a mere cognitive exercise. We are speaking of that act of atonement wrought in Jesus through which we are brought into a loving obedience to the will of God as it is exercised through all human and cosmic history. It is not merely a matter of illumination, of new understanding; it is a matter of reconciliation, of rescue from alienation, of obedient response to the divine initiative of love. It is illumination and new understanding only because it is first a divine action of reconciliation through which we are brought to that state in which we can say and know that God works all things together for good to those who love him. It is only through this act of atonement that Jesus becomes for us the clue to history.[46]

Newbigin did not much go in for theological speculation concerning the inner being and life of the Holy Trinity. It sufficed that the Nicene *homoousion* should safeguard the Gospel message that the incarnation was the personal revelation of *God*, and that the price of redemption was paid by *God*; it sufficed that, with the Nicene-Constantinopolitan creed, the Church should recognize that the life-giving and transformative Spirit is utterly *God*. Based on his reading of the divine economy of salvation, Newbigin's practical trinitarianism showed itself in the structure of *The Household of God*, where the Church appears, even through the distortions of historical divisions, as the people called by the Father, incorporated into Christ, and indwelt by the Holy Spirit; and in the structure of *The Open Secret*, in which the mission of the Church is described as "Proclaiming the Kingdom of the Father (Faith in Action)," "Sharing the Life of the Son (Love in Action)," and "Bearing the Witness of the Spirit (Hope in Action)." Moreover, this is no *mere* "economic trinitarianism," for the cooperation of the divine Persons toward the world rests on, and testifies to, their mutual coinherence *in se*, and it is in being drawn into their communion that human salvation consists. Time and time again, Newbigin describes salvation as the gift of participation in the trinitarian life of God. Even at his most "Protestant," in the chapter on justification by faith in *The Reunion of the Church*, Newbigin wrote:

> The Church is the extension to creatures of the life of the Blessed Trinity. In the response of penitent faith which is the soul's Amen to Christ's redeeming work, and in the life of self-offering to the Father in union with Him, the Christian is caught up into the very life of the Godhead. . . . Justification is the means whereby we are admitted into the very fellowship of the Holiest Himself, receiving the love with which the Father loves the Son and united with the love which the Son perpetually offers the Father. . . . The gift of the

Spirit is an "earnest." It is at the same time a real sharing in the life of God Himself and also a foretaste of the perfect life in Him which is to come. . . . Those who are in Christ are caught up into that perpetual self-offering of the Son to the Father in the Spirit which is the life of the Godhead.[47]

And similarly in the profoundly trinitarian chapter of *The Household of God* entitled "Christ in You, the Hope of Glory," we find:

Within the eternal being of God, love is a never-ceasing self-emptying and out-pouring, forever met by the same out-poured love, the love of the Father and the Son in the unity of the Spirit. Eternal life is no motionless serenity, but love meeting love, the rapture of mutual love forever poured out and forever received. . . . In the final consummation of God's loving purpose, we and all creation will be caught up into the perfect rapture of that mutual love which is the life of God Himself. What is given to us now can only be a foretaste, for none of us can be made whole till we are made whole together.[48]

Ecumenically, and with appeal to John 17:21, the triune Godhead provides not only the pattern but also the source and impetus for ecclesial "unity in diversity":

The God whose being is holy love, uniting the Father, Son and Holy Spirit, draws us by the work of the Spirit into participation in the Son's love and obedience to the Father. This same holy love draws us to one another. . . . The reason why we can never rest content in our separation is the unlimited grace of God the Father, who has accepted us in the beloved Son and bound us together in his own life by the power of the Holy Spirit—a life in which we are called to reflect both the unity and diversity of the Godhead.[49]

And, as a final example, even (or precisely) in such a worldly context as his 1984 lecture on "The Welfare State," Newbigin would utter as a Christian claim to public truth that

human beings are created in love and for love, created for fellowship with one another in a mutual love which is the free gift of God whose inner life is the perfect mutuality of love—Father, Son and Spirit; that happiness consists in participation in this love which is the being of God; and that participation in it is made possible and is offered as a gift to sinful men and women by the justifying work of Christ and the sanctifying work of the Holy Spirit.[50]

Given the eminent concern in his Reformed tradition for God's sovereignty and glory, it is not surprising that the Kingdom of God should have figured as a prominent theme in Newbigin's theology, setting its historical and eschatological direction. The theme runs from at least the Bangalore lectures of 1941 on "The Kingdom of God and the Idea of Progress" through Newbigin's work in connection with the WCC Evanston assembly of 1954 on "Christ the Hope of the World" to his missiological writings *The Open Secret* (1978) and *Sign of the Kingdom* (1980) and beyond. God's eternal rule impinges on human history, Newbigin insists, in the shape of judgment and mercy, offering to sinful men and women a redemptive new beginning in Christ that then invites them to free cooperation in the divine purposes through the Holy Spirit. God has proceeded by way of the historically manifest election of the people of Israel, then a Man among them, and finally a Church in Him—and all in the service of God's plan, through which benefits are given in order to be shared with others.[51] Since Pentecost, the historic Church exists in the Spirit as the firstfruit, and therefore the foretaste, of God's final Kingdom and serves in that capacity as both a sign of the Kingdom inaugurated by Christ and an instrument of its further proclamation and achievement, even while its works are "acted prayers" for a consummation that God will accomplish only by the radical deed of the general resurrection and the creation of new heavens and a new earth. Newbigin remained unwilling to speculate on the eternal destiny of those who did not become disciples of Christ in this earthly life; without reference to the Calvinist notion of the "hidden will" of God, he held that Christian thought and practice had properly to live in a presently unresolved tension between the universally good purpose of God and the possibility that some, perhaps many, would be lost. Certainly the New Jerusalem will include in transfigured and transgenerational form all in individual lives and historic cultures that has been in accordance with God's will and may there contribute to the ceaseless glorification of God the Holy Trinity and the endless enjoyment by redeemed creatures of Him.

Newbigin's vision of the saving work of the Triune God in history and beyond is painted with the broadest of brushes, and under the inspiration of Romans 8 and John's Apocalypse, in a short piece on "The Christian Hope" prepared for the Evanston assembly of the WCC:

The starting point is in what God has done once and for all. He has sent His only-begotten Son Jesus Christ to take upon Him our human nature, to enter into the entail of our sins, to die for us upon the cross, to carry upon His own self the whole burden and curse of our sins, and to rise again from the dead in the glory of a new life. That is the place where hope is born. . . .

That is the only starting point. But it is only the starting point. A single isolated event in the increasingly remote past could not by itself sustain the Christian hope. . . . The story of Christ's incarnation, death and resurrection comes to us not as a piece of remote history, but as the secret of the present experience of a living fellowship which spans the nineteen centuries which separate us from Pontius Pilate. What we say here we speak from out of that experience and that fellowship. We know Christ as our living and present Lord, and our fellowship with Him and with the Father *through* Him. This experience and this fellowship were born on the day of Pentecost and have been perpetually renewed ever since. Christ's finished work of atonement has so broken the dominion of evil that God's own Spirit could enter in and take possession of those who had been brought under the judgment of the mercy of the Crucified. It is in the unbroken fellowship which His Spirit has created that the Gospel story has come down to us and it is out of the experience of that fellowship that we speak. We know the risen Christ today as Lord and Saviour. . . .

What God has done in Christ is final and complete as the revelation of Himself and as the breaking of the power of sin. But yet it remains to be completed. All things are not yet subject to Him. Sin, pain, and death still exercise their rule. Even we who have received the first-fruits of the Spirit still long for our full freedom. The whole created world is in bondage to corruption and waits for release. But Christ has given us the assurance that He will complete what He has begun. . . . Yet we do not merely wait. The very reason for which the full unveiling of His victory is delayed is that He wills to give time to all men everywhere to acknowledge Him and to accept freely His rule. The time that is given to us is a time in which His victory is to be proclaimed and acknowledged in every corner of the earth and in every sphere of human life. And we are to carry out that task in complete confidence and eager hope, because we know that the final issue is not at all in doubt. . . .

The apostolic witness confidently assures us that all that opposes His will, all that is evil, will be finally destroyed, that sorrow and pain will be done away, that God's people will dwell in the perfect joy of His presence and in the perfect fellowship of His love. Such a vision carries us beyond the present conditions of earthly life, in which death and destruction are an inescapable element. Christ's final victory must mean a new heaven and a new earth, new conditions of existence, a resurrection to a new life in a body fitted to be the vehicle of such a transformed existence. It is to this glorious consummation of God's work in Christ that the hope of the Christian is directed. . . .

The Gospel . . . is a message from beyond death, the message of One who has conquered death and lives for ever, and who will in Himself consummate both the life of the world and the life of every individual. . . . He who was dead and is alive for ever more . . . has the keys of death and hell. We commit everything *now* into His hands who is Himself the End. We can do this with complete confidence, knowing that death and destruction have been robbed of their power, that even if our works fail and are buried in the rubble of human history, and if our bodies fall into the ground and die, nothing is lost, because He is able to keep that which we commit to Him against that Day. And we must work not merely with complete confidence but with vigour and eagerness, because we know that—in His mysterious wisdom—He has allowed the consummation of His purpose to wait upon our obedience, and entrusted to us the task of making His victory known and effective in every nation and in every sphere of life.[52]

10

The Christian Apologist

Always be prepared to make a defense to any one who calls
you to account for the hope that is in you.

(1 Peter 3:15)

The Modern World

For the last quarter century of his life, from his return to Britain in 1974
until his death in 1998, Lesslie Newbigin devoted himself principally to the
diagnosis and treatment of the crisis of the Christian faith in the modern
world, particularly the Western world. He sought by the Gospel to remedy
both the Church and the culture. It is as an apologist to the doubting and to
the unbelieving that he now became chiefly known.

The great issue, then, was that of "modernity." On the one hand, Newbigin
was happy to acknowledge the dazzling successes of the modern West in the
natural sciences and in technology, and to approve in many respects the
political gains made in the realms of personal freedom, human dignity, social
justice, and material welfare. Indeed, he claimed a historically Christian basis
for some of the achievements of modernity: the notion of a created universe
that was both regular and yet not itself divine provided both the possibility
and the permission for scientific investigation and technical use of the material world; the notion of humankind as persons created by a loving God for
freedom and for mutual care provided a grounding for individual liberties and
communal responsibilities. On the other hand, however, epistemological distortions and ideological degenerations had entered Western culture and were
affecting even the churches: the scientific and technological emphasis on efficient causality had squeezed out the notion of final causes or purpose in
existence; and liberties had turned into license, so that social and economic
chaos eventually attracted authoritarian responses and left a civilization sus-
pended between the horns of individualism and collectivism. As the problems
of modernity became more obvious, what some then started to call postmod-
ernity was looked on by Newbigin rather as late or advanced modernity, or
a civilization imploding. Certainly he found in the briefly fashionable ideology
of postmodernism—with its social fragmentation, its intellectual skepticism,
its moral cynicism, and its spiritual despair—no remedy for the crisis of modernity. Indeed, he often alluded in later years to the devil who returned with

335

seven worse of his kind to reoccupy the vacated house, as Jesus warned (Matthew 12:43–45; Luke 11:24–26). In this context, Newbigin saw the task of the Christian apologist as to contend for the "public truth" of the Gospel, to represent "the Gospel in a pluralist society" (to follow the title of his book from 1989). Facing the ideological pluralism of a night in which all cats are gray and the factual pluralism of competing accounts of reality, it was the apologist's business to maintain the validity of the claims of Christ and the Gospel and to defend and advocate their universal range and scope. "It is surely possible," he wrote in an essay on "Mission in a Pluralist Society," "to envision, and therefore also obligatory to work for, a society that is pluralist in the sense that the scientific community is pluralist, a society that believes in the possibility of knowing the truth about human nature and destiny and that is committed to seeking further understanding. Within such a society the Christian Church would be free and would be in duty bound to put forth its belief with the fullest confidence into the public argument about all human affairs. There would always be room for other views, but they too would have to sustain their part in the public debate."[1]

The modest beginnings of Newbigin's apologetical work go back, in fact, to an essay on "science and religion" from his student days at Westminster College, Cambridge, and to an article he wrote in 1938 for a series entitled "Can I be a Christian?" on the "Under Thirty" page of the London intellectual weekly *The Spectator*; I shall consider these in a moment. The worldly reference of the Gospel, the social location of the Church, the cultural interface of the Christian faith, and the public side of theology were already on display in two more substantial early works that have been considered in the chapter on Newbigin as a social visionary, namely, his first book, *Christian Freedom in the Modern World*, and his Bangalore lectures of 1941 on "The Kingdom of God and the Idea of Progress" which remained unpublished on account of wartime conditions. In his postwar missiological writings, he contributed, as we saw, to the recognition of the increasingly evident fact that the tasks of evangelism and service bore worldwide dimensions: Christian thinking and practice had now to deal not only with the consequences of the earlier spread and impending demise of Western colonialism but also with the decline of the faith in the older Christendom that made the West also a mission field again. From the late 1950s to the mid-1960s, Newbigin engaged in what I call in this chapter a mild flirtation with a secular reinterpretation of the Gospel that sought, somewhat overoptimistically, to find an accommodation between Christianity and certain movements in recent and contemporary history. By the 1968 Uppsala assembly of the WCC at the latest, Newbigin became thoroughly disillusioned with the secularizing trends in theology and Church, and he found himself haunted by the question overheard from the retired Indonesian general, T. B. Simatupang, at the 1973 Bangkok conference on "Salvation Today": "Can the West be converted?" To reflection and action on that theme the retired bishop consecrated his mature wisdom and practical vigor throughout his remaining years. There was an intellectual battle to be fought both within the churches and in the broader culture. There were

Christians needing to be strengthened and equipped for the witness that was required from the Church, humanly speaking, if Simatupang's question was to receive an affirmative answer. Certainly the answer, whether positive or negative, would affect the future face of Christianity and therefore, in God's good providence, the shape to be taken by the *missio Dei* in the world.

The first hints, then, of Newbigin's apologetic concerns and approach are to be found in his student paper—awarded an alpha-plus—entitled "The Relation of Theology's Claim to be a Science to Its Dependence on the Religious Life of the Theologian."[2] Although Newbigin would later have been more wary in his definition of "religious experience" as the basis for a "truly scientific" theology, this essay already adumbrates some of his abiding epistemological themes and presages the welcome that he would give to Michael Polanyi's Gifford Lectures published in 1958 under the title *Personal Knowledge*. The young Newbigin will neither concede the monopoly of the title *science* to a narrowly quantitative approach to the world nor permit religion to be confined to the realm of the private and individual, the esoteric and incommunicable. Positively put, Newbigin insists on "the necessity of keeping the experience of the religious life in the context of experience as a whole," and he stresses that a defining mark of all the various sciences is that their methods are to be determined in accordance with the nature of the object to be studied. Herein resides, however, a specific difference between the natural sciences and theological science: whereas natural science as a whole seeks "absolute rational consistency in all its statements," apparently operating on the assumption that "it is, in principle, within the power of man to hold all things within the grasp of his mind," theology by contrast seeks knowledge of a personal reality, and "it is the mark of a personal relation that in it the mind cannot grasp the totality of the other person's being in this way": "We know a person truly only in direct confrontation and response; if we try to know him in the scientific sense of reaching a complete understanding and assessment of his whole being without remainder, we fail in the deepest sense to know him at all." Nevertheless, it is Newbigin's assertion that, whether mutatis mutandis in the natural sciences or in religion, all "advance in knowledge" depends procedurally on a "passion for truth" in which there is "a blend of honesty and interest": "It takes honesty to recognize a fact for what it is, but it takes interest to find it at all." The subjective and the objective sides of knowledge can be distinguished but not separated.

The article in *The Spectator* of 1938 begins with the oblique claim that "in the Christian view of the world," there is to be found "an interpretation of the whole of human experience more reasonable than any other"; that "in the Christian understanding of man's nature and destiny, and in the practical experience of a common life of worship and mutual responsibility shared as a member of the Christian community," there resides "the only answer to totalitarianism which does not resolve itself into a defence of futilitarianism"; and that "in Christ," one may find "the answer to such personal problems as fear and worry." Yet, the writer declares, "it is not as an answer to the problems of philosophy that I believe in the Christian Gospel," "it is not as

the 'way out' for European civilisation that I turn to the Christian faith," and
"I was not drawn to Christ as one among many purveyors of personal success."[3] Newbigin clearly announces the kinds of apologetics that he will *not*
engage in (at least in the first place!):

> If these claims can be vindicated, are they not sufficient ground for being a
> Christian? The answer is that none of these claims can be vindicated if we
> go to the Christian faith simply for an answer to our problems. To the modern
> man who simply wants an answer to his questions the New Testament has
> nothing helpful to say—until he has first heard and answered the question
> which it puts to him. For the Gospel is something more serious than a so-
> lution to man's problems; it is a fresh and original word addressed to him
> from beyond the range of his problems by God, his maker.

If, then, the Gospel appears "irrelevant" to the immediate situation, that
seeming irrelevance is precisely a sign of the "tragedy" of existence in una-
wareness of a vaster and more terrifying environment and the ultimate issues
of life and death. The Gospel must first be heard on its own terms, for what
it says about our human situation. The Gospel, says Newbigin, is about "guilt
and forgiveness." The word guilt causes us offense: it conveys that we are
"misfits in the world," "at odds with the final authority of the universe,"
condemned as "mean and corrupt" by "the thing we are bound to acknowledge as good," "fit objects only for the wrath of God." How, Newbigin asks,
does all that impinge on modern Western man? In recent philosophical and
political history, "the Romantic identification of ourselves with the highest
we know" has ended up (it is 1938, and yet many of the cadres in the West
are still in denial with regard to Stalin) in "the Marxist identification of the
highest we can know with the most sordid of immediate political expedien-
cies—a view more dismal, but not more false." In a relatively comfortable
Britain, many have sought to evade the ultimate issues by saying that "ideals
are a matter of taste"; but "no one really believes that the difference between
truth and falsehood is of the same kind as the difference between black and
white coffee. No one is without some awareness of the authoritative claim of
goodness and truth to be obeyed. When we ignore it, it haunts us; yet if we
turn to face it, it condemns us. This is our situation, and not all the protests
of our outraged dignity, nor all our enthusiastic concentration upon futilities,
can alter it by one hairsbreadth."

The one thing that can alter the human situation—in its perennial and in
its contingent forms—is "that God, whose will is the personal reality behind
our ideals, against whom our treachery has been directed, should act so as
to make it possible for us to turn back again and face Him." That is where
the Gospel as forgiveness comes in:

> The Gospel is the witness of men to the fact that God has done just this, by
> the coming into the world at a certain point in history of Jesus of Nazareth,
> the Son of God, to share the humiliation of this situation of ours, and its
> culmination in a despairing death, and so to establish with us at the point
> of our deepest tragedy a secure bond of trust and love with Him against

whom we have been, and are, traitors. For us who have believed this witness, and have accepted Jesus as Saviour, His coming makes it possible for the first time to look clearly at our real situation, and to acknowledge that we are in truth rebels against God.

Without the knowledge of forgiveness this truth is too terrible to acknowledge, for it implies the sentence of annihilation upon ourselves. But in the light of the Cross we are driven to acknowledge with the deepest shame the extent of our treason, for it is measured by the costliness of God's forgiveness. And at the same time we acknowledge with unspeakable gratitude the love which came down to forgive us at such a cost. In this unique act of God, comparable only with creation itself, we meet judgement and mercy, wrath and sacrificial love, the forgiveness of a God who is both perfectly righteous and infinitely loving. And by it we are enabled again to face Him without subterfuge or make-believe, and to serve Him as those who would pay back an unpayable debt of gratitude.

Newbigin was well aware that "the majority of [his] contemporaries"—still in the thralls of the Enlightenment or Idealism—regarded this Gospel of guilt and forgiveness as "intolerable," either because it was "too humiliating" or because "their philosophical views prevent[ed] them from attaching such unique significance to any single historical event." The writer had no space to refute those views, he said; he concluded rather by reiterating his conviction that when confronted squarely with the Gospel, "one is facing the choice as to one's final destiny, and that for ever afterwards one must be either Peter or Judas, either disciple or traitor."

In September 1939 Newbigin returned to evangelistic work in India, where he spent the time of the Second World War: "Through all these years when the world was convulsed by war, our life as a family in Kanchipuram was so calm and peaceful as sometimes to make it hard to visualize what the rest of the world was suffering."[4] There is little record of Newbigin's political or theological reflections on contemporary events, perhaps because, as he coyly put it for the censor in his letter of October 1942 to friends in Britain, there was no chance for written communication "beyond what is suitable for transmission to the marines and other members of the forces" (*qui legit intellegat*, as Mark 13:14 advises). The war over, however, the rapid revival of the movement toward independence from the British Imperial Crown made India a precursor in the process of decolonization that would be such a prominent feature of the geopolitical scene for the next two or three decades. In Europe, the Nazi Germany that perpetrated the Jewish Holocaust and occupied large tracts of the Continent had been defeated by an Alliance that included not only the uninvaded United States, Britain (with its imperial forces), and the Free French but also the Soviet Union, which now proceeded to extend its empire westward as far as an iron curtain that came to symbolize a cold war between "the liberal democracies" and "the socialist lands." In 1949 the Chinese revolution brought Maoism into dominance. By that time Bishop Newbigin, consecrated in 1947, was in the thick of these events as an ecclesiastical statesman engaged in the World Council of Churches: he attended the inaugural assembly held at Amsterdam in 1948 under the banner of

"Man's Disorder and God's Design," and he chaired the heavyweight committee of twenty-five that was charged with the theological preparation of the second assembly at Evanston in 1954 and its theme of "Jesus Christ, the Hope of the World." How, then, in concrete terms did Newbigin see the Gospel of guilt and forgiveness impinging on the world at this particular point in human history?

The paper that Newbigin contributed to Amsterdam 1948 was entitled "The Duty and Authority of the Church to Preach the Gospel."[5] It offers an elegant and vigorous statement of the unique and perennial Gospel—its content and the responsibility for its proclamation—with which the readers of this book will by now be familiar, but Newbigin of course recognized that "in approaching any particular group of people with the Good News we have to relate our presentation of it to the place where they stand. We have both to state the Gospel in the language of the hearer and also to show his precarious foothold." The address to the particular situation of Church and world in 1948 comes through at five points especially, and all will remain important for Newbigin's thinking in the years directly ahead. First, there is the reaffirmation of the universal scope of Christ as creator and redeemer: "If we think and behave as though there were any created person to whom the Gospel message is not relevant, we deny the deity of Christ and treat him as though He were but a sectional or tribal demigod." Second, and consequently, "claiming the right to preach the Gospel from governments which deny it" may and must find its basis, not in a putative privilege the like of which might then be turned against Christians by others but rather in "the belief that all men are so created in God's image that they can only find their humanity in a freely given obedience to Him, and the belief that in Christ the Creator of all men has come among men in order that through His redeeming work all men may be enabled freely to give that obedience." The Church's claim that "the State should respect the freedom and responsibility of every man to make the decision of faith" is thus grounded in the Gospel itself *and* entails universal religious liberty. In a footnote, Newbigin recognizes that "there are many forms in which the issue of the freedom of the individual *vis-à-vis* the State is being pressed on our world. I speak here," he says, "only of the freedom of religious minorities to profess and propagate their faith. Where this specifically religious freedom is denied, all other forms of freedom are in danger." The Christian claim to freedom of faith may at times involve a readiness for martyrdom.

Third, to assert the Church's duty and authority to preach the Gospel, inalienably derived from Christ, is "not to deny that God is at work in manifold ways outside the bounds of the Church—every missionary knows in what wonderful ways men are prepared for their meeting with Christ in His Church (cf. Acts 10:1–8)—but it is to assert that the clue to all God's dealings with His human family is to be found in the Church, the particular, visible, historical society in which men and women are bound together in the communion of the Holy Spirit, and which grows through history by holding up Christ before men in Word and Sacraments, and by ministering His love to them in its common life." The discernment and interpretation of God's operation in the world as a whole will become an ever more pressing matter with the development of a global system of communications and commerce, of (in some sense) a universal culture.

Fourth, because the Gospel is "the message that the eternal Lord of history has revealed Himself in history in order to confront man with the final issue of his life on earth," there "is not an infinity of time either for the race or for the individual," and there is therefore an urgency about the proclamation and reception of the Gospel. Says Newbigin:

> History moves to a real climax, away from the social equilibrium which belongs to man's natural inheritance, and towards the final crisis where heaven shall stand nakedly revealed and men must enter on their heavenly inheritance or perish. The Church is bound by her own faith to take history seriously, and in this hour of history when on the one hand the sin of man threatens the utter destruction of human life, and on the other the Church has been granted a new vision of her world-wide unity, Christians will look up in hope knowing that their redemption draws near. This is an hour when the Lord is forcing us to see the whole destiny of the human race in the light of His eternal purpose, and when there is laid upon the Church, through which He has willed to make His purpose known, the duty and authority to proclaim to all men his saving acts. "Behold, now is the day of salvation."

"This hour," for Newbigin in 1948, meant ecclesiastically the twin ecumenical concerns of unity and mission. Geopolitically, it meant the threat of worldwide atomic war. In the years ahead, Newbigin would ponder the relation between the West as the source and vehicle now of a spreading but always ambiguous scientific, technological civilization and the West as for so long the principal home base of a Christianity whose missionary spread had helped to propagate a sense of history, indeed world history, and of freedom and responsibility, even while being mediated by culturally limited and sinfully inadequate carriers.

Fifth, the eschatological context of permanent crisis before the final judgment is the setting for what we have already found Newbigin saying on the matter of service as distinguished from evangelism: the Church, he writes in the Amsterdam article, "has also to do what is in its power—corporately and through its individual members—to bring all the common life of men, their economic and political systems, their family life and their social customs, under obedience to Christ."[6] The status of these areas of human existence and endeavor—in relation to God's activity, the Church's mission, and the divine Kingdom—will be matters for discussion when Newbigin starts to engage the notion of the secular.

The Secular Flirtation

While Newbigin was active in the theological preparations for the WCC Evanston assembly of 1954 on "Jesus Christ, the Hope of the World,"[7] he was also playing a part in the debates launched at the Willingen conference of the International Missionary Council in 1952.[8] At Willingen itself he was called on to redraft the text proposed by the theological group that had been swayed by "the attempt, led chiefly by Hans Hoekendijk and Paul Lehmann, to swing missionary thinking away from the 'church-centred' model which had dominated it since Tambaram and to speak more of God's work in the secular world, in the political, cultural and scientific movements of the time." Where, in particular, the group spoke of discerning by faith God's "carrying out [of] His judgement and redemption in the revolutionary movements of our time," the conference as a whole "was not ready to accept these ideas." Nor (yet, or quite ever) was Newbigin, but, as Newbigin himself later remarked, "their time was to come a few years later."[9]

A key point for Newbigin's thinking in the 1950s and 1960s occurred in 1957 during an all-night flight from India to Europe, when he worked through every mention of "the world" in the New Testament. In the resultant lecture delivered to a conference of missionaries and pastors at the Ecumenical Institute of Bossey, near Geneva, he proposed a biblical way of reading the sense of a "unitary history" that was developing across the globe and was practically embodied in "such demands as the demand for certain fundamental human rights and the demand and the expectation that this world shall be made a place more secure and more comfortable than it has been for our ancestors." These things were observable also in India, he said, for all the persistence of caste and of Hindu religion. Newbigin's thesis was that "what we are witnessing is the process by which more and more of the human race is being gathered up into that history whose centre is the Cross and whose end is the final judgment and mercy of God."[10] The ambiguities of that process—as to its source and its course—were hinted at in the following passage: "The ferment of change which arises from the impact of the Gospel, or at least of that kind of life which has its origin within Christendom, is the force which is giving an irreversible direction to that which was static or merely cyclical. When I say impact of the Gospel or of that kind of life which has its origin in Christendom, I include technology, western political ideas, Communism—all those things which have come into the eastern world from the West and have their roots in the Christian tradition." Newbigin later reported that his thesis "was taken by one of the participants, Arendt van Leeuwen, as the starting point for a very ambitious and influential book on *Christianity and World History*. As far as I was concerned," he went on, "this was the beginning of a shift in perspective which enabled me to understand the concern of people like Hoekendijk and Paul Lehmann which I had failed to understand at Willingen. It meant that I began the 'secular decade' of the 1960s with some enthusiasm for the 'secular interpretation of the Gospel,' and was the more ready to see its weaknesses before that decade ended."[11] Newbigin came to consider that the influence exercised in turn on him by the book of the Dutch missionary and theologian, A. T. van Leeuwen, was excessive;[12] and he would finally write that there never was, nor could

or should be, a "secular society" in the strong sense of that inherently ambiguous and even incoherent term.[13]

Newbigin's use of these ideas to do with "the secular" and "secularization"
was always much more dialectical than that of their fashionable exponents.
He remained aware of the six "paradoxes" that he had discerned in the New
Testament's interpretation of "the world" and "the nations" during his air-
borne study of the text. First, "the world belongs to God and yet it is in the
power of the devil" (contrast Matthew 2:1–11, in which the wise men from
the East acknowledged on the world's behalf the kingship of Christ, with
Matthew 4:1–11, in which the devil apparently had it in his power to offer
Christ the kingship of the world); "the world was made by Christ but the
world knew him not" (John 1:10). Second, "God was in Christ reconciling
the world to himself" (2 Corinthians 5:19), and Christ indeed came "to save
the world," yet "his coming is the judgment of this world" (cf. John 3:16–
21; 6:66–71). Third, Christ "came to gather all into one" (cf. John 10:16;
11:52; 12:32), "and yet his coming provokes the hatred of the world which
hates him and his disciples" (cf. John 15:18f.; 17:14), and there emerges the
figure of the antichrist, the "counterfeit of power and grace and wisdom,
gathering multitudes, deceiving even the elect," a false "universal saviour"
with whom Christ will come into "increasingly acute conflict" (cf. 2 Thessalonians 2:1–12). Fourth, "Christ calls people out of the world, but he sends
people into the world" (cf. John 17:14–21), as "salt of the earth" (Matthew
5:13) and "the bearers of God's purpose" (cf. Matthew 28:16–20); and "the
end is not a restored church but a new heaven and a new earth, a restored
world." Fifth, the world may bring judgment upon God's people for their
apostasy (cf. Matthew 12:41f.); "God uses the obedience of the heathen to
provoke his own disobedient people" (cf. Romans 10:18–21). Sixth, "all
men and all nations are ultimately judged by their relationship to Christ. And
yet Christ is hidden in the world, hidden so that even his own people do
not recognize him. 'When saw we thee hungry . . . ?' " (cf. Matthew 25:31–
46);[14] "to meet Christ we have to go into the place where apparently he is
not, i.e. the world which 'lies in the hands of the evil one' " (cf. 1 John 5:
19).

It remains that "the secular" and "secularization" were important categories for Newbigin in the 1960s; and it will be not only biographically but
also theologically instructive to relate what he learned through his adoption
and abandonment of them. The prime text must be his Firth Lectures, given
in 1964 at the University of Nottingham and published in 1966 as *Honest
Religion for Secular Man*.[15] From "secularism" ("a system of belief, or an attitude, which in principle denies the existence or the significance of realities
other than those which can be measured by the methods of natural science")
Newbigin distinguished "secularization" as a current "historical process of
which the writer and his readers are a part." Negatively, secularization may
be described as "the withdrawal of areas of life and activity from the control
of organized religious bodies, and the withdrawal of areas of thought from
the control of what are believed to be revealed religious truths"; positively,

as "the increasing assertion of the competence of human science and technics to handle human problems of every kind." Biblically, Newbigin affirms, "this can be seen as man's entering into the freedom given to him in Christ, freedom from the control of all other powers, freedom for the mastery of the created world which was promised to man according to the Bible"; and "at its best, the secular spirit claims the freedom to deal with every man simply as man and not as the adherent of one religion or another, and to use all man's mastery over nature to serve the real needs of man"—"a positive evaluation of the secular" which has won "increasing recognition among Christians." It does not necessarily deny all the claims of religion; nor is Newbigin willing, although fully recognizing "how powerful a source of evil religion can be," to accept quite all of Barth's attack on "religion" in the name of the Gospel or Bonhoeffer's tantalizing call for "a religionless Christianity." Rather, he wants to ask. what must be the—honest—"religion of a Christian who accepts the process of secularization and lives fully in the kind of world into which God has led us."

In his first and decisive chapter, Newbigin describes "the process of secularization" as "a universal fact" in a world that is being "unified" into a single, urbanized "network of interdependent thought and activity, linked together by innumerable commercial, political and cultural relationships, so that a movement in every part immediately affects every other." The emergent sense of "a common human history" does not find a basis in a common religious faith or a common ideology; rather, its substance and mood are inspired by "a shared secular terror and a shared secular hope"—on the one hand, the fear of global nuclear war, and on the other, the political and economic expectations associated at the time with the United Nations "Development Decade." As a theologian, Newbigin asks the question: "What is the relation of a secular, this-worldly unification of mankind to the biblical promise of the summing up of all things in Christ? Is it a total contradiction of it? Is it some sort of reflection of it? Or perhaps a devil's parody of it? Or has it nothing to do with it at all?" The question is unavoidable because the Bible "is in its main design a universal history," "an outline of world history"—and all historiography (history as *disciplina*) occurs by "selecting out of the almost infinite mass of recorded or remembered facts" (the *res gestae*) "that tiny proportion of them which is believed to be significant for the story." As long as we are still in the middle of it, we can tell the story of the human race "only on the basis of some belief, however provisional, about the point of the story as a whole." Newbigin discerns three links between "the biblical faith about the nature and destiny of man" and "the beliefs about the nature and destiny of man which are drawing all nations today into the sense of participation in a common, universal history." In each case he makes a positive point and then issues a warning.

First, Newbigin invokes the German physicist C. F. von Weizsäcker's *The Relevance of Science* (1964) in support of the view that the Christian concept of creation as law-abiding but nonsacral lay at the root of the tree on which the fruits of modern science have grown.[16] But then he recalls a conversation with a Chicago physicist who spoke of the "sudden swing from an exultant sense of mastery to an appalled feeling of guilt and anxiety" among the team that produced the first atomic bomb. According to Newbigin, to say in Bonhoeffer's fashionable phrase that man has "come of age" is to tell only half the truth: "To see the whole truth of the situation you must read the fiction of our time, as well as the scientific and technical journals. You must attend the theatre as well as the seminar. You must consult the psychiatrists as well as the cyberneticians. . . . One does not need to be a cynic to notice that the suicide rate varies from nation to nation in something like a direct ratio to what is called development."[17] According to the New Testament, says Newbigin on the explicit basis of Galatians 4:3–5, the only alternative to "slavery to the elemental spirits of the universe" is not an autonomous "mastery of the created world" but rather "responsible sonship of the Father in whose hands all created things, all so-called powers and forces, and all history lie": "Man is invited, if he will, to become God's son and heir and to have the freedom of the whole estate subject only to his obedience to the Father."

Second, the secular belief that the conditions of human life can be radically bettered—that "it is possible to create a new order of human existence in which poverty, disease and illiteracy are banished and all men can enjoy the privileges of what are called the developed nations"—could not possibly have sprung from any of the ancient religions of Asia or Africa; it is, says Newbigin, "a secularized form of the biblical idea of the Kingdom of God," "rooted in that understanding of human history as the sphere of God's redeeming acts which sets the Bible apart from all the other sacred literature of mankind." But once the biblical eschatology of a transgenerational community in a new heaven and a new earth has been removed, the dilemma entailed by the hope for a new order entirely within worldly history is how to "avoid the devaluation of the actual human person as he is now" for the sake of "a state of society yet to be realized." There will be a constant pressure "in the direction of some sort of messianism, either of the nation, of the leaders, or of the communist revolution."

Third, and in acknowledged dependence on A. T. van Leeuwen, Newbigin asserts that "the dissolution of the 'ontocratic' pattern of society in the non-western world can be understood as a new phase in the history of the fight of prophetic religion against the total claims of a sacral society, that is, a society completely unified around a religion and a cosmology." Van Leeuwen had argued for the central theme of the Bible as the prophetic attack on the total identification of the orders of society with the order of the cosmos, an attack made in the name of the living God whose rule is in no way to be identified with any earthly rule and whose will is not completely embodied in any human pattern of society. This was a constant struggle that extended beyond ancient Israel into the history of the Christian Church as the sacral pattern kept being broken open again by the living power of the prophetic tradition, nourished by the Bible; and the present worldwide process of secularization was a decisive and irreversible moment as, in particular, the "ontocratic societies of Asia which had endured with little break for four or five millennia are being disrupted and opened up to influences which challenge their very existence." This time, Newbigin's caveat concerns the lopsidedness of "a permanent principle of revolution": What is the positive ground on which it is possible to sustain the perpetual questioning of all settled social structures? Biblically, "the positive basis of the prophets' critique of society in their day was the word of the living God: 'Thus says the Lord.' Only from that affirmation could they proceed to negation. Only because God is higher and greater, and only because God *is*, could the prophet speak about negation, and announce even the total destruction of the society to which he belonged." Newbigin questions "whether the truly secular spirit can be sustained if it loses contact with that which gave the prophet his authority to speak— namely a reality transcending every human tradition and every earthly society, a God who is for man against all the 'powers.' "

Newbigin's summary theological evaluation of what in 1964 he and others were calling secularization ran thus:

> In so far as it rests upon the freedom of man to exercise a delegated authority over the natural world without fear of any "powers" other than the Creator himself; in so far as it seeks the freedom, dignity and welfare of man as man and challenges all authorities which deny this common dignity; in so far as it brings all mankind into a growingly interdependent unity of life: this movement of worldwide secularization is a genuine continuation of that liberation- history which is the central theme of the Bible. Just for that reason I am also driven to believe that this movement is misunderstood if it is seen out of that context; that it will recoil in self-destruction. Specifically I suggest that if the mastery which is given to man through the process of secularization is not held within the context of man's responsibility to God, the result will be a new slavery; that if the dynamism of "development," the drive to a new kind of human society, is not informed by the biblical faith concerning the King- dom of God, it will end in totalitarianism; and that if the secular critique of all established orders is not informed and directed by the knowledge of God, it will end in a self-destructive nihilism.[18]

Still in that first chapter, Newbigin rejects the move of those Christian "the- ologians" who, in a radical interpretation of the later Bonhoeffer, say that "the process of secularization must be carried through to the end. The reli- gious ideas and images of the Bible, even the idea of a God who is other than man and sovereign over man, must be given up. The Christian, too, must deal with the world *etsi Deus non daretur*. The process of secularization will not stop short with the dissolution of the pagan religions; it must dissolve what Christians have understood by religion itself. Man has come of age and has no need of the idea of God to help him deal with his environment." Newbigin insists that "questions about personal destiny, about the meaning and purpose of human life, will always be asked, whatever the umpires of the language game may say. If there is no doctrine of divine providence then the vacuum will be filled by some kind of belief in luck, in fate, or in the stars." If the West abandons what it had learned from the revelation of the Triune

God—namely, that "what man had to deal with was not an impersonal fate, but the One whose mind and purpose had been made manifest in Jesus, and that this same mind and purpose could be given to man through the Spirit to work as an inner principle guiding and sustaining him"—then "it is inevitable that some form of the ancient belief in fate should come in again to answer the questions which cannot be silenced as long as man remains human." Newbigin was already concerned about the rise of astrology in the dechristianized West, and he had not yet seen what its proponents would designate by the purloined term New Age.

In the following chapter of *Honest Religion for Secular Man* Newbigin offered a critique of several of the more affirmative "Christian responses to secularization," having already dismissed those which, on the other side, simply condemned the process out of hand. Among writers attempting a restatement of the Gospel in terms supposed to be intelligible to modern secularized man, we find Newbigin taking on a heavyweight, a bantamweight, and a featherweight. First, the existentialist individualism of Rudolf Bultmann is criticized as an "escape from history"; and, in an allusion to Bultmann's notorious essay of 1941 on "The New Testament and Mythology," Newbigin roundly declares that "it is no more and no less difficult to believe in the resurrection after the invention of electric light than before." Rather, in a move he would often repeat in his later apologetics, Newbigin conceded—and claimed!—that "it has never been possible to fit the resurrection of Jesus into any world view except a world view of which it is the basis. The resurrection is an event which you only really believe if every world view based on any other starting-point has collapsed. It was so for the first apostles, and it has never been otherwise for any generation since." The resurrection of Jesus, Newbigin asserts, is "the mighty act of God *par excellence*," and as such it is the clue to God's redemptive purpose ·for humankind and makes possible an obedient alignment with history's meaning and direction.[19]

Next, Newbigin takes on Paul Van Buren and his book *The Secular Meaning of the Gospel* (1963). Besides, of course, reducing the resurrection to an event in the disciples' minds, Van Buren turned "God," borrowing from R. M. Hare and R. B. Braithwaite, into a "non-cognitive *blik*," not a statement of "how things are" but rather a "perspective" indicating the user's intention to act in a certain way (say, loving the neighbor). Newbigin agrees that God is not an object among other objects (such would be an idol), but he maintains that Christian language referring to God is a matter of "confessing that one has been known, loved, called, redeemed by Another whom one only knows because He has so acted"; and the prophetic "Thus says the Lord" cannot be blandly altered to "The following is my program" without change of meaning. Because my behavior, says Newbigin, "is a matter not merely of my intention, but of God's will, the will expressed in Jesus Christ, there is room and need for the whole relationship of repentance, forgiveness, and asking for fresh strength, so that even my perversities become the way by which I am cleansed of self-love and enabled with a more consistent intention to love my neighbour."

Newbigin deals more gently with Harvey Cox and his "stimulating" book *The Secular City* (1965), but he denies that the technical model by which God would be made "our fellow team member in doing what needs to be done in the world" captures adequately "the truth of the biblical picture of the human situation, namely that at every point in his life man is confronted by and accountable to One who is not himself, but who is his maker and Lord." This latter point is indeed all the more important in a technologically advanced society:

> If, as we are often told today, thinking has to be functional rather than ontological, what stands between us and a society in which human beings are treated simply according to their usefulness to society? During World War II, Hitler sent men to the famous Bethel Hospital to inform Pastor Bodel-schwingh, its director, that the State could no longer afford to maintain hundreds of epileptics who were useless to society and only constituted a drain on scarce resources, and that orders had been issued to have them destroyed. Bodelschwingh confronted them in his room at the entrance to the hospital and fought a spiritual battle which eventually sent them away without having done what they were sent to do. He had no other weapon for that battle than the simple affirmation that these were men and women made in the image of God and that to destroy them was to commit a sin against God which would surely be punished. What other argument could he have used?[20]

Precisely in regard to secularization and the greater personal freedom it may bring, Newbigin makes the corresponding point that "in a secular society much more depends upon the personal responsibility of the individual than in a sacral society," so that the question of "the authority for my choices" becomes "all the more urgent." The Christian, for whom the authority is "the will and nature of God revealed in Jesus Christ," is bound to warn that, without the recognition of an authority "beyond the will of the strongest power," nothing will be able to prevent the pressures of political conformity from turning the secular state into "the demonic caricature of a sacral society, namely a society ruled by a post-Christian totalitarian ideology."

The remaining chapters of *Honest Religion for Secular Man* are devoted to epistemology, ecclesiology, and ethics, expounding what "knowing God," "being God's people," and "living for God" could "honestly" mean for "secular man" in the sense in which Newbigin was then defining him. In the first case, Newbigin does not address the "irreligious atheist" who "has never tried to enter into the religious experience" but rather the "honest believer" who is either overly impressed by the hegemonic claims to knowledge sometimes made on behalf of the natural sciences or feels desolate in the seeming absence of God. Arguing that "all knowledge is of a piece," the author begins by establishing the similarities and continuities between knowledge of God and knowledge of the world. With indebtedness to Michael Polanyi's *Personal Knowledge* (1958), Newbigin shows that all knowing is a "skill" that has to be learned; that all knowing is "an activity of persons in community," involving mutual trust and accountability to certain standards; that all knowing entails at least a provisional commitment to an existing framework of thought and knowledge, but that advances in knowledge occur only when the risk is taken that one may be proved wrong; that the natural scientist also has "faith"—which "is not 'knowledge' of the kind that could be fed into a computer"—but nevertheless "faith" in "the validity of the scientific method over against its predecessors." And as reality is "that which does not submit to our rules but requires us to submit to its," so "knowledge of another person involves the recognition of another centre of decision which it is not in my power to control." What is true of the mutual knowledge of persons at the level of humanity, Newbigin goes on to argue, is eminently true of our knowledge of the self-revealing God. And because "even our most intimate personal knowledge of one another is possible only through our sharing together in a common world of things and persons," so as creatures "it is in, with, and under this shared world of things and persons that we can know God." Just as, for us to know another person, that person "must meet us, and we must learn by speech, action, event, to know that person in the concreteness and particularity of his person," so "the Christian testimony is that God has so acted, so spoken, so given himself to us in Jesus, that we may know that he loves us, and that that knowledge is constantly confirmed and enriched through the events of daily life." The determinative self-revelation of God took place "in that bush burning in the desert, in that storm sweeping aside the waters and making a path for the escaping slaves, in that man hanging upon a gallows"; and, through word and sacrament, "the whole believing community goes back again and again to the place where the disclosure was made." Yet, given the living God's freedom and the need for our "continually fresh exposure to and encounter with his infinite creativity in the life of the world," the "tent of meeting [Numbers 9:15–23], the place where God's glory dwells and where God meets with man, the place of religion, has to be moved on as God's people follow their Lord through the world." That will provoke at times a sense of God's withdrawal, but "this desolation has to be accepted as the only gateway to renewed communion," for God is "utterly consistent and yet endlessly original." The life of faith means, in Evelyn Underhill's phrase, "total commitment to the will of God as it is disclosed in circumstances"; it means, in Dietrich Bonhoeffer's phrase, "enduring reality before God." Newbigin ends the chapter with Bonhoeffer's poem from prison:

> Who am I? They mock me, these lonely questions of mine.
> Whoever I am, Thou knowest, O God, I am Thine!

In the chapter on "Being God's People," Newbigin notes that regnant ecclesiologies were shaped during the centuries of Christendom, when "the Church had become the religious department of European society rather than the task force selected and appointed for a world mission." The process of secularization is changing that. Domestically, "the sacral unity of the Christendom society has been broken," thus allowing for "the recovery of a biblical, that is to say, a pre-Constantinian, understanding of the Church as a missionary community" even on what had been its own territory. Overseas, after

Western expansionism had circumvented the near-encirclement by Islam, there was an initial period in which the "mission station" functioned as an "outpost of Christendom"; but now, Western missionaries, "working in pagan sacral societies and finding themselves, to their own surprise, to be agents of secularization," have discovered that indigenous congregations and their evangelistically minded members "can be a true leaven in society, a spontaneously expanding fellowship with its own power to penetrate and grow, even in the difficult conditions of modern India." The time is ripe for the Church once more to see itself, in each and every place, as "a pilgrim people who have here no permanent quarters." As well as repeating the call of Jesus, "Come unto Me" (Matthew 11:28), the Church must again hear the command and promise, "Go, and I am with you" (Matthew 28:19f.): the Church "is itself the mission, the embassage of Christ sent to all men in his name, *going* in order to bid men *come, coming* in order to be *sent*, a gathering and a sending which is for all men."[21] Newbigin is careful to guard against the possible misunderstanding of a merely "functional" Church, for fellowship with God through the Holy Spirit makes the Church already a firstfruit of the harvest, a foretaste of the consummation; but he is most concerned to stress the Church's existence "for the sake of doing God's will in the world." From his own experience of living in an apartment block on the outskirts of the secular city of Geneva, Newbigin knows that the local congregation remains important for worship, teaching, witness, and service in the neighborhood on behalf of all;[22] but locality has become a much more complex notion in the modern world, and the Christian cells and groups which grow in all the various "sectors" of social existence should be regarded, Newbigin suggests, as equally valid "congregations," with "the full ministry of word, sacrament and fellowship as the centre of their common life while they seek to discover what God wills for their factory, their profession, their university." Moreover, "mission is not just church-extension": "God's apostolate is a more costly business than that," "there is a *kenosis*, a self-emptying involved"; "the corn of wheat has to fall into the ground and die" in order to bring forth its own fruit as fresh kinds of Christian life. That has its ecumenical implications, too: interdenominational programs of Joint Action for Mission have value as temporary expedients, but they "can only be pointers towards a fuller unity, and not a substitute for it," for finally "all the fruit is to be brought into one store." On the broadest scale, Newbigin concludes this ecclesiological chapter with a reading of secularization as an action of God who "himself scatters and gathers his Church":

> One of the things which the process of secularization is doing is to break up old patterns of community, among them venerable Christian communities, and to scatter Christians in ones and twos throughout the manifold and varied sectors of a complex society, as well as to gather a growing number of Christians all over the world in the service of technical development, government and education. If our doctrine of the Church is truly biblical, we shall recognize that here the ancient pattern is reasserting itself. God is scattering in order that he may gather, as he did with the infant Church in

Jerusalem when Herod put forth his hand to destroy it. When the fire is scattered, two things may happen: the scattered pieces may burn out, or they may start a wider conflagration. When the young Church was scattered abroad from Jerusalem this was what happened. It can happen again today. The condition is that Christians should remember that they are called to be a pilgrim people, to travel light, to leave behind, if necessary, much of the baggage accumulated during a long encampment, to follow without procrastination wherever the Spirit leads. For the promise of the Spirit is given only to those who go. And if the experience of one missionary is to be trusted, I would add that one has to run to keep up with him.[23]

In the final chapter on "Living for God," Newbigin tackles the notions of a secular society, a secular ethic, and a secular style of life for Christians, aiming to show how "a Christian must still be a religious man as well as a secular man at the same time." In the first section, a preliminary point concerns the need to distinguish among various parts of the world in relation to what is nevertheless supposed to be the near-universal phenomenon of secularization: in the western part of old Christendom, the Church still has some standing, and there remains "the half-conscious but enormously powerful influence of Christian ethical teachings on behavior"; in the communist parts of former Christendom, the Church lacks direct influence on public affairs, but by its "continued existence as a distinct entity unabsorbed by the omnicompetent State, it introduces into the life of these societies what one may call a de-sacralizing principle"; in the "new nations of Asia and Africa," where the Western impact has occurred not only through commerce, industry and political ideas but also, perhaps chiefly, through education that was often mission-based, the power of the old religions remains great but is diminishing, and the dominant problem is to find the foundations upon which a stable and coherent society can be built; in China, "where the greatest single effort of Western missionary expansion was concentrated, and where the Church is nevertheless an extremely small minority," very suddenly "the ancient sacral society has been replaced by a social order founded upon an apocalyptic and militant Marxism."

Newbigin then turns to a sustained engagement with the book of the British economist Dennis Munby, himself a Christian, *The Idea of a Secular Society and Its Significance for Christians* (1963). Although not unsympathetic to the advocacy of a positive Christian attitude toward the "secular society" that Munby presents in an "ideal" form, Newbigin signals a number of critical questions springing from the suspicion that Munby is tacitly relying on assumptions inherited from the Christian past concerning "the stability of society" and the "rationality and emotional coherence of the people about whom he is writing." Thus Munby's secular deflation of "the pretensions of politicians to be leaders of society and architects of manners and morals" will allow the avoidance of "the perils of messianism on the one hand, and of decay and dissolution on the other" only if there are in that society "enough men and women who acknowledge an obligation to the common good which has deeper foundations than those of loyalty to a political leaders or a political idea"; and "these foundations are *religious* foundations." Again, Munby's secular deflation of "the pretensions of judges who vainly attempt to preserve some relics of their former role as prophet-priests of the national conscience" will avoid the turning of judgment into an assertion of sheer power only if the earthly judge recognizes that behind him or her stands the Supreme Judge who judges all judges. When, in the admittedly sensitive field of education, Munby declares that the secular state will not enforce "a uniform attitude in respect of important matters of human behavior and values," Newbigin notices the question-begging character of "important" and thinks it impossible that particular schools, at any rate, should be able to nurture maturity without an acceptance of common aims. Again, economic organization will be, says Munby, a strictly utilitarian arrangement for achieving a limited aim; but such requires, Newbigin warns, "a highly developed sense of personal responsibility," and the question of motivation—which is that of a moral, and ultimately a religious, impetus—must be faced. Newbigin concludes that "the secular society is conceivable only if religion continues to be a living reality." More particularly, he denies that the idea of a secular society can be rightly understood "as if it were a timeless idea, a sort of blueprint for human society which, if it were adopted, would thenceforth provide the ideal conditions for human living." Newbigin was convinced that the idea of a secular society could be rightly understood only "in the context of a biblical understanding of history": "The Christian will see the struggle to make and keep society secular as part of his obedience to God who wills to preserve for men an area of freedom in which they may accept their calling in Christ, in obedience to whom alone is perfect freedom." Part of the missionary task of the Church is to interpret to others the historical process of secularization as "a calling to new responsibility before the Lord of history."

In going on to discuss "ethics in a secular context," Newbigin recognizes that the breakup of inherited behavioral patterns is "both an opportunity for new freedom and also an occasion for new strains upon the human spirit." According to Hendrikus Berkhof's *Christ and the Powers* (1962), "the law" belongs with those "powers" which the apostle Paul declares to have been disarmed by Christ of their claims to absoluteness, but in subjection to Christ they retain a positive function. In particular, "the law" supplies—even for Christians—the "guidance" without which human life is in any case impossible. Although seeing the life of a Christian as that of "an adult person in the Father's house," Newbigin dismisses as inadequate the New Morality that leaves matters at "love, and do what you will" and the Situation Ethics that would have behavior not merely conditioned but determined by circumstances. Although love is wholly positive, there are valid negatives that "fence off an area wherein we have the freedom to learn what love means," that "mark the edges of the road we have to travel," that "protect the traveller from falling over the edge into the ravine below." Invoking St. Paul's figure of the athlete in training (1 Corinthians 9:24f.; cf. Philippians 3:14), Newbigin considers that the "combination of freedom and discipline will be the mark of a truly Christian life"; secularization means that "the ethical behaviour of a Christian will be more, and not less, rooted in a religious discipline"; and the obedient following of Christ—Bonhoeffer's *Nachfolge*—entails "allowing Christ to conform us to himself, the incarnate, crucified and risen one." The "involvement in the world" that comes with the "secular life style" can properly be undertaken, says Newbigin in concluding the chapter and the book, only in responsibility before the Lord who is the world's—and the Christian's—maker, redeemer, judge, and renewer, which requires a religious "communion with God" that is focused in worship and prayer. Although half embarrassed by the term "divine transcendence," Newbigin declares that without the gracious and glorious reality of it "all talk of holy worldliness will become utterly shallow."

The dreaded outcome occurred for Newbigin at the Uppsala assembly of the World Council of Churches in 1968, when "Peter Seeger sang the well-known mockery of the Christian Gospel which affirms that 'there'll be pie in the sky when you die,' and the assembly sat in rapt silence and then applauded as though it were a new revelation of truth."[24] It was probably the Uppsala assembly that sealed Newbigin's disillusionment with secularizing theology. A final and formal renunciation took place in *The Gospel in a Pluralist Society* (1989), when Newbigin designated the notion of a "secular society" as a myth, both in the technical sense of "an unproven belief accepted uncritically to justify a social institution" and also flatly in the more popular sense of "a mistake" or "falsehood." It is simply untrue, Newbigin points out, that the further a society moves along the road of rationalization, industrialization, and urbanization, the more religion's role will (as Max Weber predicted) recede; and he instances the United States, with support from the Princeton sociologist Robert Wuthnow's contribution to *The Sacred in a Secular Age* (ed. P. E. Hammond, 1985). Then, too, the secularization theory has been used uncritically by some Christian theologians in order to "hold out the hope of peaceful coexistence between the religions and worldviews"; and Newbigin returns with a sharpened critique of Munby's *Idea of a Secular Society*: the secular society, with its putative tolerance for many worldviews and lifestyles, is in fact "committed to a very particular view of society," which "excludes the belief, shared by Islam, Judaism, and Christianity, that all human society, like all creation, is under the sovereign rule of God, and that the word 'God' is not a meaningless cipher but refers to one whose purpose for human society has been made known." There is, says Newbigin, no such thing as religious neutrality; and in the generation following Munby's book, the truth of Calvin's insight has been confirmed and emblematically displayed on the television screen, that the human mind is an idol factory: "What has come into being is not a secular society but a pagan society, not a society devoid of public images but a society which worships gods which are not God."[25]

In accentuating the positive in the secularization process, what Newbigin perhaps failed to see in the early 1960s—as he jetted between offices in London, Geneva, and New York and traveled the globe on behalf of the International Missionary Council and the WCC—was that the intensive and extensive spread of secularization may have been the last fling on the part of "the idea of progress" that he himself, in his Bangalore lectures of 1941, had subjected to criticism in light of "the Kingdom of God." Possibly, too, he had not so thoroughly digested the lesson that he later claimed to have learned from Germany in the 1930s, namely an appropriate skepticism in face of claims that "what looks like the new wave is 'God at work in the world.' "[26] Again, his thinking may have been colored by his Indian experience, in the idea that a "secular society" would both protect Christian interests and allow the free course of the Gospel in face of the Hindu nationalism of such a body as the Bharatiya Janata Party would prove to be.[27] Indeed, as late as his chapter in *The Gospel in a Pluralist Society* of (1989), Newbigin recognized that "in a country like India, long riven by interreligious tensions and struggling to create a single strong nation, the vision of a genuinely secular society was and is compelling,"[28] so that when his old friend M. M. Thomas in 1996 accused him of reneging on his earlier advocacy of a secular society, the shift in Newbigin may have been less a chronological than a geographical one, occasioned by what he had seen since his final return to the United Kingdom in 1974 of the disastrous results of Christendom's collapse in British society.[29] It seems, in any case, that in the 1960s Newbigin had still not fully realized that the technical, and perhaps political, achievements of "modernity" were not, in the concrete historical circumstances, to be had without the continuing vehicular function of a "Western civilization" that was itself in a deeper spiritual—intellectual and moral—crisis than he himself had yet perceived.[30] Even in his greatest period of enthusiasm for the secular, however, Newbigin held fast to the dimension of divine judgment that surrounded the summons to free choice for or against God's will and Kingdom in the greater and smaller affairs of historical existence in the world.

Some elements, at least, of what Newbigin valued in "the secular" would find a more satisfactory location when transposed into the category of the "public" character of the Gospel and of Christian faith which dominated his work as an apologist in the last quarter century of his life. That intellectual battle is the focus of the next section.

The Intellectual Battle

The key text is Newbigin's *Foolishness to the Greeks* (1986), which was developed from the sketch presented in *The Other Side of 1984*; it was followed by *The Gospel in a Pluralist Society* (1989) and by a host of lectures, articles, and shorter books. A number of themes recur in all these writings. Descartes is repeatedly fingered as the initiator and chief culprit in the intellectual—and finally moral and religious—error of the modern West: Newbigin would autobiographically recall the "profound and prophetic address" of J. H. Oldham, who spoke to the Edinburgh Quadrennial of the SCM in 1933 of "the radical departure of Europe from the Christian faith when it followed Descartes and the pioneers of the Enlightenment."[31] Descartes is blamed by Newbigin for setting the priority of doubt over faith in all matters of knowledge and for readmitting the dualism between matter and spirit that underlies the disastrous divorces between "facts" and "values," between "public" and "private," between "cause" and "purpose," which all tear asunder the Christian doctrines of creation, incarnation, redemption, and consummation and distort the Church's self-understanding and practices. The road by which the worm of destruction reaches the heart of congregational life is the false hermeneutic that deprives Scripture of its proper authority, says Newbigin, whether on the "liberal" or on the "fundamentalist" side of the street. To a professional historian of ideas, even if sympathetically inclined, Newbigin's narrative and judgments may appear unnuanced; but they may also be possessed of that clarity and sharpness which often characterize the insights and vision of pioneers and prophets. Newbigin's work confronts the reader with the task of discernment, less with regard to the details of his account than with regard to the truth of the Gospel that he was always seeking to clarify and apply in the concreteness of time and place.

Newbigin's Warfield Lectures, given at Princeton Theological Seminary in March 1984, formed the basis of the book *Foolishness to the Greeks: The Gospel and Western Culture*.[32] At the outset the author states his purpose: "to consider what would be involved in a genuinely missionary encounter between the Gospel and the culture that is shared by the peoples of Europe and North America, their colonial and cultural offshoots, and the growing company of educated leaders in the cities of the world—the culture which those of us who share it usually describe as 'modern.'" He declares his angle of approach to be that of a "foreign missionary" who, unlike such systematic theologians of culture as Paul Tillich or H. Richard Niebuhr, has had from India "the experience of the cultural frontier, of seeking to transmit the Gospel from one culture to a radically different one"; and the field of his attention, unlike that of the many recent missiological studies devoted to the problems of "indigenization," "adaptation," or "contextualization" in every other culture from China to Peru, is "the most widespread, powerful, and persuasive among all contemporary cultures," namely "modern Western" or "post-Enlightenment culture," in which resistance to the Gospel is now proving perhaps strongest of all and in which certainly the Churches are shrinking in contrast to many parts of Africa, Asia, and the Pacific. A culture is defined by Newbigin as "the sum total of ways of living developed by a group of human beings and handed on from generation to generation"; at the center is language as the means by which a people "express their way of perceiving things and of coping with them"; around that center cluster their visual and musical arts, their technologies, their law, their social and political organization; and fundamental to it all is the people's religion, the "set of beliefs, experiences, and practices that seek to grasp and express the ultimate nature of things, that which claims final loyalty." The Gospel is described as "the announcement that in the series of events that have their center in the life, ministry, death and resurrection of Jesus Christ something has happened that alters the total human situation." This announcement itself, from the beginning and ever since, is "culturally conditioned," yet "the Gospel calls into question all cultures, including the one in which it was originally embodied." The rest of the first chapter looks in general at the issues raised by the cross-cultural communication of the Gospel.

From the account given by the Apostle Paul in Acts 26 of his own conversion Newbigin extracts a three-point paradigm: Saul heard the divine voice addressing him in the language of his native culture ("in the Hebrew tongue"); the voice summoned him to a radical turnaround in his understanding and practice of the will of God ("Why persecutest thou Me?"); and it was only the sovereign Lord ("I am Jesus") who had the authority to do that. That same pattern, says Newbigin, is "brilliantly exemplified" in the Johannine writings, in which the idiom of Hellenistic Gnosticism is employed in order to challenge the outlook and life of its users on behalf of the Word made flesh. In subsequent missionary preaching, Jesus is first presented "as the missionary perceives him," but new converts eventually gain from the Bible a standpoint from which both to see their own traditional culture in a new way and also to observe the discrepancies between the picture of Jesus they (from within their own culture) find in the New Testament and the picture that was communicated by the missionary. This in turn may help the missionary to become aware of the cultural conditioning of his own view of Jesus.

Because such a corrective witness today takes place under the worldwide shadow of a modern culture that "has itself sprung from roots in Western Christendom and with which the Western churches have lived in a symbiotic relationship ever since its first dawning," the question becomes: "From whence comes the voice that can challenge this culture on its own terms, a voice that speaks its own language and yet confronts it with the authentic figure of the crucified and living Christ so that it is stopped in its tracks and turned back from the way of death?" In a first foray toward the desired encounter between the Gospel and modern culture, Newbigin gives a further turn to the screw in Peter Berger's argument concerning plausibility structures, a plausibility structure being "a social structure of ideas and practices that create the conditions determining what beliefs are plausible within the society in question." In *The Heretical Imperative* (1979), Berger had argued that in the current collapse of the inherited tradition and the absence of any generally acknowledged plausibility structure, all are now obliged to make a purely "individual choice"—in line with the original meaning of *hairesis*—concerning ultimate questions of belief and conduct. Newbigin argued that the ideological pluralism thereby implied was itself a plausibility structure that might and should be challenged by the Gospel. Christians could not allow the Gospel to be treated as one option on the plane of "comparative religion." In an ad hominem move against Berger, Newbigin further argued that by locating religious experience in an "enclave" that nevertheless was subject to "sober rational assessment" according to the valid but (according to Newbigin) incomplete rationality of the natural sciences, Berger was exemplifying a typically modern split between private and public, between value and fact. Moreover, there was an internal inconsistency in the position of those who

favored pluralism in the matter of "personal values" while maintaining a
hard-nosed insistence in the public world of the sciences that "a fact was a
fact was a fact." The Protestant churches, at least, have largely accepted these
dichotomies, Newbigin observed; and the task is to recover ways of letting
the Gospel claim be heard—not as "invincible ignorance" but rather "in all
its winsomeness and awefulness"—that "in the man Jesus there was actually
present the one who is the Creator and Sustainer and Lord of the entire
universe, that he is the light of the world, and that it is only in that light
that both the world religions and the whole structure of modern science will
ultimately be seen for what they truly are."

Whereas modern Christian apologetic has sought to "explain the Gospel in
terms of our modern scientific worldview," Newbigin's aim is to find a way
of reversing the criteriological priorities so as to "explain our modern scientific
worldview from the point of view of the Gospel." In the second chapter of
Foolishness to the Greeks, he undertakes the "profile of a culture."[33] He starts
by looking at "the genesis of our modern culture where it becomes fully
conscious of itself, the point which those who experienced it called 'the Enlightenment.' " This "collective conversion" of the European mind—Newbigin
invokes Paul Hazard's classic title *La crise de la conscience européenne* (1935)—
was immediately prepared by "the new method in philosophy opened up by
Descartes" and by "the new developments in science associated with the
names of Bacon, Galileo, and Newton": it was the conviction of Europeans
that they "now knew the secret of knowledge and therefore the secret of
mastery over the world." Whereas medieval thought had seen the world of
nature as manifesting everywhere the divine purpose that had been revealed
in the events confessed in the Church's creed, the new explanatory framework
drew on the work of science that disclosed a world "governed not by purpose
but by natural laws of cause and effect"; "efficient causality" sufficed without
teleology. Science, so understood, worked from the analysis of observed phenomena to a mathematical reconstruction that enabled all reality to be quan-
tified and arranged in a comprehensible structure; and "the geometric spirit"
was applied to all forms of human knowledge. "Reason," so understood, was
sovereign, recognizing "no authority other than what it called the facts."
Kant's challenge "dare to know" was addressed to the rational individual,
whose right to exercise his reason in the search for reality implied the right
to life, liberty, and property. Whereas medieval society had been held together
by a complex web of reciprocal rights and duties, the new "rights of man"
were individually oriented, and even "the pursuit of happiness" came to be
so defined—with the extra pathos that because "the methods of modern science provide no grounds for belief that there is anything beyond death," "the
whole freight of human happiness has to be carried in the few short and
uncertain years that are allowed to us before death ends it all," and "the
quest for happiness becomes that much more hectic, more fraught with anxiety than it was to the people of the Middle Ages." Moreover, rights demand
a juridical basis, a legal and social structure that guarantees them. In contrast
to the complex network of mutuality in medieval society, modernity invested

the duty to honor claims in the nation-state, which, given especially the infinite nature of the quest for happiness, finds itself overdemanded and thus—given now the expectations of mundane progress raised by technology coupled with the decline of a teleological view of creation and history culminating in the transcendent Kingdom of God—is exposed to the totalitarian temptation of a paradoxical sacrifice of the present and passing generation for the sake of the supposed happiness of those yet unborn. At the very least, "the young become symbols of hope, while the old can be neither objects nor subjects of hope but only an increasingly burdensome embarrassment," so that "the transmission of traditional wisdom in families from the old to the young is replaced by systems of education organized by the state and designed to shape young minds toward the future that is being planned."

Although Newbigin's account of the birth of modern Western culture began by concentrating on the realm of ideas, he was clearly aware that ideas develop in the context of social and political life, in which they may find stimulus, support, and validation. He presents a further display of such interaction. By the extension of analytical and mathematical reason, "work" gets reduced to "labor": where the purposeful work of the traditional craftsperson spanned the whole process from raw material to finished product, the new division of labor breaks up the process and, although the quantity of finished articles is greatly increased, the contribution of any operative in the chain is assimilated to the repetitive action of a machine, and "the individual worker does not know whether his product is going to make a family car or a fighter plane"; and, rather than work being directed toward an enduring achievement, "built-in obsolescence" is needed to keep the system going in "an unending cycle of production and consumption." Thus a further consequence of the division of labor is the growth of the market economy: whereas money as a means of exchange had earlier been only a minor and marginal part of the economy, now the market moved into the central place as the mechanism that linked all the separate procedures with each other and with the consumers; and whereas economics had been subject to ethical considerations about the requirements of justice and the dangers of covetousness, now it became "the science of the working of the market as a self-operating mechanism modeled on the Newtonian universe," its "law of gravitation" being "the law of covetousness assumed as the basic drive of human nature." Yet another consequence of the division of labor that came with the removal of work from home to the factory was the division of family life, a sexual fissure in society: it became "the men who operated the public world of the factory and the market, and the women who were relegated to the private sector"; "the man dealt with public facts, the woman with personal values." And yet again, the mechanization of work led to the growth of huge cities for the sake of concentrated production and distribution; such urbanization breaks up the single human milieu of traditional rural societies that embraces work, leisure, family relationships, and religion and instead introduces people into a multiplicity of human networks where they are compelled to choose their identity and often fall into anxiety, doubt, and even despair. In sum, "the division and mechanization of labor, the development of a market economy, the dichotomy of public and private worlds, and the growth of big cities" are all "key characteristics of modern culture," which "rest upon and in turn reinforce the new view of the human individual that marked the birth of the modern world at the Enlightenment." Nor can Newbigin resist adding bureaucratization to the list of woes: bureaucracy applies a mechanical model to the organization of society, turning each individual into an anonymous, replaceable unit, analyzing every situation into the smallest possible components, and recombining these elements in terms of logical relationships that can be expressed in mathematical terms and fed into a computer; "bureaucracy is the rule of nobody and is therefore experienced as tyranny."

Newbigin concludes that "the primary clue to understanding the whole of these vast changes in the human situation" is to be found in "the abandonment of teleology as the key to the understanding of nature," for it is this that underlies "that decisive feature of our culture that can be described as the division of human life into public and private, and as the separation of fact and value."[34] Since modern science methodologically eliminated the idea of purpose from astronomy, physics, and chemistry, its enormous achievements have disposed many to exclude the category also from explanations regarding both animal and human behavior—"and yet purpose remains an inescapable element in human life." The "strange fissure [that] runs right through the consciousness of modern Western man" is concretely seen in the fact that "the immense achievements of modern sciences themselves are, very obviously, the outcome of the *purposeful* efforts of hundreds of thousands of men and women dedicated to the achievement of something that is valuable—a true understanding of how things are." At the intellectual level, the fissure expresses itself in "the search for 'value-free' facts"; and the paradoxical ideal that says "the only really valuable things are value-free facts" has enormous power in the public life of modern societies. On Enlightenment terms, there is no logical move possible from a statement of fact ("This is the case") to a judgment of value ("This ought to be approved or done"); for if the assumption is that statements of fact do not include statements of purpose, then "no moral law of universal validity can be founded upon the view of what-is-the-case that post-Enlightenment science taught people to hold."[35] But "if purpose is not a feature of the world of 'facts,' and if people [nevertheless] entertain purposes, that is their personal choice and they will have to create these purposes for themselves"; their purposes will, however, have no authority beyond the strength of conviction with which they hold them, for they are simply "personal opinions" belonging to "the private world." Newbigin points to the dilemma which this poses for public education: whereas children are taught "scientific facts" as "public truth," how are they to be taught "values," which—in the absence of an agreed vision concerning the ultimate nature (and purpose) of things—are a matter of "private opinion"? In this whole context, then, "religion" is reduced to "inner experience," and "theology" to "anthropology"—whereas the Bible "is dominated by the figure of the living God who acts, speaks, calls, and expects an answer" and is "as much about God, about the created cosmos, and about the world of public events as it is about what can be called 'religious experience.' " If the Bible is true, says Newbigin, then, contrary to the modern illusion, it is not a matter of our choice whether "the one by whose will and purpose all things exist, from the galactic system to the electrons and neutrons, has acted and spoken in certain specific events and words in order to reveal and effect his purpose and to call us to respond in love and obedience." To show that that even *might* be the case, says Newbigin, he must next do two things: first, "look at the strange book we call '*the* Book' (the Bible) and ask what it is and how we can understand its authority"; then, "inquire what would be involved in both theory and practice in such a direct challenge to the very foundations of the culture of which we are ourselves a part."

Accordingly, the third chapter of *Foolishness to the Greeks* is entitled "The Word in the World."[36] The author notes that liberal Protestant apologetics since Schleiermacher in the early nineteenth century have sought to save the Gospel by locating it firmly on one side of the divide between the world of public facts and the world of private values ("Christian doctrines," wrote Schleiermacher, "are accounts of the Christian religious affections set forth in speech"). But such a strategy is readily exposed to the quickly supervening critique of Feuerbach that the very idea of God is the projection of an image of the human ego onto the cosmos. The Bible, by contrast, has been surrendered by liberal Protestants to the world of public facts, in the sense that it has been subjected to critical investigation by the tools of a "modern historical science" that has itself been left uncriticized. The believing reader may then "draw illumination from the text for his own faith. But his faith does not rest on the authority of the text. It is rather that he perceives a congruence between the faith to which the text bears witness and his own." Or else the modern reader may extract from the Bible principles for conduct or concepts that enable one to deal with reality in distinctive ways; but again it is not clear, with regard to such concepts or principles, why their provenance from the Bible "should give them any authority other than the authority that their intrinsic rightness may give them to the reason and conscience of modern men and women." Even those theologians of "salvation history" who locate "God's revelation of himself not in the text itself but in the events reported and interpreted in the text" are not always clear whether "the series of divine acts that constitute the *Heilsgeschichte* is to be understood as forming the central thread of universal history, thus replacing the world history taught in secular academies, or whether it is understood as the clue to the specifically religious experience that is available as a personal option within the public history." When, as with Rudolf Bultmann, the biblical text is indeed allowed to address the reader, it can do so "only in the pure immediacy of subject to subject," for "faith is not faith if it seeks security in what are called facts—whether metaphysical or historical," and so "Bultmann and his followers can cheerfully accept the dissolution of most of the historical material in the gospels in the powerful acids of scientific criticism and yet find in the New Testament that which summons them to faith understood as authentic existence," but in such a way that "the Christ of faith could, it would seem, function very well on Bultmann's terms without being confused by any sort of association with the so-called Jesus of history." Sadly, those on the fundamentalist wing of Protestantism who seek to defend both text and history remain themselves trapped, says Newbigin, in an "Enlightenment concept of factuality that is foreign to the Bible," as though there were "a world of so-called objective facts that can be 'scientifically' known apart from any faith commitment on the part of the knower." Newbigin returns in the next chapter to the question of scientific epistemology; meanwhile he continues with his discussion of the nature of the Bible and the appropriate way to read it.

The problem for modern readers resides in the "chasm" that separates the Bible from the pre-understanding that they bring to it from modernity. That chasm is not so much, for Newbigin, a matter of chronologically separated epochs (we shall see that he has a hermeneutical way of dealing with that) as rather the qualitative difference signaled by "the many passages of Scripture that emphasize the incomprehensibility of its message by the wisdom of this world, the radical discontinuity between all human wisdom, even the most profound, and the revelation with which Scripture is concerned." "Foolishness to the Greeks" (1 Corinthians 1:25f.)! Yet the discontinuity, although radical, cannot be total, for otherwise there could be no awareness of it on either side. Newbigin proposes an analogy with the insight concerning "paradigm shifts" that remains valid from Thomas Kuhn's book *The Structure of Scientific Revolutions* (1962): "While there is radical discontinuity in the sense that the new theory is not reached by any process of logical reasoning from the old, there is also a continuity in the sense that the old can be rationally understood from the point of view of the new. In Einstein's physics, Newtonian laws are still valid for large bodies in slow motion. Newtonian physics is still valid for mechanics. Thus, to recognize a radical discontinuity between the old and the new is not to surrender to irrationality. Seen from one side there is only a chasm; seen from the other there is a bridge." Analogously, Newbigin suggests, the "conversion" brought by the novelty of the Gospel may allow "a place for the truth that was embodied in the former vision"— the "old" in this case being "modernity"—"and yet at the same time offer a more inclusive rationality than the older one could."[37] Again, that is a possibility that is tested in Newbigin's next chapter.

Meanwhile, a rather less dramatic matter of hermeneutics is treated. Modern—or, if one prefer, postmodern—hermeneutics allows the recognition that "the Bible comes into our hands as the book of a community, and neither the book nor the community are properly understood except in their reciprocal relationship with each other":

> Quite clearly, the community as it now exists is being continuously shaped by the attention it gives to the Bible. Equally clearly, the community's reading of the Bible is shaped by a tradition that has been developed through the experience of previous generations of believers in seeking to understand and put into practice the meaning of the book. . . . Every Christian reader comes to the Bible with the spectacles provided by the tradition that is alive in the

community to which he or she belongs, and that tradition is being constantly modified as each new generation of believers endeavors to be faithful in understanding and living out Scripture. This is the hermeneutical circle operating *within the believing community.*[38]

And this living process corresponds precisely to the nature of the Bible itself, for—as one of its positive achievements—"modern scholarship, using the tools of historical and literary criticism developed since the Enlightenment, has enabled us to see that the present text of Scripture as we have it is the result of just such a continuous reshaping of tradition in the light of new experience." Accordingly, "the Bible functions as authority only within a community that is committed to faith and obedience and is embodying that commitment in an active discipleship that embraces the whole of life, public and private. This is the plausibility structure within which the faith is nourished."

Now Newbigin recognizes that "although it may be very shocking to a certain kind of post-Enlightenment Protestant conscience, it is not the Bible by itself but the Church confessing the mystery of faith that is spoken of as the pillar and bulwark of the truth (1 Timothy 3:15f.)." To maintain the primacy of canonical Scripture in the reciprocal relationship between Scripture and tradition, Newbigin turns for help to Hans Frei's book, *The Eclipse of Biblical Narrative* (1974), from which he has learned to speak of the Bible as "that body of literature which—primarily but not only in narrative form—renders accessible to us the character and actions and purposes of God": "The way in which we must read the Bible today is controlled by the fact that we are, from moment to moment in the complex events of our time, dealing with and being dealt with by the same living God who meets us in Scripture, seeking his will, offering our obedience, accepting the share he allots to us of suffering, and looking for the final victory of his cause." Admittedly, "to discern God's purpose and to be obedient to it among all the ambiguities and perplexities of life is always a struggle. We may often be wrong both in our understanding of what God is doing and in our attempted obedience, just as it is made clear in Scripture that the people whose stories it tells were often wrong, or only partially right, in their discernment of God's purpose." Therefore, "as part of the community that shares in the struggle, we open ourselves continually to Scripture, always in company with our fellow disciples of this and former ages," and "we constantly find in it fresh insights into the character and purpose of the one who is 'rendered' for us in its pages."

In transition to the next chapter, Newbigin returns to the clash between the old plausibility structure of modernity and the novel plausibility structure of the Gospel. The flashpoint is the resurrection of Jesus. The community of faith "makes the confession that God raised Jesus from the dead, and that the tomb was empty thereafter." On the terms of modernity, the "Easter event" is interpreted as a "psychological experience" on the part of the disciples. The Gospel that "the living God who was present in the crucified Jesus is now and always the sovereign Lord of history" demands and makes possible "the development of a new plausibility structure in which the most real of all realities is the God whose character is 'rendered' for us in the pages of Scripture."

The fourth chapter of *Foolishness to the Greeks* is entitled "What can we know? The dialogue with science."[39] "The public philosophy" of "our culture," Newbigin asserts, is "atheist": "For the ordinary educated person in our society," under the influence of "popular science," "the real world is not the world of the Bible but a world that can be explained, and is being more and more fully explained, without reference to the hypothesis of God." Some Christians cope with the debate between science and religion by regarding the two as different ways of "seeing as," but this merely reflects the dichotomy between the public world of facts and the private world of values, and there should be no long-term future for this kind of peaceful coexistence, for "if we are talking as the Bible talks about God, who is Creator and Governor of all things, who acts in specific ways, and whose purpose is the criterion for everything human, then there is an inevitable conflict." "Is it or is it not the case," asks Newbigin rhetorically,

> that every human being exists for the joy of eternal fellowship with God and must face the possibility of missing that mark, forfeiting that prize? If it is the case, it ought to be part of the core curriculum in every school. It will not do to say that the determination of character by the structure of the DNA molecule is a fact that any child must learn to understand, but that the determination of all proper human purposes by the glory of God is an opinion that anyone is free to accept or reject. The question of which is the real world cannot be permanently evaded.

Several more recent developments in the history, philosophy, and practice of the natural sciences, Newbigin points out, have opened the door for Christian theology to engage in a more substantial dialogue. First, it has been plausibly argued that a decisive factor in the origin of modern science was the biblical vision of the world as both rational (otherwise consistent investigation would be impossible) and contingent (here the point of contrast with regarding the universe as, say, "the emanation of Brahma" is not so much that the latter renders scientific investigation sacrally impermissible as rather that it renders it uninteresting and unnecessary, because it makes the universe part of "the eternal cycle of evolution and involution" and "its ultimate secrets are to be discovered within the recesses of the human soul, where it makes direct contact with the cosmic soul"). Insofar as western science later took on a sheerly mechanistic cast, it was falling back into the idea of a *completely* immanent rationality; but this fetter on the further development of genuine science has been broken, Newbigin argues, by some twentieth-century advances that restore the notion of contingency: "Contemporary physics recognizes a finite and therefore contingent universe; it acknowledges limits beyond which its own axioms do not operate; and in the Gödelian theorems, it recognizes that mathematics itself does not consist of absolute and eternally necessary truths but has in it an element of contingency." And contingency, he further argues, allows for the reintroduction of the notion of purpose.

At the subjective end, the very deliberate character of scientific investigation lets the notion of purpose into scientific knowing. The scientific enterprise is "impregnated through and through by commitment to a purpose" (and hence is not "value free"). Indeed, it depends on "a preliminary act of faith," "faith that the enterprise is worthwhile." It depends, too, on the scientist's ability to recognize significant patterns in the object of study: "Our recognition of a significant pattern is an act of personal judgment for which there are no rules. It is a judgment of value: the pattern represents something a human being finds meaningful in terms of intrinsic beauty or purpose. And although rules have been devised for quantifying the regularity in a series that may or may not be random, the application of these rules by the scientist to a particular case is a matter of personal judgment that depends on skills acquired by practice and is not capable of quantification or of verbal definition."[40]

Moving, then, to purpose at the objective end, Newbigin at first appears to suspend judgment on the question of the presence of purpose at the levels of physics and chemistry; but it is "absurd," he claims, to forfeit the notion of purpose once biology is reached, given "demonstration of the capacity of even very lowly animals to recognize and solve problems, in other words, to engage in purposeful activity." Jumping from earthworms to humankind, how much more absurd is it to apply reductively mechanistic models to sociology, economics, and (*reductio ad absurdissimum*) public administration! It is actually the machine, in the everyday sense of that word, that supplies Newbigin with a homely example to make his basic point about purpose: "Not even a machine can be explained by the chemical and physical analyses of its component wheels and shafts and pulleys. It is possible to show how the functioning of each part contributes to the operation of the whole, but it would be absurd to say that we have 'explained' the machine as a whole if we have no idea of the purpose for which it was designed and built"; thus, "in seeking to understand a machine, we employ the concepts of both efficient cause and final cause."

Newbigin's formal argument proceeds by ascending through a hierarchy of "levels of explanation, stretching through physics, chemistry, and mechanics to biology"—and beyond. Thus:

All chemical reactions are conditioned by the molecular changes that are the subject of physics, but chemistry as a distinct discipline cannot simply be replaced by physics. All mechanical operations are conditioned by the chemical and physical operations of the component parts of the machine; but mechanics is still a necessary form of knowledge and cannot be replaced by physics and chemistry. All animal life is conditioned by the successful working of the limbs and organs, which is in turn conditioned by the laws of chemistry and physics and mechanics. But biology is still a proper study in its own right. The Laplacean ideal, which pretends that by a complete knowledge of the smallest elements we would know everything, is absurd.

The next level is "our understanding of other human beings. Here the new factor entering in is the possibility of full, or at least growing, reciprocity." In a mature relationship, we "attend to the other person, not as a physical or chemical or biological entity but as the subject of beliefs, experiences, and purposes similar to our own"; such attention is "a purposeful effort to understand, and it is evoked by the purposeful effort of the other party to communicate." Furthermore, in case of conflict, appeal to the proper objective of purposeful action is irrelevant if it means only "what I want for myself"; it must aim more widely, and in the end universally, at the "good absolutely, good for all." The mutual relationship between two mature human beings "can be sustained only if we both acknowledge something that has authority over both and if each trusts the other to acknowledge this." This notion of "the good" as having authority for the assessment of conflicting purposes is a "pointer" to the fact that "we cannot stop with the human level"; it also reaches "the limit of what is usually called natural theology." The next stage is to ask whether "the good" is determined by the character and purpose of "a supernatural personal reality" that has communicated itself to us. Here "another kind of enterprise begins, and another kind of language has to be used—the language of testimony":

> The Christian Church testifies that in the actual events of this finite, contingent, and yet rational world of warped space-time there are words and gestures through which the Creator and Sustainer of the world has spoken and acted. It is not that the events are anything other than part of the unbroken nexus of happenings within space-time that can be analyzed and classified along with all the rest. They are not "interventions" by someone who is otherwise absent. And—even more important—it is not that we are talking about something called religious experience as a separate form of cognition. That the word *religion* points to a kind of experience that is widely diffused throughout human history is an obvious fact. But that what is called religion is the only or the primary form of contact between the human race and its Creator is a mere assertion that has no logical foundation. It is simply one of the unexamined assumptions of our culture. As a member of the Christian Church and from within its fellowship, I believe and testify (and the shift to the first person singular is, of course, deliberate) that in the body of literature we call the Bible, continuously reinterpreted in the actual missionary experience of the Church through the centuries and among the nations, there is a true rendering of the character and purpose of the Creator and Sustainer of all nature, and that it is this character and purpose that determines what is good. Because I so believe and testify, I reject the division of human experience into a private world, where the "good" is a matter of personal taste, and a public world, where "facts" are regarded as operative apart from any reference to the good. I believe that all created beings have a sacramental character in that they exist by the creative goodness and for the redeeming purpose of God, that nothing is rightly understood otherwise, and that, nevertheless, God in creating a world with a measure of autonomy and contingency has provided for us a space within which we are given freedom to

search, to experiment, and to find out for ourselves how things really are. I believe that the whole of experience in the natural world, in the world of public affairs, of politics, economics, and culture, and the world of inward spiritual experience is to be seen as one whole in the light of this disclosure of the character and will of its Creator.[41]

Yet more: at the deepest levels of interpersonal relationships between human beings, there is always the longing for complete mutual understanding, which is never attained. Is this "a mirage or a reality that can be reached"?

The Christian testimony is that it is a reality within the being of the Triune God. This testimony rests on the fact that in a life lived as part of our human history, Jesus manifested a relationship of unbroken love and obedience to the one he called Father, a love and obedience sustained by the unfailing love and faithfulness of that same Father, and that those who believe and follow have been enabled through the Spirit actually to participate in this shared life of mutual love, which is the being of the Trinity, by being made one in the sonship of Jesus. This given reality of participation is most succinctly expressed in the words of the prayer attributed to Jesus by John: "The glory which thou hast given me I have given to them, that they may be one even as we are one, I in them and thou in me, that they may become perfectly one, so that the world may believe" (John 17:23). Here is the reality of a fully reciprocal relationship between the Father and the Son within the being of the Godhead, into which believers are drawn by the power of the Spirit, and out of which they can bear witness to the world of that reality from which all things proceed, for which all things exist, and by which all things are to be understood. It is a reality within which they can seek and summon others to seek that full reciprocal understanding between persons that we can only approximate in this life but which we hope to attain fully in the life to come, when we shall know as we are known (1 Corinthians 13:12).[42]

Thus the "twin dogmas of Incarnation and Trinity" constitute "the starting point for a way of understanding reality as a whole, a way that leads out into a wider and more inclusive rationality than the real but limited rationality of the reductionist views that try to explain the whole of reality in terms of the natural sciences from physics to biology, a wider rationality that in no way negates but acknowledges and includes these other kinds of explanations as proper and necessary at their respective levels." It is from this point of view, writes Newbigin,

that I can begin to understand and cope with a world that is both rational and contingent. For at the center of this disclosure, providing the clue to the whole, there stands the cross, on which the one whose purpose is the source and goal of all was slain in shame and dereliction, and the resurrection, in which that very death became the source of life. This precludes any shortcuts to meaningfulness that would ignore the radical contingency of things. The sort of immanent rationality that supposes everything can be explained in mechanical, organismic, or mathematical terms is excluded, and so is whatever supposes (after the manner of some kinds of religion) that everything is controlled in the interests of the good as I conceive it. The meaningfulness of things in this light is compatible with the recognition of mystery that can only be borne in the course of a resolute following on the way of the cross. On the one hand, one is protected from a sheer irrationalism, for which there is no meaning in the world and everything is incomprehensible accident. On the other hand, following the way of the cross in the light and power of the resurrection, one is able to acknowledge and face the reality of evil, of that which contradicts God's good purpose, in the confidence that it does not have the last word. Here, in the responsible acceptance of this communication of a personal purpose of good, is the ground upon which it is possible to believe that the world is both rational and contingent.[43]

From that summit, Newbigin argues, one may now come back down "the continuous ladder that connects human experience through the animal and plant world to the world of molecules, atoms, protons, and electrons" and, "with the faith that there is a good purpose that can be known through the data of experience in the space-time world, namely, those events that are the subject of the Gospel message," one can see both "why the category of purpose cannot be eliminated from our total understanding of how things are" and also "how purpose may be recognized throughout the whole range of nature, and not merely at the point where *homo sapiens* emerges." Newbigin himself offers a few tentative remarks to the effect, for instance, that "biologists now think in terms of populations sharing a pool of genes, rather than of individuals, so that they are not dealing with the random behavior of individual units but with the behavior of very large numbers in which the randomness of individual units loses its importance"; that (with reference to W. H. Thorp's *Purpose in a World of Chance*) "there is more attention paid to the role of purpose in the ways by which animals adapt to their environment, which can play a role in the evolution of the species"; and that the clue to the apparent clash between the continuing biological evolution of more and more complex organisms and the physical law of relentless descent into entropy or total randomness may perhaps lie in the fact "that is familiar to us in human life and that we now find to be operative at least in the higher levels of animal life—the fact that life moves towards its proper conclusion not automatically by any purely mechanical or organic process but in response to a loving purpose, which draws out and makes actual powers that were otherwise only latent and potential." Newbigin ends by admitting—and I have to join him—that "whether or not there is anything of validity in these suggestions is something that must be left to others to discuss."[44]

In the fifth chapter of *Foolishness to the Greeks* Newbigin moves on to "What is to be done? The dialogue with politics."[45] He begins by dismissing as unbiblical the dichotomy between body and soul which would confine the Church's business to the inner world of "private" experience and "spiritual" values: "From its beginning and throughout, the Bible views the individual person realistically as someone always involved in relationships with other human beings and with the world of nature"; in the Old Testament, "faith, obedience, repentance, and love" are "embodied in ways of behaving that cover much of what we would describe as jurisprudence, public health, education, welfare, and economic policy," and the same concreteness is implied in what Jesus says and does concerning the Kingdom of God and then, after his death and resurrection, in the mission of his witnesses "to proclaim and to embody in their common life the victory of Jesus, the reality of the reign of God." Consequently, the earliest Church did not claim protection under Roman law as a *cultus privatus* but called itself "the *ecclesia tou theou*, the public assembly to which God is calling all men everywhere without distinction." Although "the God-given—and therefore limited—authority of Caesar is acknowledged in the Bible," a collision with the imperial power becomes "inevitable, as inevitable as the Cross," when political institutions are placed at the service of a lie, and then "the Church, in the power of the crucified and risen Jesus, bears witness to the truth and pays the price with its blood." But what was the Church to do when, in the fourth and fifth centuries, "the imperial power lost its will to continue and the emperor turned to the Church to provide the spiritual cohesion for a disintegrating society"? In Newbigin's judgment, the Constantinian risk had to be taken if the Church was to be "faithful to its origins in Israel and in the ministry of Jesus." For all the ease with which many in the Church fell into the temptations of worldly power, Newbigin cannot allow that "God's purpose as it is revealed in Scripture" would have been "better served if the Church had refused all political responsibility, if there had never been a 'Christian' Europe, if all the churches for the past two thousand years had lived as tolerated or persecuted minorities."

In any case, we are willy-nilly "the heirs of the Christendom experiment": "We who belong to the Western world live in societies that have been shaped by more than a thousand years during which the barbarous and savage tribes of Europe were brought, slowly and with many setbacks, into a community conceived as the *corpus Christianum*, a single society in which the whole of public and private life was to be controlled by the Christian revelation. Much of what we take for granted about normal human behavior is the fruit of that long schooling. However much we rebel against it, we are its products." It is also the case, however, that "the religious wars of the seventeenth century marked the final destruction of Christendom's synthesis of Church and society," and "from the eighteenth century onward, Europe turned away from the Christian vision of man and his world, accepted a radically different vision for its public life, and relegated the Christian vision to the status of a permitted option for the private sector." For the Church to acquiesce would be to "abandon its calling," for it would be to "deny the kingship of Christ over all of life, public and private," to "deny that Christ is, simply and finally, the truth by which all other claims to truth are to be tested." However, there are no ways either "back to the *corpus Christianum*" or—in a kind of " anarchistic romanticism"—"back to a pre-Constantinian innocence." Rather, Christians must learn "how to embody in the life of the Church a witness to the kingship of Christ over all life—its political and economic no less than its personal and domestic morals—yet without falling into the Constantinian trap."

Newbigin looks for lessons to St. Augustine, who, at a time "when the inward and spiritual disintegration of the classical world view was matched in the realm of outward and visible events by Alaric's sack of the Eternal City," set himself his greatest task, "the interpretation of secular history in the light of the Gospel." Turning especially to the nineteenth book of *The City of God*, Newbigin latches on to the notion that love, as the foundation of justice, is what holds even the earthly commonwealth together, creating order first in the family and among neighbors and then, by extension, in the city and in the nation. Newbigin concludes from Augustine that Christians,

> who—as citizens of the city of God—are resident aliens in the earthly city, must nevertheless seek its good order, and, when called to responsibility as rulers, must accept it in the spirit of servants of the common good. This is required by obedience to the law of God, which is love. Thus the citizens of the heavenly city will actively seek the peace and good order of the earthly city, not seeking to forestall, but patiently awaiting, the final judgment when the two will be visibly separated and the heavenly city will appear in all its beauty. Meanwhile, the monastic communities, such as the one to which Augustine belonged, are a visible sign and preliminary realization of a world ruled solely by the love of God in the midst of a world ruled by the love of self.[46]

Newbigin considers that it is in the realm of economics that people most need "the reminder that every man stands under the law of God and will be accountable to God for his treatment of his neighbor." The "geometric spirit" of the eighteenth century turned economics into an "autonomous science" that was to develop "on the basis of the assumption that self-interest is a universal, natural, and calculable force"; and whereas "traditional Christian ethics had attacked covetousness as a deadly sin, and Paul had equated it with idolatry" (cf. Colossians 3:5), "the eighteenth century, by a remarkable inversion, found in covetousness not only a law of nature but the engine of progress by which the pupose of nature and nature's God was to be worked out"—in the words of Alexander Pope:

> Thus God and Nature formed the general frame
> And bade self-love and social be the same.

In 1984–86, Newbigin could write that "the Enlightenment's vision of the heavenly city has failed," whether in the form of "the liberal capitalist dream of inevitable progress toward a more and more enlightened, liberated and happy world" or in the reactive form of "the Marxist dream of the apocalypse of freedom in a cataclysm that would abolish both private property and the state and create a society of perfect harmony."[47] The events of 1989–90 in Eastern Europe would prove him right with regard to Soviet Marxism, but the seeming victory of unfettered free-market enterprise gives all the more point to Newbigin's sharp critique of Michael Novak's *The Spirit of Democratic Capitalism* (1982), which boldly claimed that the latter was the form of economic organization that Christians must espouse, according to the "law" that "the free operation of rational self-interest will alone secure general well-being."[48]

Where Novak declared that in the world of economic values "the central shrine is empty," because no image is adequate to express what is ultimately good, Newbigin chided him with denying the Incarnation:

> The Church can never accept the thesis that the central shrine of public life is empty, in other words, that there has been no public revelation before the eyes of all the world of the purpose for which all things and all peoples have been created and which all governments must serve. . . . It cannot accept the idea, so popular twenty years ago, of a secular society in which, on principle, there are no commonly acknowledged norms. We know now, I think, that the only possible product of that ideal is a pagan society. Human nature abhors a vacuum. The shrine does not remain empty. If the one true image, Jesus Christ, is not there, an idol will take its place.

The caveat is that the doctrine of original sin forbids a total identification of the laws of a state with the law of God, so that "the sacralizing of politics, the total identification of a political goal with the will of God, always unleashes demonic powers":

> The project of bringing heaven down to earth always results in bringing hell up from below. The full revelation of the heavenly city lies beyond the horizon of earthly history. But the vision of it must control Christian action within history, and such action can admit no separation of private from public life. While the Church can never identify itself with the Kingdom and must seek only the role of a servant, witness, and sign of the Kingdom, yet the Church can never admit any limitations of its role to the private sector. The Church witnesses to that true end for which all creation and all human beings exist, the truth by which all alleged values are to be judged. And truth must be public truth, truth for all. A private truth for a limited circle of believers is no truth at all. Even the most devout faith will sooner or later falter and fail unless those who hold it are willing to bring it into public debate and to test it against experience in every area of life.

Because "there can neither be a total identification of the Church and political order, nor a total separation between them, there is room for much discussion of the ways in which their relationship is to be ordered."

Meanwhile, Newbigin delivers a blistering judgment on the concrete historical results of the modern shift of attention "from distribution to production": "Growth is for the sake of growth and is not determined by any overarching social purpose. And that, of course, is the exact account of the phenomenon which, when it occurs in the human body, is called cancer. In the long perspective of history, it would be difficult to deny that the exuberant capitalism of the past 250 years will be diagnosed in the future as a desperately dangerous case of cancer in the body of human society—if indeed this cancer has not been terminal and there are actually survivors around to make the diagnosis. . . . The myth of the 'invisible hand' that ensures that the untrammeled exercise of covetousness by each individual will produce the happiness of all is surely one of the most malignant falsehoods that has ever deceived the human race."[49]

Before moving at last to what Newbigin proposes as the ecclesiastical witness to the late modern world, a brief final look must be taken at his analysis of the fundamental issues of faith, doubt, truth, and authority over which the Gospel and modernity clash. The material is found in its most detailed form in the opening chapters of *The Gospel in a Pluralist Society* (1989).[50]

The first five of the lectures that became *The Gospel in a Pluralist Society* seek to establish the similarities—despite the differences in the respective epistemic objects—between the procedures of scientific knowledge, properly understood (and here Newbigin relies heavily on Michael Polanyi's works), and the procedures of evangelical knowledge, properly understood (that is to say, without engaging in the "tactical retreats" whereby much modern theology ended up succumbing to the "scientism" of the Enlightenment that lingers on as "the scientific outlook" in the popular perception).[51] In *The Gospel in a Pluralist Society*, Newbigin displays—with the aim of overcoming it—the false dichotomy between "knowing" and "believing" implicit in the common distinction between "We all know" and "Some people believe," as though there were "a world of facts without values and a world of values which have no basis in facts." Guided by Polanyi, Newbigin undertakes a "critique of doubt." In the modern history of ideas, a "systematic skepticism" was set up, first, by Descartes' doubting of everything but the *cogito*, which reintroduced an ancient—and perhaps unbridgeable—dualism between the *res cogitans* (thinking reality) and the *res extensa* (reality extended in space); the split and the dubiety were reinforced by Kant's denial of the knowability of the real or noumenal world, the *Ding an sich*. Nietzsche in turn realized that the loss of a factual, ontological basis for speaking of right and wrong left all up to "personal choice"; therefore, the strong would prevail, so that "the language of 'values' "—says Newbigin—"is simply 'the will to power' wrapped up in cotton wool." Newbigin argues that the "critical principle," valuable as it may be to the advancement of knowledge, is secondary to a more fundamental act of trust in a reality that is *not* doubted. Thus scientific investigation proceeds in the faith that the universe is in fact "rational." Dogma—or the taking of something as given—is not peculiar to religion or to Christianity. And scientific, as well as religious or evangelical, knowledge has both its subjective and its objective poles as the knower intuits and discerns the shape and significance of the realities that present themselves. The Christian goes beyond the modern scientist in response to a confrontation with events that are interpreted as the self-revelation of a transcendent personal will with a purpose for things and, more particularly, for the human race. Conformity to that will and purpose provides the criterion for rebuttal of moral relativism and the nihilism that underlies it.

If Christians are to resist and counter the plausibility structures of modernity—basically the drive "to understand everything in terms of the fundamental laws of physics"—because these structures diminish or exclude the claims of the Christian faith, they will need to understand better the working of the alternative way of construing reality that the Gospel establishes. That requires in particular, according to Newbigin, a grasp of the proper relation between reason and revelation, which becomes possible only through a due appreciation of the social reality and epistemological importance of tradition. Science, too, creates and depends on a body of transmitted knowledge that is initially accepted but may be corrected, reconfigured, developed, and expanded by skilled and imaginative investigators in ever-new encounters with the objects of study that occur and are tested within a community committed to research and reflection—"with universal intent" (Polanyi)—in the cause of truth. "The authority of science," says Polanyi, "is essentially traditional."[52] Newbigin expounds the point that the authority of the scientific tradition "is maintained by the community of scientists as a whole" and "by the free assent of its members." Innovation "can only be responsibly accepted from those who are already masters of the tradition, skilled practitioners of whom it could be said both that the tradition dwells fully in them and that they dwell fully in the tradition." Nor is the authority of the scientific tradition "something apart from the vision of truth which the tradition embodies": "If the scientist is a pioneer who has reached the point where he has to challenge the tradition and to propose a drastic innovation, it is not in order to undermine the authority of the tradition, but to strengthen it by making it more truly congruent with the truth. Insofar as his innovation proves acceptable to the scientific community, it will itself become part of the authoritative tradition."

For one engaged in countering the Enlightenment's move to disparage the authority of tradition as such, the "traditional" structure and procedures of science open up an apologetic possibility for arguing in favor of a structurally and procedurally similar "authoritative tradition in Christian believing": "When we are received into the Christian community, we enter into a tradition which claims authority. It is embodied in the Holy Scriptures and in the continuous history of the interpretation of these Scriptures as they have been translated into 1,500 languages and lived out under myriad different circumstances in different ages and places. This tradition, like the scientific tradition, embodies and carries forward certain ways of looking at things, certain models for interpreting experience." The Christian believer has to learn to indwell the tradition—and that in a personal way, though always "with universal intent," for the Gospel makes a claim to be "public truth." The tradition remains dynamic as successive generations struggle to respond to "new experiences," "whether these come from outside or from within." Proposed modifications in the tradition "must be submitted to the judgment of the Christian community as a whole" and may be "the subject of debate and dispute for many years"; and in such cases the purpose "should always be that the community as a whole should advance toward a more complete understanding of and living by the truth." A crucial difference from the scientific tradition, at least in its present form, resides in the fact that the Christian tradition addresses the larger questions about "the ultimate meaning and purpose of things and of human life": it has "the same presupposition about the rationality of the cosmos as the natural sciences do, but it is a more comprehensive rationality based on the faith that the author and sustainer of the cosmos has personally revealed his purpose." The revelatory actions of

God in history are what faith seeks to understand, so that the Christian tradition is "a matter of dwelling in a story of God's activity, activity which is still continuing."

Tradition is exactly the reality, says Newbigin, which will enable Christians in modernity to clarify for themselves the proper relation between reason and revelation, for a certain misunderstanding of that relation has put them at a loss in the face of the Enlightenment from which they have adopted it. First, after centuries of internal controversy between Catholics and Protestants, it has now become ecumenically possible to see in tradition "not a separate source of revelation from Scripture" but rather "the continuing activity of the Church through the ages in seeking to grasp and express under new conditions that which is given in Scripture. The study of Scripture takes place within the continuing tradition of interpretation."[53] Next, "no one can grasp and make sense of what is given in Scripture except by reason, and—similarly—reason does not operate except within a continuing tradition of speech which is the speech of a community whose language embodies a shared way of understanding." Therefore "reason" is *not* to be understood as "a separate source of information about what is the case," as Enlightenment theologians made it and thereby imported a whole set of substantive assumptions derived from the science and philosophy of the time and running in many ways counter to the Gospel; reason is rather "a faculty with which we seek to grasp the different elements in our experience in an ordered way so that, as we say, they make sense."[54]

There exist different "traditions of rationality," says Newbigin, borrowing from Alasdair MacIntyre's *Whose Justice, Which Rationality?* (1988). Reason is exercised within historic communities whose respective traditions are originated or renewed by contingent events. In science there are such moments of disclosure where "I have discovered" stands at the head of a new tradition of reasoning; in religion, and particularly in Christianity, the starting point is "God spoke and acted." Such revelation is possible, Newbigin affirms with Karl Barth, because it has in fact occurred: "It is from this self-revealing of God that men and women can learn to discern the evidences of his presence and work through their daily experience of the created world. In doing so, we use our reason." Thus "the true opposition is not between reason and revelation as sources of and criteria for truth. It is between two uses to which reason is put." Between the rival claims of Christian belief and modernity there is "no disembodied 'reason' which can act as an impartial umpire": the "reason" of modernity is nothing more nor less than the plausibility structure of the "cosmopolitan culture" of "most of the educated and urbanized peoples of the world" which "uses the European languages as its medium of reasoning and which makes claims to universal validity—claims which are made more plausible by the success of this culture in establishing itself throughout the world as the standard of what is called 'modernization.' " Nevertheless, we are not left without the possibility of dialogue over the veracity of different traditions of rationality. The possibility resides in the acquisition of "a second first language" (MacIntyre).[55]

In envisaging how a dialogue between different traditions of rationality may take place, Newbigin draws on his experience in South India: "There are many Indians for whom English is (in MacIntyre's phrase) a second first language, and some (alas few) English for whom Tamil is a second first language. Both of these will in some measure have come to be at home in both worlds. The English missionary can feel the force and beauty of the worldview embodied in the Tamil poetry [the Saivite devotional poetry of the Tamil poets]. He can set it beside the worldview in which as an English person he has been trained and the biblical worldview into which he seeks to grow." Then, although the ways of reasoning are mutually translatable only to a limited degree, there may take place "an internal dialogue" that is "about truth." In this dialogue the "traditions of rationality are compared with one another in respect of their adequacy to the realities with which all human beings have to deal. And, obviously, this internal dialogue is the necessary precondition for the external dialogue which is at the center of a missionary's proper concern."[56] Mutatis mutandis this supplies Newbigin with a policy for the procedure of Christians in relation to the rival tradition of modernity:

> One learns to live so fully within both traditions that the debate between them is internalized. As a Christian I seek so to live within the biblical tradition, using its language as my language, its models as the models through which I make sense of experience, its story as the clue to my story, that I help to strengthen and carry forward this tradition of rationality. But as a member of contemporary British society I am all the time living in, or at least sharing my life with, those who live in the other tradition. What they call self-evident truths are not self-evident to me, and vice versa. When they speak of reason, they mean what is reasonable within their plausibility structure. I do not live in that plausibility, but I know what it feels like to live in it. Within my own mind there is a continuing dialogue between the two. Insofar as my own participation in the Christian tradition is healthy and vigorous, both in thought and in practice, I shall be equipped for the external dialogue with the other tradition. There is no external criterion above us both to which I and my opposite number can appeal for a decision. The immediate outcome is a matter of the comparative vigor and integrity of the two traditions; the ultimate outcome is at the end when the one who alone is judge sums up and gives the verdict.[57]

That there are ethical consequences to the epistemic clash between the two traditions of rationality—the modern and the Christian—is brought out by Newbigin toward the end of *Truth and Authority in Modernity*:

> The centuries since Newton have seen the project of the Enlightenment carried to the furthest parts of the earth, offering a vision for the whole human race of emancipation, justice, material development, and human rights. It was, and is, a noble project. Yet it has failed disastrously to deliver what was promised. Forces of darkness, irrationality, and violence are perhaps more devastating throughout the world today than they have ever been. And in Europe itself, the birthplace of the Enlightenment and long regarded as the bastion of its values, there is disintegration. Those who fought to overthrow

the dark forces of fascism and national socialism in the Second World War and believed that Europe would never sink again into such barbarism have lived to see these same forces once more taking the stage. Even where such violent forms of irrationality are only on the margins of society, the great visions for the future that inspired the social legislation of the nineteenth and twentieth centuries are now widely rejected. Rational planning for human welfare is widely abandoned in favor of leaving everything to the irrational forces of the market.

It would seem that the splendid ideals of the Enlightenment—freedom, justice, human rights—are not "self-evident truths," as the eighteenth century supposed. They seemed self-evident to a society that had been shaped for more than a thousand years by the biblical account of the human story. When that story fades from corporate memory and is replaced by another story—for example, the story of the struggle for survival in a world whose fundamental law is violence—they cease to be "self-evident." Human reason and conscience, it would seem, do not operate in a vacuum. Their claim to autonomy is unsustainable. They are shaped by factors that are in operation prior to the thinking and experience of the individual. They are shaped most fundamentally by the story that a society tells about itself, the story that shapes the way every individual reason and conscience works.[58]

In those circumstances, the ecclesiastical witness must be to "tell and enact the story"—of God and the world, as it is found in Jesus Christ; to "affirm the truth and therefore the authority of the Gospel . . . by preaching it, by telling the story, and by our corporate living of the story in the life and worship of the Church." Newbigin concludes, "We have to tell and live the story faithfully; the rest is in God's hands. What matters is not that I should succeed, but that God should be honored."[59]

The Ecclesiastical Witness

The volume that included Newbigin's contribution to the inaugural assembly of the World Council of Churches at Amsterdam in 1948 was entitled "The Church's Witness to God's Design."[60] Within that universal frame Newbigin could in 1988 expound "the congregation as hermeneutic of the gospel."[61] Theologically, Newbigin had, from his early Indian days on, viewed the local church as a manifestation—an instance and a cell—of the Church catholic and therefore as bearing evangelistic responsibility. This section proceeds from the testimony of the smallest assembly of Christians through the urban church as the presence of "faith in the city" and the role of the Church in proffering a "vision for society" at the national and regional levels to the ecclesial dimensions of the most general theme signaled by "the Gospel and our culture."

"I have come to feel," wrote Newbigin in *The Gospel in a Pluralist Society*, "that the primary reality of which we have to take account in seeking for a Christian impact on public life is the Christian congregation. How is it possible

that the Gospel should be credible, that people should come to believe that
the power which has the last word in human affairs is represented by a man
hanging on a cross? I am suggesting that the only answer, the only hermeneutic of the Gospel, is a congregation of men and women who believe it and
live by it." All other means of evangelism, including the work of apologetics,
can "accomplish their purpose only as they are rooted in and lead back to a
believing community."[62] From the sound of that, there is a good chance that
what Newbigin is now about to propose should be considered as the mature
form of what he had hoped from the—to his mind, abortive—WCC project of
the mid-1960s on "the missionary structure of the congregation."[63]

The tone and authority for the Church's representation of God's Kingdom
in the life of society are set, according to Newbigin, by the "combination of
tender compassion and awesome sovereignty" which Jesus displays in the
feeding of the multitude and the subsequent discourse as related in John 6.
For the Church to "be fully open to the needs of the world and yet have its
eyes fixed always on God," a congregation will be marked by six features that
make it both the interpreter and the interpretation of the Gospel: it will be a
community of praise, truth, concern, service, mutual responsibility, and
hope.[64]

First, the congregation will be a community of praise, which may be "its
most distinctive character." In contrast to the "hermeneutic of suspicion"
that is the current manifestation of the "disenchantment" of modern society
(Max Weber), the Christian congregation functions as "a place where people
find their true freedom, their true dignity, and their true equality in reverence
to One who is worthy of all the praise that we can offer." The Church's praise
includes thanksgiving, for the assembled community "acknowledges that it
lives by the amazing grace of a boundless kindness": "In Christian worship
we acknowledge that if we had received justice instead of charity, we would
be on our way to perdition. A Christian congregation is thus a body of people
with gratitude to spare, a gratitude that can spill over into care for the neighbor. And it is of the essence of the matter that this concern for the neighbor
is the overflow of a great gift of grace and not, primarily, the expression of
commitment to a moral crusade." In Christian worship, says Newbigin, "the
language of rights is out of place except when it serves to remind us of the
rights of others."

Second, the congregation will be a community of truth. "Every person living in a 'modern' society is subject to an almost continuous bombardment of
ideas, images, slogans, and stories which presuppose a plausibility structure
radically different from that which is controlled by the Christian understanding of human nature and destiny." To challenge the reigning plausibility
structure effectively requires that one be informed through the "constant remembering and rehearsing of the true story" that takes place in the faithful
congregation. Moreover, that community's "manner of speaking the truth
must not be aligned to the techniques of modern propaganda, but must have
the modesty, the sobriety, and the realism which are proper to a disciple of
Jesus."

Third, the Christian congregation "does not live for itself but is deeply involved in the concerns of its neighborhood"; its members "are willing to be *for* the wider community." In the New Testament, Newbigin points out, the word *ekklesia* is qualified only in two ways: it is "the Church of God" or "of Christ," and it is the church of a place. Hence "a Christian congregation is defined by this twofold relation: it is God's embassy in a specific place." Negatively put, there is distortion if either of these vital relationships be neglected: "The congregation may be so identified with the place that it ceases to be the vehicle of God's judgment and mercy for that place and becomes simply the focus of the self-image of the people of that place. Or it may be so concerned about the relation of its members to God that it turns its back on the neighborhood and is perceived as irrelevant to its concerns."

Fourth, the congregation will be a place where Christian men and women are prepared for, and sustained in, the exercise of their royal priesthood in the world: "It is in the ordinary secular business of the world that the sacrifices of love and obedience are to be offered to God. It is in the context of secular affairs that the mighty power released into the world through the 2work of Christ is to be manifested." There is "a need for 'frontier groups' of Christians working in the same sectors of public life, meeting to thrash out the controversial issues of their business or profession in the light of their faith." There is a need also that the congregation recognize the diversity of God's gifts to the members of the body, and of the services to which God calls them.

Fifth, the congregation will be a community of mutual responsibility. "If the Church is to be effective in advocating and achieving a new social order in the nation," says Newbigin, "it must itself be a new social order"—or at least a "foretaste" of it. "The deepest root of the contemporary malaise of Western culture is an individualism which denies the fundamental reality of our human nature as given by God—namely that we grow into true humanity only in relationships of faithfulness and responsibility toward one another." When, by the grace of God, a local congregation becomes such a community of mutual responsibility, "its members will be advocates for human liberation by being themselves liberated; its actions for justice and peace will be, and will be seen to be, the overflow of a life in Christ, where God's justice and God's peace are already an experienced treasure."

Sixth, the congregation will be a community of hope. Newbigin is struck by "the virtual disappearance of hope" in contemporary Western culture: the general literature of the West, he observes, is "full of nihilism and despair," and even Christian writers speak in tones of "embarrassment, guilt, and shame." The Gospel of the crucified and risen Christ, he says, "offers an understanding of the human situation which makes it possible to be filled with a hope which is both eager and patient even in the most hopeless situations." But again, it is necessary to indwell the Gospel story. If the Gospel is to challenge the public life of society, "it will only be by movements that begin with the local congregation in which the reality of the new creation is present, known, and experienced, and from which men and

women will go into every sector of public life to claim it for Christ, to unmask the illusions which have remained hidden and to expose all areas of
public life to the illumination of the Gospel. But that will only happen as
and when local congregations renounce an introverted concern for their
own life, and recognize that they exist for the sake of those who are not
members, as sign, instrument, and foretaste of God's redeeming grace for
the whole life of society."

What Newbigin held to be the vocation of the local congregation was extended and concretized as part of a project of the middle and late 1980s
entitled "Faith in the City of Birmingham." In 1983, the then Archbishop of
Canterbury, Dr. Robert Runcie, had appointed a Commission on Urban Priority Areas (UPAs), and its report was published in 1985 as *Faith in the City:
A Call for Action by Church and Nation.* In the wake of the national commission,
the diocese of Birmingham conducted its own study, again with ecumenical
awareness and some ecumenical participation. Lesslie Newbigin, then pastor
of the United Reformed Church in Winson Green, was a member of the Birmingham commission and chaired the group that produced the sixth chapter
of the 1988 report, whose overall title was precisely *Faith in the City of Birmingham;* he is generally acknowledged to have been the principal writer of
this so-called "theological chapter," which is entitled "Christian Perspectives
on the City."[65] The social location is "a cosmopolitan, economically divided
city as it strives for unity and renewal"; the standpoint is the tradition shaped
by "those who, in the past of our City, have been inspired by God's action
for all people in Jesus Christ"; and the address is "to our fellow Christians
and all our fellow citizens for reflection and debate." The authors seek to
"interpret for this present time God's word of warning and promise for our
City."

In both the Greek and the biblical traditions, the report notes, the city is
"the place where human life, for better or for worse, is concentrated, the
place to which people come together for protection, for commerce and industry, the place where peoples, cultures and creeds meet and mingle, where
new ideas, new arts, new skills are born and nurtured. It is the place where
both human greatness and human wickedness flourish." In the Bible the
double character of the city is represented on the one hand by Babel, Babylon,
and imperial Rome as the great harlot in the Apocalypse and on the other
hand by the Jerusalem that both the prophets and Jesus love and over which
they weep and by the new Jerusalem, the holy city coming down as a gift
from God, the place of beauty into which all the nations will bring their
treasures. The City of Birmingham has mirrored the ancient pattern and now
figures in the worldwide trend to urbanization. People have always come
there—and finally from almost every part of the globe—in search of work;
and Birmingham has exemplified both "the virtues of the city—its craftsman-
ship, its entrepreneurial skills, its pioneering work in municipal government,
its rich cultural tradition, and its role in the political life of the nation" and
also "the darker side of urban life and, very specially at this time, the problems
of decay in the inner city areas and in some housing areas."

In the power of the Holy Spirit and under the Spirit's guidance, the nature and calling of the Church is to be, in Newbigin's familiar threesome, "a sign, instrument, and foretaste" of God's Kingdom, both pointing people to the "open secret" of Jesus in whom the Kingdom is present and constituting a place where victory may be sensed in the midst of the struggle with evil and where, at least as a "starter," "the freedom and fellowship and happiness of God's home are enjoyed." In Birmingham, as in many other cities, the Church has existed from the earliest days and has, despite its grievous sins and failures, contributed significantly to the life of the city. "Our present separation into different ecclesial communities," it is confessed, "is contrary to our calling"; but, in line with the long history of cooperation among the Birmingham churches, "we are earnestly seeking to overcome these divisions," especially through the life and work of the Birmingham Council of Christian Churches. Some of the more recent Evangelical and Pentecostal congregations, often embodying the Christian traditions of West Africa and the Caribbean and having "learned to live in the world of the Bible," are in the thick of the struggle to liberate "the victims of multiple deprivation."

Under the heading "Sinned Against and Sinning," there follows an analysis of the battle with "the enemy of God, the power that enslaves and dehumanizes the children of God": "The ultimate enemy is not any human person or agency but that power which is the source of sin and death. The redemption wrought by Jesus was first of all deliverance from the power of sin. The Gospel has to address both the sinner and the one who is sinned against. In fact all of us are both." The report continues with the refusal, characteristic of Newbigin's thought, to allow a reductive and seductive "secular" reading of the situation which puts all the blame on "the system"; yet, again in Newbigin's line, the social and public implications of the Gospel are strongly affirmed:

It is profoundly demeaning to the "oppressed" to suggest that they have no personal responsibility for the total situation of which their suffering is a part. Any honest description of the breakdown of human well-being in our cities must be in terms which are both personal and structural. The breakdown of family life, the sexual promiscuity which so often produces it, the wholesale delivery of pornography and violence into the living rooms where parents and children pass their time, the massive increase in the practice of abortion, the failure of parents to discipline their children—all of these are the fruit of a philosophy which accepts self-seeking as the norm of human conduct and pleasure as the goal of human living. This is in turn fuelled by powerful interests which depend on the multiplication of new wants among those whose basic material needs are already met. This complex web of evil cannot be understood in terms of personal sin alone nor in terms of systemic evil alone. Both are involved. There are commercial, social and economic structures which embody evil forces and which make it easier to sin than not to sin. But individual persons are responsible for consenting or resisting. . . .

It is wrong to suggest that solutions are to be found simply by "changing the system," and it is also wrong to suggest that the solution lies entirely in personal conversion. Both are involved, for true conversion has systemic implications. We are responsible persons within a network of relationships which together constitute "the system." The call to follow Jesus is indeed a call to conversion, to a radical change of direction for one's whole life. But true conversion will involve not only the direction of one's personal relationships but also the direction of one's public, civic, political and cultural activities. It is society as a whole, the rich and the poor, who are called to radical conversion. And the teaching of Jesus consistently suggests that it is the rich who are in the greatest need of a radical change of direction.

Having themselves acknowledged the light of God as it shines fully in Jesus, Christians will "welcome, cherish, and rejoice in every reflection of that light wherever it is seen." But the Church alone, in spite of its own sins, remains the only body with the specific vocation to be "sign, instrument, and foretaste of the Kingdom, the Kingdom which is for all." How may the Church authentically fulfill its calling? The report lists a number of ecclesial characteristics which, in their unfolding, closely resemble Newbigin's description of "the congregation as hermeneutic of the Gospel," though here with a close application to the Church in the City of Birmingham. The Church will be a community of praise to God overflowing in love and care for others, a community of civic and social responsibility to and with its neighbors, a community of intercultural reconciliation enriched by the results of patience and perseverance, and a community of witness by word and deed to the truth of God in prophetic service to those political agencies which have their own accountability before God. Recognizing that the Church is "a community among other communities" (for "the members of all the Christian churches put together make up only a small minority of the population of the City"), Christians need guidelines for their attitudes and behavior toward not only those who retain "residual allegiances" to a Christianity that "is no longer their controlling belief" but also "the many adherents—more or less faithful—of one or other of the great world religions."

First, Christians are advised to welcome wholeheartedly "the evidences of the work of God's grace in the lives of people of other faiths and people of no religious faith"; it is "not our business to ferret out the sins of our non-Christian neighbours," for Christ alone is judge, and "our business, as fellow-sinners, is to recognize and rejoice in the light that enlightens every person of whatever faith or no-faith." Second, and consequently, Christians should "seek out and develop those areas of our civic life in which people of all faiths can cooperate for the common good"; in particular, friendly contacts with Muslims, Hindus, and Sikhs can initiate collaborative enterprises to restore hope in the deprived areas of the City. Third, local congregations should be places "where people of all faiths can find a welcome," for "the good news of which we are the bearers is for all," and "it would be an intolerable sort of racism to suggest that the Gospel is only for people of a certain ethnic origin." Christians have much to learn from their willing Muslim and Sikh interlocutors, even while testifying to the good news that, in Jesus Christ, "the sovereign Lord of all creation has acted in infinite love and humility to deliver all humankind from the power of sin and death and to open for us the gate of life." Fourth, in the field of public education "the present danger is that the ultimate effect of the school-experience for most children will be to lead them to conclude that religious faith—Christian or otherwise—is an optional but not essential part of understanding the world"; here Muslim concerns in particular should be shared by the churches, for "no issue could be more vital for the future of our society than this question of the role of religious teaching in the schools, and the presence of the other faith communities in Birmingham is challenging us to look at this in a new light."[66]

Without "either lapsing into platitudes or else claiming transcendent authority for positions that are by no means impregnable," the Church fails in its service to the world unless it speaks to "those who have responsibility for the government, industry, commerce and culture of the City." The commission therefore offered, in conclusion, five "affirmations for public policy." First, "human wellbeing is not to be measured simply by the abundance of possessions" (cf. Luke 12:15–21). That has implications for production and distribution and for "the balance between private enterprise and public spending, and between manufacturing and the service industries"; and "we know, to our bitter cost, that where wealth accumulates, men and women may decay." Nor, second, is human well-being to be found outside relationships to others "in bonds of love, faithfulness and mutual trust." It is "an illusion of our culture that fulfilment and happiness can be reached by maximizing the opportunities for the individual to make individual choices"; rather, the clue is to be found in the doctrine of the Trinity that is at the heart of the Christian faith, that "the glory of God is not that of a solitary potentate, but the glory of love forever poured out and forever shared." Third, "trust is created only by speaking truth." In face of the "communications explosion" and the "widespread cynicism" toward the words of public figures, the Church "needs a vigilant concern for truthfulness, first in its own life and then in the life of city and nation"; Jesus issued a drastic warning against "the inflation of verbal currency," when he said "Let what you say be simple 'Yes' or 'No,' for anything more than that comes from evil" (Matthew 5:37). Fourth, in face of the contemporary "explosion of expectations" there must be a recognition of the limits to growth, for the rising spiral of demand for "necessities" that were once luxuries "deflects productive resources from the provision of the basic needs of all—housing, drainage, schools, and hospitals"; true happiness "does not come from the satisfaction of our wants but from the knowledge that God's family of mankind, all our fellow citizens, have access to the support of their needs." Fifth, "human wellbeing is not possible without hope." Against a nostalgia for the past, a lingering belief in progress, or a fear of the future, "the faith which springs from the resurrection of the crucified Jesus gives birth to a confident hope which no disappointment can destroy." The promise for both the individual soul and the world resides in the coming City of God; and because "the ultimate future belongs to Christ and his kingly rule," all the development and use of radically new technologies "must be shaped by the knowledge that in the end we shall be judged by that rule, by whether or not our use of these powers has served the needs of the least of the brothers and sisters of the King (Matthew 25:31–46).

That judgment is the ultimate horizon for all our activity whether in the Church or in the public life of the City. It must determine the direction of everything we attempt now."

Moving from the City of Birmingham to the level of the nation, we recall Lesslie Newbigin's prominent participation in the program of the British Council of Churches (now the Council of Churches for Britain and Ireland) on "The Gospel and Our Culture" (that title was his own suggestion). His conceptual contribution to this desired "missionary encounter with modernity" has already been presented through several of his successive writings: *The Other Side of 1984: Questions for the Churches* (see pp. 256–61), *Foolishness to the Greeks: The Gospel and Western Culture* (pp. 355–70), *The Gospel in a Pluralist Society* (pp. 313–17 and 371–78), and *Truth to Tell: The Gospel as Public Truth* (pp. 72–75). With his Birmingham friend Dan Beeby, the first coordinator of the program and disarmingly self-described as "the monkey to Lesslie's organ-grinder," Newbigin worked unstintingly toward the preparation of a national consultation on "The Gospel as Public Truth" that was finally held at Swanwick in July 1992. The consultation brought together some four hundred academic, ecclesiastical, and public leaders around the eight themes that had been set out by specialists in a study volume edited and introduced by Hugh Montefiore, quondam bishop of Birmingham (and my Cambridge tutor), *The Gospel and Contemporary Culture*: "The Gospel and History" (Eric Ives), "Strange Contest: Science versus Religion" (Mary Midgley), "The Gospel, the Arts, and our Culture" (Jeremy Begbie), "Knowledge and Culture: Towards an Epistemology of the Concrete" (Colin Gunton), "Contemporary Culture and the Role of Economics" (Jane Collier), "Education and the Gospel" (Brenda Watson), "Health, Healing, and Modern Medicine" (John Young), "Mass Media, British Culture, and Gospel Values" (Jim McDonnell).[67] In his keynote address to the consultation—which he began after the manner of a British Rail conductor with "Welcome to customers joining the programme at Swanwick! This is the delayed 1984 Nottingham conference!"—Newbigin concentrated on the epistemological and the politicoeconomic, hammering home points with which the reader of this book will now be familiar.[68] The interests and activities aroused by the program and the consultation were then pursued nationally in various ways, through the "Gospel and Culture" organization (with Andrew Walker) and through integration in the "Open Book" initiative of the British and Foreign Bible Society (again with Dan Beeby and with David Kettle); especially significant among the international parallels and derivatives have been the "Gospel and Our Culture Network" in North America (with George Hunsberger and others) and the "Gospel and Cultures Trust" in New Zealand (with Harold W. Turner).[69]

The persistence of Newbigin's concern for his own country and its society finds demonstration in the book *Faith and Power: Christianity and Islam in "Secular" Britain*, written with Lamin Sanneh and Jenny Taylor and published posthumously in 1998.[70] As a man of wide experience and vision, Newbigin was, of course, no "little Englander," and at an advanced age he continued to take part in conferences on the European Continent and in Scandinavia, where similar issues were being raised in similar cultural and ecclesiastical situations. He found a positive hearing among Evangelicals in particular, although his historical analyses and theological emphases did not pass—any more internationally than nationally—entirely without criticism even in some circles sympathetic to his concerns. He spoke in Germany in 1988 on "Our Missionary Responsibility in the Crisis of Western Culture," in the Netherlands in 1990 on "Evangelism in the Context of Secularization," in Germany again in 1992 on "Learning to Live in the Spirit in Our European Home," and in 1994 on "The Cultural Captivity of Western Christianity as a Challenge to a Missionary Church."[71] In 1993 he took part in a conference on "Faith and Modernity" in Uppsala, Sweden, convened by the Lausanne Committee for World Evangelism; in 1994 he visited Finland at the invitation of the national missionary council; and in 1995 he addressed a meeting in Denmark on "Gospel and Culture."[72] General Simatupang's question, "Can the West be converted?" had been echoed by Pope John Paul II's summons to "The Re-evangelization of Europe."[73] Here I pick up, by way of recapitulation, three of Newbigin's recurrent themes: the "domestication"—the German might almost be *Verharmlosung*—of the Gospel; the claim to "public truth"; and the question of a "Christian society."

On the first point, Newbigin recounted to his Stuttgart audience in 1994 that since returning to live in England after a lifetime as a foreign missionary, he had the "unhappy feeling" that "most English theology" was falling into the second of the two perennial dangers in cross-cultural mission, not irrelevance but syncretism:

> Ours is an advanced case of syncretism. In other words, instead of confronting our culture with the Gospel, we are perpetually trying to fit the Gospel into our culture. In our effort to communicate, we interpret the Gospel by the categories of our culture. But how can we avoid this? How can we, who are a part of this culture, find a standpoint from which we can address a word, the word of the Gospel, to our culture? . . . Can the experience of cross-cultural mission help us in the task?
>
> . . . I want to argue the need for a certain boldness that was evidently a characteristic mark of the first apostles. Some time ago I happened to have the privilege of sitting next to Cardinal Suenens at a conference, and he asked me what I thought of contemporary English theology. I replied "timid syncretism." Perhaps that was unfair. I am sure it cannot be true of German theology. What I am pleading for is the courage to hold and proclaim a belief that cannot be proved to be true in terms of the accepted axioms of our society, that can be doubted by rational minds, but that we nevertheless hold as the truth. . . . Our modern scientific culture has pursued the ideal of a completely impersonal knowledge of a world of so-called facts that are simply there and cannot be doubted by rational minds, facts that constitute the real world as distinct from the opinions, desires, hopes, and beliefs of human beings. . . . The Gospel is not a set of beliefs that arise or could arise from empirical observation of the whole human experience. It cannot be based upon inductive reasoning. It is the announcement of a name and a fact that

offer the starting point for the whole lifelong enterprise of understanding and coping with experience. It is a new starting point. To accept it means a new beginning, a radical conversion.[74]

Second, then, Newbigin remained willing and eager to claim and advocate as public truth the doctrine which many consider the most recondite in the Christian faith: the Trinity. In "The Trinity as Public Truth," a paper given at an Edinburgh dogmatics conference in 1993, Newbigin asserted that

the development of the doctrine of the Trinity was not the result of any kind of theological speculation within the tradition of classical thought. It was the result of a new fact (in the original sense of the word *factum*, something done). God had done those things that are the content of the good news that the Church is commissioned to tell, the Gospel. This fact required a complete rethinking of the word "God." One could, of course, decline to believe the "facts" alleged in the Gospel. This is always a possibility. But if one believes that they are true, then this has to be a new starting point for thought. . . . For nearly a thousand years—the years that shaped the barbarian tribes of this western extension of Asia into a cultural entity that we call "Europe"—it was this way of thinking that shaped public discourse. The liturgy, the preaching, the drama, and the art of Christendom all took this apostolic record as the framework within which public discourse took place."[75]

Much modern Christianity has only an enfeebled grasp of trinitarianism. And where "God" has not been entirely banished from public discourse as a threat to human autonomy, the "shadowy survival of a unitarian God in the area of public discourse corresponds to (and is perhaps responsible for) two very obvious elements in the reigning public truth," namely, "our prevailing individualism" that matches this "solitary" God, and an "ontology of violence," where (as argued by Jürgen Moltmann, in *The Trinity and the Kingdom of God*, 1981) "a model of ultimate reality in terms of a monarchical figure of unlimited power tends to validate a conception of human affairs in which sheer power is the ontological basis of everything." Instead, Newbigin proposes, "Christian doctrine, with its prime model in the doctrine of the Trinity, ought to be playing an explicit and vigorous part in the public debate that makes up the life of the public square." The terms of the discourse, and finally the social reality itself, could be changed by the trinitarian understanding of God, in which "relatedness is constitutive of the divine being" and "the ultimate reality is the eternal mutual self-giving-in-love of the three persons of the Blessed Trinity."

Third, then, there comes the question of "a Christian society." Newbigin is adamant that there can and must be no return to "Christendom," insofar as that may mean "use of coercion to impose belief." Yet "there is no 'secular' neutrality" in the shaping of the common life, and "Christians cannot evade the responsibility which a democratic society gives to every citizen to seek access to the levers of power."[76] Here is what Newbigin told his Dutch listeners in 1990:

Evangelism is not just the call to personal conversion, although it is that. It is not just a program for church growth, although it is that also. It is not just preaching, although it is that, and it is not just action for changing society, although it is that too. It is not a program for the reestablishment of the *Corpus Christianum* in Europe with the Church in the supreme position. Most certainly it is not that. But I believe it is possible to hope for and to work for something different—a Europe (a "common European home") that is a Christian society, not in the sense that it is ruled by the Church, and not in the sense that everyone is a Christian, but in another sense which I would indicate as follows. It is possible to envision a society in which Christians have engaged so seriously over several decades with the consequences of the Enlightenment (good and bad) and with the kind of society that has developed at the end of the twentieth century that those who achieve the highest standards of excellence in all the sectors of public life—politics, industry, learning, and the arts—may be shaped in their public work by the Christian story. Then the worship of the triune God as he is made known to us in Jesus may again be the focus of ordinary life in our towns and villages

Whether or not that is the purpose of God for our continent, the main point is quite simple. We are entrusted with good news, the news that God reigns. That must be the starting point of all our thinking, and our evangelism will be an overflow of that joyful faith. Who knows, perhaps God has in store for our poor old secularized Europe a new birth of faith in the twenty-first century.[77]

A Dutch Reformed theologian who participated in the conversations with Newbigin has wondered whether Newbigin was not feeding a "nostalgia" for either "an influential Christian establishment or a widely convincing *status confessionis*, in which ideologies are beaten by faith." L. A. Hoedemaker objects to making the Enlightenment "the scapegoat" in a polarization between Christian and modern rationalities. "First," says the Groningen missiologist,

Newbigin underestimates the degree to which faith itself is part of the problem, an accomplice in the development of a culture that produced the Enlightenment, and is unable to dispose of the Enlightenment in its inescapable rational functions. Faith cannot be rescued and purged from a complex history of configurations of religion, rationality, and faith. Second, he also underestimates the degree to which the Enlightenment has been an ally of the Christian faith. It has stimulated Christianity to develop and refine its view of universal history and of eschatology. Even though Newbigin is undoubtedly right when he draws attention to basic incompatibilities in regard to the concept of history, there is more than just opposition here. Third, when faith is presented as another species of rationality, it almost automatically follows that the problematic aspects of rationality, the points where it elicits contradiction and protest because it tends to neglect and violate essential aspects of human life, remain underexposed. In Newbigin's case, it implies that he concentrates much more on the battle for truth than on the struggles for justice and liberation, which have revealed the dark sides of the history of rationality. And it is precisely on those dark sides that faith has to come to life again. Its major business is not the rational fight against modern unbelief but the exposure of the crisis of rationality with regard to full humanity. Newbigin would reply that both are necessary and that the second task can be performed adequately only after the first has been dealt with. Basically, however, they present different preoccupations that may ultimately work at cross-purposes.[28]

The reader of this book may in turn wonder whether Hoedemaker's account does justice to the fact that the positions taken by Newbigin in his later years were reached only through a lifetime's intellectual and practical exploration during which the explorer had had the humility and the courage to correct his missteps and retreat from blind alleys.

There is one more level in Newbigin's engagement with these questions, that of the World Council of Churches. In 1994, the central committee of the WCC inaugurated a long-term study on "Gospel and Cultures." Some account of the project, setting it within a longer ecumenical history, is provided by Wesley Ariarajah, who had been director of the WCC subunit on "Dialogue with People of Living Faiths," in a booklet entitled *Gospel and Culture: An Ongoing Discussion within the Ecumenical Movement.*[79] The WCC had taken up the publication of Newbigin's *The Other Side of 1984* and *The Gospel in a Pluralist Society.* To the former, Wesley Ariarajah had added a postscript in which he endorsed many of Newbigin's questions and concerns, even while raising a couple of critical points as a "non-Western Christian." First, Ariarajah called attention to the continuing attractiveness of the modern fiduciary framework in many parts of the world on account of "the humanizing effects of science and technology" in combating superstition, ignorance, and servitude and helping people of diverse culture and religion to live together in a "secular" context; and if Newbigin was in earnest about "a dialogue with modern culture," then "it should be noted that in a dialogue no person has the right to assume that all the truth is only on his or her side." Second, Ariarajah highlighted the situation of "churches in cultures dominated by other living faiths":

> In Sri Lanka, for example, there is constant pressure, precisely for the kind of reasons that Bishop Newbigin gives for the recovery of the biblical faith, to return to the *Buddha dhamma* as the basis of society. In many Muslim countries there are relentless attempts to reorganize society on the basis of the Quran. There is increasing pressure to make Hinduism the official religion of India so that it can become the basis of society in a more acknowledged way. . . . In a Muslim, Buddhist or Hindu nation there can be no question of replacing their scriptures with the Bible. At the same time one sees the need for a faith perspective and recognizes the limitations of a rational scientific framework. . . . The churches living in other religious cultures must theologically evaluate the faiths of others, their fiduciary frameworks, and the life-affirming values in them. . . . If it is obvious that in the foreseeable future, the only kind of meaningful national life is one which is inextricably bound up with the life of people of other faiths, and if it is also obvious that any fiduciary framework based on faith for the whole of life must be a common framework

which can serve many religious communities, what does it mean for the churches' relationship with people of other faiths? It is obvious that all these questions point to the need for a much fuller, more genuine and more committed dialogue between faiths.

In a gracious and generally positive foreword to *The Gospel in a Pluralist Society*, Christopher Duraisingh—a successor of Newbigin's as director of the WCC Commission on World Missions and Evangelism—hinted at the criticisms which some might bring, notably concerning "the measure of integration between the epistemological insights and the theological formulations that follow," and "a certain tension" between, on the one hand, "the perspectival and the story character of the gospel," and, on the other, "the absolute claims that are made for the gospel."

In late 1996, Lesslie Newbigin addressed for the last time a world conference on mission and evangelism. It was held under WCC auspices in Salvador de Bahia, Brazil, under the title "Called to One Hope: The Gospel in Diverse Cultures." In a two-part speech Newbigin made a short, simple, and strong statement of the final position that he had come to on the themes of "Gospel" and "culture" and their interrelation. The Gospel, he said, is *not* "Christianity" (for that is "what generations of us have made of the Gospel and we know that we have often made a mess of it"); nor is the Gospel "religious experience" (which is "a very ambivalent affair"); rather, the Gospel is "a factual statement," namely, "that God, who is the author, the sustainer, the goal of all that exists, of all being and all meaning and all truth, has become present in our human history as the man Jesus, whom we can know and love and serve; and that by his incarnation, his ministry, his death and resurrection he has finally broken the powers that oppress us and has created a space and a time in which we who are unholy can nevertheless live in fellowship with God who is holy." It is possible not to believe this fact, or to say that it is just one of many stories that people tell to explain the human situation. But if the Gospel is true, then it is certainly the most important fact in the world, and we must communicate it. Its implication is that final authority lies with Jesus, as declared in Matthew 28:18. All of us need to know who is ultimately in charge. For many in the West, the free market is the "sovereign power," against which even powerful governments are powerless; we talk about "moral values," but they do not have final power in the real world. If the Gospel is true and we as the Church—who have the exclusive rights to tell this story—refrain from publishing it, that is not only betrayal of the Lord but collusion with the deceptive power. There are many more things that we can and must do with people of all faiths and ideologies as part of our common human responsibilities in such areas as politics and economics, but our specific responsibility as Christians, given to no one else, is "to bear witness to the reality of Jesus' victory."

The Gospel story must be told in a language, and there the questions about culture flood in. So, for example, in English the simplest version of the Gospel is "Jesus is Lord." That does not mean that he can be compared to other existing English "lords"; rather, our whole conception of lordship has to be revised in the light of Jesus. In street preaching in the Tamil language, among people who had no idea of Jesus, it was necessary to pick one of the names for God in Tamil, which would in fact convey quite different pictures; then, said Newbigin, one had to tell stories about the God of Jesus Christ that did not fit Shiva or Vishnu or Ganesh, until gradually—in a long process that is never complete—a new picture of God is built. The most pervasive culture at the present time, however, is the "modernity" that is based on science and technology and channeled through the ideology of the free market, and the chief rival to the Christian faith for the challenging of that culture is Islam.

"In the century ahead," Newbigin forecast, "Islam, the free market, and Christian faith will remain in contention." Like none of the other world faiths, Islam makes a claim of universal truth and allegiance. In seeking control of the political order, Islam punishes dissent (and Newbigin confessed shame at the silence of the British media about the sufferings of Christians in some Muslim countries); by contrast, the Christian Gospel affirms that God's sovereignty was manifested not by power or might but in the humiliation of the Cross and that the victory of that seeming defeat was made known not as a great public demonstration, which would mean the end of human history, but as a secret to a very small community chosen to be witnesses, so that the Kingdom of God could come through freely given love and obedience. How can Christians challenge the idolatry of the market? Only God can create a genuinely free and just society. The Gospel provides space and freedom for dissent, and only that faith can sustain a truly free society and lead to salvation. Salvation, Newbigin interjects, is not a privatized commodity but the final and glorious consummation of God's purpose for his whole creation. It is pointless to argue about whether other people will be saved; that is not our business, and Jesus makes it quite clear that there will be surprises. What, then, is the point of mission? Quite simply: the glory of God. If God has done what the Gospel story tells us, the only response can be praise and thanksgiving, and mission is the work of sharing that response with others. Why, Newbigin asked his conference audience in conclusion, are mission conferences so often guilt-ridden, as though we had failed to carry out "our program"? The Resurrection was like a huge explosion of joy, and Christians are called to carry it further.

There were two particularly moving points in Newbigin's speech. The first came when he said that he knew all about "the sins of the old missionaries": "I am an old missionary, and I have committed most of those sins." It would, however, be a strange response to conclude "I will refrain from talking about Jesus and will instead offer my own life as a witness that will enable people to believe." The second moment came when Newbigin recalled the service two days earlier on the dockside in repentance for the slave trade. The Portuguese had domesticated the Gospel and so acted in ways that turned it into bad news (though in fairness one might remember the centuries of Muslim occupation and the struggle to get rid of the invaders). But when we stood in the old slave market, on Saturday morning, on those stones which had felt the weight of the bare and bruised and shackled feet of countless of our fellow human beings, when we stood in that place so heavy with human sin and human suffering and were told to spend two minutes in silence waiting for what the Spirit might say to us, I thought first how unbelievable that Christians could have connived in that inhuman trade. And then there came to my mind the question: Will it not be the case that our great-grandchildren will be equally astonished at the way in which we in our generation, in our so-called modern, Western, rich, developed culture, connive at the wholesale slaughter of unborn children in the name of the central idol of our culture: freedom of choice?

In raising that painful issue, Newbigin had done what he "was told to do," and he had "discharged a commission" that had been laid on him.

On the journey home from Brazil, his traveling companion reports, Newbigin settled into his seat, took his Walkman from his pocket, and proceeded to listen to a reading of the Psalms, and then to pray in absorbed silence for half an hour or so at a time during the long flight to London.[80]

Conclusion

THE MAN IN HISTORY

I know whom I have believed, and I am sure that He is able
to guard until that Day what I have entrusted to Him.

(2 Timothy 1:12)

"Like a Father of the Church"

When I first informed Lesslie that I was going to portray in patristic terms
his significance as a bishop-theologian, he modestly demurred but then con-
fided that after his address to the world conference on mission and evangelism
in Salvador de Bahia in 1996, a Russian Orthodox bishop told him he had
spoken "like a Father of the Church." Five themes may be advanced in order
to display the similarities and continuities between Bishop Newbigin and the
great bishop-theologians in early ecclesiastical history.

First, Newbigin's heart and mind, his pastoral work, his ecumenical endeavors, his missionary strategies, and his social vision were decisively shaped
and constantly nourished by Holy Scripture. He prayed with the Bible, he
preached with the Bible, he thought with the Bible, he wrote with the Bible.
In broad outline and in verbal detail, the scriptural narrative and vocabulary
provide the substance and the basic language of his sermons, his treatises,
and his shorter writings, just as they do with a Chrysostom or an Augustine;
and, as with them, so also with Newbigin, one can sense the situations and
the people being addressed. The biblical story of the world's creation, redemption, and consummation are the "spectacles"—and here Newbigin used
the trope favored by his Reformed progenitor John Calvin—through which
he read the world and went about his and the Lord's business in it: "The
Christian story provides us with a set of lenses, not something for us to look
at, but for us to look *through*." One does not so much notice the biblical
glasses, Newbigin would say, once one has become accustomed to them, but
they certainly correct the vision, so that "we are able confidently, though not
infallibly, to increase our understanding of the world and our ability to cope
with it."[1] Newbigin was sometimes suspected by theological liberals of "fundamentalism," but the term is as anachronistic in his case as it would be if
applied to the patristic theologians: fundamentalism, he himself often said, is

a position that itself presupposes the modern, secular disjunction between "facts" and "values"; the integrated vision of the Scriptures and of classic Christian doctrine is what he is aiming to retrieve.

Second, Newbigin held to the ancient creeds—the Apostles' Creed and particularly the Nicene Creed with its *homoousion*—as confessions of faith safeguarding both the identity and the ontology of the Godhead. That is to say, the God of the biblical story is Father, Son, and Holy Spirit, the one true God who has entered personally into the world by the incarnation of the Son and the pentecostal gift of the Spirit. Only so are revelation, redemption, and consummation secure. Only so is the ancient and perennial dichotomy between fate and virtue overcome, as the Holy Spirit brings responsible humankind freely into the Father's plan that has been disclosed, and his reign that has been proclaimed and inaugurated, by the Son. The conciliar achievement of the doctrine of the Trinity, with Athanasius in the lead, was the basis on which, according to Newbigin, Augustine formulated a worldview that served Europe for more than a millennium and that keeps its universal potential provided only the modern reversions to paganism on its original territory can be overcome through a "reconversion of the West." By his own writings—particularly *The Household of God, Trinitarian Faith and Today's Mission,* and *The Open Secret*—Newbigin contributed significantly to the practical revival of the doctrine of the Trinity in the second half of the twentieth century.[2]

Third, Newbigin reckoned the Church to be the visible, tangible, social community that had been constituted by Jesus Christ's choice of his apostles and friends and empowered by his bestowal of the Spirit on them after his death and resurrection. Hence his rejection of a notionally spiritual, actually docetic Church. The Church and its members were in the midst of history, seeking to align themselves with the will of God in the concrete particularities of time and place. That entailed a commitment to "the unity we seek" as palpable, organic unity, such as the Fathers sought to maintain or recover. In apparent contrast to the prevalent view of the Fathers, however, Newbigin considered existing divisions among Christians as somehow within the Church (rather than as splitting a delinquent party off from an easily identifiable continuing body); in spite of that, or because of it, he had no doubt about the sinfulness of divisions, and the call to unity was as urgent as the call to holiness. The ecclesiology of schism is a matter to which I return shortly. In any case, Newbigin understood—and practiced—the episcopal ministry as a personal and institutional, and therefore visible, focus of unity, whether to preserve unity or to facilitate its restoration.

Fourth, Newbigin, like many of the early bishops, exercised a very comprehensive ministry. As a shepherd of Christ's flock, he fed by word and sacrament the sheep directly committed to his charge and care. As both a working evangelist and a missionary strategist, he led his Christians by personal example, and all the churches by his contributions to policy, in their common responsibility to spread the Gospel. In the ecclesiologically abnormal circumstances of a divided Christendom that was yet looking to become reunited, Newbigin took a prominent part in such inadequate and provisional forms of conciliar life as were still or already possible. In the midst of all this, preparing for it and pursuing its consequences, Newbigin through his writings—and now also of course through the newer means of communication—deliberately reached after the widest attainable audience for the divine Word entrusted to him. In his later years in particular, he exercised a ministry of intellectual apologetics toward many on the edges of the Church, who, under the pressures of late modernity, either seemed to be lapsing from the faith they once shared or else, from the outside, were looking with interest for better possibilities than the world otherwise held.

Fifth, there was the sheer stature of Newbigin as a man of God. Conversion to Christ, wrote Newbigin in *The Open Secret*, "is primarily and essentially a personal event, in which a human person is laid hold of by the living Lord Jesus Christ at the very center of his being and turned towards him in loving trust and obedience." To confess that "Jesus is Lord of all" is possible

> only because I have been laid hold of by Another and commissioned to do so. It is not primarily or essentially my decision. By ways which are mysterious to me, which I can only faintly trace, I have been laid hold of by one greater than I and led into a place where I must make this confession and where I find no way of making sense of my own life or of the life of the world except through being a disciple of Jesus. I have therefore to say with Paul: "Necessity is laid upon me. Woe to me if I do not preach the gospel. For if I do this of my own will, I have a reward; but if not of my own will, I am entrusted with a commission" (1 Cor. 9:16f.).[3]

Lesslie Newbigin benefited from a lasting conversion; he interpreted that blessing as for the sake of others. His life in the Spirit from whom he received many gifts found outward expression in powerful testimony and in compassionate service. This was a holy man whose plain and humble character attracted many—not, ultimately, to him, but rather through him—to the Source of his and all holiness.

As already hinted, there is a matter of ecclesiology that may separate Newbigin from the Fathers in theology and, to that extent, detract from his standing in the eyes of the Orthodox and the Catholics. The thesis underlying his book *The Reunion of the Church* is that it is the historic Church's condition as "both holy and sinful" that makes reunion both necessary and possible. Now, both Orthodox and Catholics hold that the Church in its essential character as the matrix of all holiness cannot simultaneously be sinful—even though, of course, particular Christians and even particular congregations at certain times and places may sin. Newbigin believed his view to rest on the writings of the apostle Paul. Here, then, is a matter for that "fuller study" which Pope John Paul II, in his encyclical *Ut Unum Sint*, judged to be needed on "the relationship between Sacred Scripture, as the highest authority in matters of faith, and Sacred Tradition, as indispensable to the interpretation of the Word of God." Meanwhile, it may well be that the real ministry of Lesslie Newbigin as bishop and as theologian will turn out to have been one of those signs that were obliging both Catholics and Orthodox in the latter part of the twentieth century to reflect ecclesiologically on the presence and activity of the Holy Spirit beyond their own respective canonical bounds. The spontaneous comment of the Russian bishop at Salvador de Bahia may prove prophetic.

Unto the Third and the Fourth Generation

In appraising my original project on behalf of Oxford University Press, an anonymous reader remarked that part of my task would be to explain how someone who was in the *avant-garde* of the theological mainstream in the '40s and '50s "has since been marginalized despite the fact that he has remained remarkably up-to-date intellectually. This suggests that the theological mainstream itself is now intellectually marginalized in a way that was not true in Newbigin's youth (when the theological mainstream was defined by people like the Niebuhr brothers, Tillich, Barth)." Insofar as that may be an accurate reading of the situation, I would suggest that a clue resides in the fact that many theologians in the intervening years, in their chase to remain abreast of fashions in the secular academy, have distanced themselves from the body of the faithful, which has thus itself been diminished in its intellectual life. If the discipline of theology now appears peripheral to the "higher culture" of the West and even to many Christians, a reason may be that it has in its recent exercise forfeited its constituency in the Church and therefore also in the academy and among the intelligentsia—both of which (since Michel Foucault) recognize the lack of a power base when they see one. By contrast, Newbigin—both as pastor and as thinker—stayed firmly located in the Church and, while "remaining intellectually up-to-date," brought to developments in contemporary thought and culture both a sharply critical eye and an offer to show how some of their interests and concerns, at least, could be better met within the comprehensive worldview provided by the unique Gospel of Jesus Christ. This is what has attracted to Newbigin a younger generation of theologians conscious of their ecclesial and evangelical commitments, even if they differ somewhat among themselves over the appropriate form of the relationship between Church and world and over the structural forms that the embodied Church may, should, must, and does take. Although the Church's general loss of standing in large parts of Western society is a complex matter, neither to be explained by a single cause nor to be remedied by a single solution, the intellectual strengthening of a Church that retains or regains its fidelity to the Gospel would appear to be a requisite factor in the missionary encounter with late modernity that Newbigin both desired and promoted.

"That amazing man," said David Mole of Birmingham about Newbigin, "was able to communicate with three or more generations and with well-educated and non-educated alike."[4] In a posthumous tribute, the American missiologist Wilbert Shenk analyzed thus the types of insight that nourished Newbigin's skills in communication: "Lesslie Newbigin was a frontline thinker because of an uncommon ability to sense the emerging issue that must be addressed at that moment. . . . What makes Newbigin consistently compelling is his keen sense of context and his ability to identify with his audience. He had the ability to articulate what for others remained only subliminal until he expressed it for them."[5]

Generations are tricky to discern: the starting date may be arbitrary, and there are always transitions and overlaps and internal differences. Newbigin was born in 1909. Among the theological masters of the immediately preceding generation, he clearly sided with Karl Barth (born 1886) over Rudolf Bultmann (born 1884) or Paul Tillich (born 1886), despite his tardiness in coming to terms with the massive form of Barth's work. He avowedly learned from the Gifford Lectures of Reinhold Niebuhr (born 1892) delivered around the outbreak of World War II on *The Nature and Destiny of Man*. Newbigin clearly respected his own immediate teachers at Westminster College, John Oman (born 1860), and Oman's pupil and successor Herbert Farmer (born 1892), even though later coming to see their teaching as short on explicit trinitarianism. Among the pioneering generation of the ecumenical movement, Newbigin was directly inspired by the long-lived John R. Mott (born 1865), by Joe Oldham (born 1874), and by William Temple (born 1881), the latter two of whom took the young Newbigin under their respective wings in the 1930s.

Among ecumenical leaders of Lesslie Newbigin's own generation, the only ones who, at his level of prominence, could match his range and grasp—in Faith and Order, Mission and Evangelism, Church and Society—were his friends W. A. Visser 't Hooft (born 1900) and M. M. Thomas (born 1916). The careers of the three of them were very different. Thomas was a lay theologian largely based in his home country of India and in his own Mar Thoma Church. The Dutchman Visser 't Hooft was the general secretary, first, of the World's Student Christian Federation, and then of the World Council of Churches, a consummate administrator of ecumenical organizations headquartered in the international city of Geneva. Both "Wim" and "M. M." were, of course, far larger than these capsule descriptions suggest. But only Lesslie integrated his ecumenical interests and activities with a diocesan episcopate in an alien land among people whom he had taken to his heart.

In the late 1940s and the 1950s, fresh from the achievement of church union in South India and increasingly engaged in the life of the newly inaugurated World Council of Churches, Newbigin sought and—with whatever resistance—gained a hearing among the leadership of those churches and denominations of the Reformation traditions that supported the ecumenical causes of mission and unity. His book *The Household of God* did not so much sum up as rather creatively synthesize a vision of the Church that was trinitarian in its divine reference and eschatological in its historical direction. It was a Church struggling to be reborn as "all in each place" became united in the things that mark the apostolic company according to Acts 2 and thus united also with "the whole Christian fellowship in all places and all ages"—a Church thereby better enabled to fulfill "the tasks to which God calls his people" (to use the language of the New Delhi description of "the unity we seek" drafted by Newbigin). These were perhaps the golden years of twentieth-century ecumenism.

It was, in fact, something very much like Newbigin's vision which—for all the difficulties surrounding the theological evaluation of division—made it possible for the Roman Catholic Church to make its official appearance on the ecumenical scene with the Second Vatican Council. The influence of New-bigin's *Household of God* on the council's dogmatic constitution on the Church, *Lumen Gentium*, has been informally acknowledged by several people in the know. Having first met Lesslie Newbigin at the Ecumenical Institute of Bossey in 1965, Basil Meeking—who was to join the Roman Secretariat for Promoting Christian Unity and later become Bishop of Christchurch, New Zealand—wrote twenty-five years later of Newbigin's "ecumenical leadership" in these terms:

> He is able to bring to it a freshness of thought and strategy. Yet it is so solidly rooted in the Christian tradition. And in these times of weakened identity, both Christian and confessional, when there is confusion and uncertainty in any amount of Christian teaching, Lesslie Newbigin emerges to put the case for fidelity to Scripture, the Church and Tradition in a convincing way. In doing so he is in the original and central stream of the ecumenical movement. It is there and from people like Bishop Newbigin that we may look for the new flowering of ecumenical responsibility when other more exotic and apparently exciting approaches shall have disappeared.[6]

Among my own generation (I was born in 1939), Newbigin was already a hero in our student days for those of us attracted by the ecumenical vision and reality. His *South India Diary* sparked a missionary call for some, even though far fewer foreign missionaries were being sent overseas now that the colonial period was ending and new understandings and strategies of mission were being developed—with precisely Lesslie Newbigin in the forefront. Mission at home and abroad—in six continents—was now being viewed as a single, though still complex, enterprise, albeit Newbigin was again among those who saw that cross-cultural missions (deliberately in the plural)—now multidirectional—remained essential to the prosecution of *the* mission if the "strangeness" of the Gospel was to be signified. Some of us again were to glimpse, from the example of ecclesiology in *The Household of God*, how partial emphases of particular traditions might with imagination and hard work possibly be united into a coherent theological pattern.

My generation, however, was a conflicted one, and many took the direction of the secular. In his 1994 draft, "What Kind of Britain?" Newbigin wrote:

> Most of those who now shape public opinion were intellectually formed in the decade of the 1960s. This was a period in which the Max Weber hypothesis [concerning the irreversible 'disenchantment' of public life in modern society] enjoyed a brilliant Indian summer. During the agony of the struggle with fascism, T. S. Eliot had written 'The Idea of the Christian Society'. The 1960s swept this idea aside. In a series of books such as Harvey Cox's 'The Secular City', Paul Van Buren's 'The Secular Meaning of the Gospel' and—

above all—John Robinson's 'Honest to God', we were persuaded that belief in God as this had been understood in the Christian tradition, is no longer possible for modern secular people.[7]

As was seen in chapters 7 and 10, Newbigin himself, at least partially, guardedly, and transiently, tried out the secular direction as a solution to the crisis of faith on which "the Christian West"—or at least many people hitherto more or less actively part of the "mainstream" churches—had entered. Unless the perception occurred soon after his return to India as CSI bishop in Madras in 1965, it became evident to Newbigin at the Uppsala assembly of the World Council of Churches in 1968 that those elements in the complex notion of the secular which he approved were being absorbed into an ideological relativism that ate away at the very foundations of the Christian faith on which they had rested. The theologians were sawing away at the branches on which they were sitting. As a missionary in Africa, I never set foot in Europe or North America during the revolutionary year of 1968; and I do not know whether I should be grateful to have been spared the battle or sorry to have encountered only its consequences later on.

In a 1994 exchange with Konrad Raiser (born 1938), since 1992 general secretary of the World Council of Churches and a leading advocate for the "Uppsala 1968 paradigm," Lesslie Newbigin wrote: "The [intellectual] products of the 1960s who now provide leadership in most areas are easily recognizable. I have the strong impression that the next generation, now in their twenties and thirties, have turned away from this paradigm. There is considerable fear that the WCC may be trapped in a paradigm that is already losing its power."[8]

Although the sample is neither large nor, perhaps, fair, I thought to test Newbigin's hypothesis about the rising theological generation by inviting two of my *Doktorkinder* to play a part in this book by assessing Newbigin's potential contribution to theology and Church in the opening decades of the twenty-first century. Here is Philip Butin, author of *Revelation, Redemption, and Response: Calvin's Trinitarian Understanding of the Divine-Human Relationship* (1995), pastor of Shepherd of the Valley Presbyterian Church, Albuquerque, and cofounder and teacher in the Ecumenical Institute for Ministry, New Mexico Conference of Churches:

Lesslie Newbigin's *thought*, as indicated in his writings, cannot be separated from the incredible breadth of his *life* in all its aspects. Where the renewal of the Church and the world in the twenty-first century is at stake, the significance of this remarkable "perichoresis" of life, worship, and theology in this one human story cannot be exaggerated. In an ostensibly post-modern era in which the forces of fragmentation seem largely to prevail, it is my hope that the sheer force of this astonishing human life—in which were integrated so many of the chief concerns of the Christian Gospel—may be a beacon pointing the way forward.

Among the many possible theological contributions I might emphasize are: (a) Newbigin's consistent assumption and articulation of an intrinsically trinitarian understanding of God's being and work as the theological matrix of his understanding of the Church and its mission; (b) the generosity, catholicity, and global scope of his ecclesial vision; and (c) his persistent appeal to history and biblical eschatology in order to avoid the dissolution of the Gospel of the triune God's universal love for all humankind in the direction of either a parochializing pluralism or an imperialistic exclusivism.

My fondest hope, however, for Newbigin's ongoing influence is that Christian theology in the twenty-first century would pattern itself after Newbigin's lifelong embodiment of the historic conviction that Christian theology at its most genuine is practical, pastoral theology. As this book's narrative theological synthesis of Newbigin's life and work shows, Newbigin's theological writings display a vision that is both broad and deep, coherent, and timely. I suggest that these distinctive features derive specifically from their uniquely practical and pastoral context, focus, and intent.

Rather than sitting down self-consciously to produce something called "theology," Newbigin simply and constantly reflected upon the practical and pastoral challenges of the Church's ministry for the world in the light of the Christian Gospel. This, I submit, is theology at its most genuine. Given the inherited modern Western dichotomy of theory and practice, in which the theological task is typically assumed to begin with the former and enlighten the latter, Newbigin's is a model for the theological task that the churches urgently need, both now and in the challenges that will face us in the coming years.

Throughout the many issues in world and Church, the interests, phases, and refinements that his writings reflect, Newbigin's richly variegated theological perspective was chiefly developed and articulated from the vantage point of the active practice of the servant-role of a missionary, diocesan bishop, and parish pastor. For Newbigin, Christian theology was precisely and intrinsically "working theology"—theology constantly developed and refined and formulated within and addressed to the daily lives of Christians and non-Christians, both in the Church and in the world. For Newbigin, theology was not an activity to be pursued for its own sake, or for the sake of the academy, or for the sake of impressive theoretical formulation, or for the sake of self-understanding. Rather, theology was pursued for the sake of the Church, its ministry, and its mission in and for the world. Theology was essentially *practical* theology.

In North American churches, we are just beginning to challenge prevailing Enlightenment "theory-praxis" models of theological method and ministry. Academic institutions concerned with Christian theological education for ministry are just starting to perceive that if, as Christians have always believed, the focus of God's activity is in and through the Church, then the actual faith, worship, and practice of visible communities of believers where God is at work must provide much of the subject matter of theology. It is my hope that future generations will recognize in the figure of Lesslie Newbigin an important precursor, inspiration, and impetus for a significant theological shift in this direction.

Telford Work completed his doctorate at Duke University in the Spring of 1999 with a dissertation that set forth a constructive trinitarian account of the nature, authority, interpretation, and use of the Bible under the title *Living and Active: The Christian Vision of Scripture.* He is teaching at Westmont College, Santa Barbara. Here is how he acknowledges his own debt to Newbigin and estimates what his peers might also gain:

> How might my generation's fellow theologians benefit from attending to Lesslie Newbigin's work? He has affected my theological life in many, surprising ways. Newbigin's contributions are numerous and impressive, but I recount one basic contribution that drives my appreciation of the others.
>
> Before my exposure to Newbigin, I had a fairly typical North American attitude towards Christian denominationalism: first, that differences in *polity* between denominations are by and large adiaphora, no more relevant to Christian life than the differences between California's and Nevada's political structures are relevant to U. S. citizenship; second, that *theological* differences (defined of course in terms of doctrine rather than mere polity) between denominations necessitate a search for the One True Church and emigration to it (after all, God must have provided one for diligent seekers to find).
>
> Many of my fellow evangelical Protestants at Fuller Seminary were engaged in similar quests for the ultimate denomination. Our role as enquirers was to study the traditions' various polemics, in order to declare a winner of the ecclesiological debate. Some found what they were searching for. One friend's laborious search led him powerfully to the fundamentalistic Reformed tradition, then to a reformed Episcopalian splinter group, then finally into Eastern Orthodoxy, where he lives an entirely satisfied life in the priesthood. Others have never quite finished their quest, and remain unsatisfied with both their present location and their other denominational options. Still others have given up, concluding that there simply *is* no One True Church. For these the greatest temptations, both fatal to Christian theologians, are either to settle for ecclesiastical mediocrity or to give up on organized Christianity entirely. I myself switched allegiances many times in my heart. But unlike my Orthodox friend, I could never find a tradition with which I was entirely comfortable.
>
> Newbigin's ecclesiological vision, developed in *The Household of God* and elsewhere, saved me from my search for the One True Church, by offering me an alternative I had never considered. "The Holy Catholic Church has not ceased to exist, defaced and divided though it is by our sin," he claims in *The Reunion of the Church* (p. 113). However, like the Corinthian body, circumstances have divided the universal Church *not* into one true fellowship and many counterfeits, nor even one Church and other mere "ecclesial bodies" or "vestiges of the Church," but into mutually compromised factions with continuing, legitimate ecclesiological claims on each other.
>
> Schism does not annihilate God's presence to the divided fellowships, for "God in His mercy has not allowed our sinful divisions to destroy the operations of His grace" (ibid.). Yet schism *does* compromise God's presence throughout the Church, for no denominational camp can live up to the full promise of the Church of Jesus Christ. So the factions' ecclesiological justifications afflict their internal health and their external witness. Furthermore, as Newbigin brilliantly argues in *The Household of God*, they frustrate the very divisions they seek to justify, by revealing the Holy Spirit's work in supposedly illegitimate rivals and pointing the factions beyond themselves and towards each other. My fellows and I were feeling the effects: Appreciation of the partly incompatible insights of more than one tradition, frustration at each

tradition's own inadequacy, and restlessness at the prospect of accepting the failings of any one of these as God's will, when life together in Christ seems to promise so much more than the *status quo*.

My fellows and I had failed to understand that these flawed Christian fellowships were compromised not simply because of the positions they had taken, but in part because of the way they had taken up these positions *against* others. We let the factions judge each other as Johannine children of light and darkness, rather than childish Corinthians. We had bought into their common claim that one tradition could be entirely right, or even simply be fundamentally sound, apart from the resources of the others. This mistake led us either into the overrealized eschatology implicit in the various denominations' claims to be the One True Church (even those of traditions that in other respects championed futurist eschatologies!), or to its abandonment for an utterly futurist eschatology where the current institutional fellowships of Christians would have only a weak relationship to the invisible Church of Christ (an easy move for those of us with strong premillennial heritages).

Newbigin's diagnosis decisively refutes these false opposites. It resists the smug exclusivism of any one position—"Catholic," "Protestant," "Pentecostal/Free Church"—while simultaneously resisting both the facile inclusivism that forces all these traditions under one pseudo-ecclesiological umbrella, and the convenient pluralism that considers each of them self-sufficient or essentially commensurate. After Newbigin, I have stopped searching for the One True Church, for he has helped me see that I already belong to it.

Yet this insight is not a license for ecumenical complacency, for my local church and its denomination are paradoxically neither one, nor true, nor even Church, insofar as we fail to practice Christian unity on the local and global levels. I cannot dismiss the important claims that divide the Christian traditions. In fact, now that I understand how division harms those even on the right sides of the debates, I must take them more seriously than ever. The indicative-imperatives Paul applied to the Church in Corinth apply also directly to the Church in Los Angeles, as they apply to the universal Church: Be one, as you really are one (cf. 1 Cor. 5:7, 2 Cor. 7:1). Many of the issues that divide Christians are genuine issues. Some are crucial enough to warrant prolonging the visible disunity of Christ's Church until they are settled (for instance, those facing the Church in Galatia). Yet the Church's unity is no less pressing. In its absence, no theological dispute that has led to schism can truly be resolved.

Thus Newbigin has transformed how I understand my task as a Christian theologian. Because a reunion of churches "is a reunion of divided parts of the Church, not the return of dissident brethren to the one Church" (*The Reunion of the Church*, p. 108), my task is to *resolve* debates rather than to *win* them, to reconcile all sides rather than to beat the opposition. Newbigin has also reformed my evangelical "church-shopping" habit. Rather than looking for one true denomination or local church, I have started simply discerning where God has put my family and me. Frustration turned to relief as my criterion went from doctrinal blackballing to fruits-testing: Where among God's divided people can we bear the fruit of the Holy Spirit and best exercise our spiritual gifts? As a worshiper and teaching pastor, where can I take joy in the holiness of my own tradition, and lead others to appreciate the holiness of Christ's traditions around us? Where can I work most productively for our local and global reconciliation? Ironically, it is by pointing out the ecclesiological *incoherence* of contemporary Christianity that Newbigin lends ecclesiological *coherence* to my work in one of Jesus' estranged churches, on behalf of all of them.

I stress this one argument of Newbigin's because many today so need to appreciate it. Denominational partisanship is losing its appeal, as ecumenists had hoped. Sadly, so is the theological confidence that produced the hard-won strengths of the denominations in the first place. They are being replaced not by Christocentric, evangelical, ecumenical ecclesiology, but by pragmatism, consumerism, pluralism, relativism, and theological apathy. These have little to offer hungry disciples, and even less to offer the unchurched. In their own ways, all such ecumenical heresies accept a divine household divided against itself. They settle either for ecclesiological anarchy, or for a "reconciled diversity" which is institutionalized ecclesiological incoherence and denominational pride. Consequently, afflicted traditions are suffering in every other area of Newbigin's lifetime witness and achievements: faith, evangelism, ecumenism, pastoral leadership, mission, dialogue with the religions, social vision, liturgical and homiletical power, scriptural teaching, and apologetics.

Like the WCC itself, Newbigin's ecclesiological vision was inspired by frustration at the impotence of divided and competing missionary efforts in the mission field. As the years have gone on, it has only become more obvious that that mission field is the whole world, including even the churches that occupy it, and the WCC itself. How long will it be before not only the world, but even the churches themselves, fail to see the sonship of Jesus on account of their own divisions (cf. John 17:23)?

Yet here too, Newbigin has something to teach us. Where phenomenology sees mainly centrifugal forces that atomize Christians and further splinter and hollow out their traditions, faith and hope still confess one holy catholic Church with Christ as its center, and work to manifest it. Newbigin's account is finally eschatological, his vision of organic churchly unity "a credible sign of that eschatological unity when it is moving toward it, and when it is already embodying a foretaste of it in its own actual life" (as *In Each Place* claims). The goal is forever burned in the Christian consciousness by Luke's image of Pentecost evening: All believers together, having all things in common, growing in number and in favor with all the people (Acts 2:42–47). "The central and simple fact of redemption into Christ makes outward division intolerable," writes Newbigin in *The Reunion of the Church*, "and it is this central certainty which makes us sure that . . . we shall be led forward into unity of heart and mind and into the full riches of the inheritance of the Church." Such a vision of the unseen will never settle for an endless postponing of the fulfillment promised and required now; nor for a veneer of interconfessional conciliarity; nor for illusory utopias built on theological sand; nor for the lure of *In Each Place*'s "monolithic imperialism which, in the name of unity, crushes that blessed variety which God the Father has so lavishly bestowed on his creation."

There is no question that "sinful self-will operates to keep us separated," and that only the Day of the Lord Jesus will see its final defeat. I have no idea how episcopal, presbyterian, congregational, and other structures might work together in my local context following the "death and rebirth of many forms of church life as we have known them" (New Delhi 1961). But if God has intended these structures to function properly in the age for which they are ordained, then so they will. My generation should pay attention to Newbigin, if only to avoid being left behind when that extraordinary work of the Holy Spirit finally comes.

During the last years of his life Newbigin would risk looking into the proximate future, sometimes with explicit mention of "the twenty-first century." One important instance was the "missionary's dream" contributed at the invitation of the editor of the *Ecumenical Review*.[9] Other hints are scattered through the later writings. These prospective forays scout areas of his enduring concern: apologetics, the life of society, the claims of competing religions, the evangelical mission, the unity of the Church, and the nature and identification of a tradition and a community that keep fidelity to the Scriptures.

On the terrain of apologetics, Newbigin foresaw the Christian faith as offering a new-old rationality that could take over again from the Enlightenment rationality which had temporarily replaced it but was now crumbling. Thus already in *Foolishness to the Greeks*:

> When the ultimate explanation of things is found in the creating, sustaining, judging, and redeeming work of a personal God, then science can be the servant of humanity, not its master. It is only this testimony that can save our culture from dissolving into the irrational fanaticism that is the child of total skepticism. It will perhaps be the greatest task of the Church in the twenty-first century to be the bastion of rationality in a world of unreason. But for that, Christians will have to learn that conversion is a matter not only of the heart and the will but also of the mind.[10]

Or again, in *Truth and Authority in Modernity*: "With the widespread breakdown of confidence in the universal applicability of the 'reason' of the eighteenth century and the growth of movements like astrology and the New Age, I suspect that one of the main functions of the Church in the twenty-first century will be to defend rationality against the hydra-headed *Volksgeist*," and:

> Forces of darkness, irrationality, and violence are perhaps more devastating throughout the world today than they have ever been. And in Europe itself, the birthplace of the Enlightenment and long regarded as the secure bastion of its values, there is disintegration. Those who fought to overthrow the dark forces of fascism and national socialism in the Second World War and believed that Europe would never sink again into such barbarism have lived to see these same forces once more taking the stage. Even where such violent forms of irrationality are only on the margins of society, the great visions of the future that inspired the social legislation of the nineteenth and twentieth centuries are now widely rejected. Rational planning for human welfare is widely abandoned in favor of leaving everything to the irrational forces of the market.[11]

With the political and the economic we arrive back at Newbigin the social visionary.

In that area, Newbigin forecast that "the exuberant capitalism of the past 250 years" will be diagnosed in the long run as "a desperately dangerous," and perhaps terminal, "case of cancer in the body of human society," if indeed there are "actually survivors around to make the diagnosis."[12] Unfettered growth, he held, was driven by that covetousness which St. Paul labeled idolatry.[13] "Justice for the poor" and "responsibility for the environment"— both interests of the World Council of Churches in its major concern of "Justice, Peace, and the Integrity of Creation"—needed therefore to be set within a more profound understanding of sin and redemption than appeared to Newbigin so far to be the case with the WCC. On "the calling to seek justice," he wrote this in his "dream" of 1991:

> Christian involvement in issues of justice for the poor has been considerably influenced by Marxism. This influence is likely to decrease. There will be a new urgency in clarifying the Christian belief about the possibilities and the limits of human well-being on this side of death, about the relation between God's justification and human justice, and about the role of the local eucharistic community in every place as a foretaste and sign of God's justice, as well as an instrument of that justice. Marxism has not been able to deliver what it promised—a human society that overcame the evils of capitalism and created justice and freedom on earth. Capitalism has not delivered such a society. Adam Smith himself was clear that free markets would not work except in the presence of a certain moral framework, and when modern capitalism began to develop in the Western world in the eighteenth and nineteenth centuries, it very quickly became clear that free markets could not ensure a minimum of humane treatment for workers. The market had to be controlled in the interests of human good. The market is the best means available for continuously balancing supply and demand, but it cannot be the ultimate authority over human life. Everything depends upon the fundamental beliefs about human nature and destiny which permeate the society in which the market operates. There will always be need for controls of the market. We certainly cannot seek the kind of theocratic society which Islam represents. But we can and must affirm that every local eucharistic community in which we celebrate the acts through which we are enabled to participate in God's justice and God's mercy is a centre from which we can radiate the kind of human behaviour in which markets can operate for the common good. They can be places where people are delivered from the ideology of capitalism and can make markets human. To *multiply* such centres throughout the world must surely be the first priority for a world council of churches. In other words, the question "How can modern people be enabled to know Jesus and put their trust in him?" must become the very central issue on the agenda of the Council.[14]

On "the calling to care for creation," Newbigin noted that the threat to the human environment had only recently emerged in its full proportions and urgency, for "until recently there seemed to be ample room on the surface of our planet for all its inhabitants, and room to dispose of all our waste." The answer to the question "Why should I put the care of the creation above my own present advantage?" has to be "so based in reality that it can halt the accelerating rush of modernity to carry to the limit the human power to exploit the natural world." Lacking transcendental reference, no purely secular ethics—whether capitalist, Marxist, or scientific—can find valid reasons for "curbing our own desires for the sake of remote descendants who have no power to exert sanctions on us as our contemporaries do." Whence, then, can come the motive for caring for the planet?

> It cannot come only from nostalgia for a lost security in the womb of nature. It is understandable that modern people feel this nostalgia. We have treated the natural world as something at our disposal. We have forced it to answer our questions and used the answers to manipulate nature in accordance with our whims. We have therefore become alienated from nature, and we feel the pangs of bereavement when we see "primitive" peoples who have escaped modernization. So it is understandable that there are "New Age" movements which invite us to turn back and become again part of nature, seeking to unite ourselves again with the cosmic forces in ways that bypass our arrogant rationality. Astrology and transcendental meditation become big industries, and long-forgotten pagan rites are celebrated again in Europe. But the New Age is a very ancient blind alley. Nature is not a source of ethics. There is no right and wrong in nature. Its governing realities are power and fertility. To make nature our ultimate is to be delivered to death. Nature's smile can be charming, but her teeth are cruel.

To the question of why we should care for the planet the Christian answer is,

> because it is the place which God has created to be cherished and husbanded by his human family as the theatre of his glory; because God delights in it and has created human beings to share his delight; because in his incarnate Son Jesus Christ he has taken created nature upon himself to fulfill and glorify it; and because in the bodily resurrection of Jesus from the dead he has given us the pledge and proof of his purpose to bring a new creation out of the death and decay of the old.[15]

In the area of religion, Newbigin declared his opinion that "in the twenty-first century the main global alternative to Christianity will be Islam." Newbigin respected Islam for the seriousness of the Muslims' commitment to their faith and morals, but as a Christian he found them lacking in their rejection of the atoning work and the final authority of Christ with all the consequences of those. The challenge that Islam posed for Christianity he formulated thus:

> Islam is now, with a renewed confidence and with great material resources, making a global claim to offer a kind of society in which God is affirmed as sovereign, and all human life, public and personal, is ruled by revealed law. This claim comes into head-on collision with the claim of modernity to provide an open society in which all creeds are tolerated but none except its own is allowed into the public domain. Islam will not accept relegation to the private sector as Christianity has—in many societies—tamely done. Islam, like Marxism, seeks to identify ultimate truth with actual political power. The union of truth with power lies beyond death, and in that sense Christi-

anity has to be other-worldly. The City of God cannot be built by human hands on earth but is a gift from heaven. But the Muslim challenge will compel Christians to question the privatization of their faith and to challenge also the idea that public life is an arena from which the truth-claims of the Gospel are excluded.[16]

At the close of the twentieth century, the "clash of civilizations" which some foresaw was already being adumbrated in the Balkans, the Caucasus, the East Indies, and parts of Africa.[17] The form that such a clash may take will vary geographically with the forms of Islam and with the vitality or otherwise of Christianity in its own various forms. For the West, Newbigin's "vision of a Christian society" can only be the framework—whether as anticipation or accompaniment or aftereffect—of a deeper "reconversion" to the Gospel on the part of (some of) the people.

What, then, of the future in Newbigin's lifelong fields of mission and evangelism? Already in 1947, Newbigin was writing that "the Churches of old Christendom, conscious of the paganism of their lands, are painfully struggling back to the truth that mission is the task of the Church, and that a Church which is not a mission is not a Church."[18] From the integration of the International Missionary Council with the World Council of Churches in 1961 Newbigin had hoped for an increasing infusion of evangelistic concern into the entire awareness and activity of the "main-line" churches of western Europe and North America. In 1990, however, he read the current situation thus:

While the old "Christendom" has been in decline, new and powerful centres of Christian culture have developed in other parts of the world. To an astonishing extent the call for "the evangelization of this generation" has been honoured—if not in one generation, at least in one century. The vigorous missionary outreach is now mainly from the churches of the "third world." Not only is the rapid growth of the churches in many areas the result of the evangelistic outreach of the local churches, but in the field of international and cross-cultural mission new and powerful thrusts are coming from such burgeoning churches as those of Korea. By contrast, it is now typical to find in the old "main line" churches an acute embarrassment about missions, partly the result of guilt about the wrongs of colonialism, partly a fundamental loss of nerve which manifests itself in all aspects of Western culture outside of its science and technology. The traditional "main-line" missionary societies are now mainly agencies of interchurch aid. The vast new missionary challenge, namely that presented by modernization, is one that they find hard to respond to because they are part of it.[19]

Newbigin still desired that "the WCC should be and should be seen to be an enabler of the Church's universal mission to make Christ known, loved, and obeyed throughout this entire global city of which we are all a part. And I am asking that the WCC recognize that it is not enough to address the *symptoms* of modernization; we have to address the causes, the underlying belief systems which sustain it. We need a theological clarification of the issues involved in a global missionary encounter with modernity."[20] Elsewhere Newbigin envisaged all this in 1990 as a task for at least "several decades."[21]

Where is ecclesial unity to figure in this future prospect? Admitting that much progress had been made in the twentieth century in mutual understanding and collaboration among the existing churches, Newbigin remained deeply disappointed by the many failures to achieve the visible, tangible, organic unity that he believed belonged to the credibility of the Gospel. Perhaps "the ecumenical moment" had been missed.[22] By the end of the twentieth century the ecumenical scene was taking on new configurations. The Protestant churches belonging to the World Council of Churches, for instance, now accounted for fewer than half the Protestants in the world. There were, moreover, growing signs of splits within some of the Western churches. "Lesslie died," said Dan Beeby, "in conflict with his own Church": the issue was the liberalizing moves in the United Reformed Church in the matter of homosexual practices; Newbigin registered his protest in the assembly and sought by letter to mobilize support for the scriptural and traditional teaching on men lying with men and women lying with women; he stayed to fight on what was not only the matter of a surrender to claims of "individual choice" but also the case of a substantial abandonment of the divine order made known in Scripture. At the turn into the twenty-first century, some of the most interesting efforts—in the West, at least—at the preservation and renewal of the classic Christian faith are, it strikes me, in the hands of those who, across ecclesiastical and denominational lines, represent an "evangelical catholicism" or a "catholic evangelicalism." What this may eventually mean, institutionally and confessionally, is not yet clear. But if Newbigin's ecumenical vision is to be followed, the result will have to serve the Church as a network of local churches, truly united in themselves, joined in a global fellowship by word, sacraments, and a universally recognized ministry and bearing through proclamation and service—and their very existence—the mission entailed in being created by the Spirit as the firstfruits, sign, and instrument of God's Kingdom.

The ecclesiological issue remains crucial, for it is a matter of being able to identify and locate the tradition and the community that embody the charge laid by Jesus on his followers to transmit and enact the Gospel message. Any Western Christian, at least, has to face the presence and the claims of the Church of Rome. Few theologically educated Protestants in Lesslie Newbigin's generation took the path to Rome: many invested their energies and their hopes in an ecumenical movement toward which official Rome showed first hostility and then at least suspicion until mid-century and even beyond. In my generation, a few more have taken the Rome-ward track, perhaps because they saw many concerns of the sixteenth-century Reformation finally taken up by the Second Vatican Council. In the next generation, the numbers seem to increase, conceivably from disappointment with the leadership of the mainstream Protestant churches in my generation. If such seekers were to be influenced by Newbigin, they would certainly be willing to engage in what

Pope John Paul II called "a patient and fraternal dialogue" on "the ministry of universal unity" which the Roman see wishes to offer to all Christians, especially when that ministry and its cause are geared—as declared in *Ut Unum Sint*—to the task of evangelization. Students of Newbigin would also wish to treat with even-handed seriousness both parts of the relationship, which John Paul II saw as needing further exploration, between "Sacred Scripture as the highest authority in matters of faith" and "Sacred Tradition as indispensable to the interpretation of the Word of God." With that, of course, would have to go consideration of the teaching authority—a function which Newbigin affirmed as necessary in the Church—which the Pope saw as located in the Magisterium "entrusted to the Pope and the Bishops in communion with him, understood as a responsibility and authority exercised in the name of Christ for teaching and safeguarding the faith." The free assent of the company of the faithful—in obedience to the living Lord encountered in the Church—would remain important in Newbigin's perspective. Recognizing also with Newbigin the sin that remains in Christians and in the Church, there would be a need to affirm with Vatican II the realization of *Ecclesia semper purificanda*. And anyone with a Reformed streak in him would doubtless keep Lesslie's limerick in mind:

> *Full Circle*
>
> The Church of St. Peter in Rome
> has a vast and magnificent dome.
> It's spectacular, but
> in a fisherman's hut
> I think Peter would feel more at home.

In an eightieth-birthday tribute to Newbigin's personal, pastoral, and institutional concern for ecclesial unity, Cardinal Jan Willebrands, head of the Pontifical Council for Promoting Christian Unity, took the risk of an "indiscretion" in order to say that "for Lesslie Newbigin the source of the coherence in his efforts for unity is to be found in his familiarity with the Word of God, read and reread, meditated on, prayed over, listened to with the desire to put it into practice in his life and word. May the Lord multiply the docile servants of his Word."[23]

It would be impertinent of me, and baseless, to suggest that Newbigin himself considered a move to the Church of Rome; but that these speculations on Rome are not merely gratuitous is shown by a speck on Newbigin's horizon—admittedly in a vision of corporate reunion—in 1948: "However far-reaching may be the transformation required both of the Protestant Churches and of the Roman and Eastern before union can be a matter even of discussion, there ought to be nothing to prevent our looking now towards the restoration to the whole Church of a visible unity with a central organ of unity such as Rome was for so many vital centuries of the Church's history."[24] Admittedly also, Newbigin sharply criticized in *The Finality of Christ* the Romanocentric cosmos of Pope Paul VI's encyclical *Ecclesiam Suam*.[25] But in a paper on "Ministry" in the late 1980s, he said in connection with "the right balance of personal and conciliar elements in the government of the Church at every level—local, regional, national, universal": "That means that Protestants have to take seriously the Roman Catholic witness about primacy, that Catholics have to take seriously the testimony of Protestants about the role of the Church meeting and the synod or council."[26] Newbigin's thoughts on a "Petrine ministry" from that same paper are also interesting, based as they are on John 21:

> In the first part Peter is the fisherman who (if only he is obedient to the Lord) is able to catch not only a vast number of fish, but also (unlike the "evangelists" who leave as their legacy a litter of mutually competing sects) is able to bring them all to the feet of Jesus as one, with no "schism" in the net (21: 11). Then Peter is the shepherd to whom the Lord entrusts his sheep, but only because he is assured that Peter loves him, the one to whom the sheep belong. But finally—and this is where the chapter comes to its crucial point— Peter is a disciple. The words "follow me," in the context of all that has gone before (see 13:36–38), constitute the punch-line of the whole chapter. But this decisive word can only be spoken because Peter has learned what following means—not his own programme, but the way of the cross (21:18f.). Peter in other words can be a shepherd only if he is a disciple. He can bring others to Jesus and guard them in his ownership only if he is himself following Jesus on the way of the Cross. He can be a leader only as he is a follower—a follower on the way of the cross. Following Jesus on the way of the cross in such wise that others are enabled to follow: this, I believe, is the heart of what the New Testament has to say about ministry.[27]

But to return directly to the generation game and play it for one more stage, let us imagine a theological descendant of Lesslie Newbigin born in 1999. Where will such a theological great-granddaughter find herself in, say, 2029, and to what will she commit her life? Will she be a cross-cultural missionary, experiencing what her great-grandfather wrote during a visit to the Congo in October 1960?

> While we are engaged in the search for a biblical theology of mission, we shall not be able to escape the fact that in the New Testament, suffering certainly plays a very central part in the picture. . . . In the end of the day, there is nothing so important as the coming to the Congo of missionaries who know that the one thing they bring is the Gospel which they share with the Congolese Christians, and who are ready to disappear into the Church in the Congo and become part of it, dying that it may live. I am expressing this badly, because it is late at night, but these days in the Congo have sharpened for me a feeling which has been growing through all these discussions in Africa so far—the feeling that the sending of missionaries who understand their task in those terms is the greatest thing that can be done for any people.[28]

If she is in Africa, will she find it by now a "Christian continent"—though racked by internecine wars? What, ecclesiologically, will she make of those communities that started life as "African independent churches," where theological and practical "syncretism" threatened and where a "universally recognized ministry" was lacking?[29] Or if she has followed in her great-grandfather's footsteps to India, where will she stand in the theological and practical tensions between Christian evangelism and interreligious dialogue that have been more acutely felt in that country than anywhere else? Or will China—its weight and shadow having long lurked in Lesslie Newbigin's mind—have been "opened up" for perhaps the fourth time in its history to the possibility of the Gospel?

Or will this imaginary theological great-granddaughter stay somewhere "in the West"? To what extent will she find it "reconverted" to the Gospel? Will she come—perhaps from an educational background primarily in the natural sciences rather than in the humanities or the social sciences—to engage as a Christian in a continuing intellectual and public debate over the culture? Will there be a continuing Christian missionary witness from overseas for her to welcome? Will she have to live under the *shariah* law of Islam? Or will neopaganism have run rife? Where will she be exercising the ancestral concern for society and care for the poor? What Church will she belong to? Is it too soon to envisage a "Western Orthodoxy," composed of catholic, evangelical, pentecostal Christians, in full communion with Eastern Orthodoxy, Oriental Orthodoxy, and perhaps an "African Orthodoxy," a complex family living in a single household of God, all confessing one apostolic faith in the Holy Trinity, and all bearing a common witness as one body to the whole Gospel of Jesus Christ before the entire world? Might Newbigin's imaginary great-granddaughter have joined one of those "monastic communities, such as the one to which Augustine belonged," of which her great-grandfather spoke as "a visible sign and preliminary realization of a world ruled solely by the love of God in the midst of a world ruled by the love of self"?[30] Might she be another Scholastica, not Benedict this time, showing her contemporaries "how to create the living cells for a new kind of body politic"?[31]

"Amid the Rubble of History"

Newbigin was well aware that there is no direct, uninterrupted road from this earthly life to the heavenly City and the divine Kingdom, either for the individual or for the Church or for the human race. Death always intervenes and leaves behind "the rubble of history." That was a phrase Newbigin used from the Bangalore lectures of 1941 on "The Kingdom of God and the Idea of Progress" onward, and Christians have the privilege and responsibility, he said, of raising amid this transience "acted prayers," "signs of hope."[32] What has proved acceptable to God will be preserved and will, transfigured, be taken into his eternal Kingdom, for "He is able to guard until that Day what has been entrusted to Him."

If any in the next generations should rummage through the rubble of the twentieth century, they might half-see, where Lesslie Newbigin passed, a glint of something very precious, a lingering reflection of a man who sparkled in the Light that had shined on him, the words he spoke and wrote, the deeds he did, the life he lived, the person he was and is.

Epilogue

From Dan Beeby's address at Lesslie Newbigin's funeral

Lesslie never touched anything that he did not adorn, illuminate, and advance. In a faltering age with hope run low, he swung the lamp of resurrection over increasing gloom. We can no longer leave it to Lesslie; his farewell is also a call, almost a command. Our agenda, things to be done.

From the end of Gerard Manley Hopkins' poem "That Nature is a Heraclitean Fire, and Of the Comfort of the Resurrection"

Man, how fast his firedint, his mark on mind, is gone!
Both are in an unfathomable, all is in an enormous dark
Drowned. O pity and indignation! Manshape, that shone
Sheer off, disseveral, a star, death blots black out; nor mark
Is any of him at all so stark
But vastness blurs and time beats level. Enough! the Resurrection,
A heart's-clarion! Away grief's gasping, joyless days, dejection.
Across my foundering deck shone
A beacon, an eternal beam. Flesh fade, and mortal trash
Fall to the residuary worm; world's wildfire, leave but ash:
In a flash, at a trumpet crash,
I am all at once what Christ is, since he was what I am, and
This Jack, joke, poor potsherd, patch, matchwood, immortal diamond
Is immortal diamond.

Notes

Introduction

1. The last mentioned may have been Gray's *The Christian Adventure* (1920) or, more likely perhaps, his *With Christ as Guide: An Apprehension of Christianity* (1927).

2. *Unfinished Agenda: An Autobiography* (London: SPCK, 1985), p. 7 [updated ed. Edinburgh: St. Andrew Press, 1993, p. 7].

3. Ibid., p. 13 (1993, p. 12f.).

4. Ibid., p. 40 (1993, p. 38).

5. "Dear Friends," in Selly Oak box 1, document no. 1/2/44.

6. Circular letter of October 1947, in Selly Oak box 2, document no. 2/1/6.

7. See chapter 4, this volume.

8. "My dear Friends" (October 26, 1947), typescript in Selly Oak box 2, document no. 2/1/14.

9. "Dear Friends" (October 13, 1948), printed letter, Selly Oak box 2, document no. 2/1/69; cf. *Unfinished Agenda*, p. 103 (1993, p. 98).

10. *Unfinished Agenda*, p. 114 (1993, p. 108); cf. pp. 111–113, 128, 162, 231 (1993, pp. 105–107, 121f., 153, 218). Selly Oak box 2 contains a batch of "Anglican correspondence" amounting to fifty-seven documents, including some biting epistolary exchanges with Archbishop Fisher. On one face-to-face occasion—on March 24, 1961—Newbigin was on the point of being "thrown out of Lambeth Palace"; see *Unfinished Agenda*, p. 181 (1993, p. 171), though Lesslie would narrate the incident orally in livelier terms.

11. A (British) Methodist may find cause for a similar sense of frustration, especially given that his own Church was an original party to the South Indian union and was the sole positive respondent to the invitation issued in Archbishop Fisher's Cambridge sermon of 1946 to conversations about unity in England. In 1969 and 1972 the governing bodies of the Church of England twice narrowly

failed to secure the requisite majority for a plan of union which the Methodist Conference had twice approved. In 1982 the Church of England was again among those rejecting a wider (and looser) "covenant" between several churches, while the Methodists voted in favor. The Lambeth Conference of 1988 issued, with some gusto (as I observed), an invitation to dialogue, which the World Methodist Council immediately took up. During the next few years the Anglican-Methodist International Commission—of which I was a member—produced *Sharing in the Apostolic Communion*. The report concluded with a proposed enabling resolution that would have allowed and encouraged the churches of the two families to take positive steps toward "fuller communion." But as an "ecumenical participant" at Lambeth 1998 I detected little interest and less enthusiasm; and it became clear, already at the subsectional and sectional stages, that the Conference could not be asked to give, with whatever theological and moral weight it possessed ("legislation" was never in question, any more than it had been when the World Methodist Council passed its side of the resolution in 1996), a straightforward "recognition" that "Methodists belong to the one, holy, catholic and apostolic Church of Jesus Christ" (the word "acknowledge" was, for instance, substituted for "recognize" with the stated intention of somehow diminishing the import, and other changes were unilaterally introduced into the resolution submitted from the Commission). I am tempted to declare that some of my own best friends are Anglicans.

12. For more on these travels, see *Unfinished Agenda*, pp. 176–191, 194f. (1993, pp. 166–180, 183f.). Selly Oak box 2 contains detailed "travel diaries"—marked "private and confidential" and written by Newbigin for IMC and WCC staff—on the African and Latin American journeys (documents no. 2/4/72–82 and 120, 125, 128–130).

13. "Africa Travel Diary" IV, p. 4. Newbigin himself published this passage in *Unfinished Agenda*, p. 179 (1993, p. 169).

14. I was put on to this testimony by Hans-Ruedi Weber, who had himself been an overseas contributor to the Australian conference. He kindly sent me a photocopy of an otherwise inaccessible text.

15. *Unfinished Agenda*, pp. 174–176 (1993, p. 164f.). Telling an insider's story deriving from a later moment in the decade, Risto Lehtonen, former general secretary of the World's Student Christian Federation, concluded thus: "After the initial stage of protest movements which increased awareness of questions of social and economic justice among Christians in a healthy way, the detrimental effects of the ideological orientation of the sixties became more marked. New Left ideologies continued to appear in the thought patterns, language, and theological views of many ecumenical leaders, causing tensions within the ecumenical movement and distancing the constituency from its leaders. The current crisis of confidence of the ecumenical movement, which is felt acutely in many member churches and which is reflected in the recurring financial problems of the WCC, stems significantly from the influence of these ideological 'germs.' " R. Lehtonen, *Story of a Storm: The Ecumenical Student Movement in the Turmoil of Revolution, 1968–1973* (Grand Rapids: Eerdmans; Helsinki: Finnish Society of Church History, 1998), p. 323f.

16. *Unfinished Agenda*, p. 231f. (1993, p. 219). See pp. 128–129, 353, this volume.

17. *Unfinished Agenda*, p. 252 (1993, p. 239).

18. *"The Good Shepherd": Meditations on Christian Ministry in Today's World* (Grand Rapids: Eerdmans, 1977), p. 9f.

19. Ibid., p. 10f.

20. In the autobiographical *Unfinished Agenda*, see chapter 17, "Madras: Mission in Metropolis," pp. 214–238 (1993, pp. 202–225).

21. *Unfinished Agenda*, p. 248 (1993, p. 234f).

22. Letters of February 25 and March 4, 1999, from Simon Downham to me.

23. Letter from Colin Gunton to me, May 21, 1998.

24. Respective sources: BBC, "Prayer for the Day," February 26, 1985; *Unfinished Agenda*, 1993 ed., p. 261.

25. See *"The Good Shepherd,"* p. 40

26. Letter of Hans-Ruedi Weber to me, March 20, 1998.

27. Letter from the Right Reverend Leslie Brown to me, March 4, 1998.

28. Letter from the Reverend H. B. S. Rahi to me, August 22, 1997.

29. Text in the publication of the Church of England's Council for Christian Unity, *Unity Digest*, no. 18 (April 1998), pp. 17–20. Newbigin's account of the incidents in Birmingham is found in *Unfinished Agenda*, 1993 edition, pp. 257–260.

30. Bernard Thorogood, "Apostolic Faith: An Appreciation of Lesslie Newbigin, Born 8 December 1909," in *International Review of Mission* 79 (1990), pp. 66–85; Martin Conway, "Profile: Lesslie Newbigin's Faith Pilgrimage," in *Epworth Review* 20/3 (September 1994), pp. 27–36, also in *Mid-Stream* 34 (1995), pp. 21–33; Tim Stafford, "God's Missionary to Us," in *Christianity Today*, December 9, 1996, pp. 24–33.

31. T. Dayanandan Francis and Israel Selvanayagam (eds.), *Many Voices in Christian Mission: Essays in Honour of J. E. Lesslie Newbigin, World Christian Leader* (Madras: Christian Literature Society, 1994).

32. *International Review of Mission* 79 (1990), p. 88.

33. *International Review of Mission* 79 (1990), p. 94f.

34. All quotations in this paragraph come from Newbigin's sixtieth birthday tribute to M. M. Thomas, typescript in Selly Oak box 10; no publication discovered.

35. Newbigin wrote a long chapter for a composite book on W. A. Visser 't Hooft that was never in fact published; his typescript is lodged in Selly Oak box 10. A much shorter version of Newbigin's text appeared as "The Missionary Legacy of W. A. Visser 't Hooft" in the *International Bulletin of Missionary Research* 16 (1992), pp. 79–82.

36. E-mail letter from N. T. Wright to me, April 5, 1998. For Newbigin, the work of James Barr was emblematic of the breakup of "biblical theology" in the early 1960s, but he considered that "Barr can be answered"; see *The Gospel in a Pluralist Society* (Grand Rapids: Eerdmans; Geneva: WCC, 1989), pp. 68, 74–77, 94.

37. Letter of May 7, 1994. On occasion he could address me at "Duje Unicersity."

38. "Africa Travel Diary" VI, p. 2.

39. *Unfinished Agenda*, p. 154 (1993, p. 145).

40. Two further theological examples will be given later; see chapter 7, note 53, and conclusion. The collection was published posthumously as *St. Paul in Limerick, and Other Missionary Journeys He May Have Made* (Carlisle, Cumbria: Paternoster/Solway, 1998).

41. In the "selected bibliography" she prepared for *Many Voices in Christian Mission* (1994), Eleanor Jackson listed 219 numbered items; but Newbigin continued to write, and older pieces also came to light, so that at least 247 titles

figure, as far as 1995, in the (avowedly incomplete) "annotated bibliography" of the "Writings of Lesslie Newbigin" in George R. Hunsberger, *Bearing the Witness of the Spirit: Lesslie Newbigin's Theology of Cultural Plurality* (Grand Rapids: Eerdmans, 1998), pp. 283–304). Greater bibliographical completeness is promised in T. F. Foust, J. A. Kirk, and W. Ustorf (eds.), *A Scandalous Prophet: The Way of Mission After Newbigin* (Carlisle, Cumbria: Paternoster Press, forthcoming).

42. Letter from Hans-Ruedi Weber to me, March 20, 1998.

Chapter 1

1. *Sin and Salvation* (London: SCM Press, 1956). The opening phrases come from pages 62 and 99, respectively.

2. *Unfinished Agenda* (London: SPCK, 1985), p. 6 [updated ed. Edinburgh: St. Andrew Press, 1993, p. 6]. Newbigin was still citing William James's essay in *Proper Confidence* (Grand Rapids, Eerdmans, 1995), p. 102.

3. *Unfinished Agenda*, p. 11f. (1993, p. 11f.).

4. *Unfinished Agenda*, p. 24f. (1993, p. 23f.).

5. *Unfinished Agenda*, p. 30f. (1993, p. 28f.).

6. James Denney, "St. Paul's Epistle to the Romans" in *The Expositor's Greek Testament*, ed. W. Robertson Nicoll, volume 2 (New York: George H. Doran Company, no date), p. 608. See pp. 555–725, especially 591–595, 608–613.

7. Paper in Selly Oak box 7.

8. "Revelation," in Selly Oak box 7.

9. The reference is to the *Contra Celsum* I. xi.

10. Text in Selly Oak box 7.

11. *Truth and Authority in Modernity* (Valley Forge, Pa: Trinity Press International, 1996), pp. 15f., 39. In context, Newbigin is differentiating his position from what he understands as "natural theology"; see, in this volume, chapter 10, note 55.

12. The very image of the citadel recurs in *A Faith for This One World?* (London: SCM Press, 1961): "The dying of the Son of God for my sins means the end of any claim of mine to a standing before God. In the face of that fact, I can have no standing ground except what is given to me by his dying for me. The life that was mine is forfeit; the life that I now have is his. The citadel that I kept against him, and over which my flag flew, has surrendered. He is now the rightful Lord. He is free to come in and take control" (p. 86).

13. *Sin and Salvation*, p. 16f.

14. Ibid., p. 98f.

15. Ibid., p. 99f.

16. How Newbigin dealt with the question about the possibility of salvation for those who never heard the Gospel is discussed in chapter 6.

17. *Proper Confidence: Faith, Doubt and Certainty in Christian Discipleship* (Grand Rapids: Eerdmans, 1995); "Certain Faith: What Kind of Certainty?" in *Tyndale Bulletin* 44.2 (1993): 339–350.

18. The phrase comes from Locke's "Third Letter on Toleration."

19. *Proper Confidence*, pp. 25, 49, 96.

20. Ibid., p. 66f.; cf. "Certain Faith," p. 346. 2 Timothy 1:12 was a favorite text of Newbigin's. He was well aware of the exegetical ambiguity; and he took whichever alternative suited his argument at the time—either "I am sure that He

is able to guard until that Day what has been entrusted to me" or "what I have entrusted to Him."

21. *Proper Confidence*, p. 104.

22. Ibid., p. 54.

23. The respective historical references are as follows. Thomas Aquinas, *Summa Theologiae* II/1.112.5. Martin Luther, 1531 Commentary on Galatians, ad 4:6, WA 40:575; Preface to Romans, WA/DB 7:10. The Council of Trent: in Denzinger-Schönmetzer, *Enchiridion Symbolorum*, 1520–1583.

24. Calvin: *Institutes* III.24. Wesley: *Explanatory Notes upon the New Testament*, ad Hebr. 6:11; letter of April 10, 1781, to Hetty Rowe; treatises *Predestination Calmly Considered* and *Serious Thoughts upon the Perseverance of the Saints*.

25. For example, *Sin and Salvation*, p. 118; *The Open Secret* (London: SPCK; Grand Rapids: Eerdmans, 1978), p. 80 (rev. ed. 1995, p. 72).

26. At the annual conference of his preachers in 1745, Wesley described this as coming "to the very edge of Calvinism." For the sense in which Newbigin rejects merit, see *Sin and Salvation*, p. 110: "There is absolutely no place in the Christian life for the idea of merit. It is not because of any good that we do that we are accepted by God. There is no possibility of earning His favour. If we have even a little of that thought we shall find ourselves outside with the elder brother, we shall find the feasting of heaven as unpleasant as he found the feasting for the prodigal son. The greatest saint cannot earn his place in God's home. We are there simply because of His grace. We are ready to come in there when we have the new mind that is created by Christ's death, when we know, at the same moment, how hateful we are to God, and how precious we are to Him."

27. Text in *Reformed World* 39 (1986–1987): 821–829.

28. A. Mitchell Hunter, *The Teaching of Calvin* (Glasgow: Maclehose, 1920), p. 129, quoted by A. P. F. Sell, *The Great Debate: Calvinism, Arminianism and Salvation* (Grand Rapids: Baker, 1983), p. 125. This is what Newbigin wrote toward the end of his life, in *Truth and Authority in Modernity* (1996): "If the faith with which the believer follows Jesus is itself the gift of God, is not God arbitrary in his granting of this gift to some and not to others? I think that the response to this must be along the following lines. If those whom God so calls and to whom is given the gift of faith to respond to the call were called in order that they might be simply the beneficiaries of this calling, there would be ground for making accusation of arbitrary action. But if, as the Bible makes clear, those so called are called not [only?] for themselves but that they may be the messengers of his calling for others, then the charge does not stand. Second, although we must acknowledge that we are here seeking to probe something beyond our powers, namely, the inner freedom of God himself to call whom he will, nevertheless those who have been made part of the new creation in Christ would never seek to claim any personal credit for their calling or their faith. If I, at least, interrogate my own experience, I can only confess that the ways by which I was brought to Christ are very mysterious and beyond my own capacity fully to understand. I can only say that it was the immeasurable grace of God. It is true that there is a personal decision—or series of decisions—involved. But these pale into insignificance in comparison with the vast and immeasurable grace of God" (p. 21f.; the insertion of "only" seems justified by the "simply" in the previous sentence).

29. "The Gospel in Today's Global City: An Address Delivered at the Launch of the Selly Oak Colleges' School of Mission and World Christianity, in the Chapel

of St. Andrew's Hall, Saturday 11 May 1996, by Bishop Lesslie Newbigin" (Birmingham, England: Selly Oak Colleges, 1996), p. 9. The Pauline text is, of course, Ephesians 6:10–20.

Chapter 2

1. *What Is the Gospel?* (Madras: Christian Literature Society). The copy I had access to bears no mention of the author on the cover, and the closing date for printing is 1942. An annotation in Newbigin's hand reads "by L. N., 1936," but in a letter to me of January 1998 he corrected the date to 1942. He mentions his authorship in *Unfinished Agenda* (London: SPCK, 1985), p. 73 (updated ed. Edinburgh: St. Andrew Press, 1993, p. 68).

2. *Christ Our Eternal Contemporary* (Madras: Christian Literature Society, 1968).

3. *Truth to Tell: The Gospel as Public Truth* (Grand Rapids: Eerdmans, 1991).

4. *Unfinished Agenda*, p. 12 (1993 ed., p. 12).

5. Ibid., p. 32 (1993, p. 30).

6. *Unfinished Agenda*, p. 58 (1993, p. 55).

7. *Unfinished Agenda*, p. 61 (1993, p. 57).

8. Selly Oak box 1, document no. 1/2/44; quoted also in *Unfinished Agenda*, p. 63f. (1993, p. 59f.).

9. *Unfinished Agenda*, p. 102 (1993, p. 97). Again I am reminded of my introduction to the life of the village churches in Ivory Coast in particular, although the allegiance there—apart from the Roman Catholics and the independent "Harristes"—was largely Methodist and there was no "church union" to celebrate or explain.

10. *Unfinished Agenda*, p. 248f. (1993, p. 235).

11. Letter from the Reverend H. B. S. Rahi to me, August 22, 1997.

12. See chapters 1 and 10, this volume.

13. *Proper Confidence* (Grand Rapids: Eerdmans, 1995), p. 4; cf. p. 93: "The affirmation that the One by whom and through whom and for whom all creation exists is to be identified with a man who was crucified and rose bodily from the dead cannot be accommodated within any plausibility structure except one of which it is the cornerstone." On the notion of "background" theories or beliefs, see F. Fiorenza and others, *Systematic Theology* I (Minneapolis: Fortress Press, 1991), pp. 74–77. Interpretative "frameworks" is the terminology of the Canadian philosopher Charles Taylor; "plausibility structures," of the American sociologist Peter Berger.

14. *What Is the Gospel?* p. 5.

15. Ibid., p. 10.

16. Ibid., p. 11.

17. *Christ Our Eternal Contemporary*, p. 5.

18. Michael Polanyi, *Personal Knowledge: Towards a Post-Critical Philosophy* (Chicago: University of Chicago Press, 1958). Newbigin had already cited Polanyi in *Honest Religion for Secular Man* (London: SCM Press, and Philadelphia: Westminster Press, 1966), pp. 80–83.

19. See chapter 1, this volume.

20. *Christ Our Eternal Contemporary*, p. 72.

21. *Christ Our Eternal Contemporary*, p. 6.

22. This is a sideswipe at Rudolf Bultmann's essay "New Testament and Mythology" (1941). For Newbigin directly on Bultmann, see chapters 9 and 10, this volume.

23. *Truth to Tell*, p. 28.

24. Ibid., p. 86f.

25. "What is 'a local church truly united'?" in *In Each Place: Towards a Fellowship of Local Churches Truly United* (Geneva: WCC, 1977), pp. 14–29, especially p. 17f.; cf. the strong use of "for" recalled by Newbigin from the sermon he preached at his installation as bishop in Madras in 1965 (*Unfinished Agenda*, p. 215 [1993 ed., p. 203]).

26. So Newbigin, in his foreword to Hubert J. B. Allen, *Roland Allen: Pioneer, Priest, and Prophet* (Cincinnati, Ohio: Forward Movement Publications; Grand Rapids: Eerdmans, 1995), p. xiii. Allen's name is mentioned in *Unfinished Agenda* only at p. 166 (1993 ed., p. 156), from 1959; but Newbigin had been struggling with him from the early years of his episcopate in Madurai.

27. Some shorter and abbreviated texts of Allen's are gathered, together with a bibliography, in *The Ministry of the Spirit: Selected Writings of Roland Allen*, ed. David M. Paton (London: World Dominion Press, 1960).

28. To the first American edition of *The Spontaneous Expansion of the Church* (Grand Rapids: Eerdmans, 1962), Lesslie Newbigin contributed a foreword, here cited from p. xiv.

29. *Unfinished Agenda*, pp. 165f., 206 (1993, pp. 156, 194f.). As is indicated in chapter 5, Newbigin came to consider that the WCC program had been hijacked by the advocates of secularization.

30. Newbigin's foreword to *The Spontaneous Expansion of the Church*, p. iii.

31. *Trinitarian Faith and Today's Mission* (Richmond, Va.: John Knox Press, 1964), pp. 71–73.

32. Foreword to H. J. B. Allen, *Roland Allen*, p. xiv-xv.

33. *Unfinished Agenda*, p. 157f. (1993, p. 149), emphasis added.

34. Ibid., p. 166f. (1993, p. 157).

35. Ibid., pp. 42–44 (1993, pp. 40–42).

36. *Sin and Salvation* (London: SCM Press, 1956), p. 7f.

37. *Christ Our Eternal Contemporary*, p. 51. I ascertained from Newbigin himself the everyday meaning of *aavi* as steam.

38. *Unfinished Agenda*, p. 215f. (1993, p. 203f.).

39. Ibid., p. 218f. (1993, p. 206f.); cf. "Personal Recollections of South India: 1936–1974," in *Indo-British Review* 14/1. A contrast is provided by Newbigin's story of the conflict-arousing tactics employed by left-wing American and Australian "community organizers" who, causing "the one really unhappy time" of his life in India, muscled in on an intervillage dispute with no regard for the situation and language of the people (*Unfinished Agenda*, p. 222f.; 1993 ed., p. 210f.).

40. *Unfinished Agenda*, p. 235f. (1993, p. 222f.).

Chapter 3

1. The world "ecumenical" itself was actually avoided in connection with Edinburgh 1910 lest it carry legislative associations from the ancient councils of the Church. See William Richey Hogg, *Ecumenical Foundations: A History of the International Missionary Council and Its Nineteenth-Century Background* (New York: Harper, 1952), pp. 45–48, 102–109.

2. Composite quotation from *The Reunion of the Church* (London: SCM Press, 1948; 2d rev. ed. 1960), pp. 18, 11, 19. The 1960 edition contained a lengthy new introduction (pp. ix–xxxvi), to which extended reference will be made later; otherwise the book and its pagination were unchanged.

3. Bengt Sundkler, *The Church of South India: The Movement Towards Union 1900–1947* (London: Lutterworth Press, 1954), p. 115.

4. L. Newbigin in the brief history offered in his *South India Diary* (London: SCM Press, 1951), pp. 6–12. An American edition was published as *That All May Be One: A South India Diary—The Story of an Experiment in Christian Unity* (New York: Association Press, 1952). Curiously, the U.S. edition replaced the author's original foreword (pp. 5–16 of the U.K. edition), with an editorial "prologue" (pp. 7–20), so that the historical survey is not contained in the American publication; in pagination the original pp. 21–125 became pp. 23–127.

5. Sundkler, p. 339.

6. Sundkler, pp. 302, 324.

7. *Unfinished Agenda* (London: SPCK, 1985), p. 75f. (updated ed. Edinburgh: St. Andrew Press, 1993, p. 70).

8. *The Reunion of the Church*, p. 103.

9. Ibid., p. 101f.

10. Ibid., p. 86, emphasis added.

11. Georges H. Tavard, *The Catholic Approach to Protestantism* (New York: Harper, 1955), p. 81f. ("peculiarities" is presumably to be taken in the sense of "particularities"); cited by Newbigin, *The Reunion of the Church*, 1960 edition, p. xxxiv.

12. *The Reunion of the Church*, p. 134.

13. Ibid., p. 136 and p. 52, respectively.

14. Ibid., p. 131, emphasis added.

15. Ibid., 1960 edition, p. xix.

16. *The Reunion of the Church*, p. 108f.

17. Ibid., p. 188f.

18. *The Reunion of the Church*, 1960 ed., p. xxxi (cf. pp. xxviii–xxix). In the 1994 report of the third phase of the Lutheran–Roman Catholic international dialogue, "Church and Justification: Understanding the Church in the Light of the Doctrine of Justification," the Lutherans showed themselves disposed to accept the historic episcopate provided it was not made "necessary" for reception of salvation and "the church's being the church," for that would be to elevate "ecclesial structures, which emerged in history" to "the same level with the gospel proclaimed in word and sacrament, which alone is necessary for salvation and the church" (paragraphs 174–204). For the full text, see *The Pontifical Council for Promoting Christian Unity: Information Service*, No. 86 (1994/ii–iii), pp. 128–181.

19. See Sundkler, pp. 305–315.

20. *The Reunion of the Church*, 1960 ed., pp. xx–xxvii.

21. *The Reunion of the Church*, pp. 107–114, here p. 113f. Cf. also pp. 161–167, as part of a polemically pointed chapter on "the ministry" (versus K. E. Kirk, T. Jalland, L. Thornton, G. Dix, et alios).

22. *The Reunion of the Church*, 1960 ed., pp. xxxiii–xxxiv. On the precise matter of the unification of ministries, North India and Pakistan proceeded by way of a mutual imposition of hands with prayer for "whatever of the fullness of Christ's grace, commission and authority each may need for the performance of his proper office in the Church of North India/Pakistan" (see *Plan of Church Union in North*

India and Pakistan, 4th rev. ed. [Madras: Christian Literature Society, 1965], pp. 49–57); the plans for union in Ceylon and West Africa broke down over a variety of issues. In 1988 and 1998 the Lambeth Conference appeared finally to recognize that a state of full communion existed between the CSI and the provinces of the Anglican Communion, which was all the more remarkable for the fact that in 1977, at the end of the "thirty year period" covered by the initial agreement, the CSI had decided *not* to reconsider the method by which ministers were received from the nonepiscopal churches. Nearer home, the Church of England has maintained episcopal ordination as a condition for recognition of ministries in its various discussions and relations with the Methodists, the Reformed, and the Moravians in Britain, and with the Evangelical Church in Germany (the "Meissen Agreement"); but it has shown just a touch of flexibility in recognizing the ministry in some national Lutheran Churches in Scandinavia and the Baltic, where for one reason or another the succession had been kept up only through a presbyteral line (the "Porvoo Agreement"). See Geoffrey Wainwright, "Is Episcopacy a Matter of Dogma for Anglicans? The Evidence of Some Recent Dialogues," in *Community, Unity, Communion: Essays in Honour of Mary Tanner*, ed. Colin Podmore (London: Church House Publishing, 1998), pp. 164–179.

23. *The Reunion of the Church*, pp. 122, 187.

24. *The Reunion of the Church*, 1960 ed., pp. xxxv–xxxvi.

25. *The Reunion of the Church*, pp. 44, 39.

26. Quotations from *The Reunion of the Church*, pp. 62, 66. Newbigin chooses to address his criticisms to Roman Catholicism because the "Catholic" position is there at its most consistent. Anglo-Catholicism, faced with the split that occurred at the Reformation, reduces the thread of historical continuity to the episcopate in isolation from its institutional setting (p. 189; cf. p. 82f.). A "branch" theory of the Church—say, "Greek, Latin, Anglican"—cannot be used to rationalize schism (p. 105).

27. *The Reunion of the Church*, p. 44.

28. Ibid., pp. 24f.; cf. pp. 105 and 123 for other statements of these two "typical" ecclesiologies and their inadequacies as accounts of division and reunion.

29. Ibid., chapter 4, pp. 44–54 ("The Spirit, the Body and the Flesh").

30. Ibid., pp. 49f., 51, 54.

31. Ibid., p. 81.

32. Ibid., p. 50f.

33. Ibid., p. 48.

34. Ibid., pp. 73, 76.

35. Ibid., p. 81.

36. Ibid., pp. 105, 123.

37. Ibid., p. 12f.

38. Writing in 1947, Newbigin confessed that "the picture which I have drawn is over-simplified because I have omitted mention of the Roman Catholic Church, which has very widespread work in South India and does not observe 'comity.' This qualifies, but does not invalidate, the points I have tried to make. In the villages—which is where the Church has its roots—it is normal to have only one congregation; and where—as in larger towns—the Roman and non-Roman Churches are side by side, their methods of expansion and their customs of life and worship are so different as to make them appear to the common man both inside and outside their membership as almost two separate religions" (*The Reunion of the Church*, p. 20). That sad footnote dates, of course, from well before

the Second Vatican Council and its renewal of the Roman Catholic Church and the official entry of that Church into the ecumenical movement. Newbigin was not blind to the fact that, even among Churches in the Reformation traditions, work on theological differences was both relativized and yet also made more significant by moves toward unity (ibid., pp. 181–188).

39. *The Reunion of the Church*, p. 182.

40. Ibid., p. 20f.

41. Ibid., p. 182.

42. Ibid., p. 188.

43. Ibid., p. 189. See also, in this volume, pp. 405–407.

44. *The Household of God* (London: SCM Press, 1953; New York: Friendship Press, 1954). Inconveniently, the American edition underwent repagination.

45. *Unfinished Agenda*, p. 136f. (1993 ed., p. 128f.).

46. Ibid.

47. *The Household of God*, p. 18 (U.S. ed., p. 9).

48. Ibid., p. 21 (U.S. ed., p. 13f.).

49. Ibid., p. 22 (U.S. ed., p. 14). By 1959–60, in the preface to the second edition of *The Reunion of the Church*, Newbigin would be quite forthright concerning the bureaucratization of ecclesial unity: "I cannot doubt that there is already discernable a 'shift of the centre of gravity for many of the most serious Christians, from the total sacramental and congregational life of the Church, to the conference room and the program, from the priest or pastor to the 'secretary,' from the sermon to the 'agreed statement,' from Church to 'movement.' It is already difficult in many places to secure the services of the ablest young men for the ministry, because it appears that opportunities more spiritually significant (and more financially rewarding) are open to the secretary of some branch of ecumenical activity than to the pastor of a congregation. . . . There is here a profound change in the traditional understanding of what our being-together in Christ means" (p. xii–xiii).

50. *The Household of God*, p. 25f. (U.S. ed., p. 18f.).

51. Ibid., pp. 57, 51 (U.S. ed., pp. 57, 49).

52. Ibid., p. 56 (U.S. ed., p. 56).

53. Ibid., p. 85 (U.S. ed., p. 91f.).

54. Ibid., p. 79 (U.S. ed., p. 84f.). The Second Vatican Council allowed that the churches and communities separated from the Roman communion were "not without significance in the mystery of salvation" (*Unitatis Redintegratio*, 3), even though "the sole Church of Christ subsists in the Catholic Church" and ecclesial elements beyond its visible confines belong by right to that Church (*Lumen Gentium*, 8). In his ecumenical encyclical of 1995, Pope John Paul II wrote that "to the extent that these elements are found in other Christian Communities, the one Church of Christ is effectively present in them," this being the "objective basis of the communion, albeit imperfect, which exists between them and the Catholic Church" (*Ut Unum Sint*, 11).

55. *The Household of God*, p. 123 (U.S. ed., p. 138).

56. Ibid., p. 152 (U.S. ed., p. 174).

57. See *The Household of God*, in particular p. 144 (U.S. ed., p. 164).

58. See *The Ecumenical Review* 14 (1961–62): 351–379.

59. See *Unfinished Agenda*, pp. 160–162, 171–172 (1993 ed., pp. 151–153, 160–162). The record of the Spittal meeting is contained in WCC Commission on Faith and Order, *Minutes of the Working Committee 1959, Spittal, Austria*, Faith

and Order Paper No. 27 (Geneva: WCC, 1959), with p. 23 being particularly important for the "Newbigin minute." Newbigin's paper "Churchly Unity" exists only in typescript in the Faith and Order archives under the cipher "FOC/WC, July 1959."

60. WCC Commission on Faith and Order, *Minutes of the Commission Meeting held at St. Andrews, Scotland, August 3rd to 8th, 1960*, Faith and Order Paper No. 31 (Geneva: WCC, 1960), pp. 10–17, 28–30, 34–38. Archbishop Michael Ramsey, whom Newbigin acknowledged as having exercised crucial influence on his own thinking at an earlier stage, seems to have provoked the insertion of the phrase "holding the one apostolic faith." The New Delhi text itself, which has often been anthologized, appeared originally in *The New Delhi Report: The Third Assembly of the World Council of Churches 1961* (London: SCM Press; New York: Association Press, 1962), pp. 116–135, crucially p. 116f.

61. Outler's drafting was confirmed to me in a letter of February 13, 1998, from Dr. Lukas Vischer, secretary (1961–1965) and then director (1965–1979) of Faith and Order at the WCC.

62. Letter of Lukas Vischer to me, January 16, 1998.

63. Lesslie Newbigin, "The Quest for Unity through Religion," in *The Journal of Religion* 35 (1955) 17–33, in particular p. 31.

64. See Newbigin's article "Unity of 'all in each place' " in *Dictionary of the Ecumenical Movement*, ed. Nicholas Lossky and others (Geneva: WCC; Grand Rapids: Eerdmans, 1991), pp. 1043–1046.

65. "Unity of 'all in each place,' " p. 1044.

66. *Unfinished Agenda*, p. 172 (1993, p. 162).

67. "Unity of 'all in each place,' " p. 1044.

68. *Unfinished Agenda*, p. 233 (1993, p. 220). For the Louvain text, "Conciliarity and the Future of the Ecumenical Movement," see *Faith and Order, Louvain 1971: Study Reports and Documents*, Faith and Order Paper No. 59 (Geneva: WCC, 1971), pp. 225–229. For arguments on this matter from the Lutheran side, see Harding Meyer, " 'Einheit in versöhnter Verschiedenheit,' 'konziliare Gemeinschaft,' 'organische Union': Gemeinsamkeit und Differenz gegenwärtig diskutierter Einheitskonzeptionen," in *Ökumenische Rundschau* 27 (1978): 377–400.

69. *Breaking Barriers, Nairobi 1975: The Official Report of the Fifth Assembly of the World Council of Churches, Nairobi, 23 November–10 December, 1975*, ed. David M. Paton (London: SPCK; Grand Rapids: Eerdmans, 1976), p. 60.

70. See *In Each Place: Towards a Fellowship of Local Churches Truly United*, Geneva: WCC, 1977. Newbigin's paper occupies pp. 14–29; it was also printed in *The Ecumenical Review* 29 (1977): 115–128.

71. "Nairobi 1975: A Personal Report," dated December 30, 1975 (Selly Oak box 10).

72. "What is 'a local church truly united'?" in *In Each Place*, p. 17f.

73. Ibid., p. 25.

74. Chapters 2 and 4 in this book show Newbigin at work a decade later in a local congregation amid the inner suburbs of Birmingham.

75. See *In Each Place*, pp. 20f., 23, 28f.

76. Ibid., p. 29.

77. *Unfinished Agenda*, p. 249 (1993, p. 236).

78. Ibid., p. 243 (1993, p. 230).

79. Document coded CCC/39, dated July 1979 (Selly Oak box 5).

80. "Which Covenant?" (Selly Oak box 5).

81. *Unfinished Agenda*, p. 249f. (1993, p. 236f.)

82. *God's Reign and Our Unity: The Report of the Anglican-Reformed International Commission 1981–1984*, London: SPCK, and Edinburgh: St. Andrew Press, 1984.

83. Copies of the two papers are lodged in box 9 of the Selly Oak archive; the second paper will be drawn on in chapters 4 and 8.

84. *God's Reign and Our Unity*, paragraph 17.

85. *God's Reign and Our Unity*, paragraph 18.

86. The chapter on ministry does not contain such a strong affirmation of the historic episcopate as Newbigin had been accustomed to make since his South India days. Newbigin hinted to me that this may be due to the role of his old Swiss Reformed friend Lukas Vischer in shaping this section of *God's Reign and Our Unity*. The notion of "bishops-in-presbytery" makes a comeback among the practical suggestions of the final chapter.

87. *God's Reign and Our Unity*, paragraph 110. Note—remembering the vicissitudes of the New Delhi definition—that the local and the wider levels are here typographically "run on"!

88. *Towards a Statement on the Church* (in *Secretariat for Promoting Christian Unity: Information Service*, no. 62, 1986/4, pp. 206–216), paragraphs 22–28.

89. See pp. 387–389, this volume.

90. *Unfinished Agenda*, p. 231f. (1993, p. 219).

91. Konrad Raiser, *Ökumene im Übergang: Paradigmenwechsel in der ökumenischen Bewegung?* (Munich: Kaiser, 1989); *Ecumenism in Transition: A Paradigm Shift in the Ecumenical Movement?* (Geneva: WCC, 1991).

92. See *One in Christ* 29 (1993): 269–275; *International Bulletin of Missionary Research* 18/1 (January 1994): 2–5, and 18/2 (April 1994): 50–52. Typescript copies of Raiser's LMS address and Newbigin's reflections on it were supplied to me by Bishop Newbigin in November 1996. All the following quotations come from these various sources.

93. Roland Allen has already figured in chapter 2 of this book, and "the missionary structure of the congregation," as well as Newbigin's own trinitarian missiology, appears in chapter 5. Some events at the seventh assembly of the WCC at Canberra in 1991 revealed the dangers of a "pneumatology" let loose from Christ; see the criticisms made by the Orthodox and Evangelical participants or observers, recorded in *Signs of the Spirit: Official Report, Seventh Assembly, Canberra, Australia, 7–20 February 1991*, ed. Michael Kinnamon (Geneva: WCC; Grand Rapids: Eerdmans, 1991), pp. 279–282, 282–286 (cf. pp. 15f., 37–47 for the "events"). In a lecture given at the Selly Oak Colleges ecumenical summer school in July 1990, Newbigin had welcomed the theme of the upcoming Canberra assembly, provided that it were interpreted in the strongly redemptive, genuinely trinitarian ("christocentric" though not "christomonist"), and profoundly eschatological way for which Romans 8 would lay the basis; see *Come Holy Spirit—Renew the Whole Creation*, Occasional Paper No. 6 (Birmingham, England: Selly Oak Colleges, 1990).

94. For Newbigin as religious interlocutor, see chapter 6.

95. Chapter 7 shows Newbigin as a lifelong social critic and builder.

96. See his book *To Be the Church: Challenges and Hopes for a New Millennium* (Geneva: WCC, 1997). My reviews of the German and English editions of his earlier book appeared respectively in *The Expository Times* 102 (1990–1991): 332f. and in *Mid-Stream* 31 (1992): 169–173.

Chapter 4

1. *"The Good Shepherd": Meditations on Christian Ministry in Today's World* (Grand Rapids: Eerdmans, 1977), p. 13.

2. *The Household of God* (London: SCM Press, 1953; New York: Friendship Press, 1954), p. 146 (U.S. ed., p. 166f.).

3. *God's Reign and Our Unity* (London: SPCK; Edinburgh: St. Andrew Press, 1984), paragraphs 78 and 76.

4. *The Reunion of the Church* (London: SCM Press, 1948; 2d rev. ed. 1960), p. 13f.

5. *Unfinished Agenda* (London: SPCK, 1985), p. 15f. (updated ed. Edinburgh: St. Andrew Press, 1993, p. 15).

6. See, for the Kanchipuram period, *Unfinished Agenda*, pp. 51–69 (1993 ed., pp. 48–64), and the annual circular letters in which Newbigin reported home to friends in Britain (Selly Oak box 1).

7. Circular letter, April 1940.

8. See J. E. L. Newbigin, "The Ordained Foreign Missionary in the Indian Church," in *International Review of Missions* 34 (1945): 86–94.

9. *Unfinished Agenda*, p. 67 (1993 ed., p. 63); circular letter of October 1942, and a missing earlier one of "15 months ago."

10. *Unfinished Agenda*, p. 64f. (1993 ed., p. 60f.); letter to his mother, September 13, 1942.

11. Circular letter of October 1942.

12. *"The Good Shepherd": Meditations on Christian Ministry in Today's World* (Leighton Buzzard, England: The Faith Press; Grand Rapids: Eerdmans, 1977). The first edition was by the Christian Literature Society, Madras. For the circumstances of the original delivery of the addresses, see the preface to the British and American editions, as well as *Unfinished Agenda*, p. 227 (1993 ed., p. 215).

13. A footnote expounds the Hindu notion of "karma" in such a way as to illuminate powerfully the redemptive scope of Christ's work. "Karma" entails that "a man's actions form a sort of indestructible reality the consequences of which a man must enjoy or endure through an indefinitely prolonged succession of lives."

14. That dual experience was also mine during my years in Cameroon: the Gospel made its power felt both in Yaoundé jail and when spoken to those in the upper echelons of public life in the capital city.

15. On the theme of the parish, see the transcript of an address given by Newbigin in Scotland in 1985: "Does Society Still Need the Parish Church?" in his collection *A Word in Season: Perspectives on Christian World Missions* (Grand Rapids: Eerdmans; Edinburgh: St. Andrew Press, 1994), pp. 48–65.

16. The meditations in *The Good Shepherd* conclude with some themes that recur in other places and stages of Newbigin's work and that are given attention particularly in chapters 6 and 10 of this book: "Jesus, Saviour of the World," "The Particularity and the Universality of the Gospel," and "The Gospel and Our Culture."

17. Letter from Lukas Vischer to me, January 16, 1998.

18. *Unfinished Agenda*, p. 210f. (1993 ed., p. 198f.).

19. Letter from Frank Davies to me, November 20, 1997.

20. "Ministry," in Selly Oak box 9, bearing Newbigin's handwritten notation "Late 1980s."

21. Dated June 1994, this typescript was given to me by Lesslie Newbigin in November 1996.

22. Circular letter of October 1947, Selly Oak box 2, document no. 2/1/6.

23. The undated typescript "Reflections on the Ministry of a Bishop," lodged in Selly Oak box 9, probably dates from around 1980, when the English churches were considering the establishment of a covenant for unity. See chapter 3.

24. Letter of March 4, 1998, to me from Dr. Leslie W. Brown, formerly missionary in South India (1938–1943, 1945–1953), bishop in Uganda (1953–1965), and bishop of St. Edmondsbury and Ipswich (1966–1978).

25. See *Unfinished Agenda*, pp. 90–92 (1993 ed., pp. 85–87).

26. *A South India Diary*, pp. 61–64 (U.S. ed., pp. 62–66).

27. Cf. the parallel account in *Unfinished Agenda*, p. 215 (1993 ed., p. 203) and the entire chapter "Madras: Mission in Metropolis (1965–74)."

28. See *The Reunion of the Church*, p. 162f. The argument runs through pp. 148–167.

29. *God's Reign and Our Unity*, paragraph 80.

30. *The Reunion of the Church*, p. 177f.; cf. *God's Reign and Our Unity*, paragraphs 81–83.

31. *God's Reign and Our Unity*, paragraph 83.

32. *The Reunion of the Church*, p. 177; cf. *God's Reign and Our Unity*, paragraph 83.

33. *The Reunion of the Church*, p. 178; cf. *God's Reign and Our Unity*, paragraph 83. When, by 1996, even some Anglicans had begun to move in favor of "Lay Presidency at the Eucharist," Newbigin refuted the notion in an article under that title in the Anglican journal *Theology* (vol. 99, no. 791, September-October 1996: 366–370). For "a rule of order" in this connection, order being "one necessary expression of love," Newbigin invoked the phrase's use by "Edwin James Palmer, the saintly Bishop of Bombay, who was the main architect of both the fundamental statutes of the Anglican province of India, Burma and Ceylon (CIBC 1927) and of the Church of South India (CSI 1947)."

34. *Unfinished Agenda*, p. 124f. (1993 ed., p. 117f.), quoting from a letter to Raymond Dudley, "the shrewd and far-sighted India secretary" of the American Board in Boston; cf. p. 147f. (1993 ed., pp. 138–140). Note further Newbigin's pamphlet, *The Ministry of the Church—Ordained and Unordained, Paid and Unpaid* (London: Edinburgh House Press, 1953).

35. *Unfinished Agenda*, p. 68 (1993 ed., p. 64).

36. See the late 1980s paper "Ministry" (cited in note 20), p. 9.

37. *The Constitution of the Church of South India, with Amendments up to and Approved by the Synod of January 1972* (Madras: The Christian Literature Society, 1972), p. 48f.

38. "How Should We Understand Sacraments and Ministry?" (in Selly Oak box 9), pp. 5, 8.

39. "Which Covenant?" (in Selly Oak box 5), p. 2.

40. "Reflections on the Ministry of a Bishop" (in Selly Oak box 9), p. 1.

41. "Reflections . . . .," p. 2; cf. *The Reunion of the Church*, pp. 167–169, and, in the 1960 edition, pp. xxvii–xxviii.

42. See "Episcopacy and the Quest for Unity," which was Newbigin's address to the annual conference of CCLEPE (Consultative Committee for Local Ecumenical Projects in England) and ecumenical officers at Swanwick, September 1978, and "How Should We Understand Sacraments and Ministry?" which was the paper prepared for the meeting of the Anglican-Reformed International Commission in January 1983 (both in Selly Oak box 9).

43. *God's Reign and Our Unity*, paragraph 92.

44. "How Should We Understand Sacraments and Ministry?" pp. 10–13.

45. Chapter 19 in *The Gospel in a Pluralist Society* (Grand Rapids: Eerdmans; Geneva: WCC, 1989), pp. 234–241.

46. Ibid., p. 240.

47. Ibid., p. 241.

Chapter 5

1. For Newbigin's early years in India, see *Unfinished Agenda* (London: SPCK, 1985; updated ed. Edinburgh: St. Andrew Press, 1993), chapters 5–7; passages drawn on here occur on pp. 40–42, 61f., 67f. (1993 ed., pp. 38–40, 57f., 63f.).

2. *International Review of Mission* 34 (1945): 86–94.

3. See *Unfinished Agenda*, pp. 70–72 (1993 ed., pp. 65–67). It was while he filled the "superior administrative post" that Newbigin transferred his canonical allegiance from "the Church of Scotland, Presbytery of Madras" to the South India United Church, so that when in fact he was later elected among the first bishops of the new Church of South India, he was not a minister of the Church of Scotland.

4. See Newbigin's chapter, "Mission to Six Continents," in *A History of the Ecumenical Movement: Vol. 2 (1948–1968)*, ed. Harold E. Fey (Philadelphia: Westminster Press, 1970), pp. 171–197, here pp. 176–178.

5. *Missions Under the Cross*, ed. Norman Goodall (London: Edinburgh House Press, 1953), p. 14. There long remained a tension between those who favored the plural "missions" and those who favored the singular "mission." Both can be justified according to historical and theological context, but the preferred usages came to signal a difference in approach.

6. See *Unfinished Agenda*, pp. 131–134, 148–150 (1993 ed., pp. 123–126, 140f.); and pp. 333–334, this volume.

7. *Unfinished Agenda*, p. 138 (1993 ed., p. 130). Their views are expressed in the unadopted report printed in *Missions Under the Cross*, pp. 238–245.

8. Text in *Missions Under the Cross*, pp. 188–192.

9. Newbigin had proffered a more discursive version of this confession in his contribution to the second of the preparatory volumes for the First Assembly of the World Council of Churches at Amsterdam in 1948: "The Duty and Authority of the Church to Preach the Gospel," in *The Church's Witness to God's Design: An Ecumenical Study Prepared under the Auspices of the World Council of Churches* (New York: Harper, 1948), pp. 19–35, especially pp. 24–35; see p. 322, this volume.

10. On the prehistory and posthistory of the notion of "missio Dei," see David J. Bosch, *Transforming Mission: Paradigm Shifts in Theology of Mission* (Maryknoll, NY: Orbis, 1991), pp. 389–393. Its modern origins were Barthian. Newbigin later complained of its hijacking by the secularists; see later in this chapter.

11. See *Unfinished Agenda*, pp. 138, 152f., 254 (1993 ed., pp. 130, 144, 241); later in this chapter, and chapter 10.

12. In "The Duty and Authority of the Church to Preach the Gospel," p. 21; again in *One Body, One Gospel, One World* (1958), p. 42.

13. *The Household of God* (London: SCM Press, 1953; U.S. ed., New York: Friendship Press, 1954), p. 147f. (U.S. ed., p. 168f.).

14. Ibid., p. 148 (U.S. ed., p. 169).

15. *Unfinished Agenda*, pp. 133f., 137f. (1993 ed., p. 125f., 129f.); for the respective texts, see *The Ecumenical Review* 4 (1951–52), 66–71 ("The Calling of the Church to Mission and to Unity," received by the central committee and commended for study and comment in the churches), and *Missions Under the Cross*, p. 193f. ("A Statement on the Calling of the Church to Mission and Unity," prepared in group one and adopted by the full meeting).

16. *Unfinished Agenda*, pp. 150f., 153f., 156–158, 163–165 (1993 ed., pp. 142, 145, 147–149, 153–155).

17. *One Body, One Gospel, One World: The Christian Mission Today* (London and New York: The International Missionary Council, 1958).

18. *Unfinished Agenda*, p. 164 (1993 ed., p. 155). Newbigin's own two-sentence summary of the shilling booklet is found there.

19. These ideas were taken up by D. T. Niles in *Upon the Earth: The Mission of God and the Missionary Enterprise of the Churches* (London: Lutterworth Press, 1962).

20. *One Body, One Gospel, One World*, p. 40.

21. Newbigin's point could be made linguistically in various ways: in German, *Mission* was used for the specific activity of "the missions" and *Sendung* for the broader "mission" of the Church (*One Body, One Church, One World*, p. 43); to ensure continuing attention to the former within the wider range of the latter, Newbigin successfully insisted on retaining the final *s* in the title of *The International Review of Missions*, though it was dropped after his own departure from Geneva (*Unfinished Agenda*, p. 200; 1993 ed., p. 189).

22. *Unfinished Agenda*, p. 200f. (1993 ed., p. 189f.); cf. pp. 150f., 163f., 168f., 203 (1993 ed., pp. 142, 153f., 158f., 192). In Newbigin's personal notes and drafts lodged in box 1/3 of the Selly Oak papers, there is clear evidence that he argued at the meeting of the joint committee between the IMC and the WCC in Nyborgstrand, Denmark, in the summer of 1958 for a single "Division of World Mission and Inter-Church Aid" in the integrated Council; but he lost the debate and dropped the proposal from the draft paper that became the basis of *One Body, One Gospel, One World*. That draft, dated "Edinburgh, June 1958," also spoke (p. 12) of "the work of explicit evangelism" as "central"—and needing to "be seen to be central"—"to the whole mission"; but that precise formulation of the claim ceded in *One Body, One Gospel, One World* (p. 22) to the statement that "evangelism" and "service" each "has its proper dignity within the wholeness of the mission, and neither should be subordinated to the other." In this recurrent discussion, Newbigin's basic instinct was to stress the mutual indispensability of evangelism and service within what he formulated, in a much later writing, as "the prior reality, the givenness, the ontological priority of the new reality which the work of Christ has brought into the world"—"the gift of a real foretaste, pledge, *arrabôn* of the Kingdom, namely the mighty Spirit of God"; see *The Gospel in a Pluralist Society* (Geneva: WCC; Grand Rapids: Eerdmans, 1989), chapter 11, pp. 128–140 ("Mission: Word, Deed, and New Being"), in particular p. 136.

23. *One Body, One Gospel, One World*, p. 55f.

24. See *The New Delhi Report: The Third Assembly of the World Council of Churches*, ed. W. A. Visser 't Hooft (New York: Association Press, 1962), pp. 3–7, 56–60. Newbigin's speech on the occasion, under the title "The Missionary Dimension of the Ecumenical Movement," appeared in January 1962 in *The Ecumenical Review* 14 (1961–62): 207–215.

25. *Unfinished Agenda*, p. 198 (1993 ed., p. 187).

26. The text of this "zettel" is given in *Unfinished Agenda*, p. 197 (1993 ed., p. 186).

27. *Unfinished Agenda*, pp. 196, 206f. (1993 ed., pp. 185f., 194f.).

28. On Newbigin's travels at this time, see the introduction, this volume. For his being *au fait* with developments worldwide, see "A Survey of the Year 1962–3" and "A Survey of the Year 1963–4" in *International Review of Missions* 53 (1964): 3–82 and 54 (1965): 3–75, respectively.

29. For "mood" and "substance" see Charles W. Ranson, "Mexico City 1963" in *International Review of Missions* 53 (1964): 137–145. For the official report see *Witness in Six Continents: Records of the Meeting of the Commission on World Mission and Evangelism of the World Council of Churches held in Mexico City December 8th to 19th, 1963*, ed. Ronald K. Orchard (London: Edinburgh House Press, 1964). Extracts from Newbigin's report to the conference as divisional director are found in Robert O. Latham, *God for All Men* (London: Edinburgh House Press, 1964), pp. 58–61.

30. *Unfinished Agenda*, p. 206 (1993 edition, p. 195). For Visser 't Hooft's text, see Orchard, pp. 20–28, or *The Ecumenical Review* 16 (1963–64): 249–257.

31. Lesslie Newbigin, "Mission to Six Continents," in *A History of the Ecumenical Movement: Vol. 2 (1948–1968)*, ed. Harold E. Fey (Philadelphia: Westminster Press, 1970), pp. 171–197 (on Mexico City, pp. 193–195). These pages are drawn on in the next paragraphs.

32. *Unfinished Agenda*, p. 206; cf. p. 166 (1993 ed., p. 194f.; cf. p. 156); cf. also the Newbigin collection edited by Eleanor Jackson, *A Word in Season: Perspectives on Christian World Missions* (Grand Rapids: Eerdmans; Edinburgh: St. Andrew Press, 1994), p. 145f. Chapters 7 and 10 in this volume show much more of Newbigin's attitudes and practice toward "the world." The latter chapter in particular shows Newbigin tracing—under the rubric of "the congregation as hermeneutic of the Gospel"—the local church's vital function of witness in the late modern world.

33. In his foreword to Robert Latham's *God for All Men*, p. 4.

34. Fey, pp. 173, 197.

35. *Unfinished Agenda*, pp. 192, 198f. (1993 ed., pp. 181, 187f.).

36. *The Relevance of Trinitarian Doctrine for Today's Mission* (London: Edinburgh House Press, 1963). Newbigin later described the original title as "appalling" (*Unfinished Agenda*, p. 199; 1993 ed., p. 187). For the American edition the title was improved to *Trinitarian Faith and Today's Mission* (Richmond, Va.: John Knox Press, 1964). The U.S. edition is cited henceforth.

37. Many of the same themes recur also in *The Gospel in a Pluralist Society* (1989), in which chapters 6–19 are the most explicitly missiological.

38. *Trinitarian Faith and Today's Mission*, p. 25.

39. Ibid., p. 32.

40. Ibid., p. 33.

41. Ibid., p. 78.

42. *The Open Secret: Sketches for a Missionary Theology* (London: SPCK; Grand Rapids: Eerdmans, 1978); rev. ed., *The Open Secret: An Introduction to the Theology of Mission* (Grand Rapids: Eerdmans, 1995).

43. Ibid., p. 43 (1995, p. 39).

44. Ibid., p. 72 (1995, p. 65).

45. Ibid., p. 101 (1995, p. 89f.).

46. Ibid., p. 120f. (1995, p. 107).

47. Ibid., p. 123–127 (1995, pp. 109–113).

48. Ibid., pp. 127–134 (1995, pp. 113–120). In reference to the indebtedness of Latin American liberation theology to Marxist theory, Newbigin would suggest in *The Gospel in a Pluralist Society* (1989) that it is not "intellectually coherent to use one conceptual framework for diagnosis and another for treatment" (p. 59).

49. *The Open Secret* (rev. ed., 1995), p. 94f.

50. John V. Taylor, *The Growth of the Church in Buganda* (London: SCM Press, 1958), pp. 45–49.

51. *The Open Secret* (1978 ed.), p. 161 (1995 ed., p. 144). Readers of the revised edition should be warned that at around line 27 of page 145 the entire page 163 of the original edition appears to have been accidentally lost.

52. A broad missiological discussion of "the Gospel and cultures" is found in Newbigin's *The Gospel in a Pluralist Society*, chapter 15, pp. 184–197.

53. *Mission Agenda* (no place, no date, but in fact Dublin 1992). The text is also found in a collection of Newbigin's missiological papers, especially from his later years: *A Word in Season: Perspectives on Christian World Missions*, edited by Eleanor Jackson (Grand Rapids: Eerdmans; Edinburgh: St. Andrew Press, 1994), pp. 177–189.

54. *Your Kingdom Come* (Leeds: John Paul the Preacher's Press, 1980); *Sign of the Kingdom* (Grand Rapids: Eerdmans, 1981).

55. Lesslie Newbigin, *Mission in Christ's Way: Bible Studies* (Geneva: WCC, 1987).

56. See *International Bulletin of Missionary Research* 13 (1989): 102.

57. *Mission Agenda*, p. 11f. (cf. *A Word in Season*, p. 188f.). Newbigin's understanding and practice of the worship life of the Church and of the ministry of word and sacrament will is treated in chapter 8, in which he appears as liturgist and preacher.

58. Typescript "Our Missionary Responsibility in the Crisis of Western Culture" (Selly Oak box 8), p. 2; cf. *A Word in Season*, pp. 98–112, in particular p. 100. In 1994 Newbigin spoke to another German missionary conference in Stuttgart under the title "The Cultural Captivity of Western Christianity as a Challenge to a Missionary Church"; see *A Word in Season*, pp. 66–79.

59. "Mission in the 1980s" in *Occasional Bulletin of Missionary Research* 4 (1980): 154f.

60. "Mission in the 1990s" in *International Bulletin of Missionary Research* 13 (1989): 100–102.

61. The "recovery of confidence" was taken up again in the Dublin lecture of 1992, "Mission Agenda," and, of course, in the book *Proper Confidence* (Grand Rapids: Eerdmans, 1995); see chapter 1, this volume.

62. *Unfinished Agenda*, 1993 ed., p. 243.

63. Hendrik Kraemer, *The Christian Message in a Non-Christian World* (New York and London: Harper, for the International Missionary Council, 1938).

64. See *The World Mission of the Church: Findings and Recommendations of the Meeting of the International Missionary Council, Tambaram, Madras, India, Dec. 12–29, 1938* (London and New York: International Missionary Council, 1939), in particular pp. 46–55.

65. Newbigin's sermon was printed in the issue of *International Review of Mission* devoted to Tambaram 1988: volume 78, no. 307, July 1988, pp. 325–331.

66. See Jean Stromberg, "Christian Witness in a Pluralistic World: Report on a Mission/Dialogue Consultation," in *International Review of Mission* 78 (1988): 412–436.

67. *International Review of Mission* 78 (1988): 417. See also chapter 10, this volume. That the ancient Greek civilization perished through "a failure of nerve" was a favorite allusion of Newbigin's; he tentatively attributed the insight to Gilbert Murray (see *Mission Agenda*, p. 10).

68. "Reflections on the History of Missions," in *A Word in Season*, pp. 132–147, in particular p. 137. The affirmation commended by Newbigin is found in *International Review of Mission* 61 (1982): 427–451.

69. In the 1990s, calls multiplied for the WCC to ground itself in its scriptural, christocentric, trinitarian basis and pursue the original ecumenical vocation to ecclesial unity and to the mission of evangelism and service. The principles were already laid out in the affirmation of 1982!

70. Newbigin's address is excerpted in *The San Antonio Report: Your Will Be Done—Mission in Christ's Way*, ed. Frederick R. Wilson (Geneva: WCC, 1990), pp. 162–166 ("A Mission to Modern Western Culture").

Chapter 6

1. *Mission Agenda* (no place, no date, but in fact Dublin, 1992), p. 9; contained also in the collection of Newbigin's papers edited by Eleanor Jackson, *A Word in Season: Perspectives on Christian World Missions* (Grand Rapids: Eerdmans; Edinburgh: St. Andrew Press, 1994), pp. 177–189, here p. 185f.

2. *Trinitarian Faith and Today's Mission* (Richmond, Va.: John Knox Press, 1964), p. 27f.

3. Newbigin knew, of course, that "Hinduism" was in a sense the creation of the West. As he would much later put it in a foreword written for Chaturvedi Badrinath's *Dharma: India and the New World Order* (unpublished), Hinduism "is a word invented by invaders to describe what they wrongly took to be 'the religion' of the people of the subcontinent." Elsewhere (in a generally favorable review of Eric J. Sharpe's *Faith Meets Faith: Some Christian Attitudes to Hinduism in the Nineteenth and Twentieth Centuries*) he called "Hinduism" a "European idea" and likened the usage to "a professor in Tokyo offering a course of study on all the philosophical and religious ideas and practices which have occurred in Europe from Pythagoras to Tillich and entitling it 'Europeanism.' " The beginnings of what Newbigin in his scholarly writings calls "modern Hinduism" or "the higher Hinduism"—in the sense of a mystical, philosophical, theological "system"—are credited to Ram Mohun Roy in nineteenth-century Bengal (see Newbigin, "The Quest for Unity through Religion," in *The Journal of Religion* 35 (1955), in particular p. 17.

4. *A South India Diary* (London: SCM Press, 1951), p. 27f. (U. S. ed., *That All May Be One*, New York: Association Press, 1952, p. 29f.).

5. *Unfinished Agenda* (London: SPCK, 1985), pp. 142, 146f., 220–222 (updated ed. Edinburgh: St. Andrew Press, 1993, pp. 133f., 137f., 208f.)

6. *Unfinished Agenda*, p. 57f. (1993 ed., p. 54f.).

7. See chapters 2 and 7, this volume.

8. "Our Missionary Responsibility in the Crisis of Western Culture," annotated in Selly Oak box 8 as "Arnoldshain, May 1988." See *A Word in Season*, pp. 98–112, in particular p. 109.

9. Selly Oak box 2, document no. 2/2/6.

10. See later in this chapter.

11. "The Quest for Unity through Religion" in *The Journal of Religion* 35 (1955): 17–33.

12. *A Faith For This One World?* (London: SCM Press, 1961).

13. See chapter 3, this volume.

14. See chapter 5, this volume.

15. *The Finality of Christ* (London: SCM Press; Richmond, Va.: John Knox Press, 1969).

16. *The Finality of Christ*, p. 16. Newbigin had already invoked the story–and rejected its implications–in the Chicago lecture of 1954 (*Journal of Religion* 35 [1955], 19) and would do so again in *The Gospel in a Pluralist Society* (Geneva: WCC; Grand Rapids: Eerdmans, 1989), p. 9f.

17. The more detailed epistemological and ecclesiological discussion occurs on pp. 74–80.

18. In *A Faith For This One World?* (p. 75f.), Newbigin had written with regard to "the spiritual experience of the Vaishnava saint": "I cannot believe that God turns a deaf ear to these outpourings of devotion from men made in his image, or that they arise otherwise than through his witness in their hearts. I cannot believe that there is no contact between the soul and God in these prayers. And yet you only have to get into close contact with a good and godly man of the school of faith we are considering to discover that you are in a totally different world from the world of Christian faith"—a world in which you may switch gods according to your needs, rather than the world of the holy, redeeming, and historically active God of the Bible.

19. For the issue being addressed here, see *The Finality of Christ*, pp. 43, 46f.

20. Thus: "Rightly understood, the process of secularization is an extending of the area of freedom wherein man has the opportunity to understand and respond to what God has done for the world in Jesus Christ" (*The Finality of Christ*, p. 63).

21. *The Finality of Christ*, p. 69.

22. Ibid., p. 83f.

23. Ibid., pp. 80, 86.

24. Ibid., pp. 35–38, 57–60.

25. Ibid., pp. 60–62 and 112–115.

26. See *Unfinished Agenda*, 1993 ed., p. 245f.

27. *Unfinished Agenda*, p. 244 (1993, p. 231f.).

28. Typescript dated March 1989, lodged in Selly Oak box 10.

29. Similar thoughts are expressed in an undated typescript, "How can I teach a faith to which I am not fully committed?" (Selly Oak box 10).

30. This text appeared in June 1976 as a pamphlet from the New York office of the Lutheran Church in America under the department "World Mission Interpretation." It was also published as "The Basis, Purpose, and Manner of Interfaith Dialogue" in *Scottish Journal of Theology* 30 (1977): 253–270.

31. Lesslie Newbigin, *The Open Secret* (London: SPCK; Grand Rapids: Eerdmans, 1978) pp. 181–214 (rev. ed., Grand Rapids: Eerdmans, 1995, pp. 160–189).

32. *Keeping the Faith: Essays to Mark the Centenary of "Lux Mundi,"* ed. Geoffrey Wainwright (Philadelphia: Fortress Press, 1988; London: SPCK, 1989), pp. 310–340.

33. In *Christian Uniqueness Reconsidered: The Myth of a Pluralistic Theology of Religions,* ed. Gavin D'Costa (Maryknoll, New York: Orbis, 1990), pp. 135–148. Newbigin had engaged with the Hick-Knitter book, *The Myth of Christian Uniqueness* (1988), in an article entitled "Religious Pluralism and the Uniqueness of Jesus Christ" in the *International Bulletin of Missionary Research* 13 (1989), 50–54. He also reviewed the Hick-Knitter book in *The Ecumenical Review* 41 (1989), 468f., where an editorial note explained that "in view of the controversial nature of this book, we are pleased to offer two reviews from different perspectives"; Newbigin's was followed by one from A. J. van der Bent (pp. 469–471).

34. "Theology of Religions," i.e., *Studia Missionalia*, vol. 42 (1993), pp. 227–244.

35. *The Gospel in a Pluralist Society*, pp. 171–183 and 155–170, respectively.

36. That Newbigin kept abreast of the current debates is illustrated by the reviews he wrote of books by authors of various tendencies: Eric J. Sharp, *Faith Meets Faith: Some Christian Attitudes to Hinduism in the Nineteenth and Twentieth Centuries* (1977), in *Theology* 81 (March 1978), 142–143; Wilfred Cantwell Smith, *The Meaning and End of Religion* (1978), in *Theology* 82 (July 1979), 294–296; Gerald H. Anderson and Thomas F. Stransky, eds., *Christ's Lordship and Religious Pluralism* (1981), in *International Bulletin of Missionary Research* 6 (January 1982), 32; Ninian Smart, *Beyond Ideology* (1981), in *Theology* 85 (September 1982), 381–383; M. M. Thomas, *Risking Christ for Christ's Sake: Towards an Ecumenical Theology of Pluralism,* (1987) in *Ecumenical Review* 39 (1987), 494–496; Carl E. Braaten, *No Other Gospel! Christianity Among the World's Religions* (1992), in *First Things* no. 24 (June–July 1992), 56–58.

37. See especially *Interfaith Dialogue*, pp. 3–7; *The Open Secret*, pp. 191–197 (1995 ed., pp. 169–174); *Keeping the Faith*, pp. 315–331.

38. See especially *The Open Secret*, p. 195f. (1995 ed., p. 172f.), and *Keeping the Faith*, pp. 323–327.

39. See *Keeping the Faith*, pp. 327–329.

40. Ibid., pp. 321–323.

41. *Christian Uniqueness Reconsidered*, p. 147.

42. *Keeping the Faith*, pp. 331–339; cf. *Interfaith Dialogue*, pp. 7–11; *The Open Secret*, pp. 197–205 (1995 ed., pp. 174–182).

43. *Interfaith Dialogue*, pp. 1–3.

44. The handwritten text of the three Henry Martyn Lectures is lodged in Selly Oak box 8. The cited passage occurs on p. 26f. of the first lecture, which was entitled "Authority, Dogma and Dialogue." The second and third lectures were entitled "Conversion, Colonies and Culture" and "Church, World, Kingdom."

45. *Studia Missionalia*, vol. 42 (1993), p. 243.

46. *Interfaith Dialogue*, pp. 9, 12–16; *The Open Secret*, pp. 203, 206–212 (1995 ed., pp. 179, 183–188).

47. *Interfaith Dialogue*, p. 15; *The Open Secret*, p. 211 (1995 ed., p. 187).

48. See *International Bulletin of Missionary Research* 13 (1989), 50f., 54; *Christian Uniqueness Reconsidered*, p. 138.

49. Newbigin makes a sharp criticism of Samartha in *The Gospel in a Pluralist Society*, p. 164f.

50. John Hick, "Christian Theology and Inter-Religious Dialogue," in *World Faiths*, no. 103 (Autumn 1977), 2–19; cf. Newbigin, *The Open Secret*, pp. 184–191 (1995 ed., pp. 162–169).

51. J. H. Hick, *God and the Universe of Faiths* (New York: St. Martin's Press, 1973), p. 131.

52. *Christian Uniqueness Reconsidered*, p. 142.

53. Ibid., p. 139; cf. *Keeping the Faith*, p. 337; *International Bulletin of Missionary Research* 13 (1989), 50; *Studia Missionalia*, vol. 42 (1993), p. 234.

54. *Studia Missionalia*, vol. 42 (1993), p. 235.

55. *The Open Secret*, p. 190 (1995 ed., p. 167f.).

56. See *The Gospel in a Pluralist Society*, p. 3; and *Christ Our Eternal Contemporary* (Madras: Christian Literature Society, 1968), p. 4.

57. *Studia Missionalia*, volume 42 (1993), p. 237.

58. "Africa Travel Diary" I, pp. 2 and 5; II, p. 8; III, p. 4; VIII, p. 4 (in Selly Oak box 2).

59. Conversation with the author, November 1996.

60. Henry Martyn Lecture I, "Authority, Dogma and Dialogue," manuscript page 17 and facing (Selly Oak box 8).

61. In *Christian Uniqueness Reconsidered*, ed. G. D'Costa, p. 143; for the moribundity of Western culture in this connection, cf. further "Religious Pluralism and the Uniqueness of Jesus Christ," in *International Bulletin of Missionary Research*, 13 (1989), 50–54.

62. *Mission Agenda*, p. 8 (*A Word in Season*, p. 185).

63. *Studia Missionalia*, vol. 42 (1993), pp. 227–244, here p. 236. After an article in *Foreign Affairs*, Francis Fukuyama published the book *The End of History and the Last Man* (New York: Free Press, 1992).

64. Samuel P. Huntington, *The Clash of Civilizations and the Remaking of World Order* (New York: Simon and Schuster, 1996). See especially pp. 209–218.

65. Henry Martyn Lectures I, manuscript p. 28f. (Selly Oak box 8).

66. From a brief article by Newbigin under the heading "A Time to Speak" in *GO* (the URC mission magazine), April–June 1989; typescript in Selly Oak box 8.

67. *The Gospel in Today's Global City: An Address Delivered at the Launch of the Selly Oak Colleges' School of Mission and World Christianity in the Chapel of St. Andrew's Hall, Saturday 11 May 1996, by Lesslie Newbigin* (Birmingham, England: Selly Oak Colleges, 1997).

68. Ibid., p. 4f. I quote from the printed version rather than the typescript that Newbigin supplied to me.

69. Ibid., p. 8f.

70. One of Lesslie's last mailings to me included a copy of the typescript of his chapters.

71. Lesslie Newbigin, Lamin Sanneh, and Jenny Taylor, *Faith and Power: Christianity and Islam in "Secular" Britain* (London: SPCK, 1998). The published version, in its table of contents (p. vii), mistakenly attributes part 1 to all three authors. Page 1 correctly shows Newbigin's authorship of part 1.

72. *Faith and Power*, p. 19; quoted according to the slight variant in the typescript of part 1, p. 17.

73. *Faith and Power*, p. 22. The reference to *dharma* is due to a previous citation of Newbigin's Indian Marxist friend and interlocutor Chaturvedi Badrinath.

74. Ibid., p. 22.

Chapter 7

1. See *Unfinished Agenda* (London: SPCK, 1985), pp. 1–3, 6f., 11f. (updated ed., Edinburgh: St. Andrew Press, 1993, pp. 1–3, 6f., 10–12).

2. Ibid., p. 22f. (1993 ed., p. 21f.).

3. Ibid., p. 22 (1993, p. 21).

4. Ibid., pp. 23–25, 34–36 (1993, pp. 22–24, 32–34).

5. "Exegesis of Exodus XXX, 11–16," in Selly Oak box 7; see chapter 1, this volume.

6. *Unfinished Agenda*, pp. 31, 33, 37f. (1993, pp. 29, 31, 35f.).

7. Ibid., p. 48f. (1993, p. 46).

8. *Christian Freedom in the Modern World* (London: SCM Press, 1937).

9. See chapter 1, this volume.

10. *Christian Freedom in the Modern World*, p. 82.

11. Ibid., p. 83.

12. Ibid., p. 86f.

13. Ibid., p. 66f.

14. Bangalore manuscript II/9–10. With the positive reference to a "service beyond death" rendered by the faithful departed, Newbigin seems to be hinting that—unless perhaps you have been a Protestant!—you may on leaving this world "be asked to go on praying for those who are still in the midst of the struggle." So at least it appears, much later (1983), from *The Other Side of 1984* (Geneva: WCC, 1984), p. 35.

15. Bangalore manuscript IV/2f., 8f.

16. Bangalore manuscript, IV/14f.

17. "What Bishop Newbigin Has Meant To Me": text supplied by Dr. Thomas with an updating letter to me of September 24, 1996.

18. On all this, see M. M. Thomas, "Nation," in *Dictionary of the Ecumenical Movement*, ed. N. Lossky and others (Geneva: WCC, 1991), pp. 709–711.

19. See *Unfinished Agenda*, pp. 121f., 140–142 (1993, pp. 114f., 132–134). The letters testify in more detail to drought and famine between 1948 and 1953 and floods in 1956. The "My Dear Friends" letter of November 1, 1949, contains these observations on the political situation: "The young democracy faces fearful tasks. It has been born out of a struggle in which for decades opposition could only mean sedition. It is not possible in a few months to create that combination of unity on fundamentals with conflict on policies which is taken for granted in a stable democracy and which makes genuine parliamentary opposition possible. Hardly anyone of the ordinary artisan or merchant classes can understand opposition [on the part of an uprooted urban proletariat] as other than sedition. The powerful and ruthless challenge of Communism tends to drive those who oppose it more and more into policies which are totalitarian in direction, and these in turn make it more certain that all opposition will be seditious in character. The only hope lies in a tremendous birth of moral energy to tackle the fundamental problems of society—caste, destitution, and corruption in public life. Many of the leaders and faithful workers in the Congress party have that moral energy and

show it in their lives. The achievements of the Madras Government in carrying through and enforcing prohibition, in tackling the great *zemindari* estates, and in their program of village reconstruction, are truly wonderful. Yet no one could be more frank than the national leaders themselves in confessing that corruption, black-marketing, and nepotism are paralysing the nation in its terrific struggle with its real enemies" (Selly Oak box 2, document no. 1/86).

20. See *Christian Participation in Nation-Building: The Summing Up of a Corporate Study on Rapid Social Change*, ed. P. D. Devanandan and M. M. Thomas (Bangalore: The National Christian Council of India and The Christian Institute for the Study of Religion and Society, 1960), especially pp. 2f., 48f., 154f., 209f., 227–242, 266–289, 290–305.

21. See again the "My Dear Friends" letter of November 1, 1949.

22. On India as a "secular state," see *Christian Participation in Nation Building*, pp. 39–41, 51, 259f., 282–287.

23. Letter of November 1, 1949.

24. *Unfinished Agenda*, p. 152f. (1993, p. 144). For the medium-term effects on Newbigin's thinking, see *A Faith For This One World?* (1958/1961), pp. 99–103; *Trinitarian Faith and Today's Mission* (1963/1964), pp. 35–51; *Honest Religion for Secular Man* (1964/1966), passim; *The Finality of Christ* (1966/69), pp. 46–64.

25. In: *The Church's Witness to God's Design*, volume II of the Amsterdam Series (New York: Harper, 1948), here p. 19.

26. *Mission in Christ's Way* (Geneva: WCC, 1987), pp. 10–12.

27. See chapter 6, this volume. That Newbigin himself was still in 1959 having difficulties with the relation between evangelism and service may be seen from the change between a draft and the final version of a text written in an IMC context; see chapter 5, this volume.

28. See chapter 4, this volume. See also from the Madras period the presentations on *Christ Our Eternal Contemporary* (see chapter 2, this volume) and *Journey into Joy* (see chapter 9, this volume.) For a direct account of those years, see also chapter 17 of *Unfinished Agenda*: "Madras: Mission in Metropolis, 1965–1974."

29. *The Open Secret* (London: SPCK; Grand Rapids: Eerdmans, 1978), p. 122f. (rev. ed. 1995, p. 109).

30. "Not Whole Without the Handicapped," in *Partners in Life: The Handicapped and the Church*, Faith and Order Paper No. 89, ed. Geiko Müller-Fahrenholz (Geneva: WCC, 1979), pp. 17–25. Newbigin had come to "a quite new realization of the vital role of the incurably handicapped in the life of the Church" through his participation in the pertinent section of the meeting of the Faith and Order Commission at Louvain in 1971 (see *Unfinished Agenda*, p. 233f.; 1993 edition, p. 220f.).

31. The principal documents of the debate are: M. M. Thomas, *Salvation and Humanisation: Some Crucial Issues of the Theology of Mission in Contemporary India* (Madras: Christian Literature Society, 1971); L. Newbigin, review article, in *Religion and Society* 18/1 (March 1971), pp. 71–80; letters from Thomas to Newbigin (October 21, 1971), from Newbigin to Thomas (November 18, 1971), and from Thomas to Newbigin (December 20, 1971), all three of which were published in *Religion and Society* 19/1 (March 1972), pp. 61–90, and again in *Some Theological Dialogues*, based on the correspondence of M. M. Thomas (Madras: Christian Literature Society, 1977), pp. 110–137; a comment from Paul Loeffler of the Near

Eastern School of Theology, originally in a letter of January 30, 1973, published in *Some Theological Dialogues*, pp. 139–144; and a response by Newbigin to Loeffler, dated July 1972 (but actually 1973), under the title "The Church and the Kingdom" (typescript in Selly Oak box 10). The last item appears to have remained unpublished; a note from Newbigin suggests that it was meant for a book on the whole debate, planned by T. K. Thomas of the Christian Literature Society in Madras, but both Newbigin and T. K. Thomas left Madras before the project could be completed.

32. See *Unfinished Agenda*, p. 232 (1993, p. 219).

33. "The Church and the Kingdom," typescript p. 4f.

34. The last formulation—"nucleus" is an addition to Newbigin's long-familiar triad—is found in *Religion and Society* 18/1 (1971), p. 73.

35. "The Church and the Kingdom," typescript p. 3.

36. Already in *A Faith For This One World?* (London: SCM Press, 1961), Newbigin had invoked the novel *Nineteen Eighty-Four* in connection with false ideas of progress and the emergence of the antichrist, "Big Brother"; see pp. 213–214, this volume.

37. Quotations are taken from the edition published in Geneva by the WCC.

38. *The Other Side of 1984* (Geneva: WCC, 1984), pp. 60–62.

39. Ibid., p. 56f.

40. Ibid., p. 57.

41. Ibid., p. 58f.

42. Ibid., p. 59f.

43. Ibid., pp. 37–43.

44. "Church, World, Kingdom," Henry Martyn Lecture III, handwritten text in Selly Oak box 8.

45. *The Other Side of 1984*, p. 37.

46. Henry Martyn Lecture III, manuscript p. 16. In practical British politics, within the endemically limited range of options, Newbigin threw in his lot with the Labor Party and was known during his Birmingham years to distribute leaflets door to door on its behalf at election times.

47. *The Other Side of 1984*, pp. 28–37.

48. Ibid., p. 31. I have borrowed the epexegetical insertion from Newbigin's review of M. M. Thomas in *Religion and Society* 18/1 (1971), p. 75.

49. *The Other Side of 1984*, p. 43.

50. See chapters 9 and 10 and the conclusion, this volume.

51. *Unfinished Agenda*, 1993 ed., p. 250.

52. The Gore Lecture is quoted in the following paragraphs from the full version, printed as *The Welfare State: A Christian Perspective* (Oxford: Oxford Institute for Church and Society, 1985). An abbreviated and otherwise slightly altered version was preached as the University Sermon at Cambridge on March 10, 1985. Some of the same material was also used, in a different setting, in an address given to the Churches' Council on Health and Healing at Swanwick in the summer of 1988 under the title "Human Flourishing in Faith, Fact and Fantasy." The notion of the welfare state was carried from Britain to India and adapted there after independence: see *Christian Participation in Nation-Building*, ed. M. M. Thomas, pp. 1–23.

53. *The Welfare State*, p. 11. On family and sexual ethics, Newbigin would later give his support to the "Presbyterians Pro Life" organization in the United States. I am indebted to Mrs. Terry Schlossberg for making available to me copies of

several pieces of correspondence in that connection (Newbigin's letters of January 30, 1992, February 25, 1993, and March 8, 1993). Later still, a mordant limerick expressed Newbigin's views on abortion:

Techno-speak

Said an angry young man of Miletus,
"These doctors use jargon to cheat us.
They're quite reconciled
to killing a child
'cos they're only 'aborting a foetus.' "

54. *The Welfare State*, p. 11.

55. Ibid., p. 14f.

56. "Human Flourishing in Faith, Fact and Fantasy," p. 411 (part of pp. 400–412, from an unidentified record, lodged in Selly Oak box 10, of the address given to the Churches' Council on Health and Healing, Swanwick, Summer 1988).

57. Cambridge University Sermon, March 10, 1985. The hope for "another St. Benedict" echoes the ending of Alasdair MacIntyre's *After Virtue* (Notre Dame, Ind.: University of Notre Dame Press, 1981; 2nd ed., 1984). Drawing "certain parallels" between "our own age in Europe and North America and the epoch in which the Roman Empire declined into the Dark Ages," MacIntyre concluded that "what matters at this stage is the construction of local forms of community within which civility and the intellectual and moral life can be sustained through the new dark ages which are already upon us. And if the tradition of the virtues was able to survive the horrors of the last dark ages, we are not entirely without grounds for hope. This time however the barbarians are not waiting beyond the frontiers; they have already been governing us for quite some time. And it is our lack of consciousness of this that constitutes part of our predicament. We are waiting not for a Godot, but for another—doubtless very different—St. Benedict" (p. 244f.; 1984, p. 263). Thereby the mood is set for Newbigin's late work in Christian apologetics that is treated in chapter 10.

58. *Foolishness to the Greeks: The Gospel and Western Culture* (Grand Rapids: Eerdmans; London: SPCK, 1986), pp. 124–150. Another version of these themes is found in *The Gospel in a Pluralist Society* (Grand Rapids: Eerdmans; Geneva: WCC, 1989), pp. 222–241.

59. *Foolishness to the Greeks*, p. 125.

60. Ibid., pp. 126 and 128. For more detailed thinking of Newbigin's on "the powers," see *The Gospel in a Pluralist Society*, pp. 198–210 (chapter 16: "Principalities, Powers, and People"). Newbigin was indebted to Hendrikus Berkhof, *Christ and the Powers* (1962). The present grounding of "the powers" in the sovereignty of the victorious and exalted Christ is more characteristic of the Reformed tradition than of, say, the Lutheran tradition with its view of the continuing "orders of creation," though Newbigin was also willing to draw on the favorite Lutheran text of Romans 13.

61. *Foolishness to the Greeks*, p. 129.

62. See *Foolishness to the Greeks*, p. 130f.; *The Gospel in a Pluralist Society*, pp. 222–224.

63. See p. 118, this volume.

64. *Foolishness to the Greeks*, pp. 134–150; cf. *The Gospel in a Pluralist Society*, pp. 227–233.

65. *Faith and Power: Christianity and Islam in "Secular" Britain* (London: SPCK, 1998). Newbigin was the author of part 1 (chapters 1–4) and part 4 (chapters 17–19). See p. 235 and p. 432, note 71, this volume.

66. *Faith and Power*, preface (p. ix–x).

67. Typescript dated November 1994, supplied to me by Bishop Newbigin. This version, too, will be freely drawn on in what follows.

68. *Faith and Power*, p. 6.

69. *Faith and Power*, p. 20f.

70. For Muslim expansionism, see "What Kind of Britain?", p. 5, citing "The Islamic Movement and the West," a document of the Islamic Foundation from the 1980s. For the official statistician, see "What Kind of Britain?", p. 2.

71. "What Kind of Britain?", p. 9.

72. Ibid., p. 10.

73. Ibid., p. 7; cf. *Faith and Power*, p. 155f.

74. "What Kind of Britain?", pp. 7, 9; *Faith and Power*, pp. 135–143.

75. "What Kind of Britain?", p. 10.

76. "What Kind of Britain?", p. 11; *Faith and Power*, p. 157f.

77. "What Kind of Britain?", p. 11; *Faith and Power*, pp. 158–160.

78. "What Kind of Britain?", p. 12.

79. *Faith and Power*, p. 163f.

80. Ibid., pp. 140–142, 148.

81. "What Kind of Britain?", pp. 6–8; cf. *Faith and Power*, p. 149.

82. *Faith and Power*, pp. 147f., 162f.

83. Ibid., p. 164.

84. Ibid., p. 164f.

Chapter 8

1. Writing approvingly of the structure and the phraseology of the eucharistic prayer, Bouyer said everything would depend on the ecclesiological and theological context in which it was placed, but "if that develops along the lines of Bishop Newbigin's book on the Church, *The Household of God*, one will then be able to regard this very sober eucharistic prayer (itself no small merit) as satisfactory from a traditional point of view" (*Eucharistie: Théologie et spiritualité de la prière eucharistique* [Tournai: Desclée, 1966], pp. 420–423).

2. C. O. Buchanan, *Modern Anglican Liturgies 1958–1968* (London: Oxford University Press, 1968), p. 5; *Further Anglican Liturgies 1968–1975* (Bramcote, Nottingham, England: Grove Books, 1975), pp. 15, 279–288, 416.

3. The Scots D. Forrester, J. I. H. McDonald, and G. Tellini rank the CSI eucharist among "the most interesting and influential of the new wave of liturgies" (*Encounter with God*, Edinburgh: T. & T. Clark, 1983, p. 124).

4. Many of the particular features were present in the Syrian Orthodox liturgy of the ancient churches of India. A generation previously (1920), an almost entirely Syrianized liturgy had been prepared by J. C. Winslow, E. C. Ratcliff, and others with the blessing of the Anglican bishop of Bombay, E. J. Palmer; but despite repeated authorizations, this *Eucharist in India* had remained something of a dead (Bombay) duck.

5. Eric J. Lott, "Historic Tradition, Local Culture: Tensions and Fusions in the Liturgy of the Church of South India," in *The Sunday Service of the Methodists:*

Twentieth-Century Worship in Worldwide Methodism, ed. Karen Westerfield Tucker (Nashville: Abingdon Press, 1996), pp. 53–66.

6. Marcus Ward, *The Pilgrim Church: An Account of the First Five Years in the Life of the Church of South India* (London: Epworth Press, 1953), in particular pp. 127–148; T. S. Garrett, *Worship in the Church of South India* (London: Lutterworth Press; Richmond, Va.: John Knox Press, 1958, revised 1965); L. W. Brown, "The Making of a Liturgy," in *Scottish Journal of Theology* 4 (1951) 55–63. Brown was certainly familiar with the worship of the Syrian-Indian Orthodox; see his *The Indian Christians of St. Thomas: An Account of the Ancient Syrian Church of Malabar* (Cambridge: Cambridge University Press, 1956), pp. 213–288.

7. *Unfinished Agenda* (London: SPCK, 1985), pp. 77, 96 (updated ed. Edinburgh: St. Andrew Press, 1993, pp. 72, 90).

8. Selly Oak box 2, document no. 2/1/69.

9. *Unfinished Agenda*, pp. 91f., 100–102, 103f., 106f., 143f. (1993 ed., pp. 86f., 95–97, 98f., 101f., 135).

10. Ibid., p. 107 (1993, p. 101f.).

11. Selly Oak box 2, document no. 2/ 1/86.

12. Selly Oak box 2, document no. 2/1/101.

13. *Unfinished Agenda*, p. 107 (1993, p. 102).

14. *Sin and Salvation* (London: SCM Press, 1956), p. 86f. Later (p. 116f.), Newbigin cites the same CSI service for evidence that the Church both "has" and "hopes for" salvation: "Thy death, O Lord, we commemorate; thy resurrection we confess; and thy second coming we await."

15. On the "rule of faith" in Newbigin, see pp. 166, 212–213, 317–326, this volume.

16. See Michael J. Hill, *The Formative Factors in the Compilation of the Eucharistic Liturgy of the Church of South India between 1949 and 1954* (postgraduate thesis, United Theological College, Bangalore, 1978), pp. 55–59, especially p. 57.

17. Letter from Conjeeveram/Kanchipuram to "dear friends," October 1944, Selly Oak box 1, document no. 1/2/48 (cf. *Unfinished Agenda*, p. 64f.; 1993 edition, p. 60f.). For Newbigin's love of the Tamil lyric, see pp. 77 and 374, this volume.

18. *Unfinished Agenda*, pp. 139, 149, 162, 181 (1993 ed., pp. 131, 140, 153, 170). The typescript of the San Francisco homily is lodged in Selly Oak box 9.

19. *Unfinished Agenda*, pp. 207, 209, 235 (1993 ed., pp. 196, 197f., 222).

20. See chapter 3, this volume.

21. See Eric J. Lott, "Faith and Culture in Interaction: The Alternative CSI Liturgy," in *Reflections* [Festschrift for the Rt. Revd. Sundar Clarke, Bishop in Madras], ed. Sathianathan Clarke (Madras: Poompuhar Pathipagam, 1987), pp. 120–140.

22. Israel Selvanayagam, "With the Cross and the Lotus: The Church of South India in Fifty Years," in *Epworth Review* 25/1 (January 1998), pp. 107–114.

23. Letter of Dr. Eric Lott to me, July 17, 1998. This had long been a concern of Newbigin's: "The name of Jesus is a stumbling-block in a situation such as India, because it is concrete and refers to a human being who cannot be dissolved away. People find it easier to use the word Christ, because that can be detached from particularity and made into a general idea. But our message is 'Jesus come in the flesh' "; see "The Gathering Up of History into Christ," in *The Missionary Church in East and West*, ed. Charles C. West and David M. Paton (London: SCM Press, 1959), pp. 81–90, here p. 89.

24. Letter of March 11, 1992, from the Reverend David Devairakkam to the newly elected moderator of the CSI, the Most Reverend Ryder Devapriam.

25. See chapter 7, this volume. The eucharistic liturgy in the Bangalore booklet also allowed that "on occasions such as National Days, Harvest Festival, etc. there may also be a suitable reading from scriptures other than those of the Christian tradition"; and samples of such readings were in fact provided for use in other liturgies on special occasions.

26. Letter of August 22, 1997, from the Reverend H. B. S. Rahi to me.

27. Martin Conway, "Profile: Lesslie Newbigin's Faith Pilgrimage," in *Epworth Review* 20/3 (September 1994), 27–36. Elsewhere Conway says of the London Tamil occasion that he "witnessed a respect and attention in the hearers matching what I can only call a 'majesty' in Newbigin's speaking, a calm, a poise, an inner authority that was unmistakable again in the last public address I heard him give, now in English at the World Mission Conference in Salvador de Bahia, Brazil, in November 1996."

28. Typescript in Selly Oak box 9.

29. Typescript in Selly Oak box 8; extracted in Newbigin's *A Word in Season*, ed. Eleanor Jackson (Grand Rapids: Eerdmans; Edinburgh: St. Andrew Press, 1994), pp. 1–6.

30. Typescript in Selly Oak box 10.

31. See p. 435, n.53, this volume.

32. Typescripts in Selly Oak box 9.

33. Typescripts in Selly Oak boxes 9 and 8, respectively.

34. In 1979 I, too, had sought to fulfill in changed conditions the same obligation to Mrs. Ramsden's original mid-nineteenth-century endowment for an annual sermon on "Church Extension over the Colonies and Dependencies of the British Empire."

35. As an observer at the Lambeth Conferences of 1988 and 1998, I witnessed the continuing rise of the African bishops and their churches within the Anglican communion, representing the faith of historic Christianity on such matters as the primacy and centrality of Holy Scripture, the bodily resurrection of Christ, and sexual morality. But the civil wars and ethnic turmoil in various regions of sub-Saharan Africa render the notion of a Christian continent as ambiguous as ever.

36. Typescripts in Selly Oak box 10.

37. See p. 151, this volume.

38. Text in Selly Oak box 8.

39. Manuscript in Selly Oak box 8. See *Concise Encyclopedia of Preaching*, ed. William H. Willimon and Richard Lischer (Louisville: Westminster John Knox, 1995), p. 335f.

40. *The Reunion of the Church* (London: SCM Press, 1948; rev. ed. 1960), p. 70; cf. 102f.

41. See *The Household of God* (London: SCM Press, 1953), pp. 17f., 103, 138, 143, 145–147, 149–152; and then, for example, *A Faith For This One World?* (London: SCM Press, 1961), p. 93, *The Open Secret* (London: SPCK; Grand Rapids: Eerdmans, 1978), pp. 124, 127, 163, 169 (1995 ed., pp. 110, 113, 150), and *Foolishness to the Greeks* (London: SPCK; Grand Rapids: Eerdmans, 1986), pp. 124, 133. In the case of *The Open Secret*, the equivalent to the entire page 163 of the original edition was accidentally omitted from the revised edition.

42. *Sin and Salvation*, p. 95.

43. Ibid., p. 102.

44. *The Reunion of the Church*, p. 69.

45. *The Finality of Christ* (London: SCM Press; Richmond, Va.: John Knox Press, 1969), pp. 88–115.

46. Ibid., p. 109f.

47. Typescript in Selly Oak box 10. See p. 435, n.31, this volume.

48. In his interpretation of "the one baptism," Newbigin is probably indebted to the Church of Scotland's *Biblical Doctrine of Baptism* (1958); cf. J. A. T. Robinson, "The One Baptism as a Category of New Testament Soteriology," in *Scottish Journal of Theology* 6 (1953): 257–274.

49. cf. *The Household of God*, pp. 65–68.

50. *Sin and Salvation*, p. 94f.

51. *The Household of God*, p. 67f.

52. *Christ Our Eternal Contemporary* (Madras: Christian Literature Society, 1968), p. 79f.

53. Selly Oak box 2, document no. 2/1/69.

54. *The Open Secret*, pp. 123–127 (1995 ed., pp. 109–113).

55. See p. 124, this volume. The typescript of Newbigin's paper is lodged in box 9 of the Selly Oak papers.

56. This is naturally gratifying to me, having worked with the small writing group on *Baptism, Eucharist and Ministry* in the final years and chaired the definitive redaction at Lima itself. See Geoffrey Wainwright, *Worship with One Accord* (New York: Oxford University Press, 1997), pp. 65–83 ("The Lima Text in the History of Faith and Order").

57. *The Christian Prospect in Eastern Asia. Papers and Minutes of the Eastern Asia Christian Conference, Bangkok, December 3–11, 1949* (New York: Friendship Press, 1950), pp. 77–87, here p. 83f.

58. Ibid., p. 84.

59. See p. 170, this volume.

60. "Religious Pluralism: A Missiological Approach," in *Studia Missionalia*, vol. 42 (1993) 227–244, here p. 242.

61. *The Household of God*, p. 147f. See p. 167, this volume.

62. "Religion in the Marketplace," in *Christian Uniqueness Reconsidered: The Myth of a Pluralistic Theology of Religions*, ed. Gavin D'Costa (Maryknoll, New York: Orbis, 1990), pp. 135–148, here p. 146.

63. See pp. 54 and 242, this volume.

64. See p. 331–332, this volume.

65. *God's Reign and Our Unity: The Report of the Anglican-Reformed International Commission 1981–1984* (London: SPCK; Edinburgh: St. Andrew Press, 1984), paragraph 38.

66. *Proper Confidence* (Grand Rapids: Eerdmans, 1995), pp. 52f., 87.

67. Ibid., p. 53.

68. *Foolishness to the Greeks*, p. 42f.

69. *The Gospel in a Pluralist Society* (Geneva: WCC; Grand Rapids: Eerdmans, 1989), p. 227f.

70. *Foolishness to the Greeks*, p. 149f.; cf. "Religious Pluralism: A Missiological Approach," in *Studia Missionalia*, vol. 42 (1993), in particular p. 243f.

Chapter 9

1. Samples of Newbigin's Bible studies from the mid-1990s are available on audiocassette recordings made at Holy Trinity Brompton (Brompton Road, London SW7 1JA). Note also the booklet *A Walk through the Bible* (London: SPCK, 1999).

2. *A Word in Season* (Grand Rapids: Eerdmans; Edinburgh: St. Andrew Press, 1994), p. 204f.

3. *Proper Confidence: Faith, Doubt and Certainty in Christian Discipleship* (Grand Rapids, Mich.: Eerdmans, 1995), pp. 79–92.

4. Ibid., p. 86f.

5. Ibid., p. 88.

6. Ibid., p. 90. Because Newbigin was sometimes accused by liberals of being a fundamentalist, and by fundamentalists of being a liberal, it may be as well to quote another passage in which he rejects both "fundamentalism" and "liberalism" as based on common mistaken presuppositions and then sets out what he considers the appropriate approach to Scripture. Noting the "deep division between those who label each other as 'fundamentalist' and liberal,' " he argues that "this split is simply a surface manifestation of the deeper split in our culture between what we call "facts" and what we call "values." If the spectacles we wear (supplied freely to all through our educational system) cause us to see "facts" and "values" as two quite different things, then we shall ask, "Is the Bible a book of facts or a book about values?" It must be either one or the other. And so we have on the one hand those who treat the Bible as a book of certain and indisputable facts such as we imagine a textbook of physics to be. There is no room for human subjectivity, no room for the influence of human culture, no room for the human subject. And we have on the other hand those who see the Bible as part of the history of religious experience. It is all subjective. Human religious experience is infinitely various, and the Bible can only represent a very small sample of this vast variety. Part of it may be "meaningful" for me; I can neglect the rest. What both these points of view have in common is that they relieve me of personal responsibility. The true understanding of the Bible is that it tells the story of which my life is a part, the story of God's tireless, loving, wrathful, inexhaustible patience with the human family, and of our unbelief, blindness, disobedience. To accept this story as the truth of the human story (and so of my story) commits me personally to a life of discernment and obedience in the new circumstances of each day. When I accept this as the true story and begin to live within the story that the Bible tells as my own story, then the Bible becomes the spectacles through which I see the world. I do not examine the Bible through the spectacles provided by our modern "culture"; I begin to see the world (the "modern" world) through the spectacles that the Bible provides." See *A Word in Season*, p. 203f.

7. *Proper Confidence*, p. 91.

8. Paper dated April–May 1985, in Selly Oak box 10.

9. Newbigin put this point a little more carefully in a 1991 address to a regional meeting of the Bible Societies at Eisenach, Germany; and went on to develop a linguistic analogy for what he meant by "indwelling" the Bible as the condition of a faithful encounter with the world: "A Latin American theologian has said that the important thing for the student of the Bible is not to understand the text but to understand the world through the text. Of course, the second is not possible without the first. In this respect the Bible functions in the life of the Church like

the language we use. Of course, we have to learn the meaning of words and the rules of grammar and syntax. But when we are actually speaking, writing or reading, we do not attend to these things. We attend through them to the meaning, through which we deal with the situation 'out there.' All knowing, and all human dealing with the world is conducted by means of a language. We do not think about the language so much as live in it. It is part of ourselves. In an analogous fashion we need to live in the Bible so that its language, its images, its histories, its prayers, its songs become our way of understanding and dealing with the world" ("The Bible: Good News for Secularised People," typescript in Selly Oak box 8, p. 7).

10. *The Open Secret* (London: SPCK; Grand Rapids: Eerdmans, 1978), pp. 34–36 (rev. ed., Eerdmans 1995, p. 32f.).

11. *The Open Secret*, pp. 84–86 (1995 edition, pp. 75–77).

12. The text of *The Sending of the Church* was published in pamphlet form by the Church of Scotland's Board of World Mission and Unity. Newbigin's copy is lodged in Selly Oak box 8.

13. See p. 194, this volume.

14. *The Sending of the Church*, p. 3; cf. *Mission in Christ's Way* (Geneva: WCC, 1987), p. 17.

15. *Mission in Christ's Way*, p. 26f.

16. See Nicholas Lash, *Theology on the Way to Emmaus* (London: SCM, 1986), pp. 37–46.

17. *Mission in Christ's Way*, p. 38f.; cf. *The Sending of the Church*, p. 13f.

18. *The Light Has Come: An Exposition of the Fourth Gospel* (Grand Rapids: Eerdmans; Edinburgh: Handsel Press, 1982).

19. "The Bible: Good News for Secularised People," in Selly Oak box 8.

20. *The Gospel in a Pluralist Society* (Grand Rapids: Eerdmans; Geneva: WCC, 1989), especially pp. 66–115.

21. See chapter 6, this volume.

22. *The Gospel in a Pluralist Society*, p. 67f.

23. Ibid., p. 85.

24. Ibid., p. 86f.

25. Ibid., pp. 94f., 77–79.

26. *The Gospel in a Pluralist Society*, p. 97. For the "turning point," see the Arnoldshain paper of May 1988, "Our Missionary Responsibility in the Crisis of Western Culture," typescript in Selly Oak box 8, p. 10 (cf. *A Word in Season*, p. 110); and the June 1989 PCUSA sermon, typescript in Selly Oak box 10, p. 6 (see p. 281, this volume).

27. *The Gospel in a Pluralist Society*, p. 115.

28. *The Gospel in a Pluralist Society*, p. 89; see p. 208, this volume; cf. the Arnoldshain paper of May 1988, "Our Missionary Responsibility in the Crisis of Western Culture," typescript in Selly Oak box 8, p. 9 (also in *A Word in Season*, p. 109); PCUSA sermon of June 1989, p. 5f..

29. See chapter 7, this volume.

30. See pp. 217–218, this volume.

31. *The Reunion of the Church* (London: SCM Press, 1948; rev. ed. 1960), pp. 124–147 (chapter 8: "The Standard of Faith").

32. *The Reunion of the Church*, p. 146. The last phrase hints perhaps at Tertullian's "Christ did not call himself custom but truth (*Christus veritatem se, non consuetudinem cognomavit*" ("On the Veiling of Virgins," 1; PL 2:937).

33. But see pp. 278–279, this volume, for Newbigin's later worries about the CSI's treatment of the creeds.

34. *Trinitarian Faith and Today's Mission* (Richmond, Va.: John Knox Press, 1964), p. 32f.; see p. 179, this volume.

35. See *The Open Secret*, pp. 26–31 (1995 edition, pp. 24–29).

36. Ibid., p. 28f. (1995, p. 26f.)

37. "Religious Pluralism: A Missiological Approach," in *Studia Missionalia*, vol. 42 (1993), pp. 227–244, here p. 228f.

38. *The Open Secret*, p. 29 (1995, p. 27).

39. *Truth to Tell* (Grand Rapids: Eerdmans; Geneva: WCC, 1991), p. 65, citing Romano Guardini, *The End of the Modern World: A Search for Orientation* (New York: Sheed & Ward, 1956), p. 128f.

40. See p. 166, this volume.

41. See chapter 1, this volume.

42. *Journey into Joy* (Grand Rapids: Eerdmans, 1972), p. 13f. See chapters 1 and 7, this volume.

43. See p. 30, this volume.

44. In 1996, the general assembly of the United Reformed Church considered an "alternative statement of faith" which referred to God "whom Jesus called Father." Seemingly, for the assembly, poor benighted Jesus was a man of his time, whereas the assembly was better placed. . . . Newbigin lost a motion to say rather "whom, through Jesus, we know as Father." In a subsequent note (the text of which he gave me in November 1996), Newbigin wrote that "the very heart of the Gospel is that Jesus, who is the beloved Son of the Father, has adopted us as sisters and brothers so that, with and in him, we also can know God as our own Father with the intimacy of a beloved child" (cf. Matthew 11:27; Luke 10:22); he declared it heartrending that, in the interests of "inclusive language" and the avoidance of "patriarchy," "we should want to throw away this most precious of privileges and substitute words which any pagan or atheist can repeat." Moreover, God alone defines fatherhood, and human "patriarchy" is thereby excluded (cf. Matthew 23:9).

45. "The Trinity as Public Truth," in *The Trinity in a Pluralistic Age: Theological Essays on Culture and Religion*, ed. Kevin J. Vanhoozer (Grand Rapids: Eerdmans, 1997), pp. 1–8, here p. 2.

46. *Truth and Authority in Modernity* (Valley Forge, Pa.: Trinity Press International, 1996), pp. 15f., 39f.

47. *The Reunion of the Church* (1948), pp. 98–100; cf. pp. 31, 47f., etc.

48. *The Household of God* (1953), pp. 111–134, here p. 130.

49. *God's Reign and Our Unity: Report of the Anglican-Reformed International Commission 1981–1984* (London: SPCK; Edinburgh: St. Andrew Press, 1984), paragraph 25 (p. 16); cf. paragraph 43 (p. 28). Newbigin was the principal, practically the sole, drafter of the text; see chapter 3, this volume.

50. *The Welfare State: A Christian Perspective* (Oxford: Oxford Institute for Church and Society, 1985), p. 11.

51. George Hunsberger considered election to be the controlling theme in Newbigin's theology. See *The Missionary Significance of the Biblical Doctrine of Election as a Foundation for a Theology of Cultural Plurality in the Missiology of J. E. Lesslie Newbigin* (Ph. D. diss., Princeton Theological Seminary, 1987). Newbigin considered Hunsberger's doctoral dissertation to be the best devoted to him so far but disagreed with the thesis. Conversation with the author (October 1994).

52. "The Present Christ and the Coming Christ," in *Ecumenical Review* 6 (1953–1954): 118–123; cf. the text of a radio talk given by Newbigin on the BBC Third Program, "What is the Christian Hope?" in *The Listener*, September 20, 1951, 464f. In his autobiography, Newbigin offers glimpses of his mediating role as chairman of the pre-Evanston theological "committee of twenty-five," in which sharp clashes occurred between the Continental Europeans of Barthian or Lutheran disposition and the Anglo-American representatives of a "western liberal establishment" that "was unwilling to face the issue of eschatology"; see *Unfinished Agenda*, pp. 131–133, 148–150 (1993, pp. 123–125, 140f).

Chapter 10

1. "Mission in a Pluralist Society," in *A Word in Season: Perspectives on Christian World Missions* (Grand Rapids: Eerdmans; Edinburgh: St. Andrew Press, 1994), pp. 158–176, here p. 169f. The word "pluralism" is slippery, and some clarification of Newbigin's usage may be useful. In his later writings, Newbigin sometimes used the phrase "committed pluralism." It was not his coinage, and one might wish that he had never picked it up. But to lessen the risk of its being misunderstood if encountered in isolation, I quote at some length the opposition which Newbigin draws in this same essay between "committed pluralism" and "agnostic pluralism." "Agnostic pluralism" assumes that "ultimate truth is unknowable, and that there are therefore no criteria by which different beliefs and different patterns of behavior may be judged. In this situation one belief is as good as another and one lifestyle is as good as another." "Committed pluralism," by contrast, can be illustrated from "the scientific community": "The scientific community is pluralist in the sense that it is not controlled or directed from one center. Scientists are free to pursue their own investigations and to develop their own lines of research. They are free to differ from one another and to argue with one another. . . . There is a commitment to search for the truth, a commitment that implies that the truth can be known—not fully and completely, but in part and with increasing depth and range and coherence. It is therefore not an anarchic pluralism, but a directed and committed one. It follows that the freedom to explore is exercised with recognition and respect for the limits established by the work of previous scientists. Some things have been learned and are accepted as true. They provide the guidance for what is still to be discovered. . . . Because truth is at stake, the differences become a matter of argument. Experiment, testing, and further argument continue until one of the two views prevails or else some fresh way of seeing things enables the two views to be reconciled" (ibid., p. 168f.).

2. Text in Selly Oak box 7.

3. *The Spectator*, May 6, 1938, p. 800.

4. *Unfinished Agenda* (London: SPCK; Geneva: WCC, 1985), p. 81f. (updated ed. Edinburgh: St. Andrew Press, 1993, p. 76f.).

5. In *The Church's Witness to God's Design*, volume 2 in the Amsterdam Assembly series (New York: Harper, 1948), pp. 19–35; see pp. 212 and 322, this volume.

6. See p. 252, this volume.

7. For Newbigin's own contributions on the theme, see chapter 9, this volume.

8. See pp. 165–168, this volume.

9. *Unfinished Agenda*, p. 138 (1993, p. 130).

10. "The Gathering Up of History into Christ," in *The Missionary Church in East and West*, ed. Charles C. West and David M. Paton (London: SCM Press, 1959), pp. 81–90.

11. *Unfinished Agenda*, p. 152f. (1993, p. 144); see p. 251–252, this volume.

12. *Unfinished Agenda*, p. 254 (1993, p. 241).

13. "The Myth of the Secular Society," chapter 17 in *The Gospel in a Pluralist Society* (Grand Rapids: Eerdmans; Geneva: WCC, 1989), pp. 211–221.

14. A different exegesis of that parable emphasizes that it is "the nations" who will be judged according to their behavior toward the followers of Christ; see J. Mánek, "Mit wem identifiziert sich Jesus (Matt. 25:31–46)?" in *Christ and Spirit in the New Testament*, ed. B. Lindars and S. S. Smalley (Cambridge: Cambridge University Press, 1973), pp. 15–25. But Newbigin is at one with a broad tradition in finding in the parable (also) an encouragement of Christians to engage in the "corporal works of mercy" toward (all) the needy.

15. *Honest Religion for Secular Man* (London: SCM Press; Philadelphia: Westminster Press, 1966).

16. The later Newbigin would appeal to the theologically more sophisticated work of Stanley Jaki, *Science and Creation* (1974) and *The Road of Science and the Ways to God* (1978) [see *Foolishness to the Greeks* (1986), p. 70] and of Christopher Kaiser, *Creation and the History of Science* (1991) [see *Proper Confidence* (1995), p. 7f.].

17. *Honest Religion for Secular Man*, p. 31. Here Newbigin was anticipating what he would find in the observations of the Chinese thinker Carver T. Yu concerning the "technical optimism and literary despair" of the West; see p. 73, this volume.

18. *Honest Religion for Secular Man*, p. 38f.

19. Ibid., pp. 47–53.

20. Ibid., p. 62.

21. Ibid., p. 109.

22. See p. 147, this volume.

23. *Honest Religion for Secular Man*, p. 122.

24. *Unfinished Agenda*, p. 231f. (1993, p. 219); see p. 128, this volume.

25. *The Gospel in a Pluralist Society*, pp. 211–221. Later still, Newbigin disallowed "religious neutrality" even with respect to the sciences: "The dependence of all systematic thought upon assumptions that are accepted by faith has been well documented in the work of the American philosopher Roy Clouser. In his book *The Myth of Religious Neutrality* (1991), he examines major theories in the areas of mathematics, physics, and psychology and shows how all such theories involve a prior decision as to what is fundamental in the area studied" (*Proper Confidence*, Grand Rapids: Eerdmans, 1995, p. 50; cf. *Truth and Authority in Modernity*, Valley Forge, Pa.: Trinity Press International, 1996, p. 10).

26. *Unfinished Agenda*, p. 24f. (1993, p. 23f.). See pp. 30–31, this volume.

27. There were reports in the Raleigh (N. C.) *News and Observer* of November 26, 1998, concerning rapes of nuns, desecration of graves, and the demolition of churches in India following the BJP's sweeping election victories.

28. *The Gospel in a Pluralist Society*, p. 212.

29. Shortly before his death, Dr. M. M. Thomas kindly sent me the text of his Westminster College, Oxford, lecture of July 1996 on "The Gospel, Secular Culture, and Cultural Diversity." In it Thomas himself acknowledges that "with the

dehumanizing effects of modernization on the western and non-western peoples becoming stronger," a "positive theology of modern secular culture as an ally of the Christian mission in the world has got weakened considerably." He still favors an "open secularism" as permitting "a culture of dialogue among religions, secular ideologies, and the sciences to evolve a common holistic anthropology, at least a common body of anthropological insights on the basis of which they can undertake public actions for social and ecological justice"; and he maintains that "a syncretism at the level of culture as distinct from a syncretism at the level of faith should be welcomed."

30. Note, however, by 1968 his contribution to the second volume of the *History of the Ecumenical Movement*; see pp. 176–177, this volume.

31. *Unfinished Agenda*, p. 26 (1993, p. 25).

32. *Foolishness to the Greeks: The Gospel and Western Culture* (Grand Rapids: Eerdmans; London: SPCK, 1986).

33. The earlier sketch appears in *The Other Side of 1984: Questions for the Churches* (Geneva: WCC, 1984), pp. 5–27.

34. *Foolishness to the Greeks*, p. 34.

35. Newbigin refers to Alasdair MacIntyre's *After Virtue* (Notre Dame, Ind.: University of Notre Dame Press, 1981), pp. 35–59 (1984 edition, pp. 36–61).

36. A preliminary treatment of Scripture and the modern world is found in *The Other Side of 1984*, pp. 43–54. See also in this book chapter 9.

37. *Foolishness to the Greeks*, pp. 52–54.

38. Ibid., p. 55f.

39. Earlier hints are found in *The Other Side of 1984*, pp. 8–11, 18–21, 60–62.

40. *Foolishness to the Greeks*, p. 81. Here Newbigin is relying on M. Polanyi, *Personal Knowledge* (London: Routledge; Chicago: University of Chicago Press, 1958), pp. 22–24, who was in turn quoting from Ronald A. Fisher, *The Design of Experiments* (1935).

41. *Foolishness to the Greeks*, p. 88f.

42. Ibid., p. 89f.

43. Ibid., p. 90f.

44. In a historical article in *Mind* 43 (1934) 446–468, Michael Foster argued that "the Christian doctrine of creation" made possible "the rise of modern natural science" precisely by its elimination of the "Greek" notion of final causality. There need be no contradiction with Newbigin at the normative level provided the latter means by purpose something other than entelechy. Foster himself speaks of creation as a *voluntary* activity of God.

45. The earlier sketch is found in *The Other Side of 1984*, pp. 32–43.

46. *Foolishness to the Greeks*, p. 104f.

47. Ibid., p. 106; cf. p. 110.

48. Ibid., pp. 111–114.

49. *Foolishness to the Greeks*, pp. 110, 114, 121.

50. Much the same ground is covered in a short book that was drawn on for a particular purpose in chapter 1, namely, *Proper Confidence: Faith, Doubt, and Certainty in Christian Discipleship* (Grand Rapids: Eerdmans, 1995). The themes recur also in *Truth and Authority in Modernity* (Valley Forge, Pa.: Trinity Press International, 1996), a booklet published as part of a series on Christian Mission and Modern Culture. The second chapter in that case is structured as a discussion of the relations among Scripture, tradition, reason, and experience; and this was

the tack Newbigin had already taken in a paper—"By What Authority?"—written in the development of the "Gospel and Our Culture" project described subsequently; see, for the early paper, *A Word in Season*, pp. 80–97.

51. It is, of course, necessary to be careful in speaking of God as an epistemic "object": "God is not an object for our investigation by scientific methods in the style of Descartes. God is the supreme Subject who calls us by grace to put our faith in him" (*Truth and Authority in Modernity*, p. 78).

52. *Knowing and Being* (London: Routledge, 1969), p. 66, quoted by Newbigin, *The Gospel in a Pluralist Society*, p. 43.

53. *The Gospel in a Pluralist Society*, p. 52f. Newbigin cites from the Vatican II constitution on Divine Revelation: it is in the tradition that "the Church's full canon of the sacred books is known, and the sacred writings themselves are more profoundly understood and unceasingly made active in her" (*Verbum Dei* II. 8).

54. Thus, as Newbigin explicitly argues in *Truth and Authority in Modernity* (pp. 58–63), experience also—even "religious experience"—is not to be seen "as a distinct source of authority for Christian believing." Rather, "the Christian gospel provides a framework within which all experience is interpreted in terms of the wise and loving purpose of God"; and what is sometimes called "Christian experience" is "the experience of the contemporary power of the Holy Spirit of God, who is the Spirit of Jesus, to bring the atoning work of Christ home to the heart and conscience."

55. It is Newbigin's refusal of "reason" as a separate source of knowledge that explains his opposition to what he understands as "natural theology." "Natural theology" appears to cover any attempt to start—or even to prepare for—Christian faith or theology anywhere else than in God's personal self-revelation in the history of Israel and finally in Jesus Christ (see *The Gospel in a Pluralist Society*, p. 61f.). In the second chapter of *Proper Confidence* (1995, pp. 16–20) and in the first chapter of *Truth and Authority in Modernity* (1996, pp. 1–24), Newbigin's attack becomes quite sharp. He invokes the thesis put forward by the Jesuit Michael Buckley in his book *At the Origins of Modern Atheism* (1987) concerning the deleterious effects of Aquinas' use of Aristotle to establish "truths of reason" (the existence of God and of the soul) before and apart from what can be known only by revelation and faith (the Trinity, the Incarnation, the Atonement): "If one thing is obvious," writes Newbigin (p. 18f.), "it is that the 'god' whose existence natural theology claims to demonstrate is not the God whose character is rendered in the pages of the Bible, not the God and Father of our Lord Jesus Christ, not the blessed Trinity. It is hard to deny that this 'god' is a construct of the human mind and therefore has the essential character of an idol. One has to ask whether idolatry is a step on the way to the worship of the true God, or a threat to it. If our starting point is the kind of reasoning provided by 'the Philosopher' or his many successors, it becomes difficult to accept the possibility of a true incarnation and almost impossible to regard the blessed Trinity as anything other than a piece of mystification. If this is so, must we not say that the knowledge of God given through 'natural theology' is not merely partial knowledge but is a distorted and misleading knowledge?" Nevertheless (p. 22f.): "The territory that natural theology explores may quite properly be explored in the reverse direction. That is to say, it is both possible and necessary, starting from the revelation in Jesus Christ, to explore all its implications in the realm of philosophy. Indeed this is often a very necessary part of the task of Christian witness. Any mind that has been shaped by modernity will be fully furnished with beliefs and assumptions that seem to make Christian

faith untenable or at least very questionable. It is part of the business of Christian testimony to uncover the hidden assumptions that lie behind these beliefs and to show how God's action in Christ in redeeming and revealing opened the way for a truer understanding of the things that had been seen as calling it into question. This kind of activity can have a very important role in helping others on the journey of faith. In that sense they may form part of the pathway to faith. But one must make a distinction between the ways by which people are drawn to faith (which are as various as the varieties of human nature and experience) and the foundation on which faith rests. This foundation cannot be anything provided by the philosopher. It can only be the action of God himself. The only ultimate authority in the new creation is its Author." It is on these terms that Newbigin himself can be called—as in the title of this chapter—an apologist. Whether Buckley was right to push the blame as far back as Aquinas is doubted by more sympathetic interpreters of Aquinas, but the moves Buckley criticizes were certainly being made by the later Middle Ages.

56. *The Gospel in a Pluralist Society*, p. 56; cf. *Truth and Authority in Modernity*, p. 42f.

57. *The Gospel in a Pluralist Society*, p. 65.

58. *Truth and Authority in Modernity*, p. 73f.

59. Ibid., pp. 80f., 83.

60. See pp. 339–341, this volume.

61. Such was the title of chapter 18 in *The Gospel in a Pluralist Society* (1989), the book of Newbigin's 1988 Alexander Robertson Lectureship in the University of Glasgow.

62. *The Gospel in a Pluralist Society*, p. 227. The chapter, "The Congregation as Hermeneutic of the Gospel," covers pp. 222–233.

63. See pp. 76 and 175, this volume.

64. The list comes from *The Gospel in a Pluralist Society*, pp. 227–232. Newbigin rings the changes somewhat in other places. See, for instance, "Evangelism in the Context of Secularization," in *A Word in Season*, pp. 148–157.

65. Only a few changes did he accept against his will! See *Unfinished Agenda*, 1993 edition, p. 257. Those reluctant sentences are rather easily discernible, and I have left them out of account in what follows. The "theological chapter" occupies pages 111–129 of the final report.

66. On the subject of religious education, see pp. 208 and 220–221, this volume.

67. *The Gospel and Contemporary Culture*, ed. Hugh Montefiore (London and New York: Mowbray, 1992).

68. I have copies of this address in various typewritten forms, all given to me by Newbigin. The final title appears to have been "The Gospel as Public Truth."

69. Newbigin's own account of his engagement in the British Council of Churches program is found in the 1993 edition of his *Unfinished Agenda*, pp. 251–256. His response to some liberal criticisms that had appeared in the quarterly of the aptly named *Modern Churchpeople's Union* is found in that same publication, MC 34/2 (1992), pp. 1–10: "The Gospel and our Culture: A Response to Elaine Graham and Heather Walton." For further reflections on the themes of the Swanwick consultation and its aftermath, see Lawrence Osborn, *Restoring the Vision: The Gospel and Modern Culture* (London and New York: Mowbray, 1995).

70. See pp. 266–269, this volume.

71. These texts are printed in *A Word in Season*, respectively pp. 98–112, 148–157, 201–205, and 66–79.

72. Typescripts from these occasions were given to me by Newbigin in November 1996. Material by Newbigin in connection with the Uppsala conference is found in *Faith and Modernity*, eds. P. Samson, V. Samuel, and C. Sugden (Oxford, England: Regnum/Lynx, 1994), and in a booklet co-authored with John Reid and David Pullinger, *Modern, Postmodern and Christian* (Carberry, Scotland: Handsel Press, 1996).

73. Newbigin refers to the Pope's call in *A Word in Season*, pp. 172–176.

74. "The Cultural Captivity of Western Christianity as a Challenge to a Missionary Church," in *A Word in Season*, pp. 66–79, here pp. 67f., 78f. The remark about German theology may have been made tongue in cheek. Certainly there has even been a theoretical resurgence of *Kulturprotestantismus* in some academic and ecclesiastical circles in Germany; see, for instance, *Das protestantische Prinzip: Historische und systematische Studien zum Protestantismusbegriff*, eds. A. von Scheliha and M. Schröder (Stuttgart: Kohlhammer, 1998).

75. "The Trinity as Public Truth," in *The Trinity in a Pluralistic Age: Essays on Culture and Religion*, ed. Kevin J. Vanhoozer (Grand Rapids and Cambridge, England: Eerdmans, 1997), pp. 1–8. For Newbigin's trinitarian theology, see especially chapter 9, this volume.

76. *The Gospel in a Pluralist Society*, pp. 222–224.

77. "Evangelism in the Context of Secularization," in *A Word in Season*, pp. 148–157, here p. 157. Newbigin preferred the implications of "a common European home" (did the phrase originate with M. Gorbachev?) to those of "a single European market": see his address to a mission congress in Hanover in 1992, "Learning to Live in the Spirit in Our European Home," in *A Word in Season*, pp. 201–205.

78. Bert Hoedemaker, *Secularization and Mission: A Theological Essay* (Harrisburg, Pa.: Trinity Press International, 1998), pp. 42–52.

79. Wesley Ariarajah, *Gospel and Culture: An Ongoing Discussion within the Ecumenical Movement* (Geneva: WCC, 1994).

80. Letter from Martin Conway to me, April 20, 1999. Newbigin's address at Salvador de Bahia was never published. I have been able to reconstruct it and its circumstances from a tape recording and from Martin Conway's notes taken at the time. The speech was unscripted on account of Newbigin's failing eyesight. When the time-keeping moderator of the first session passed him a note to stop, he was—much to the delight of his audience—unable to read it.

Conclusion

1. *The Gospel in a Pluralist Society* (Geneva: WCC; Grand Rapids: Eerdmans, 1989), pp. 35f., 38; cf. pp. 97–99. Calvin wrote: "Just as eyes, when dimmed with age or weakness or by some other defect, unless aided by spectacles, discern nothing distinctly, so, such is our feebleness, unless Scripture guides us in seeking God, we are immediately confused" (*Institutes* I. 14. 1; cf. I. 6. 1). Newbigin contrasts the scriptural spectacles with the spectacles of modernity "which we use in public life" and which "give us a quite different view of things": "Now the figure of God has disappeared into the shadows. He may exist or he may not; the question is

not vital. We have learned to understand things in a different way." Moderns often forget that the spectacles of modernity are spectacles too.

2. See Geoffrey Wainwright, "The Ecumenical Rediscovery of the Trinity," in *One in Christ* 34 (1998): 95–124.

3. *The Open Secret* (London: SPCK; Grand Rapids: Eerdmans, 1978), pp. 156 and 19 (1995 edition, pp. 140 and 19).

4. Letter of the Reverend Dr. David Mole to me, December 1998.

5. Wilbert R. Shenk, "Lesslie Newbigin's Contribution to the Theology of Mission," in a special issue of the [British and Foreign] Bible Society's journal, *The Bible in TransMission* (1998): "A Tribute to Lesslie Newbigin (1909–1998)," 3–6.

6. From the *International Review of Mission* 79 (1990), p. 95.

7. "What Kind of Britain?" (typescript made available to me by Newbigin), p. 3.

8. From the *International Bulletin of Missionary Research* 18 (1994), p. 52.

9. "A Missionary's Dream" in *Ecumenical Review* 42 (1991): 4–10; reprinted as "The Ecumenical Future and the WCC: A Missionary's Dream" in *A Word in Season*, pp. 190–200.

10. *Foolishness to the Greeks: The Gospel and Western Culture* (Grand Rapids: Eerdmans; London: SPCK, 1986), p. 94.

11. *Truth and Authority in Modernity* (Valley Forge, Pa.: Trinity Press International, 1996), pp. 54 and 73f.

12. *Foolishness to the Greeks*, p. 114. See p. 370, this volume.

13. See p. 261, this volume.

14. *Ecumenical Review* 42 (1991), 8; cf. *A Word in Season*, p. 196f.

15. *Ecumenical Review* 42 (1991), 8f.; cf. *A Word in Season*, pp. 197–199.

16. *Ecumenical Review* 41 (1991), 7f.; cf. *A Word in Season*, p. 196.

17. On little-noticed Africa, see the observations of the veteran Africanist Roland Oliver on the two "major religions of Africa, with Islam long entrenched throughout the northern half of the continent and Christianity still rapidly consolidating to the south": "Both religions have strongly political overtones. Where the two meet and interact, as they do in Ethiopia, Sudan, Chad and Nigeria and other countries as far west as Senegal, any potential or actual threat of civil war is greatly accentuated. It is the geopolitics of the two world religions that have been mainly neglected; and, at least in the case of Christianity, the role of the Churches in the mediation of aid and relief, as well as in exercising a certain licence to criticize the excesses of authoritarian governments" (in *The Times Literary Supplement*, February 5, 1999, p. 6).

18. *The Reunion of the Church* (London: SCM Press, 1948), p. 10f.

19. *Ecumenical Review* 41 (1991), 5; cf. *A Word in Season*, p. 192f.

20. *Ecumenical Review* 41 (1991), 6; cf. *A Word in Season*, p. 194.

21. See *A Word in Season*, p. 157.

22. See Geoffrey Wainwright, *The Ecumenical Moment: Crisis and Opportunity for the Church* (Grand Rapids, Mich.: Eerdmans, 1983).

23. See *International Review of Mission* 79 (1990), 100. Conversely, Newbigin had noted that Willebrands "carries a New Testament in his wallet"; see *Unfinished Agenda*, p. 207f. (1993 ed., p. 196).

24. *The Reunion of the Church* (London: SCM Press, 1948), p. 189; see chapter 3, this volume.

25. *The Finality of Christ* (London: SCM Press; Richmond, Va.: John Knox Press, 1969), pp. 43f., 73f.

26. "Ministry" (part typescript, part manuscript, bearing Newbigin's later handwritten annotation "Late 1980s"), p. 9; in Selly Oak box 9.

27. Ibid., p. 4; see pp. 160–161, this volume.

28. "Africa Travel Diary" IV, p. 6f., typescript in Selly Oak box 2.

29. See Geoffrey Wainwright, "Christianity in (South) Africa: Ecumenical Challenges in the Twenty-first Century" in *Nederduitse Gereformeerde Teologiese Tydskrif* 41 (2000).

30. *Foolishness to the Greeks*, p. 105.

31. Cf. the conclusion to Newbigin's Oxford University sermon, March 10, 1985 (pp. 264–265, this volume).

32. For relevant passages: "The Kingdom of God and the Idea of Progress," manuscript lecture IV, p. 2f., p. 8f. (see chapter 7); *A Faith For This One World* (London: SCM Press, 1961), pp. 98–102; *Honest Religion for Secular Man* (London: SCM Press; Philadelphia: Westminster Press, 1966), p. 150; *Christ Our Eternal Contemporary* (Madras: Christian Literature Society, 1968), p. 47f.; *The Other Side of 1984* (Geneva: WCC, 1984), p. 37; *Faith and Power: Christianity and Islam in "Secular" Britain* (London: SPCK, 1998), p. 154f.

Index

Printed in the United States
19441LVS00001B/145-156